SAMUEL TAYLOR COLERIDGE:

A Bondage of Opium

The Ancient Mariner: Samuel Taylor Coleridge, *aet* forty-two, "In all but the Brain . . . an *old* man!"
Portrait by Washington Allston, Bristol, 1814
(*National Portrait Gallery, London*)

SAMUEL TAYLOR COLERIDGE:

A Bondage of Opium

by

MOLLY LEFEBURE

𝔰𝔡

STEIN AND DAY/*Publishers*/New York

First published in the United States of America in 1974
Copyright © 1974 by Molly Lefebure
Library of Congress Catalog Card No. 74-80899
All rights reserved
Printed in the United States of America
Stein and Day/*Publishers*/Scarborough House, Briarcliff Manor, N. Y. 10510
ISBN 0-8128-1711-7

This book is for Keith Simpson, M.D., Professor and head of the Department of Forensic Medicine, Guy's Hospital, who instructed me in the elements of investigation and reconstruction. I shall always be grateful for the privilege of having worked with him.

CONTENTS

Contents

Part Three

SHOOTING THE ALBATROSS

Part Four

THE COURTS OF THE SUN

Part Five

ALONE ON A WIDE SEA

EPILOGUE

LIST OF ILLUSTRATIONS

painted by Matilda Betham in 1809. (*By permission of Mr A. H. B. Coleridge*)

The Exile: S.T.C. in Rome, 1805. Unfinished portrait by Washington Allston. (*Courtesy of the Fogg Art Museum, Harvard University, Loan — The Washington Allston Trust*)

ACKNOWLEDGMENTS

There survives in Bristol Central Library Samuel Taylor Coleridge's letter of rebuke to a Mr Catcott, Sub-Librarian of Bristol Library Society, who, in 1797, was directed by the Committee of that Society to send Coleridge a succession of notes reminding him that books borrowed from the library were overdue. Stirred at last to reply, Coleridge wrote:

> Mr Catcott,
> . . . when I received your first letter on this subject, I had had the two Volumes *just three* weeks. Our learned & ingenious Committee may read thro' two quartos—i.e. two thousand and four hundred pages of close printed Greek & Latin in three weeks, for aught I know to the contrary: I pretend to no such intenseness of application or rapidity of Genius . . . I subscribe to your Library, Mr Catcott! not to read novels, or books of quick reading & easy digestion— but . . . books of massy knowledge . . . so that if I be not allowed a longer period of time for the perusal of such books, I must contrive to get rid of my subscription, which would be a thing perfectly useless, except as far as it gives me an opportunity of reading your little notes and letters—.
>
> Yours in christian fellowship
S.T. COLERIDGE   (CL 187)

My thanks are especially due to Lambeth Public Library and Bromley Central Library for the great help and kindness shown to me both in procuring books and for permitting me to retain them for lengths of time truly Coleridgean.

I am also indebted to the Bristol Central Library; the British Museum; the British Tourist Authority; the Records Office, Carlisle; Mr A.H.B. Coleridge; Miss S.T. Macpherson, Archivist-in-Charge, Joint Archives Committee for the Counties of Cumberland and Westmorland; the Keswick Branch of the Cumberland County Library; Dove Cottage Trustees; Mr George Fisher; Fogg Art Museum, Harvard University; Miss Ann Innes Meo; the National Portrait Gallery, London; Westminster City Central Reference Library; Westmorland County Library.

Quotations from *Collected Letters of Samuel Taylor Coleridge*, edited by Earl Leslie Griggs: © vol. 1 1785–1800 (1956), vol. 2 1801–1806 (1956), vol. 3 1807–1814 (1959), vol. 4 1815–1819 (1959) Oxford University Press, by permission of the Clarendon Press, Oxford.

I should also like to thank Mrs Kay Hasler and Mrs Olive Garrood for much hard and high-pressured typing, Miss Natasha Rogai for helping to check manuscript and Messrs Hilary and Nicholas Gerrish for valued assistance with illustrations and transport.

I have also received invaluable help and advice from others who, for professional or personal reasons, choose not to be named. I am exceedingly grateful to them all.

Finally I must thank my husband who has tolerated the Esteesian invasion of his domestic peace with exceeding patience.

M.L.

To any one who may protest . . . that the intimate examination of an artist's life is irreverent, or worse, we may answer with Sainte-Beuve: "*Quand on fait une étude sur un homme considérable, il faut oser tout voir, tout regarder, et au moins tout indiquer.*" We must not pay so much attention to momentary exclamation of satisfied curiosity . . . as to the more general aim of casting some light upon the most profound instincts of humanity.

Mario Praz

PREFACE

COLERIDGEAN CRITICISM has always tended to divide itself into two opposing camps. On the one hand have stood S.T.C.'s prosecutors: among them notably De Quincey, Ferrier, Stirling, Ingleby, Robertson in the nineteenth century; Beach, Bonjour, Wellek and Schneider in the twentieth. Their charge is plagiarism (that is, intellectual dishonesty and theft). Chief among S.T.C.'s defenders stand Gillman, Green, Arnold, Richards, Read, Lowes and, recently, McFarland.

The evidence of unacknowledged borrowings by S.T.C. from other authors, chiefly of the German Romantic school, must now be seen as virtually incontrovertible. Nevertheless, we have not yet been given any convincing explanation of the true reason for these apparently wholly unscrupulous borrowings.

It is easy and obvious enough to say that S.T.C.'s ambition and vanity were involved: but why did this man, who was intellectually endowed beyond all his contemporaries (as they themselves were perfectly prepared to admit) need to promote his ambition and flatter his vanity by passing off as his own the writing and thinking of others?

During the course of the heated discussion that has taken place throughout the years upon the vexed subject of S.T.C.'s plagiarisms, one vitally important, indeed the most important factor of all, has consistently been underestimated and misunderstood. This factor is his drug addiction.

It would be correct to say, of course, that until the past two decades much of the most important evidence of his addiction has not been readily available. With the full edition of the Coleridge letters and the publication of the early Coleridge notebooks a mass of immensely revealing material has been released. With further publication of the notebooks and of the collected works still to come, it would be rash indeed to suppose that we have yet reached the ultimate point in our knowledge of this extraordinary being. Nevertheless, sufficient material is now available for us to reconstruct a detailed history of his life which was not within the grasp of his earlier biographers. Certainly there is now ample material to leave us in no doubt whatever of the salient part which opium played throughout the life story of Coleridge.

Yet, even today, S.T.C.'s 'opium habit' is dismissed as having been neither so extensive nor so damaging as the poet himself contended in self-justification for his failures.

It is upon this point that criticism of Coleridge falls down. S.T.C. was not simply a dreamy Romantic, sprawled upon his couch, raptly 'eating opium' (whatever that is supposed to mean). Study of his letters and notebooks—above all of the notebooks—reveals that S.T.C.was a classical case of nineteenth-century morphine-reliance.

His predicament was not simply a matter of a sapped will. S.T.C.'s imaginative powers and concentration were literally destroyed by the drug: his intellectual capacity was fearfully eroded: his sense of truth hopelessly distorted (one of the major effects of morphine addiction).

The present study is an attempt to present Samuel Taylor Coleridge as it seems that he really was—a junkie.

At this point it is perhaps necessary to explain why I have attempted such a study. As a writer I had long been interested in the Wordsworths and Coleridge as a group providing material for a fascinating relationship study. I began to work on a play based upon this relationship. This was before I had grasped the true implication of S.T.C.'s drug habit. I then became involved in researching material for a book on Lake Country life in the eighteenth and nineteenth centuries, in the course of which I examined S.T.C. as a pioneer fell-walker. This work almost imperceptibly led to more and more attentive reading of the letters and notebooks. I began to realise the true nature and significance of S.T.C.'s drug addiction, dropped my other work and turned my full attention to research for this present book.

The reader may now be wondering why a writer like myself should know anything about drug-addiction. For nearly six years (at some considerable distance in time, now) I worked as private secretary to Professor (then Dr) Keith Simpson, the Home Office pathologist, and head of the Department of Forensic Medicine at Guy's Hospital. This work was essentially that of investigation, reconstruction and research. Since we were largely dealing with criminal cases in our daily work I learned a considerable amount about drugs and poisons.

Since then I have worked fairly extensively with young people, many of them confronted with serious social and personality problems. Inevitably, over recent years, I have, through this work, become only too well-acquainted with problems of drug-addiction.

How does this view of S.T.C. as junkie affect our ultimate assessment of him? For my part I think it must greatly, very greatly increase our respect for him. The number of persons, today, who are cured of morphine addiction is given at less than 2 %. It is true that our modern drug, heroin, administered intravenously, cannot really be compared with tincture of opium, taken orally. But with the latter, the ultimate establishment of addiction and reliance resulted in problems of drug-slavery, as S.T.C. called it, just as binding and dreadful, if not so dramatically lethal, as those we encounter today.

Coleridge was one of the small number of people to succeed in breaking a truly fearful bondage. The story of how he succeeded is a tremendous tribute to his courage, his deep basic integrity and his enormous and wonderful reserves of . . . what shall we call it, his unquenchable spirit of faith and endeavour?

Peer Gynt found that he, himself, resembled an onion: he could be peeled away in layers until at last nothing remained. S.T.C. too can be peeled away in several layers of deceptions and lies and weaknesses. But then one arrives at the core of the man. And that is great.

This book was written and in the hands of the publisher before Norman Fruman's *Coleridge, The Damaged Archangel,* his extensive study of Coleridge as plagiarist, appeared in England. His book has provided most important further knowledge of the *extent* of Coleridge's borrowings from other authors, but it in no way diminishes the observation made in these present pages that unscrupulous plagiarism should not be confused with an advanced case of morphine reliance.

SAMUEL TAYLOR COLERIDGE
A Bondage of Opium

I pass, like night, from land to land;
I have strange power of speech;
The moment that his face I see,
I know the man that must hear me:
To him my tale I teach . . .

O Wedding-Guest! this soul hath been
Alone on a wide wide sea:
So lonely 'twas, that God himself
Scarce seemed there to be . . .

S. T. Coleridge, *The Rime of the Ancient Mariner* (1797–1834)

PROLOGUE

Enter Samuel Taylor Coleridge
Himself and Alone

IN THE YEAR of 1816 the following letter was sent by Joseph Adams, physician, of Hatton Garden, London, to James Gillman, surgeon, of Highgate:

Hatton Garden, 9th April, 1816

Dear Sir,

A very learned, but in one respect an unfortunate gentleman, has applied to me on a singular occasion. He has for several years been in the habit of taking large quantities of opium. For some time past, he has been in vain endeavouring to break himself off [sic] it. It is apprehended his friends are not firm enough, from a dread, lest he should suffer by suddenly leaving it off, though he is conscious of the contrary; and has proposed to me to submit himself to any regimen, however severe. With this view, he wishes to fix himself in the home of some medical gentleman, who will have courage to refuse him any laudanum, and under whose assistance, should he be the worse for it, he may be relieved. As he is desirous of retirement, and a garden, I could think of no one so readily as yourself. Be so good as to inform me, whether such a proposal is absolutely inconsistent with your family arrangements. I should not have proposed it, but on account of the great importance of the character, as a literary man. His communicative temper will make his society very interesting, as well as useful. Have the goodness to favour me with an immediate answer; and believe me, dear sir, your faithful humble servant,

JOSEPH ADAMS[1]

James Gillman was later to describe the results of this letter:

"I had seen the writer of this letter but twice in my life, and had no intention of receiving an inmate into my house. *I however determined on seeing Dr Adams, for whether the person referred to had taken opium from choice or necessity, to me he was equally an object of commiseration and interest.* Dr Adams informed me that the patient had been warned of the danger of discontinuing opium by several eminent medical men, who, at the same time, represented the frightful consequences that would most probably ensue. I had heard of the failure of Mr Wilberforce's case, under an eminent physician at Bath, in addition to which, the doctor gave me an account of several others within his own knowledge. After some further conversation it was agreed that Dr Adams should drive Coleridge to Highgate the following evening. On the following evening came Coleridge *himself* and alone. An old friend, of more than ordinary acquirements, was sitting by the fireside when he entered. We met, indeed, for the first time, but as friends long since parted, and who had now the happiness to see each other again. Coleridge took his seat—his manner, his appearance, and above all, his conversation were captivating. We listened with delight and upon the first pause, when courtesy permitted, my visitor withdrew, saying in a low voice, 'I see by your manners, an old friend has arrived, and I shall therefore retire.' Coleridge proposed to come the following evening, but he *first* informed me of the painful opinion which he had received concerning his case, especially from one medical man of celebrity. The tale was sad, and the opinion given unprofessional and cruel—sufficient to have deterred most men so afflicted from making the attempt Coleridge was contemplating, and in which his whole soul was so deeply and so earnestly engaged. In the course of our conversation, he repeated some exquisite but desponding lines of his own. It was an evening of painful and pleasurable feeling, which I can never forget. We parted with each other, understanding in a few minutes what perhaps under different circumstances, would have cost many hours to arrange; and I looked with impatience for the morrow, still wondering at the apparent chance that had brought him under my roof. I felt indeed almost spell bound, without the desire of release. My situation was new, and there was something affecting in the thought, that one of such amiable manners, and at the same time so highly gifted, should seek comfort and medical aid in our quiet home. Deeply interested, I began to reflect seriously on the duties imposed upon me, and with anxiety to expect the approaching day."[2]

On April 14th arrived the following letter from S.T.C.:

42, Norfolk Street, Strand, Saturday noon.
[April 13, 1816]

My Dear Sir,

The first half hour I was with you convinced me that I should owe my reception into your family exclusively to motives not less flattering to me than honourable to yourself. I trust, we shall ever in matters of intellect be reciprocally serviceable to each other . . .

With regard to the Terms, permit me to say, that I offer them as proportioned to my *present* ability, and least of all things to my sense of the service. But that indeed cannot be *payed* for: it must be returned in kind by esteem and grateful affection.—

And now of myself. My ever-wakeful Reason, and the keenness of my moral feelings will secure you from all unpleasant circumstances connected with me save only one: Viz.—*Evasion*, and the cunning of a specific madness. You will never *hear* anything but truth from me—Prior Habits render it out of my power to *tell* a falsehood, but unless watched carefully, I dare not promise that I should not with regard to this detested Poison be capable of *acting* a lie.—

No sixty hours *have yet passed* without my having taking [taken?] Laudanum, tho' for the last week comparatively trifling doses. I have full belief that your anxiety will not need to be extended beyond the first week; and for the first week I shall not, *I must not be permitted* to leave your House, unless I should walk out with you. —Delicately or indelicately, this *must* be done: and both the Servant and the young Man must receive absolute commands from you on no account to fetch anything for me. The stimulus of Conversation suspends the terror that haunts my mind; but when I am alone, the horrors, I have suffered from Laudanum, the degradation, the blighted Utility, almost overwhelm me—. If (as I feel for *the first time* a soothing Confidence it will prove) I should leave you restored to my moral and bodily Health, it is not myself only that will love and honour you— Every friend, I have (and thank God! in spite of this wretched vice* I have many and warm ones who were friends of my Youth & have never deserted me) will think of you with reverence.

I have taken no notice of your kind apologies—If I could not be comfortable in your Home & with your family, I should deserve to be miserable . . .

If you could make it convenient, I should wish to be with you by Monday Evening, as it would prevent the necessity of taking fresh Lodgings in Town.

With respectful Compliments to Mrs Gillman & her sister, I remain, dear sir,/your much obliged

S. T. COLERIDGE[3]

On the evening appointed, Monday, April 15, S.T.C. arrived at Highgate, the arrangement being that he should stay with the Gillmans for a month. He remained domiciled with them until his death in 1834—a period of eighteen years.

*Gillman's footnote:
"This is too strong an expression. It was not idleness, it was not sensual indulgence, that led Coleridge to contract this habit. No, it was latent disease, of which sufficient proof is given in this memoir."

INTRODUCTION

A preliminary scrutiny of S.T.C.'s reputation as an opium-eater, of his medical history, of his drug-reliance, of his family background, of his earliest recorded personality traits and of the shaping years of infancy, boyhood and adolescence.

I

*"God Protect Me from My Friends . . ."**

DURING S.T.C.'s LIFETIME it was common knowledge that he was an
'opium-eater'. By the second decade of the nineteenth century his addiction
had become a favourite topic for scandal-mongering in literary circles.
S.T.C. was increasingly incapable of fulfilling either social or professional
commitments; his existence became a never-ending squalor of procrastination, excuses, lies, debts, degradation, failure.

He was far from being the only distinguished figure of his day to be
reliant upon morphine (commonly taken in the form of opium), but the
very exuberance of his personality and his celebrity as a Romantic poet
exposed him to particular attention. As he observed to his publisher, Rest
Fenner, in a letter of mid-September, 1816;

> the anguish of my mind concerning . . . [opium addiction], my anxiety to
> warn others against the like error in the very commencement, and the total
> absence of all concealment, have been, far more than the thing itself, the
> causes of its being so much and so malignantly talked about. (For instance,
> who has dared blacken Mr Wilberforce's† good name on this account?
> Yet he has been for a long series of years under the same necessity. Talk with
> any eminent druggist or medical practitioner, especially at the West End of
> the town, concerning the frequency of this calamity among men and women
> of eminence).[1]

It was not strictly true that there was "total absence of all concealment;"
S.T.C., in the earlier stages of his "slavery to poison," as he called it, had
made desperate attempts to keep his condition secret. Even so late as 1816,
he was still emphatically and loudly insisting that opium had originally
been resorted to for purely medicinal reasons and that he had been seduced
into the accursed habit innocently (this was not the excuse that he had
always used, but it was a respectable one for public consumption).

The constant procurement of opium was a drain on his pocket that kept
him chronically short of money and, in 1816, he succumbed to the irresistible temptation (more correctly, perhaps, the necessary evil) of exploiting

---

*God Protect Me from My Friends—From My Enemies I can Protect Myself.
Anon. First encountered in the fifteenth century and then found in an anthology of
popular seventeenth-century sayings.
†William Wilberforce (1759–1833): parliamentarian, eminent social reformer and
abolitionist.

his opium habit as a sales gimmick for some of his poems. He required money, quickly and urgently, to help his formerly prosperous friends the Morgans, who for the greater part of the preceding five years had housed and fed him, supported and cherished him through a series of drug crises, and were now themselves, through no fault of their own, bankrupt. In April, 1816, Charles Lamb told William Wordsworth:

> Coleridge is printing 'Christabel' by Lord Byron's recommendation to Murray, with what he calls a vision, 'Kubla Khan', which said vision he repeats so enchantingly that it irradiates and brings heaven and elysian bowers into my parlour when he sings or says it.[2]

S.T.C. was to describe this transaction with Murray, thus:

> Mr Murray called on me, in consequence of some flashes of praise, which Lord Byron had coruscated respecting the . . . Christabel. Murray urged me to publish it, and offered me 80 pounds . . . The publication was utterly against my feelings and my Judgement—But poor Morgan's Necessities, including his Wife & Sister, were urgent & clamorous . . . With many a pang & many a groan . . . I concluded the bargain—and gave the 80£ to Morgan.[3]

The sum actually paid, eighty guineas, included *Christabel, Kubla Khan* and *The Pains of Sleep.* They were published on May 25, 1816, as an octavo pamphlet of sixty-four pages. *Kubla Khan* was no more than a fragment. *Christabel,* too, was an unfinished poem, albeit in two parts—677 lines in all, including the *Conclusion* to Part II (according to S.T.C. he envisaged the completed poem as consisting of five parts; but the final three parts were never written).

Whether publication was really utterly against S.T.C.'s feelings and judgement it is impossible to say: he may have made this subsequent observation in a mood of hindsight, arising from a belated realisation of the extent to which these particular poems had contributed to damage of his personal reputation.

Mrs Coleridge, writing on May 24, 1816, to Thomas Poole about S.T.C.'s decision to publish the poems, said: "He has been so unwise as to publish his fragments of 'Christabel' & 'Koula-Khan' . . . we were all sadly vexed when we read the advertisement of these things."[4] Presumably her opinion (doubtless, also, that of S.T.C.'s brother-in-law, Robert Southey, Poet Laureate) was that the appearance of unfinished poems could only reinforce the popular view of S.T.C.; that want of inclination and exertion prevented him from giving full scope to his mind, and of completing anything that he began.

S.T.C.'s family and well-wishers must have been even more seriously perturbed when they saw the actual publication and discovered the guise in which S.T.C. had deliberately offered the three poems. He described, explicitly, how *Kubla Khan* (sub-titled *A Vision in a Dream*) had come to him "without any sensation or consciousness of effort" during a sleep following "an anodyne"[5] (which, in the public mind of that era, could only mean opium). *Christabel*, similarly, he claimed, came to him "with the wholeness, no less than the liveliness of a vision."[6] *The Pains of Sleep* he offered as describing "the dream of pain and disease."[7]

The publication of these three poems together in a single context, the description of them all as, in some kindred measure, visionary and the mention of sleep resulting from an anodyne had the inevitable (and, judged by S.T.C.'s own prefaces to the poems, calculated) result that the poems were universally accepted as opium-inspired.

The public, then as now, neither could nor wished to comprehend that writing good, let alone great poetry is labour as hard and exhausting as road-building. People love to believe, and therefore do believe, that poets work effortlessly, their poems borne to them on wings of an extraordinary something called inspiration. The sweating, grim, relentless process of fighting for the right word, the terrible struggles to make the thing come and, when it comes, the fearsome tenacity of concentration required to hold on to it and work it through, are stringencies unknown to non-composers.

S.T.C. was desperate for success with his poetry, after years of silence (years during which, significantly, he had become increasingly reliant upon morphine). The drug had extinguished him as a poet, not turned him on; but this hard truth was not in accordance with popular myth and so, in order that his poems might have a better chance of receiving an enthusiastic reception, S.T.C. (who is on record by his brother poets as having worked and re-worked his compositions more meticulously than any other man of their knowledge and from whom Wordsworth and Robert Southey constantly sought professional advice), presented himself as a slothful, opium-steeped dreamer who had had the poems miraculously given to him, "without any . . . consciousness of effort."

The qualities of magic and music, fantasy and dream which *Kubla Khan* and *Christabel* possess in such extraordinary degree (the calculated effects of a supreme technician working with a subtlety that comes only from intensive control), convinced delighted readers that here indeed were spontaneous products of bedrugged trance;

> Where Alph, the sacred river, ran
> Through caverns measureless to man
> Down to a sunless sea.[8]

From this it may be seen that it was S.T.C. himself who attached to his name, for eternity, the label OPIUM. But it is one thing to be known to the world as an opium-dreamy poet inspired by magical visions; it is quite another to be revealed in detail as a squalid addict. To do S.T.C. justice, he did include, with *Kubla Khan* and *Christabel*, *The Pains of Sleep*—an almost clinical description of what happens to the junkie when his sweet drug-honeymoon turns sour and horror takes the place of delight:

> . . . yester-night I prayed aloud
> In anguish and in agony,
> Up-starting from the fiendish crowd
> Of shapes and thoughts that tortured me:
> A lurid light, a trampling throng,
> Sense of intolerable wrong . . .
> Desire with loathing strangely mixed
> On wild and hateful objects fixed.
> Fantastic passions! maddening brawl!
> And shame and terror over all!

The poetry-reading public in the main is not, however, knowledgeable upon drugs and so the merciless self-exposure of *The Pains of Sleep* went, and goes, unheeded.

In 1816, therefore, S.T.C. openly established a public image of himself as romantic opium-eater. Opium played a not unimportant rôle in the mystique of the Romantic Period; drugs were simultaneously glamourised and proscribed, as they are today; for the public mind, as now, they exercised a morbid fascination. The respectable bourgeois, confident that he had never resorted to a drug in his life, was intrigued by the subject's aura of taboo and derived from the dreadful appellation, 'opium-eater', a spine-chilling bogeyman-shock that was exceedingly gratifying.

In 1821, Thomas De Quincey, whose gifts as a journalist approached genius and whose underworld (today's underground) experiences as an adolescent had equipped him with valuable material for copy (besides leaving him reliant upon morphine), published in the *London Magazine* an essay, *Confessions of an English Opium Eater* (produced the following year as a small book). The sensational personal revelations and powerful dream-painting of the *Confessions* attracted much notice. Its observations about S.T.C. as an addict brought the latter (now, after relentless struggle, successfully emerging from desperate opium-bondage) publicity of a kind that was most unwelcome and which exceedingly annoyed and distressed his family and friends. From Rydal Mount the Wordsworths expressed the opinion that De Quincey, in this essay, had transferred his own opium habits to Coleridge, in exculpation of himself.

How far this really was the case it is impossible to say; in view of what we know of the extent of S.T.C.'s addiction, it seems improbable that he could have been any less of "a real opium-eater"[9] than was De Quincey. What can be in no doubt at all is the fact that the *Confessions* did S.T.C.'s reputation grave harm.

His addiction had been brought most heroically under control by 1821; his career was in a second, and impressive, flowering; even poetry returned to him—not in the fantastic vein of *Christabel*, but with equal control and beautifully subtle technical expertise. Yet his public image was irrevocably steeped in opium. Acquaintances who learned that he still took drugs (although under strict and highly expert medical supervision) winked and nodded at one another and, knowing nothing of the long-term effects of drug-reliance upon the body's chemistry, muttered gleefully that poor Coleridge was still too weak to be able to conquer entirely his craving for opium.

By the date of his death, in July, 1834, S.T.C. was a Grand Old Man of English letters and, in the opinion of many young liberal-minded English clergy, the foremost religious thinker of the time. For a circle of devout admirers he was enshrined as the guru of Highgate; men of eminence came to pay homage; over Americans, particularly, he exerted a profound fascination. He had become wise, loving, forgiving; even visits from his wife passed off benignly. The past seemed forgotten; he had apparently achieved his sworn ambition of living it down. The present was serenely golden; Heaven, assuredly, was the future.

A bare two months after S.T.C.'s death, De Quincey launched an attack upon him in *Tait's Edinburgh Magazine* for September, 1834. This article was the first of a series by De Quincey;[10] the attack was based chiefly on S.T.C. as a plagiarist. Julius Hare retaliated on S.T.C.'s behalf in the *British Magazine* in January, 1835.[11]

Although the Wordsworths considered De Quincey's attacks on S.T.C. to be "infamous,"[12] these were mild in comparison with those subsequently launched by a bevy of academics, led by Professor J. F. Ferrier, in 1840, in *Blackwood's Edinburgh Magazine*. These attacks concentrated upon S.T.C.'s activities as a plagiarist, upon the quality of his intellectual integrity and the real extent of his contribution to learning. It is a debate which has continued intermittently for a hundred and thirty years and, though it has afforded serious Coleridgeans considerable excitement and one or two passionate enmities have been engendered thereby, it has scarcely been a controversy which the general public has followed with bated breath.

The common reader, with a fondness for poetry and an interest in the lives of poets, has invariably carried in his mind an image of Samuel Taylor Coleridge as an opium-dreamy individual who abandoned himself to drugs and indolence, deserted his wife and children, wrote nothing of importance after *Christabel*, made no attempt to pull himself together and, the despair of all who knew him, finally settled in semi-private custody in Highgate, where he held occasional conversational tea parties and, every now and again, having contrived to give his custodians the slip, shuffled round to a chemist to buy further secret supplies of opium.

The first attempt to draw, in derogatory vein, an allegedly fictional but nonetheless recognisable portrait of S.T.C. was made by Charles Lloyd, S.T.C.'s pupil, disciple, lodger and supposed friend. His novel, *Edmund Oliver*, appeared in 1798, published by Joseph Cottle of Bristol. Cottle was also S.T.C.'s publisher and friend. Lloyd, an epileptic who was prone to bouts of acute mental derangement, was clearly motivated in his authorship by an irrational jealousy. His portrait of Coleridge, alias Edmund Oliver, not only caused Coleridge much distress but undoubtedly set the precedent for all subsequent popular biographical sketches of him:

> I have at all times a strange dreaminess about me . . . with that dreaminess I have gone on . . . from day to day; if any time thought troubled, I have swallowed some spirits, or had recourse to my laudanum.

Thus spake Edmund Oliver.

It is interesting to note that the title of the novel was supplied by Robert Southey, with whom Lloyd was living at the time of writing the book. Some of the biographical material may also have been provided by Southey who, though in 1798 estranged from S.T.C., had earlier been his closest friend.

Thomas Carlyle, writing of S.T.C. in *The Life of John Sterling*, remarked; "To the man himself Nature had given, in high measure, the seeds of a noble endowment; and to unfold it had been forbidden him." Carlyle claimed that S.T.C.'s "contribution to poetry, philosophy, or any specific province of . . . literature or enlightenment, had been small and sadly intermittent. . . ."[13]

The word 'sadly' is interesting. It is one of pity, rather than of condemnation or reproach; the whole tone of Carlyle, on the subject of Coleridge, is in fact pitying, condescending. It was the Wordsworths, more specifically Dorothy Wordsworth, who, as Coleridge himself complained, set a pattern of pity for him: "poor Coleridge" was her favourite epithet for him from *circa* 1801 and thereafter. To 'poor' Coleridge was a fashion that quickly caught on, at last drawing an explosive objection from Charles Lamb:

> He is a fine fellow, in spite of all his faults and weaknesses. Call him Coleridge—I hate 'poor Coleridge'. I can't bear to hear pity applied to such a one.
>
> (Charles Lamb talking with
> Crabb Robinson. August 3, 1811)[14]

In 1836, Joseph Cottle, who no doubt had noticed the degree of excitement and attention which De Quincey's *Confessions* had aroused as well as the subsequent article in *Tait's*, decided to leap on the bandwagon himself and write a book of recollections about his old friend, S.T.C.* Cottle was in

---

*Joseph Cottle, *Early Recollections*; *Chiefly Relating to the Late Samuel Taylor Coleridge During his Long Residence in Bristol* (London, 1837).

possession of several sensational letters from S.T.C., confessing to and bewailing his "slavery to opium." These letters Cottle was greatly desirous to publish; the Coleridge family was, naturally, equally anxious to prevent publication.

Cottle's avowed reasons for wishing to write his recollections were admirable enough; as he explained in his later *Reminiscences*:

—Neither to clothe the subject of biography with undeserved applause, nor unmerited censure, but to present an exact portraiture, is the object which ought scrupulously to be aimed at by every impartial writer.

The problem here was that presentation of "exact portraiture" of the late S.T.C. would necessitate making disclosures which could only have a devastating effect upon his reputation and cause deep distress and embarrassment to his surviving relatives. Cottle ruminated:

whether it be best or not . . . to throw a mantle over these dark and appalling occurrences, and . . . consign to oblivion the aberrations of a frail mortal? . . . If the individual were alone concerned, the question would be decided; but . . . the world is interested in the disclosures connected with this part of Mr Coleridge's life. His example forms one of the most impressive memorials the pen ever recorded; so that thousands hereafter, may derive instruction from viewing in Mr C. much to approve, and in other features of his character, much also to regret and deplore. Once Mr Coleridge expressed to me, with indescribable emotion, the joy he should feel, if he could collect around him all who were "beginning to tamper with the lulling, but fatal draught," so that he might proclaim as with a trumpet "the worse than death that opium entailed." . . . if he could now speak from his grave . . . he would doubtless utter, "Let my example be a warning!"[15]

It did not take long for Cottle to persuade himself that it was his duty to give publicity to the detailed, intimate and hitherto private facts of S.T.C.'s reliance upon opium.

He went ahead in drawing a picture of Coleridge:

spell-bound by his narcotic draughts; deploring . . . in his letters, the destructive consequences of opium: writhing under its effects . . . who can estimate the beneficial consequences of this undisguised statement to numerous succeeding individuals? It is consolatory to believe, that had I written nothing else, this humble but unflinching narrative would be an evidence that I had not lived in vain . . .

The most expressive and pungent of all Mr Coleridge's self-upbraidings, is that, in which he thrills the inmost heart, by saying with a sepulchral solemnity, 'I have learned what a sin is against an infinite, imperishable being, such is the soul of man!'[16]

Both Cottle and the bosom-beating S.T.C. constitute classical examples of two leading drug-scene characters: firstly, the intrigued and excited lay onlooker, violently titillated by the sordid drama of addiction but endeavouring to cloak his morbid curiosity by posing as a public benefactor out to protect society by uncovering and denouncing a great evil in its midst; and, secondly, the addict himself, loving nothing better than an opportunity to bruit his addiction, deriving almost as much satisfaction, it seems, from larger-than-life-sized self-exhibitionism, as he does from the immediate sensation of the drug itself.

Cottle, by a trick, contrived to get even more sensational letters from Josiah Wade, S.T.C.'s Bristol friend who had supported him during a particularly acute opium crisis and had possibly been instrumental in saving his life at that time.

It seems highly probable that it was Thomas Poole, S.T.C.'s old and dearly loved friend from Nether Stowey, Somerset, who first alerted the Coleridge family to the seriously damaging nature of the proposed volume of recollections.

Poole, requesting it as a favour, visited Cottle in order to read the manuscript and the letters under dispute. Cottle was later to say that he had good reason to believe that Poole "communicated a report to C.'s relations."[17]

Poole also informed Southey that, in his opinion, what Cottle had to say about S.T.C.'s opium habits "would operate less to deter others from the practice, than it would lead them to flatter themselves in indulging in it, by the example of so great a man."[18] This wise observation made some initial impression upon Southey:

> That there is some probability in this I happen to know from the effect of De Quincey's book; one who had never taken a drop of opium before, but took so large a dose, for the sake of experiencing the sensations which had been described, that a very little addition to the dose might have proved fatal. There, however, the mischief ended, for he never repeated the experiment.[19]

Unhappily, Southey had not truly forgiven S.T.C. for his rebukes made in the course of their youthful quarrel of nearly half-a-century earlier. S.T.C., when the spirit moved him, could be the very incarnation of indignant wrath, with a tongue like Toledo steel, and in 1795 he had rent Southey from head to foot. These wounds had never wholly healed. Southey, to be sure, during the long decades of S.T.C.'s chronic ill-health and drug-reliance had generously fathered and largely supported S.T.C.'s family, but S.T.C. had never ceased, through the dark dejections of his years of dilemma, to accuse Southey of being the man who had ruined his life by forcing him into a calamitous marriage.

It may now be seen that it was not S.T.C.'s marriage that brought him disaster; on the contrary, it was his disturbed personality and opium-habits that had plunged his marriage into chaos. Nonetheless, Southey had been accused often and passionately enough to have developed a lurking guilt-complex towards S.T.C., and sensations of guilt breed, after all, resentment. Southey's resentment of S.T.C. now came to the fore and resulted in some extremely ungenerous behaviour.

The Coleridge family, learning that Cottle intended going ahead with publication, became increasingly perturbed. The head of the family approached Southey who, as a very old friend of Cottle's, might perhaps be able to persuade him to agree to some omissions? Southey's attitude towards the whole matter was a cool one; as he wrote to Cottle, on October 10, 1836 (Cottle's dating), "I have long foreseen that poor S. T. Coleridge would leave a large inheritance of uneasiness to his surviving friends, and those most nearly connected with him."[20]

Cottle, thus under pressure, was now contemplating withdrawing the work entirely, but Southey visited him at Bristol, read the manuscript himself and gave unqualified approval for publication of all the opium letters (as they came to be called), "for the sake of faithful biography and for the beneficial effect they . . . must inevitably produce."[21]

To Southey, therefore, must be accorded much of the responsibility for the decision to publish the letters, against the express wishes of the Coleridge family. At that date S.T.C.'s widow and three children were all living; S.T.C. himself had been dead barely two years; it was fully understandable that exposures such as Cottle intended making could only have painful and seriously damaging repercussions.

These letters were, of course, bound to be published ultimately, but there is a wealth of difference between the publication of letters as part of a scholarly corpus of material presented as serious documentation and scrupulously devoid of mutilation or gratuitous and prejudicial editorial comment, and the wholly unscrupulous sub-editing methods which were unhesitatingly applied by Cottle. Encouraged (however subconsciously) by Southey, he proceeded to do an unabashed hatchet-job on S.T.C., in spite of his introductory contention that his aim was "impartial and exact portraiture." Cottle, in preparing S.T.C.'s letters for the public eye, interpolated passages from one letter to another, altered dates, inserted footnotes into the main body of text, printed fragments of letters as separate and complete entities and even did not hesitate to resort to improvisation of fact where it suited him. In sum, he behaved with a complete lack of either literary or moral responsibility. This documentary mish-mash was later further enlarged and enhanced by letters from Southey written to Cottle during the period of the opium-letters and dealing with S.T.C.'s tragic predicament. The tone of Southey's letters, needless to say, was one of moral righteousness and indignation. Cottle himself added his own comments, in similar key.

Neither Southey nor Cottle knew anything factual about drug-reliance; they were wholly ignorant of the effects which prolonged morphine dosage has upon the body. They neither of them possessed gifts of psychological insight. Both of them were inflexible in their general attitudes and judgement; Southey was entrenched in his views to the point of rigidity; while Cottle combined a not over-intelligent mind with an essentially provincial outlook.

Their basic reaction to S.T.C.'s drug addiction was that it had constituted a gross self-indulgence which might have been abandoned, categorically, by a simple, if powerful, effort of will, whenever S.T.C. had summoned the strength of purpose so to do. Moral cowardice alone had prevented him from extricating himself from the opium habit.

The contention of Mr Gillman, made on S.T.C.'s behalf (and confirmed by post-mortem examination), that S.T.C. had been an often agonised sufferer from chronic disease resulting from rheumatic illness in early life, was dismissed by both Southey and Cottle with scorn. Mr Gillman, in their opinion, was simply whitewashing S.T.C., whose illness, declared Southey roundly, had resulted from excessive opium, the reverse process of what Mr Gillman urged.

Between 1800 and 1813 Cottle had virtually lost all personal contact with S.T.C., save for a brief encounter when S.T.C. had visited Bristol in 1807. At the time of his transference in 1800 from the West Country to Greta Hall, Keswick, in the Lake Country, S.T.C. had been apparently healthy, strong and buoyant; he was privately already addicted to opium, but symptoms of reliance had not yet overtly manifested themselves. Although, before meeting Cottle in 1807, S.T.C. had sent his old friend an account of himself as "a wretched wreck of what you knew me, rolling, rudderless,"[22] when he finally appeared Cottle found him "quite an improved character . . . about, I thought, to realise the best hopes of his friends."[23]

Another seven years intervened; S.T.C. next appeared in Bristol in the autumn of 1813 to give a repeat of the series of exceedingly successful lectures on Shakespeare that he had given at the Royal Institution. The first course of Bristol lectures, of which six were on Shakespeare and two on Education, began in Bristol on October 28, at the White Lion Hotel (which charged S.T.C. £2 for the hire of its main large room for each session of two hours, the price of candles included). These lectures (admission, 5s.) were given twice weekly, on Tuesdays and Thursdays, until November 23.

A brief trip to London in late November, and an acute opium crisis with moral and physical collapse at Bath, followed by a prolonged convalescence at Josiah Wade's home in Bristol, intervened between this first course of lectures and a second. This series, on Milton and *Paradise Lost*, poetic taste, and a philosophical analysis of *Don Quixote*, commenced, again at the White Lion, on April 5, 1814.

During these lectures, according to Cottle, it was remarked by many of S.T.C.'s friends:

> That there was something unusual and strange in his look and deportment. The true cause was known to few, and least of all to myself. At one of the lectures, meeting Mr Coleridge at the inn door, he said, grasping my hand with great solemnity, "Cottle, this day week I shall not be alive!" I was alarmed and speaking to another friend, he replied, "Do not be afraid. It is only one of Mr C's odd fancies." After another of the lectures, he called me on one side and said, "My dear friend, a dirty fellow has threatened to arrest me for ten pounds." Shocked at the idea, I said, "Coleridge, you shall not go to gaol while I can help it," and immediately gave him ten pounds.[24]

This seems to have been a true account of S.T.C. at that time: visibly affected by his drug, desperately short of cash to the point of being troubled by duns and envisaging possible debtor's-prison and extracting money from sympathetic friends and acquaintances (one suspects that S.T.C. found the essentially naive Cottle an easy touch).

Once he had discovered S.T.C.'s financial desperation, Cottle asked him for permission to approach a few friends, in an endeavour to raise an annuity of one hundred a year for him so that he might pursue his literary objects without pecuniary distraction, and produce great things.

The account given by Cottle, in his *Recollections*, of his discovery that S.T.C. was taking opium and of the occurrences arising from the discovery is, like the quoted letters themselves, mangled.

Apparently Cottle, while brooding over this idea of the annuity, took S.T.C. to Barley Wood to introduce him to Hannah More. Although the meeting was mutually agreeable, with no lack of conversation, Cottle observed S.T.C. to be "extremely paralytic, his hands shaking to an alarming degree, so that he could not take a glass of wine without spilling it, though one hand supported the other!"[25]

Cottle described S.T.C.'s condition to a friend shortly after. The friend said: "That arises from the immoderate quantity of opium he takes."[26]

Cottle went on to ascertain from others, "not only the existence of this evil, but its extent, so as to render doubt impossible."[27] One of these others who enlightened him upon S.T.C.'s habits was Southey.

Although Cottle, in publishing Charles Lloyd's *Edmund Oliver*, must surely have recognised that novel's laudanum-sipping hero as a scantily disguised portrait of S.T.C., he was to maintain that, until this April of 1814, he had known nothing of S.T.C.'s opium habit:

> It is remarkable, that this was the first time the melancholy fact of Mr Coleridge's excessive indulgence in opium had come to my knowledge. It

astonished and afflicted me. Now the cause of his ailments became manifest.[28]

Southey was much against the idea of the annuity. All S.T.C.'s miseries
arose, Southey categorically maintained, "from one accursed cause—excess
in opium." He pointed out the costliness of drugs, adding that S.T.C. also
consumed frightening quantities of spirits. Southey attributed all S.T.C.'s
financial embarrassments and ill health to his "most culpable habits of sloth
and self-indulgence," and argued that: "There are but two grounds on
which a subscription can proceed; either where the object is disabled from
exerting himself—or when his exertions are unproductive. Coleridge is in
neither of these predicaments. He is at this moment as capable of exertion
as I am." S.T.C.'s salvation lay within his own power; he had but "to leave
off opium, and devote a certain portion of his time to the discharge of his
duty." He should return to Greta Hall and apply himself to steady daily
writing, raising money by lecturing at Birmingham and Liverpool *en route*
for Keswick (Southey added that this letter must not be shown to Wade,
for he would only repeat its contents to S.T.C. and "make mischief").[29]
As a result of Southey's letter, said Cottle:

> I now saw it was mistaken kindness to give him money as I had learned that
> he indulged in his potions according to the extent of his means, so that to be
> temperate, it was expedient that he should be poor.[30]

In fact, of course, S.T.C.'s means bore no relationship to the extent of
his opium consumption; regular opium was essential to him, in ever-
increasing quantity, and in order to obtain it he was prepared to beg,
borrow or lie, possibly even to steal: "What crime is there scarcely which
has not been included in or followed from the one guilt of taking opium?"[31]
S.T.C. exclaimed to Morgan, in a passionately remorseful confessional
letter of May 14, 1814.
Still wishing to assist S.T.C., Cottle next considered the idea of administering the proposed annuity through friends, so that S.T.C. would have all
his bills for board and necessities paid for him and would not find himself
with any actual sums of money at his disposal. However Southey obviously
believed that it was only sloth which prevented S.T.C. from working gain-
fully, and sloth was not a sin that should be encouraged with a dole from
kind friends. Therefore Cottle, "with indescribable sorrow" and "under
the full impression that it was a case of 'life and death' and that if some
strong effort were not made to arouse him from his insensibility, speedy
destruction must inevitably follow", wrote a long and dramatic appeal to
S.T.C.: "All around you behold the wild eye! the sallow countenance! the
tottering step! the trembling hand! the disordered frame! And yet will you
not be awakened to a sense of your danger, and I must add, your guilt? . . .

Is it a small thing, that one of the finest of human understandings should be lost? . . . What you have already done, excellent as it is, is considered by your friends and the world, as the . . . mere promise of the harvest."[32]

He went on to remind S.T.C. of his domestic duties:

Let me sincerely advise you to return home, and live in the circle once more, of your wife and family. There may have been faults on one, possibly on both sides: but calumny itself has never charged criminality. Let all be forgotten, a small effort for a christian . . . If I can become a mediator, command me. If you could be prevailed upon to adopt this plan, I will gladly defray your expenses to Keswick, and I am sure, with better habits, you would be hailed by your family, I was almost going to say, as an angel from heaven. It will also look better in the eyes of the world, who are always prompt with their own constructions, and these constructions are rarely the most charitable . . .

And now let me conjure you, alike by the voice of friendship, and the duty you owe yourself and family: above all . . . by the fear of God, and the awfulness of eternity, to renounce from this moment opium and spirits, as your bane! . . . My dear Coleridge, be wise before it is too late! I do hope to see you a renovated man! and that you will still burst your inglorious fetters, and justify the best hopes of your friends . . .

Excuse the freedom with which I write. If at the first moment it should offend, on reflection, you will approve at least of the motive, and perhaps, in a better state of mind, thank and bless me. If all the good that I have prayed for, should not be effected by this letter, I have at least discharged an imperious sense of duty.[33]

To this S.T.C. made his famous and tragic response:

You bid me rouse myself—go, bid a man paralytic in both arms rub them briskly together, & that will cure him. Alas! (he would reply) that I cannot move my arms is my Complaint & my misery.[34]

He gave Cottle a detailed account of how he had fallen into the clutches of opium:

I was seduced into the ACCURSED Habit ignorantly.—I had been almost bed-ridden for many months with swellings in my knees—in a medical Journal I unhappily met with an account of a cure performed in a similar case . . . by rubbing in of Laudanum, at the same time taking a given dose internally—It acted like a charm, like a Miracle! . . . At length, the unusual Stimulus subsided—the complaint returned—the supposed remedy was recurred to—but I can not go thro' the dreary history—suffice it to say, that effects were produced, which acted on me by *Terror & Cowardice* of PAIN & sudden Death . . . Had I but a few hundred Pounds, but 200£, half to send to Mrs Coleridge, & half to place myself in a private madhouse, where I could procure nothing but what a Physician thought proper, & where a medical attendant could be constantly with me for two or three months (in less than that time Life or Death would be determined) then there might be Hope. Now there is none!— ... for my Case is a species of madness, only that it is a derangement, an utter impotence of the *Volition*, & not of the intellectual Faculties.[35]

(Statements by drug-casualties should never be taken at their face value, even when originating from S. T. Coleridge; there can now be no doubt that, several years before the date of this specific illness mentioned in this letter, he was resorting with frequency to opium when under nervous stress and pressure of work.)

Cottle, understandably, was horrified by S.T.C.'s letter. He concluded that S.T.C.'s "passion for opium had so completely subdued his *will*, that he was carried away, without resistance."[36] Deeply perturbed, he wrote again to S.T.C.:

> Dear Coleridge,
> I am afflicted to perceive that Satan is so busy with you, but God is greater than Satan. Did you ever hear of Jesus Christ? That he is come into the world to save sinners? Leave your idle speculations: forget your vain philosophy. Come and be healed ... I believe that you will still be as "a brand plucked from the burning" ... Pray! Pray earnestly.[37]

S.T.C. replied with ready unction: "O if to feel how infinitely worthless I am, how poor a wretch ... so far I am a Christian—."[38] He followed it up with a thoughtful treatise on what Christians might expect from prayer, and a brief, but savage dismissal of Socinianism (which he had formerly embraced) as "not only not Christianity, it is not even *Religion*."[39] Cottle, encouraged by this response, enquired if this rejection of Socinianism meant that S.T.C. now embraced the Trinity? Swiftly came back an exceedingly lengthy and profound letter, stating S.T.C.'s views on the Trinity (which he said he now accepted, as "the clear revelation of Scripture"),[40] and exploring "some floating ideas on the *Logos*." This letter, or more properly sermon, was wholly in his very best vein. One wonders if Cottle, upon reading it, recalled to mind a shrewd observation that he had earlier made about Coleridge, that he "was somewhat in the habit of accommodating his discourse to the sentiments of the person with whom he was conversing."[41]

It is certainly a little shattering, after perusing S.T.C.'s apparently heartfelt theological letters to Cottle, to read what he subsequently (in early June) wrote to Morgan about this particular correspondence:

> poor Jo. [Cottle] ... instead of applying his Conscience to himself ... has taken it into his skull (heaven knows! there is *room* enough for any alien guest) to turn it all on me—& I have had some 4 or 5 letters, arm's length each, & (except the occasional bad spelling, very finely *sentenced*) the object of all which is to convince me, that it has not been Opium, quoad Opium, that has injured me; but—(what think you?—) the DEVIL. Yes, says he,

the Devil, depend upon it, has got possession of you. —'A strong man armed (that is, the said *Devil*) has the mastery of you; but a stronger than he will not suffer him, I hope, to keep possession. —Do not deceive yourself about opium, &c: it is the . . . DEVIL, that is in you.'— . . .
God bless him! he is a well-meaning Creature; but a great Fool.— . . .
P.S. Quere. As I COULD not have swallowed the Devil with his antlers dispreading, whether it does not follow, that he must have *pocketed his Horns*: consequently, that the Devil is a poor cowardly Wittold? Indeed, I never had a good opinion of him.[42]

In one of his letters (CL 921), S.T.C. had asked Cottle if a group of friends might not be persuaded to club together in order to raise the money required to place him under medically supervised restraint in a private asylum. S.T.C. was correct in thinking that this was the sole method by which he might achieve at least partial cure. Unfortunately Cottle, not certain whether S.T.C.'s case was desperate enough for such action to be taken, sent his letters to Southey, with a request for advice. Southey, as usual, had no doubts about the best course of action:

> Shocking as his letters are, perhaps the most mournful thing they discover is that while acknowledging the guilt of the habit, he imputes it still to morbid bodily causes, whereas . . . every person who has witnessed his habits, knows that for . . . infinitely the greater part—inclination and indulgence are the motives. It seems dreadful to say this . . . but it is so and I know it to be so, from my own observation and that of all with whom he has lived . . . This, Cottle, is an insanity of that species which none but the Soul's physician can cure . . . [Southey did not think that any cure brought about by restraint would be permanent.] The restraint which would effectually cure him is that which no person can impose upon him. Could he be compelled to a certain quantity of labour for his family every day, the pleasure of having done it would make his heart glad, and the sane mind would make the body sane.[43]

Southey's advice was as before: Coleridge should visit Poole for two or three weeks to freshen himself and recover his spirits and should then return to Greta Hall, lecturing to raise money as he went. Southey concluded by saying that he had not shown the letters to Mrs Coleridge, whose spirits and health were beginning to sink.

Thus, thanks to Southey's upright-downright opinions on a subject of which he knew worse than nothing, the one course of action which might have saved S.T.C. was dismissed as useless.

Coleridge remained at Josiah Wade's home and became a patient of Henry Daniel, a Bristol physician. Wade, says Cottle, "engaged a respectable and decayed tradesman, constantly to attend Mr C and . . . placed him even in his bed-room: and this man always accompanied him whenever he went out." But every precaution was unavailing. By "unknown means and dexterous contrivances" S.T.C. (as he subsequently confessed) still obtained his "lulling potion."[44]

A letter of guilty remorse from Coleridge to Wade (written on June 26, 1814, following the poet's defection from Wade's supporting restraint and devoted rescue attempt) was obtained from Wade by Cottle, who misrepresented the facts in order to obtain possession of the letters (as Wade subsequently explained to Henry Nelson Coleridge). This letter was published by Cottle in *Recollections* and, indeed, its contents were used by him to urge his contention that S.T.C. himself would have wished his 'opium-letters' to be placed before the public:

Bristol, June 26th 1814

Dear Sir,

For I am unworthy to call any good man friend—much less you, whose hospitality and love I have abused; accept, however, my intreaties for your forgiveness, and for your prayers.

Conceive a poor miserable wretch, who for many years has been attempting to beat off pain, by a constant recurrence to the vice that reproduces it. Conceive a spirit in hell, employed in tracing out for others the road to that heaven from which his crimes exclude him! In short, conceive whatever is most wretched, helpless, and hopeless, and you will form as tolerable a notion of my state, as it is possible for a good man to have.

I used to think the text in St. James that 'he who offended in one point, offends in all,' very harsh; but I now feel the awful, the tremendous truth of it. In the one CRIME of OPIUM, what crime have I not made myself guilty of!—Ingratitude to my Maker! and to my benefactors—injustice! *and unnatural cruelty to my poor children*! self-contempt for my repeated promise—breach, nay, too often, actual falsehood!

After my death, I earnestly entreat, that a full and unqualified narration of my wretchedness, and of its guilty cause, may be made public, that at least some little good may be effected by the direful example!

May God Almighty bless you, and have mercy on your still affectionate, and in his heart, grateful—

S. T. COLERIDGE[45]

In September Coleridge went back to live with the Morgans: first at Box, near Ashley, Bath; then, with them, he moved to Calne, in Wiltshire.

S.T.C.'s subsequent remark to Cottle, in a letter of March 7, 1815— "I would die, after my recent experience of the cruel & insolent Spirit of Calumny, rather than subject myself as a slave to a Club of Subscribers to my Poverty,"[46] strongly suggests that Cottle had divulged to the Bristol circle Southey's bitter and damaging criticism of S.T.C. It is extremely interesting that, in this same letter of March 7, S.T.C., describing his current financial position, informed Cottle that his expenses were two pounds ten shillings a week (this Cottle translated, in his book, into the firm statement that for years S.T.C.'s expenses for the purchase of opium had amounted to "nearly two pounds ten shillings per week").[47]

S.T.C. asked Cottle if he would be prepared to advance him thirty or forty pounds upon receipt of some manuscripts and poems which were ready for the press. Cottle, under the conviction that S.T.C. would spend this money on opium, declined his request "in the kindest manner, but enclosing a five pound note."[48]

In point of fact, S.T.C. did not want the money for opium, but to assist the Morgans. The letter of March 7 was followed by an even more desperate appeal for help, on March 10. To this second letter, Cottle replied with another five-pound note, by return of post, urging S.T.C. to come at once to Bristol, where his friends would do all they could to advise and assist him. To this S.T.C. made no reply, nor did he reappear at Bristol.

In spite of bitter opposition Cottle reproduced the opium-letters in full in *Early Recollections*, which appeared in 1837, in two volumes. Ten years later he re-issued this work as *Reminiscences of Samuel Taylor Coleridge and Robert Southey*; in this Cottle additionally quoted at length from Southey's letters, to prove that Southey had fully supported him in his decision to publish the opium-letters.

This 1847 collaboration (for as such it can only be called) between Cottle and Southey in their loaded presentation of S.T.C. as moral reprobate and slothful ne'er-do-well, undoubtedly made a more profound and lasting impression upon the public imagination than did any other portrayal of him. Typically of this persistent reaction to the Coleridge dilemma was a review which appeared in *The Times* of April 27, 1895, on the occasion of the publication of Ernest Hartley Coleridge's edition of the *Letters* of his grandfather. In this unsigned review it was categorically stated, in bravest Southey vein:

> The perpetual cry of ill-health seems to echo through the volumes from end to end, and this being interpreted means little less than opium and Indolence. There is no getting over this unfortunate truth.

Truth and opinion are easily confused, especially when biographers of S.T.C. turn to Cottle as a source. In the past he was a mainstay of students of Coleridge; even today he is still consulted and quoted with surprisingly little hesitation. S.T.C.'s personality, behaviour and history are still interpreted in terms of Cottlean perspective; a perspective which assumes that a man reliant upon morphine can be subjected to the same kind of biographical scrutiny and critical analysis as a man uninvolved in drugs. That perspective should by now stand as wholly outdated. Opium is assuredly the theme that echoes throughout S.T.C.'s life and letters, but our scrutiny and understanding of his dilemma should have changed radically since *Early Recollections* of 1837 and *Reminiscences* of 1847.

II

The Tyranny of the Body

... Coleridge ...
The rapt One, of the godlike forehead
The heaven-eyed creature ...[1]

William Wordsworth

IN 1838 MR GILLMAN published the first volume of his *Life of Samuel Taylor Coleridge*, intended as a rebuttal of *Early Recollections*. Gillman made no reference by name to either Cottle or Southey, but it was clear enough to whom he was referring when he launched forthrightly into his old friend and patient's defence, against

> .... men who, though possessing great worldly reputation never gave him their support; but, on the contrary, were sometimes even ready to whisper down his fair name ...
> Some of these might be well meaning enough to believe that in giving publicity to what they erroneously considered moral infirmities, (not possessing the knowledge to discriminate between moral and physical infirmities), they were performing a religious duty—were displaying a beacon to deter others from the same course. But in the case of Coleridge, this was a sad misconception. Neither morally nor physically was he understood. He did all that in his state duty could exact: and had he been more favoured in his bodily constitution, he would not have been censured for frailties which did not attach to him.[2]

Gillman had, and still has, one enormous advantage over all other biographers of Coleridge: he lived in the same house as his subject for eighteen years, having him daily under his observation, not only as companion and friend, but as a patient. Gillman's keenly appraising and detailed scrutiny was coupled with a penetrating grasp of psychology, much in advance of its day. He was not likely to be seriously wrong in the portrait that he ultimately drew of S.T.C.

His attitude towards drug-addiction was excellently illustrative of his professional stance—coolly objective, entirely free of moral prejudice or prejudgement: "Whether the person referred to [S.T.C.] had taken opium from choice or necessity, to me he was equally an object of commiseration and interest."

The true meaning of drug reliance, indeed the difference between addiction and reliance, was not understood by S.T.C.'s critics.

Addiction might be defined as the derivation of an extreme degree of pleasure from something: television, rock-climbing, fox-hunting, football, digestive biscuits, fishing, ice-cream, opera, bull-fighting, bridge, stamp-collecting, knitting; to all of these, to specify but a few possibilities, do people become addicted. Although a stage may be reached where to give up the obsession is both painful and difficult, upon none of these things can an addict become, strictly speaking, reliant. But when an addiction has been formed for, say, nicotine, in the shape of cigarettes, the case is different. By constant smoking, the addict introduces quantities of nicotine into his chemical system. Gradually his body learns to adjust to, or in other words, to tolerate these regular quantities of nicotine. This adjustment involves a highly complicated chemical process, but at length it is achieved; the body is now not only tolerant of nicotine, but requires regular nicotine to be kept smoothly adjusted. If and when nicotine is denied, the body sets in motion a series of distress signals, technically described as withdrawal symptoms. A further supply of nicotine is essential if chemical balance is to be restored. It is no longer a matter of cigarettes being a gratifying indulgence; nicotine has become integral to the addict's personal chemistry; he has become reliant upon it to maintain a sense of well-being.

It is, of course, possible for the body's nicotine-adjusted chemistry to readjust back to a nicotine-free regime, although to achieve this may involve a sharp struggle. The body objects to being switched from one chemical programme to another.

In the case of morphine, the process is very much more dramatic. Once the body has become tolerant to this drug the process is literally impossible to reverse (the number of morphine addicts who are 'cured' is placed by some optimists at 2 per cent: sterner realists place the figure at nil).

A small category of drug-casualties consist of persons who initially received a drug (usually morphine) for medicinal purposes and resultantly became reliant upon it. The larger category consists of those persons who are attracted towards drugs for reasons (usually combined) of personality disorder and pressure.

There can now be very little doubt that some kind of personality disturbance or inadequacy must be present for a person to resort seriously to drugs. The well-orientated and undisturbed person, even though under severe pressure, will not do so; the disturbed person will resort to them, if they are accessible. Hard-drug reliance is an indication of desperation; people who are not desperate do not go for the hard-stuff.

In his study of S.T.C., Gillman, in the language of his day, described the poet as possessing "a mind remarkably sensitive, so much so, as at times to divest him of that mental courage so necessary in a world full of vicissitudes and painful trial." In today's vocabulary, this means a degree of inadequacy.

S.T.C. maintained, of course, that he had become "seduced" into the drug habit through innocently dosing himself with laudanum during a prolonged bout of painful illness in the opening years of the nineteenth century. The evidence of drug-casualties concerning their own history, or indeed concerning anything, must always be regarded with the utmost suspicion; truth and drugs do not keep company. There is sufficient material available now to indicate, almost beyond doubt, that S.T.C. became reliant upon morphine for a complexity of reasons; his was far from being a simple case of reliance resulting from medical treatment. His addiction may well have had its roots in an illness during his last year at school, for which laudanum was prescribed, but there are important additional factors to be taken into consideration. S.T.C. was a highly neurotic personality. His history is one of repeated collapse under pressure. He had easy access to laudanum. He became closely involved with a circle of persons who were decidedly drug-orientated and contained several recognised 'opium-eaters'. All in all, S.T.C. might accurately be seen as a young man who, in the drug context, was definitely at risk.

Gillman fully realised that in studying a case of drug habit the personality of the patient was of the utmost importance. He was under no misapprehension about S.T.C.'s quality of genius. Here was one, Gillman judged, who "surely . . . could not be compared to the generality of his fellows." One who was "Born a poet, and a philosopher by reflection" and for whom "the mysterious depths of nature and the enquiry into these depths were among his chief delights."

Grave personal and social problems frequently arise in cases of that mysterious abnormality which we call genius:

> It has been observed, that men of genius move in orbits of their own; and seem deprived of that free will which permits the mere man of talent steadily to pursue the beaten path . . . Coleridge . . . was made to soar and not to creep.

This truly Esteesian phrase, "to soar and not to creep," is reminiscent of S.T.C.'s own fragmentary exclamation of impatience, in one of his notebooks, at the total inability of common-clay to comprehend the nature and phenomenal power of genius:

> Men of Genius not believed clever because cleverness . . . [?incapable] of making rapid & sudden [Insight/Delight] . . . —man intoxicated with Genius makes large Strides[3]

But the same personality that is so magnificently equipped in one sphere of activity may be markedly inadequate in others. Coleridge, the genius who could soar higher than Icarus, was neurotically "susceptible and sensitive, requiring kindness and sympathy, and . . . support."[4]

In rebutting the view of S.T.C. as incurably slothful, the commonest accusation made against him, Gillman became vehement in tone: "Coleridge never was an idle man . . . when his health permitted, he would drudge and work more laboriously at some of the mechanical parts of literature, than any man I ever knew."

Lesser men reproached S.T.C. constantly for not producing *more*. The tragedy of his predicament was his own private conviction that, in fact, he *could* have achieved much more.

But though he reserved the right to reproach himself, he deeply (and justifiably) resented the ignorant and presumptuous reproaches of others:

> My character has been repeatedly attacked . . . as of a man incorrigibly idle . . . who, intrusted not only with ample talents, but favoured with unusual opportunities of improving them, had nevertheless suffered them to rust away without any sufficient exertion, either for his own good or that of his fellow-creatures . . . By what I have effected, am I to be judged by my fellow-men; what I *could* have done, is a question for my own conscience.[5]

To add injury to insult, in spite of his vast output he never earned more than a pittance from literature (journalism paid, but his health was not good enough to stand the strain of unremitting newspaper work). Fortunately S.T.C. was blessed with an inextinguishable sense of the comic, well revealed in the following wry excerpt from a letter to John Murray, the publisher, dated August 31, 1814:

> the Quarterly review attacks me for neglecting & misusing my Powers!—
> I do not quarrel with the Public—all is as it must be—but surely the *public* (if there be such a Person) has no right to quarrel with *me* for not getting into Jail by publishing what they will not read!—[6]

Finally he was to conclude, with a nice touch of practical philosophy: "I dare believe that in the mind of a competent Judge what I have performed will excite more suprise than what I have omitted to do, or failed in doing."[7]

Dr Adams appears to have recommended James Gillman as S.T.C.'s physician-custodian on the strength of a retired situation and a pleasant garden: Highgate in 1816 was a leafy hill-top village of wholly rural character. Luckily for S.T.C., Gillman was not only the owner of a very charming house and garden, he was also an exceptionally skilled practitioner. The conditions were further rendered favourable for S.T.C.'s at least partial recovery by the fact that patient and doctor found themselves mutually sympathetic from the first moment of their meeting. This undoubtedly must have played a rôle in the success that Gillman had in his handling of S.T.C.'s case; Coleridge responded to him as he had never done to any of the several eminent medical men whom he had consulted previously.

These included Carlisle (1810), Tuthill (1811?), Gooch (1812), Parry (1813), Daniel (1814), Brabant (1815), and Adams (1816).

S.T.C. probably saw Tuthill at the recommendation of Mary Lamb, who had been his patient in 1810; while Dr Adams was an old acquaintance of J. J. Morgan (S.T.C.'s devoted friend and supporter) and had attended S.T.C. when he had been taken seriously ill with what was almost certainly valvular heart disease in London in March, 1816.

S.T.C. was forty-four when he went to live with the Gillmans: "in *all* but the Brain . . . an *old* man! Such ravages do anxiety and mismanagement make,"[8] he had written despairingly to Washington Allston.

S.T.C., since childhood, had suffered from intermittent attacks of illness, but his basic chronic condition of impaired health was masked by joyous qualities of buoyancy and resiliency and his essentially hypermanic traits of endless energy, endless talk, insatiable restlessness of body and curiosity— qualities in dramatic contrast with the abysses of dejection into which he fell when under pressure.

His usual tearing high spirits, enormous charm, beautiful manners, inherent sweetness of nature and goodness of heart, dazzling conversation, overwhelming intellectual capacity and vast erudition made it seem incredible that this gifted "Heaven-eyed creature" should possess feet of a substance not so much resembling clay, as pulp.

His almost incessant complaints of ill-health were all too easily attributed to hypochondria. As an undergraduate, when he was still amused by a life that was turning out to be a chapter of accidents, S.T.C. levelled the charge of hypochondria against himself; he was, he said, "of the Race of Grumbletonians . . . my hypochondriac gloomy Spirit *amongst blessings* too frequently warbles out the hoarse gruntings of discontent."[9] But in his middle years, when he was truly a chronically sick man, he wrote differently of his complaints, sighing over "the Hardheartedness of healthy People."[10]

Gillman traced S.T.C.'s history of ever-intensifying ill-health back to rheumatic fever contracted as a schoolboy at Christ's Hospital, stating categorically that this was the origin and cause of all the poet's subsequent bodily sufferings.

S.T.C.'s medical history commenced in 1778 when, aged six, he had a "dangerous putrid fever."[11] No further details are available concerning this illness. At the age of seven S.T.C. spent a wet autumnal night in the open, on a river-bank, and was carried home unable to stand with stiffness and cold. Since that occasion, he was prone to colds and agues. In his eighteenth year he had rheumatic fever.

Rheumatic fever, formerly common in children and young people (but now become comparatively rare in Britain), is thought to be a hypersensitivity disease. Physical stress, malnutrition and exposure to cold all seem to predispose towards acute rheumatism (because living conditions have greatly improved in the West over the last century this may partly explain why the disease has become much less common).

The disease initially reveals itself in a sore throat; the haemolytic streptococci, or "strep throat." This is quickly followed by a high temperature and acute pains in the knees, wrists and ankles: pain that flits from joint to joint, sometimes with actual swelling of the large joints. The lining membrane and the muscle of the heart are almost always both affected (endocarditis and myocarditis).

Rheumatic pain may return intermittently, indicating that the rheumatic process has become reactive; but often the patient appears to have grown out of this aftermath of rheumatic pain. S.T.C. seems to have enjoyed respite from it during his first year or two at Bristol; but his medical history is never easy to unravel because of the complication of opium. (For instance, Wordsworth recalled that when he and S.T.C. walked together in Somerset in 1797 and 1798, S.T.C. was sometimes seized with violent attacks of internal pain that caused him to throw himself down and writhe like a worm upon the ground.[12] Coleridge by that date was certainly resorting with frequency to opium and may have been getting attacks of colic.)

By his early mid-twenties the rheumatic disease patient may develop shortness of breath, the sign of mitral stenosis; the mitral valve of the heart has become scarred and deformed by the endocarditis of the early illness; in short, the patient has become a sufferer from valvular disease of the heart.

Auricular fibrillation is a common late consequence of chronic rheumatic heart disease. Congestion and oedema accompany this condition. Gradually, over the years, the victim becomes increasingly short of breath, with a puffy, congested appearance. The feet and legs swell. Congestion of the lungs may encourage bronchitis and cough. The ultimate cause of death may be a stroke, or, as in pre-antibiotic days, broncho-pneumonia.

S.T.C.'s progress followed this clinical outline closely. His years of apparent good health, during his early and mid-twenties in the West Country, were followed by spectacular deterioration when he moved to the Lake Country in 1800, at the age of twenty-eight; the damp climate was the worst that he could have chosen. Finally, chronic illness drove him to Malta in 1804 (it should be added that opium, too, played a vital part in his determination to seek a complete change of scene).

By this time he was complaining of shortness of breath and "heart flutterings." On his return from Malta his friends remarked upon his puffy appearance: Dorothy Wordsworth, more right than she supposed, compared it to a dropsy. S.T.C.'s feet and legs swelled, his breathlessness and rheumatism increased markedly. About the year 1809, while ascending Skiddaw with his younger son, he was suddenly seized with pain in the chest, becoming so overpowered that it attracted the notice of the child.

The period 1810–1816 was one during which S.T.C.'s morphine reliance particularly overlaid and obscured what Gillman was to describe as years of "much bodily suffering. The *cause* of this was the organic change slowly and gradually taking place in the heart itself." In London, in March, 1816, S.T.C. succumbed to a serious attack of his heart disease; he wrote to Morgan, pleading with him to join him:

> My *heart*, or *some part* about it, seems breaking, as if a weight were suspended from it that stretches it, such is the *bodily feeling*, as far as I can express it by words.[13]

It was for this illness that Dr Adams was consulted. But, continued Gillman in his account of S.T.C.'s disease, this actual physical process "was so masked by other sufferings . . . and was so generally overpowered by the excitement of animated conversation, as to leave its real cause undiscovered."

> his own familiar mode of describing his sensation was, 'that as to his head he did not know he had one' but placing his hand over . . . the situation of the *caput coli* . . . 'here I have a misery'.

S.T.C., stated Gillman roundly, began the use of opium to relieve bodily pain arising from his chronic rheumatic disease. This, of course, was S.T.C.'s own excuse for his reliance. It was only part of the truth.

Gillman was deprived of the extra sources of information now available to us in the letters, but he had some access to the very revealing notebooks. Most properly, he exercised a certain degree of professional discretion in writing the *Life*; it is highly probable that he understood more of the complexities of S.T.C.'s opium habits than he chose to disclose.

Tranquillity, the release from pressure, a steady and gratifying increase of reputation as poet and philosopher (which, nonetheless, was not permitted to interfere with his serene routine), above all, loving, skilled and unremitting medical attention, kept S.T.C. alive until the age of sixty-two. His body had become too reliant upon morphine for him to be able to relinquish it entirely, but his addiction was brought under control and he only received carefully supervised quantities of the drug in a degree necessary to maintain him on an even keel.

In the last two or three years of his life his health deteriorated markedly, although his mind lost none of its vigour. For the final month or so he was confined to his bed, virtually dying by degrees, with great suffering. The end came on July 25, 1834.

An autopsy was performed by anatomists appointed by J. H. Green, philosopher, disciple and friend of S.T.C. and Professor of Anatomy at the Royal College of Surgeons. No one would have been better pleased by this than S.T.C. himself. Twenty years earlier he had remarked to Dr Sainsbury:

Have you ever heard of a man whose Hypochondriasis consisted in a constant craving to have himself opened before his own eyes? . . . Wounded by the frequent assertions—"all his complaints are owing to the use of opium" . . . if I could but be present while my Viscera were laid open![14]

The autopsy thoroughly vindicated him. It revealed that:

The left side of the chest was nearly occupied by the heart, which was immensely enlarged, and the sides of which were so thin as not to be able to sustain its weight when raised.
The right side of the chest was filled with fluid enclosed in a membrane having the appearance of a cyst, amounting in quantity to upwards of three quarts, so that the lungs on both sides were completely compressed.[15]

A present-day specialist's interpretation of this is given as:

Hypertrophy and dilatation of the left heart due to either aortic disease or high blood pressure. In view of the history of rheumatic fever and the adherent pericardium, almost certainly, the former. The cause of death would have been left heart failure and right pleural effusion.

In the autumn of 1835, Gillman learned, no doubt through the Coleridge family, that Cottle had determined to publish his *Recollections* and that in these he was alleging that S.T.C.'s ill-health had been solely due to self-indulgent opium habits. As a result, Gillman sent a copy of the autopsy report to Cottle, together with a letter dated November 2, 1835:

Mr Coleridge's . . . sufferings were agonising to himself and those about him . . . his bodily sufferings, which were almost without intermission during the progress of the disease . . . will explain to you the necessity of subduing the sufferings by narcotics, and of driving on a most feeble circulation by stimulants which his case had imperatively demanded.
This disease, which is generally of slow progress, had its commencement in Coleridge nearly forty years before his death.
To the general observer his disease masked itself, and his personal sufferings were hidden and concealed by his fortitude and resignation, and by the extraordinary power he had of apparently overcoming and drowning them as it were in 'fervid colloquy'.[16]

In 1895 came the above-quoted review in *The Times* of E. H. Coleridge's edition of his grandfather's letters. James Gillman's niece, Mrs Lucy E. Watson, sent to *The Times* a copy of the autopsy report and her late uncle's letter to Cottle. These were reprinted in *The Lancet* for June 15, 1895, together with an editorial comment:

Introduction II

The tyranny of the body finds its most striking examplification in the subjects of chronic disease which without actually threatening life so restricts vitality as to modify the whole character of the individual . . .
The case of Coleridge is an illustration of this . . .
The account given of the post-mortem examination . . . suffices to prove that this intellectual giant must have suffered more than the world was aware of, and it can be understood that his 'indolence' as well as his opium habit had a physical basis!
It can only add to the marvel with which his achievements are justly regarded, that one so physically disabled should have made such extra-ordinary and profound contributions to Philosophy and Literature.
It is one more instance of *the triumph of mind over body*.

S.T.C., in his last year of life, composed his own epitaph, typically working it through several drafts. He completed it nine months before his death:

> Stop, Christian Passer-by!—Stop, child of God,
> And read with gentle breast. Beneath this sod
> A poet lies, or that which once seem'd he.—
> O, lift one thought in prayer for S.T.C.;
> That he who many a year with toil of breath
> Found death in life, may here find life in death!
> Mercy for praise—to be forgiven for fame
> He ask'd, and hoped, through Christ. Do thou the same!
>
> 9th November 1833.

III

The Bondage of Opium

Of all words I find it most difficult to say, *No.*
> S.T.C., Letter to William Godwin,
> January 21, 1802.

At times it would be more delightful to me to lie in the
Kennel . . . (as Southey said) 'unfit to be pulled out by
any honest man except with a pair of Tongs'.—
> S.T.C., Letter to J. J. Morgan, May 15,
> 1814.

OPIUM IS THE dried juice of the poppy (*Papaver somniferum*). The unripe
heads are incised and the milky juice which exudes is collected and allowed
to evaporate. The crude drug contains a large number of alkaloids (some
twenty in all), of which the principal, and most notable, is morphine—
about 10 per cent of the total alkaloid content. The narcotic effects of
opium poisoning are due to the combined action of several of the more
potent alkaloids, above all of morphine.

The symptoms of opium addiction reveal themselves in grave physical
and mental deterioration. The alimentary canal is rapidly affected and
chronic constipation and nausea result, together with loss of appetite and
loss of weight. There is a serious decline in the addict's sense of self-respect;
he becomes careless in his habits, displays want of purpose and impaired
powers of concentration, lack of sense of responsibility and consideration
for others. Lying and, indeed, deception of all kinds become habitual.
Nothing that he says can be believed; he cannot be relied upon to fulfil any
commitment or honour any obligation.

In 1814 S.T.C. admitted to his friend John Morgan the extent to which
opium had undermined him, morally and socially:

> in *exact proportion* to the *importance* and *urgency* of any *Duty* was it . . .
> sure to be neglected . . . In exact proportion, as I *loved* any person or persons
> more than others, & would have sacrificed my life to them, were *they* sure to
> be the most barbarously mistreated by silence, absence, or breach of
> promise.— . . . What crime is there scarcely which has not been included in
> or followed from the one guilt of taking opium? Not to speak of ingratitude
> to my maker for the wasted Talents; of ingratitude to so many friends who
> have loved me I know not why; of barbarous neglect of my family . . . I have
> in this one dirty business of Laudanum an hundred times deceived, tricked,
> nay, actually & consciously LIED. —And yet *all* these vices are so opposite
> to my nature, that but for this *free-agency-annihilating* Poison, I verily

believe that I should have suffered myself to be cut in pieces rather than have committed any one of them.[1]

This statement in itself was not strictly true, so far as S.T.C.'s habit of lying was concerned. The collected letters, dating back to adolescence, expose him (to put it bluntly) as an inveterate liar; his lying pre-dated opium-addiction and therefore cannot be wholly attributed to the effects of the drug, although these effects undoubtedly accentuated the habit. Lying, then, must be seen as an essential facet of S.T.C.'s personality, indeed, as a trait which orientated him towards opium in the first instance. The purpose of his lying was not deception, in the popularly understood sense, but the evasion of stress. He shrank from confrontations with harsh reality. "No" was for him the most difficult word in the language (as he confessed to Godwin). Inevitably, this attitude led to delusion—of himself, as well as of others. Opium, the supposed path-smoother, was the greatest delusion of all.

But if the letters are those of a man who could not prevent himself from practising deception, the notebooks, on the other hand, show S.T.C. paradoxically engaged in a lifelong pursuit of the truth. He was obsessed by an attempt to preserve the integrity of his I-ship, as he called it, and navigate it at last to harbour, out of the tumult of existential shipwreck. The notebooks are the logbooks of this hazardous life's voyage. *The Rime of the Ancient Mariner* is an autobiographical epic based on this circumnavigation; with the baffling clairvoyance of genius he wrote it before he actually experienced it.

S.T.C.'s notebooks (or, as he himself called them, pocket-books) cover a period of over forty years, from the occasion of his undergraduate walking-tour in Wales in 1794 until within a few weeks of his death. When he first started keeping them they were in the normal nature of a writer's notebook: jottings of things that interested him, ideas that he didn't want to forget, simple daily memos, recipes, fragments of verse, quotations from his reading, schemes for projected work and so forth.

But, as time went on, they became more and more a form of private dialogue with himself. At the turn of the century S.T.C. was trying to use his notebooks as a species of scrupulously honest self-scrutiny, analysis and resultant control; in 1804 he referred to his pocket-book as "the history of my own mind for my own improvement."[2] Later, they became essential to him in his period of most acute isolation. A poignant entry in 1808 reveals their rôle:

Ah! dear Book! Sole Confidant of a breaking Heart,
whose social nature compels some Outlet.[3]

Fortunately the notebooks were not burned; they remain to enrich posterity. Other virtually life-long journals have survived; but the singularity of the Coleridge notebooks is that they are not quotidian detailings of events, or even thoughts, but a life-cycle revelation of the intellectual and emotional progress of one of the select handful of history's poet-philosophers of genius, who happened also to be a classic case of morphine-addiction.

Henry Nelson Coleridge, S.T.C.'s nephew and son-in-law, wrote in 1835, in his preface to his late uncle's *Table Talk*:

> It would require a rare pen to do justice to the constitution of Coleridge's mind. It was too deep, subtle and peculiar, to be fathomed by a morning visitor . . . Mere personal familiarity with this extraordinary man did not put you in possession of him; his pursuits and aspirations, though in their mighty range presenting points of contact and sympathy for all, transcended in their ultimate reach the extremest limits of most men's imaginations.

The notebooks, nakedly revealing as they are, create for the reader a feeling of personal acquaintance with S.T.C., but they do not put the reader in possession of him; indeed, the reverse occurs. There can be few scholastic experiences more moving than reading the actual notebooks themselves: many of them worn with carrying in S.T.C.'s pocket, scarred and scraped, some blotched with the rain of Skiddaw Forest and Eskdale, others wine-dribbled and candle-greased and ink-smeared, thumb-marked and tear-blotted, redolent of S.T.C. as if it were only two hours, and not two centuries, since he put them down. From their pages, Phoenix-like, he rises, the whole man resurrected: his laughter, his puns and conundrums, his tears, gaieties and glooms, tantrums and jealousies and hypochondria; his quarrels and nightmares; all his endearing humdrum of laundry-lists and laxatives and hints for boiling eggs; his jottings of travelling-expenses, addresses, designs for mountaineering footwear, and random comments upon the night-sky viewed as he empties his urine-pot out of his study window. All this juxtaposed with the working notes of a poet, the reveries of a philosopher, the shrieked-aloud torments of a soul in purgatory. The reader draws almost unbearably close to S.T.C. in one sense; but, as with a mountain, the nearer one approaches, the greater the feeling of bedwarfment, the sense of unattainability. The stature of S.T.C. increases upon acquaintance until he looms as a giant indeed.

Even the endless passages of squalid writhing in the tentacles of opium have a culminative effect of inducing profound respect for the disintegrated being who sprawls in the kennel "unfit to be pulled out by any honest man except with a pair of Tongs." The notebooks provide a searing, blow-by-blow account of S.T.C.'s terrible struggle for survival, a self-portrait of a drug victim which at times is repellent in its remorseless exposure of the obscenities of addiction. Yet, again paradoxically, there is an element of sublimity in this battle for emancipation. An entry for 1796, when the fight against opium was as yet in an early phase, echoes with cadences of other, more stupendous contests:

> O man, thou half-dead Angel—
> a dusky light—a purple *flash*
> crystalline splendor—light blue—
> *Green* lightnings.
> in that eternal & delirious misery
> wrathfires—
> inward desolations—
> an horror of great darkness
> great things that on the ocean
> couterfeit infinity—[4]

The dark decades still lay ahead when S.T.C. wrote this, but already he seemed to be shuddering over something sensed, rather than actually seen, in the shadows that were gathering. There is a preludial ring to the passage, uncannily linking it to the famous stanzas that were to come:

> Alone, alone, all all alone
> Alone on the wide wide Sea;
> And Christ would take no pity on
> My soul in agony.
>
> The many men so beautiful
> And they all dead did lie!
> And a million million slimy things
> Liv'd on—and so did I.[5]

Drug experiences vary greatly, according to the extent to which the person concerned has been resorting to the drug and the degree of reliance that has been established. Idiosyncratic responses of the individual concerned have also to be taken into account. But most notable is the great gulf of difference between the experiences of the addict who is still in the sweet honeymoon phase of his drug and the addict who has entered the reliant stage and is experiencing consequent disillusionment, despair and disintegration.

During the honeymoon the addict is positively elated by his drug experience; he is in control, or management, of the drug and of his dreams or trips, and on top of the world, convinced that he is possessed of greater wisdom in the art of living than any non-addict around him.

This management, or construction, of 'dreams' arising from narcosis is a kind of subconscious, remote control, but it is nonetheless definitely exercised. The addict dreams the kind of dream that he wants and avoids unpleasant or frightening sequences. S.T.C. described this process, in his notebooks. When dozing (which he always spelled 'dosing', which has led to confusion in some readers, so that a 'deep dose' has been misinterpreted as meaning a big dose of laudanum), day-dreaming or half-asleep fantasy building, he was still sufficiently conscious to be able to *construct* his dreaming. A notebook entry for April 1805 explains the process:

> I humbly thank God, that I have for some time past been more attentive to the regulation of my Thoughts . . . There are few Day-dreams that I dare allow myself at any time; and few & cautiously built as they are, it is very seldom that I can think myself entitled to make lazy Holiday with any one of them. I must have worked hard, long, and well, to have earned that privilege. So akin is Reason to Reality, that what I could *do* with exulting Innocence, I can not always *imagine* with perfect innocence/ for Reason and Reality can stop and stand still, new Influxes from without counteracting the Impulses from within, and *poising* the Thought. But Fancy and Sleep *stream on* . . . I have done innocently what afterwards in absence I have likewise day-dreamed innocently, during the being awake . . . the Reality was followed in Sleep by no suspicious fancies, the Day-dream *has* been. Thank Heaven! however/ Sleep has never yet desecrated the images . . . of those whom I love and revere.[6]

The day-dreams, or fantasies, were founded on real events and situations, upon which he invented themes of gratification, often masochistic, since he derived intense satisfaction from mental and psychological torture. Ugly incidents and images of torture could be controlled during "the being awake," but they defied inhibition in his night sleep.

Fantasy-building is, of course, also commonly encountered in persons having no resort whatever to drugs; indeed, it is probably an essential process, in some degree, for a happily balanced frame of mind. But when indulged in to excess, either without or with drugs, it is a sign of inadequacy of some kind; it is being used as compensation for a personality that cannot measure up to reality.

Opium is a great aid to the process of fantasy-building, because opium opens the mind; it removes barriers of memory and inhibition; it releases a tide (S.T.C. repeatedly used the word *stream*) of memories of persons, situations, things actually experienced, or even read. All come thronging from where they have previously lain dormant, apparently totally forgotten; they manifest themselves in such vibrating urgency of detail that they appear more real than reality.

The honeymooning addict, not yet too disorientated in personality, nor too ill physically, not yet depressed or frightened by his drug-predicament, not too stressfully involved in what might be termed his life-dilemma, will find in these fantasies a world of enchantment; he will revel in the essence of his sweetest private imaginings; he will explore landscapes of delight.

To George Coleridge who himself resorted occasionally to laudanum during illness and who, clearly, had discussed opium experiences with S.T.C. the latter wrote, in March, 1798, after a painful tooth-abscess:

> Laudanum gave me repose, not sleep: but YOU, I believe, know how divine that repose is—what a spot of enchantment, a green spot of fountains, & flowers & trees, in the very heart of a waste of Sands![7]

This is exceedingly reminiscent of one of S.T.C.'s earliest notebook entries, made in the autumn of 1794:

> A subject for a romance—finding out a desert city & dwelling there/
> —Asia—[8]

without doubt, an inspiration drawn from his reading at that time. It lay in his mind as a germ for opium-dreaming and for *Kubla Khan*, that sweet green Xanadu:

> A damsel with a dulcimer
> In a vision once I saw.[9]

The building up of tolerance to the drug means, automatically, that increasingly frequent and massive doses are required for the desired effects to be felt. The chemistry of the body changes under this kind of saturation; complete reliance upon the drug is established. The happy honeymooner becomes horrifyingly aware of the fact that he is hooked. He no longer controls the drug; it controls him.

Attempts to give it up result in severe withdrawal symptoms which include violent sweating and trembling, nervous irritability, restlessness, gastritis, hyperacidity, sleeplessness, and terrifying, if vague, sensations of oppression and apprehension. S.T.C. himself described a withdrawal attack as,

> the dire moment . . . when my pulse began to fluctuate, my Heart to palpitate, & a dreadful *falling-abroad*, as it were, of my whole frame . . . with intolerable Restlessness and incipient Bewilderment.[10]

And, in another account:

> From the disuse [of opium] my spirits and pleasurable feelings used gradually to increase to the very Hour, when my circulation became suddenly disturbed, a painful and intolerable Yawning commenced, soon followed by a violent Bowel-complaint.[11]

Attempts to break the habit are doomed, except in rare and isolated instances. The addict becomes particularly skilful at deceiving those persons who attempt to bar his access to drugs. S.T.C. became an adept at procuring opium on the sly, as several letters show (Cl 927, 986, 987, 989, 1004n2, among other references). Even his doctors were duped by him. He told Dr Daniel: "Plainly (for I had skulked out the night before & got Laudanum) . . . while I was in my own power, all would be in vain—I should inevitably cheat & trick *him*, just as I had done Dr Tuthill—."[12]

At last the drug victim, realising the total nature of his bondage, becomes profoundly dejected and feels mounting terror at the thought of the future:

> there was no prospect, no gleam of Light before, an indefinite indescribable Terror as with a scourge of ever restless, ever coiling and uncoiling Serpents, drove me on from behind.—[13]

S.T.C. admitted that even he was unable to find the words precisely right to convey the full horror of

> a Slavery more dreadful than any man who has not felt its iron fetters eating into his very soul, can possibly imagine.[14]

The victim's acute anxiety and depression over what is happening to him, the ensuing disruption of all his personal relationships, his inability to keep a job—the breakdown, in fact, of his life—are reflected in the changed nature of his dreams; visitations of terror replace the former delights. This process, the so-called drug 'mismanagement', should more correctly be described as a loss of ability to approach the drug in the optimistic frame of mind required for successful dream manipulation.

The victim's body chemistry finally is so radically affected by the drug that he develops an organic psychosis, entering an entirely irrelevant and irrational private world of his own, a world of delusion and chaos. He can no longer connect properly with the exterior world. His mind lies wide open to Bosch-like terrors; he is whirled, as S.T.C. said, into a maelström of dreadful night.

Intravenous injection of morphine and heroin has so speeded up and dramatised the process that, today, the junkie has, on an average, an estimated two years between serious resort to the drug and death. In S.T.C.'s day the process was very much more prolonged and although it ended in total shipwreck of the addict, it did not necessarily end fatally. Opium, taken by the mouth, was far less noxious and acted upon the system by a less direct, and therefore much slower, much less drastic, method.

S.T.C.'s natural, spontaneous and exceptional powers as a creative composer greatly complicate attempts to determine when, in his early years, he was fantasising under opium and when he was not. Clearly, he could daydream marvellously without opium: he required no drugs to turn himself on.

Again, idiosyncratic responses condition the nature of the stimulus required to turn an individual on. It can be done by contemplation, prayer, administered or self-flagellation, certain sound rhythms, with or without hypnotically repetitive physical movement as in certain kinds of dancing, certain colour combinations, and a wide variety of other methods.

The artist, like the religious, is particularly endowed with an ability to turn on; the creative writer, especially, is able to "open the mind" without opium. The experience of imaginative writing is, indeed, almost the identical process of mind-opening experienced under opium; a sudden throng of persons and incidents and scenes, inevitably based on personal acquaintances, experiences and reading; a mass of material which has long lain buried, seemingly quite forgotten, rises, as if by magic, when required, surfacing in full-colour and perfect detail, to inhabit the upper reaches of the mind. There the characters talk, perform and activate apparently spontaneously. Yet they are controlled, nonetheless, by the author from, as it were, the sidelines. Thus, when a character says something out of character, or the action takes an undesired twist, the author intervenes, scrubs what has just been done or said, and changes dialogue or action. There is, however, the danger of too much control; the writer is being carried along ("streaming" along, as S.T.C. said) and while he must not be carried too headlong so that he loses control, on the other hand if he interferes too heavily, he may kill the thing stone dead, after which no kiss of life can be conjured to revive the creative spark of that particular story, or poem. Above all, it may be dangerous to kill off (in the interests of the plot) one specific character; for, as E. M. Forster has remarked, with him may die the whole book; the unwary author did not realise that this particular character was acting, as it were, as a medium, feeding the entire stream of creation of that book into the author's mind.

How all this happens is impossible for the writer to explain; all he can do is to say (as Hemingway did) that "the juice is up." S.T.C. came as near as anyone to defining the process, again in a notebook entry:

> Poetry, a rationalised dream dealing (? manipulating/ ? organising ? composing) —to manifold Forms our own Feelings, that never perhaps were attached by us consciously to our own personal Selves. —What is the Lear, the Othello, but a divine Dream/ all Shakespere, & nothing Shakespere. —O there are truths below the Surface in the subject of Sympathy.[15]

Solitude amongst certain kinds of scenery proved a particularly potent turning-on agency for S.T.C. "Solitude and solitary Musings do of themselves impregnate our Thoughts perhaps with more life & Sensation, than will leave the Balance quite even,"[16] he wrote to William Sotheby in 1802, when he was living in the heady atmosphere of the Lake Country and revelling in strenuous solitary fell-walking. What poet requires opium when he has Skiddaw on his doorstep?

In fact, S.T.C. required opium not to turn himself on, but to turn himself off.

In S.T.C.'s day laudanum (the alcoholic tincture of opium) was as widely used for a variety of complaints, and as easily obtainable, as aspirin in our era. Fact and fiction of the period repeatedly reveal the extent to which it was employed both under medical direction and as a home-cure. During the final decades of the eighteenth and the greater part of the nineteenth centuries laudanum was used in almost every ailment, from trivial indispositions to severe contagion.

An especially revealing allusion to laudanum is found in a letter of August 23, 1826, written from Rydal Mount by Sara Hutchinson to Edward Quillinan. Miss Hutchinson described how S.T.C.'s daughter, the young and very beautiful Sara, had left Keswick to visit her father in London, but "unluckily her mother accompanied her to Kendal & there persuaded her that she was not fit for the journey, dosed her with laudanum to make her sleep . . . and brought her back."

Miss Hutchinson's criticism was not of the dosing with laudanum, but of Mrs S.T.C.'s eternal fussing over Sara *fille*. "Oh how I do pity her!" rattled on the tartly witty Sara Hutchinson, "& hope that if she gets rid of her Mother that she may turn out something useful before she ceases to be ornamental."

That Mrs S.T.C., whose marriage and family life had been wrecked by opium, should unhesitatingly give the drug to her cherished only daughter, indicates how automatically it was turned to as a sedative, even by those who had good reason to know that it held hidden dangers.

Mrs H. Sandford, in her book *Thomas Poole and His Friends*, describes how, in 1772, a "malignant fever" broke out in the district of Nether Stowey, Somerset, where lived the Poole family. John Poole, Thomas's valued uncle, died of this fever on August 30 of that year; in September his eldest son John, who had just gained a Fellowship at Oriel, was taken ill with the same disease. For a fortnight he was in a state of raving delirium. The only prescribed remedy was large doses of opium and these the patient, "suffering from such spasms of the throat it was feared lock jaw would ensue" (to quote from the journal kept by Charlotte Poole, his sister) resisted violently, so that those about his sick-bed despaired.

" 'What!' said Tom Poole, 'let a fine young man *die*, for want of a little resolution?' " Whereupon (to continue quoting Charlotte), "calling in the strongest men from the farm, he administered the required medicine by main force." The sick youth thereafter recovered.

The real difficulty in any estimation of the pharmaceutical power of an opium preparation of around that time is that the extracts varied so much; they were never standardised. De Quincey and S.T.C., for instance, could take what would now be fatal doses of laudanum, because it contained so much less morphine then than now, when the quantity has become standardised. For this reason, to state that they drank this or that quantity of laudanum is of little purpose. De Quincey described taking 8000 drops of laudanum; the probable equivalent of some 300 or more grains a day; but everything that he has to say upon the subject of opium should be accepted with reservation, if we heed Wordsworth's cautionary advice on the celebrated 'opium-eater'. At one time S.T.C., so he told Morgan, was taking four to five ounces of laudanum a day; once, he said, he took nearly a pint (there are twenty fluid ounces in an English pint). Again, this tells us nothing factual about the extent of his tolerance, except that it must have been high.

Today laudanum has a carefully controlled strength, set by the British Pharmacopœia at 1 per cent w/v.* Black Drop has about three times that strength. The minimal adult fatal dose of morphine is probably about two to three grains (or two drachms of the tincture); for children the quantities are much less. The effect of the drug on different individuals is variable; death has occurred in adults unused to the drug from as little as one grain.

Britain imported 22,000 lb. of opium in 1830, not all for use in a strictly medical context. Opium was the agent with which the workers of the Industrial Revolution, particularly in the cotton-spinning areas, dulled themselves against the remorseless drudgery of their lives. In 1808 S.T.C. informed T. G. Street (co-proprietor, with Daniel Stuart, of the *Courier*) that laudanum:

> Throughout Lancashire & Yorkshire . . . is the common Dram of the lower orders of People—in the small town of Thorpe the Druggist informed me, that he commonly sold on market days two or three Pound of Opium, & a Gallon of Laudanum—all among the labouring Classes.[17]

Calkins[18] states that in 1843, in one Lancashire town, there were one thousand six hundred regular purchasers of Godfrey's Cordial, a soothing syrup containing opium. Teething and sedative preparations of this kind, all containing opium, accounted, it is said, for a high proportion of infant deaths among the families of cotton-mill workers: the babies were dosed to keep them drowsy and lethargic, so that they might be left unattended while their mothers were at work.

At the other end of the social scale, amongst what we would call the liberal intelligentsia, there existed an undoubted drug-scene—taking that expression to mean an esoteric culture based on a mystique.

The opium mystique had revealed itself tentatively as early as 1700, when Dr John Jones teased readers with *The Mysteries of Opium Revealed*. It was not, however, until the Romantic School began to burgeon into full flower

* Weight/Volume.

in the second half of the eighteenth century that opium found its real disciples and advocates.

Opium, with its aura of mystery, strange excitements and depravity, epitomised much that the Romantic School especially loved: veiled eroticisms, travellers' tales, spells and visions and frenzies, the forbidden entertainments of a thousand and one scented Arabian nights, freneticism of all kind.

John Brown (1735–1788), a highly unorthodox Scottish physician, having quarrelled with all his colleagues, founded his own, Brunonian theory of medicine which he expounded in his *Elementa Medicinae* of 1780, one of the theories explored therein being that opium was highly beneficial as a means of maintaining a state of excitability necessary to nourish what he vaguely termed the "vital process." This book was translated and edited by Dr Thomas Beddoes, an almost equally unorthodox Bristol specialist in pulmonary ailments.

Bristol, at the close of the eighteenth century, was the centre of a limited but distinct drug-circle revolving around Dr Beddoes. He included among his friends and patients Tom Wedgwood, James Mackintosh (the politician and publicist), Charles Lloyd, De Quincey and Coleridge; all were known, to lesser or greater degree, as opium-eaters. S.T.C. settled in Bristol in 1795 and was introduced to Beddoes some time in the latter half of that year.

Although no excuses of ill-health were ever advanced on behalf of millhands who resorted to opium in order to blunt the edges of harsh existence, this excuse was almost always offered for more distinguished addicts. Thus Robert Clive, an early celebrated opium-casualty (whose addiction almost certainly arose out of his years in India), was said to have required opium for serious bowel disorders. Wilberforce, S.T.C.'s favourite example of addiction, allegedly first resorted to opium for digestive disorders; Isaac Milner, Dean of Carlisle, was similarly supposed to have developed an opium-habit through taking the drug for alimentary trouble; Tom Wedgwood, Dr Beddoes' most distinguished patient and in due course S.T.C.'s close companion, was described as a chronic sufferer from a diseased lowergut. Since opium itself promotes chronic alimentary disturbance, one cannot help wondering which came first in these cases.

Tom Wedgwood was, no doubt, a chronically sick man from disease which at that date in medical history defied successful diagnosis. There is nonetheless evidence, as there is with S.T.C., that his interest in drugs extended beyond the purely medicinal.

It is not known for certain who it was that persuaded the Wedgwoods that Coleridge, as poet and intelligence, was a worthy object for their patronage; there is reason to suppose that James Mackintosh may have played a leading part in the moves which made the Wedgwoods patrons of S.T.C. early in 1798.

Mackintosh was married to Tom Wedgwood's sister-in-law and was well known to be seriously addicted to opium. His son's biography of him refers to "self-indulgent habits which prevented him ever finishing the major work of philosophy which he projected for so many years."[19] Mackintosh, who was medically qualified, in his youth had studied under Dr Brown.

A lifelong friend of Mackintosh's was Robert Hall, the celebrated Baptist divine who, after studying at Aberdeen University, was appointed tutor in classics at the Bristol academy. In 1790 he became minister of a church in Cambridge where he made a great name for himself as a preacher. S.T.C. was an immense admirer of his style and in April, 1796, sent him copies of some of his political pamphlets, through the agency of a Cambridge friend, Benjamin Flower, editor of the *Cambridge Intelligencer*. Hall had a reputation for 'opium-eating'; it was said that the drug was responsible for the stirring quality of his sermons.

Beddoes, with generous financial support from the Wedgwoods, in 1798 opened, in Clifton, his celebrated Pneumatic Institution, where both in-patients and out-patients were treated for various diseases by the inhalation of different gases, referred to by Beddoes, in the jargon that he made fashionable, as "factitious airs." For the preparation of these gases Beddoes used pneumatic apparatus invented for him by James Watt.

Beddoes also engaged in experimental treatments with drugs (he was particularly interested in digitalis).

While in some quarters he was positively revered, in others he was held to be little better than a quack (S.T.C.'s excellent military brother, James, was one who entertained this latter view). The Pneumatic Institution, at this distance in time, certainly sounds to have been little better than an expensive exercise in rank quackery, but it did produce one outstanding achievement. Beddoes employed the young Humphrey Davy as his superintendent of experiments, and it was in the Institution laboratory that Davy discovered 'laughing gas' (nitrous oxide). This was not only administered to patients with symptoms of melancholy; it became popular with persons anxious to try it for kicks. S.T.C. was among these enthusiasts.

Over thirty years later, at Highgate, he became unexpectedly animated when recalling 'laughing-gas':

It is said that every excitation is followed by a commensurate exhaustion. The excitation caused by inhaling nitrous oxide is an exception at least; it leaves no exhaustion on the bursting of the bubble. The operation of the gas is to prevent the decarbonating of the blood; and consequently, if taken excessively, it would produce apoplexy . . . The voluptuous sensation attending the inhalation is produced by the compression and resistance.[20]

Extremely important evidence has survived which shows that Tom Wedgwood was greatly desirous to sample *Bhang* (otherwise *cannabis resin,*

Indian hemp, hashish, pot, and a dozen other names). He first asked Humphrey Davy to get him some; Davy replied that he could not procure any and advised Wedgwood to try Dr Beddoes, as he had recently had a present of some from a friend from the East Indies. S.T.C., learning early in 1803 that Tom Wedgwood was endeavouring to get some of this drug, resorted to his own initiative and finally obtained a small package of it through the good offices of Sir Joseph Banks.

On February 17, 1803, S.T.C. wrote gaily to Tom Wedgwood: "We will have a fair trial of *Bang*—Do bring down some of the Hyoscyamine Pills—& I will give a fair Trial of opium, Hensbane, & Nepenthe. Bye the bye, I always considered Homer's account of the *Nepenthe* as a *Banging* lie.—"[21] It was also proposed there should be "red Sulfat" (sulphate) and "Compound Acid" at their disposal.[22]

The suggestion, sometimes made, that these two invalids were proposing to embark upon an intensive medical cure together can only be dismissed as impossibly naive.

It is important to note that S.T.C. was anxious to keep Wedgwood, the recipient of the *Bhang*, anonymous so far as possible: "you may be vexed at Purkis's having mentioned your name"[23] he remarked apprehensively to Wedgwood. Had the *Bhang* been required solely on medicinal grounds, would there have been any reluctance in disclosing for whom it was intended? The correspondence concerning this parcel of *Bhang* indicates that all parties involved comprehended perfectly that the drug would not be used in the normal sense of a medicinal dose.

The Coleridge letters contain many light passing references to narcotics, specifically opium. These sallies are only passed to certain individuals, presumably persons involved in the opium mystique.

S.T.C. was indulging in little jokes of this nature from undergraduate days. The first one of its kind to survive appeared in a letter to Mary Evans in February, 1793. At the end of a screed of rigmarole and a poem, S.T.C. concluded;

> Are you asleep, my dear Mary?—I have administered
> rather a strong Dose of Opium—: however, if in the
> course of your Nap you should chance to dream, that
> > I am with the ardour/ of fraternal
> > friendship/ Your affectionate
> > S. T. Coleridge
> you will never have dreamt a truer dream in all *your born days.*[24]

This does not mean that little Miss Evans (about whom, at that time, he was highly sentimental) was herself involved with drugs; but she was an avid reader of Romantic gothic-horror novels, and opium, together with wild dreams, was one of the favourite ingredients of mystery and terror in these tales.

It should be borne in mind that two years earlier S.T.C. had spent the greater part of twelve months in the school medical-ward, a very sick youth, and that without doubt he had received quantities of regular laudanum during the course of his illness. It is highly possible that this had left him orientated towards opium, in fact, addicted to it in the strictly proper sense of the word.

Early in 1794, after his flight from Cambridge (under pressure from debts and looming academic failure), S.T.C. wrote to George Coleridge a long letter of an autobiographical nature, confessing to indolence at Cambridge (it is worth noting here that "indolence" was to become S.T.C.'s favoured euphemism for opium):

> the time which I should have bestowed on the academic studies, I employed in dreaming out wild Schemes . . . It had been better for me if my imagination had been less vivid . . . How many and how many hours have I stolen from the bitterness of Truth in these soul-enervating Reveries—in building magnificent Edificies of Happiness on some fleeting Shadow of Reality![25]

This is precisely the dream-process which we know he experienced under opium.

The opium-joke to Mary Evans was made during the period when S.T.C. was escaping from "the bitterness of Truth in . . . soul-enervating Reveries." But even more significant is evidence provided by William Wordsworth in this context of S.T.C.'s undergraduate opium addiction.

It is important to bear in mind that, upon his own admission, S.T.C. confided the full facts of his opium habit to Wordsworth and to Wordsworth alone (below, p. 397). At the time of writing Book Six of *The Prelude*, describing his own undergraduate experiences beside "Cam's silent waters," Wordsworth was already in possession of these Coleridge confidences.

Musing in *The Prelude*, upon the possible course of events had he and S.T.C. been up at Cambridge together, Wordsworth addressed S.T.C. thus:

> . . . had we met
> Even at that early time, needs must I trust
> In the belief, that my maturer age,
> My calmer habits, and more steady voice,
> Would with an influence benign have soothed,
> Or chased away, the airy wretchedness
> That battened on thy youth.[26]

It is impossible to think of a better or more accurate euphemism for opium addiction than "the airy wretchedness that battened on thy youth."

If this seems somewhat tentative ground, there is undeniable documentary and circumstantial evidence available to establish beyond doubt that S.T.C. was most certainly opium-addicted at least some four to five years prior to the winter of 1800–1801, upon the events of which he ultimately blamed his "slavery." In short, there is sufficient evidence to discredit entirely the accounts that he gave Cottle, Gillman and innumerable other persons, of:

> the habit into which I had been ignorantly deluded by the seeming magic effects of opium, in the sudden removal of a supposed rheumatic affection . . . by which I had been bedridden for nearly six months. Unhappily, among my neighbour's and landlords' books were a large parcel of medical reviews and magazines . . . [elsewhere S.T.C. says that he borrowed a load of old medical journals from his doctor] and in one of these reviews I met a case, which I fancied very like my own, in which a cure had been effected by the Kendal Black Drop. In an evil hour I procured it: —it worked miracles . . . Alas! it is with a bitter smile, a laugh of gall and bitterness, that I recall this period of unsuspecting delusion, and how I first became aware of the Maelström, the fatal whirlpool, to which I was drawing just when the current was already beyond my power to stem.[27]

It is possible that S.T.C. had not experimented with the Kendal Black Drop before coming to the Lake Country. This celebrated and allegedly noxious draught, a solution of opium in vegetable acids (App. I), popularly supposed to be four times as strong as laudanum, was resorted to by S.T.C. in what might be termed massive quantities during the course of his first winter at Keswick (and thereafter). Undoubtedly, this 1800–1801 winter of the Black Drop clinched his process of reliance: from that date onward all attempts to dispense with opium were followed by violent withdrawal symptoms.

The excuses and explanations offered by drug-addicts can never be accepted with the slightest degree of confidence, because truth is one of the major casualties in the addict's long list of casualties; truth melts from under him; he stands precariously perched on an ever-dwindling floe of reality which at last vanishes altogether.

The addict's excuses vary according to whom he is addressing. They do, however, sustain certain key notes. It is never his own fault that he has become addicted; somebody else is always blamed; if not any one person in particular, then 'society' at large is identified as the scapegoat. He is always 'seduced' into use of the drug in the first place, by an already addicted friend, or a 'pusher', or by sheer force of cruel circumstance (the eager acceptance by a drug-riddled society of the myth of the 'pusher' is an indication of the guilt which society feels in the face of its drug-problem).

The classic excuse of the drug-victim is to blame his addiction upon the unsympathetic and unloving behaviour of those nearest to him; the youthful addict hurls accusation, recrimination and violent verbal abuse at his parents; the married addict turns his guilty virulence upon his spouse. S.T.C., following this pattern, made Mrs Coleridge his scapegoat. In a frenzy of remorse over the suffering which his opium habit was inflicting upon her, he denounced her, to all who would listen, as a heartless virago, whose terrible tantrums and total lack of feeling had driven him to laudanum.

There was no love lost between the Wordsworths and Mrs Coleridge with whom, from early in their acquaintance, they had been involved in a strenuous tug-of-war for S.T.C.'s heart. The Wordsworths were as ready to suspect Mrs Coleridge of undermining her husband's health, spirits and genius as she was to suspect them of the same; each side blamed the other for the disintegration of Coleridge. He, for his part, found the Wordsworths and their circle highly receptive to his tormented allegations that his hideously intensifying drug-slavery and consequent miseries were due to "my marriage—constant dread in my mind respecting Mrs Coleridge's Temper."[28]

Her tantrums and rages, declared S.T.C., precipitated his violent bowel attacks, which, he claimed, arose from his mental agitation. He took more and more opium to quell the bowel attacks and, in due course, increasing quantities of spirits, mainly brandy, to keep the opium upon his rebelling stomach.

Opium, of course, was not only the true cause of the bowel attacks, but without doubt also the indirect reason for Sara Coleridge's impassioned rages. As S.T.C. himself observed, outbursts of violent anger are frequently prompted by fear. There can be no experience more frightening than that of watching a close relative or beloved companion succumb to drugs. If the addict is also the family bread-winner, as was the case in the Coleridge household, then the situation cannot be more dire. Sara's outbursts may be seen as perfectly understandable, given the dilemma that she found herself facing. Upbraidings and reproaches of the most vehement and despairing kind are inevitable in such a situation; the guilty party, impelled by his very guilt, responds with equal energy; horrible quarrels and fights are the un-avoidable pattern of the partnership. No marriage can survive drug addiction.

The Romantic liberalism of the Wordsworths prompted them, for a long time, to be very much more sympathetic about S.T.C.'s opium-habit than was Southey. They believed that if S.T.C. would only separate from Mrs Coleridge, he could, with their sympathetic guidance, find strength to wean himself from drugs and brandy. It is clear enough, from their subsequent reaction to S.T.C.'s reliance and their comments upon it, that they had no real comprehension of the true meaning of his dilemma: like Southey they were absolutely convinced that lack of will-power alone prevented S.T.C. from giving up the drug.

Encouraged by the reaction of the Wordsworths, S.T.C. continued, for nearly a decade, to throw all the blame for his opium predicament upon his wife; but in Bristol, in 1807, he was obliged to change his tune, for here he was among people who had known both himself and Sara in the days of their highly romantic and ardent courtship and the loving first years of their marriage.

Therefore, in confidences to Cottle and other Bristol friends, S.T.C. blamed his opium excesses wholly upon ill-health; his sufferings had demanded opium and he, in innocence, had been seduced into dreadful slavery.

Occasionally he made a different, more ingenious excuse:

> the fear of dying suddenly in my Sleep, which and, heaven only knows! which alone had seduced me into the fatal habit of taking enormous quantities of Laudanum.[29]

The causes truly motivating any case of drug addiction are always too manifold and complex for categorical definition. In S.T.C.'s case his history of chronic rheumatic disease undoubtedly played an important part in his recourse to narcotics, but his addiction cannot be attributed to this factor alone. As he had confessed to George Coleridge, as early as 1794, his over-ruling inclination, always, was to evade "the bitterness of Truth in . . . soul-enervating Reveries." Opium was his vehicle for this evasion.

However, we should hesitate to attach the word 'guilt' to drug-addiction. Samuel Taylor Coleridge, in common with the rest of us, had no real choice in the matter of deciding who, and what, he was fundamentally to be. We none of us select for ourselves those mysterious congenital blueprints which we bring into the world as individual, computer-programmed pilot-guides to our future: directives irrevocably built in to each of us before we are expelled into orbit from the amniotic launch-pad. Nor do we select the environment or incidents of our shaping early years.

S.T.C. was responsible neither for his predisposition towards certain kinds of disease, nor for his neurotically inadequate personality which required constant propping. Treatment for the disease brought him into contact with morphine, that most insidious of props.

Opium cannot be dismissed as a tragic habit which is but briefly mentioned as one of the darker passages in Coleridge's life and then put aside as irrelevant to Coleridge the poet-philosopher, Coleridge the thinker, Coleridge the Christian, Coleridge the plagiarist, Coleridge the friend of Wordsworth, and all the other facets of him which are wrenched out of the context of the whole man and subjected to isolated scrutiny. Although we insist upon drawing categorical distinctions between the body and the mind, thought and feeling, intellect and instinct, these distinctions are the products of popular prejudice. Man is total, every part of him integrated; he cannot be divided into isolated provinces. If the balance of his chemistry is disturbed by massive invasion by a drug, then his entire system and every process controlled by that system, including his mind and his personality, will reflect the influence of that drug. To study Coleridge from any aspect without taking opium into constant consideration is to ignore the clue without which there can be no correct understanding or interpretation.

Opium was an essential part of Samuel Taylor Coleridge. He and opium travelled literally as blood-brothers for close on forty years of his entire sixty-two. The central action of the greater part of these forty years was almost unremitting struggle against a devastating tyranny and an even more devastating burden of guilt arising from his obsessive self-reproach for wasted gifts and ingratitude to the Maker who had so liberally endowed him, all to such abortive purpose:

> I languish away my Life in misery, unutterably wretched from the gnawing of the Disease, and almost equally miserable from the Fear of the Remedy. —or—harassed by the Disease, and miserable from the Fear of the Remedy.

> While by the Delay not only the Remedy becomes more difficult, & the Fear consequently greater, in addition to the growing exacerbation of the Disease, but there is regularly annexed to it the pangs of Self-reproach & blackning Despair from the Delay.
> And sapp'd Resolves, the rotten Banks of Fools against the swelling Tide of Habit.[30]

It was a servitude beyond description, a burden of intolerable torment. Added to it was the knowledge that he was to be seen not only by the world at large but, much more distressingly, by his own children as an abject failure. He developed a festering sense of isolation, feeling himself a social outcast. Years previously he had prophetically described the fate that had now overtaken him:

> Ah! well-a-day, what evil looks
> Had I from old and young!
> Instead of the Cross the Albatross
> About my neck was hung.[31]

IV

The Shaping Years
(October 1772–October 1791)

> The entire man . . . is to be seen in the cradle of the child.
>
> Gillman, *Life*

> Samuel Taylor Coleridge was the youngest child of the Reverend John Coleridge, Vicar of the parish of Ottery St Mary, in the county of Devon, and master of Henry the Eighth's Free Grammar school in that town. His mother's name was Ann Bowdon. He was born at Ottery on the 21st of October 1772, "about eleven o'clock in the forenoon" as his father the Vicar has, with a rather curious particularity, entered it in the register.
>
> Henry Nelson Coleridge, S.T.C.'s nephew and son-in-law, in his preface to *Table Talk of Samuel Taylor Coleridge* (1835).

IN 1797 S.T.C., then aged twenty-five, commenced a series of autobiographical letters[1] to Thomas Poole, who was to receive a letter every Monday morning. Needless to say, his correspondent being S.T.C., he didn't. Five letters in the series arrived, all told, over a period of twelve months and got S.T.C. up to 1782 and the start of his schooldays at Christ's Hospital. There the experiment in autobiography stuck; S.T.C. had become infatuated by William Wordsworth and engulfed in *The Ancient Mariner*.

The Reverend John Coleridge was twice married. By his first wife he had three daughters; by his second, Ann Bowdon, who came from an ancient family of Exmoor yeomen, he had ten children, of whom S.T.C. was the youngest.

S.T.C., who grew up to dislike his mother, described her tersely to Poole, thus: "My Mother was an admirable Economist, and managed exclusively." He also referred briefly, in passing, to her pride and spirit of aggrandising her family. But upon the memory of his father he dwelt long and tenderly in the autobiographical letters, and during his years of residence with the Gillmans he loved to recount anecdotes about him, repeating these "till the tears ran down his face, from the fond recollection of his beloved parent."[2]

According to S.T.C., his father was distinguished by his learning, good-heartedness, absentness of mind, and excessive ignorance of the world (S.T.C. added that, when occasion demanded, his father could be a good man of business). He was spoken of in his parish as a dear, good old man, devoted to his books, his flock and his scholars. Although desperately absent-minded he was a most valuable pastor, celebrated for his sermons, in the course of which he not infrequently lapsed into Hebrew which greatly impressed his rural congregations. As a schoolmaster he manifested the same simplicity and honesty of purpose that he did as a pastor. "My father was not a first-rate Genius—he was however a first-rate Christian," S.T.C. liked to tell Gillman.

From which parent S.T.C. inherited a predisposition towards neurosis it is impossible to say; the information about his background is far too scanty. Undoubtedly his was a highly neurotic personality. He emerged as the family genius, but he was also the family embarrassment. Once he left school he quickly developed into a black sheep and there is clear evidence in letters that, in his early twenties, his behaviour appeared so irrational that his brothers entertained grave doubts of his sanity and at one point considered having him placed under restraint in a private asylum.

It is significant, genetically, that of S.T.C.'s own three surviving children, two, the brilliant Hartley and the even more brilliant Sara, were markedly neurotic; Hartley became an alcoholic, albeit a most scholarly and poetic one, while Sara, in the wake of the strain of child-bearing, was severely incapacitated for a lengthy period by what would probably be described today as an acute anxiety-neurosis.

S.T.C.'s account of his brothers and one sister deserves quotation because it provides such an excellent portrait of a family of the professional class of that period:

My eldest Brother's name was John: he went over to the East Indies in the Company's Service; he was a successful Officer, & a brave one, I have heard: he died of consumption there about 8 years ago. My second Brother was called William—he went to Pembroke College, Oxford; and afterwards was assistant to Mr Newcome's School, at Hackney. He died of a putrid fever the year before my Father's death, & just as he was on the eve of marriage with Miss Jane Hart, the eldest Daughter of a very wealthy druggist in Exeter. —My third Brother, James, has been in the army since the age of sixteen—has married a woman of fortune—and now lives at Ottery St Mary, a respectable Man. My Brother Edward, the wit of the Family, went to Pembroke College; & afterwards, to Salisbury, as assistant to Dr Skinner; he married a woman 20 years older than his Mother. She is dead: & he now lives at Ottery St Mary, an idle Parson. My fifth Brother, George, was educated at Pembroke . . . and from thence went to Mr Newcome's, Hackney, on the death of William. He stayed there . . . [ten] . . . years [after which he became Chaplain Priest and Master of the King's

School, Ottery St Mary] . . . and has lately married Miss Jane Hart, who with beauty, & wealth, had remained a faithful Widow to the memory of William for 16 years. —My Brother George is a man of reflective mind . . . He possesses Learning in a greater degree than any of the family, excepting myself. His manners are grave, & hued over with a tender sadness. In his moral character he approaches every way nearer to Perfection than any man I ever knew—indeed, he is worth the whole family in a Lump. My Sixth Brother, Luke (indeed the seventh, for one Brother, the second, died in his Infancy, & I had forgot to mention him) was bred as a Medical Man— he married Miss Sara Hart: and died at the age of . . . [25] . . . The 8th Child was a Sister, Anne—she died a little after my brother Luke—aged 21 . . . The 9th Child was called Francis: he went out as a Midshipman, under Admiral Graves—his Ship lay on the Bengal Coast—& he accidentally met his brother John—who took him to Land, & procured him a Commission in the Army. —He shot himself . . . in a delirious fever brought on by his excessive exertions at the siege of Seringapatam: at which his conduct had been so gallant, that Lord Cornwallis payed him a high compliment in the presence of the army, & presented him with a valuable gold Watch, which my Mother now has. —All my Brothers are remarkably handsome; but they were as inferior to Francis as I am to them. He went by the name of 'the handsome Coleridge'.

The discrepancy in age between himself and his brothers, save Francis, with whom he did not get on well, prevented S.T.C. from forming close and early family ties which would have helped to train him in the important art of personal relationships. He suffered throughout his adult life from the effects of an emotionally isolated childhood, as is not infrequently the case with the youngest member of a large family.

My Father was very fond of me, and I was my Mother's darling—in consequence, I was very miserable. For Molly, who had nursed my Brother Francis, and was immoderately fond of him, hated me because my mother took more notice of me than Frank—and Frank hated me, because my mother gave me now & then a bit of cake, when he had none—quite forgetting that for one bit of cake which I had & he had not, he had twenty sops in the pan & pieces of bread & butter with sugar on them from Molly, from whom I received only thumps & ill names.

Frank had "a violent love" of beating S.T.C., looking with a strange mixture "of admiration & contempt" upon his precociously clever younger brother (Frank "hated books, and loved climbing, fighting, playing, & robbing orchards, to distraction"). As a result of bullying by Molly and beatings from Frank, together with what was clearly a situation of mutual jealousy between the two youngest members of the family, S.T.C. became "fretful, & timorous, & a tell-tale."

He was not helped by his remarkably scholastic precocity. In his second year he went to Dame School, his schoolmistress being Old Dame Key, a close relative of Sir Joshua Reynolds. By the end of 1775, S.T.C. could read the Bible. Because he was a timorous tell-tale he was constantly tormented by his father's schoolboys, so he avoided their company and consoled himself with books. By the age of seven he was steeped in the tales of Tom Hickathrift, Jack the Giant-killer and similar stories, and had read Belisarius, Robinson Crusoe and Philip Quarll. He then discovered the *Arabian Nights' Entertainments*, which made so keen an impression upon him that "I was haunted by spectres, whenever I was in the dark . . . My Father found out the effect, which these books had produced—and burnt them."

There can be little doubt that from this source sprang the monstrous Ebon Ebon Thalud and, with the greatest deference to Lowes,[3] almost certainly the obsessive fascination which Kubla Khan himself and Tartary held for S.T.C.:

> And all should cry, Beware! Beware!
> His flashing eyes, his floating hair!
> Weave a circle round him thrice,
> And close your eyes with holy dread . . .[4]

Enchantment of this potency springs from sources more profoundly rooted in the subconscious than from travel books read in early maturity.

One story from the *Arabian Nights* which S.T.C. recalled as having had an inordinate effect upon him, childhood dreamwise, was that of a man who was compelled to seek for a pure virgin. The effect that this tale had upon him may well have been even more profound and lasting than he realised. Throughout his life, S.T.C.'s ideal woman was a mild maiden of total innocence. It was, he declared, "the perfection of woman to be characterless. Everyone wishes a Desdemona or Ophelia for a wife,—creatures who, though they may not always understand you, do always feel you, and feel with you."[5]

Throughout his life he attempted to pour flesh-and-blood women into the vapid mould of meek-eyed, characterless "creatures." The results were inevitably catastrophic, both for himself and the women concerned. With men, too, he blundered for the same reason; his hopeless romanticism betrayed him into viewing people not as they really were, but as he wished them to be; he was always making "Romances out of men's characters,"[6] as he called it.

S.T.C. developed into what he described as a mopey, dreamy, lonely child, indisposed to communal games and play. Sometimes when (as he put it to Poole) his spirits came upon him suddenly in a flood he would run up and down the church-yard, acting over all the roles that he had been reading, fighting hectic duels with the docks, nettles and rank grasses.

I was fretful, and inordinately passionate, and as I could not play at anything, and was slothful, I was despised & hated by the boys; and because I could read & spell, & had, I may truly say, a memory & understanding forced into almost unnatural ripeness, I was flattered & wondered at by all the old women—& so I became very vain, and despised most of the boys, that were at all near my own age—and before I was eight years old, I was a *character*—sensibility, imagination, vanity, sloth, & feelings of deep & bitter contempt for almost all who traversed the orbit of my understanding, were even then prominent & manifest.

He continued at Dame School until 1778, because he was too small in size to go to his father's grammar school (where, doubtless, his unpopularity with the other boys would have exposed him to bullying). In his seventh year he was finally admitted to grammar school and soon outstripped all his contemporaries.

During that year he caught "a dangerous putrid fever" which his brother George, eight years his senior, had at the same time. S.T.C.'s mother related a story of him, belonging to this period of illness, which S.T.C. repeated to Poole as his first witticism; it has greater significance as an indication of his ineradicable imprinting with the Christian faith:

During my fever I asked why Lady Northcote (our neighbour) did not come and see me. —My mother said, she was afraid of catching the fever— I was piqued and answered—Ah—Mamma! the four Angels round my bed ain't afraid of catching it. —I suppose you know the old prayer—

> Matthew! Mark! Luke! & John!
> God bless the bed which I lie on . . .

This prayer I said nightly—& most firmly believed the truth of it. Frequently have I, half-awake and half-asleep, my body diseased & fevered by my imagination, seen armies of ugly Things bursting in upon me, & these four angels keeping them off.

Round about the time of his eighth birthday there occurred the episode which was probably the most important single incident in S.T.C.'s life:

I had asked my mother one evening to cut my cheese *entire* so that I might toast it; this was no easy matter, it being a *crumbly* cheese—My mother however did it— / I went into the garden for some thing or other, and in the mean time my Brother Frank *minced* my cheese, 'to disappoint the favorite.' I returned, saw the exploit, and in an agony of passion flew at Frank—he pretended to have been seriously hurt by my blow, flung himself on the ground, and there lay with outstretched limbs—I hung over him moaning & in a great fright—he leaped up, & with a horse-laugh gave me a severe blow in the face—I seized a knife, and was running at him, when my Mother came in & took me by the arm — / I expected a flogging— & struggling from her ran away, to a hill at the bottom of which the Otter flows—about one mile from Ottery. —There I stayed; my rage died away; but my obstinacy vanquished my fears—and taking out a little shilling book which had, at the end, morning and evening prayers, I very devoutly repeated them—thinking *at the same time* with inward & gloomy satisfaction, how miserable my Mother must be!—I distinctly remember my feelings when I saw a Mr Vaughan pass over the Bridge, at about a furlong's distance—and how I watched the Calves in the fields beyond the river. It grew dark—& I fell asleep—it was towards the latter end of October—& it proved a dreadful stormy night— / I felt the cold in my sleep, and dreamt that I was pulling the blanket over me, & actually pulled over me a dry thorn bush, which lay on the hill—in my sleep I had rolled from the top of the hill to within three yards of the River . . . I awoke several times, and finding myself wet & stiff, and cold, closed my eyes again that I might forget it.

The memory of this night never left him. Twenty-four years later, when he was living at Keswick, he entered in his notebook:

Tuesday Night, July 19, 1803—Intensely hot day—left off a waistcoat, & for yarn wore silk stockings—about 9 o'clock had unpleasant chillinesses—heard a noise . . . listened anxiously, found it was a Calf bellowing—instantly came on my mind that night, I slept out at Ottery—& the Calf in the Field across the river whose lowing had so deeply impressed me—Chill + Child + Calf-lowing.[7]

In the meantime his mother waited about half-an-hour, expecting his return when his sulks had evaporated; but the child did not return and so an alarm was raised by the now distracted parents. At ten that night he was cried by the Ottery town-crier and also in two nearby villages and a reward was offered for his recovery. Half of Ottery stayed up all night, combing the district. The ponds and the river were dragged, but all without result. At about five the following morning Sir Stafford Northcote, who had been out all night, resolved to make one more search and, as he crossed the fields above the river, he heard S.T.C. crying. The child was so stiff with cold and exposure that he could not walk. He was carried home and put to bed and within a day or two appeared to have recovered; but his health had been impaired by the adventure and he was weakly and "subject to the ague for many years after."

This adventure was not only of vital importance because of the undermining damage to his health; it was also significant because it laid down the blueprint, as it were, of his lifelong pattern as an incurable bolter.

Thus the first, vital, seven to eight years of S.T.C.'s life were fraught with experiences, impressions and developments which virtually guaranteed a rough passage for him through the years that lay ahead.

My Father . . . had . . . resolved that I should be a Parson . . . he used to take me on his knee, and hold long conversations with me . . . I walked with him one evening from a farmer's home . . . & he told me the names of the stars—and how Jupiter was a thousand times larger than our world— and that the other twinkling stars were Suns that had worlds rolling round them—& when I came home, he shewed me how they rolled round.

This close and loving relationship came abruptly to an end when, within three weeks of S.T.C.'s tenth birthday, the Reverend John Coleridge collapsed and died suddenly, from what appears to have been a classic coronary attack, on the night of October 4, 1781. The effects of his death were calamitous for the security of S.T.C. From that date onward he embarked upon a Stephen Dedalus-like search for a substitute father, which lasted until he entered the Gillmans' home thirty-five years later.

The funeral took place on October 10 and shortly afterwards the Coleridge family moved house. S.T.C. remained living at Ottery with his mother, as a day-scholar to his father's successor, until the spring of 1782, when Judge Buller, whose own father had been the Reverend John Coleridge's patron, procured S.T.C. a Christ's Hospital Presentation.

Accordingly, S.T.C. travelled to London, where he lived for ten weeks with an uncle, his mother's brother, a tobacconist by trade and a great tavern man by inclination, who was very proud of his precocious little nephew and took him from coffee-house to coffee-house and tavern to tavern, where S.T.C. drank, talked and disputed as if he had been a man, and was exclaimed over as a prodigy. Thus, having his head turned, he spent the summer.

He was entered in the books of Christ's Hospital on July 8, 1782. The day came when he donned the famous uniform of long blue habit and yellow stockings which gave the Christ's Hospital scholars their name of "Blue-coat boys" and he was sent down to Hertford, where there were then schooled about three hundred of the younger boys. There, on the whole, he was happy, for the children were well fed and cared for. He remained in Hertford six weeks. In September 1782 he was drafted up to the great school in London.

On arrival at the London school S.T.C. was placed in the second ward, or dormitory, then called Jefferies's Ward, in the lower Grammar School. There were five schools; a mathematical, a grammar, a drawing, a reading, and a writing school. "All very large Buildings," remembered S.T.C., recapturing for a moment the scale of an undersized ten-year-old, newly plunged into a great public school.

After Hertford's homely atmosphere the child found his change in surroundings traumatic. The discipline at Christ's Hospital in those days was ultra-Spartan, the mood monastic. All domestic ties were to be put aside. Once, when young S.T.C. was crying, on the first day of his return after the holidays, Mr Boyer (or as S.T.C. sometimes wrote it, Bowyer), the splenetic head of the upper Grammar School, descended upon him with: "Boy! the school is your father! Boy! the school is your mother! Boy! the school is your brother! the school is your sister! the school is your first cousin, and your second cousin, and all the rest of your relations! Let's have no more crying!"[8]

S.T.C., drawing a portrait of his early years for Gillman, saw himself in retrospect as a "Depressed, moping, friendless, poor orphan, half starved (at that time the portion of food to the Bluecoats was cruelly insufficient for those who had no friends to supply them)."

Charles Lamb, one of the boys at school with S.T.C., was an example of a lucky Bluecoat, for, with family and friends near the school, he was able to visit them almost as often as he wished and had all kinds of extras in the way of food and small comforts sent in.

S.T.C. was less fortunate; his closest relatives were a long way distant and could not keep him supplied with a steady flow of daily comforts. Nonetheless, his letters written to his mother and brothers from school in the years 1785–1789 make it clear that, when he was reminiscing to the Gillmans, he must have overdrawn his schoolboy plight, for in these family letters he mentions a food box, gifts in money and kind, and refers to his London uncle and aunt in a manner which suggests that they, at least, saw him sometimes, while, "Miss Cabrier [sic] and my Cousin Bowdon behave more kindly to me than I can express. I dine there every Saturday."[9] (Miss Cabriere was his cousin Betsy Bowdon's companion).

It is extremely unlikely that the relatives and friends who took such a kindly and, apparently, continuous interest in S.T.C. during his last four years at school would have neglected him during his first three years there.

During his first two years at the school, however, S.T.C. had none of his immediate Ottery family in London and it was those two years, between the ages of ten and twelve, that were for him probably the most traumatic of his schooldays. In 1784 his brother George, eight years his senior, took his degree at Pembroke and soon after joined the teaching staff of Newcome's Academy, Hackney. He was now strategically placed to keep a fatherly eye on S.T.C. and this he did; obviously, as the letters show, with a sympathetic understanding and wise tolerance rather remarkable in a young man himself only in his early twenties. S.T.C. told his brother Luke: "I can never sufficiently express my gratitude to my Brother George. *He* is father, brother, and every thing to me."[10] Upon George, S.T.C. bestowed all his pent up affections. The older brother found himself proxy parent to one of the most entertainingly endearing and, in due course, hair-raisingly troublesome characters conceivable.

The earliest known letter of S.T.C., written from Christ's Hospital in 1785 and dated February 4, is to his mother, in acknowledgment of a letter from her and of gifts from friends:

Dear Mother,—I received your letter with pleasure on the second instant
. . . I also with gratitude received the two handkerchiefs and the half-a-
crown from Mr Badcock, to whom I would be glad if you would give my
thanks. I shall be more careful of the somme, as I now consider were it not
for my kind friends I should be as destitute of many little necessaries as
some of my schoolfellows are; and Thank God and my relations for them!
My brother Luke saw Mr James Sorrel, who gave my brother a half-a-crown
from Mrs Susendon, but mentioned not a word of the plumb cake . . . My
aunt was so kind as to accommodate me with a box.[11]

The stiff formality of the letter must in part be attributable to the dutiful
respect which children displayed towards their parents in those days, but
nonetheless a certain note of cold dislike creeps through (the letter should
be compared with those which S.T.C. presently wrote to Mrs Evans, the
widowed mother of Tom Evans, one of S.T.C.'s school-fellows). It would
be most helpful to know why S.T.C. so disliked his mother, but we have
no real information on this score. Possibly he resented the fact that she had
sent him away from home, following his father's death, regarding this as a
gesture of rejection. But the active dislike of a parent usually has earlier
roots.

S.T.C.'s worst school memories were of the Whole Day Leaves, as they
were called, when the scholars were turned out of school for the entire day,
whether they had homes or friends to go to, or not. S.T.C.'s London
relatives were not prepared to entertain him on every occasion that he was
off school, so he, with companions in a similar plight, was obliged, on winter
day holidays, to prowl aimlessly about the streets, standing nose pressed to
shop-windows or, as a last resort, visiting the dreary lions in the Tower
menagerie, to whose levée the Bluecoat boys were by ancient privilege
admitted.

In the summer things were better, for the boys could go swimming in the
New River; but the joys of the day's freedom were marred by hunger, for
between meagre breakfast and meagre supper the boys had nothing to eat
and their young appetites were painfully sharpened by the swimming and
exercise.

There is a significant notebook entry for April–May, 1802, commenting
upon:

The great importance of breeding up children *happy* to at least 15 or 16
illustrated in my always dreaming of Christ Hospital and when not quite
well having all those uneasy feelings which I had at School / feelings of
Easter Monday &c—[12]

Mr Gillman, with his trained medical eye, was to describe S.T.C. as
blessed by nature with buoyancy of spirits, so that "even when suffering, he
deceived the partial observer." This joyousness of temperament became

almost wholly obscured in S.T.C.'s tragic middle-age, lost to him during the blackness of severe ill-health and drug-reliance; while as a child and early adolescent it was partially eclipsed by his constant sense of isolation. He took refuge from this in a fantasy world and remained what, essentially, he had been from his eighth year; a book-worm and day-dreamer.

A friendly adult made him a gift of a subscription to a circulating library in Cheapside. "I read," said S.T.C., "through the catalogue, folios and all, whether I understood them, or did not understand them, running all risks in skulking out to get the two volumes which I was entitled to have daily. Conceive what I must have been at fourteen . . . My whole being was, with eyes closed to every object of present sense, to crumple myself up in a sunny corner, and read, read, read; fancy myself on Robinson Crusoe's island, finding a mountain of plumb-cake, and eating a room for myself, and then eating it into the shapes of tables and chairs—hunger and fancy!"[13]

His talents and intellectual capacity placed him, without endeavour, at the head of every class at school; for although he was an undisciplined, even an idle scholar, his calibre was such that he could not help but outshine the other boys. "But the difference between me and my form-fellows, in our lessons and exercises, bore no proportion to the measureless difference between me and them in the wide, wild, wilderness of useless, unarranged book-knowledge and book thoughts."[14]

The headmaster, the Reverend James Boyer, known by the boys (behind his back) as 'Jemmy Boyer', was a fine classical scholar and gifted teacher, and a man of keen discernment in matters of scholastic potential. He was, in addition, of highly choleric disposition and an ardent flogger. His favourite adjuration, "'Ods my life, man, what d'ye mean?" was more often than not followed by a bellow of "Sirrah! I'll flog you!" or, "Bring that boy here, and I'll flog him!" Indeed, these words were said to be so habitual to him that on one occasion, when some female relation or retainer entered his classroom enquiring for one of the boys and, being told to go from the room immediately, still lingered in the doorway, Boyer roared, "Bring that woman here, and I'll flog her."[15] It is possible that the female in question was Mrs Boyer herself—an apparently imperturbable woman whose kindness S.T.C. still remembered some fifty years later. She was not afraid of intervening on the part of the boys, but it had to be done in an oddly *Looking Glass* manner. To quote S.T.C. on the subject:

> No tongue can express good Mrs Bowyer. Val Le Grice and I were once going to be flogged for some domestic misdeed, and Bowyer was thundering away at us by way of prologue, when Mrs B looked in, and said, "Flog them soundly, sir, I beg!" This saved us. Bowyer was so nettled at the interruption that he growled out, "Away, woman! away!" and we were let off.[16]

Boyer was more highly inflamed on some days than others and these, the boys declared, were the days when he wore his 'Passy wig' (passionate wig).

Flogging, being then so prevalent and accepted as both proper and necessary by almost everyone from high to low, aroused little of the aversion that
it does today and none of the suspicion. Whether it was the floggings
that did it, or not, it is certain that the much-flogged S.T.C. grew up
to be a practitioner of a subtle yet hopeless masochism and the inevitable
accompanying sadism: he never resorted to physical violence, but he
inflicted exquisite mental tortures upon all those persons whom he most
loved.

That S.T.C. himself associated the floggings of his adolescence with
some of the troubles of his nightmare-haunted maturity is clear from the
euphemistic tribute to Boyer in *Biographia Literaria*: S.T.C. referred to his
old headmaster as

> a man, whose severities, even now, not seldom furnish the dreams by which
> the blind fancy could fain interpret to the mind the painful sensation of
> distempered sleep, but neither lessen nor diminish the deep sense of my
> moral and intellectual obligations.

We all have our Black Museums, where lie rusty and dusty mementos of
violence inflicted both upon ourselves and others; disturbing objects repos-
ing half-forgotten on the dim shelves of the inner cabinets of our subconscious minds. The passy wig was, it seems, one of the blackest items of
S.T.C.'s museum furniture.

According to his own account he was brought early to the special attention of the febrile Boyer because, while still in the lower grammar school, he
precociously read Virgil for pleasure. Boyer made enquiries about the down-
at-heel child who mooned about, always glued to a book, his rough black
hair unkempt and the knees of his breeches unbuttoned. S.T.C.'s master
reported that the boy was markedly lethargic in class, invariably unable to
repeat a single parrot-learned rule of syntax, although he could give a rule
fluently in his own way. Boyer henceforth made S.T.C.'s classical education
a matter of personal concern, fortifying this individual tuition with un-
stinted floggings, generally with an extra cut at the end, "for," said he, to
the slovenly embryonic genius, "you are such an ugly fellow."[17]

In October, 1784 Coleridge's brother Luke, then aged nineteen, was
admitted to the London Hospital to walk the wards. Hospitals were very
much less formal places than they are now; S.T.C., visiting his brother,
apparently was allowed to play part-time medical student. "Every Saturday
I could make or obtain leave, to the London Hospital trudged I. O the bliss
if I was permitted to hold the plasters, or to attend to the dressings . . . I
became wild to be . . . a surgeon."[18]

But this was not to be, although Gillman, in his *Life*, observed that, in
his opinion, had S.T.C. entered the medical profession "he must have been
pre-eminent."

Introduction IV

With Luke, in spite of the age discrepancy, S.T.C. seems to have experienced, at last, some interchange of relaxed brotherly friendship and affection. But the period of training for medical students in those days was very much shorter than now; after twelve months Luke was finished with the wards of the London Hospital. In due course he entered medical practice at Thorverton, near Exeter (his career was but a short one, he died in 1890). After his departure from London, S.T.C. wrote to him: "I doubly lament your absence, as I now have no one, to whom I can open my heart in full confidence. I wish you would *remedy* that evil in keeping up an epistolory [sic] correspondence with me. It would in some measure supply the place of conversation."[19]

With his appetite thus whetted for, and then deprived of, the pleasures of an informal fraternal relationship, S.T.C. added a search for a brother to the search for a father. To be sure there was George, but he, as aforesaid, was more father than brother. Indeed, at this stage of S.T.C.'s career the father-search fell into a place of less importance than the brother-search; George was there to be father.

At the age of sixteen S.T.C. became Graecian, Christ's Hospital jargon for going into the top class of the Upper Grammar School. Graecians had studies of their own and this might explain S.T.C.'s sudden budding as a poet at this particular point. Poetry demands seclusion.

At the age of seventeen S.T.C. came heavily under the influence of the work of William Lisle Bowles (1762–1850), whose sonnets, first published in 1789, filled the boy with enthusiastic admiration. From Bowles he picked up bad habits of gush which it took him some time to lose. It was, as S.T.C. acknowledged in *Biographia Literaria*, from Boyer that he learned some of the basic, and toughest, truths about poetry: "I learnt from him that Poetry, even that of the loftiest, and, seemingly wildest odes, had a logic of its own, as severe as that of science; and more difficult, because more subtle, more complex, and dependent on more, and more fugitive causes."

S.T.C. was rightly to observe that his own juvenile verse did not contain anything that any other schoolboy might not have written.

By this time S.T.C. had received what he was to regard as the one just flogging of his career. Metaphysics had become passionately interesting to him; before long he had come under the influence of Voltaire on atheism, and the pantheism of Jacob Boehme's *Aurora*. The result was that he informed Boyer that he hated the thought of becoming a clergyman (the profession for which he was destined by the wish of his father). Boyer enquired "Why so?" "Because, to tell you the truth, sir," said S.T.C., "I am an infidel!" For this, without more ado, Boyer flogged him: "wisely, as I think,—soundly as I know. Any whining or sermonising would have gratified my vanity, and confirmed me in my absurdity; as it was, I was laughed at, and got heartily ashamed of my folly."[20]

The pious imprinting of his early childhood, reinforced by the most violent flogging of his career, confirmed S.T.C. in the Christian faith for life. Not that he did not expose his belief to the most rigorous intellectual probing; but there was in him a core of gut blind acceptance of Christianity which all the intellectual scrutiny in the world could never entirely dissipate. Matthew, Mark, Luke and John had taken up their stations at his infant bedside and there they would remain until he drew his last breath.

By his sixteenth year the quintessential S.T.C. was clearly emerging. He now always referred to himself by his initials, which he often wrote phonetically as Esteese, Esteesee or Esteesi. Only his own immediate family and his wife and her mother and sisters seem to have called him Samuel; it was a name that he detested and he did all he could to discourage its use:

> from my earliest years I have had a feeling of Dislike & Disgust connected with my own Christian Names: such a vile short plumpness, such a dull abortive smartness in the first Syllable, & this so harshly contrasted by the obscurity & indefiniteness of the syllable Vowel, and the feebleness of the uncovered liquid, with which it ends—the wabble it makes, & staggering between a diss—& a tri-syllable—& the whole name sounding as if you were abeeceeing. S.M.U.L.—altogether it is perhaps the worst combination, of which vowels & consonants are susceptible.[21]

The name Coleridge, on the other hand, pleased him greatly (his comments upon it give a very clear and accurate idea of how it should be pronounced):

> I think, that the word Cō lĕ rīdge (amphimacron = long on both sides) has a noble *verbal physiognomy* . . . it is one of the vilest Belzebubb cries of Detraction to pronounce it Col-ridge, or Cŏllĕridge, or even Cōle-ridge. It is & must be to all honest and honorable [sic] men, a trisyllabic Amphimacer, — — ![22]

Charles Lamb and other friends of his schooldays and youth called him Col. The Wordsworths seem always to have referred to him as Coleridge, with rare exceptions, such as when Wordsworth, in Book Six of *The Prelude*, writes

> Share with us thy fresh spirits, whether gift
> Of gales Estesian or of tender thoughts.[23]

By sixteen S.T.C. was certainly already a great talker, in best Esteesian philosophical vein, and verse flowed almost incessantly from his pen. George was the recipient of Latin odes, languishing sonnets, verses gay, scholarly, mildly bawdy. A letter to Luke Coleridge, of May 12, 1787, is in every way typical of S.T.C., either at fifteen or fifty. It commences with an elaborate apology for not having written before: "Five times have I sat down with fixed resolution to write to you; and five times have I torn it before I have writ Half."[24] It contains personal news, a digression on atheism and a quotation from Addison, a refusal of the offer of Burke's *Art of Speaking* because S.T.C. had already made himself acquainted with it and did not think much of it, a request for Young's *Night Thoughts*; and, as conclusion, S.T.C. transcribed two of his own poems.

He was already, in Charles Lamb's famous phrase, "Samuel Taylor Coleridge—Logician, Metaphysician, Bard!"[25] He fascinated chance passers-by in the school cloisters with his talk.

At the age of sixteen, or thereabouts, he fell in love; or, more accurately, imagined himself to have fallen in love. This first affair might stand as a blueprint for his subsequent ones; it was, according to him, desperate; it was, as he much later confessed in his notebook, almost wholly of his own romantic invention; his wooing was conducted almost exclusively in literary form; and it ended disastrously for both parties, but particularly so for the girl.

She was Mary Evans, the oldest of the three sisters of S.T.C.'s friend, Tom Evans, who entered Christ's Hospital on May 7, 1784. S.T.C., as an upper boy, had the responsibility of "protecting" him. In due course Tom took S.T.C. home and introduced him to his mother and his sisters; they received him into their family circle with unaffected kindness. Gradually he came to regard Mrs Evans as somewhat more of a mother than his real mother, while with Mary he inevitably fell sentimentally in love. The attachment was in the nature of an uncontrollable explosion of bewildered excitement: reared in an exclusively single-sex society he had no idea of how to confront a young girl of his own class without emotional confusion. As he was to muse some twenty years later:

> so it would be with a man bred up in a Wilderness by unseen Beings . . .
> how beautiful would not the first other man appear, whom he saw . . . he
> would . . . attribute to the man all the divine attributes of humanity, tho'
> haply it should be a very ordinary or even almost ugly man, compared with
> a hundred others. Many of us have felt this with respect to women, who
> have been bred up where few are to be seen.[26]

A letter survives, probably written by S.T.C. just before Whitsun, 1789, to Brother George:

> You will excuse me reminding you that, as our Holidays commence next
> week, and I shall go out a good deal, a good pair of breeches will be no
> inconsiderable accession to my appearance. For though my present pair
> are excellent for the purposes of drawing Mathematical Figures on them . . .
> yet they are not so well adapted for the female eye . . . P.S. Can you let me

have them time enough for readaption before Whitmondy, I mean, that they may be made up for me before that time?[27]

At least half of S.T.C.'s eighteenth year was spent in the Christ's Hospital sick ward, seriously ill with jaundice and rheumatic fever; the latter following upon an escapade during one of the whole day leaves when he swam, fully dressed, across the New River and wandered about for the rest of the day with his sodden clothes drying upon his back. From this attack of rheumatic fever, as Gillman rightly pointed out, "could be dated all his bodily sufferings in future life."

During this illness laudanum was certainly administered to him. There is his categorical observation to George, made in November 1791: "Opium never used to have any ill effects upon me—but it has upon many."[28] This suggests an acquaintance with laudanum in regular and not inconsiderable quantities, over a sustained period of time—precisely the kind of experience of the drug that we would expect for a person of that era who had undergone medical treatment for a severe and protracted illness. It was, of course, also the kind of experience which would leave the patient orientated towards if not addicted to the drug; certainly, it was the kind of experience which, classically, would act as a prelude to drug addiction given a certain type of vulnerable personality.

Knowing, as we do, S.T.C.'s insecurity and emotional inadequacy and taking into further consideration the fact that he was now emerging as an embryonic poet in the Romantic vein and, furthermore, bearing in mind the part which opium and wild dreams and kindred extravagances of fancy played in the climate of the time, it is not irresponsible to assume that he, in great probability, became addicted to opium (in the strictest meaning of the term) during his final terms at school. Most certainly he went up to Cambridge as an undergraduate orientated towards opium and drug experience.

During his nineteenth year, in his last months at school, S.T.C. had his first active sexual experience (not, it goes without saying, with Mary Evans, or any other girl of his own class or kind). His farewell sonnet to Christ's Hospital hints at this experience, while a letter to Humphrey Davy, dated May 20, 1801, states that his nineteenth to his twenty-second year was the period that, as S.T.C. put it, comprised his unchastities.

Davy had asked if S.T.C. recalled anything of a "woman called Hays *or* Taylor." S.T.C. replied:

No Lady of either of these names do I recollect . . . I went first thro' all the names of *virtuous* Women, I had ever known, as far as my Memory would assist—but it was all Blank. Then (& verily I, a Husband & a Father, & for the last seven years of my Life a very Christian Liver, felt oddly while I did it) then, I say, I went as far as memory served, thro' all the loose women I had known, from my 19th to my 22nd year, that being the period that

83

comprizes my Unchastities; but as names are not the most recollectible of
our Ideas, & the name of a loose Woman not that one of her adjuncts, to
which you pay the most attention, I could here recollect no *name* at all—
no, not even a face nor feature. I remembered my vices, & the times
thereof, but not their objects.[29]

S.T.C. was admitted to Jesus College, Cambridge, as a sizar on February
5, 1791 and began his residence in October of that year. His farewell to
Christ's Hospital was genuinely a melancholy one. The years there had
developed in him all the classical symptoms of what might be termed the
English public-school syndrome. In his worst nightmares he was to dream
that he was back there; his outstanding memories of the place included
savage floggings, semi-starvation, acute home-sickness, loneliness, and very
possibly some kind of forcible experience of homosexuality. Yet he wept
when he left, returned there repeatedly during his undergraduate days,
remained in lifelong touch with old schoolfellows, never ceased to show
avid interest in school news and, when a nephew was left fatherless, did all
that he could to get "poor dear little Robert Lovell" into Christ's Hospital.
He marked his departure from school with a sonnet:

> Farewell parental scenes! a sad farewell!
> To you my grateful heart still fondly clings,
> Tho' fluttering round on Fancy's burnished wings
> Her tales of future Joy Hope loves to tell.
> Adieu, adieu! ye much lov'd cloisters pale!
> Ah! would those happy days return again,
> When 'neath your arches, free from every stain,
> I heard of guilt and wonder'd at the tale!
> Dear haunts! where oft my simple lays I sang,
> Listening meanwhile the echoings of my feet,
> Lingering I quit you, with as great a pang,
> As when ere while, my weeping childhood, torn
> By early sorrow from my native seat,
> Mingled its tears with hers—my widow'd Parent lorn.[30]

Thus Samuel Taylor Coleridge, nineteen-year-old philosopher-poet, left
the scenes of childhood and adolescence; bidding them goodbye with
nostalgic reluctance, yet turning towards the future with confidence:

> O the Joys, that came down shower-like,
> Of Beauty, Truth, and Liberty,
> When I was young.[31]

So he leapt forward into a future that seemed bright with good omens:
great gifts of mind, high ambition, activity of body. His health seemed
recovered; his spirits were high; all was right with his world:

The ship was cheered, the harbour cleared,
Merrily did we drop
Below the kirk, below the hill,
Below the light house top.

The sun came up upon the left,
Out of the sea came he!
And he shone bright, and on the right
Went down into the sea.[32]

No Graecian ever left Christ's Hospital with a better prospect of good wind and fair weather. But, concealed by the fog of the future, the albatross already circled on great pinions; the ice floated mast-high; all the beauties and terrors and mysteries of the incredible circumnavigation awaited S.T.C.

PART ONE

A Country in Romance

Bliss was it in that dawn to be alive,
But to be young was very heaven!—Oh, times,
In which the meagre, stale, forbidding ways
Of custom, law, and statute, took at once
The attraction of a country in Romance!
When Reason seemed the most to assert her rights
When most intent on making of herself
A prime enchantress—to assist the work,
Which then was going forward in her name! . . .
Not in Utopia . . .
But in the very world, which is the world
Of all of us.

French Revolution as it Appeared to
Enthusiasts at its Commencement
William Wordsworth

INTERLUDE

Portraits of S.T.C. as a young man:

Random entry in his notebook; possibly an observation that he had over-heard about himself:

> Remark that young Man's Eyebrows too very beautiful—
> NB 292 G.289

Self portrait in November 1796:

my face, unless when animated by immediate eloquence, expresses great sloth, & great, indeed almost ideotic, good nature. 'Tis a mere carcase of a face: fat, flabby, & expressive chiefly of inexpression. —Yet, I am told, that my eyes, eyebrows, & forehead are physiognomically good . . . As to my shape, 'tis a good shape enough, if measured—but my gait is awkward, & the walk, & the *Whole man* indicates *Indolence capable* of *energies*. I am, and ever have been, a great reader—& I have read almost everything—a library-cormorant—I am *deep* in all out of the way books . . . Metaphysics, & Poetry, & 'Facts of mind'—(i.e. Accounts of all the strange phantoms that ever possessed your philosophy-dreamers . . .), are my darling Studies. —In short, I seldom read except to amuse myself—& I am almost always reading. — . . . .
I cannot breathe thro' my nose—so my mouth, with sensual thick lips, is almost always open. In conversation I am impassioned . . . but I am ever so swallowed up in the thing, that I perfectly forget my *opponent*. Such am I.

> Letter to John Thelwall,
> November 19, 1796.

He is pale and thin, has a wide mouth, thick lips, and not very good teeth, longish loose-growing half-curling rough black hair . . . His eye is large and full, not dark but grey . . . He has fine dark eyebrows and an overhanging forehead.

> Dorothy Wordsworth, letter to Mary
> Hutchinson, June, 1797.

CHAPTER ONE

JESUS MAN

(October 1791–December 1793)

"HERE I AM—*videlicet*—Jesus College,"[1] S.T.C. wrote triumphantly to George, on October 16, 1791.

Term had scarcely begun, Cambridge seemed deserted. On arrival S.T.C. went to Pembroke to enquire for the only man he knew in Cambridge, a former Bluecoat boy, three years S.T.C.'s senior and revered by him when at school—Thomas Fanshaw Middleton, a classical scholar of brilliance. Fortunately Middleton was in residence and proved amiable; he gave S.T.C. breakfast and conversation and in due course conducted him to Jesus.

Here things were very quiet—no Tutors, no lectures, no anything. Until a Tutor arrived to appoint S.T.C. rooms, he kept in the vacant rooms of an absent undergraduate; in Hall he knew nobody, so he ate alone and in silence, and then walked round to Pembroke and the company of Middleton.

This was a sober start. S.T.C., as usual brimming with admirable intentions, matched the solitude of these early days with inspired dedication to study. Brother George, *in loco parentis*, received encouraging progress reports; once a day S.T.C. had a mathematics lecture and in addition he read mathematics three hours a day (he had no affinity whatever for this subject, but a respectable degree in mathematics was necessary for anyone hoping to become a candidate for the classical medal). Classical lectures were rarely given, but, S.T.C. assured George, he read classics every evening, after tea, until he went to bed at eleven o'clock. He was reading Pindar, and composing Greek verse "like a mad dog".[2] In his leisure hours he translated Anacreon. A formidable scholastic timetable! Even S.T.C. himself had doubts about keeping it up, as he admitted to George: "If I were to read on as I do now—there is not the least doubt, that I should be Classical Medallist, and a very high Wrangler—but *Freshmen* always *begin* very furiously."[3]

In November 1791 S.T.C. was awarded a Rustat Scholarship, worth to him, he estimated, some twenty-seven pounds a year. He also had a Christ's Hospital exhibition of forty pounds a year. Mr Boyer had planned things so that ten pounds of the exhibition money was held back and S.T.C. was scarcely installed at Jesus before he ran short of cash and was trying to get George to advance him the ten pounds: "one feels cold, and naked, and shivering, and gelid, and chilly and such like synonimes—without a little money in one's pocket."[4]

Theoretically, S.T.C. should have been almost self-supporting, buttressed as he was with his exhibition and the Rustat, but things didn't work out that way. He quickly entangled himself in debts. Predominant were his Tutor's bills and a bill from the upholsterer who had furnished his college rooms for him a trifle over-lavishly.

It was easy to get into debt at Cambridge. Life was gay, with incessant wine-parties and suppers. Dr Pierce, the Master of Jesus, was on a protracted leave and S.T.C., with injudicious flippancy, informed George that: "There is no such thing as *discipline* at our college—There was once, they say—but so long ago, that no one remembers it."[5]

George, who had, after all, been an undergraduate himself, scented what was afoot and wrote a brotherly warning. This prompted a suspiciously over-hearty reply:

> My dear Brother, I assure you, I am an Œconomist. I keep no company—that is, I neither give nor receive invitations to wine parties . . . I eat no suppers. Middleton acts to me with great friendship . . . After he has taken his degree, he has promised to read Mathematics with me.[6]

Cambridge is a damp, bleak place, "the very palace of the winds,"[7] to quote S.T.C. Within a month of going up he had caught a violent cold and this rapidly had him confined to bed with a "fit of the Rheumatism."[8] George, too, was ill at this time and must have mentioned to S.T.C. that he had been dosed with laudanum, for S.T.C., in a sympathetic letter in late November, passed the significant remark: "Opium never used to have any ill effects upon me—but it has upon many."[9] (Above p. 83.)

Over Christmas of that year S.T.C. spent a fortnight with the Evans family at their London home in Villiers Street, a visit which proved "very potently medicinal."[10] Much of the magic of this cure doubtless lay in the charms of little Mary Evans.

A euphemistic letter to George made it pretty clear how things stood:

> I wish, my dear Brother, that sometime when you walk into town, you would call at Villiers Street—and take a dinner or dish of tea there. Mrs Evans has repeatedly expressed her wish, and I *too* have made a half promise, that you would. I assure you, you will find them not only a very amiable, but a very sensible family.[11]

Since George, later, seems to have been in personal touch with the Evanses it is not unreasonable to suppose that he availed himself of this invitation. Certainly he was soon perfectly aware of his brother's interest in Mary.

A veritable spate of letters now began to sparkle and gurgle between Jesus College, Cambridge, and Villiers Street. S.T.C. had not only discovered the charms of Mary; even more importantly he had found a family circle to which he could belong.

A letter of February 17, 1792, officially addressed to Mrs Evans, but quickly throwing aside that pretence and gaily exhorting the entire female Evans force, assured them that they had "the very first row in the front box of my Heart's theatre—and—God knows! *you are not crowded.*" Prophetically he told them: "There, my dear Spectators / you shall see what you shall see—Farce, Comedy, & Tragedy— . . . Come Ladies! will you not take your seats in this play house? Fool that I am! Are you not already there? Believe me, You are,—"[12]

He would lay his whole heart open to them, he said, and thereafter did— or almost. One thing he had to restrain himself from, an open declaration of love to Mary; this he was in no position to make. The whole family, however, comprehended the situation; and, as S.T.C. was a gentleman, and at Cambridge, and brilliant, and destined for the church and absolutely bound to become a bishop at least, his attentions to Mary were not discouraged.

Obviously, the Evans ladies found him tremendous fun apart from anything else, and he let himself go with gusto in his efforts to amuse. Some of his humour was decidedly earthy, in the literal as well as the figurative sense, as for example when he told them of his pipe-dream to hire a Cambridge garden for the summer; assuming, as he wrote, a comic mock-genteel semi-Cockney voice, unmistakable even two centuries later:

> It will be nice exercise. Your Advice. La! it will be so charming to walk out in one's own *garding*, and sit and drink Tea in an arbour, and pick pretty nosegays—To plant and transplant . . . Foh! Oh! 'twill be very *praty* to make water—I meant to say—to water the *garding* morning and eve—O La! give me your advice.

Then, resuming his own voice:

> Now suppose I conclude something in the manner, with which Mary concludes all her Letters to me—'*Believe me your sincere friend*, and dutiful humble servant to command'—
> Now I do hate that way of concluding a letter—'Tis as dry as a stick, as stiff as a poker, and as cold as a cucumber. It is not half as good as my old God bless you and / Your affectionately grateful
>
> S. T. Coleridge[13]

There is no doubt that S.T.C. kept Villiers Street far more exactly informed about his activities than he did Hackney. The Evans sisters learned about wine-parties, suppers, outings, concerts, jollities galore. To George, S.T.C. simply hinted, in veiled fashion, at his social whirling: "Philanthropy generally keeps pace with Health—my acquaintance becomes

93

more general."[14] He described one of his new friends, George Caldwell; a prudent youth, said S.T.C., pursuing nearly the same line of study as himself. To the Evanses was given a rather different portrait of Caldwell; it was true that he and S.T.C. were pursuing much the same line of study, but that study included "suppers and two or three other little unnecessaries."[15]

Anne Evans learned from S.T.C. that "the Gods have not made me a drawer (of anything but corks)."[16] Mary was informed that he had invested in a swan-skin waistcoat as an indispensable item of fashionable attire. George, in March, heard that S.T.C. had successfully matriculated; this news being followed in the same breath with a request for "ten or five pounds, as I am at present cashless."[17] S.T.C. dashed to London to visit the Evanses, briefly, after Easter; he explained to George that he needed this respite for health reasons, he was "villainously vapoured."[18]

He had now made the Villiers Street family to all intents and purposes his own; "My sisters . . . Mama! . . . Right Reverend Mother in God."[19]

In spite of this social whirling he had written for all the prizes: the Greek Ode, the Latin Ode, and the Epigrams. To his immense gratification he learned, in June, that he had won the Browne Gold Medal with his Greek Ode on the slave trade; an autographed copy, dated June 10, 1792, S.T.C. proudly sent to George.

S.T.C. came down shortly after for the Long Vacation, which he spent in the West Country, visiting his family. Upon the whole the vacation went off rather well, although S.T.C. found his brother Edward's puns very bad, while Mrs Coleridge disapproved of her youngest son's wine-drinking, upon which she placed a ban: "Not a single drop."[20] S.T.C., in preparation for the Craven Scholarship for which he was due to sit the following term, wrote reams of family gossip, in Latin, to George, who corrected the letters for him. On his return to Cambridge S.T.C. allegedly commenced to work very seriously indeed for the Craven.

But he was beset by equally serious distractions. Duns were now pressing for his debts and, additionally, his unpaid Tutor's bills weighed with increasing heaviness upon his conscience. These financial pressures, combined with the tension of the looming examination, proved too much for S.T.C. He succumbed to the temptation of side-tracking the stringencies of his predicament by abandoning himself to day-dreams: "The time I should have bestowed on . . . academic studies, I employed in dreaming out wild Schemes."[21] (Above, p. 64). Later he was to say that as his affairs became more and more involved he fled to debauchery: "fled from silent and solitary Anguish to the uproar of senseless Mirth!"[22] If we can believe him, he did not read three days uninterruptedly for the Craven and, "for the whole six weeks that preceded . . . [it] . . . was almost constantly intoxicated!"[23]

Although there is abundant evidence that S.T.C. at no time in his career might have been described as abstemious, this tale of uproar and almost chronic intoxication is not convincing, for the simple reason that the college authorities would have noticed had S.T.C. been in this condition. The Master then would certainly not have voiced commiseration (as he subsequently did) at S.T.C.'s failure to get the scholarship. Neither, had S.T.C. truly been a drunken sot, would the University have had him back after his bolt (which it did). Drunkenness of this flagrant nature would not have been overlooked or condoned.

Addiction to alcohol is much more readily detectable than addiction to narcotics, however, and (as already discussed above) it is a highly probable possibility that S.T.C., during this period of pressure and anxiety prior to the Craven, resorted to opium.

That S.T.C. found it all too much for him he virtually confessed to George (who had now got wind of the debts). On November 11, S.T.C. wrote to his brother:

A fortnight from the date hereof I shall be entering the fray. You can scarcely imagine how weary I am of this business, how I abhor, my dear George, living under this strain. My prospects are almost hopeless—in fact quite hopeless . . . As to what you wrote to me about the accounts, I do realize your friendliness and love towards me—for you have always been a brother to me in kindness and a father in wisdom, as I well know. But I am too worried and tired out to reply; please believe me, though, that I will reply soon—and reply very fully.[24]

(This letter, in common with all the correspondence between the brothers at that period, was in Latin.)

The examination for the scholarship extended over the last days of 1792 and the first of 1793. Seventeen candidates entered; these were reduced to a short list of four, comprising "Bethel and Keate of King's, Butler of St John's, and myself."*[25] After further examination Butler was awarded the scholarship.

S.T.C. sent George this disappointing news in a letter postmarked January 14.[26] To this was added the promised financial statement: S.T.C. owed some fifty pounds to his Tutor and about eight pounds upon unspecified items (doubtless of a frivolous nature that he preferred not to detail to George). On the credit side, S.T.C. hastened to add, he had the forty pounds from Christ's Hospital and about twenty-three from the Rustat; furthermore, Dr Pierce had just awarded him the Chapel clerkship, worth an annual thirty-three pounds. This entailed an immense amount of chapel-going, "but all good things have their contingencies of evil," commented S.T.C. (it should be noted that this award of the Chapel clerkship may be seen as additional evidence that S.T.C. could not have been a proverb to the University for intoxicated idleness; had such been the case, he would not

*Christopher Bethell (1773–1859), later Bishop of Bangor; John Keate (1773–1852), later Headmaster of Eton; Samuel Butler (1774–1839), later Bishop of Lichfield.

95

have been awarded what was, in effect, a consolation prize for missing the Craven).

Continuing to reassure George about the financial situation, S.T.C. added that as he ate no supper, nor tea, and kept little company, he expected to be able to save nearly twenty-six pounds during the coming year, not counting the profit that he hoped to make from translations of classical verse, to be published by subscription. "By means of Caldwell, Tucket, & Middleton I can ensure more than two hundred subscribers—so this and frugality will enable me to pay off my debts." And then, in case George read the letter aloud to the rest of the family: "I have been lesson'd by the wholesome discipline of Experience, that *Nemo felix qui debet*—: and I hope, I shall be the happier man for it.—"

The scheme to make translations of classical verse, although harboured by him over a period of many months to come and frequently referred to with optimism in moods of financial desperation, never materialised. Had S.T.C. produced them, it is doubtful whether they would have made him any profit. As it was, the translations remained a dream.

Although S.T.C. put a brave public face on his disappointment over the Craven, there can be little doubt that he was deeply depressed by his failure; especially as he knew that he would in all likelihood have won it, had he worked for it so hard as he had claimed.

Mental depression almost invariably had dramatic effects upon his physical state; now he became ill with a gum abscess and finally had to have a tooth extracted. For this he would almost certainly have been pre-scribed laudanum.

Whether under the stimulation of opium, or his own natural effervescence (for the very act of taking pen or pencil in his hand was stimulation to him), he wrote a flamboyant letter[27] to Mary Evans in the second week of February; in this very long epistle he gave her an hilarious account of his decision to learn to play the fiddle, and added a song of his own:

here comes my fidling Master . . . Twit-twat-twat twit—pray, Mr de la peuche, do you think I shall ever make anything of this Violin?—do you think, I have an ear for Music?—'Un Magnifique! Un superbe! / Par honeur, sir, you be a ver great genius in de music. —Good morning, Monsieur!' This Mr de la peuche is a better judge, than I thought for— . . . This new whim of mine is partly a scheme of self-defence—three neighbours have run Music-mad lately—two of them fiddle-scrapers, the third a flute-tooter . . . Now I hope by frequently playing myself—to render my ear callous . . . And why should *not* a man amuse himself sometimes? . . .

There is an old proverb—of—a river of words, and a spoonful of sense—and I think, this letter has been a pretty good proof of it—: but as Nonsense is better than blank paper, I will fill this side with a song, I wrote lately—my friend, Charles Hague, the composer, will set it to wild music, I shall sing it, and accompany myself on the violin. —Ca ira!—

There followed one of his own poems, in imitation of Ossian (at that time all the Romantic rage). S.T.C. explained to Mary that his verses were intended as the complaint of Ninathóma, daughter of Cathlóma, allegedly monarch of the Scottish Highlands:

> How long will ye round me be swelling,
> O ye blue-tumbling waves of the Sea?

Finally he concluded:

> Are you asleep, dear Mary?—I have administered rather a strong Dose of Opium—: however, if in the course of your Nap you should chance to dream that
> I am with the ardour / of fraternal friendship / Your affectionate
> S. T. Coleridge,
> You will never have dreamt a finer dream in all *your born days*.

This highly significant passage has already been discussed above (p. 63). Whether he had in fact been resorting to opium to ease his tension prior to the Craven, or whether (as we may assume with a very high degree of certainty) he had been taking it for his jaw abscess, or whether (as is very possible) he had had recourse to it for both tension and toothache, the established fact is that S.T.C. by early 1793 was distinctly orientated towards opium.

In mid-February the news reached S.T.C. of the death of his brother Francis at Seringapatam: an event which had occurred almost twelve months previously, but which was not known to the family until early in 1793. S.T.C. could not pretend to a grief that he did not feel. However, it was traditional to wear mourning at the death of a brother and so mourning he wore, George sending him money with which S.T.C. might buy what was needed. He seems to have received one or two extra bank-notes from the loving and ever-understanding George; S.T.C.'s reply (in Latin) commenced with thanks for the money and continued with solemn affirmation of his intention to devote the coming spring and summer to classical studies, or, as he put it, the more austere Muses. Then, his irrepressible high spirits bursting from him, he broke into verse; "Ite mordaces, procul ite, Curae!" ("Begone afar, ye gnawing cares!").[28]

A further reason for S.T.C.'s academic failure at Cambridge must have been the increasing amount of time that he was now devoting to radical political activity.

At school, as a Graecian, he had had his head filled with classical studies, philosophy and verse to the exclusion of all else. 1789 had seen him succumb in poetic hero-worship of the newly-published sonnets of Bowles:

> . . . those soft Strains
> That on the still air floated tremblingly[29]

murmuring to the adolescent S.T.C. of Fancy, Love and Sympathy. But 1789 witnessed, also, the fall of the Paris Bastille and from then on Fancy, Love and Sympathy were challenged by the clamour of *Liberté, Égalité, Fraternité*.

Early in 1790 S.T.C. wrote an ode on the *Destruction of the Bastille* (he could not have written it before that date because, addressing Freedom, he intoned: "Lo, round thy standard Belgia's heroes burn," and the Belgians did not rise against the Emperor Joseph II until January 1790). This ode concluded with an interesting (and typically Esteesian) combination of enlightened international sentiment and unswerving John Bullism:

> . . . every land from pole to pole
> Shall boast one independent soul!
> And still, as erst, shall favor'd Britain be
> First ever of the first and freest of the free!

By the time S.T.C. went up to Cambridge, the universities were in a ferment of enthusiasm for France and the Revolution.

It is important to bear in mind that the Revolution, in its first phase, not only had the fullest support of the majority of the French *bourgeoisie* (using the word in its late eighteenth-century sense), but also aroused passionate interest and sympathy among radical intellectuals throughout Europe. English democrats were particularly ardent in their support.

The paramount objective advanced by the deputies of France's Third Estate, in 1789, was to replace the *ancien régime* by a progressive society founded on the economic and political thinking of the Enlightenment, and upon British experience of representative government. English democrats who visited France in the halcyon period between the autumn of 1789 and September 1792, (especially, of course, those who travelled as fraternal delegates from the republican, or patriotic societies at that time proliferating in England), were received with reciprocative rapture.

The Revolution, with the roots of much of its dialectical idealism embedded in the thinking of the Romantic Movement, naturally had an irresistible attraction for the poets of the period. To them revolutionary France of pre-September 1792 appeared, as poetess Helen Maria Williams was to put it, "a country in romance,"[30] a phrase which Wordsworth, who visited France in 1791–1792, was later to echo.

The French Legislative Assembly, which replaced the Constituent Assembly, opened its session on October 1, 1791 (only a few days before S.T.C. went up to Cambridge). The most talented members of the Legislative Assembly came from the Left wing—notably, the Girondins, a group formed round a nucleus of deputies from the Gironde, the majority of them drawn from the intellectual *bourgeoisie*.

Idealistic, enlightened, although activated by very different, indeed sometimes conflicting, motives, the Girondins approached (at least theoretically) "the shield of human nature from the golden side;"[31] they believed that all things were possible if inspired by fraternal sentiment and controlled by Reason. At the same time, their leaders in the Legislative Assembly seem to have been implacably determined to destroy the opponents of the Revolution's objectives, even if such destruction entailed using violence.

It was with the Girondins that so many English enthusiasts, including Wordsworth, were to identify themselves, and it was the Girondin-influenced period of the French Legislative Assembly, from October 1791 to August 1792, that was to provide these enthusiasts with their "very heaven."

Tutoiement in France became universal, accompanied by a general abandoning of formality in all directions; everyone used the *égalité* form of address, *Citoyen* or *Citoyenne*; powdered hair was discarded in favour of carelessly flowing locks; fastidious dress succumbed to casual attire. In England these democratic habits and fashions caught on like wildfire. Portraits of S.T.C. in his youth show him with a dark mane that not only never saw powder, but apparently never saw brush or comb, either. A cravat of excessively liberal dimensions, loosely and casually wound, contrasts with a tightish dark jacket, perhaps "the short black coat (like a shooting-jacket) which hardly seemed to have been made for him" which Hazlitt described,[32] or the "blue cloaths,"[33] that is, the blue jacket with the brass buttons, that was the recognised costume of a radical Dissenter. During the course of his public lecturing at Bristol in 1795 it was commented that S.T.C. would do better if he appeared "with cleaner stockings in public, and if his hair were combed out."[34] His scruffiness was, of course, all part of his democratic image and matched the habit which radicals had adopted of addressing each other as Citizen John, Citizen Robert, Citizen Samuel, and so on.

During 1791 popular and fraternal societies began to appear in Paris to which—revolutionary innovation indeed—women as well as men were admitted. The basic rôle of these societies was the education of an urban "small man" (*sans culotte*) population in Revolutionary doctrine and the results of these societies began to be visible in Paris in the late summer of 1792 when, following the capture of the Tuileries by a well-organised, indoctrinated body of *sans-culottes* (a very different episode from that of the rabble-seized Bastille), the Paris Commune began practising the direct democracy of Rousseau. The influence of the fraternal societies extended far beyond the French frontiers. The sanctity of fraternal love, the brotherhood of man, had already been made fashionable by the disciples of

Rousseau; it was a happy creed that could be all things to all men. The example of the Paris societies in openly including women in fraternal comradeship had a galvanising effect upon sexual relationships. Progressive young women abandoned chaperones and appeared boldly in public places of entertainment, as well as at political meetings. A women's society, *Républicaines Révolutionnaires*, was formed, led by the actress, Rose Lacombe: these impassioned feminists joined the ranks of the *enragés*, or supporters of the Abbé Roux, representative of the Grevilliers section of the Paris Commune, and darling of the *sans-culottes*. 1792 also saw the publication, in England, of Mary Wollstonecraft's *A Vindication of the Rights of Women*. It was the start of Women's Lib.

"Fraternal friendship" between the sexes covered a wide range of possibilities, from William Wordsworth getting Annette Vallon pregnant, to S.T.C. amending his felicitations to Mary Evans from the

> "Yours with sincerity of friendship
> Samuel Taylor C"[35]

of February 1792, to the

> "I am with the ardour/of fraternal friendship
> Your affectionate
> S. T. Coleridge"[36]

of February 1793

In his undergraduate days, S.T.C. expressed enthusiasm for the Revolution, because that Revolution was the visible manifestation of the political and social democratic principles which he was now so ardently extolling. But, fundamentally, his attitude to France as a nation was, from first to last, implacably John Bullish: a compound of Anglo–Saxon contempt and Protestant low-church fear of all things French as the "scarlet woman" incarnate. Frenchmen, as individuals, S.T.C. declared to be "smutty," while in the mass they were blood-thirsty, unpredictable and terrible.[37]

In a letter to George Coleridge, written in March, 1798, S.T.C. assured George that: "my own opinions . . . are utterly untainted with French Metaphysics, French Politics, French Ethics, & French Theology.—"[38] The significant word here is untainted. On another occasion S.T.C., in expressing his definition of a useless individual, chose a "man frenchified in Heart . . . the whole Seine with all its filth and poison flows in his Veins and Arteries—."[39]

Radical political activity in England in the late eighteenth century had its grass-roots in religious non-conformity. S.T.C. was drawn into serious democratic politics during his first year at Cambridge, not through Romantic francophiliac channels, but by his awakening interest in Unitarianism, the writings of Hartley and the polemics of William Frend.

During his first term at Cambridge S.T.C. had been greatly influenced by the company of Middleton (a future Bishop of Calcutta and always orthodox in his faith), who was far removed from Unitarian thinking, even as an undergraduate. But, as S.T.C. moved increasingly in radical circles, so did Middleton fade from his scene, until the time came for him to leave the University. S.T.C. was subsequently to remark: "How much misery should I have escaped, in all human probability, if he had been but one year my Senior, instead of three."[40]

George Coleridge first had real occasion to worry about S.T.C. when he learned, through the academic grape-vine, early in 1792, that his brother kept occasional company with William Frend, a Fellow of Jesus, who had been removed from his office of Tutor in 1788 because of his dissenting religious views. George wrote to S.T.C. suggesting that Frend's company was invidious; S.T.C. replied that the Master of Jesus himself was very intimate with Frend. Neither should George worry about the possible influence that Frend's views might have upon S.T.C.: "Tho' I am not an *Alderman,* I have yet *prudence* enough to *respect* that *gluttony of Faith* waggishly yclept Orthodoxy."[41]

With this somewhat uneasy joke, the matter appeared to be dropped. But in May, 1793, as a result of his pamphlet, *Peace and Union recommended to the Associated Bodies of Republicans and Anti-republicans,* Frend was tried before the Vice-Chancellor of the University for "sedition and defamation of the Church of England, in giving utterance to and printing opinions, founded on Unitarian doctrines, adverse to the established Church." After a stormy hearing, during which the undergraduates, including S.T.C., made clear their enthusiastic support for him, Frend was found guilty of having violated the statutes of the University by his pamphlet, and was ordered to retract. This he refused to do, whereat he was banished from the University. S.T.C., who had made himself especially conspicuous by his behaviour during the trial, apparently ran very close to being sent down.

The year 1792-3 was a traumatic one for radicals. Following the fall of the Tuileries on August 10, 1792, the Girondins had continued to get all the ministries into the hands of their own nominees, with the exception of the Department of Justice, which went to Danton. A Republic was declared; dues to seigneurs were abolished; the deportation of refractory priests was ordered; *emigré* property was put up for sale. These measures were greeted with enthusiastic approval by English democrats:

> . . . a glorious time,
> A happy time that was . . .
> For battle in the cause of Liberty.[42]

But, ominously, the Paris Commune reacted to these radical Girondin measures by denouncing the Girondins as conservatives and crypto-royalists; middle-class ministerial reserve found itself eyeball-to-eyeball with the uncontrollable pressures of popular enthusiasm for total revolution. Between the factions of the political left (Girondins and Montagnards, the Jacobin Opposition in the Assembly) there now appeared open rupture. Paris society had, hitherto, not been greatly changed by the Revolution; the *salons*, although increasingly political in their tone, had not ceased to function; but now the Parisian scene underwent abrupt transformation; the prisons became choked with what remained of the liberal lesser nobility and the refractory priesthood, while the *salons* became silent, with the exception of those kept by extremist ladies like Madame Roland and Miss Williams.

On August 16 the Prussian army crossed the French frontier and by the end of the month had reached Verdun. On September 2 the citizens of Paris were called to arms. In the Assembly Danton thundered his famous battle cry: *"De l'audace, encore de l'audace, toujours de l'audace, et la France est sauvée!"* Within three weeks, 20,000 volunteers marched from Paris for the defence of the Revolution.

This, for many, was the Revolution's finest hour. For Wordsworth, the Romantic *voyeur*, as for Miss Williams,

> . . . Elate we looked
> . . . saw, in rudest men,
> Self-sacrifice the firmest; generous love,
> And continence of mind, and sense of right,
> Uppermost in the midst of fiercest strife.[43]

Meantime, in Paris, a rumour was started of a counter-revolutionary plot; the reactionaries now cramming the prisons were, it was alleged, planning to escape, seize Paris and hold it until the Prussians arrived. On the afternoon and evening of September 2 the prison massacres, probably organised and set in motion by the Commune's *Comité de Surveillance*, reorganised to include Marat, began. *Sans-culottes* broke into the prisons and butchered the occupants. These excesses continued for several days before firm action by the authorities, backed by horrified public reaction, put a stop to them; but not before some 1400 prisoners, including many priests, had been slaughtered.

It is important to bear in mind that the *sans-culottes* who formed these butcher squads were drawn from precisely the same lower-middle-class population-group of urban artisans, shop-keepers, clerks, master-craftsmen and so on, as were the 20,000 volunteers who had marched away to the waving flags, patriotic tears and slogans, fervent embraces and the *Ça Ira* as described by an ecstatic Miss Williams. Indeed, to those who carried them out, the massacres doubtless seemed an integral part of the general defence of the Revolution.

An incident of significance, during the time of the massacres, had been the attempt by Robespierre and Billaud-Varenne, both members of the

Commune, to have the Girondin leaders arrested and imprisoned, which would have been tantamount to a death-sentence. This scheme was foiled; but henceforth there was open rupture between the Montagnards and Girondins.

While the Montagnards might dismiss the massacres as "an abominable incident in a sublime drama,"[44] a demonstration of *élan populaire*, the Girondins, together with the entire French *bourgeoisie*, were appalled by them. Henceforth, for them, the *sans-culottes* were to be associated with anarchy and murder.

The effect of the massacres upon English democrats and Romantics was traumatic; the "cause" had been betrayed.

Further shocks were in store. By the close of 1792 France's policy of revolutionising her neighbour-states and her offer of help to all peoples prepared to fight for their liberty had thoroughly alarmed neutral opinion and especially the British Government. On January 21, 1793, Louis XVI went to the guillotine; the British made it clear that they took a very serious view of this act of regicide. *"Toujours de l'audace"*: France, on February 2, 1793, declared war on England and Holland and, on March 7, upon Spain too.

> What, then, were my emotions, when in arms
> Britain put forth her freeborn strength in league,
> Oh, pity and shame! with those confederate Powers!
> Not in my single self alone I found,
> But in the minds of all ingenuous youth,
> Change and subversion from that hour . . .
>
> Oh! much have they to account for, who could
> tear,
> By violence, at one decisive rent,
> From the best youth in England their dear pride,
> Their joy, in England . . .[45]

wrote Wordsworth, speaking for all British democrats of the period, but particularly for the radical young, for whom the war between England and France gave rise to an agony of mental conflict. They felt, or at least felt it proper to maintain that they felt, a burning sense of betrayal at their Government's opposition to the forces of international liberty. (Pitt, in the summer of 1793, was denounced in France as the enemy of the human race.)

For S.T.C., whose retrospective view of the French Revolution was a cryptic, "it had all my wishes, none of my expectations,"[46] the massacres and the war presented problems, but no trauma.

One of the main clues to S.T.C.'s character, a clue that is often over-looked, is his complete Englishness. S.T.C. was an Englishman from the crown of his head to the soles of his feet. His immense intellectual capacity enabled him to break through the parochialism of the English climate of his day, but his basic social attitudes and responses were traditionally die-hard English. Hence the reason why, when it came to the final count, he always chose to do the illogical thing, the romantic thing, the bloody-minded thing. It could be said of S.T.C. that, deep in the grain, he, like his brother James Coleridge, was "of the old cavalier stamp."[47] Thus, the French prison massacres failed to shake S.T.C. because it really could have come as no surprise to him to learn that these wretched foreigners were butchering one another.

His democratic stance impelled him to condemn the British Government for its aggression against the French Republic; while later, when in his full seditionist guise, S.T.C. was to denounce, even more energetically, Britain's part in the conflict with France. Yet, this flamboyant Jacobinism notwithstanding, S.T.C. was cheerfully prepared to enlist in the British Army to fight the French himself if given the order.

It is revealing that James Coleridge had no hesitation in passing unerringly penetrative judgment upon S.T.C.'s alleged Jacobinism: "Samuel is no Jacobin, he is a hot-headed Moravian!"[48] This was the matter in a nutshell.

The summer of 1793 saw S.T.C. becoming progressively involved in the university political scene, albeit in typically convivial fashion. His Christ's Hospital and Cambridge crony, Val le Grice, has left a vivid portrait of the poet-philosopher and democrat at this stage of his career:

> he was ready at any time to unbend his mind in conversation, and for the sake of this, his room (the ground-floor room on the right hand side of the staircase facing the great gate) was a constant rendez-vous of conversation-loving friends, I will not call them loungers, for they did not come to kill time, but to enjoy it. What evenings have I spent in those rooms! What little suppers, or *sizings* as they were called . . . when Aeschylus, and Plato, and Thucydides, were pushed aside, with a pile of lexicons &c., to discuss the pamphlets of the day . . . Frend's trial was then in progress. Pamphlets swarmed from the press. Coleridge had read them all; and in the evening, with our negus, we had them *viva voce* gloriously.[49]

S.T.C.'s intense and persistent intellectual curiosity impelled him, during his early manhood, in the direction of religious unorthodoxy although inevitably he always found himself stranded on a bar of conflict between intellectual daring and a basic psychological adherence to the Christian indoctrination of his infancy.

By March, 1794, S.T.C. was already a convert to the necessitarian philosophy of David Hartley; yet he still harboured reservations. We find him trying to explain his position to the deeply concerned, wholly orthodox, yet undoubtedly perceptive and highly intelligent George, in a letter of March 30, 1794, which is of relevance here:

my creed bore and perhaps bears a correspondence with my mind and heart—I had too much Vanity to be altogether a Christian—too much tenderness of Nature to be utterly an Infidel. Fond of the dazzle of Wit, fond of subtlety of Argument, I could not read without some degree of pleasure the levities of Voltaire, or the reasonings of Helvetius—but tremblingly alive to the feelings of humanity, and susceptible to the charms of Truth my Heart forced me to admire the beauty of Holiness . . . forced me to *love* the Jesus, whom my Reason (or perhaps my *reasonings*) would not permit me to worship— . . . who can say, *Now* I'll be a Christian—Faith is neither altogether voluntary, or involuntary—We cannot believe what we choose— but we can certainly cultivate such habits of thinking and acting, as will give force and effective Energy to the Arguments on either side—[50]

S.T.C. had therefore, by the age of twenty-two, established the major tenet of his personal creed, corresponding to his mind and his heart; for him the reconciliation of opposites had already become of primary importance and his lifelong intellectual and emotional endeavour was to accommodate all facts and viewpoints, however at variance. It was an endeavour which may be seen essentially as an intellectual expression of his overwhelming psychological reluctance to say 'no'.

That summer of 1793 S.T.C. again submitted a Greek ode for the Browne Medal, this time on *The Praise of Astronomy*. He was but runner-up for the award, not the winner; John Keate carried off the medal.

S.T.C. spent the Long Vacation with his relations, first with Ned at Salisbury, then with James at Tiverton and Sidmouth (a charming little watering-place where James took his wife and young family for sea air). In James, S.T.C. recognised "a man of reflection, and *therefore* of virtue— but . . . [with] . . . a too great attention to external appearance."[51] Upon the subject of Ned, S.T.C. was less charitable: "I soon perceived that Edward never thought."[52] Both James and Ned expected to be shown a deference from their young brother which he, "conscious of few obligations to *them*, aware of no *real* inferiority, and laughing at the artificial claim of primogeniture . . . felt . . . little inclined to pay."[53]

S.T.C. arrived at length at Ottery and found his mother and other relatives well. There was the usual small country town gossip to be amused by, attractive girls to flirt with and flatter with verses. ("Do you know Fanny Nesbitt? She was my fellow-traveller in the Tiverton diligence from Exeter.—I think a very pretty girl.—")[54] There was Luke Coleridge's young widow, Sally, and her little boy, Will. There was ripe fruit to pick and there was sunshine and sleepy tranquillity; but in spite of this bucolic atmosphere S.T.C. was on tenterhooks. The vacation, which should have been so relaxing, proved just the reverse, for real crisis was now upon him. Far from being "nearly 26£ plus" in pocket, as he had assured George that he expected to be by the summer, S.T.C.'s debts had now grown to £148 17s 1¼d and he was awaiting a show-down with his brothers. James had already read to S.T.C. a few unnerving lines from a letter on the subject which George had sent to Tiverton. S.T.C. attempted to forestall the looming family wrath: "what is left for me to do—but to grieve? The Past is not in my Power—for the follies, of which I may have been guilty, I have been greatly disquieted—and I trust, the Memory of them will operate to future consistency of Conduct—."[55] This to George, shortly after S.T.C.'s arrival at Ottery.

Finally, confrontation with his family arrived. S.T.C. was bluntly censured. But the brothers of whom he had been so critical, James and Ned, proved to be exceedingly decent; together with George, they raised the money to pay S.T.C.'s debts: "a fair Road seemed open to extrication—."[56]

S.T.C. returned to Cambridge via London; he frittered money away as he travelled, and more when he reached London. On arrival at Cambridge he found himself deluged by a multitude of petty, but pressing, debts which he had overlooked and by the time he had settled these, he was quite unable to meet the Tutor's bills. In a typical gesture of inadequacy, S.T.C. rushed back to London with a party of friends and spent what money remained on a wild spree. He then returned to Cambridge intending suicide (or so he was later to allege to George). But he did not kill himself. After a week of agonised remorse (and very possibly opium) he packed a few things and fled again to London.

It was not only his debts that drove him to such extremes of behaviour. He was convinced that he, who had gone to Cambridge so smugly confident of dazzling success, would now, in all likelihood, be doomed to failure. His hero Middleton had left Cambridge without a sufficiently good degree to be able to try for a Fellowship; if this fate had overcome the brilliant Middleton, who had worked hard at mathematics in his attempt at a classical medal, what hope of a Fellowship had S.T.C., with no aptitude whatever for mathematics and little, if any, effort made to grapple with that unappetising subject?

Mary Evans too, or rather, the idea of Mary Evans, had a good deal to do with his by now extremely disturbed condition. S.T.C. had passed through the common enough adolescent phase of vaguely defined fears from sex[57] and had, apparently successfully, enjoyed a series of "unchastities" (as he always referred to them) with university harlots. So long as the sexual object was inferior to him and could be picked up, used and dropped, without involvement, all was well. But mature involvement with a woman who was socially his equal confronted him with insurmountable difficulties.

His writings provide ample evidence that, fundamentally, he regarded sexual activity as degrading. For it to be otherwise, it had to be linked with a special, intellectualised 'pure' love. A kind of chemical action then occurred (in theory), which transformed the unwholesomeness of lust (which he compared with a "marsh reek"[58]) into a spiritual happening. The bride of his dreams, with whom alone this chemistry could work, was, of course, the "maiden mild" of absolute purity of mind and exquisite sensibility of whom he had day-dreamed since infancy. The whole point about her, however, was that for some reason or other she was always hopelessly beyond his reach. This enabled him to go through the torments of unconsummated love without having to face the terrors of sexual intimacy.

Like so many men who are privately scared of intimacy with women, S.T.C. was an incurable philanderer. He made it a golden rule never to get to know a woman properly; he created an image, and stuck to it. Around any unfortunate who seized his imagination as "an angel", symbol of perfect innocence and tenderness, he wove endless fantasies; a "strange passion . . . of fervent tho' wholly imaginative and imaginary love uncombinable by my utmost efforts with . . . Hope"[59] was how he was to describe the Mary Evans episode. Later, for Sara Hutchinson, he was to nurse an "appetiteless heart-gnawing Passion"[60] which he could not reveal.

So far as Mary Evans was concerned, there was no reason why his "fervent . . . love" should have been hopeless. S.T.C. was of respectable, professional background; he had no fortune, but a brilliant career was predicted for him. Mrs Evans did not find his attentions to her daughter unwelcome. Mary would have had to wait for him; but such a proposition was not outrageously unreasonable. Yet S.T.C. decided, categorically, that his love for Mary (or what he at the time imagined to be love for Mary) was without hope, and this hopeless love inspired him with all the effects of "direct Fear;" he lay "awake at night, groaning and praying."[61]

The masochistic satisfaction of luxuriating in a hopeless passion was to be repeated at greater length and with intensified morbidity when he met Sara Hutchinson. "The Joy of Grief! A mysterious Pleasure" as he described it to Southey.[62]

This avoidance of physical consummation with women might be taken to imply that S.T.C.'s real sexual inclination lay towards men. It is true that he was capable of exceptionally deep emotional friendships with men; but there is nothing in the letters and notebooks of Coleridge (and it is in the notebooks, above all, that we discover him bared) to indicate that he was not basically sexually orientated towards females; indeed, there is abundant evidence that he was so orientated. His horror was of the sexual act. He regarded it as a flagrant violation of his personal integrity, his decent self. Homosexual incidents certainly occurred in his nightmares, but these were no more, nor less, repugnant to him than the images of the aggressive women who thronged upon him. Women grabbed at his penis: boys snatched at his scrotum. He was, in either case, equally outraged and terrorised.

Mary Evans, visionary bride and sexual threat, was keeping S.T.C. awake at nights, "groaning and praying." The dread of academic failure also loomed over him; the unpaid Tutor's bills harried his conscience. Reduced to a condition approaching nervous collapse, unable to face these pressures any longer, S.T.C. bolted back to his dear London, to the studies of the Graecians, the tap-room of the Angel Inn, the "Ale-house by courtesy called 'a Coffee House'—the 'Salutation & Cat', in Newgate Street."[63] In these undemanding City haunts he felt more at home and more nearly secure than anywhere else on earth.

He bought a ticket in the Irish lottery and wrote a poem, *To Fortune*, which he sent to the *Morning Chronicle*. It appeared on November 7, 1793:

TO FORTUNE

On Buying A Ticket In The Irish Lottery.
Composed during a walk to and from the Queen's Head, Gray's
Inn Lane, Holborn, and Hornsby's and Co., Cornhill.

> Promptress of unnumbered sighs,
> O snatch that circling bandage from thine eyes!
> O look, and smile! No common prayer
> Solicits, Fortune! thy propitious care!
> For, not a silken son of dress,
> I clink the gilded chains of *politesse*,
> Nor ask thy boon what time I scheme
> Unholy Pleasure's frail and feverish dream;
> Nor yet my view life's *dazzle* blinds—
> Pomp!—Grandeur! Power!—I give you to the winds!
> Let the little bosom cold
> Melt only at the sunbeam ray of gold—
> My pale cheeks glow—the big drops start—
> The rebel *Feeling* riots at my heart!
> And if in lonely durance pent,
> Thy poor mite mourn a brief imprisonment—
> That mite at Sorrow's faintest sound
> Leaps from its scrip with an elastic bound!
> But oh! if ever song thine ear
> Might soothe, O haste with fost'ring hand to rear
> One Flower of Hope! At Love's behest,
> Trembling, I plac'd it in my secret breast:
> And thrice I've viewed the vernal gleam,
> Since oft mine eye, with Joy's electric beam,
> Illum'd it—and its sadder hue
> Oft moisten'd with the Tear's ambrosial dew!
> Poor wither'd floweret! on its head
> Has dark Despair his sickly mildew shed!
> But thou, O Fortune! canst relume

Its deaden'd tints—and thou with hardier bloom
May'st haply tinge its beauties pale,
And yield the unsunn'd stranger to the western gale!

More than one reader must have had difficulty in deciding what this meant.

What it really meant was that S.T.C. had made a strenuous public signal in the hope that somebody who knew him would see it and come to his rescue. However, no rescuer appeared, not even George, let alone blind-folded Dame Fortune. S.T.C. hung about the City until November 20, when the lottery draw took place. Of course his number had not come up. Somehow he managed to survive another ten days, perhaps by selling some of his clothes. He never gave any real clues about this odd stay in London, apart from his mumble to George that it was done in "a strange way."[64] It was typical of him that, reduced as he was to his very uppers, he carried with him all the time, and refused to part with, a valuable 1759 Barbou edition of *Casimir*, a 1567 Canterus edition of *Synesius*, with Greek and Latin text, and Richard Bentley's 1711 quarto edition of *Horace*. It was his intention to translate the first two (he did manage to translate a few odes of the Casimir), but, not very surprisingly, his circumstances proved unpropitious for that type of literary activity.

This sojourn of concealment in London was equivalent to that childhood runaway vigil spent on the cold hillside of Ottery "thinking . . . with inward & gloomy satisfaction, how miserable my Mother must be!"[65] Doubtless, now, S.T.C. thought with similar relish of how miserably anxious Brother George must be. At last, after a night spent on the steps of a house in Chancery Lane, where he was accosted by a procession of beggars to whom he gave the last few pence remaining to him, S.T.C. arrived at his moment of truth. Either the time had come for "the dernier resort of misery,"[66] or he had to decide how he proposed to survive. Although there were two or three times in his life when he toyed with the idea of suicide, it seems never to have been more than a toying; S.T.C., despite his many neuroses and fallibilities, was fundamentally a fighter. Whatever he was subsequently to tell George, S.T.C.'s ideas of suicide on this occasion of his 1793 bolt were pure self-dramatisation. In point of fact, his main preoccupation was with evolving a scheme of survival.

S.T.C., in his time-killing wanderings about the streets, had noticed and noted a recruiting poster for the Light Dragoons. He now went to the enlisting place and presented himself to an elderly recruiting sergeant who, doubtless perceiving at one experienced glance that this was not dragoon material, did his utmost to persuade S.T.C. to change his mind. But S.T.C. had reached a point of no return. He persisted and so, on December 2, 1793, he was enlisted in the 15th, or King's Regiment, of Light Dragoons.

He gave his name as Silas Tomkyn Comberbache, which fitted the initials

S.T.C. on his clothing. He selected *Silas Tomkyn* as names suitably clownish for a Trooper in Dragoons, while he is thought to have taken *Comberbache* from a name that he noticed above a door either in Lincoln's Inn or the Temple.

Prior to leaving London for Reading, where he was to be sworn in, S.T.C. took the precaution of dispatching a letter, containing details of his regimental address, to his Graecian cronies at Christ's Hospital, all, of course, "under the most solemn Importation of secrecy."[67] He was then, with other new recruits, marched away to Reading, fervently praying that "the young men at Christ's Hospital"[68] would betray the solemn secret of his whereabouts before the 15th Regiment of Light Dragoons was ordered to active service.

CHAPTER TWO

AN INDOCILE EQUESTRIAN

(December 1793–June 1794)

THE COMBERBACHE EPISODE[1] is a particularly revealing demonstration
of the extent of S.T.C.'s personality disorder. As such, it calls for attentive
scrutiny.

The process of attempting to turn raw-recruit Comberbache into an
action-ready cavalry-man proved hair-raising for all parties involved.
S.T.C. quickly discovered that he had no affinity whatever with a horse. As
an equestrian he never progressed beyond the "awkward squad."[2] He was
constantly either being thrown—"Silas is off again!"[3]—or carried from the
parade-ground at full gallop by his bolting steed, to the accompaniment of
the drill-sergeant's frenzied bellows: "Take care of that Comberbache,
take care of him, for he'll ride over you!"[4] It is not surprising to learn that
the sergeant's despairing conclusion was that he would never succeed in
making a dragoon out of Comberbache.

The men spent a prodigious amount of time in grooming their mounts,
an activity which filled S.T.C. with repugnance. "A horse," he is on
record as saying, "should rub himself down, and shake himself clean, so to
shine in all his native beauty."[5] Horses, unfortunately, are not so obliging.
But S.T.C. soon found other ways of avoiding grooming chores. His
amiable and unassuming manners quickly endeared him to his fellow
troopers and when they discovered his literacy they arranged a British
compromise; S.T.C. wrote their letters home for them and they groomed
his horse and cleaned his accoutrements for him.

On enlistment Comberbache had received a bounty of six-and-a-half
guineas, but, as he pointed out, "a Light horseman's bounty is a mere
lure—it is expended for him in things which he must have had without a
Bounty—Gaiters, a pair of Leather Breeches, Stable Jacket and Shell,
Horse Cloth, Surcingle, Watering Bridle, Brushes, and the long etcetera of
military accoutrement."[6]

It was out of the question for a Dragoon trooper to carry a small but
weighty classical library about with him in addition to all this equipment.
So the Casimir, Synesius, and Bentley's *Horace* were sold to a Reading
bookseller for fourteen shillings, less than half their value.

S.T.C.'s comrades soon came to regard him as "a natural, though of a
peculiar kind—a talking natural."[7] During off-duty periods he entertained
his barrack-room companions with tales from classical history; the Pelo-
ponnesian wars, the campaigns of Alexander the Great, the crossing of the

Hellespont by Xerxes, the heroics of Thermopylae, and so on—all recited with such verve that his listeners were convinced that these were anecdotes of contemporary, or very recent, military exploits. Clearly S.T.C. found the naive ignorance of his audience privately diverting, but, since he never let his listeners guess this, they continued to enjoy his flow of talk as greatly as he enjoyed talking.

Shortly after his arrival at Reading, S.T.C. experienced a vivid sensation of *déjà vu*; while exercising on horse-back with the rest of his squad, as he and his fellow blue-uniformed troopers rode into a field, he suddenly recognised the reality of "my Dream of going into a Field with men on horseback all in blue which made me, then a Child of 7 years old, burst into tears in a corner of the Parlour at Ottery."[8]

There are several romantic versions of how S.T.C.'s true identity was at length revealed. What really happened was simple enough; his careful advance-planning of a rescue ultimately came into anticipated operation.

In January (1794) the annual Reading horse fair was held—an occasion always for much drinking, brawling and general disturbance. The army was called upon to stand by to preserve some semblance of law and order; S.T.C.'s regiment was dispersed in and about the towns within a ten-mile radius of Reading. S.T.C. found himself at Henley.

He was suffering from a severe eruption of boils upon his posterior, which placed his saddle temporarily out of bounds and so, when one of his fellow troopers was seized with smallpox and carried to the pest-house of Henley workhouse, S.T.C. was detailed to accompany him thither, to act as sick-nurse.

The pest-house was a minute brick building of one apartment, "four strides in length, and three in breadth,"[9] with four windows, one set in each wall. It stood in the workhouse grounds, about a hundred yards from the main building. Here S.T.C. spent a vigil of great strain and isolation: the almost total loss of sleep, the putrid smell and the fatiguing struggles with his violently delirious comrade proving almost too much for him in his boil-weakened condition.

Meantime, his disappearance from Cambridge had become the topic of much University gossip and dire Coleridge family agitation. News of this had percolated through to Christ's Hospital and at last an old scholar, G. L. Tuckett, one of S.T.C.'s contemporaries, contrived to worm from the Graecians the "secret" of S.T.C.'s whereabouts. This information Tuckett passed on to George Coleridge. Tuckett also got into contact with one of the Light Dragoon officers (possibly at the London recruiting centre) and finally wrote a long letter to S.T.C., enclosing another letter, this one from George. These were delivered to the pest-house on Thursday night, February 6, 1794.

S.T.C. was, without doubt, relieved beyond measure that his prudent steps to ensure ultimate rescue had worked out so well, but, in order to save face, he had to counterfeit great annoyance:

Tuckett! . . . In an hour of extreme anguish under the most solemn Imposition of secrecy I entrusted my place & residence to the young men at Christ's Hospital—the intelligence, which you extorted from their Imbecility, should have remained sacred with you—it lost not the obligation of secrecy by the transfer.

One senses that Tuckett was the proper English public-school prefect type. S.T.C. went on to take a few good Upper Sixth jabs at him, spiced with an Esteesian element of Jacobean drama:

You have acted, Tuckett! so uniformly well, that reproof must be new to you—I doubtless shall have offended you—I would to God, that I too possessed the tender irritableness of unhandled sensibility—mine is a sensibility gangrened with inward corruption . . . Your gossip with the commanding officer seems so totally useless and unmotivated, that I almost find a difficulty in believing it—
A letter from my Brother George! . . . it lies unopened . . . The anguish of those who love me— . . . does it not plant my pillow with thorns, and make my dreams full of terrors?—Yet I dare not burn the letter—it seems, as if there were a horror in the action . . . Alas! my poor Mother! What an intolerable weight of guilt is suspended over my head by a hair on one hand —and if I endure to live—the look ever downward—insult—pity—and hell. God or chaos defend me! What but infinite Wisdom or infinite Confusion can do it![10]

Exeunt S.T.C., too overwhelmed even to sign the letter. (It is worth noting that Tuckett, not altogether surprisingly, never entertained much of an opinion of S.T.C. after this.)

George Coleridge's letter to the miscreant was so full of real love, relief and concern, that S.T.C. was clearly at somewhat of a loss how to reply. So he fell back upon *Hamlet*, followed up by a Biblical style tinctured with Webster:

My more than Brother What shall I say—what shall [I] write to you? . . . O my wayward soul! I have been a fool even to madness. What shall I dare to promise? My mind is illegible to myself—I am lost in the labyrinth, the trackless wilderness of my own bosom. Truly may I say—I am wearied of being saved . . . one wish only can I read distinctly in my heart—that it were possible for me to be forgotten as tho' I had never been! The shame and sorrow of those who loved me—the anguish of him who protected me from my childhood upwards—the sore travail of her who bore me— intolerable Images of horror! . . . O that the shadow of Death were on my

Eyelids! That I were like the loathsome form, by which I now sit! . . .
My Brother—my Brother—pray for me.[11]

George replied immediately: "I was comforted by the sight of your own
hand-writing."[12] He went on to try to veer S.T.C. away from rhetoric and
down to brass-tacks: what plans had he, should it prove possible to get him
out of the army?

George's generosity of spirit touched S.T.C. to the quick; indeed, S.T.C.
found it almost more than he could bear. His masochistic instincts yearned
for a berating; George refused to berate. S.T.C.'s spirits wilted:

> I am indeed oppressed—oppressed with the greatness of your Love . . .
> my heart is sick and languid with this unmerited kindness. I had intended
> to have given you a minute history of my thoughts, and actions for the last
> two years of my life . . . But I am so universally unwell—and the hour is so
> late—that I must defer it till tomorrow.[13]

George, doubtless, was thankful for this respite; he had a lot of organising
and letter-writing to do if Samuel were to be extricated from this ridiculous
mess.

It was not until Sunday night, February 23, that S.T.C. summoned the
energy to pen an account of the events which had led to his flight from
Cambridge:

> I laugh almost like an insane person when I cast my eye backward on the
> prospect of my last two years—What a gloomy *Huddle* of eccentric Actions,
> and dim-discovered motives! To real happiness I bade adieu from the
> moment, I received my first Tutor's Bill—since that time my Mind has
> been irradiated by Bursts only of Sunshine—at all other times gloomy with
> clouds, or turbulent with tempests. Instead of manfully disclosing the
> disease, I concealed it with a shameful Cowardice of sensibility, till it
> cankered my very Heart.

He then went on to outline his idle and dreamy behaviour at Cambridge
(already discussed above) and to make confessions of chronic intoxication,
adding with smug satisfaction: "My Brother, you shudder as you read." He
continued with a description of the sequel—the squandering of most of the
money which his family had given him with which to repay his debts,
until: "So small a sum remained, that I could not mock my Tutor with it—
My Agitations were delirium . . . Where Vice has not annihilated Sensibility, there is little need of a Hell!" As a result, he had fled to London,
where he had

> staid about a week in a strange way, still looking forwards with a kind of
> recklessness to the dernier resort of misery—An accident of a very singular
> kind prevented me—And led me to adopt my present situation—.[14]

This incredible epistle concluded with a memorised six-line quotation from Claudianus, *In Eutropium*, ii, 13.

Whether the effect of the whole amazing thing was to make George laugh like an insane person himself, pray, or beat his head against the wall in desperation, we shall never know.

Mr Plampin, S.T.C.'s Tutor at Jesus, made it clear that the prodigal would be welcomed, should he wish to return to Cambridge. "Your decision," advised George, passing on this news to S.T.C., "should be certainly to return."

"Undoubtedly—my Brother! I would wish to return to College—I know, what I *must suffer* there—but deeply do I feel, what I *ought* to suffer."

"Such steps if agreeable to yourself may still secure to you your Christ's Hospital allowance & Rustat Scholarship, full now 70£ per annum . . . Mr Bowyer (I hear) insinuates that you [had] leave of him to leave College—God bless him—for a man of his disposition to descend to so amiable a fraud demands no trifling respect from us."

"Mr Bowyer!—indeed—indeed—my heart thanks him! how often in the petulance of Satire, how ungratefully have I injured that man!"

"A handsome Sum shall be gotten ready for the liquidation of your College debts."

"I owe my Shoemaker at Cambridge 3£—and I owe my Taylor a Bill—of what amount, I am not positively accurate—but to the best of my remembrance it is about 10£ . . . Besides these, I owe nothing."*

"The business of your discharge shall be commenc'd immediately—Write to me swift as wind—that I may take every step for restoring you to happiness & myself."

S.T.C. could only fall back on repeating: "Pray for me my Brother."[15]

George was able to arrange with Mr Plampin for the Tutor's bills to be paid by the Coleridge family in instalments over the next few months. James Coleridge, being a retired army officer, had the unenviable task of conducting the negotiations to get S.T.C. out of the Dragoons—a much more devious and protracted business than had been the enlistment. S.T.C. had prudently investigated the best method of going about getting released, so that no time might be wasted once rescue operations commenced; he passed this information on to James:

With regard to my Emancipation, every enquiry I have made, every piece of Intelligence, I could collect, alike tends to assure me, that it may be done by *Interest*, but not by negociation without an Expence, which I should tremble to write—Forty guineas were offered for a discharge the day after the young man was sworn in—and were refused—His friends made

*S.T.C. omits to mention his Tutor's bills which amounted to £132. 6s. 2d. by Lady Day, 1794, the income from the Rustat, Christ's Hospital Exhibition, etc, having reduced the arrears of the previous midsummer.

Interest—and his discharge came down from the War Office—If however negociation *must* be first attempted, it will be expedient to write to our Colonel . . . My assumed name is Silas Tomkyn Comberbache 15th or King's Reg. of Light Dragoons—G. Troop—My *Number* I do not know—it is of no Import . . .

. . . there will be a large draught from our Regiment to complete our Troops abroad—the men were picked out today—I suppose, I am not one—being a very indocile Equestrian.[16]

James immediately made application for the release of S.T.C., without, however, receiving any reply whatsoever. Meantime, letters passed to and fro between members of the Coleridge family, the University, friends in Ottery; everyone was writing letters "full of wisdom, and tenderness, and consolation"[17] as S.T.C. described them.

The sick comrade being now well on the way to recovery (a tribute to S.T.C.'s devoted nursing) S.T.C. was removed to join his regiment at High Wycombe, Buckinghamshire. He was conveyed there on an army baggage cart, in a "mizzley rain," so that he caught, inevitably, a bad cold and developed what he nicely termed "a feverette."[18] He was quartered at a pot-house, The Compasses; there, as he struggled with his illness, he enjoyed diverting company of a very mixed sort. It was typical of S.T.C. that, feeling freedom to be near at hand, he began to shake down very well in the Army. He wrote cheerfully, even blithely, to George, describing life at the Compasses:

I met yesterday—smoking in . . . a chimney corner . . . a man of the greatest information and most original Genius, I ever lit upon. His Philosophical Theories of Heaven & Hell would have both amused you, and given you hints for much speculation—he . . . kept me awake till 3 in the morning with his Ontological Disquisitions . . . I have little *Faith*, yet am wonderfully fond of speculating on mystical schemes.[19]

A Captain Ogle, just returned from abroad, always found time at night, during stable inspection, to have a conversation with Trooper Comberbache and, on learning from the corporal's report that Comberbache was unwell, Ogle handsomely sent him a couple of bottles of wine.

Robert Allen, S.T.C.'s earliest friend and almost exact contemporary, now at University College, Oxford, was perpetually sending gifts of money and tea and sugar, and a variety of other small things, and twice visited S.T.C. in person after he had been moved from High Wycombe back to Reading. Letters came from Cambridge bearing the heart-warming assurance that the Jesuites (as S.T.C. termed them) were looking forward to S.T.C.'s return "as to that of a lost Brother."[20] Trooper Comberbache, in fact, would have been almost happy had it not been for his horse, with whom he continued to have the most alarmingly indocile experiences:

"within this week I have been thrown three times . . . and run away with to the no small purturbation [*sic*] of my nervous system almost every day."[21]

It was now mid-March and James Coleridge had had no notice whatever taken of the letter that he had written a month previously to General Gwynne. George Coleridge, knowing that S.T.C. could retain his Rustat Scholarship only by appearing at the Easter Week examinations, decided to see what an urgent letter from himself to the General would achieve and wrote asking for an interview to plead his brother's case for discharge. A Captain Hopkinson, now in command of the King's Light Dragoons, replied with unexpected promptitude; there was an interview. It emerged that a substitute recruit must be found; this could not be arranged under twenty-five guineas. There was much family discussion.

Meantime, S.T.C. was beginning to lose his nerve. It was one thing to sit snug in a pot-house, writing letters of ever-growing confidence; it was quite another to confront his brothers and mentors face to face. Finally he confessed to George: "I am afraid to meet you." In the same letter he continued:

> When I call to mind the toil and wearisomeness of your avocations, and think how you sacrifice your amusements, and your health—when I recollect your habitual and self-forgetting Economy, how generously severe—my soul sickens from its own guilt.[22]

This is wrenched from the heart. And it is extremely important; it explains S.T.C.'s subsequent behaviour towards his family.

S.T.C. now had the visible jitters. He quite lost grip on himself, becoming increasingly muddled and increasingly reliant on George:

> I mean to write Dr Pearce—the letter I will inclose to you— perhaps it may not be proper to write—perhaps it may be necessary—you will best judge. The discharge should, I think, be sent down to the Adjutant—yet I don't know—it would be more comfortable to me to receive my dismission in London were it not for the appearing in these Cloaths.

For, of course, he had to be kitted out for his return to civilian life. He had breeches and waistcoats at Cambridge, together with three or four shirts, some neck cloths, and a few pairs of stockings. The clothes which he had sold in Reading, upon enlisting, he could recover, but not "my Coat and Hat—they are gone irrevocably—My Shirts which I have with me are all but one worn to rags, mere rags—their texture was ill adapted to the Labor of the Stables."[23]

Poor George! Within four days came another letter from young Samuel:

> I find that I was too sanguine in my expectations of recovering all my Clothes—My Coat, which I had supposed gone, and all the Stockings

viz—4 pair of almost new silk stockings, and 2 pair of new silk & cotton
I can get again—for 23 Shillings—I have ordered therefore a pair of Breeches,
which will be 19 Shillings, a Waistcoat at 12 Shillings, a pair of Shoes at
7s-4d. Besides these I must have an Hat, which will be 18 Shillings, and two
Neckcloths which will be 5 or 6 Shill.—These things I have ordered—My
travelling expenses will be about half a guinea—Have I done wrong in
ordering these things? Or did you not mean me to do it by desiring me to
arrange what was necessary for my personal appearance at Cambridge? I
have so seldom acted right, that in every step I take of my own accord I
tremble lest I should be wrong. —I forgot in the above account to mention
a flannel Waistcoat—it will be 6 shillings—The military dress is almost
oppressively warm—and so very ill as I am at present, I think it impudent
to hazard cold—
I will see you at London—or rather at Hackney—
There will be two or three trifling Expences on my leaving the Army—I
know not their exact amount.—
The Adjutant dismissed me from all Duty yesterday.—
My head throbs so, and I am so sick at Stomach that [it] is with difficulty
I can write—[24]

George, having coped with all this, now seems to have had a most alarming afterthought of his own. Much as he looked forward to seeing Samuel in
London, suppose if he lingered there, worshipping at Mary Evans's shrine,
thereby missing the Easter Week examinations at Cambridge after all? It
was quite possible; indeed, knowing S.T.C., it was distinctly probable that
this might happen.

Tuckett, who was still in correspondence with George, pooh-poohed this
notion, writing confidently: "He must, I am conscious, feel too much shame
to entertain even a wish of having an interview with Mrs Evans's family."[25]
But George was not prepared to risk it; he wrote to S.T.C. instructing him
categorically to go direct from Reading to Cambridge, immediately following discharge. He also spoke severely about the meaning and duty of
economy and the necessity of Faith in order to regulate virtues. S.T.C.
replied with the assurance: "If I receive my discharge by Thursday, I will
be—God pleased—in Cambridge on Sunday—."[26]

A week later, on April 5th or 6th, in spite of, or, perhaps, because of
further severities from George, S.T.C. wrote one of his bloody-minded
notes: he had changed his plans; he had had the offer of a horse and the
company of a fellow-rider for the journey to London on Wednesday next
and, if his discharge had come through by then, he intended to embrace this
offer.

S.T.C.'s discharge at last came through on April 10th; his commanding
officer had abandoned the demand for a substitute recruit and had seized
upon an alternative method (permitted by Regulations) of obtaining a discharge for Trooper Comberbache upon grounds of insanity.

The muster roll of the regiment reads: "discharged S. T. Comberback/

Insane/10 Apl." The regimental monthly return for May, 1794, signed by Captain Nathaniel Ogle, reiterates this: "the other Man was dischd. being Insane."[27]

Letter to George Coleridge, at Hackney, London. Postmarked 12 April, 1794.

> My dear Brother,
> On Wednesday night I arrived from Reading—I took my place immediately in the Cambridge Fly—went there half past 7, found the horses not put to— so walked on before—saw another Coach go up a different road—pursued it under a false supposition—in the mean time the Fly passed by—I missed it —so went to Cambridge on the outside of the Mail—and have arrived safe. I have not yet seen Dr Pearce—he is gone out to Dinner—I wrote to him as soon as I got up this morning—From violent pain in my Limbs, I am not able to write distinctly what I would wish to say—only that I am with excess of warmest gratitude & affection.
> Your Brother
> S. T. COLERIDGE[28]

S.T.C.'s return to Cambridge was noted in the Jesus College Register, succinctly: "1794 Apr: *Coleridge admonitus est per magistrum in praesentia sociorum.*"

To George, S.T.C. gave an account of the episode in greater detail (letter postmarked 1 May, 1794):

> My dear Brother
> I have been convened before the fellows—Dr Pearce behaved with great asperity, Mr Plampin with exceeding and most delicate kindness—My Sentence is a Reprimand (not a public one, but *implied* in the sentence), a month's confinement to the precincts of the College, and to translate the works of Demetrius Phovareus [sic] into English . . . All the fellows tried to persuade the Master to greater Lenity, but in vain— without the least affectation I applaud his conduct—and think nothing of it—The confinement is nothing—I have the fields and Grove of the College to walk in—and what can I wish more? Nothing. The Demetrius is dry . . . Besides this, I have had a Declamation to write in the routine of College Business—and the Rustat Examination—at which I got credit—. I get up every morning at 6 o'clock—.
> Every one of my acquaintance I have dropped solemnly and for ever except those of my College with whom before my departure I had been least of all connected—who had always remonstrated with me against my Imprudences —yet have treated me with almost fraternal affection—Mr Caldwell, particularly. —I thought, the most *decent* way of dropping acquaintances, was to express my intention openly and irrevocably . . .

I have been engaged in finishing a Greek Ode—I mean to write for all the Prizes—I have had no time upon my ha [nds]. I shall aim at correctness & perspicu [ity], not *genius*—My last ode was so *sublime* that nobody could understand it—*if* I should be so *very lucky* as to win one of the Prizes, I could *comfortably* ask the Dr's Advice concerning the *time* of my degree—I will write tomorrow—
God bless you—my Brother—my Father!

S. T. COLERIDGE[29]

It is scarcely surprising to learn that George's onerous burden of responsibility had now impaired his never very robust health; he sought respite in a country holiday. S.T.C. wrote solicitously; he also made solemn vows to refund the money which his family, not without difficulty, had got together to pay his debts, and once again swore to practise stringent economy: "Every enjoyment—except of *necessary* comforts—I look upon as criminal."[30] A note to a fellow undergraduate, Samuel Butler (he who had won the Craven), inviting him to a supper of bread and cheese, strikes an impressively abstemious key. No mention is made of negus.

On June 15, or thereabouts, S.T.C. commenced his Long Vacation. He and his friend, Joseph Hucks, planned a pedestrian tour together; first to Oxford for a few days, to visit Robert Allen, to be followed by a month's walking among the mountains of North Wales. After which S.T.C. proposed to resume frugal living and dedicated study at Cambridge.

An admirable-sounding scheme. George, informed of it, could have had no qualms. Samuel, rescued, admonished, forgiven, had turned over a new leaf. His feet were set in the right direction. After a false start, all would now be well.

INTERLUDE

Data: The Adorable I Am

WHEN S.T.C. WROTE, in 1798, to his Bristol Dissenting minister col-
league, the Reverend John Prior Estlin, to tell him, as he was constantly
telling everyone, what a marvellous man his new friend William Wordsworth was, he added: "On one subject are we habitually silent—we found
our data dissimilar, & never renewed the subject."[1]

S.T.C. was not, as has sometimes been supposed, referring to the theory
of poetic diction. On the poetic level the two men discussed their differences
at length and frequently and with mutual understanding of the other's
point of view. The basic difference dividing the friends lay in their personal
philosophies. The dissimilarity of data dividing S.T.C. and Wordsworth
was, in fact, the central philosophical controversy of the Romantic era, the
argument over pantheism, or so-called *Pantheismusstreit*.

This controversy provided S.T.C. with the major intellectual struggle of
his life and was the inspiration behind his great masterwork, *The Ancient
Mariner*. He had become involved in the struggle long before he met
Wordsworth. He was involved in it, if but tentatively, by the time he bolted
into the Dragoons and there can be little doubt that he and Hucks must
have had some, albeit woolly, discussion on the matter as they tramped
together from Cambridge to Oxford. The controversy pivoted upon that
mystery of mysteries, existence. One can imagine S.T.C. putting to Hucks
an immature version of the question which, some fifteen years later, he was
to pose to his readers, in *The Friend*:

> Hast thou ever raised thy mind to the consideration of existence, in and by
> itself, as the mere act of existing? Hast thou ever said to thyself thoughtfully,
> It is! heedless in that moment whether it were a man before thee, or a
> flower, or a grain of sand—without reference, in short, to this or that
> particular mode or form of existence? If thou hast indeed attained to this,
> thou wilt have felt the presence of a mystery, which must have fixed thy
> spirit in awe and wonder. The very words—There is nothing—are self-
> contradictory. There is that within us which repels the proposition with as
> full and instantaneous a light as if it bore evidence against the fact in the
> sight of its own eternity.
> Not to be then, is impossible: to be, incomprehensible. If thou hast
> mastered this intuition of absolute existence, thou wilt have learned
> likewise, that it was this, and no other, which in the earlier ages seized the
> nobler minds, the elect among men, with a sort of sacred horror . . .

But let it not be supposed that it is a sort of knowledge: no! It is a form of BEING, or indeed is the only knowledge that truly *is*, and all other science is real only as far as it is symbolical of this.[2]

S.T.C. was to say of himself: "I feel strongly, and I think strongly, but I seldom feel without thinking, or think without feeling . . . My philosophical opinions are blended with, or deduced from, my feeelings."[3]

His feelings were grounded in an innate need for religious faith. His family background and upbringing had determined that that faith should be Christian and Protestant. But intellectually he found himself, in late adolescence and young manhood, profoundly attracted by a philosophy which, if followed through, logically, without self-deception, could only be interpreted as atheistic. This was Spinozistic Pantheism.

Coleridge, like Goethe, divided all men into either Platonists (where philosophy embraces the intuitive knowledge 'I am'), or Aristotelians (where philosophy embraces the intuitive 'It is'):

> Schools of real philosophy there are but two, best-named by the arch-philosopher of each, Plato and Aristotle. Every man is born an Aristotelian, or a Platonist. I do not think anyone born an Aristotelian can become a Platonist; and I am sure no one born Platonist can ever change into an Aristotelian . . .
> The difference between Aristotle and Plato is that which will remain as long as we are men and there is any difference between man and man in point of opinion . . . Aristotle . . . affirmed that all our knowledge had begun in experience, had begun through the senses, and that from the senses only could we take our notions of reality. But Plato demanded that we should go into ourselves and in our own spirits to discover the law by which the whole universe is acting.[4]

The psychological gulf dividing the two types is well recognised. It is the focal point of irreconcilability between today's two major philosophies: the existentialist *I think, therefore I am*, and the postive-analytic, which, essentially, insists upon the *It is*.

During the Romantic era this eternal controversy took the form of a conflict between the philosophy of Spinoza (*it is*) and that of Kant (*I am*) which ultimately crystallised itself as a conflict between Spinoza and Christianity.

Spinoza postulates that: "The first element which constitutes the actual being of the human mind, is the idea of some *particular thing* actually existing." This places him, fairly and squarely within the 'It is' category of philosophers.

In complete opposition to this, the point of departure for the affirmation of the 'I am' philosophy is the subjectivity of the individual. "There cannot be," states Sartre, "at such a point of departure, any truth but this one: *I think, therefore I am,* which is the absolute truth of consciousness attaining itself."[5]

Individual things, said Spinoza, are nothing but modifications of the attributes of God. The more we know of particular things, therefore, the more we know of God. Hence, all things are God and God is all things—not the cause of All, but the All itself.

The individual is engulfed in a universal Oneness; the human mind is seen as but merely part of Nature; man has no free will, no final control over his destiny, no real freedom of choice. At death, man merely becomes re-absorbed into the All—"made one with Nature," as Shelley expressed it. Obviously, Spinozism is the antithesis of the individual 'I am' and, further, of Christian belief in the survival of the individual soul.

During the century following his death in 1677, Spinoza's reputation sank increasingly into theological and philosophical ignominy. The philosophy of the 'I am' and the integrity of the Christian individual soul triumphed.

Early Romanticism rediscovered Spinoza in the late eighteenth century with a kind of delighted astonishment which rapidly swelled into a crescendo of enthusiasm. Goethe described his reaction when he turned to Spinoza's works: "I gave myself to the reading and felt . . . that I had never seen the world so clearly."[6]

The emotional and intellectual climate of the times was fundamentally Spinozistic. Kant alone raised his voice in warning. "Spinozism," he said, "leads straight to gush!" Lawless speculative reason, he urged, caused devastation in morals as well as in religion.

Despite Kant, pantheism gushed onward into the nineteenth century, sweeping all before it. Only a few rare individuals, notably Jacobi, Coleridge and Kierkegaard, spoke up as advocates of the integral 'I am'.

Wordsworth was, virtually automatically, an ardent disciple of Spinoza. Spinoza's contention that the more we know of individual aspects of nature, the more we know of God, was the message fundamental to Wordsworth's poetry. "Let Nature be your teacher," was his basic theme, expressed in a series of poetic variations, such as these in *The Tables Turned*:

> Books! 'tis a dull and endless strife;
> Come, hear the woodland Linnet,
> How sweet his music! On my life,
> There's more of wisdom in it.

> And hark! how blithe the Throstle sings!
> He, too, is no mean preacher:
> Come forth into the light of things,
> Let Nature be your teacher . . .

> One impulse from a vernal wood
> May teach you more of man,
> Of moral evil and of good,
> Than all the sages can . . .

While in his great passage on the Simplon Pass he expresses Spinoza's "All is One and One is All":

> Winds thwarting winds, bewildered and forlorn
> The torrents shooting from the clear blue sky,
> The rocks that muttered close upon our ears,
> Black drizzling crags that spake by the wayside
> As if a voice were in them . . .
> The unfettered clouds and region of the Heavens,
> Tumult and peace, the darkness and the light—
> Were all like workings of one mind, the features
> Of the same face, blossoms upon one tree;
> Characters of the great Apocalypse,
> The types and symbols of Eternity,
> Of first, and last, and midst, and without end.[7]

Wordsworth might, as a Spinozist, venerate Christianity as a social code which produced virtue and therefore happiness, but clearly, as S.T.C. lamented, to Estlin, he could not be a Christian:

> It is his [Wordsworth's] practice and almost his nature to convey all the truth he knows without any attack on what he supposes falsehood, if that falsehood be interwoven with virtues or happiness—he loves and venerates Christ & Christianity—I wish he did more.[8]

Thus, from the first, an immense psychological abyss yawned between the two men; but, in the first glow of their friendship, it was possible for them to ignore it, as honeymooners are able to be ignorant of the differences which will eventually bring them to the divorce-court.

Moreover, the fundamental discrepancies between the intellectual stances of the two men could, in the early years, easily be glossed over because S.T.C.'s attitude to Spinoza was far from being one of categorical rejection.

S.T.C. adored Nature and much of his response to it was spontaneously in the Romantic key. There is, in illustration of this, Hazlitt's account of him, while staying at Lynton, rushing, bare-headed, out into a raging thunderstorm so that he might savour the ferocity of the elements amongst the picturesque scenery of the Valley of Rocks.[9]

Again and again in his poetry S.T.C. bears testimony to intuition and responses that are purely pantheistic. Thus, in *Fears in Solitude* (April, 1798) he speaks of "Religious meanings in the forms of nature" and of "the God in nature." Natural scenery provides him with:

> . . . my sole
> And most magnificent temple, in the which
> I walk with awe . . .

In the exquisite *Frost At Midnight* (February, 1798) S.T.C. promises the slumbering infant, Hartley, that he shall be reared, not in a city, but in the open countryside, where he shall

> . . . see and hear
> The lovely shapes and sounds intelligible
> Of that eternal language, which thy God
> Utters, who from eternity doth teach
> Himself in all, and all things in himself.

Pantheistic responses to the natural world about him come instinctively to the creative artist; poets, above all, are susceptible to this kind of response. Indeed, S.T.C. declared emphatically that:

A Poet's Heart & Intellect should be *combined*, intimately combined & unified, with the great appearances in Nature.[10]

He believed passionately in what he called "the sense of the heart." The heart did not for him mean his sentimental region, as it popularly does; the heart symbolised for him his moral nature; it was "the beginning and the end." Truth, knowledge and insight were comprehended in its expansion. "The faith, which saves and sanctifies, is a collective energy, a total act of the whole moral being . . . its living sensorium is in the *heart*; and . . . no errors of the understanding can be morally arraigned unless they have proceeded from the heart."[11]

"Heart-withering" was an expression which S.T.C. used frequently. "Heart-withering sensations" meant, not the blighting of romantic love, but the frosty blighting, or, worse, the atrophy, of the moral nature—that half of the man that was living Angel—The Esteesee in Coleridge. "Esteesee" became his code-name for his unique and individual self-awareness; the I-am-ness, or as he once called it, the "I-ship," "the adorable I AM."[12]

> —and the deep power of Joy
> We see into the *Life* of Things—

i.e. By deep feelings we make our Ideas dim—& this is what we mean by our Life—ourselves. I think of the Wall—it is before me, a distinct Image—here. I necessarily think of the *Idea* & the Thinking I as two distinct & opposite Things. Now [let me] think of *myself*.—& the thinking Being—the Idea becomes dim whatever it be—so dim that I know not what it is—but the Feeling is deep & steady—and this I call *I*—identifying the Percipient & the Perceived—[13]

Contemplating suicide, or, more correctly, contemplating the contemplation of suicide, while in Malta, he mused in his notebook whether Death was what he groaned for. He envisaged death not as an end, but as a "transfiguration of Consciousness;" "of annihilation I cannot by the nature of my Imagination have any idea / Yet it may be true."[14]

Here stands the core of his dilemma. In his heart he was convinced of the eternal survival of the I-ship, the I AM, the Esteesee. Yet the sense of the heart alone was not enough; there also had to be the thinking of the head. And, as he expressed it, for many years although his heart was with John and Paul, his head was with Spinoza.[15]

Indeed, over a period of forty years S.T.C. attempted to reason his way through this problem, struggling with it interminably, in solitude: Jacob wrestling with the angel.

In old age S.T.C. explained to his nephew, Henry Nelson Coleridge:

> I am by the law of my nature a reasoner. A person who should suppose I meant by that word, an arguer, would not only misunderstand me, but would understand the contrary of my meaning. I can take no interest whatever in hearing or saying anything merely as a fact . . . It must refer to something within me before I can regard it with any curiosity or care . . . I require in everything . . . a reason, why the thing *is* at all.[16]

This revealing Esteesian self-appraisal should be compared with Matthew Arnold's well-known evaluation of S.T.C.:

> that which will stand of Coleridge is this; the stimulus of his continued effort . . . to get at and lay bare the real truth of his matter in hand, whether that matter were literary, or philosophical, or political or religious; and this in a country where at the moment such an effort was almost unknown.[17]

S.T.C.'s almost life-long struggle to lay bare the real truth of his intuition of absolute existence probably started shortly after his arrival at Cambridge when he began reading the arch-priests of Socinianism, Doctors Hartley and Priestley.

The central teaching of Socinianism (or Unitarianism, as it was then more popularly known), denied the Trinitarian concept of "God the Father, God the Son and God the Holy Ghost," maintaining instead that Christ was a "mere man." "*Jesus of Nazareth was* a man approved of God . . . the same kind of being with yourselves . . . *a mere man*, as other Jews, and as we ourselves also are,"[18] wrote Joseph Priestley (1733–1804), republican, theologian and scientist, whom S.T.C. was to describe as "the author of . . . modern Unitarianism."[19]

Priestley's unorthodoxy and republicanism finally forced him to emigrate to the United States. S.T.C., during his Pantisocratic period, positively revered Dr Priestley and for a while even entertained hopes that he might become a fellow Pantisocrat on the banks of the Susquehannah.[20]

But, over and beyond Priestley, S.T.C. attached importance to the philosophy of David Hartley, whose *Observation on Man, his Frame, His Duty, and His Expectations* (1749) was a strange hotch-potch of associational psychology, necessitarianism, and Christianity. Such a fetish of Hartley did the youthful S.T.C. make that, when Shuter painted his portrait in 1798, he showed him ostentatiously clasping a volume of Hartley, although, by that date, S.T.C. had, strictly speaking, passed beyond his influence. How ardently he had felt himself to be a dedicated disciple of Hartley is demonstrated by the fact that he named his first-born child (1796) after the Master.

Hartley and Priestley, together with Godwin (whose treatise on anarchical and utopian society, *On Political Justice*, was all the rage in British radical intellectual circles when S.T.C. was at Cambridge), shared a common Spinozistic conviction that human action was determined, or necessitated, by reality located in external circumstance; hence their creed was known as "Necessitarianism."

Necessitarianism was very fashionable with young radicals of that period. Wordsworth, for one, "was even to Extravagence a Necessitarian."[21] S.T.C. for the greater part of a decade, called himself a Necessitarian; as Comberbache, he made it clear to George that he subscribed to necessitarian views;[22] and ten months later he was boasting of being "a compleat Necessitarian" who understood the subject almost as fully as Hartley himself.[23]

Hartley's enormous appeal for S.T.C. undoubtedly lay in the fact that his philosophy continued to fuse Necessitarianism with Christianity. William Godwin, an atheist, inspired respect in S.T.C. for only a very brief period. By the close of 1794, Coleridge was proclaiming: "I set him at Defiance—tho' if he convince me [of atheism] I will acknowledge it in a letter to the Newspapers."[24]

The boot ultimately proved to be on the other foot; Godwin was to say, in due course, that it was S.T.C. who had led him to Theism.

By 1796, S.T.C. had thought through, and seen through Dr Priestley. From close scrutiny of Priestley's writings the unavoidable inference had to be drawn that he was, in fact, as much of an atheist as Godwin, without Godwin's frank avowal of the fact. The Priestley system, as S.T.C. explained in *Aids to Reflection*, had "no advantage over Spinosism."

Abandoning Priestley, S.T.C. turned for a while to George Berkeley, Bishop of Cloyne (he who once commenced a dissertation with Tar Water and ended with the Trinity). "The sublime system of Berkeley" so enraptured S.T.C. for a while that he mused upon the idea of composing a cycle of:

Hymns to the Sun, the Moon, and the Elements—six hymns. —In one of them to introduce a dissection of Atheism—particularly the Godwinian

System of Pride—Proud of what? An outcast of blind Nature ruled by a fatal
Necessity—Slave of an ideot Nature! . . .
In the last Hymn a sublime enumeration of all the charms or Tremendities
of Nature—then a bold avowal of Berkeley's System!!!!!![25]

Like so many of S.T.C.'s ideas, this one came to nothing. He compensated by naming his second son (1798) after the Bishop.

But the Bishop's system, too, when subjected to hard study and the thinking-through process, proved to be invalidated by Spinozistic implications and was therefore accordingly rejected.

S.T.C.'s Wedgwood-financed visit to Germany in 1798–9, during which he studied the German language and read German philosophy, resulted, as the Wedgwoods had hoped, in a broadening of his horizons, releasing him from the provincialism that had threatened his development. S.T.C.'s removal to the Lake Country, after his return to England, was followed by several months of severe illness. As a form of therapy S.T.C. embarked upon a philosophical study, commencing with an examination of the relationship of Locke and Descartes and continuing to an analysis of Newton. The results of this study he described to his patron, Josiah Wedgwood, in a series of letters, copies of which S.T.C. sent to Thomas Poole.[26]

By March, 1801, S.T.C. was telling Poole:

The interval since my last letter has been filled up by me in the most intense Study. If I do not greatly delude myself, I have . . . overthrown the doctrine of Association, as taught by Hartley, and with it all the irreligious metaphysics of modern Infidels—especially, the doctrine of Necessity.[27]

Poole was interested in metaphysics, but, like many Englishmen of his period, he had been taught to revere Locke. To discover S.T.C. taking Locke apart was a shattering experience which prompted Poole to warn him: "Think before you join the herd of *Little-ists*, who, without knowing in what Locke is defective, wish to strip the *popular mind* of him, leaving in his place *nothing*—darkness, total darkness."[28]

The Wedgwood reception of S.T.C.'s philosophical letters was even more disappointing; Josiah Wedgwood gave no acknowledgment of them to S.T.C., but he did write to Poole: "As to metaphysics, I know little about them, and my head is at present so full of various affairs that I have not even read the letters Coleridge has written on those subjects." His brother, Tom Wedgwood, himself a philosopher, was too ill "to pursue his own speculations," let alone to "attend to those of others."[29]

S.T.C. at this time claimed also to have essayed a study of sensory perception, in a bid to "solve the process of Life & Consciousness."[30] Together with these experiments went a study of Newton's treatise on optics.

S.T.C.'s abandonment of Unitarianism took place several years before he was prepared to accept the Trinity. He was not ready for the embracement of Trinitarian Christianity until the close of his sojourn in Malta and his return to England in August, 1806. An important letter to Thomas Clarkson, the abolitionist, written in October, 1806, states categorically, "the Idea of God involves that of a Tri-unity."[31]

Even now, his struggle was far from over. Crabb Robinson, in a diary entry for October 3, 1812, gives an unforgettable glimpse of the Esteesian dilemma; S.T.C. borrowed a copy of Spinoza from Crabb Robinson and, while standing in the room with him,

> kissed Spinoza's face in the title-page, and said, "This book is a gospel to me." But in less than a minute he added, "His philosophy is nevertheless false, but only by that philosophy which has demonstrated the falsehood of all other philosophies. Did philosophy commence with an *it is*, instead of an *I am*, Spinoza would be altogether true." And without allowing a breathing time, Coleridge asserted, "I however, believe in all the doctrines of Christianity, even the Trinity."[32]

S.T.C.'s cherished, but unrealised dream, was to achieve a systematic reconciliation of the 'I am' with the 'It is'. "The theory of natural philosophy would then be completed, when all nature was demonstrated to be identical in essence with that, which in its highest power exists in man as intelligence and self-consciousness."[33]

This completed theory of natural philosophy was envisaged by S.T.C. as the core of a philosophical *magnum opus* which he for so many years projected, but never succeeded in producing, for the simple reason that the 'I am' and the 'It is' refused to be systematically reconciled.

Coleridge's period saw the close of the great era of systematic thinking, a major disciplinary approach to intellectual activity from which we ourselves are now so far removed that we no longer properly understand its aims.

An organised, systematic fusing of varied elements of knowledge and of thought, so that they might be presented as an harmoniously unified structure, was accepted by S.T.C. and his contemporaries as the necessary condition for serious intellectual pursuit.

Here then, lies the explanation of S.T.C.'s prolonged struggle to demonstrate, intellectually, the reconciliation of the 'It is' and the 'I am'. Unless he could show system in his philosophical thinking, he could not hope for serious acclaim as a philosopher.

At last he had to admit failure: he could not find a systematic solution to the problem of the polarity of 'It is' and 'I am'; but the very fact that he admitted his dilemma should be seen as a tribute to the scrupulous integrity which always motivated his objective intellectual activity, as opposed to the deception which he was prepared to practise upon the world in his publications and the subjective lies which, for many years, he told in an attempt to smooth his path through day to day existence. As McFarland[34] has pointed out, S.T.C. could have engaged in the subterfuges of the transcendental systematists like Schelling, Hegel and Schopenhauer, who managed to convince themselves that 'I am' and 'It is' could exist within a single system. S.T.C. could not convince himself, and said so.

This ambiguity implied that there must always be a moment of truth hanging over him—the moment when a final choice had to be made between the 'It is' and the 'I am'. S.T.C. had a pathological dread of final decisions; he postponed this one until, literally, the last moment. On his death-bed, during the final evening of his life, S.T.C. dictated to his friend and disciple in philosophy, Dr J. H. Green, the following statement, which he articulated with the utmost difficulty, although his mind was still clear and powerful: [35]

> And be thou sure in whatever may be published of my posthumous works to remember that, first of all is the Absolute Good whose self-affirmation is the "I am," as the eternal reality in itself, and the ground and source of all other reality.
> And next, that in this idea nevertheless a distinctivity is to be carefully preserved, as manifested in the person of the Logos by whom that reality is communicated to all other beings. [36]

Beyond doubt, if S.T.C. had not had this profound heart-sense of the 'I Am', he could not have survived his terrible middle passage. He knew himself to be an old man by the time he was forty, prematurely aged by chronic ill-health and, as he put it, mismanagement. He was hopelessly dependent upon the drug which was destroying him; scarcely a relationship in his life had survived; his intellectual and literary powers were at their lowest ebb; his crises of despair were catastrophic. He was, indeed, a shipwrecked mariner, caught in the eye of the tempest with but the one solid plank of his 'I Am' to which to cling.

That he virtually fought his way out of his bondage of opium, resumed a life of distinguished literary activity, emerged as the Grand Old Man of English Literature and the guru of Highgate and (most important of all, as an indication of the extent of his recovery) succeeded in establishing a circle of secure personal relationships, was nothing short of miraculous. Only a man with an exceptionally strong personal philosophy, or faith, could have achieved this. In Coleridge's case it was a triumph for belief in Esteesee, the 'I-ship', the integrity of the individual soul.

It would be true to say that at no time did S.T.C. wholly abandon his faith. Even at Cambridge, when under the direct influence of Frend, S.T.C. retained, as he explained to George, a species of vague conviction, a "Faith . . . made up of the Evangelists and the Deistic Philosophy—a kind of *religious Twilight*." [37]

When considering S.T.C.'s progression from childhood baptismal Christian faith to near loss of all belief, moving through Dissension back to the fold of Christian orthodoxy, it is of the greatest importance to bear in mind the undoubted link that exists between drug-addiction and religious fervour.

After S.T.C. had worked his way through his (exceptionally prolonged) period of adolescent rebellion he found himself instinctively returning towards his nursery-conditioned Christian orthodoxy; but instinct was tempered by thinking and, intellectually, S.T.C. discovered the Trinity to be a virtually impassable obstacle. Nonetheless, unable as he was to accept it intellectually, neither could he ignore it. There may well be considerable significance in the fact that his ultimate acceptance of the Trinitarian concept coincided with the nadir of his morphine reliance.

The terrors of drug enslavery and the emotional and social isolation attendant upon the condition stimulated in S.T.C. the desire, indeed the need, for spiritual comfort and sanctuary. Finally an appalling drug crisis in 1813 precipitated him into an ardent, not to say desperate, embracement of full Christian orthodoxy (below pp. 475–9).

It is true that S.T.C., as he aged, might equally well, without the experience of morphine reliance, have found it increasingly satisfying to exchange objective metaphysical speculation in favour of orthodox Christianity. However, in view of the evidence now available to us in letters and notebooks, it is clear that drug experience played a major rôle in S.T.C.'s final emergence as a most profoundly devout orthodox Christian, for whom the saving of his immortal soul became a paramount concern.

CHAPTER THREE

THE PANTISOCRATS I

(June–August 1794)

S.T.C. AND HUCKS received an enthusiastic welcome from Robert Allen at Oxford; he lost no time in introducing them to his friends, among them a twenty-year-old Balliol man who had a reputation both as an ardent democrat and a rising poet. For these reasons S.T.C. must have been most interested to meet him. His name was Robert Southey.*

Southey, the son of an unsuccessful Bristol linendraper, had from infancy been brought up in Bath by his aunt, Miss Elizabeth Tyler. At the age of fourteen he had been sent to Westminster School, his education being paid for by his uncle, the Reverend Herbert Hill, who was determined that the boy should take Holy Orders. During his last year at school Southey entered a period of acute adolescent rebellion, finally being expelled for a school-magazine essay condemning flogging. As a result of this expulsion Southey was refused entrance at Christ Church, Oxford; he was ultimately admitted to Balliol, where he matriculated in November 1792.

Southey's political views contrasted violently with his poetry. The former were uncompromisingly jacobin; the latter sweetly lyrical, to the point of cloying, with the exception of his blank verse, which was highly rhetorical.

S.T.C. was greatly impressed and delighted by Southey's poems; (it must be remembered that, at this time, S.T.C. was still a slavish admirer, and imitator, of Bowles). Politically he summed Southey up: "He is truly a man of perpendicular Virtue—a downright upright Republican!"[1]

Southey, for his part, was immediately and immensely impressed by S.T.C. He found Coleridge "of most uncommon merit, of the strongest genius, the clearest judgments, the best heart."[2]

The friendship, therefore, was mutually impetuous, admiring and warm; S.T.C. perhaps especially hurling himself at Southey with impassioned abandon because such leaps forward into emotional involvement were, in his case, virtually pathological:

> . . . from the spot where first I sprang to light
> Too soon transplanted, ere my soul had fixed
> Its first domestic loves; and hence through life
> Chasing chance-started friendships.[3]

*Pronounced, as Southey himself was at pains to point out, *not* as the south in *southern*, but as the south in *south* wind.

Southey introduced S.T.C. to a circle of friends, all burning democrats. They included Robert Lovell, a visitor from Bristol, the son of a rich Quaker. Robert Lovell had six months earlier greatly annoyed his family by marrying a beautiful young actress named Mary Fricker. Another of Southey's friends, a fellow undergraduate, was George Burnett, the son of a Somerset farmer. Burnett, like Southey, was intended for the Church. Good-natured, trusting and transparently honest, he now found himself completely out of his depth, drowning in a tidal wave of furious republican talk which Southey, S.T.C., Lovell and the circle that they had attracted round them loosed in Southey's rooms in Balliol that intoxicating June.

All were agreed that the prevailing system of society was rotten, worthless, ruled by avarice and self-interest, riddled with hypocrisy and its attendant evils. Even France, upon which they had earlier pinned such extravagant hopes, had betrayed the cause. Terror had become an official weapon of the Revolution; fraternity lay, a mutilated corpse, upon the steps of the guillotine.

A fresh start must be made. It was decided that a small and dedicated brotherhood would cross the Atlantic and pioneer an experimental community, embracing the principles of abolition of personal property, fraternal equality and a participatory government by all, for all. The "prejudices and errors" of contemporary society would be eschewed. Fear, Selfishness and their "necessary offspring . . . Deceit, and desultory Hatred"[4] would be banished. For this experiment S.T.C. invented the name Pantocracy (later changed to Pantisocracy).

The "three or four"[5] day stay of S.T.C. and Hucks at Oxford protracted itself into one of three weeks, during which the "leading features of a Pantisocracy"[6] were worked out. The spot tentatively selected for the experiment was the Susquehannah—chosen, S.T.C. was much later to confide to Gillman, principally because the name was pretty and metrical.

The fullest account to survive of this Pantisocratic scheme is that given by Thomas Poole in a letter of September 22, 1794, to a Mr Hoskins, who had asked for details:

Twelve gentlemen of good education and liberal principles are to embark with twelve ladies in April next. Previous to their leaving this country they are to have as much intercourse as possible, in order to ascertain each other's dispositions, and firmly to settle every regulation for the government of their future conduct. Their opinion was that they should fix themselves at—I do not recollect the place, but somewhere in a delightful part of the new back settlements; that each man should labour two or three hours in a day, the produce of which labour would, they imagine, be more than sufficient to support the colony. As Adam Smith observes that there is not above one productive man in twenty, they argue that if each laboured the twentieth part of time, it would produce enough to satisfy their wants. The produce of their industry is to be laid up in common for the use of all; and a good library of books is to be collected, and their leisure hours to be spent in study, liberal discussions, and the education of their children . . . The regulations relating to the females strike them as the most difficult; whether the marriage contract shall be dissolved if agreeable to one or both parties, and many other circumstances, are not yet determined. The employments of the women are to be the care of infant children, and other occupations suited to their strength; at the same time the greatest attention is to be paid to the cultivation of their minds. Every one is to enjoy his own religious and political opinions, provided they do not encroach upon the rules previously made, which rules, it is unnecessary to add, must in some measure be regulated by the laws of the state which includes the district in which they settle. They calculate that each gentleman providing £125 will be sufficient to carry the scheme into execution. Finally, every individual is at liberty, whenever he pleases, to withdraw from the society. . . [7]

Forging Pantisocracy, reading aloud one another's poetry, S.T.C. and Southey commenced their friendship in an euphoric cloud of utopian politics, plans and prospects. When S.T.C. finally left Oxford he was in a state of elation and stimulation which made the process of being 'turned on' by drugs pallid in comparison. "America really inspired Hope, & I became an exalted Being."[8]

S.T.C. and Hucks resumed their pedestrian tour on July 5; it was made to the sound of loud, almost non-stop, joyous laughter. S.T.C. preached Pantisocracy as he went to anyone who would listen to him, thereby causing a good deal of indignation and confusion among loyal Britishers, who did not understand most of what he said, but, grasping that he was republican, reached for their own glasses exclaiming, "God Save the King!" He kept up an ebullient running commentary on the tour in a flow of dazzlingly high-spirited letters to Southey, who wrote back dismally from his aunt's house in Bath, where he had returned for the vacation. S.T.C. responded to Southey's dejection with sympathetic understanding:

> of all Habits the Habit of Despondence is the most pernicious to Virtue and Happiness. I once shipwrecked my bark on that rock—a friendly plank was vouchsafed me . . .These Dreams of Despair are most soothing to the Imagination—I well know it. We shroud ourselves 'in this mantle of Distress, And tell our poor Hearts, This is Happiness!' There is a *dignity* in all these solitary emotions, that flatters the pride of our *Nature*.[9]

While Southey languished in Bath, S.T.C. and Hucks walked in scorching heat among the Welsh hills. On the road from Bala to Llangollen they met two other Jesus men, Brookes and Berdmore, "rival pedestrians . . . vigorously persuing their tour—in a post chaise!"[10] The excuse of this rival pair was that Berdmore had worn himself out with his exertions. There was tremendous laughter from both parties; then Brookes and Berdmore whirled away in a cloud of dust; S.T.C. and Hucks tramped on to Wrexham. Here S.T.C. had a jolting experience. He had forgotten (or so he claimed) that Eliza Evans, Mary's sister, was in residence at Wrexham with her grandmother.

Mary Evans, by this date, was either actually betrothed to, or in the course of becoming betrothed to, a suitor named Fryer Todd, a young man of good fortune (whom she married on October 13, 1795). There is indirect evidence that she privately harboured a warm attachment to S.T.C. (in all likelihood her affection for him was more real than his for her); but common-sense, and her family, must have convinced her that to hanker after him was both fruitless and pointless. But whether she had come to this conclusion by July of 1794, or whether the event which occurred at Wrexham finally made up her mind for her, we do not know.

Clearly, S.T.C. had heard that she was being woo'd by Todd, but he had no idea of whether or not she had become officially betrothed (four months later we find him writing to Mary asking her to confirm or deny her rumoured engagement).

In spite of this, in July he was behaving as if her betrothal to Todd were virtually a certainty: it was the kind of situation from which he derived exquisite masochistic satisfaction. To Southey he wrote, with delicious melancholy, in Latin verse: "She lives, but not for me; as a loving bride perhaps—ah, sadness!—she has thrown her arms round another man's neck. Farewell . . . oh, beautiful Mary!"[11]

On the morning of Sunday, July 13, during service in Wrexham church, S.T.C. found himself exchanging a startled glance with Eliza Evans. The service concluded, he hurried back to his inn; it seems he was now anxious to avoid Eliza (which substantiates his claim that he had forgotten that she resided at Wrexham). To his amazement, not long after, Eliza appeared in the street outside the inn, with Mary at her side. The sisters walked back and forth past the inn, several times (as Hucks, instructed to keep sentinel, afterwards informed S.T.C., who had retired into hiding).

There was nothing to prevent him from rushing into the street and making ardent avowal of his love. No chaperones were present to deter him. There can be no doubt that Mary was giving him the opportunity to speak to her. But so fearfully ignorant was he of female psychology that he supposed that the sisters were simply trying to ascertain whether or not Eliza truly *had* seen him in the church, or had been deceived by a very similar face! This misunderstanding of Mary's behaviour was, nonetheless, no reason for his failure to seize the opportunity of resuming contact with the girl whose Image, he swore to all his male friends, "is in the Sanctuary of my Bosom—and never can it be torn from thence but with the strings that grapple my heart to Life.—"[12]

Instead, confronted by this moment of truth with Mary Evans, S.T.C. fled and remained hidden from view until poor Mary had ceased to walk up and down outside the inn.

S.T.C. sent two friends, Southey and Henry Martin, highly-coloured and somewhat differing accounts of this episode. To Martin he described how the sisters had first spied him in the inn window and had both uttered shrieks; he, for his part, had almost fainted. "But Love is a local Anguish— I am 16 miles distant, and am not half so miserable—"[13] he told Southey; these two letters go far to support S.T.C.'s subsequent statement that his love for Mary Evans was a matter of his imagination.

The pedestrian tour continued into Snowdonia. At Aberconway the travellers ran into Brookes and Berdmore again, with whom they joined forces for the tramp to Caernarvon and an ascent of Snowdon. By August 5, S.T.C. was in Bristol seeking Southey in order to organise further the Pantisocratic venture.

One of their major calculations was that each gentleman of the party should provide £125. Southey and S.T.C. decided to raise money by writing a drama. Robespierre had fallen from power and had been guillotined on July 24: *The Fall of Robespierre* was therefore written by the two co-dramatists, at top speed, in tremendous blank verse with a sublime disregard for action. As S.T.C. explained, in the dedication to Henry Martin: "intricacy of plot could not have been attempted without a gross violation of . . . facts."[14] Nonetheless, the work merits attention if for no other reason than that it is the earliest surviving attempt at modern political drama.

S.T.C. wrote the first act, Southey the remaining two. *Act One, Scene: The Tuileries* cradles some tantalisingly prophetic flashes of other work to come:

> And love and friendship on his coward heart
> Shine like the powerless sun on polar ice.

This anticipates that magical mast-high ice which, in a short span of years, was to come floating by, as green as emerald.

S.T.C. was superbly confident of the play's success. "It will repay us amply."[15]

Meantime Pantisocracy was preached to a circle of the democratically inclined in and about Bristol. This included Robert Lovell's friend, Joseph Cottle, a young bookseller and printer and Tom Poole of Nether Stowey.

Cottle, although flattered to be asked by Lovell if he would care to join the Pantisocrats, could not conceal doubts about the feasibility of the scheme and finally declined to participate. Poole proved warmly enthusiastic about Pantisocracy as an idea, but was sceptical of its viability.

Poole was a democrat of action. A man of considerable resources of intellect, he had been destined from birth to carry on his family's long-established and prosperous tanning business. Unlike his younger brother and cousins he had not been sent to grammar school but had been apprenticed straight into the trade. He was therefore largely self-educated, so far as scholarly attainments were concerned.

His knowledge of the tanning industry was extensive and in 1790 he was sent by the West of England tanners to London as their delegate at a conference to discuss the distressed state of the industry. The conference, in turn, elected Poole as its representative to interview Pitt, the Prime Minister, in 1791. Poole, who was twenty-six at the time, returned to Stowey inflamed with democratic views which his family and neighbours found alarming. He went about with his hair ostentatiously unpowdered, learned French, studied Paine's *Rights of Man* and started the Stowey Book Society.

His cousin, Charlotte Poole, noted in her journal for December 18, 1792: "Everybody at this time talks politicks, and is looking with anxiety for fresh intelligence from France, which is a scene of guilt and confusion."[16]

As a result of his democratic activities and opinions Poole, to his great amusement, was warned that he was considered by the Government to be the most dangerous person in the county of Somerset, which was regarded, thanks chiefly to Poole himself, as "a gravely disaffected area."[17]

The first visit of S.T.C. and Southey to Nether Stowey took place on August 18, 1794, according to the journal kept (in Latin) by Tom's cousin, John Poole. The translated entry for this date reads:

About one o'clock, Thomas Poole and his brother Richard, Henry Poole, and two young men, friends of his, come in . . . One is an undergraduate of Oxford, the other of Cambridge. Each of them was shamefully hot with Democratic rage as regards politics, and both Infidel as to religion. I was extremely indignant. At last, however, about two o'clock, they all go away. After dinner I betake myself to the *Life of Johnson*. About seven o'clock Mr Reekes comes from Stowey; he is very indignant over the odious and detestable ill-feeling of those two young men, whom he had met at my Uncle Thomas's. They seem to have shown their sentiments more plainly there than with us. But enough of such matters.[18]

Poole himself, attracted as he was by the Pantisocratic ideas of his visitors, commented:

Could they realize . . . their Scheme . . . they would, indeed, realize the age of reason; but, however perfectable human nature may be, I fear it is not yet perfect enough to exist under the regulation of such a system.[19]

Pantisocracy became a popular topic of conversation with Bristol's radical intelligentsia, but there were no useful offers of financial assistance, nor were there volunteers eager to join the Susquehannah-bound party, with the exception of the ladies of the Fricker family, to whom S.T.C. had been introduced without delay by Robert Southey.

The widowed Mrs Fricker had five daughters: Mary Lovell, and the as yet unwed Sarah, Edith (the betrothed of Southey), "the Angel of the Race, self-nibbling Martha,"[20] and Little Eliza, who was scarcely more than a child, as was the son of the family, George.

S.T.C., a pathological philanderer, was in his element with the pretty, intelligent, lively Fricker girls. Bursting with laughter, puns and conundrums, brilliant with elation and marvellously pleasing (he prided himself on his gallantry with attractive young women), he became wholly carried away. He blithely made increasingly warm advances to Sarah, who responded delightedly. The inevitable happened; within a matter of days S.T.C. had convinced himself that he was in love. He proposed and was accepted.

Everyone was astonished, particularly Southey, who was under the impression that S.T.C. still nursed the image of Mary Evans in the sanctuary of his bosom, as he had sworn was the case only a few weeks previously.

The whirlwind courtship was not really so very remarkable when S.T.C.'s personality is borne in mind. "The lamentable difficulty I have always experienced in . . . abstaining from what the people around me were doing"[21] goes far to explain the betrothal to Sarah Fricker. Lovell and Southey had already chosen Fricker brides; George Burnett proposed to Martha (and was refused). With all this Fricker wooing in the air, S.T.C. was bound to follow suit.

Among the *dramatis personae* of the Wordsworth-Coleridge circle the two wives, Sarah Coleridge and Mary Wordsworth, remain the least known to us. Mary was overshadowed by her sister-in-law, Dorothy; while Sarah, or Sara (as S.T.C. always called her, dropping the *h*), has been handed down to posterity mainly through the medium of the loaded pens of Dorothy Wordsworth and S.T.C. himself.

When a marriage founders, or simply goes through a bad patch, the friends and acquaintances of the couple concerned all too often find themselves taking sides: the Wordsworths, understandably, stood foursquare behind S.T.C. He complained bitterly and incessantly to his friends about the behaviour of his wife; Dorothy, who was devoted to him, gave a ready ear to his criticism of Sara, accepting without hesitation all that he had to say. It is always flattering to a woman to be told by a man that she can give him greater sympathy and understanding than can his own wife; it is an ancient spiel, but it nearly always works. The women of the Wordsworth household showered upon S.T.C. the love and tender reciprocation which Mrs Coleridge, so her husband alleged, was incapable of giving him.

The ladies of the Wordsworth "fireside Divan" (as Keats put it)[22] were noted above all for their exquisite sensibility. Mrs Coleridge, according to S.T.C. and his echo, Dorothy, was wholly lacking in sensibility; indeed, if we believe them, she was devoid of all feeling whatsoever, apart from emotions of social pride. Dorothy took her cue for criticism of Sara Coleridge from S.T.C. and would certainly not have been so acrid had it not been for his example (though, equally, it is doubtful whether he would have criticised his wife so bitterly had he not had the encouragement of

Dorothy's sympathetic ear). She, for her part, further enlarged in her journal and letters the unflattering portrait of Sara Coleridge as a sad fiddle-faddler, a foolish mother who reared her children to be namby-pamby, puny and nettle-rashy—a light, stupid, frivolous personality, fat, rather vulgar and thinking only of her personal vanity and social position.

Against this should be set the Greta Hall portraiture of the Grasmere ladies: Dorothy with her "dirty scotchy ways"[23] and total lack of discretion, Mary Wordsworth's deplorable cooking, the undisciplined, rowdy upbringing of the Wordsworth children, Southey's comment that Wordsworth and his sister were, of all human beings whom he had ever known, the most intensely selfish.[24] In short, an active rivalry existed between Grasmere and Keswick and in retrospect we may now well feel that it was six to the one and half a dozen to the other. However, the Wordsworth writings have received much greater publicity than the letters and journals stemming from Greta Hall; what Grasmere thought of Keswick is infinitely better known than is Keswick's opinion of Grasmere.

The bitter accusations, amounting to vilification, hurled by S.T.C. at his wife, both directly and indirectly, are classical examples of the ranting upbraidings and indictments directed by the drug-addict at those who are nearest and intrinsically dearest to him, to whom he stands most in debt, to whom he also knows that he has behaved most cruelly. Tortured by guilt, the addict, in reaction, lashes with his tongue his parents, or marriage-partner, circulating fearsome portraits of them as polar-hearted and full of positive dislike and ill-natured feeling, if not downright hatred for him. As S.T.C. himself at one point confessed:

> In exact proportion, as I *loved* any person or persons more than others, & would have sacrificed my *Life* for them, were *they* sure to be the most barbarously mistreated.[25]

S.T.C.'s diatribes against his wife are suitable for inclusion in a textbook on drug-addiction; they tell us a great deal about his condition, but, as portraiture of Sara Coleridge they are valueless, apart from providing evidence that she reacted to his addiction in the bewildered, frightened, desperate, despairing, and at last hopelessly resigned pattern to which the tragic close relatives of addicts must inescapably adhere.

The Coleridge children have left us material which affords a glimpse of a dearly loved and loving mother, naturally cheerful, immensely loyal, both in word and deed, to the husband, their father, who was almost always absent from home. Sara never permitted herself a syllable of criticism of S.T.C. in the presence of the children; indeed, she was always at pains to impress upon them his distinction as a man and love for them as a father.

(It is equally touching and impressive to read the letters that S.T.C. wrote to his children, emphasising their mother's devotion to them and reminding them of their loving duty towards her. The Coleridges had a sacred pact that they would do nothing to denigrate each other in the eyes of their children; to this they adhered scrupulously.)

The handful of Sara's own letters which survive are not over-revealing; she was reticent as a personality and, furthermore, had been reared to maintain a discreet social front. Her letters are those of a fluently literate woman, entertainingly gossipy and not unwitty; her proclivity for prattle concealed (one suspects, and Southey himself confirmed it) an often heavy heart. Hers is an over-brightness that suggests a person gallantly determined to remain cheerful at all costs, or, as the Cockney succinctly expresses it, "to keep her pecker up." That she was a proud and dedicated mother is spontaneously demonstrated in almost every line that she writes; deep feelings of love and loyalty lie below the somewhat affectedly brittle façade. She is at pains to make it clear that she holds a secure and respected social position and for this she has been much criticised; but when her unhappy and frequently perilous background, the difficulties of her early years and the traumata of her married life are taken into consideration, her anxiety to be seen to have an established position in respectable society must appear a perfectly understandable preoccupation. In the happier days of early womanhood, under the heady influence of Pantisocracy, she had revealed a much freer spirit. Given different circumstances Sara Coleridge must have developed potentialities which marital disaster blighted.

The Frickers, in fact, were in almost every respect a family of misfortune. They had not always been poor; Mrs Fricker, an educated woman, had brought a marriage dowry of "up to 10,000£ . . . & yet . . . drank up the Cup of affliction . . . to the very dregs."[26] Her husband, a tinsmith and sugar-mould maker of Westbury (a suburb of Bristol), who had died in 1786 leaving his family impoverished, had been an unsatisfactory spouse; Mrs Fricker had emerged from the ordeal of marriage pious, miserable and martyr-like, to face the further ordeal of poor widowhood with a large and still young family.

Her daughters all had looks and charm. Sarah, like her sister Mary, was a beauty: small, dainty, dark, vivacious, flower-like. A tribute to her is paid (in a typically back-handed way) by Sara Hutchinson, writing in middle-age from Rydal Mount:

I often congratulate myself upon never having been a beauty—for Mrs Coleridge says she cannot come to look at herself—and that it is not a bit matter what one puts on when one is grown such a [torn] . . . [? fright].[27]

The Fricker girls had brains as well as beauty. Their mother gave them educations well above those usually received by females at that time. Mary was remarkably studious (she could read both Latin and Greek); she was sufficiently accomplished for S.T.C. to have been prepared, at one point, to have considered recommending her to the Wedgwood family as a governess. He hesitated, not on the grounds of her intellectual unsuitability, but because of her proud and unreliable temperament.

Edith taught in a small school before her marriage. Sara and Martha were milliners. It must be remembered that the range of occupations open to respectable girls, however well educated, was strictly limited and that, for the Frickers, reduced by poverty to a station in life well below that appropriate to their natural endowments and acquirements, the horizon was bleakly restricted.

Sara was, according to S.T.C.'s considered and frequently repeated judgement, of "considerable intellect."[28] She was able to educate her own daughter, Sara, so that by the age of ten the child could read French tolerably well and Italian fluently and had an acquaintance with the English language which astounded and impressed S.T.C. when he met her after a period of absence. Even Dorothy Wordsworth had to admit that Mrs Coleridge was "an excellent teacher by *books*."[29] Dorothy, of course, was a disciple of the "spontaneous wisdom" taught by Nature:

> Books! 'tis a dull and endless strife:
> Come, hear the woodland linnet . . .

The Frickers were undoubtedly handicapped (and this must have been Dorothy's implication when she jibed, as she constantly did, at Mrs Coleridge's stupidity) by certain miserable inhibitions and obsessions consequent upon their social predicament as adolescent girls. The tensions imposed by straitened circumstances upon families of small income, the ever-present wary sense of a fight for survival (a campaign waged incessantly not only to maintain meagre living standards, but to preserve a good name amongst one's peers, to keep intact one's social pride), constituted a species of battle of social attrition which our own era virtually does not know and therefore fails to take into account when considering the psychology (especially the female psychology) of the time. Both sexes, below a certain income belt, were exposed to severe insecurity, but upon females particularly this insecurity had far-reaching and crippling effects. The world was a most perilous place for women of restricted circumstance who, like the Frickers, had to find a way of supporting themselves, yet at the same time to remain respectable. They suffered a sense of ever-lurking danger; the consequences of an unguarded moment or a single false step could be calamitous. For those young women who, like the Frickers, lacked the protection of a father or older brothers, the situation was rendered increasingly dire; their vulnerability was alarming indeed.

All this emerges clearly from novels of the period. Dickens (drawing upon his own childhood and family for source material) has left us several imperishable portraits of early nineteenth-century shabby gentility. He exposes the inevitable results of genteel poverty—among them an exaggerated regard for all the trappings of respectability, an even more exaggerated sense of personal importance and an edgy irritability lest this importance should not be accorded proper acknowledgement, a desperate eye always watching for real or imagined social slights, and a prickly, all too easily injured pride.

The traits which S.T.C. found so unrewarding in his wife, and which Dorothy Wordsworth attributed to stupidity, must almost certainly have resulted from the stresses of an impoverished and unprotected girlhood, which had been survived only by unremitting vigilance, wearisome thrift and wary attention to the everlasting keeping up of appearances. It was not a background which promoted a relaxed and liberated spirit.

These tensions Dorothy (and her friends the Hutchinson girls) were spared. They at no time in their lives stood unprotected or were obliged to step out into the world to earn their own bread. Dorothy's parentless adolescence was not, it is true, always happy, but to insecurity, in the real sense, she was unexposed.

In any case, the true issue between herself and Sara Coleridge was not one of stupidity, but of class distinction. Dorothy was not alone in regarding Sara as somewhat of a social inferior. The Ottery Coleridges seem to have behaved courteously and kindly to "Mrs Sam" but we know that the Poole family (with the exception of Tom and his mother) was rude to Mrs Coleridge when she went to live at Nether Stowey; other women in the neighbourhood followed suit. Mrs Sandford herself, in her biography of Poole, indicates that Sara Coleridge was of inferior social status.

The Wordsworths, upon arriving in the Stowey locality, would soon have heard this kind of talk. In spite of their democratic views they were both nicely aware of their status as gentlefolk. The social nuances of Dorothy's comments upon Sara Coleridge are exceedingly delicate, but to the trained ear they are unmistakably present.

Sara must have known only too well that she was condescended to by S.T.C.'s two most valued Stowey friends (Tom and old Mrs Poole apart) and this would have exacerbated her own aggressive attitudes.

The element of Fricker social inferiority may well have been a factor in encouraging the Pantisocrats to favour Fricker brides; by marrying a little beneath them Lovell, Southey and Coleridge were practising the equality which they preached. That in two cases the family of the bridegroom objected to the bride would have served only to stimulate democratic fervour.

For S.T.C. the suggestion of social inferiority in his bride may well have been an essential ingredient for any chance of marital happiness. It has been pointed out that he regarded sexual activity as degrading, unless intellectually sublimated into spiritual significance, or frankly indulged in as an overt vice, with a whore. Sara was to prove to be the only woman who was not a professional harlot from whom he did not run, in a physically sexual context; his sexual union with her seems to have been, while his health permitted it, entirely satisfactory. The fact that he could always look down on her a little socially may well have been an important contributing factor here.

During their early years together he found much in her to admire, also. He took enormous delight and pride in her beauty and dainty elegance. His letters contain tributes to her wit and perception and what he called her "polished understanding." Indeed, he went so far as to endow her with those mysterious attributes of specialness which he later reserved exclusively for the Wordsworths and the Hutchinson sisters. Writing to John Thelwall, in 1797, upon the subject of a Mrs Evans of Darley, whom S.T.C. held in almost extravagant esteem and with whom he and Sara had once spent a blissful five weeks stay, he explained: "She is no common Being who could create so warm & lasting an interest in *our* hearts: for *we* are no common people."[30]

Even in the darkest days of estrangement from Sara, S.T.C. never ceased to pay tribute to her dedicated and tireless devotion as mother to his children and her exceedingly capable management of the always meagre financial resources. Her absolute purity of mind won enduring tribute from him, as did her discretion.

Sara's personal style was almost diametrically opposed to that of the Wordsworths and when S.T.C. came under their influence (prostrating himself in admiration of them, many of his old friends complained) it was inevitable that he should commence to scrutinise Sara with a cooler eye. Dorothy affected the Romantic stance as a child of Nature: Sara modelled herself on the provincial drawing-room elegances of middle-class Bristol. The tone of voice revealed in her letters is unmistakably that of a calculatedly trivial rattle; a sprightly, careless gaiety, a smart flippancy was her cultivated keynote. Yet her lightness of touch, her "dancing, frisking high-spirits"[31] were obviously inherent personality traits and must have been most baffling to Dorothy Wordsworth who was fundamentally of an earnest disposition.

Highly revealing is Sara Hutchinson's comment upon Sara Coleridge's impulsive, fly-away, surface-skimming aspect (a comment made in a letter to Edward Quillinan, after Mrs Coleridge's removal from Keswick to Hampstead in 1829):

We . . . have lost the amusement derived from poor Mrs Coleridge's *Sibyllines*, as we used to call her flying letters written on scraps of paper.*[32]

Undoubtedly this somewhat giddy, gad-fly, happy-go-lucky accident-

Sibylline Leaves, S.T.C.'s collected poems, published in 1817.

proneness was one of Sara Coleridge's predominant features; it was adorable in the eyes of a man in love with her, infuriating once disenchantment
had set in. She knew this well and when she could at last stomach no more
of Samuel she resorted to a feather-on-the-breeze levity which maddened
him (precisely as she had intended that it should). One such occasion was
when, having received from S.T.C. yet another of an endless string of
letters all assuring her that he faced imminent death (intelligence that he
had been drumming into her for over a decade), she returned the blithe
comment: "Lord! how often you are ill! You must be MORE careful about
Colds!"[33] "O shocking!" groaned S.T.C., reacting as she had hoped, "it is
too clear, that she is glad that her Children are about to be fatherless!"[34]
This was in 1808, twenty-five years before his demise.

She was always delightfully vague about dates. We find S.T.C. scribbling
to Southey: "I received . . . your head piece to Mrs Coleridge's Letter,
which, as usual, she has not dated."[35] Her first-born arrived when she was
not in the least expecting him, so that she had to deliver herself. S.T.C.
informed Thelwall:

> My little David Hartley is marvellously well, & grows fast—I was at
> Birmingham when he was born—I returned immediately on receiving the
> unexpected news (for my Sara had strangely miscalculated).[36]

She lacked persistence and not infrequently required prompting. A husbandly letter, written to her from Somerset when she was racked with
rheumatism in the cold and damp of a Lake Country January, in 1802, is
worth quoting:

> I hope to God you will make you[rself] flannel Drawers, &c, as I advised
> —[and] instantly, get the fluid Essence [of] Mustard—& that you have
> already [begun] to take the Mustard Pills, night & morning. Do it regularly
> & perseveran[tly], or it will not signifiy a farthing.—[37]

She was, as aforesaid, accident-prone; sometimes with unfortunate consequences for Samuel, as when:

> dear Sara accidentally emptied a skillet of boiling milk on my foot . . . [38]

It was no laughing matter; he was laid up for several days, and just when
the Lambs had come to stay. On other occasions it was a misfortune which
provoked hilarity. Southey, in later years, described how:

> Yesterday I took Miss Betham, Edith and Mrs C. up Skiddaw . . . Coming
> home Mrs C. got into a bog some way above her knees, and I saved her life!
> . . . Afterwards I washed her petticoat in one of the gills, and carried it
> home upon my stick.[39]

S.T.C.'s birthplace; the vicarage, Ottery St. Mary, Devon.
(*British Tourist Authority*)

Easedale Tarn, the Wordsworths' "Black Quarter" and favoured place for
expeditions. The scene pictured here in a photograph of
c. 1890 can be little changed from their day.
(*George Fisher Collection*)

Pantisocrat: S.T.C. in 1795. Portrait by P. Vandyke.
(*National Portrait Gallery, London*)

Lapsed Pantisocrat: Robert Southey in 1798. Sketch
in pencil and chalk by R. Hancock.
(*National Portrait Gallery, London*)

"Alfoxden's musing tenant": William Wordsworth in 1798.
Sketch in pencil and chalk by R. Hancock.
(*National Portrait Gallery, London*)

"The maid . . . who with fraternal love sweetens his
solitude": Dorothy Wordsworth, *c.* 1800. Silhouette by
artist unknown.
(*Courtesy Dove Cottage Trustees*)

It is not altogether surprising to learn that Southey referred to Sara (to her slight annoyance, we are told) as "Bumble-cum-Tumble," taking this name from the nursery rhyme:

> All I have left as company now
> Are Bumble-cum-Tumble and Doggy Bow-Wow.[40]

Yet Sara had her practical side, too. We have S.T.C.'s unwavering testimony to her as an excellent mother and a skilled manager in household economy. She was obviously flexible and adaptable, well able to cope when left to all intents and purposes husbandless for long periods at a time, with very little money and no exact idea of S.T.C.'s whereabouts. She was called upon to make tedious moves about the country, with small children and much baggage. Her life, by twentieth-century standards, was physically hard; she lived in a succession of cold, damp, draughty, comfortless houses, coping with an infant family, a chronically sick and drug-reliant husband, and all the wearing daily chores of early nineteenth-century domestic life, assisted by only one small servant-girl. Somehow, on next to nothing, she contrived to raise three children to educated and physically healthy maturity; she kept herself neat and well turned out. She was, as we have seen, a cultivated woman. She shared Greta Hall with a Poet Laureate and his family, was long and intimately acquainted with the Wordsworths, was the wife of Samuel Taylor Coleridge and hostess to many distinguished and eminent people. It would be foolish to dismiss her as a fat, tedious, weak little person who was nothing but a burden to a man of genius; she was a highly accomplished, spirited and, indeed, exceptional personality, in her own right. (It is worth noting that the Gillmans greatly liked her.)

Without doubt, when S.T.C. was courting her in a state of Pantisocratic euphoria, he preached to her the doctrine of sexual equality. If Sara had not already made acquaintance with *A Vindication of the Rights of Woman* she must soon have done so. Her behaviour during her engagement showed a surprising disregard for the conventions of female modesty prevailing among respectable young ladies of her day, despite all the inhibitions and prohibitions of Fricker upbringing. One of S.T.C.'s letters to his Sara, written in 1802 during a period of violent marital strife, indicates that she had embraced, too enthusiastically for his real liking, the creed of women's rights:

> Permit me, my dear Sara! . . . to say—that in sex, acquirements, and in the quantity and quality of natural endowments whether of Feeling, or of Intellect, you are the Inferior.[41]

Opium apart, it is not difficult to see why they fought.

This, then, was the spirited (and according to S.T.C. at times fiery), gallant, obstinate, highly intelligent, tough, maddening, loyal, beautiful, not altogether predictable little woman to whom S.T.C. got himself betrothed in his twenty-third year, mistaking "the ebullience of *schematism* for affection"[42] as he subsequently expressed it. His scheming now included domestic bliss in a humble cottage in some picturesque rustic spot (a stock Romantic idyll, this); the only difference, in his case, being that the dream was to be realised, he hoped, on the other side of the Atlantic, in a Brave New World which, obviously, he visualised as precisely like the English West Country—green, cosy, tranquil. Here he would turn over a new leaf and, with spade in hand, start anew. As he had told Tom Poole, his "aberrations from prudence" had been great; but he now vowed to be "as sober and rational as his most sober friends could wish."[43] What more sober and rational than a scheme for a self-supporting utopian community upon the banks of the Susquehannah?

> No more my visionary soul shall dwell
> On joys that were; no more endure to weigh
> The shame and anguish of the evil day,
> Wisely forgetful! O'er the ocean swell
> Sublime of Hope, I seek the cottage'd dell
> Where Virtue calm with careless step may stray,
> And dancing to the moonlight roundelay,
> The wizard Passions weave an holy spell . . .[44]

By the end of August S.T.C. was on his way back to Cambridge, via London, where it was proposed that he should recruit support for the Pantisocratic scheme and get a handbook written and through the press, describing how "A small but liberalised party" of persons "all highly charged with that enthusiasm which results from strong perceptions of moral rectitude, called into life and action by ardent feelings" had formed "a scheme of emigration on the principles of an abolition of individual property." The proposed site for the community was, tentatively, "a convenient distance from Cooper's Town on the banks of the Susquehannah." The date of departure was fixed for the following March and, in the course of the ensuing winter "those of us whose bodies, from habits of sedentary study or academic indolence, have not acquired their full tone and strength, intend to learn the theory and practice of agriculture and carpentry."[45]

Bearing the draft outline of the handbook, the not yet completed *Fall of Robespierre* and his beloved Casimir, S.T.C. left Bristol to a flutter of Fricker handkerchiefs and the republican salutes of his fellow Pantisocrats.

CHAPTER FOUR

THE PANTISOCRATS II

(August 1794–August 1795)

S.T.C. REACHED LONDON in a dejected state. For one thing, he had lost his beloved Casimir on the road and, for another, he was already beginning to have gnawing doubts about recent events in Bristol.

In London he lived by day in the studies of friendly Graecians; at night he slept in the Angel Inn, off Butcher Hall Lane behind Newgate Street, and every evening he spent at the Salutation and Cat, an alehouse in Newgate Street. Here he drank porter and punch round a good fire in a private room, with various cronies, including a young man, a former Christ's Hospital boy, who had been to North America and had now returned as an agent for an American firm selling land to would-be immigrants. S.T.C., a most innocent Martin Chuzzlewit, reported back to Southey:

> He says, two thousand Pound will do—that he doubts not, we can contract for our Passage under 400£.—that we shall buy the land a good deal cheaper when we arrive at America,—than we could do in England—or why (adds he) am I sent over here. That 12 men may *easily* clear *three hundred* Acres in 4 or 5 months—and that for 600 Dollars a Thousand Acres may be cleared, and houses built upon them—He recommends the Susqusannah [sic] from its excessive beauty, & its security from hostile Indians . . . That literary Characters make *money* there—He never saw a *Byson* in his life—but he has heard of them—They are quite backwards.—The Musquitos are not so bad as our Gnats—and after you have been there a little while, they don't trouble you much.[1]

This sounded encouraging enough, but others took a less optimistic view. S.T.C. found that he could drum up no more volunteers for Pantisocracy, with the exception of two Bluecoat boys, Samuel Favel and the younger Le Grice, who both vowed to hasten Susquehannahwards immediately upon coming down from Cambridge (they had not yet left school).

S.T.C., during this sojourn in London, made no contact with Sara Fricker. He had promised her that he would write upon his return to Cambridge; this return he delayed. One gains the impression that he was endeavouring to hide from the events which were overtaking him. There is strong indication that he took refuge in laudanum; by September 11 he was unwell, "heavy of head, turbulent of Bowell, and inappetent"[2]—ominous symptoms. He postponed his return to Cambridge for a further week because of this illness.

On September 17 he arrived back in his familiar room at Jesus. "My God! . . . since I quitted this room what and how important Events have been evolved! America! Southey! Miss Fricker!"[3] With an attempt at a confidence that he did not feel, he declared: "I certainly love her. I think of her incessantly & with unspeakable tenderness—with that inward melting away of Soul that symptomatizes it."[4]

In this mood he sat down and wrote to Sara ("my Sally"),[5] an ardent love letter, "pouring forth the Heart."[6] This was the fatal letter, the writing of which S.T.C. would subsequently describe to Southey as "the most criminal action of my life . . . I had worked myself to such a pitch, that I scarcely knew I was writing like an hypocrite."[7] He had barely finished it before a furious missive arrived from Southey, upbraiding S.T.C. for not having written to Sara and accusing him of neglecting her. S.T.C. at once wrote a second letter (of apology and explanation) to Sara and a letter to Southey.

Southey, doubtless, had acted with the best of motives in spurring S.T.C. to greater attention to Sara; but it was the worst possible way of furthering the courtship. S.T.C.'s immediate reaction was to experience a marked cooling of the "unspeakable tenderness" which, until then, had been melting his Soul. As he was to observe most truly of himself, to himself:

> you have some small portion of pig-nature in your moral idiosyncracy, and, like these amiable creatures, must occasionally be pulled backward from the boat in order to make you enter it.[8]

Southey, not understanding this but scenting that S.T.C. was experiencing chilling second thoughts over Sara, proceeded now, most energetically, to shove S.T.C. towards the Fricker boat, while Coleridge revealed increasing signs of reluctance: "My heart is very heavy." "I am labouring under a waking Night-mair of Spirits." "I am in the queerest humour in the world—and am out of love with everybody—."[9]

It is clear that he did not mention his engagement to Sara Fricker to anyone, not even, it seems, to his own family. In an attempt to forget his troublesome involvement S.T.C. plunged into a whirling social life. The Norwich Theatre company was at Cambridge on tour; the undergraduates flocked to pay homage to the leading-lady, Elizabeth Brunton, daughter of the actor-manager of the company, John Brunton. S.T.C. and his close comrades, Francis Wrangham and George Caldwell, were particularly enthusiastic in paying their respects and competed in composing Bruntoniads to the actress. S.T.C. declared himself "Bewitched. I have indeed incautiously drank too deeply from the bowl of the blameless Circe—the sweet intoxication, that makes the Heart forget its duties & its cares."[10]

The passion was a deliciously hopeless one; the actress married and became Mrs Merry upon the close of her Cambridge tour. This did not really worry S.T.C. who had been simultaneously pursuing a gay flirtation with her very pretty sister, Ann. Indeed, he probably created an impression of genuine interest and attachment in this quarter, for Mr and Mrs Brunton invited him to visit Norwich in the New Year. Furthermore, this invitation he accepted.

Naturally, in mentioning these social activities to Southey, S.T.C. made it sound as if it were all against his personal inclination. "Much against my Will I am engaged to drink Tea and go to the play with Miss Brunton (Mrs Merry's Sister). The young lady and indeed the whole Family have taken it into their heads to be very much attached to me—tho' I have known them only 6 days."[11]

Meanwhile, thanks initially to Brookes and Berdmore, who had returned from Wales with mangled accounts of Pantisocracy, the Scheme had become a favourite topic of Cambridge conversation; though almost everyone agreed with Caldwell that the strength of S.T.C.'s imagination had intoxicated his reason.

Whether S.T.C. himself informed George Coleridge of the Scheme or whether news of it leaked through the academic grape-vine we do not know, but by October the senior Coleridge brothers were in agitated correspondence with S.T.C., a correspondence that was "all remonstrance, and Anguish, & suggestions, that I am deranged!!—."[12]

Clearly, the senior Coleridges had reminded themselves of the Army's verdict upon Samuel. If they had not paid serious attention to it at the time, they were doing so now.

It seems probable that George Coleridge, in desperation, at last asked Mary Evans to approach S.T.C. in an attempt to dissuade him; a letter, unsigned but unmistakably in her writing, reached S.T.C. in early October. It began abruptly and dramatically:

Is this handwriting altogether erased from your Memory? . . . For whom am I now violating the Rules of female Delicacy? Is it for the same Coleridge, whom I once regarded as a Sister her best-beloved Brother, Or for one who will RIDICULE that advice from me, which he has rejected as offered by his family? I will hazard the attempt . . . I conjure you, Coleridge! earnestly and solemnly conjure you, to consider long and deeply, before you enter into any rash Schemes. There is an Eagerness in your Nature, which is ever hurrying you into the sad Extreme. I have heard that you mean to leave England: and on a Plan so absurd and extravagant, that were I for a moment to imagine it *true*, I should be obliged to listen with a more patient Ear to Suggestions, which I have rejected a thousand Times with scorn and anger—yes! whatever Pain I might suffer I should be forced to exclaim—'Oh what a noble Mind is here o'erthrown. Blasted with Exstacy!". . . . [She went on to point out the duties that he owed to his country, his friends, his God] . . . you have too much Sensibility to be an Infidel . . . [Finally she became touchingly personal, reminding him of the time when] . . . you used to say, We thought in all things alike. I often reflect on the happy hours we spent together, and regret the Loss of your Society. I cannot easily forget those whom I once loved— . . . If you value my peace of mind, you must *on no account* answer this Letter . . . Farewell—Coleridge—! I shall always feel that I have been your *Sister*.[13]

This letter flung S.T.C. into a wretchedly confused humour: "My thoughts are floating about in a most Chaotic State—."[14]

Southey was now upbraiding him again for neglecting to write to Sara Fricker. S.T.C. confessed to Southey that he did not love her: "a moment's reflection might have told me, Love is not a plant of so mushroom a growth."[15] He added, repeatedly, with too great a vehemence to be entirely convincing, that nonetheless he would do his duty by Sara Fricker. "I am resolved—but wretched!"[16]

Among his friends he distributed copies of a sonnet, *Thou bleedest, my poor Heart*, occasioned, he explained, "by a letter (which I recently received from a young Lady, whom for five years I loved—almost to madness) dissuasive of my American Scheme—; but where Justice leads, I will follow."[17]

The Coleridge brothers, with George as their mouthpiece, warned S.T.C. that it might prove necessary to restrain him from the ridiculous Pantisocratic venture by having him confined in a private lunatic asylum. Although S.T.C. was pretty certain that much of this was a carefully calculated pattern of tactics designed to stampede him into abandoning the Scheme, he clearly became deeply perturbed by the campaign that his family was waging against him and began to wonder to what lengths it would be carried. George affected coldness and alienation:

> mixed with involuntary bursts of ANGUISH and disappointed Affection— questions concerning the mode in which I would have it mentioned to my aged Mother.[18]

Forcibly cogent arguments against the Pantisocratic Scheme came from all directions. Late in October, for instance, S.T.C. received an invitation from Dr Thomas Edwards, "the great Grecian of Cambridge and heterodox Divine," to drink tea with him and spend the evening in discussion. With Dr Edwards was "a counsellor whose name is Lushington—a Democrat— and a man of the most powerful and Briaréan Intellect." These two challenged S.T.C. on the subject of Pantisocracy; the discussion lasted for six hours. In conclusion "Lushington and Edwards declared the System impregnable, supposing the assigned Quantum of Virtue and Genius in the first Individuals."[19] However, Lushington had also left S.T.C. with a chill prophecy to brood upon: "Your System, Coleridge! appears strong to the head and lovely to the Heart—but depend upon it you will never give your women sufficient strength of mind, liberality of heart, or vigilance of Attention—*They* will spoil it!"[20]

Not only women! Robert Southey, too, was suddenly entertaining some very dubious, indeed, downright undemocratic notions. He was now suggesting that the Pantisocrats should take one or two servants with them to America.

Not that he was not prepared to be highly democratic in his behaviour towards them: "Let them dine with us and be treated with as much equality as they would wish . . . but perform that part of Labour for which their Education has fitted them."[21] S.T.C. at once flew to pen and paper to answer this in his best forensic vein:

> Is every Family to possess one of these Unequal Equals . . .? Or are the few, you have mentioned—'with more toil than the Peasantry of England undergo—' to do for all of us 'that part of Labour which their Education has fitted them for'? If your remarks . . . are just, the Inference is, that the Scheme of Pantisocracy is impracticable.[22]

There were other vexations on hand. *The Fall of Robespierre* was not the money-spinner that S.T.C. had confidently predicted: unable to find anyone interested in publishing it, he had at last had five hundred copies privately printed at Cambridge. Ninepence a copy was charged by the booksellers and acquaintances who were prevailed upon to attempt to distribute the drama. The expenses of paper, printing and advertisements came to nearly nine pounds: "We ought to have charged 1s-6d a copy,"[23] sighed S.T.C., recounting all this to Southey. It was clear that this literary venture would not pay for Pantisocratic passages to the New World.

But now it became doubtful whether such passages would be possible even if financial resources were at hand; for war between England and America seemed inevitable, and emigration in that case would be stopped.

What with one thing and another, S.T.C. was sinking rapidly into a state of dejection. There are several indications that, finding the pressures too great for him, he resorted to narcotics; he confessed to Southey that he was taking ether for a violent throbbing of his head.[24] A letter to Francis Wrangham, joking about Pantisocracy, possibly belongs to his category of flighty letters (as he called them) written under the influence of Laudanum:

> I call my Cat Sister in the fraternity of universal Nature. Owls I respect and Jack Asses I love: for Aldermen & Hogs, Bishops & Royston Crows I have not particular partiality—; they are my Cousins, however, at least by Courtesy. But Kings, Wolves, Tygers, Generals, Ministers, and Hyaenas, I renounce them all—or if they *must* be my Kinsmen, it shall be in the 50th remove—.[25]

In a significant passage to George, S.T.C. confessed:

Anxieties that stimulate others, infuse an additional narcotic into my mind. The appeal of Duty . . . and the pleadings of affection . . . have been heard indeed—and heard with deep regard—Ah! that they had been as constantly obeyed—But . . . I have sate in drowsy uneasiness—and doing nothing have thought, what a deal I had to do![26]

The Coleridge family now decided to try a different approach. George wrote in warmer vein, to which S.T.C. responded eagerly. He repudiated democracy in a tone of voice and manner especially tailored to soothe his distraught relatives. All the evidence points to a situation where S.T.C. was now desperately endeavouring to run with the hare and hunt with the hounds; in short, he was saying "Yes" to both his family and Southey, a double-game which could only lead to disaster.

To George he intoned:

How often and unkindly are the ebullitions of youthful disputationess mistaken for the result of fixed Principles! . . . Solemnly, my Brother! I tell you —I am *not* a Democrat. I see, evidently, that the present is *not* the *highest* state of Society, of which we are *capable*—And after a diligent, I *may* say, an intense study of Locke, Hartley and others who have written most wisely on the Nature of Man—I appear to myself to see the point of *possible* perfection at which the World may perhaps be destined to arrive—But how to lead Mankind from one point to the other is a process of such infinite Complexity, that in deep-felt humility I resign it to that Being—'Who shaketh the Earth out of her place and the pillars thereof tremble'.[27]

The letter concluded with the intelligence that S.T.C. was driving up to London on Saturday morning and would, of course, see George on Sunday.

Southey also was informed that S.T.C. was coming up to London on Saturday (November 8), but to Southey S.T.C. added the information that he hoped to be in Bristol by Wednesday week.

S.T.C. travelled to London as arranged and must have met George who, at some juncture, made S.T.C. a "liberal Proposal"[28] of which we have no details, although it most certainly embodied the suggestion that S.T.C. should abandon Pantisocracy and, upon leaving Cambridge, should enter the Temple and read for the Bar. This would mean that he would remain dependent on his family for a long time to come, because:

No man dreams of getting Bread in the Law till six or eight years after his first entrance at the Temple. And how very few even then?—[29]

A period of frenetic indecision now ensued for S.T.C. His choice lay between a professional career in which he would in all likelihood gain great distinction and from which he would himself derive vast satisfaction (he had the makings of a brilliant lawyer); in choosing this career he would, furthermore, gratify his own family. On the other hand, there were his promises to Southey and to Sara Fricker.

Finally he decided upon the Temple. Not only upon the Temple; he determined to make one final, desperate bid for Mary Evans. Some time in early November he wrote to her, asking her to confirm whether or not she had become engaged to Fryer Todd. "I conjure you not to consider this request as presumptuous Indelicacy. Upon mine Honour, I have made it with no other Design or Expectation than that of arming my fortitude by total hopelessness." This was followed by an avowal of his love (which strongly suggests the same mental fantasy pattern that he was to follow with Sara Hutchinson: "your Image was blended with every idea. I thought of you incessantly"). He concluded on a harshly resolute note:

> But these are the poisoned Luxuries of a diseased Fancy! Indulge, Mary! this my first, my last request—and restore me to *Reality*, however gloomy . . . Indulge my request—I will not disturb your Peace by even a *Look* of Discontent . . . In a few months I shall enter at the Temple—and there seek forgetful Calmness—where only it can be found—in incessant and useful Activity.[30]

The mention of the Temple and "incessant and useful Activity" was doubtless included in order to show Mary that, should she still be uncommitted and fancy-free, he was of steadier purpose than had hitherto appeared and with a definite goal in view: might, in fact, be worth waiting for. It was a very remote hope, but it must have been present in his heart to some feeble degree, or he would not have written.

He made no attempt to fulfil his promise to Southey of being in Bristol by Wednesday week. After London, S.T.C. returned to Cambridge and busied himself with literary activity, probably to please George and "show" Mary. He arrived at an agreement with the *Morning Chronicle* to transmit to that paper a series of sonnets addressed to eminent contemporaries. The first, *To the Honourable Mr Erskine*, appeared on December 1.

By December 9 S.T.C. was back in London. He had had no reply from Mary Evans and his plans were in a state of fluidity verging on the nonexistent, although, deep within himself, the decision seems to have been hardening that Pantisocracy must be abandoned for the Temple. He made no categorical announcement of this to Southey (though it is very probable that he informed George that such was his decision). S.T.C. allowed himself to be wafted on the tide and the tide carried him, temporarily, back to the Angel Inn. Here he wrote verse and once more sank into dejection and, in every probability, opium—jerking himself spasmodically out of his lethargy to enjoy Charles Lamb's company, or to talk with radicals like Dyer, Holcroft and Godwin.

On arrival back in London S.T.C. had written to Southey saying, very vaguely, that he hoped "to receive a remittance from Cambridge within a day or two—and then I will set off to Bristol—though I find, they are making a row about me at Jesus."[31]

A "row at Jesus" was mentioned, it seems, simply to provide an excuse for a subsequent return to Cambridge. This he made briefly, and then once more journeyed to London. He was not, one surmises, in any condition whatever, by now, to make categorical decisions; his state was approaching breakdown. Southey, too, was becoming desperately over-tense and anxious; the initial fire was rapidly going out of the Pantisocratic Scheme. S.T.C. dragged his feet in London, while in Bristol Robert Lovell was giving indication of having second thoughts. At this juncture Southey mooted a new idea (suggested to him by his friend, C. W. W. Wynn) that Pantisocracy should first be essayed on a Welsh farm. Southey tentatively mentioned this to S.T.C., who rejected the notion out of hand: "pardon me—it is nonsense."[32]

More bother now came from Southey over S.T.C.'s lack of interest in Sara. S.T.C. responded:

> I have written 4 or 5 letters since my absence—received one. I am not conscious of having injured her otherwise, than by having mistaken the ebullience of *schematism* for affection . . . but my whole life has been a series of Blunders! God have mercy upon me—for I am a most miserable Dog— . . .
>
> However it still remains for me to be externally just though my heart is withered within me—and life seems now to give me disgust rather than pain—
>
> My Love to your Mother and to Edith—and to whomever it is right or convenient.
>
> God almighty bless you / and (a forlorn wish!)
>
> S.T. Coleridge[33]

This was followed by other letters, each successively more dejected and ambiguous in tone; they made no definite statements but somehow created, nonetheless, a decided impression that S.T.C. no longer had the slightest intention of joining Southey in Bristol, of marrying Sara Fricker, or of furthering Pantisocracy. He wrote meanderingly ("not that I have anything particular to say—")[34] about poetry—Southey's, Lamb's, his own—avoided the topic of Bristol entirely, and sent his love to Southey's mother. He enclosed copies of his sonnets for the *Morning Chronicle* and a charming *Address to a young Jack Ass & its Tethered Mother*, hailing the little ass as his Brother:

> And fain I'd take thee with me in the Dell
> Of high-soul'd Pantisocracy to dwell.

This disconcerting epistle had commenced:

When I am unhappy, a sigh or a groan does not feel sufficient to relieve the oppression of my Heart—I give a long *whistle*— / This by way of a detached Truth.—

It concluded, facetiously:

God love you & your Mother & Edith & Sara & Mary & little Eliza & & & & & & S. T. Coleridge—[35]

On December 24 S.T.C. received Mary Evans's long-awaited reply. As this was destroyed (S.T.C. assured her that he would burn all her letters and seems to have kept his word), we do not know precisely what she said, but from his reply to her, and from what he subsequently told Southey, it is clear that she must have informed him that she was indeed betrothed to Fryer Todd, but that she loved S.T.C. as a favourite brother. She blamed herself for having allowed him to dream of anything more. S.T.C. wrote back hastily, but not very truthfully: "In my wildest day-dream of Vanity I never supposed that you entertained for me any other than a common friendship."[36]

Precisely how S.T.C. spent his Christmas we do not know; certainly he saw something of the Lambs (when next he wrote to Southey he mentioned Mary Lamb's illness and her brother's devotion to her). S.T.C. also started his poem, *The Nativity*, which was to become his much-worked *Religious Musings*.

On December 29 he informed Southey that his passion for Mary was now divested of all shadow of Hope; he confessed, furthermore, his reluctance to marry Sara. Of Mary he wrote nostalgically, concluding:

To lose her!—I can rise above that selfish Pang. But to marry another—O Southey! bear with my weakness. Love makes all things pure and heavenly like itself:—but to marry a woman whom I do *not* love—to degrade her, whom I call my Wife, by making her the Instrument of low Desire—and on the removal of a desultory Appetite, to be perhaps not displeased with her Absence!—Enough!

Then came his inevitable avowal:

Mark you, Southey!—*I will do my Duty.*

And then, even more unconvincingly:

Think you, I wish to stay in Town? I am all eagerness to leave it—and am resolved, whatever the consequence, to be at Bath by Saturday—I thought of walking down.[37]

S.T.C.'s letter was postmarked 29 December, which was a Monday; Saturday, the day upon which he was "resolved to be in Bath, whatever the consequence," would therefore be 3 January. On 2 January, S.T.C., still in London, posted yet another letter to Southey. Only a fragment remains; it is inspired lunacy:

> The roads are dangerous—the horses soon knock'd up—The outside to a Man who like me has no great Coat, is cold and rheumatismferous—the Inside of a Coach to a man, who like me has very little money, is apt to produce a *sickness on the Stomach*—Shall I walk, I have a sore throat—and am not well.—
> I will dash through the Towns and helter skelter it into Bath in the Flying Waggon!
> Two miles an hour! That's your Sort—! I shall be supplied with Bread and Cheese from Christ's Hospital and shall take a bottle of Gin for myself and Tuom, the Waggoner!—Plenty of Oronoko Tobacco—Smoke all the Way—that's your Sort!
> Wrapped up in Hay—so warm! There are four or five Calves Inside—Passengers like myself—I shall fraternize with them! The folly & vanity of young men who go in Stage Coaches!—!—!—!—
> The Waggon does not set off before Sunday Night—I shall be with you by Wednesday, I suppose.—
>
> S. T. COLERIDGE[38]

In response to this Southey and Lovell walked to Marlborough, to meet the wagon, but "no S. T. Coleridge was therein!"[39] Southey himself was now becoming a prey to anxiety and nervous tension. "This state of expectation totally unfits me for anything," he wrote to Sara Fricker. "Why will he ever fix a day if he cannot abide by it?"[40] Southey, in a state of constant anticipation, was kept in exercise by walking to meet coaches and wagons; but no S.T.C. appeared.

Mid-January: still no S.T.C. At length Southey saw that there was nothing for it but either to forget S.T.C. as a Pantisocratic comrade or to go to London and haul him back to Bristol by main force. This latter Southey did.

It was an hour of drama which S.T.C. was never to cease to lament:

> I played the fool, and cut the throat of my Happiness, of my genius, of my utility, in compliment to the merest phantom of overstrained Honour!— O Southey! Southey! an unthinking man were you—[41]

Robert Southey's anxiety to have S.T.C. securely back in Bristol was based not so much on concern that he might desert Sara Fricker as anxiety lest he should abandon what Southey was now calling the DUTY of Pantisocracy.

Seeing enthusiasm for Pantisocracy fast dwindling among his fellow Pantisocrats, Southey adopted an heroic stance and declared that, even if all
others deserted Pantisocracy, he, his brother and George Burnett would
stand firm.

Meantime, S.T.C. was busy resuming his addresses to Sara. The results
were wholly unexpected.

During his absence she had rebuffed the advances of two other suitors,

> one of them of large Fortune—and by her persevent [sic] attachment to me
> disobliged her Relations in a very uncomfortable Degree . . . In short . . . so
> commanding are the requests of her Relations, that a short time must decide
> whether she marries me whom she loves with an affection to the ardor of
> which my Deserts bear no proportion—or a man whom she strongly dislikes
> in spite of his fortune and solicitous attentions to her. These peculiar circum-
> stances she had with her usual Delicacy concealed from me till my arrival at
> Bristol.[42]

The discovery that Sara had turned down two suitors (one of them rich)
in his favour completely disarmed S.T.C. He had anticipated neither such
loyalty nor fervour of attachment. He was immensely flattered and stirred
by "particular Ties of Gratitude."[43] The situation contained a further
ingredient essential to arouse his desire; the continued opposition of Sara's
family to her match with him must have afforded him every opportunity to
experience masochistic visions of Sara in another man's arms. Within a
month of his return to Bristol, S.T.C.'s feelings towards Sara had changed
radically; he wrote ecstatically: "I love and I am beloved, and I am
happy!—."[44]

A letter from S.T.C. to George Dyer, written in late February 1795,
indicates that the former had returned to Bristol with an escape-plan ready.
Dyer, it seems, had offered to help S.T.C. to procure a post as tutor to the
family of the Earl of Buchan. This would have necessitated S.T.C.'s absence in Scotland for the next two or three years, some four hundred miles
away from Sara, who might almost certainly have been counted upon, in
that case, to lose interest in such an elusive and in every respect distant
lover.

It seems that S.T.C. had not, at first, disclosed to Dyer his full reasons
for welcoming exile in Scotland, but by the end of February he was telling
Dyer, with total frankness, about Sara Fricker, the intention now being that
she should accompany him to Scotland. "To leave her for two or three
years would, I fear, be sacrificing her health and happiness."[45] Could lodgings be obtained for S.T.C. as a married man while he was tutoring the
young gentlemen?

Pantisocracy was now being dreamed of by S.T.C. rather as a romantic
idyll than as a hard proposition. The Scheme had become inextricably

interwoven for him with his Sara, a "chaste-eyed Maiden mild."[46] He visualised himself,

> In Freedom's UNDIVIDED dell,
> Where Toil and Health with mellow'd Love shall dwell,
> Far from folly, far from men,
> In the rude romantic glen,
> Up the cliff, and thro' the glade,
> Wandering with the dear-lov'd maid.[47]

It seemed likely that the glade, if it now materialised at all, would be in Wales rather than on the banks of the Susquehannah. S.T.C. remained opposed to this Welsh project, but he was outnumbered; the Lovells were backing Southey in favour of a trial period in Wales and so S.T.C., for the sake of preserving harmony, agreed to the plan likewise.

It was obvious that a Welsh farm would not immediately provide a livelihood for the Pantisocrats. S.T.C. and Southey, together with George Burnett, took lodgings in Bristol and a series of lectures was embarked upon in order to earn some ready money. S.T.C. commenced with three political lectures,* given in mid-February. These were followed, according to Cottle, by fourteen other lectures on religious and political subjects, though S.T.C., in a letter to Southey, speaks of having given only eleven in all.

Southey delivered a course of twelve historical lectures. S.T.C. gave him considerable assistance with these: "all the *Tug* of Brain was mine . . . your share was little more than Transcription."[48]

The summer of 1795 was a hot one, in physical climate as well as in Pantisocratic fervour. During those dazzling days of high summer Bristol came to know well the sight of Southey and S.T.C., "vile jacobin villains" (as they were not infrequently called), dashing, hatless, heated and frenetic from Redcliff down to the city library, from library to Cottle's, from Cottle's to Redcliff, from Redcliff to lecture-rooms. S.T.C., at any given time, might be carrying in addition to his notes and the latest political pamphlets, his own poems in manuscript, Bruce's *Travels to Discover The Source of the Nile*, Baxter's *Enquiry Into the Nature of the Human Soul*† (between lectures S.T.C. was making a study of dreams, for which his chief authority was Baxter) and a miscellany of other objects such as, on one occasion, a goose and its giblets. In addition each young man might, with gallantry, have an enthusiastic Miss Fricker clinging to his arm.

S.T.C., says Cottle, undertook his heavy programme of lecturing because he was anxious to build up "a provision for his speedy marriage."[49]

*The first and second lectures were published in November 1795 as *Conciones ad Populum*. The third lecture, *The Plot Discovered*, was published separately that same month.
†Andrew Baxter (1615–91), *An Enquiry Into the Nature of the Human Soul: Wherein the Immortality of the Soul is Evinced from the Principles of Reason and Philosophy*.

Robert Lovell, it seems, now attempted to prevent this marriage. S.T.C. reacted furiously. Cottle asked him what this outburst of violent temper meant. S.T.C. replied: "Lovell, who at first, did all in his power to promote my connexion with Miss Fricker, now opposes our union." Cottle adds that S.T.C. referred to Lovell as "a villain."[50]

This is significant. Lovell had now had opportunity to see more of S.T.C. than hitherto had been possible and his enthusiastic encouragement of the marriage was exchanged for opposition. As we know that he complained to Southey of S.T.C.'s indolent habits, this complaint, presumably, was the basis of his objection to S.T.C. as a husband for Sara (for whom, as her brother-in-law, Lovell probably felt some responsibility). That Lovell should take such an abrupt and categorical stand over habits of indolence suggests that this must have been indolence of no common degree: in short the situation points to Lovell's discovery of S.T.C.'s opium indulgence.

Southey, at this juncture, rallied to the support of S.T.C., while Sara, in spite of Lovell's warnings (buttressed, it seems, by continuing Fricker family opposition) remained as determined to wed Samuel as ever.

Meanwhile Southey's friends and family continued to do all that they could to dissuade him from Pantisocracy. Southey was, fundamentally, an exceedingly level-headed person and it was to be anticipated that his undergraduate enthusiasm for politics would evaporate once he was forced to confront the hard realities of the bread-winning world. Such now proved the case. He began to give indications of receding "from those broad Principles, in which Pantisocracy originated." He became "cold and gloomy" in manner. S.T.C. was far too perceptive not to recognise the direction in which the wind lay. "Then darted into my mind the Dread, that you were meditating a Separation."[51]

The lodgings on Bristol's Redcliff Hill became the scene of wordy and impassioned Pantisocratic disputes. For a brief period it seemed that S.T.C.'s eloquence had subdued Southey's reaction. This was revived and overt quarrelling surfaced between the two some time in June, when S.T.C., Cottle, Southey, Edith and Sara Fricker made a two-day excursion to Tintern Abbey.

These emancipated unchaperoned young women and their escorts crossed the Severn and went to the Beaufort Arms, Chepstow, to dine. After dinner Southey and S.T.C. had a lively disagreement; Cottle suggests that it arose over a matter pertaining to the lectures. S.T.C., on the other hand, in a long, retrospective letter of November 13, 1795, to Southey, stated that the dispute concerned Pantisocratic principles and Southey's changing attitude: "At Chepstow your Conduct renewed my Suspicion."[52]

Evidently the young ladies joined the controversy, Edith siding with her Robert, Sara with her Samuel. The latter became greatly agitated, "even to many Tears."[53] Joseph Cottle, for his part, was horribly embarrassed by this scene: "In unspeakable concern and surprise I retired to a distant part of the room."[54]

It is interesting to compare Cottle's account of the expedition with S.T.C.'s scantier, but more illuminating, comments. Cottle, never a very perceptive individual, supposed that the party soon regained their "accostomed spirits."[55] They left Chepstow and continued their tour to Tintern. During the journey S.T.C. and Southey had a long, intimate and agitated conversation; S.T.C. was given assurances that his suspicions were altogether unfounded; differences between himself and Southey were purely speculative; Southey would certainly remain with the Pantisocrats. S.T.C. was made glad and satisfied: "For my Heart was never bent from you Southey but by violent strength—and heaven knows, how it leapt back to esteem and love you."[56]

Not long after the expedition to Tintern Abbey came the occasion of a strawberry party at Ashton, following which S.T.C.'s suspicions of Southey flared again. George Burnett repeated to S.T.C. a conversation that he had had with Southey at this party. The latter had revealed that he had been offered, by Wynn, an annuity of a hundred-and-sixty pounds per annum, to begin as soon as Wynn came of age. Southey had added that, in spite of Pantisocracy, his private resources must remain his own; indeed, he was now proposing that the Welsh farm property should be divided amongst individual owners, with the exception of five or six acres, which should be communal.

S.T.C.'s reception of this variation upon the theme of Pantisocracy was scathing:

> we were to commence Partners in a petty Farming Trade. This was the Mouse of which the Mountain Pantisocracy was at last safely delivered! I received the account with Indignation and Loathings of unutterable Contempt.[57]

The breach between the Pantisocratic brethren now yawned wide. Southey was forced into an increasingly aggressive stance by pressure placed upon him by his aunt, Miss Tyler, and his uncle, Herbert Hill. Early in August Southey received a letter from his uncle, cogently urging him to take Holy Orders. It is possible that Southey might have agreed to do this had not S.T.C. pointed out, with impassioned vehemence, that for Southey so to do would be self-perjury: "You disapprove of an Establishment altogether—you believe it iniquitous—a mother of Crimes! . . . It is impossible that *you* could uphold it by assuming the badge of Affiliation."[58]

Southey prevaricated with agility but, shaken by S.T.C.'s assault, he did, in fact, abandon all idea of taking Holy Orders. Nevertheless he quitted the Pantisocrats, saying, lamely, that he might rejoin the movement in about fourteen years. S.T.C. exploded this limp notion with a barrage of furious invective, concluding (with intimations of *Kubla Khan*): "Heaven . . . grant that however foul your Stream may run here, yet that it will filtrate & become pure in its subterraneous Passage to the Ocean of Universal Redemption."[59]

Southey, infuriated with S.T.C., retaliated by letting it be known that he was quitting the Pantisocrats because of S.T.C.'s indolence. The Esteesian rejoinder was devastatingly to the point: "Supposing it true, it might indeed be a Reason for rejecting *me* from the System? But how does this affect Pantisocracy, that you should reject *it?*"[60]

Now came the announcement that Southey would return to Oxford and read Law. S.T.C. publicly erupted. The quarrel of the Pantisocrats became the talk of radical circles in Bristol. Cottle, who never truly understood all the ins and outs of the affair, at least has left a clear impression of S.T.C.'s seething response to Southey's defection:

a tumult of fearful intensity arose in Mr Coleridge's mind . . . Charges of "desertion" flew thick around; of "dishonourable retraction, in a compact most binding".[61]

S.T.C.'s furious indignation was understandable. Southey, whom he unhesitatingly dubbed "a specious rascal,"[62] had forced him away from Cambridge, from his own opportunity to read Law, from his family, his friends, and from "every prospect & every certainty,"[63] all in the name of honouring the very Pantisocratic duty which Southey himself was now abandoning in order to return to Oxford, read Law and assure himself of a secure professional future.

S.T.C. scornfully designated Southey, to his face, as *"one who had fallen back into the Ranks."*[64] Henceforth, when they met, S.T.C. was coldly civil, but no more. Southey was no longer a friend ("a very sacred appellation"[65] with S.T.C.), but a mere acquaintance. Southey flinched in the face of this rejection, but S.T.C. was adamant: "I *locked up* my heart from you, and you perceived it and I intended you to perceive it."[66]

CHAPTER FIVE

THE EOLIAN HARP

(August 1795-December 1795)

AUGUST, 1795 SAW not only the breakdown of Pantisocracy, it also witnessed the final arrangements for the Coleridge–Fricker marriage.

Mrs Sandford has suggested (using Poole family traditional gossip as her source) that the

> marriage was believed to have been rather hurried on, in consequence of some hostile breath of rumour that had arisen in connection with the Misses Fricker, caused partly by the unconventional manner in which they were constantly to be seen walking about Bristol with two such remarkable and well-known young men as Coleridge and Southey, and partly from the impression that Pantisocracy meant a system of things that dispensed with the marriage-tie.[1]

That there was unfavourable gossip about the behaviour of the Fricker sisters need not be doubted. Indeed, it is interesting to reflect that Sara Coleridge (whom posterity usually chooses to see as an almost tediously conventional figure) in her youth had the reputation for being precisely the reverse. There can be no question that her progressive behaviour seriously damaged her reputation in the Bristol area; whether, however, gossip really hastened her wedding is less certain. S.T.C., in his infatuation for her, could not have the wedding-day fixed soon enough, and she was equally ardent.

That he was infatuated with her his friends and contemporaries in Bristol had no doubt. The Coleridge–Fricker marriage was seen as a romantic union of the most idyllic description. S.T.C. was known to be uniting himself "with the woman he loved, regardless of every other consideration."[2] Cottle referred to them in terms of a veritable fairy-tale couple.

A cottage was rented (it would seem in late August) at Clevedon, on the Bristol Channel. The rent was five pounds a year; the cottage was one storey high and stood at the secluded western extremity of the village. It was everything that a honeymoon cottage should be:

> Low was our pretty Cot: our tallest rose
> Peeped at the chamber window. We could hear
> At silent noon, and eve, and early morn,
> The sea's faint murmur.[3]

The Eolian Harp

The betrothed couple found their future home, it seems, in midsummer, for S.T.C. (who wrote several poems centred on it) described myrtles, jasmine, roses, the song of a skylark and the scent of a beanfield—all impossible in the context of their actual residence at Clevedon, which dated from October until December of that year.

One must either allow for a great deal of poetic licence, or decide that S.T.C. and Sara spent time there together before their marriage; the former is the more probable. When one reads that S.T.C. left the low dell where his cottage lay, and climbed "with perilous toil" a stony mount, "a bare bleak mountain,"[4] and realises that he is describing some gentle protuberance of the Quantocks, the rest of this Clevedon verse must be treated with extreme caution.

We know that some time in August S.T.C. and George Burnett went to Clevedon together; perhaps the cottage was discovered then; perhaps to view it was the main purpose of their visit. S.T.C.'s poem, *The Eolian Harp*, dated August 20, 1795, and sub-titled *Composed at Clevedon, Somersetshire* may or may not be reliably autobiographical; Dykes Campbell suggests that the occasion was a preliminary visit by S.T.C. and Sara to their future home. This poem indicates that the first item of furniture which they installed in the cottage was an eolian-harp: it was at that time the rage to place one of these at a casement-window, so that winds, or draughts, played random notes upon the strings—a touch of Ossian-like romanticism. The installation of an eolian-harp in their honeymoon-home before anything so mundane as a bed, or a table, or a tea-kettle would, of course, have been in key with these two highly romantic lovers (using the term *lovers* in the sentimental sense of their day; to speak, then, of two people as lovers carried no sexual implication as it does for us).

> My pensive Sara! thy soft cheek reclined
> Thus on my arm, most soothing sweet it is
> To sit beside our cot, our cot o'ergrown
> With white-flowered jasmin, and the broad-leaved myrtle,
> (Meet emblems they of Innocence and Love!)
> And watch the clouds, that late were rich with light,
> Slow saddening round, and mark the star of eve
> Serenely brilliant (such should wisdom be)
> Shine opposite! How exquisite the scents
> Snatched from yon bean-field! and the world so hushed!
> The stilly murmur of the distant sea
> Tells us of silence.

>   And that simplest lute,
> Placed length-ways in the clasping casement, hark!
> How by the desultory breeze caressed,
> Like some coy maid half yielding to her lover,

It pours such sweet upbraiding, as must needs
Tempt to repeat the wrong! And now, its strings
Boldlier swept, the long sequacious notes
Over delicious surges sink and rise,
Such a soft floating witchery of sound
As twilight Elfins make, when they at eve
Voyage on gentle gales from Fairy-Land . . .
Which meets all motion and becomes its soul,
A light in sound, a sound-like power in light
Rhythm in all thought, and joyance everywhere— . . .

   And what if all of animated nature
Be but organic harps diversely framed,
That tremble into thought, as o'er them sweeps
Plastic and vast, one intellectual breeze,
At once the Soul of each, and God of All?
   But thy more serious eye a mild reproof
Darts, O beloved woman! . . .
And biddest me walk humbly with my God . . .
Who with his saving mercies healed me,
A sinful and most miserable man,
Wildered and dark, and gave me to possess
Peace, and this cot, and thee, heart-honoured Maid!

The poem is an important one because it shows S.T.C. already being torn between Pantheism and orthodoxy, and Sara already darting reproof at him for "vain philosophy's aye-babbling spring." The atmosphere of being in love is unmistakable in the opening lines. The line, "Rhythm in all thought, and joyance everywhere," so typical of S.T.C. in his early years, should be compared with the morphine-distorted *Ode to Dejection* of 1802, when the eolian-harp sent forth, not elfin music but "a scream of agony by torture lengthened out."

During his final year at Cambridge S.T.C. had read and had been deeply impressed by William Wordsworth's *Descriptive Sketches* and *An Evening Walk*, published in 1793. S.T.C. had recognised in these poems an entirely new voice: "seldom, if ever, was the emergence of an original poetic genius above the literary horizon more evidently announced."[5] By the spring of 1795 S.T.C. was either contemplating making contact by letter with Wordsworth or had actually done so; on the address sheet of the letter to George Dyer, postmarked March 10, is written in another hand: "Wm Wordsworth / No 15 / Chalton Street / Sommers Town."

Some time in September, 1795, there occurred the first meeting between S.T.C. and Wordsworth. Little is detailed of this most pregnant encounter. We know simply that Wordsworth was in Bristol that September; he wrote, on October 24, to his friend William Mathews that,

The Eolian Harp

Coleridge was at Bristol part of the time that I was there. I saw but little of him. I wished indeed to have seen more—his talent appears to me very great.

A week before his wedding S.T.C. paid a visit to Shurton Bars, near Bridgewater in Somerset and, while there, received a melancholy letter from Sara, in Bristol. This prompted him to write a long, highly spontaneous, poignantly naive and impassioned *Ode to Sara*. The final verses breathe the essence of a youthful bridegroom's impatience:

> How oft, my Love! with shapings sweet
> I paint the moment, we shall meet!
>   With eager speed I dart—
> I seize you in the vacant air,
> And fancy, with a husband's care
>   I press you to my heart!

> 'Tis said, the Summer's evening hour
> Flashes the golden-coloured flower
>   A fair electric flame:
> And so shall flash my love-charged eye
> When all the heart's big ecstacy
>   Shoots rapid through the frame!

S.T.C. and Sara were married at the church of St Mary Redcliff, Bristol, on Sunday, October 4, 1795; the officiating clergyman was Benjamin Spry, the vicar. The witnesses were the bride's mother, Mrs Martha Fricker, and Josiah Wade, a Bristol tradesman, who had become one of S.T.C.'s warmest friends. Robert Southey was not present. He and S.T.C. were no longer on speaking terms.

St Mary Redcliff was, and is, a beautiful Gothic building of cathedral-like dimensions and magnificence; a cantata of soaring steeple and flying-buttresses without, mediaevally splendid within; the ancient resting-place for great Bristol burghers and merchantmen and prelates and, in 1770, for the wretched and tragic boy-poet, Chatterton, whose squalid suicide by arsenical poisoning inspired S.T.C., as a schoolboy in 1790, to write an exceedingly unsuitable Monody. The thought of "poor Chatterton" gave "a tinge of melancholy to the solemn Joy"[6] which S.T.C. felt as he stood side by side with Sara in the stained-glass-illuminated twilight while Benjamin Spry pronounced them man and wife. Then S.T.C. and his bride and their small wedding-party emerged from the cavernous porch on to the windy, shallow, wide stone steps of the church, with all Bristol spread below and before them: wharves and water and roofs and ships; masts and rigging —a proud seafaring city (changed out of all recognition today and lost forever). But the steps where S.T.C. stood with his Sara on his arm are still there. The visitor to them can visualise that October wedding-group and the happy but poignant young pair; he with his shaggily abundant, glossy black locks, great grey eyes and wonderful eyebrows; she, a little beauty in her wedding-clothes.

Some time that day they left for Clevedon; then a tiny village. The weather was mild; late roses may still have bloomed in the garden; the eolian-harp sang in the casement; Sara rested her soft cheek on her Samuel's arm.

On October 1 a cart had taken their goods to the cottage; the only items actually specified by S.T.C. were some old prints. In their romantic bliss Samuel and Sara seem to have started their honeymoon singularly ill-equipped; two days after the wedding Cottle received a note from S.T.C. requesting him to dispatch to Clevedon, with as little delay as possible:

> A riddle slice; a candle box; two ventilators; two glasses for the washstand; one tin dust pan; one small tin tea kettle; one pair of candlesticks; one carpet brush; one flower dredge; three tin extinguishers; two mats; a pair of slippers; a cheese toaster; two large tin spoons; a bible; a keg of porter; coffee; raisins; currants; catsup; nutmeg; allspice; cinnamon; rice; ginger; and mace.[7]

The obliging Cottle responded without delay to this S.O.S., riding over to Clevedon in person.

The Bible bears the inscription: "Given to me by Joseph Cottle after my marriage—S. T. Coleridge." On the first fly-leaf is written: "Married at St Mary Red Cliff to Sara Fricker on the fourth day of October, 1795—I being 23 years old the twentieth day following of the same month." Later entries record the births of Coleridge's four children.

The newlyweds seemed blissfully happy. The honeymoon cottage, though pretty, was spartan in its decoration and appointments, according to Cottle; S.T.C., on the other hand, rapturously referred to it as "Our comfortablè Cot!—!—"[8] The walls were adorned, Cottle noticed, with nothing more than "dirty old whitewash" and so he ordered "a few pieces of sprightly wall-paper" for the parlour-dining-room.[9]

Cottle, leaving S.T.C. "to write verses on his beloved Sara,"[10] rode back to Bristol bearing a letter from S.T.C. to Poole, which commenced ebulliently:

> My dear Sir—God bless you!—or rather, God be praised for that he *has* blessed you—!—
> On Sunday morning I was *married*—at St Mary's, Red Cliff—poor Chatterton's Church— / The thought gave me a tinge of melancholy to the solemn Joy, which I felt—united to the woman, whom I love best of all created Beings—We are settled—nay—quite domesticated at Clevedon— Our comfortable Cot!—!—

Mrs Coleridge—MRS COLERIDGE!!—I like to *write* the name—well—
as I was saying—Mrs Coleridge desires her affectionate regards to you—I
talked of you on my wedding night—God bless you!—I hope that some ten
years hence you will believe and know of my affection towards you what I will
not now profess.

The letter continued with an outline of S.T.C.'s forthcoming projects;
he was full of high hopes. Cottle had entered into an engagement to give him
a guinea and a half for every hundred lines of poetry he wrote, "which will
be perfectly sufficient for my maintenance," while in the course of half a
year he intended to return to Cambridge "and taking lodgings there for
myself and wife finish my great work of Imitations in 2 vols." He would
then publish proposals for a school of his own, for which he had ambitious
plans.

The letter concluded:

My respectful & grateful remembrance to your Mother.—& believe me, dear
Poole! your affectionate & mindful—*Friend*—shall I so soon dare to say?—
Believe me, my *heart* prompts it—

S. T. COLERIDGE[11]

On October 10 Poole replied warmly:

I do congratulate you—most heartily I do. I wish I knew Mrs Coleridge—
remember me most kindly to her. May you both long, long be happy . . . I
cannot tell you, my dear friend, for such I am sure I may call you, how much
I am interested in everything which concerns you. The world is all before
you; your road seems yet to choose. Providence has been pleased, if I may so
express myself, to drop you on this globe as a meteor from the clouds, the
track of which is undetermined. But you have now, by marrying, in some
sense fixed yourself. You have created a rallying point. It is the threshold of
your life. It is the epocha from which you must date every subsequent
action. You now begin to live.

This was followed by advice about S.T.C.'s future career, which all his
friends were at all times only too ready to give him; Poole, like everyone
else, begged Coleridge not "to disappoint us . . . set yourself about some
work of consequence, which may give you a reputation, whether it be in
poetry or in prose . . . delight and improve us all." Finally, the letter concluded on a less elevated, but much more comfortable note:

"My dear mother begs to say she wishes you all the good that man can
know."[12]

Indirectly, S.T.C. and Sara learned, on Thursday, November 12, that
Southey was leaving for Lisbon on the coming Saturday morning (his
family had decided that a tour overseas would be beneficial in helping him
to break with his past). The rumour also reached S.T.C. that Southey

would not now read Law on his return, but maintain himself by his writings and promised annuity. S.T.C., mulling over these things, wrote to Southey the long, retrospective letter already quoted in which he reviewed the course of events, based his charges fairly upon them and levelled each charge at Southey with an accuracy of aim and passionate, yet controlled invective, which would have brilliantly distinguished S.T.C. had he been leading for the Crown. Then he summed up, displaying qualities which might well have made him Lord Chief Justice, had his stars been more propitious.

At the time of the breach between the Pantisocrats it had been Southey's flagrant disregard of Pantisocratic principles which had most distressed and enraged S.T.C.:

O Selfish, money-loving Man! What Principle have you not given up? . . . O God! that *such a mind* should fall in love with that low, dirty gutter-grubbing Trull, WORLDLY PRUDENCE!.[13]

George Burnett's plight particularly worried S.T.C. The poor youth had been "seduced" by Southey from university and the Church (to use S.T.C.'s own expression); he was not, said S.T.C., calculated for any other profession, neither was his father prepared to spend any more money on his education. What, S.T.C. asked Southey with vehemence, was George Burnett to do, now that Pantisocracy had been abandoned? "He who leaned on you with all his head and his heart? He who gave his all for Pantisocracy & expected that Pantisocracy would at least be Bread & Cheese to Him?"[14]

Finally, S.T.C. concluded:

Southey! . . . You have left a large Void in my Heart—I know no man big enough to fill it. Others I may love equally & esteem equally; and some perhaps I may admire as much. But never do I expect to meet another man, who will make me unite attachment for his person with reverence for his heart and admiration of his Genius! I did not only venerate you for your own Virtues, I prized you as the Sheet Anchor of mine! . . . But these Things are past by, like as when a hungry man dreams, and lo! he feasteth—but he awakes, and his Soul is empty!—. . . . May God Almighty bless & preserve you! And may you live to know, and feel, and acknowledge that unless we accustom ourselves to meditate adoringly on him, the Source of all Virtue, no Virtue can be permanent.[15]

For this letter Southey never really forgave S.T.C. Just as S.T.C. never really forgave Southey for what he regarded as an act of gross betrayal.

Southey was too deeply committed to Edith Fricker to be able to extricate himself from her. His family was utterly opposed to the marriage; it took place, therefore, in secret on the morning of his departure, Saturday November 14, 1795. Like the Coleridges, Southey and Edith were married at St Mary Redcliff (it was the Frickers' parish church). Joseph Cottle and his wife alone were present as witnesses. Southey and his bride parted in the church-porch immediately following the ceremony; he set sail for Lisbon; Edith returned home with the Cottles, with whom she stayed until Southey's return. A letter to Cottle from Southey, written at Falmouth before he embarked, explains the reasoning behind this rather unusual arrangement:

> I have done my duty. Perhaps you may think my motives for marrying (at that time) not sufficiently strong. One, and that to me of great weight, I believe was not mentioned to you. There might have arisen feelings of an unpleasant nature, at the idea of receiving support from one not legally a husband; and (do not show this to Edith) should I perish by shipwreck, or any other casualty, I have relations whose prejudices would then yield to the anguish of affection, and who would then love and cherish, and yield all possible consolation to my widow. Of such an evil there is but a possibility, but against possibility it was my duty to guard.[16]

Thus the upright-downright one departed, leaving his erstwhile brothers in Pantisocracy to face bleak futures.

Of all the outstanding attributes which S.T.C. possessed (and they were many), among the greatest was his courage. He had told Southey:

> I neither have or could deign to have an hundred a year—Yet by my own exertions I will struggle hard to maintain myself, and my Wife, and my Wife's Mother, and my associate [George Burnett].[17]

With the prospect of this struggle in view, S.T.C. was no longer able to remain in blissful seclusion in Clevedon. It was too far from Bristol, an inconvenience in several respects, but particularly because it cut S.T.C. off from the Bristol City Library which would henceforth be increasingly essential to him now that he had to apply himself so urgently and seriously to professional writing.

Thus, by early December he and Sara were back in Bristol, lodging temporarily and none too happily with Mrs Fricker.

PART TWO

The Milk of Paradise

And all should cry, Beware! Beware!
His flashing eyes, his floating hair!
Weave a circle round him thrice,
And close your eyes with holy dread,
For he on honey-dew hath fed,
And drunk the milk of Paradise.

Kubla Khan (1797)

INTERLUDE:

SELF-PORTRAITURE

My dear fellow! I laugh more, & talk more nonsense in a week, than most other people do in a year—

Letter to John Thelwall,
19 November, 1796.

I was thought *vain* ... it was ... heat, bustle, and overflowing of a mind, too vehemently pushed on From within to be regardful of the object, upon which it was moving—an instinct to have my power proved to me by transient evidences, arising from an inward feeling of weakness ... A sense of weakness—a haunting sense, that I was an herbaceous Plant, as large as a large Tree, with a trunk of the same Girth, & Branches as large & shadowing—but with *pith within* the Trunk, not heart of Wood/—that I had *power* not *strength*—an involuntary Imposter— that I had no real Genius, no real Depth/—This is ... a fair statement of my habitual Haunting.

Letter to Robert Southey, 1 August,
1803, describing his sensation of inadequacy as a young man.

CHAPTER SIX

ON WATCH, BUT NOT ON GUARD

(December 1795–May 1796)

> The Fox, and Statesman subtile wiles ensure,
> The Cit, and Polecat stink and are secure:
> Toads with their venom, Doctors with their drug,
> The Priest, the Hedgehog, in their robes are snug!
> Oh, Nature! cruel step-mother, and hard,
> To thy poor, naked, fenceless child the Bard!
> No Horns but those by luckless Hymen worn,
> And those, (alas! alas!) not Plenty's Horn!
> With naked feelings, and with aching pride,
> He bears th' unbroken blast on every side!
> Vampire Booksellers drain him to the heart,
> And Scorpion Critics cureless venom dart!
>
> Sonnet contained in a letter of dejection
> from S.T.C. while at Lichfield, *circa*
> February 10, 1796; the recipient,
> Josiah Wade of Bristol.

ACCORDING TO COTTLE, S.T.C. had told him despairingly, some time in the early months of 1795, that he had been unable to sell a volume of his collected poems to any of the London booksellers; all of them save one, had refused to look at them, and that one had offered a mere six guineas for the copyright. This sum S.T.C. had refused to accept, poor as he was. Cottle, on hearing this, had at once offered S.T.C. thirty guineas, payable in advance, which offer S.T.C. had at once accepted.

Throughout the latter half of 1795 and the early months of 1796, S.T.C. worked intermittently upon the task of getting this collection of poems ready for the press.

At the close of 1795 S.T.C. decided to embark, also, upon a journalistic venture; his plan was to publish a periodical. When this idea first presented itself to him he convened his Bristol friends one evening at the Rummer Tavern to discuss details. It was decided that the periodical should be named *The Watchman* and, soon after, a prospectus was circulated stating that it was to be a miscellany of two sheets, or thirty-two pages, "closely printed in 8vo., the type, long primer:" it was to be devoted to reports of the debates in both Houses of Parliament with a selection of celebrated parliamentary speeches from the past, ranging from the reign of Charles the First to contemporary times. There would also be historical and other essays and poetry and reviews of new publications.

"From its form, it may be bound up at the end of the year, and become an Annual Register," explained the prospectus, adding hopefully: "The last circumstance may induce men of letters to prefer this miscellany to more perishable publications as the vehicle of their effusions."[1]

The Watchman would appear every eighth day and would cost four pence.

Some three hundred subscribers were found in Bristol alone and on January 9, 1796, S.T.C. enterprisingly commenced a subscription-raising tour. Armed with letters of introduction to influential figures in the various towns that he proposed to canvass, he set out on a projected itinerary of visits to Worcester, Birmingham, Nottingham, Lichfield, Derby, Manchester, Sheffield, Liverpool and, lastly, London.

Worcester, his first stop, proved socially pleasant, but, as S.T.C. reported to Wade,[2] there was no chance of doing any business there. At Birmingham, if we can believe the famous account given in the *Biographia Literaria*, S.T.C.'s first interview was with

a rigid Calvanist, a tallow-chandler by trade . . . Oh that face! I have it before me at this moment. Lank, dark, very hard, and with strong perpendicular furrows, it gave me a dim notion of someone looking at me through a used gridiron . . . I commenced an harangue of half-an-hour, varying my notes, through the whole gamut of eloquence, from the ratiocinative to the declamatory, and in the latter from the pathetic to the indignant. I argued, I described, I promised, I prophesied: and beginning with the captivity of nations I ended with the near approach of the millennium . . .

My taper man of lights listened with praiseworthy patience . . . though (as I was afterwards told), it was a melting day with him. 'And what, Sir,' (he said, after a short pause) 'might the cost be?' 'Only FOUR-PENCE. (O, how I felt the anti-climax, the abysmal bathos of that four-pence!) 'only four-pence, Sir, each number, to be published on every eighth day.' 'That come to a deal of money at the end of the year,' said he. 'How much, did you say, there was to be for the money?' 'Thirty two pages, Sir! large octavo, closely printed.' 'I'm as great a one as any man in Brummagen Sir! for liberty and truth and all them sort of things, but bless me! that's more than I ever reads, Sir, all the year round!'

The general hard-headed advice received by S.T.C. at Birmingham was that *Watchman* could not succeed. Nevertheless he obtained about a hundred subscribers from that city. He then changed his proposed route, going to Derby, Nottingham, Sheffield, Manchester and Lichfield. At Sheffield alarming intelligence reached him of Sara's health. This flung him into profound dejection; the sense of freedom and hence the gaiety which had joyously impregnated the opening stages of his tour, became abruptly extinguished by a sudden terrifying realization of the fearful weight of responsibility that rested upon his shoulders. He grew panicky: "I verily believe no poor fellow's idea-pot ever bubbled up so vehemently with fears, doubts and difficulties, as mine does at present. Heaven grant it may not boil over, and put out the fire!"[3]

Wade was, at that time, S.T.C.'s father-brother figure and in a despairing letter to him S.T.C. (probably quite unconsciously) used almost verbatim the expressions that he, as Comberbache, had addressed to George Coleridge two years previously:

> I am almost heartless! My past life seems to me like a dream, a feverish dream! all one gloomy huddle of strange actions, and dim-discovered motives! Friendships lost by indolence, and happiness murdered by mismanaged sensibility! The present hour I seem in a quickset hedge of embarrassments! For shame! I ought not to mistrust God! but indeed, to hope is far more difficult than to fear.[4]

The letter concluded with the sonnet quoted at the head of this chapter.

In spite of the fact that S.T.C. did very well with subscribers at Lichfield, he cut short his tour and arrived back in Bristol on February 13. He rejoined Sara at her mother's house. Sara, in the early weeks of pregnancy, had been taken ill with a fever and was threatening miscarriage. S.T.C. became increasingly panicky.

Cottle, having a friend who much wished to meet S.T.C., sent an invitation by messenger to the latter, asking him to dine. S.T.C. was not at home, and the messenger, instead of leaving the note of invitation for him, returned with it to Cottle, who, a short space of time after, received what he called "an astounding letter" from the now near-hysterical S.T.C.:

Redcliff-hill, Feb. 22, 1796.

My dear Sir,

> It is my duty and business to thank God for all his dispensations, and to believe them the best possible—but, indeed, I think I should have been more thankful, if he had made me a journeyman Shoemaker, instead of an 'Author by Trade'!—I have left my friends, I have left plenty—I have left that ease which would have enabled me to secure a literary immortality . . . and to have given the public works conceived in moments of inspiration, and polished with leisurely solitude: and alas! for what have left them—for a specious rascal who deserted me in the hour of distress, and for a scheme of Virtue impracticable & romantic.—So I am forced to write for bread—write the high flights of poetic enthusiasm, when every minute I am hearing a groan of pain from my Wife—groans, and complaints & sickness! The present hour, I am in a quick-set hedge of embarrassment, and whichever way I turn, a thorn runs into me—. The Future is cloud & thick darkness— Poverty, perhaps, and the thin faces of them that want bread looking up to me!—Nor is this all—my happiest moments for composition are broken in upon by the reflection of—I *must* make haste—I am too late—I am already months behind! I have received my *pay* before hand!—O way-ward and desultory Spirit of Genius! ill canst thou brook a task-master! The tenderest

touch from the hand of *Obligation* wounds thee, like a scourge of Scorpions!—
I have been composing in the fields this morning, and came home to write down the first rude Sheet of my Preface—when I heard that your brother had been with a note from you.—I have not seen it; but I guess its contents —I am writing as fast as I can—depend on it, you shall not be out of pocket for me! . . . If I have written petulantly, forgive me—God knows, I am sore all over.[5]

This unfortunate misunderstanding drew from Cottle the wryly humorous comment: "An invitation to a good dinner!"[6] The incident, however, was fundamentally grim in import; it indicated the serious degree to which S.T.C. was under stress. His was not a personality equipped to withstand experience of this kind.

S.T.C. had returned from his canvassing tour with nearly a thousand names on the subscription list of *The Watchman*, yet, nonetheless, he was more than half convinced that prudence dictated the abandonment of the scheme. But for that very reason he persevered in it: "I was at that period of my life so completely hag-ridden by the fear of being influenced by self motives, that to know a mode of conduct to be the dictate of *prudence* was a sort of presumptive proof of my feelings, that the contrary was the dictate of duty."[7]

Watchman went into production. Cottle assisted with the provision of paper and printing, at reduced trade prices. S.T.C. was soon referring to his labours as "Watch drudgery," and as being "on Watch."

As the result of much struggle, the first issue appeared on March 1. It took Cottle and S.T.C. together "four full hours to arrange, reckon . . . pack up, and write invoices and letters for the London and country customers . . . This routine was repeated with every fresh number."[8] Ten numbers appeared, all told, at eight-day intervals.

On March 12, 1796, the Rev. John Edwards (a Unitarian minister of the New Meeting at Birmingham, with whom S.T.C. had become friendly), received the following significant letter from S.T.C.:

Since I last wrote to you, I have been tottering on the edge of madness— . . . the repeated blunders of the printers, the forgetfulness & blunders of my associate [George Burnett] and . . . Mrs Coleridge dangerously ill, and expected hourly to miscarry. Such has been my situation for the last fortnight—I have been obliged to take laudanum almost every night.[9]

A not unimportant point to bear in mind when examining the history of S.T.C.'s opium-addiction is that, when the Coleridges moved from Redcliff Hill to Oxford Street, Kingsdown, Bristol (which move they made in early March), Burnett went to reside with them.

We know that Burnett, by 1803, was hopelessly addicted to opium (he died in 1811 at the age of thirty-five, destroyed by the drug). When first he commenced the opium-habit is not known, but we do know that he proved worse than useless to S.T.C. as a working partner; his intelligence, it is true, was low, but opium may well already have accounted for his general inefficiency. S.T.C. was constantly complaining about his performance, as in this comment to Cottle: "the Debates which Burnet [sic] undertook to abridge for me, he has abridged in such a careless, slovenly manner, that I was obliged to throw them in the fire, and am now doing them myself!"[10]

It need scarcely be stressed that Burnett and S.T.C. would each have encouraged the other in the opium-habit.

The Coleridges supposed that, on March 19, Sara had had a miscarriage; such, in fact, was not the case. The pair seem to have been decidedly ignorant on matters concerning pregnancy. S.T.C. was of the opinion that it was the most obscure of all God's dispensations: "it seems coercive against Immaterialism—it starts uneasy doubts respecting Immortality, & the pangs which the Woman suffers, seem inexplicable in the system of optimism."[11]

Sara's thoughts on the subject have not been recorded. Fortunately, once the first three months were over, she recaptured her former excellent health and had no further trouble; neither she nor S.T.C. realised that she was still pregnant until her increasing size, in mid-April, placed her condition beyond all possible further doubt.

The Watchman was by now receiving some stiff criticism, but S.T.C. was virtually past caring. To Edwards he wrote, on March 20:

> I am perfectly callous except where Disapprobation tends to diminish Profit—there indeed I am all one Tremble of sensibility, Marriage having taught me the wonderful uses of that vulgar article, yclept BREAD—My wife, my wife's Mother, & little brother, & George Burnet—five mouths opening and shutting as I pull the string! . . . Formerly I could select a fine morning, chuse my road, and take an airing upon my Pegasus right leisurely —but now I am in stirrups all day, yea, and sleep in my Spurs.[12]

It would be wrong to suppose that *The Watchman* was a slipshod or dilettante production; the reverse was the case, it was an immensely professional piece of work. The same may also be said of the poems that S.T.C. was assembling; here again he was most thorough and professional. Letters to Cottle illustrate, time and time again, the expert interest which S.T.C. took in the actual presentation and publication of his poems; practical details concerning the paging of the book, the setting of the page-heads, the order of the poems, positioning of notes, changes in punctuation, and so forth, received meticulous attention from the poet.

The first edition of S.T.C.'s collected poems, *Poems on Various Subjects*, was ready for the press by the end of March. The most important poem in the collection was *Religious Musings*, the first draft of which, entitled *The Nativity*, had been written at Christmas, 1794. Almost a year later, while at Clevedon, S.T.C. was still at work on it: "The Nativity . . . has cost me much labour in polishing, more than any poem I ever wrote—and I believe, deserves it more—,"[13] he told Cottle, adding that he would like John Prior Estlin, a Bristol Unitarian minister friend, to read it for him. In the New Year he was still struggling with it.[14]

Of its chaotic content of musings ("soaring aloft" on "Meditation's heaven-ward wing"), S.T.C. was to remark to Cottle, eighteen years later: "I was very young when I wrote that poem, and my religious feelings were more settled than my theological notions!"[15]

Religious Musings is an incredible conglomeration of Unitarian thinking, Jacobin polemics, hero-worship, the Book of Revelations, travellers' tales, and experimental writing; but study of the poem reveals it as carefully organised, and polished to a high gloss. When first published it was heavily embellished with notes.

The poem was motivated by S.T.C.'s then all-prevailing enchantment with Unitarianism. The appeal which this sect held for S.T.C. undoubtedly lay in the intellectual freedom that it afforded him. "The *necessary* creed . . . is but short . . . to believe that Jesus Christ was the Messiah—in all other points I may play off my intellect *ad libitum*."[16]

In *Religious Musings* Jesus of Nazareth was firmly pinned down as: "Thou, Man of Woes! Despised Galilean!"[17] Working from this firm belay, as it were, S.T.C. was free to perform as many dizzy gymnastics as he chose. Fashionable Spinozistic philosophising found vent in the seven most lucid lines of the entire four hundred and twenty which comprised the whole:

> 'Tis the sublime of man,
> Our noontide majesty, to know ourselves
> Parts and proportions of one wondrous whole!
> This fraternizes man, this constitutes
> Our charities and bearings. But 'tis God
> Diffused through all, that doth make all one whole.[18]

Yet inherent belief in his "I-ship" could not be kept submerged; sixty lines further on he categorically saluted the individual soul:

> Lord of unsleeping Love,
> From everlasting Thou! We shall not die.[19]

Spinoza was deserted for Habakkuk. The family pew at Ottery always tugged him back.

Milton, Newton, Hartley and Priestley were adoringly singled out among the "mighty Dead."[20] The war against France was passionately denounced; this was a must, if S.T.C. were to preserve his public image as a fiery democrat (fortunately for S.T.C. few of his readers had heard of Comberbache).

The most arresting passages in *Religious Musings* were derived from the literature of global exploration which, for a long period of time, furnished S.T.C.'s favourite and most stimulating reading, influencing his major poetry so profoundly that some of these sources must, for a moment, be given at least glancing consideration.

Among the works of travel and voyaging which he gluttonously consumed were Captain Luke Foxe's *North-west Fox, or Fox from the North-west Passage*; Frederick Marten's *Voyage into Spitzbergen and Greenland* (1649); George Shelvocke's *A Voyage Round the World by Way of the Great South Sea* (1726); Samuel Hearne's *A Journey from Prince of Wales's Fort in Hudson Bay to Northern Ocean 1769–1772, by order of the Hudson Bay Company* (1793); Sir John Narborough's account of his exploration of the Arctic; James Bruce's *Travels to Discover the Source of the Nile*; William Bartram's *Travels Through North and South Carolina, Etc* (1791) (a great favourite, this, with S.T.C.); William Dampier's *New Voyage Round the World*; and Cook's *Voyage to the Pacific Ocean* (1789). Most seminal of all S.T.C.'s reading in this genre were the tales of travel and voyaging in the collections edited by Samuel Purchas in the early 17th century: *Purchas his Pilgrimage* (1617) and *Purchas his Pilgrims* (1625).

Two hundred years ago such reading exerted a potent fascination and excitement which our blunted society can scarcely appreciate. The printed page and the reader's imagination effect an alchemy to which television cannot aspire; a viewer might watch an entire series of programmes on the Arctic and yet never once receive an impression so brilliant and unforgettable as this glimpse of penguins given by Narborough: "they are short-legged like a Goose, and stand upright like little Children in White Aprons, in companies together."

This kind of writing stimulated S.T.C. almost beyond endurance. His poetry became flooded with images of Greenland and Africa, the Poles and the source of the Nile, alligators and Abyssinians. In *Religious Musings* we are suddenly mesmerised by a Douanier Rousseau-like glimpse of a

> ... sun-scorched waste,
> Where oft majestic through the tainted noon
> The Simoon sails, before whose purple pomp
> Who falls not prostrate dies! And where by night,
> Fast by each precious fountain on green herbs
> The lion couches; or hyaena dips
> Deep in the lucid stream his bloody jaws;
> Or serpent plants his vast noon-glittering bulk,

Caught in whose monstrous twine Behemoth yells,
His bones loud-crashing![21]

(To this was appended a typically Esteesian footnote:

Behemoth, in Hebrew, signifies wild beasts in general. Some believe it is the
elephant, some the hippopotamus; some affirm it is the wild bull. Poetically,
it designates any large quadruped.)

There is a clearly discernible Miltonic influence in *Religious Musings*, but
there are also reverberations of another voice now ringing in S.T.C.'s ears
—that of William Wordsworth. S.T.C. had learned much from his study of
Descriptive Sketches:

In the form, style and manner of the whole poem, and in the stricture of the
particular lines and periods, there is an harshness and acerbity connected and
combined with words and images all a-glow, which might recall those products of the vegetable world, where gorgeous blossoms rise out of the hard
and thorny rind and shell, within which the rich fruit was elaborating. The
language was not only peculiar and strong, but at times knotty and contorted,
as by its own impatient strength; while the novelty and struggling crowd of
images, acting in conjunction with the difficulties of the style, demanded
always a . . . [great] closeness of attention.[22]

Religious Musings reveals very clearly the new, severe standard that
S.T.C. was setting himself in "novelty of . . . images, acting in conjunction
with style." He was attempting composition where both sound and
imagery seem "ruthless, ancient, and inevitable,"[23] as Edith Sitwell observed of Dryden; where texture was becoming as important a technique to
consider as metre. In short, S.T.C., now approaching maturity as a poet,
had grasped the essential message which Blake stated bluntly when he said:
"Mechanical excellence is the only vehicle of genius."[24]

For Cottle, *Religious Musings* was a poem that badly held up the printer.
For S.T.C. the poem was not only an analysis of, and statement upon, his
religious stance: it was also a tremendous leap forward in his development
as a poet. To Benjamin Flower, a Cambridge friend and editor of the
Cambridge Intelligencer, S.T.C. observed: "I rest for all my poetical credit
on the *Religious Musings*."[25] To John Thelwall he said much the same.
When Richard Poole commented that he thought *Religious Musings* too
metaphysical for common readers, S.T.C. replied tersely that the poem
was not written for common readers.

The collected poems were at last published on April 16, 1796. A copy
was sent to George Coleridge, another to Thomas Poole. It is doubtful if
George could have been altogether reassured by *Religious Musings*: but the
dispatch of a copy of the book to him might at least be seen as a gesture by

S.T.C. in the direction of reconciliation. To Poole, on the other hand, S.T.C. wrote with true fraternal warmth:

> My very dear Friend! I send these poems to you with better heart than I should to most others, because I know that you will read them with affection however little you may admire them. I love to shut my eyes, and bring up before my imagination that Arbour, in which I have repeated so many of these compositions to you.—Dear Arbour! an Elysium to which I have so often passed by your Cerberus, & Tartarean tan-pits! God bless you my dear Poole/& your grateful & affectionate Friend
>
> S. T. Coleridge[26]

Anti-Jacobin reaction to *Religious Musings* was furious, as might have been anticipated; but, on the whole, the poems had a reception which greatly gladdened S.T.C. The *Monthly Review* placed *Religious Musings* "on the very top of the scale of Sublimity!—!—!—!"[27] as the ecstatic author repeated exultantly.

Publication day had brought S.T.C. no financial harvest; he had been paid in advance and had long since spent all the money.

By the end of April, S.T.C. was asking Cottle if he could get "25 or 30 of the *Poems* ready by tomorrow . . . Parsons of Paternoster Row has written to me pressingly about them. 'People are perpetually asking after them— All admire the Poetry in the Watchman'."[28] Accordingly, thirty copies of *Poems* were dispatched and six of *Joan of Arc*, together with a hundred copies of the first number of *Watchman*. These were apparently readily sold, for a large further order was soon received. Copies of the *Poems*, *Conciones* and *Joan of Arc* were also dispatched to the Midlands and North for sale; some of these were paid for, if we can believe Cottle, but Parsons never paid S.T.C. "one farthing" of the profits and when pressed for payment set the wretched young poet "at defiance."[29]

The Watchman, meantime, tottered towards an early and inevitable demise, in spite of all S.T.C.'s desperate efforts to keep it alive. Even at its most successful this periodical never yielded more than "a bread-and-cheesish profit."[30] By April 11, S.T.C. was writing despairingly to Poole: "I have scarcely sold enough to pay the expences."[31] Subscribers dropped away at an alarming rate, some disliking this aspect of *Watchman*, some another. To quote once more from S.T.C. himself:

> Thus, by the time the seventh number was published, I had the mortification . . . of seeing the preceding numbers exposed in sundry old iron shops for a penny apiece . . . Of the unsaleable nature of my writings I had an amusing memento from our own servant girl. For happening to rise at an earlier hour than usual, I observed her putting an extravagant quantity of paper into the grate in order to light the fire, and mildly checked her for her wastefulness. 'La Sir' (replied poor Nanny) 'why, it is only Watchman.'[32]

The last number of *The Watchman* appeared on May 13, 1796. The final page was devoted to an "Address to the readers of the Watchman:—"

> This is the last Number of the Watchman.—Henceforward I shall cease to cry the state of the Political atmosphere. While I express my gratitude to those friends who exerted themselves so liberally in the establishment of this Miscellany, I may reasonably be expected to assign some reason for relinquishing it thus abruptly. The reason is short and satisfactory.—The work does not pay its expences. Part of my subscribers have relinquished it because it did not contain sufficient original composition; and a still larger number, because it contained too much ... To return to myself. I have endeavoured to do well: and it must be attributed to defect of ability, not of inclination or effort, if the words of the Prophet be altogether applicable to me.
>
> O, Watchman! thou hast watched in vain.

To Poole, S.T.C. wryly augmented this: "It is not pleasant, Thomas Poole, to have worked 14 weeks for nothing—*for nothing*." The tradesmen's bills for the Watchman, continued S.T.C., amounted to exactly five pounds more than the whole amount of the receipts. "Meantime Mrs Coleridge asks about baby-linen & anticipates the funeral expences of her poor Mother—."[33]

Old Mrs Fricker did not die: Robert Lovell did, upon Tuesday, May 3rd, 1796, of what was described as a putrid fever. The agonised groans of his final hours drove his wife almost demented and S.T.C., who was present, at last rushed out, summoned a chairman, and had her conveyed to his own house.

What his feelings were in the presence of this young widow who, with her infant son, had been left wholly reliant on the possible generosity of a none-too-friendly father-in-law, may best be imagined. A succession of terrifying visions of Sara, and her future child, in a like predicament must have presented themselves to S.T.C. He had no money; he could make no provision for Sara; his only means of livelihood, writing, was proving a profitless deception. It was possibly the episode of this young, much-in-love married couple parted by death which prompted S.T.C. to write in his notebook: "Mem—not to adulterize my time by absenting myself from my wife—."[34]

The failure of *Watchman* set him making desperate plans for the future: these reduced themselves to two—the first, as he himself said, impracticable, and the second not likely to succeed.

The first was to perfect his study of German and then to propose to Robinson, the London bookseller, that S.T.C. be commissioned to translate the works of Schiller, on the condition that Robinson should pay the travelling expenses of S.T.C. and Sara to and from Jena, where Schiller resided. S.T.C. further proposed that at Jena he should study chemistry and anatomy, and bring back with him the works of Semler, Michaelis and Kant.

On his return he would open a school for eight young men at 100 guineas each, proposing to perfect them in the following curriculum:

1. Man as an Animal: including ... Anatomy, Chemistry, Mechanics & Optics.—

2. Man as an *Intellectual* Being: including the ancient Metaphysics, the systems of Locke & Hartley,—of the Scotch Philosophers—& the new Kantian System.

3. Man as a Religious Being: including an historic summery of all Religions & the arguments for and against Natural & Revealed Religion ... 1. The History of Savage Tribes. 2. of semi-barbarous nations. 3. of nations emerging from semi-barbarism. 4. of civilized states. 5. of luxurious states. 6. of revolutionary states. 7. —of Colonies.—[Also studies of] the knowledge of languages ... Belles Lettres & and the principles of composition.[35]

"Bright Bubbles of the aye-ebullient brain!" commented S.T.C., in subsequent review of this. "Gracious Heaven! that a scheme so big with advantage to the Kingdom, therefore to Europe, therefore to the World should be demolishable by one monosyllable from a Bookseller's Mouth!"[36]

His second plan was "to become a Dissenting Parson & abjure Politics & carnal literature."[37]

To Cottle he explained:

Preaching for Hire is not right; because it must prove a strong temptation to continue to profess what I had ceased to believe, *if ever* maturer Judgment ... should lessen or destroy my faith in Christianity. But tho' not right in itself, it may become right by the greater wrongness of the only Alternative— the remaining in neediness & Uncertainty. That in the one case I should be exposed to temptation, is a mere contingency: that under necessitous circumstances I am exposed to great & frequent temptation is a melancholy certainty.—[38]

S.T.C. did not put a name to "this great & frequent temptation," but there can be little real doubt that he was referring to opium.

CHAPTER SEVEN

THE FEELINGS OF THE MOMENT

(May–December 1796)

TOM POOLE HAD foreseen from the start that *The Watchman* would never provide S.T.C. with a reasonable livelihood if, indeed, with any. As early as March 25, 1796, he was drawing up a plan to come to S.T.C.'s assistance. He organised a group of friends to contribute five guineas each, yearly, to furnish S.T.C. with a small annuity for the next six years. Contributors to this fund included Josiah Wade, the Rev. J. P. Estlin, John Cruikshank, Charles Danvers, J. J. Morgan and, of course, Poole himself. The money was to be presented in the tactful guise of a testimonial. Cruikshank was appointed treasurer of the fund (this office later passed to Estlin). Payments were made to S.T.C. in 1796 and 1797; they were thereafter discontinued when S.T.C. accepted an annuity from the Wedgwoods in 1798. Poole contrived that S.T.C. should receive tidings of the testimonial upon the day that *Watchman* made its final appearance.

S.T.C.'s reaction to the testimonial was a burst of affectionate gratitude towards Poole, but at first he was not sure whether to accept the money or not; his financial situation was desperate enough, but pride impelled him to make a show of reluctance. He solved the problem by paying a visit to Stowey to discuss the matter with Poole in person and, once at Stowey, was quickly induced to accept the annuity.

The relationship between S.T.C. and Tom Poole had developed, within the space of six months, from mere friendly acquaintance in the autumn of 1795 to brotherly love by April 1796.

Each man had a need of the other. Poole, during 1794 and early 1795, had been confined to his room for days at a time with a nervous illness. The butt of his now dying father's chronic irascibility, in general disfavour for his democratic views, disappointed, it seems, in love, Poole had consoled himself with Latin studies and with designing and furnishing for himself a library, where he had arranged the nucleus of that fine collection of books which, twelve years later, was to arouse the great admiration of De Quincey.

The death of his father in July 1795 released Poole from his major source of pressure, but it was not until S.T.C. entered his life, with meteor-like flamboyance, that the crepuscular monotony of Poole's nervous debility was dispersed.

Poole's relatives, with the exception of his mother, objected strongly to the Esteesian invasion of Nether Stowey. On September 19, 1795, Tom Poole's cousin, Charlotte Poole, wrote in her diary:

Tom Poole has a friend with him of the name of Coldridge [sic]: a young man of brilliant understanding, great eloquence, desperate fortune, demo-cratick principles, and entirely led away by the feelings of the moment.[1]

From that visit onward, Poole's home became a place of stable refuge for S.T.C. The commonplace, comfortable brown house, with a tanyard at the back and a long garden from which there was a view of the Quantocks, Poole's draughty study, his mother's cosy parlour, all grew increasingly dear to S.T.C., and to Sara too. The pair stayed with Thomas and his mother in the final weeks of 1795 and thereafter S.T.C. was constantly discovering excuses to go to Stowey.

Between himself and old Mrs Poole there sprang up the liveliest of affections. There were, maintained S.T.C., three kinds of old women: "That old woman—That old witch—and that dee-ar old Soul."[2] Mrs Poole was a "dee-ar old soul." S.T.C. quickly appropriated her; she became "our Mother."

In Tom, S.T.C. found that perfect brother-figure of whom he had always dreamed—close in age, senior in stability and wisdom, yet sharing his own views and sympathies.

Under the combined circumstances S.T.C.'s refusal of the testimonial annuity would have been an impossibility. With heartfelt thanks he accepted it. George Dyer came to his further aid with a sum "amply sufficient" to extricate S.T.C. from his difficulties "till such time as my Literary Industry will, I trust, find employment"[3] as S.T.C. put it in a brief, but warm, letter of thanks. Shortly after, S.T.C. received a donation of ten guineas from the Royal Literary Fund.

Early in July, through Dr Beddoes, S.T.C. received an offer of employment from Perry, editor of the London *Morning Chronicle*. S.T.C. accepted this, but with a "heavy and reluctant heart . . . If I go, farewell, Philosophy! Farewell, the Muse!"[4]

But he had scarcely steeled himself to face newspaper work when an invitation arrived from a Mrs Evans of Darley, near Derby, asking him to visit her with a view to educating her two sons. S.T.C. and Sara travelled up to Darley, where the matter was arranged to the satisfaction of both parties. Mrs Evans captivated S.T.C. She appeared avid to have him as tutor for her children. S.T.C. returned to Bristol alone, leaving the eight-months-pregnant Sara at Darley as Mrs Evans' guest. Meantime S.T.C. made a flying visit to Ottery in order fully to reconcile himself with his family before moving to Derbyshire for what promised to be a long period. The visit went well, beyond all expectation; his mother received him "with transport," Brother George with "joy and tenderness" and his other brothers with "affectionate civility."[5]

But now came an incoherent note from Mrs Evans, putting an end to the tutorship scheme. The guardians of her sons were totally opposed to it; so strong were their remonstrances that she was compelled to yield to them. S.T.C. hastened back to Darley and a further stay of ten days with Mrs Evans, during which time a polite social gloss was spread over the incident by the embarrassed hostess and an ever-courteous S.T.C. who, being a gentleman, concealed his chagrin and disappointment.

Not so Tom Poole. From Stowey came an explosive note, highly typical of that impulsive democrat:

> My dear fellow, you are schooled to disappointment. I hope you bear this with steadiness . . . I am now convinced of what I doubted before, that woman is inferior to man. No man who is capable of willing as ardently as she willed, who had the heart and head she possesses, and understood the object to be attained so well, would vacillate. Woman, thou wast destined to be governed. Let us then bow to destiny.[6]

Mrs Evans at least had given the young Coleridges, particularly Sara, a much-needed rest in comfortable surroundings. "We spent five weeks at her home—a sunny spot in our life!—"[7] S.T.C. was to recall. Mrs Evans also gave Sara a generous gift of baby-clothes.

S.T.C. now had plans to open a day-school in Derby, for twelve scholars, at twenty guineas each scholar. While further considering this S.T.C. went with Sara to Moseley, near Birmingham, where they stayed as guests of Thomas Hawkes. Here they met Charles Lloyd, the twenty-one-year-old elder son of the Quaker banking family. Charles was subject to attacks of violent epilepsy (later he became insane and already he revealed clear signs of mental disturbance).

For S.T.C. Charles Lloyd held certain attraction as a Romantic figure; epilepsy and madness were both part of the Romantic mystique of tainted beauty. Added to this, Lloyd wrote (bad) poetry. He already vastly admired S.T.C. as a poet and now, upon meeting him, developed an abrupt and violent admiration for him, expressing a passionate desire to become domiciled with S.T.C. and to be tutored by him. For these benefits Lloyd proposed to pay a good price, which would relieve S.T.C. of the need to open the school in Derby.

The Coleridges returned to Bristol while this proposal underwent further consideration. There is some evidence that S.T.C. was resorting to opium throughout this period of uncertainty. A letter to his friend, John Colson, written on September 4, opened with excuses for not writing, due to disappointments and much worry over the sorrows of others (including Robert Allen, whose young wife was dying), and continued ominously:

Can you wonder then, that I have neglected *some* necessary business—and that when I have finished my 'letters of compulsion', that I have dreamt away the leisure hours—dreamt of *you*, my Colson! not unfrequently—altho' I have not written you.—[8]

On September 17, S.T.C. travelled to Bristol once more in order to complete arrangements for Lloyd's envisaged domicile at Bristol. Sara, who was not expecting to be confined for some three weeks, assured S.T.C. that she was perfectly happy for him to leave her; he would be back well in time for the arrival of the baby. S.T.C. departed; but on Tuesday morning, September 20, he received the staggering news that Sara had been delivered of a son at half-past two in the morning of the previous day: "my Sara had strangely miscalculated."[9] She had commenced labour suddenly and before either nurse or surgeon could arrive had delivered herself; the nurse came in time to remove the after-birth. Within a few hours after her delivery Sara, apart from weakness, was perfectly well; the baby, too, was thriving.

S.T.C., "quite annihilated with the suddeness of the information,"[10] hastened home, taking Charles Lloyd with him. His first view of his child was an anti-climax: "I did not feel the thrill & overflowing of affection which I expected . . . The Baby seems strong, & the old Nurse has over-persuaded my wife to discover a likeness of me in its face—no great compliment to me —for in truth I have seen handsomer Babies in my life time.—"[11]

His first reaction to the child he recalled, vividly, in conversation thirty-five years later, while discussing the differences between Dutch and Italian schools of painting:

> The Italian masters differ from the Dutch in this—that in their pictures ages are perfectly ideal. The infant that Raffael's Madonna holds in her arms cannot be guessed of any particular age: it is Humanity in its infancy. The babe in the Manger in a Dutch painting is a fac-simile of some real new-born bantling; it is just like the little rabbits we fathers have all seen with some dismay at first burst.[12]

But when, two hours after his initial, disillusioned view of his first-born, S.T.C. saw the infant again "on the bosom of its Mother; on her arm; and her eye tearful & watching its little features, then I was thrilled & melted, and gave it the Kiss of a FATHER."[13]

The moment when he first saw Sara with their baby at her breast remained for ever impressed upon his memory. On one occasion, discussing a remark by a man friend (probably Wordsworth) that love was friendship accidentally combined with desire, S.T.C. concluded that the speaker had never been in love. "For what shall we say of the feeling which a man of sensibility has towards his wife with her baby at her breast. How pure from sensual desire! yet how different from friendship!"[14]

The child was named David Hartley Coleridge, in honour of "the great master of *Christian* Philosophy."[15]

One of the first to be informed of the boy's birth was Thomas Poole, in a letter which commenced with an allusion to what was, in all probability, opium day-dreaming on a masochistic theme—that Poole did not love S.T.C. so much as formerly. S.T.C., describing this state of feeling to Poole, anticipated his self-induced sufferings of the Asra period:

> my Soul seems so mantled & wrapped round by your Love & Esteem, that even a dream of losing but the smallest fragment of it makes me shiver—as tho' some tender part of my Nature were left uncovered & in nakedness.—[16]

Poole's love, said S.T.C., had come to form an essential part of his happiness.

The letter in reply from Poole (on September 26) requires quoting in full, for it indicates the depth of the friendship:

> September 26, 1796.
> My Dearest Friend—the friend held dearest by me. *I say it thinkingly*—and say it as a *full* answer to the first part of your interesting letter. By you, Coleridge, I will always stand, in sickness and in health, in prosperity and misfortune; nay, in the worst of all misfortunes, in *vice* . . . if vice should ever taint thee—but it *cannot*.
>
> My dear, I came an hour ago from Sherborne, where I have left my mother and sister.
>
> I congratulate you on becoming a father—the father of David Hartley; on the health of his mother, to whom remember me tenderly. When I have a son, his name shall be John Hampden. If either of them should feel, what a coronet he will have to support!
>
> I have now two or three buzzing round me, and I can only simply answer your letter. I am happy Mr Lloyd is with you; I shall be more happy to see him. Come both directly, I am all alone. And we will *live*. Yes: I hope we will live.
>
> I have only ran over the poetry. When we meet we will talk of all things.
>
> Give me a line by return of post, just mentioning the day—nay, I will send horses to Bridgewater—only mention the day and the time of day. They shall be there.—Adieu most kindly,
>
> THOS. POOLE[17]

To interpret the deep affection between Poole and S.T.C. in terms of homosexual love as we understand it today would almost certainly be to distort the relationship. It must be borne in mind that for S.T.C.'s happiness it was essential that he should have intellectual friendship, overflowing with sympathy and tenderness, but devoid of any normally overt sexual content; although, intermittently, he would gratify himself by imposing masochistic images upon the basic fabric of tender sympathy. His choice of friends who fulfilled this rôle was made irrespective of sex: Sara Fricker, Poole, Sara and Mary Hutchinson, William Wordsworth, the Brent sisters, all at some time or other became his dream-loves, whom he imagined as symbols of the purest and tenderest sympathy, with occasional transposed variations of withdrawal, or transference of the love; variations improvised for purposes of (pleasurable) painful sensation.

Poole, at this period, played the part of S.T.C.'s chaste, dream-love. It was a role which Sara Coleridge had only been able to fill prior to their marriage. Sexual impregnability was an essential ingredient; she, as his sexual partner, was now debarred from being his ideal love. Poole was elevated into,

> My beloved ... dearest, and most esteemed friend—Friend of my Soul! and Brother of my Choice!"[18] "... to see you daily, to tell you all my thoughts in their first birth, and to hear your's, to be mingling identities with you as it were;—the vision-weaving *Fancy* has indeed often pictured such things, but *Hope* never dared whisper a promise![19]

This is S.T.C. writing to Poole in 1796; it could equally be S.T.C. writing to Sara Hutchinson in 1802.

Present too, with Poole, were masochistic dreams:

> My heart has been full, yea, crammed with anxieties about my residence near you. I so ardently desire it, that any disappointment would chill my faculties, like the fingers of death. And entertaining a wish so irrationally strong, I necessarily have *day* mair dreams that something will prevent it— so that ... I have been gloomy as the month which even now has begun to lower and rave on us.[20]*

This kind of writing was to be echoed, again and again, in addresses to Sara Hutchinson written in S.T.C.'s notebooks (although not, of necessity, actually sent to her in letter-form, or, indeed, even seen by her).

Financial anxiety had now been removed; Lloyd had agreed to pay £80 a year for board, lodging, and three hours' daily tuition. But S.T.C. still had to face the problem of what to do with his life.

At this point he had his mind abruptly taken off his own worries by an urgent call from Charles Lamb for succour.

On September 22, Mary Lamb who, like Charles, was highly unstable (Charles, at the close of 1795, had been a patient for a short while in a mental asylum) was seized by a fit of acute mania during which she fatally stabbed her mother. Charles himself took the knife from her. He revealed most exemplary self-control throughout this terrible family crisis, and even succeeded, with the help of friends, in obtaining his sister's release from life-long restraint in an asylum, on the condition that he himself undertook

---

*Compare with *Ode to Dejection*.

responsibility for her safe-keeping. Mary Lamb recovered her sanity (though throughout her life she from time to time had relapses into acute mania, during which she had to be temporarily removed for treatment).

Lamb, after the tragic death of his mother, wrote to S.T.C. begging him to write, "as religious a letter as possible."[21] S.T.C., it seems, sent Lamb several letters, but only one has survived, that of September 28th, 1796. In this letter S.T.C. writes with great sincerity of feeling:

> Your poor father is, I hope, almost senseless of the calamity; the unconscious instrument of Divine Providence knows it not, and your mother is in heaven. It is sweet to be roused from a frightful dream by the song of birds and the gladsome rays of the morning. Ah, how infinitely more sweet to be awakened from the blackness and amazement of a sudden horror by the glories of God manifest and the hallelujahs of angels.[22]

S.T.C. pressingly invited Lamb to visit him, but this Lamb was unable to do.

S.T.C.'s religious conviction was never doubted by his oldest and closest friends. In writing to Charles Lamb in this vein he was being wholly sincere, and Lamb knew it. Indeed, this was why he had written to S.T.C. for religious reassurance.

S.T.C.'s hints that he had, at some unspecified point in his youth, doubted the existence of God, should be taken with a very large pinch of salt indeed. (They belong to the same category as the hints of elderly virgins that they, in the distant past, have had a lover in their bed.)

In April or early May of 1796, S.T.C. entered into correspondence with John Thelwall (1764–1834), a hard-core republican seditionist and atheist, who had been imprisoned in the Tower in May, 1794, and later tried for treason. He had been acquitted in December of that same year. Shortly afterwards, in early 1795, he published *Poems written in Close Confinement in the Tower and Newgate*. He first wrote to S.T.C. in April, 1796, as a result of an article in *The Watchman*. S.T.C., in reply, sent him a copy of *Poems on Various Subjects*, begging Thelwall to overlook their 'effimacy [sic] of sentiment" and "faulty glitter of expression;"[23] it was the *Religious Musings* which S.T.C. wished to bring to Thelwall's attention.

S.T.C.'s letters to Thelwall make fascinating, at moments comic, reading. In them he unconsciously reveals the unsubstantiality of his radical pretensions. The fiery young democrat whose revolutionary views so shocked Nether Stowey is exposed as deeply orthodox, innately reactionary, a classical instance, in short, of a youth from the English ruling class who, as an undergraduate, flexes his mental muscles blithely in the open fields of radical thinking before settling down to sober adult embracement of traditional conservative opinion.

To Thelwall, S.T.C. in a long letter of May 13, 1796, declared, in his stoutest accents:

I again assert, that a Sensualist is not likely to be a Patriot.—Scott told me some shocking stories of Godwin ... of his endeavors to seduce Mrs Reevely—&— ... I have been informed by a West-Indian (a Republican) that to *his knowledge* Gerald [the seditionist] left a *Wife* there to starve—and I well know that he was prone to intoxication, & an *Whore* monger. I saw myself a letter from Gerald to one of his FRIENDS, couched in terms of the most abhorred Obsenity, & advising marriage with an old woman on account of her money—Alas! alas! Thelwall—I almost wept—& poor Lovell (who read it with me) was so much agitated that he left the room.[24]

Thelwall's reply to this was to say that he supposed that S.T.C. must industriously collect anecdotes unfavourable to atheists; why, he asked, did S.T.C. not favour him with a few slanderous stories about Christians? S.T.C., nettled and on the defensive, replied that, doubtless, he could fill a book with slander about:

professed Christians; but those very men would allow, they were acting contrary to Christianity—but, I am afraid, an atheistic bad Man manufactures his sytem of principles with an eye to his peculiar propensities;—and makes his actions the criterion of what is virtuous, not virtue the criterion of his actions. Where the *disposition* is not amiable, an acute understanding I deem no blessing— ... Let me see you—I already know a Deist, & Calvinists, & Moravians whom I love & reverence—& I shall leap forward, to realize my *principles* by *feeling* love & honour for a Atheist.[25]

The animated correspondence which sprang up between the two men during the course of the ensuing months resolved itself into arguments over atheism and poetry. The aim of S.T.C. was, obviously, to save Thelwall's immortal soul, which could not be achieved without first persuading him that he had one to save:

the religion which Christ taught, is simply 1. that there is an Omnipresent Father of infinite power, wisdom & Goodness, in whom we all of us move, & have our being & 2. That when we appear to men to die, we do not utterly perish; but after this Life shall continue to enjoy or suffer the consequences & natural effects of the Habits, we have formed here, whether good or evil.[26]

This raised the question, What is Life? S.T.C. mused:

Dr Beddoes, & Dr Darwin think that *Life* is utterly inexplicable, writing as Materialists—You [Thelwall] I understand, have adopted the idea that it is the result of organized matter acted on by external Stimuli ... Morris believes in a plastic immaterial Nature—all-pervading— ... Hunter that the *Blood* is the Life—which is saying nothing at all ... & Ferriar believes in a *Soul*, like an orthodox Churchman—So much for Physicians & Surgeons —Now as to the Metaphysicians, Plato says, it is *Harmony*—he might as well have said, a fiddle stick's end—but I love Plato—his dear *gorgeous* Nonsense! And I, *tho' last not least*, I do not know what to think about it—on the whole, I have rather made up my mind that I am a mere *apparition*—a naked Spirit! —And that Life is I myself I![27]

To further enliven thoughts on immortality, the Esteesian apparition scattered happy, inconsequential asides: "Well, true or false, Heaven is a less gloomy idea than Annihilation."[28] "If my System should prove true, we, I doubt not, shall both meet in the kingdom of Heaven, and I with transport in my eye shall say—'I *told* you so, my *dear* fellow'."[29]

Thelwall succumbed to S.T.C.'s charm, although not to his arguments. The letter-writing ripened into friendship and pressing invitations from S.T.C. to Thelwall, to pay a visit to Bristol. Thelwall's wife, Stella, also exchanged fraternal greetings with Sara Coleridge: "I should not wonder if they were to be sworn sister-seraphs in the heavenly Jerusalem,"[30] was S.T.C.'s comment.

On October 15, 1796, S.T.C. wrote to Charles Lloyd's father, Mr Charles Lloyd, Senior, outlining to him the details of an important change that he had now decided to make in his way of life. He proposed to remove himself,

> once for all and utterly from cities and towns ... My reasons are—that I have cause to believe my Health would be materially impaired by residing in a town, and by the close confinement and anxieties incident to the education of children.[31]

He was determined, he added, that his own children should be bred up from earliest infancy in the simplicity of peasants; if reared in cities they would necessarily become acquainted with politicians and politics:

> a set of men and a kind of study which I deem highly unfavourable to all Christian graces. I have myself erred greatly in this respect; but, I trust, I have now seen my error. I have accordingly snapped my squeaking baby-trumpet of Sedition, and have hung up its fragments in the chamber of Penitences.[32]

This letter should be compared with that written in 1807 to Sir George Beaumont, in which S.T.C. described how, at the age of twenty-four (in other words, in 1796), he had retired from politics, "disgusted beyond measure by the manners & morals of the Democrats ... sick of Politics."[33]

He went on to explain to Beaumont that the reason why he and Southey had not got into trouble with authority as a result of their political activities was because "the Government knew that Southey & I were utterly unconnected with any party or club or society."[34]

No evidence has been found that either S.T.C. or Southey were actual members of any known political society, but it is worth noting that in a letter to Thelwall of November 19, 1796, S.T.C. wrote:

Have you any connection with the Corresponding Society Magazine—I have not seen it yet—Robert Southey is one of its benefactors.[35]

It is important to remember that, in his letter to Beaumont, S.T.C. was anxious to minimise his early activities in republican politics. Hence his heavy insistence that the Ministers "knew that we were Boys."[36] His partnership with Southey in a career of sedition, added S.T.C., had lasted but ten months; then Southey had left for Lisbon and S.T.C. had retired into the country "sick of Politics, & sick of Democrats and Democracy, before the Ministers had ever heard of us."[37]

If this last were true, it would be surprising; S.T.C.'s published lectures and *Watchman* must almost certainly have attracted some notice from authority, even though no action had been taken against the author. Thelwall subsequently gave it as his opinion that S.T.C. must have gone to the Tower, had he continued with his political career. The salient point here is that S.T.C. did not continue with it.

To Beaumont S.T.C. explained:

tho' I detested Revolution in my calmer moments . . . yet with an ebullient Fancy, a flowing utterance, a light & dancing Heart, & a disposition to catch fire by the very rapidity of my own motion, & to speak vehemently from mere verbal associations, choosing sentences & sentiments . . . that would have made me recoil with . . . an unutterable Horror from the action expressed in such sentences & sentiments . . . I aided the Jacobins.[38]

Doubtless this self-portrait, of a young bourgeois intellectual playing at Revolution without the slightest realisation of where the road led, was true enough; it was a common occurrence in his day; it is common in ours; it is the reason why proletarian activists never place serious reliance upon radical student movements.

Neither Southey nor S.T.C. as young men were truly interested in politics, nor in social reform; they enjoyed political philosophy—a very different matter. The early stages of the French Revolution, which had so enraptured them, had been a wonderful period for philosophising. In its later stages the Revolutionary action had centred upon social legislation and class attrition; in the first, Southey and S.T.C. had revealed little real interest, if any; by the second, they were naturally appalled. The year 1794 had witnessed their complete disillusionment with France; the Terror and sans-culottism had made a mockery of the Romantic philosophy of the brotherhood of man. Yet the year which saw the height of the Terror in France saw also the introduction there of a vast scheme for providing public assistance and free medical attention for the elderly and the sick, nursing-mothers and widows, at a total annual cost to the country of nearly 15 million *livres*. An Education Act, passed in January of that year, provided three years of free, compulsory, primary education. In February slavery had been abolished. To this impressive French social legislation the newly-emergent Pantisocrats had remained surprisingly unresponsive. They preferred the cloud-cuckoo-land of the Susquehannah.

In short, their preoccupation with democratic politics had been precisely what S.T.C. was to admit that it had been; an adolescent game. His early political writing therefore remains, not as evidence of his youthful jacobin convictions (these, demonstrably, he never truly held), but of what he himself subsequently recognised as the ebullience of his fancy, the flowing utterance of his brilliantly gifted pen, his disposition to ignite himself with his own eloquence, and, above all, his fatal susceptibility to "the feelings of the moment." Personal disorientation, not socially motivated reasoning, prompted him to leap to embrace radical political views which were wholly inimical to his true nature and, indeed, his real intellectual stance. It is possible that Thelwall's hard-hitting and uncompromising attitudes finally convinced S.T.C. that he was not tough enough for serious political involvement; thus, he decided to quit.

Equally cogent was his need for as stress-free a life as possible; he had now definitely ascertained that, for him, anxiety was insupportable without opium.

A letter to John Colson, written in December 1796, renders S.T.C.'s predicament abundantly clear:

> Your long silence did indeed make me uneasy. I attributed it to your anxieties, which (Judging of your mind by my own) I supposed to have exerted a *narcotic* influence on you.[39]

(The letters to Colson are all written in a vein which strongly suggests that they came from one opium-addict to another. There is a tacit understanding, on S.T.C.'s part, that Colson will understand his veiled allusions to opium.)

To Lloyd senior, in further correspondence, S.T.C. enlarged upon the problem of temptation: "Does not that man *mock* God who daily prays against temptations, yet daily places himself in the midst of the most formidable?"[40] In sum, S.T.C. had discovered that involvement in busy city life, either in the field of politics or journalism, exposed him to pressures with which he could not cope. His instinct was, as always, to bolt from any overwhelming situation; this time he would flee into rustic seclusion, near Tom Poole, whose brother-father-figure held out promise of sympathy, guidance and support.

Above all, in secure tranquillity, S.T.C. could give his full mind to poetry.

He had at last discovered his true and ruling life's calling: he was a poet.

The seriousness of poetry; the stringent demands of total concentration that it makes upon those who give themselves to it, can be understood only by those who have dedicated themselves to a Muse. S.T.C. now knew that to be a poet he must devote his entire attention and endeavour to poetry; half of his attention would not do. To explain this to outsiders was impossible—it simply evoked the kind of response which S.T.C. had drawn from Poole's London friend, Samuel Purkis, who, approached by Poole in the summer of 1796 to interest himself on S.T.C.'s behalf (should S.T.C. go to London to do newspaper work), commented upon S.T.C.'s reluctance to abandon poetry for journalism: "as Raphael did not disdain to paint cups and vases, I think Coleridge may display his taste and genius in a paragraph or an essay."[41]

The giant strides now being made by S.T.C. as a poet are indicated by the natural tone of authority which he assumed in the discussion of poetry problems which commenced or, more correctly, was resumed between himself and Southey in September 1796. Southey had returned to England in May of that year, but reconciliation with S.T.C. appears not to have taken place until September when Southey, possibly at the prompting of Edith at the time of Hartley Coleridge's birth, made an overture towards S.T.C. to which the latter responded. The ill-feeling between the two former inseparables was now concealed rather than buried beneath a drift of letters about technical aspects of poetry (S.T.C. stuck to his policy of discussing nothing personal with Southey).

S.T.C.'s attitude to poetry had changed radically during Southey's absence; largely due to discovery of Wordsworth.

S.T.C. and Wordsworth seem not to have met in 1796, but they appear to have corresponded, if not extensively. Writing to Thelwall on May 13 of that year, S.T.C. referred to "a very dear friend of mine, who is in my opinion the best poet of the age."[42] This was Wordsworth (S.T.C. went on further to describe him as "a Republican & at least a Semi-atheist").[43] Enthusiastically as S.T.C. now admired Wordsworth's verse, it was, nonetheless, premature (although typically Esteesian) to describe him as "a very dear friend."

Wordsworth, during this year, had read and commented favourably upon *Religious Musings* and Cottle had shown S.T.C. Wordsworth's *Guilt and Sorrow: or, Incidents Upon Salisbury Plain*, which had sent S.T.C. into a fervour of admiration. It had also inspired him to do some hard and critical thinking about his own poetry. We get a glimpse of this thinking in a letter that he wrote to Thelwall:

In some (indeed in many of my poems) there is a garishness & swell of diction, which I hope that my poems in future, if I write any, will be clear of . . . In the second Edition now printing I have swept the book with the expurgation Besom to a fine tune—having omitted nearly one third . . . I do confess that . . . [my own poetry] frequently both in thought & language deviates from 'nature & simplicity'.[44]

"Nature and simplicity." The phrase is wholly Wordsworthian.

In comparison with *Guilt and Sorrow* Southey's poetry appeared as lightweight stuff and S.T.C. treated much of it with a levity which would have offended a conceited man; but Southey was fortunately too professional to be vain of his own work (the exact reverse of Wordsworth). S.T.C. had an invigorating, pugilistic attitude towards the Muse: "And now, my dear fellow! for a little sparring about Poetry."[45] This was to Thelwall, but Southey provided an equally useful sparring-partner and he now came in for a rapid succession of biffs and blows, all above the belt and completely within the rules, but with none of the punches pulled.

To the Genius of Africa provoked:

perfect, saving the last line . . . who after having been whirled along by such a tide of enthusiasm can endure to be impaled at last on the needle-point of an Antithesis? [the last stanza of the poem was, in due course, dropped] 'The poem on the Death of an old Spaniel' will, I doubt not, be set to music by angelic & arch-angelic Dogs in their state of exaltation . . . 'The Musings on a Landscape' is a delicious poem.—The words TO HIM begin the line awkwardly, to *my* ear.—The final pause at the end of the first two Syllables of a line is seldom tolerable, except when the first two Syllables form a trochee —the reason, I apprehend, is, that to the ear they with the line foregoing make an Alexandrine . . . And now for the *Penates* . . . *the five first Lines* of the Poem—they are very, very *beautiful*; but (pardon my obtuseness) have they any *meaning*? 'The Temple of Paean' does not, I presume, mean any real temple—but is only an allegorical building—expressing Poesy—either ancient or modern. If modern, how is its wall ruined? If ancient, how do *you* hang up your silent harp on it? . . . But indeed the lines sound so sweet, and *seem* so much like sense, that it is no great matter. 'Tis a handsome & finely-sculptur'd Tomb—& few will break it open with the sacrilegious spade & pick-ax of Criticism to discover, whether or not it be a *Cenotaph*.[46]

Southey, to give him his due, made many alterations to his poems in accordance with S.T.C.'s "spade-and-pick-ax" work.

The major fault with Southey, as S.T.C. commented to Thelwall, was that he failed to engage in "that toil of thinking, which is necessary in order to plan a Whole . . . he abjures *thinking*—& lays the whole stress of excellence—on *feeling*.—Now (as you say) they must go together."[47]

It is a wry comment on the popular understanding (or misunderstanding) of poetry that Coleridge, who put such toil of thought into his poems, should be known to posterity as one who did it all the easy way, on drugs.

In October of 1796 S.T.C. seemed to have found a cottage and six acres to rent at Adscombe, near Stowey. While waiting for negotiations over this property to be completed he surrendered himself to "gloomy thoughts,"[48] opium, masochistic day-dreams, indolence, and withdrawal from the anxieties pressing upon him. He commented to Poole, unguardedly: "Ah! me— I wonder not that the hours fly ... for they pass unfreighted with the duties which they came to demand!—"[49]

This ominous communication was made on November 1; two days later S.T.C. was abruptly seized by agonising pains: "A devil, a very devil, has got possession of my left temple, eye, cheek, jaw, throat and shoulder."[50]

The doctor diagnosed nervous disorder, arising either from severe overwork, or excessive anxiety. S.T.C. agreed with the latter explanation; he had, he told Poole,

With a gloomy wantonness of Imagination ... been coquetting with the hideous *Possibles* of Disappointment—I drank fears, like wormwood; yea, made myself drunken with bitterness! for my ever-shaping & distrustful mind still mingled gall-drops, till out of the cup of Hope *I almost poisoned* myself with Despair![51]

Anxiety, dejection, illness and opium formed a sequence of ruling importance in S.T.C.'s history; each factor interacting upon the other in an endless series of fugal developments.

Upon this occasion the doctor prescribed blisters, and twenty-five drops of laudanum every four hours (it should be borne in mind that we do not know the opium content of the laudanum, so this tells us nothing of the real quantity of opium prescribed). S.T.C., in his excruciating pain, ran about the house naked, "endeavouring by every means to excite sensations in different parts of my body, & so to weaken the enemy by creating a diversion."[52] The pain continued from one until five-thirty in the morning, leaving him weak and faint. It returned (but not so violently) the following day and showed signs of growing very bad at evening "but I took between 60 and 70 drops of Laudanum, and *sopped* the Cerberus just as his mouth was beginning to open."[53]

His one preoccupation now was escape to the country. Opium robbed him of inhibition in writing to Poole a letter which S.T.C. subsequently described as "flighty;" it was, he explained, written "under the immediate inspiration of *Laudanum*:"[54]

I am anxious beyond measure to be in the country as soon as possible—I would it were possible to get a temporary residence till Adscombe is ready for us.—I would ... that we could have three Rooms in Bill Poole's large House for the winter—Will you try to look out for a fit servant for us—simple of heart, *physiognomically* handsome, & scientific in vaccimulgence? That last

word is a new one; but soft in sound, and full of expression. Vaccimulgence!
—I am pleased with the word— ...

Tell me whether you think it at all possible to make any terms with
William Poole—you know, I would not wish to touch with the edge of the
Nail of my great toe the line which should be but half a barley corn out of
the circle of the most trembling Delicacy![55]

The quantities of laudanum taken at this time seem to have been large
enough for S.T.C. to have mentioned them in his letters as a dramatic
indication of the extent of his agonising pain. It is therefore equally deduc-
ible that he had, by constant use of ever-increasing amounts of opium over
a considerable period of time, built up a comparatively high degree of tolerance to the drug.

This bout of laudanum was followed by languor and exhaustion. There
was, too, total loss of appetite and "the wind & the hiccups as if the Demon
of Hurricanes were laying waste my trillibub-plantation."[56] These were the
classical symptoms of opium-addiction.

To amuse himself as he convalesced, S.T.C. read *Institutes of Hindu Law:
or the Ordinances of Menu*, translated by Sir William Jones (1794). Further
to occupy and amuse himself he got together a selection, *Sonnets From
Various Authors*, including, among others, four by himself, four by Lamb,
four by Lloyd, four by Southey and three by Bowles. S.T.C. printed two
hundred of these at sixpence each. He prefaced them with an essay of his
own and apparently just succeeded in covering the cost of the printing.

Barely a fortnight after S.T.C.'s illness, Charles Lloyd was seized with
violent epileptic fits and mania. S.T.C., still weak from his own affliction,
found himself having to struggle with Lloyd during his alarming frenzies.
At the same time, the experience held for S.T.C. a certain element of
Romanticism, epilepsy being a favoured theme of the New Sensibility.
Boulay-Paty's *Élie Mariaker*,

> Rose et pale soudain, la jeune fille frêle
> Qui tombe du haut mal, âme forte et corps grêle ...
> Cette beauté souffrante, oh! voila mon envie!

should be compared with S.T.C.'s prose description of Lloyd's attacks:

his distemper (which may ... be named either Somnambulism, or frightful
Reverie, or *Epilepsy from accumulated feelings*) is alarming. He falls all at
once into a kind of Night-mair: and all the Realities round him mingle with,
and form a part of, the strange Dream. All his voluntary powers are suspended; but he perceives everything & hears everything; and whatever he
perceives & hears he perverts into the substance of his delirious Vision.[57]

Epilepsy, in short, was romantically attributed to excess of sensibility; a spirituality too strong for the weak flesh to support. S.T.C., in keeping with this attitude, called in Dr Beddoes to see Lloyd, because Beddoes was a philosopher as well as a physician. Beddoes recommended Sympathy and Calmness and the keeping of the patient "in situations perfectly according with the tenderness of his Disposition."[58]

Lloyd made an apparently fairly good recovery, although S.T.C. found it necessary to write and warn Mr Lloyd senior that his son would never make a physician, nor a banker; both careers had been envisaged for him. S.T.C. advocated that Charles should devote himself to agriculture, marry and settle down. Agriculture at that stage appeared to S.T.C. as a panacea for all troubles.

The scheme of renting a house at Adscombe had now fallen through; the idea of taking temporary lodging at William Poole's was one which could only have occurred to S.T.C. while he was under the influence of either drink or drugs.

A small, dilapidated cottage was discovered in Nether Stowey village; it stood cheek-to-jowl by the wayside, was dark and damp, and had nothing to recommend it, save that it was near Poole. S.T.C. longed to be a close neighbour of Poole and Poole had said that S.T.C.'s residence near him would give him great pleasure; adding that he thought that the Coleridges could live happily in the cottage as a temporary abode until they found something more suitable.

Now Poole changed his mind; or perhaps, he did not so much change his mind, as change his tune, when he realised that he was positively to have as near neighbour a young man who was known by Stowey folk as "a vile jacobin villain."[59] Correctly, Poole foresaw that this might lead to embarrassment. He had had some difficulty in living down his own democratic reputation; to establish S.T.C. in Stowey would incur further odium, not least among Poole's relatives, who saw even old Mrs Poole as a Coleridgean convert to jacobinism. "Aunt Thomas exceedingly violent against the War, Ministers, etc, etc,"[60] complained John Poole after a visit to Stowey.

Finally, Poole had grave private doubts about S.T.C.'s suitability for the rôle of agriculturist.

Rather, however, than confront S.T.C. point-blank with these brutal facts, Poole took refuge behind the argument that it would be next to impossible to find S.T.C. a suitable house in, or near, Stowey; the cottage certainly would not do.

S.T.C., in reply, deluged Poole with a series of cajoling, lamenting, arguing, explaining, persuading letters:

You saw the Cottage . . . and thought we might be *happy* in it—and now you hurry to tell me we shall not even be *comfortable* in it—[61]

As for not being able to survive if he relied upon his own agricultural efforts to make ends meet, S.T.C. repeated that he had determined to adopt "a severe process of simplification."[62]

> I mean to work *very hard*—as Cook, Butler, Scullion, Shoe-Cleaner, occasional Nurse, Gardener, Hind, Pig-protector, Chaplain, Secretary, Poet, Reviewer, and omnium-botherum shilling scavenger—in other words, I shall keep no Servant, and will cultivate my Land-acre, and my wise-acres, as well as I can.[63]

He added that he had thought about all this "much and calmly" and "calculated time & money with unexceptionable accuracy."[64] All he wanted was to cultivate an acre-and-a-half of Land which "divided properly & managed properly would maintain a small family in clothes & rent."[65] Sara was entering enthusiastically into the scheme, added S.T.C. Poole continued to be extremely discouraging. He was accordingly bombarded with every strain of eloquence and heart-rending reproach that S.T.C. could muster, together with a probing for the "true reasons"[66] why he had changed his mind about the desirability of having S.T.C. as a near neighbour.

S.T.C. implored Poole either to declare his attachment to him as unaltered (in which case the Stowey plan would be adhered to) or to describe, without reservation, the circumstances that had lessened his "Love, or Esteem, or Confidence."[67] S.T.C. would await an answer "which I shall expect with a total incapability of doing, or thinking of any thing, till I have received it.—Indeed, indeed, I am very miserable—"[68]

Poole capitulated.

S.T.C. at once became full of plans to make the despised Stowey cottage snug: "If we can but contrive to make two rooms *warm*, & wholesome, we will laugh in the faces of Gloom & Ill-lookingness."[69]

The removal itself required bold Esteesian organisation:

> What with boxes of Books, and Chests of Drawers, & Kitchen-Furniture, & Chairs, and our Bed and Bed-linen, &c, &c, we shall have enough to fill a small Waggon— . . . I shall make enquiry among my trading acquaintance, whether or no it would not be cheaper to hire a Waggon to take them straight down to Stowey.[70]

All this excitement had the usual effect upon S.T.C.; he fell ill, with a sty on the eye, rheumatic pains in the head and shoulders, and a severe sore throat. His apothecary forbade him to walk to Stowey to do preliminary work in the house, as he had planned. He was obliged to take to his bed for a few days. He wrote touchingly to Poole:

> You thoroughly & in every nook & corner of your Heart forgive me for my letters?—Indeed, indeed, Poole! I know no one whom I esteem more, no one friend whom I love so much—but bear with my Infirmities![71]

Poole melted utterly.

1796 ended with a poem, *Ode To The Departing Year*. Early in December Benjamin Flower asked S.T.C. to furnish him with some lines for the last day of that year. S.T.C. agreed, but almost at once succumbed to rheumatic pains in the head, which quite prevented the possibility of poetic composition until December 24, when S.T.C. started to compose; he finished the ode within three days. The Ode was first published in the *Cambridge Intelligencer* on December 31, 1796, entitled *Ode for the last day of the Year 1796;* it was accompanied by a dedicatory letter to Thomas Poole. (S.T.C. was later to observe to Cottle that the ode would have been better had he had the advantage of Lamb's criticism; this arrived on January 2 and January 6 of 1797, too late to be of use.)

Although the poem is excessively discursive and contains many lapses into the "garishness and swell of diction"[72] which S.T.C. had recently deplored as a great fault in his poetry, it also contains several passages of controlled technical mastery and brilliant imagery which indicate how close S.T.C. was, now, to break-through to the stature of major poet; that incredible leap of genius which he was to make in a matter of months.

The ode commenced with an address to Divine Providence; moved, via the Empress of Russia, to a vision of the Image of the Departing Year and concluded with an anguished prophecy of the downfall of Britain. In the final stanza S.T.C. made it clear that he was opting out. Albion would have to collapse without him:

> Away, my soul, away!
> I unpartaking of the evil thing,
> With daily prayer and daily toil
> Soliciting for food my scanty soil,
> Have wailed my country with a loud Lament.
> Now I recentre my immortal mind
> In the deep sabbath of meek self-content;
> Cleansed from the vaporous passions that bedim
> God's Image, sister of the Seraphim.[73]

On the day of the poem's publication, the last day of the year, S.T.C., Sara, Hartley, and their little maid-servant, removed from Bristol to Nether Stowey.

CHAPTER EIGHT

HAPPY YOUNG MAN LEAPS
OVER A GATE

(*January–June 1797*)

Plucking flowers from the Galaxy
On the pinions of Abstraction
I did quite forget to ax'e
Whether you have an objaction
With us to swill 'e and to swell 'e
And make a pig stie of your belly.
A lovely limb most dainty
Of a ci-devant Mud-raker
I make bold to acquaint 'e
We've trusted to the Baker:
And underneath it Satis
Of that subterrene Apple
By the Erudite 'clep'd, *taties*
With which if you'd wish to grapple;
As sure as I am a sloven
The clock will not strike one,
When the said Dish will be out of the Oven,
And the Dinner will be a nice one . . .

> Invitation addressed to T. Poole from
> S.T.C., some time in January 1797 and
> scribbled on the back of a prospectus
> for S.T.C.'s course of six lectures on
> the English Rebellion and the French
> Revolution, to begin on June 23, 1795.

How many tales we told! What jokes we made!
Connundrum, Crambo, Rebus, or Charade;
Ænigmas, that had driven the Theban mad,
And Puns then best when exquisitely bad;
And I, if aught of archer vein I hit,
With my own laughter stifled my own wit.

> S.T.C., *Poems*, ii, 976.

We arrived safe—our house is set to rights—we are
all, Maid, Wife, Bratling, & self, remarkably well—
Mrs Coleridge likes Stowey, & loves Thomas Poole, &
his Mother, who love her—a communication has been
made from our Orchard into T. Poole's Garden, & from
thence to Cruikshank's, a friend of mine & a young
married Man, whose Wife is very amiable; & she &
Sara are already on the most cordial terms—from all
this you will conclude, *that we are happy*—.

> Letter from S.T.C. to Cottle, January 6, 1797.

AT NETHER STOWEY S.T.C. entered upon the happiest, healthiest, most creatively productive period of his life. There may have been several reasons for this, but chief amongst them must have been his comparative freedom from financial pressure, the undoubted success of his marriage, and the near presence of Poole who, combining as he did idealism with strong practical common-sense, sound business acumen with a keen and stimulating intellect, and a robust sense of humour with great delicacy of feeling, provided S.T.C. with a perfect anchor-man.

The Coleridges' new abode was, in actuality, a particularly ugly little cottage crouched hard by the roadside. Sara, in later years, was to recall it as a "miserable" habitation which only Thomas Poole's "many and so friendly exertions" had transformed into a place of passable comfort.[1] S.T.C. himself was in the habit of referring to it, retrospectively, as "the old hovel."[2] It consisted of two small, dark, damp little parlours, one upon either side of a passage which led from the front of the house to a primitive kitchen in the rear and an adjoining outhouse. There were three or four bedrooms upstairs. The cottage boasted a long strip of kitchen garden, with some fruit trees; at the bottom of it ran a narrow lane by which communication was made with Poole's garden.

It was dead of winter when the Coleridges moved to their new home; S.T.C. at once embarked upon a series of enthusiastic letters to his friends, describing his venture into rural life and agriculture. Rapturously he wrote of his "very pretty garden" and "sweet orchard,"[3] of his pigs and poultry. He outlined his daily programme:

> from seven to half-past eight I work in my garden; from breakfast till 12 I read and compose; then work again—feed the pigs, poultry &c, till two o'clock—after dinner work again till Tea—from Tea till supper *review*. So jogs the day.

He was, he claimed, already an expert gardener and could exhibit a callum on each of his hands as testimonials of his industry. "I raise potatoes & all manner of vegetables . . . & shall raise Corn with the spade enough for my family."[4] This was in early February; he had been at Stowey for just over a month. When news of these astounding Esteesian agricultural exploits reached Charles Lamb, he wrote to S.T.C. with lovingly gentle irony: "Is it a farm you have got? And what does your worship know about farming?"[5]

What the poet sees in his mind's eye is often as vivid, if not immeasurably more so, than what he sees with his actual eye. S.T.C. stood on his cottage doorstep and surveyed his wintry garden; in his imagination he saw it fair with flowers and rich with the fruits of husbandry. Through the brumous shadows of the present he glimpsed the apple-blossom and daisies of the future spring.

If S.T.C.'s accounts of his agricultural prowess strike the reader as unconvincing, his descriptions of Stowey social life ring more true:

> I have society—my *friend*, T. Poole and as many acquaintances as I can dispense with—there are a number of very pretty young women in Stowey, all musical—& I am an immense favourite: for I pun, conundrumize, *listen*, & dance. The last is a recent acquirement.[6]

Nonetheless, not all Stowey welcomed the Coleridges. With the exception of Poole's mother, his other relations revealed antipathy and this "in more than one instance led his Brother's Widow into absolute insult to Mrs Coleridge."[7] But the peaceable manners of the Coleridges and S.T.C.'s "known attachment to Christianity"[8] (or so he told Thelwall) gradually wore away most of this ill-feeling.

However unfriendly the outside world, within the cottage there was much love and joy:

> We are *very* happy—& my little David Hartley grows a sweet boy—& has high health—he laughs at us till he makes us weep for very fondness.—You would smile to see my eye rolling up to the ceiling in a Lyric fury, and on my knee a Diaper pinned, to warm.—[9]

This to Thelwall. To Wade, S.T.C. adoringly described Hartley as "a very Seraph in clouts."[10]

It is worth noting that, after the initial outburst of January and February, when not enough could be said in praise of smallholding, Esteesian references to agriculture became few and far between. For him the pen was mightier than the spade.

Over the past six to eight months S.T.C. had engaged in what seems to have been mainly speculative writing of reviews of popular novels of the day. (There can be little doubt that one of the temptations of poverty was, for him, not unnaturally, the idea of turning out fashionably romantic fiction and narrative verse, which, in his innocence, he supposed that he should find easy to write, not appreciating that his literary gift was of too valuable a currency to be debased into easy cheap money. He could no more write like Ann Radcliffe than Ann Radcliffe could write like him.) He told Bowles that he had reviewed M. G. Lewis's *The Monk*, Ann Radcliffe's *The Italian*, Mary Robinson's *Hubert de Sevrac* and

> &c & &c—in all of which dungeons, and old castles, & solitary Houses by the Sea Side, & Caverns, and Woods, & extraordinary characters, & all the tribe of Horror & Mystery, have crowded on me—even to surfeiting.—[11]

(These reviews, at the time, he felt to be "clever & epigrammatic & devilishly severe,"[12] but when he subsequently read one of them to Dorothy

Wordsworth she commented so rudely upon it that he committed the entire batch to the fire.) Only one of them seems to have been published, despite S.T.C.'s assurances to Bowles that all had been; the review of *The Monk* appeared in the February issue of the *Critical Review* for 1797.

Some time in that same February (perhaps as a result of this review) S.T.C. received from the musician William Linley, a friend of Bowles and brother-in-law of Richard Brinsley Sheridan (the dramatist and parliamentary orator), a request, originating from Sheridan, that S.T.C. should write a tragedy upon some popular subject for Drury Lane. As a result, S.T.C. abandoned digging in his garden and commenced work on a drama entitled *Osorio*, which, he informed Bowles, was "romantic & wild & somewhat terrible!"[13] The over-optimistic author confessed that he had Siddons and Kemble in mind as the leading players.

In addition to writing *Osorio* S.T.C. was also busy completing the second (1797) edition of his poems for Cottle; the first poem in this new edition was to be *The Progress of Liberty, or, the Vision of the Maid of Orleans* (later published as *The Destiny of Nations*). In this poem S.T.C. incorporated some 255 lines which he had composed the previous summer as his contribution to Southey's revised *Joan of Arc*, S.T.C. assisting him with the second part of that work. In November, 1796, S.T.C. had told Poole: "I shall alter the lines of the Joan of Arc & make a *one* poem entitled the progress of European Liberty, a vision—."[14]

Early in February, 1797, S.T.C. was writing to Cottle: "I give every moment I can spare from my garden and . . . my potatoes and meat, to the poem, but I go on slowly, for I torture the poem, and myself, with corrections; and what I write in an hour, I sometimes take two or three days correcting."[15] In a previous letter S.T.C. had already told Cottle that he was sending the poem to Wordsworth and Lamb for criticism.

S.T.C. and Wordsworth had, for some months now, been in intermittent correspondence, their subject of epistolary discourse being, presumably, poetry. It is noteworthy that this period of commencing poetic discussion with Wordsworth marked the beginning of S.T.C.'s incredible leap into full and magnificent maturity as a poet. As a poet he virtually grew, in one spectacular movement, from adolescence to manhood. There is no doubt that Wordsworth had a marked influence on S.T.C.'s style, which he now drastically simplified, compressed and disciplined, thereby strengthening and greatly expanding the development of his unrivalled technical gifts. "Study compression!"[16] he was to advise Thelwall.

Strong indications of this wonderful poetic development are to be discovered in *The Destiny of Nations*. Aware of this advancement in his art, S.T.C. was all the more depressed when he received Lamb's criticism of the poem. On February 10, S.T.C. wrote despairingly to Cottle: "The lines which I added to my lines in the 'Joan of Arc' have been so little approved by Charles Lamb . . . that . . . I have no heart to finish the poem."[17]

Although, on February 13, Lamb followed up this criticism with a letter urging S.T.C. to go on with the poem, S.T.C. did not resume it until February of the following year. He had by that time finished, or was on the point of finishing, his first version of *The Rime of the Ancyent Marinere.*

The Destiny of Nations (of which Wordsworth apparently thought even less than did Lamb) shares many important images with the *Mariner. The Destiny of Nations* reveals, fascinatingly, how a poet may use the same imagery and much of the same material, certainly the identical sources, for two different, yet almost simultaneous works, and have comparative failure with one, while with the other he achieves a masterpiece.

S.T.C., since adolescence, had been deeply engrossed in books of travel and voyaging; vivid fragments of mariners' tales were flashing before his mind's eye as he brooded over the vision of the Maid of Orleans. As a lighthouse flashes both to the ship approaching near at hand and, at the same instant and with the same beam, to the ship still far on the distant horizon, so did images of ancient circumnavigation flash inspiration to S.T.C. both for the poem that he was currently working on and the great masterpiece the tip of whose topsail was as yet barely breaking the skyline.

> "Maid beloved of Heaven! . . .
> Of Chaos the adventurous progeny
> Thou seest; foul missionaries of foul sire,
> Fierce to regain the losses of that hour
> When Love rose glittering, and his gorgeous wings
> Over the abyss fluttered with such glad noise,
> As what time after long and pestful calms,
> With slimy shapes and miscreated life
> Poisoning the vast Pacific, the fresh breeze
> Wakens the merchant-sail uprising. Night
> A heavy unimaginable moan
> Sent forth, when she the Protoplast beheld
> Stand beauteous on confusion's charmed wave.[18]

This passage had its immediate origin in James Cook's *Voyage to the Pacific Ocean,* which had appeared in 1784; these slimy shapes of the vast Pacific, emerging after "long and pestful calms" were the same "God's creatures of the great calms" that the Ancient Mariner beheld; the million million slimy things which, in an inspired flash, he was to recognise as beautiful and happy watersnakes,

> Blue, glossy green, and velvet black
> They coiled and swam . . .

In the Maid's vision the albatross hovered in the guise of:

> . . . that giant bird
> Vuokho, of whose rushing wings the noise
> Is tempest. . .[19]

Present too were the blessed troop of angelic spirits (who returned to work the Ancient Mariner's ship). In *The Destiny of Nations* these were introduced in embryonic form as

> . . . those happy spirits . . .
> Who . . . in floating robes of rosy light
> Dance sportively . . .[20]

among the "streamy banners of the North."[21]

For much of this material S.T.C. was indebted to his reading of *Leemius de Lapponibus*, in the seminal pages of which he had made acquaintance with

> . . . those legends terrible, with which
> The polar ancient thrills his uncouth throng.[22]

His other major source was Crantz's *History of Greenland*; from here derived Torngarsuck, the Good Spirit (who was male in gender) and the malignant spirit (nameless and female) who dwelt under the sea in a great house, where she had the power to detain in captivity all the creatures of the ocean by her magic. In *The Destiny of Nations* Torngarsuck armed the Greenland Wizard (or Angekok)

> . . . to unchain the foodful progeny
> Of the Ocean stream;—thence thro' the realm of Souls,
> Where live the Innocent, as far from cares
> As from the storms and overwhelming waves
> That tumble on the surface of the Deep . . .[23]

In *The Ancient Mariner* Torngarsuck becomes "the lonesome spirit from the south-pole" who "carries the ship as far as the Line," the Polar spirit who

> . . . loved the bird that loved the man
> Who shot him with his bow.[24]

The reader may well suspect that *The Destiny of Nations* was overloaded with images which could not be fitted into the magnificently compressed and disciplined *Mariner*, but which were too satisfying for S.T.C. to sacrifice entirely. Thus, the wonderful glimpse of Leviathan, who, if

> . . . weary of ease,
> In sports unwieldy toss his island-bulk,
> Ocean behind him billows, and before
> A storm of waves breaks foamy on the strand.[25]

And the unforgettable polar vignette with which *The Destiny of Nations* stops, rather than ends; a glimpse, as it were, between curtains of flying snow, of

> ... a landscape ...
> More wild and waste and desolate than where
> The white bear, drifting on a field of ice,
> Howls to her sundered cubs with piteous rage
> And savage agony.[26]

The Destiny of Nations (referred to by S.T.C. as his "Epic Slice")[27] did not appear in its entirety until *Sibylline Leaves* in 1817. Cottle, receiving the 1797 draft, commented, perhaps understandably, that "it was all very fine, but what it was all about, I could not tell."[28] The work was dropped from the projected second edition of collected poems.

S.T.C. could expend his time on poetry because his financial situation during this period was not desperate. Charles Lloyd, who had been on a visit to his home in Birmingham and from thence to London to stay with the Lambs, had arrived in Stowey early in February and had moved into the cottage with the Coleridges on the twenty-second day of that month. However, having him as a lodger was no sinecure; early in March he had another violent bout of fits and delirium. S.T.C. sat up all hours with him, wearing himself out with holding Lloyd down during his frantic seizures. By the end of March, Lloyd had made some kind of recovery and had left Stowey; soon afterwards he entered a sanatorium in Lichfield, under the care of Dr Erasmus Darwin. Mr Lloyd Senior sent S.T.C. ten pounds to cover the expenses involved during the month that Charles had lodged at Stowey with the Coleridges, who were now left with a spare room, but no immediate financial pressure.

The spare room made it possible to put friends up for the night. Some time in late March Wordsworth and his friend Basil Montagu, on their way to Bristol from Racedown (near Lyme Regis) where the Wordsworths were then in residence, visited S.T.C. at Stowey. S.T.C. also probably met Wordsworth later that month in Bristol (where S.T.C. stayed from March 23 until April 6) and it is almost certain that Wordsworth stayed briefly at Stowey with the Coleridges on his way back to Racedown during the first half of April.

William Wordsworth of that period has been best preserved for us by Hazlitt's famous pen-portrait. In this Wordsworth is seen as

> gaunt and Don-Quixote-like ... a severe, worn pressure of thought about the temples, a fire in his eye (as if he saw something in objects more than the outward appearance), an intense, high, narrow forehead, a Roman nose, cheeks furrowed by strong purpose and feeling, and a convulsive inclination to laughter about the mouth, a good deal at variance with the solemn, stately expression of the rest of his face ... He talked very naturally and freely, with a mixture of clear, gushing accents in his voice, a deep gutteral intonation, and a strong tincture of the northern *burr*, like the crust on wine.[29]

(Crabb Robinson, commenting upon Wordsworth less romantically and with the objective perception of a trained legal eye, noted that he was a sloven and that his manners were not prepossessing. His features were large and coarse and his voice unattractive. Though not arrogant, Wordsworth's mien nonetheless indicated a sense of his own worth.)

This then was the decidedly extraordinary person who made his first appearance at Stowey in the spring of 1797. Even at this very early stage in their friendship criticism of Wordsworth would have seemed a sacrilege to S.T.C. From the first he was predisposed to idolatry of William. "The Giant Wordsworth—God love him!"[30]

It is highly probable that Poole was introduced to Wordsworth during this visit. Carried away by S.T.C.'s enthusiastic conviction that Wordsworth was the greatest man whom he had ever met, Poole, too, formed a glowing first impression of the poet; an impression which he was presently to exchange for one that was rather different.

That Wordsworth's friend, Basil Montagu, should have been present on the occasion of the March visit to Stowey must be seen as singularly appropriate. He, who was to play a leading rôle in the final episode of rupture between the two poets, had a rightful place at the opening of the great and celebrated friendship.

Basil Montagu in 1797 was twenty-seven years of age and reading for the Bar, to which he was called in May of the following year. His personal background was a disturbed one. He was the natural son of John Montagu, fourth Earl of Sandwich, by Martha Ray, a well-known singer of the day, who was shot dead in 1779 by a disappointed suitor. In 1791 Basil Montagu had made an early marriage; two years later his wife died in giving birth to a son. Montagu had made an attempt to rear the child (also named Basil) with him in his chambers at Lincoln's Inn, but the task had proved too much for him and when the Wordsworths took up residence at Racedown in 1795 and offered to have little Basil with them, Montagu agreed readily to their plan.

Despite the superficial veneer of affability which S.T.C. and Montagu displayed towards one another, privately each distrusted the other.[31]

Some time during Wordsworth's Stowey visit that spring it was arranged that S.T.C. should, in due course, pay a return visit to Racedown. This he at last did in early June, travelling on foot. He had arrived at Racedown by June 8. The meeting between himself and William and Dorothy Wordsworth, so immensely looked forward to by all three, took place beneath propitiously blue skies, among the sweetly-scented long grasses and flowers of hay-time meadows. More than forty years later the Wordsworths could still remember that meeting; brother and sister walked out to greet their visitor, who, loping along the dusty lanes, spied his host and hostess in the distance, whereat, with typical Esteesian fervour, "He did not keep to the highroad, but leaped over a gate and bounded down a pathless field by which he cut off an angle."[32]

Thus, in old age, at Rydal Mount, the Wordsworths recalled that glittering morning when Coleridge, avid for friendship, sprang to clasp hands with

> William, my head and my heart!
> Dorothy, eager of soul.[33]

INTERLUDE:

THE NEW SENSIBILITY I

"I have no notion of loving people by halves; it is not my nature. My attachments are always excessively strong."

> Catherine Morland conversing with her friend, Isabella Thorpe, in the Pump Room, Bath, *circa* 1798.
> Jane Austen, *Northanger Abbey*.

"What delight! What felicity! . . . What are men to rocks and mountains! Oh, what hours of transport we shall spend!"

> Elizabeth Bennet envisaging a picturesque tour of the Lake Country, *circa* 1796.
> Jane Austen, *Pride and Prejudice*.

"My dearest Catherine, what have you been doing with yourself all this morning? Have you gone on with *Udolpho*?"

"Yes; I have been reading it ever since I woke; and I am got to the black veil."

"Are you indeed? How delightful! Oh! I would not tell you what is behind the black veil for the world! Are you not wild to know?"

"Oh! yes, quite; what can it be? But do not tell me . . . I know it must be a skeleton; I am sure it is Laurentina's skeleton. Oh! I am delighted with the book! I should like to spend my whole life in reading it, I assure you; if it had not been to meet you, I would not have come away from it for all the world."

"Dear creature, how much I am obliged to you; and when you have finished *Udolpho*, we will read *The Italian* together; and I have made out a list of ten or twelve more of the same kind for you."

"Have you indeed? How glad I am! What are they all?"

"I will read you their names directly; here they are in my pocket book. *Castle of Wolfenbach, Clermont, Mysterious Warnings, Necromancer of the Black Forest, Midnight Bell, Orphan of the Rhine*, and *Horrid Mysteries*. Those will last us some time."

"Yes, pretty well; but are they all horrid? Are you sure they are all horrid?"

"Yes, quite sure; for a particular friend of mine, a Miss Andrews, a sweet girl, one of the sweetest creatures in the world, has read every one of them."

> Catherine Morland and Isabella Thorpe, in the Pump Room, as before.

Pride and Prejudice, Jane Austen's first novel, was written between October 1796 and August 1797. *Northanger Abbey* and *Sense and Sensibility* followed in rapid succession.* In these three early books, Miss Austen

*Owing to the reluctance of publishers, *Sense and Sensibility* did not appear in print until 1811; *Pride and Prejudice*, 1813; *Northanger Abbey* posthumously in 1818.

particularly directed her subtle, yet merciless, ironies against the refined sensibilities of voguishly Romantic people of her class and day.

By 1797 William and Dorothy Wordsworth had established themselves, in the eyes of a still very small, but highly selective circle, as notable personalities in the vanguard of the fashion of picturesque taste and Romantic sensibility. They not only conformed perfectly to the established dictates of that fashion; they had advanced to a forward position where they were establishing patterns for its further development. They were now people to observe and copy; just as they themselves had observed and copied in order to achieve recognised expertise.

In one salient respect the Wordsworths differed from their modish Romantic peers. Brother and sister each possessed attributes which made them immeasurably more than mere trend setters. Yet, unless we fully understand the close adherence of the Wordsworths to the fashionable cultural ethos of their day, we are liable to misunderstand much of their personal lives.

William, in 1797, was twenty-seven years of age; Dorothy was twenty-one months his junior. Their background was middle-class and provincial (exactly that from which Jane Austen drew so many of the characters and settings of her novels).

On either side the Wordsworths came from North Country stock. Their paternal ancestry was Yorkshire, shrewdly hard-headed, conformist, Tory. Their grandfather had been Receiver-General for Westmorland; their father, an attorney, was agent to Sir James Lowther, first earl of Lonsdale, the predominant Tory power in the region. Their mother, born Anne Cookson, was daughter of William Cookson, a mercer of Penrith, Cumberland, whose wife, Dorothy, had been a Crackanthorp of Newbiggen, Westmorland.

The five Wordsworth children, Richard, William, Dorothy, John and Christopher, passed their happy infancy at Cockermouth, Cumberland, a small market-town situated where the Cumbrian hills relinquish their pastoral strength to the industrial plain. Their home was a large and, for eighteenth-century Cockermouth, somewhat ostentatious house, on what was then the edge of the town.

Following the death of their mother in 1778 Dorothy saw nothing of her brothers for the better part of a decade, an important point to bear in mind. She was sent to live in Halifax with her mother's cousin, 'Aunt' Threlkeld; the boys went away to school.

With the death of their father in 1783 the young Wordsworths were placed under the guardianship of two uncles, Richard Wordsworth and Christopher Crackanthorp. The financial prospects of the children were precarious; their father had left small provision for them, at the time of his death having been owed well over four thousand pounds by the Lowther family (claims to this money on behalf of the Wordsworth children led to years of protracted and fruitless dispute).

Meantime, in 1787, Dorothy, now aged sixteen, was removed from Halifax, where she had been happy, to Penrith, there to reside with her maternal grandparents, the Cooksons, with whom she was frustrated and miserable. Her chief solace lay in the opportunities she now had of seeing something of her brothers. She and the seventeen-year-old William particularly were each enchanted by this rediscovery of the other. Their remarkable natural sympathy was made even more exciting by the fact that an interval of nine years had elapsed since their last meeting. The encounter was therefore, to all intents and purposes, an encounter between two adolescent strangers. Whether they recognised it or not at that stage, their mutual attraction was a species of falling in love.

Dorothy sent accounts of her wonderful brothers to her bosom friend, Jane Pollard, whom she had left behind in Halifax. We glimpse Dorothy— small, slightly built, garbed in her bed-gown—scribbling long, animated letters to Jane at night, by candlelight, outpourings about the delight of holiday visits of her brothers marred only by the chagrins of life in the household of the Penrith Cooksons.

Jane received ecstatic details of William's cleverness, tender disposition and handsome looks. (Of Dorothy's adolescent self we are also given a touching glimpse: "I now wear my hair curled about my face in light curls frizzed at the bottom and turned at the ends.")[1]

The unhappy period in Penrith did not last long; a year later, in 1788, Dorothy went to Forncett, in Norfolk, to dwell with her newly-wed and congenial Uncle William Cookson, a clergyman. In this tranquil household Dorothy, for the ensuing five years, lived the life of one of Jane Austen's genteelly impoverished heroines, earning her keep in the home of relatives by assisting with household duties, lighter chores and much needle-work. Dearly fond of babies and little children, Dorothy's special rôle lay in helping to tend the infants with whom the Cooksons were soon blessed.

Her daily routine, like that of all similar young ladies, was carefully regulated into periods of domestic duty, of walking in the garden or country-side, of paying and receiving calls and of cultivating her mind. This, in Dorothy's case, meant fairly voracious reading of a wholly unselective kind, together with a mainly untutored study of French.

Dorothy Wordsworth was not, in the true sense of the word, an educated woman, judged even by the standards of her day. This was what S.T.C. was indicating, tactfully, when he remarked to Cottle that her "informa-tion" was "various."[2] De Quincey was to put it more bluntly. Her know-ledge of literature, he said, was irregular and thoroughly unsystematic; the predominant impression that she gave was not one of intellect, but of exceeding sympathy (he was here employing 'sympathy' in accordance with the usage of the time, which invested the word with the meaning of the French *sympathique*, rather than that which we give it today).

This impression of exceeding sympathy was one which all modish young women of the period were anxious to create. They also cultivated 'wildness', meaning an unspoilt and spontaneous 'child of nature' quality. Again, to quote De Quincey, Dorothy was the "very wildest [in the sense of the most natural] person"[3] he had ever known.

Like Dorothy, William never got to grips with real intellectual discipline, although, unlike her, he had plenty of opportunity to do so. He should have had a solid early grounding in classical scholarship at Hawkshead school (an ancient foundation with an excellent reputation) but he was, self-confessedly, indolent:

> On his own time . . . would he float away,
> As doth a fly upon a summer brook.[4]

He went up to St John's, Cambridge, in 1787, coming down in 1790, without sitting for his degree. It was recognised that by predisposition he was literary, but he was quite without real ambition or goal. As he confided in his friend, William Mathews, in November 1791:

> I am doomed to be an idler throughout my whole life. I have read nothing this age, nor indeed did I ever . . . My Uncle the clergyman proposed to me a short time ago to begin a course of oriental Literature, thinking that that was the best field for a person to distinguish himself in as a man of letters . . . But what must I do amongst that immense wilderness, who have no resolution, and who have not prepared myself for the enterprise by any sort of discipline amongst the Western languages? who know little of Latin, and scarce anything of Greek. A pretty confession for a young gentleman whose whole life ought to have been devoted to study. And thus the world wags.[5]

As an undergraduate Wordsworth's pose was that of the dandy, perilously close to that of the fop. He loved parties and crowded gatherings:

> . . . if a throng was near
> That way I leaned by nature; for my heart
> Was social, and loved idleness and joy.[6]

This was an ingrained inclination which remained with him throughout his life (witness the crowded summers of entertaining at Rydal Mount).

Like S.T.C. the undergraduate William ran up bills, including debts to his tutor, but without, it seems, experiencing S.T.C.'s racking qualms of conscience. Like S.T.C., also, William made acquaintance with the contemporary unorthodoxies—the philosophy of Hartley, the polemics of Godwin and Frend, republicanism, all the current intellectual and political movements agitating the universities. Wordsworth's stance was soon Spinozistic, Necessitarian, republican. But whereas S.T.C., encountering these influences, grappled in struggle with them, weighing new ideas against the old and reasoning his way through the problems with which these new ideas confronted him, revelling in the resultant intellectual tussling (having fun with his mind, he called it), Wordsworth adopted radical intellectual and political stances with the unhesitating enthusiasm of callow provincialism in combination with a lazy mind. Coleridge, the youthful polymath, greeted new ideas as a dolphin greets new waters; plunging, leaping, sparring, drenching himself and then flinging off the glittering drops, then diving again to contend joyously with more and more strenuous depths. Wordsworth, in complete contrast, basked on the surface of ideas which he found already thrown up for him.

Both he and Dorothy possessed an extraordinary gift for being able to adapt themselves wholly to the mood and modes of the day. So perfectly were they each able to assimilate Romantic taste and feeling that they came, themselves, to personify the Romantic spirit. Each guided, emulated and encouraged the other. Idle they may have been among books,* but in pursuit of the acquirement of perfect picturesque taste and Romantic sensibility brother and sister were indefatigable.

They immersed themselves in what William was subsequently to call "the strong infection of the age," assiduously studying "the rules of mimic art transferred to things above all art,"[7] shaping their imagination and taste in accordance with the dictates of the *avant garde*.

William must have passed on many of his Cambridge impressions and attitudes to Dorothy. She, for her part, also had an opportunity to make first-hand acquaintance with the world beyond Forncett, Halifax and Penrith. In the company of her relatives she was able to go to Windsor, where she saw something of the Court. She learned not only to converse easily and naturally with persons of rank; she was also able to study at first hand the cultural affectations of the rich and socially acceptable who possessed, or believed that they possessed, taste and sensibility. By combining what William was able to teach her with what she learned in drawing-rooms of social distinction Dorothy became excellently equipped to strike a highly successful note as an arbiter of picturesque taste and an example of exquisite sensibility.

---

*There are indications that they nursed an almost neurotic contempt for books. See Sara Coleridge, in a letter to Matilda Betham in 1810: "Coleridge sends you his best thanks for the elegant little book; I shall not, however, let it be carried over to Grasmere, *for there* it would soon be *soiled*, for the Wordsworths are woeful destroyers of good books, as our poor library will witness." There is also De Quincey's vignette of Wordsworth cutting the pages of a new book with a buttery knife.

The underlying philosophy of the Romantic school was that of Rousseau. Romantic sensibility (by which the taste was prompted and guided so closely that taste and sensibility were inextricably wedded) owed to him its paramount insistence upon the natural, the wild, the primitive, the instinctive. Within every person of taste and refinement there lurked a noble and innocent savage; or such, at any rate, was the impression which all persons of taste and refinement hoped to give.

The wild, the primitive, the sublime, were essential ingredients for the kind of beauty, termed picturesque, which the period so much admired. Romantic obsession with the picturesque saturated all forms of art. Its paramount popular manifestation, however, was in the fashionable rage for picturesque scenery.

There were certain recognised experts who established rules with which natural scenery had to conform in order to rank as picturesque. Scenery was subjected to rigorous criticism, together with suggestions (perhaps, fortunately, usually unrealisable) for its improvement. (Thus we find Mrs Radcliffe, author of the purple passages in Ackermann's famous guide to the English Lake Country,* commenting therein, with perfect seriousness, upon the Vale of Eden that it wanted "only a river like the Rhine or the Thames to make it the very finest in England for union of grandeur, beauty and extent.")

The cult of admiring scenery enjoyed a well-defined etiquette. Celebrated scenic views were not gazed at impulsively from any convenient spot; there were special vantage points, or stations, as they were called, which the picturesque tourist visited in strict order, obtaining from each station a different view. Camp-stools were carried so that the disciple of the wildly sublime might sit in damp-proof comfort while surveying and analysing the scene before him. Persons of particularly refined sensibility (the Wordsworths and S.T.C. among them) lay down on the ground, upon their side, and surveyed the view from this *recherché* position. Dorothy, in her Alfoxden Journal, describes how, for instance, on February 26, 1798, she, William and S.T.C. "lay sidelong on the turf, and gazed on the landscape until it melted into more than natural loveliness."

Another favoured stance of appreciation was to stand with one's back to the view, seeing it in a Claude-glass,† the object of this exercise being to isolate, or frame, some particular feature which would best epitomize the picturesque quality of the whole.

In addition to a camp-stool and a glass the picturesque tourist was equipped with a notebook in which to write criticism of the scenery. A specialist jargon was developed:

A Picturesque Tour of the English Lakes (London, 1821).
†A plano-convex mirror about four inches in diameter, on black, silver or tinted foil, selected according to light conditions.

Sublimity can scarcely exist without simplicity; and even grandeur loses much of its elevating effect, when united with a considerable portion of beauty; then descending to become magnificence. The effect of simplicity, in assisting that high tone of mind produced by the sublime, is demonstrated by the scenery of Ullswater, where very seldom a discordant object obtrudes over the course of thought, and jars upon the feelings.[8]

Wordsworth, in *The Prelude*, was to describe himself retrospectively (and with disparagement) as a disciple of this cult:

> . . . disliking here, and there
> Liking; by rules of mimic art transferred
> To things above all art; . . .
> . . . giving way
> To a comparison of scene with scene,
> Bent overmuch on superficial things,
> Pampering myself with meagre novelties
> Of colour and proportion . . .

It was, he said, a pursuit stimulated by a love of "sitting in judgment." The "bodily eye",

> The most despotic of our senses, gained
> Such strength in *me* as often held my mind
> In absolute dominion . . .
> . . . my delights
> (Such as they were) were sought insatiably . . .
>
> I roamed from hill to hill, from rock to rock,
> Still craving combinations of new forms,
> New pleasure, wider empire for the sight . . .[9]

Both William and Dorothy became acknowledged experts themselves in the field of picturesque taste in scenery. Neither hesitated to admonish firm rebukes to those who, they felt, made errors of judgement. For instance, when Dorothy's friend, Jane, was rash enough to write to Dorothy in praise of a view of Bassenthwaite Lake (seen during a honeymoon tour of the Lake Country), she received this reply:

Do not flatter yourself . . . that you have any good idea of Bassenthwaite Lake from having seen it from the top of the hill. For the credit of my own taste I am interested in undeceiving you if you suppose so, as there is nothing uncommonly beautiful in the view from that point.[10]

Romantic sensibility demanded a primitive simplicity of manner, together with an enormously exaggerated capacity for emotional response.

Persons of sensibility regarded qualities of reticence and discretion as contrived and unnatural and therefore as a form of social dishonesty. The aim of persons of sensibility was to behave always with complete spontaneity and to speak with total frankness. Discipline of the emotions was highly suspect, since it implied calculated responses which, in turn, meant that sincerity was impaired, if not destroyed (the falsity of the entire position is apparent when one compares the approved simplicity and uncontrived ardency of manners with the, equally approved, rigid rules of taste).

So extreme was the importance which the school of sensibility attached to natural simplicity and spontaneity, so great its impatience with conventional disciplines that it is highly unlikely that Dorothy Wordsworth would have applied herself to tutored study had she had any real opportunity to do so; we should remind ourselves here of her scornful comment that Mrs Coleridge was an excellent teacher by books.

In the context of personal relationships Romantic sensibility implied a special kind of sympathy: a warmth of tenderest understanding, a reciprocal feeling with, as well as for, a person, a loving more profound, more delicate, more sensitive, more innocent, more true than the love which the vulgar, lacking sensibility, were capable of experiencing.

The love relationship which the Romantics idealised above all else, however, was fraternal love. As a *cliché* term "Fraternal love" could, most conveniently, be applied descriptively to mean all things for all men. It had its roots in the all-pervading philosophy of Rousseau; from his insistence upon the Brotherhood of Man had sprung the potent cry of "Fraternity!" Fraternal love stood for democratic comradeship, international socialism, abolition of slavery, sexual equality, pure, disinterested love of one human being for another ("Love Thy Neighbour"). More subjectively, it introduced a vogue for tender, yet platonic friendship between men and women, who loved as brothers and sisters. Especially of course, fraternal love, in this subjective sense, stood for the innocent, yet blood-close love relationship between a true brother and sister.

It was a common occurrence in those days for an unmarried woman to domicile with her brother, both during his bachelorhood and, if he married, with him and his wife and children. Women who remained spinsters naturally turned to their brothers (when they had them) for social protection and financial support. It is an interesting reflection that, while maiden aunts living with a married brother or sister (and the resultant nephews and nieces) were almost universally regarded as laughable (the spinster aunt in *Pickwick Papers* is a perfect example), maiden ladies who were life-partners of bachelor brothers found themselves regarded in a different light. Such fraternal couples were sentimentalised over; the Romantics saw special virtues of devotion and purity in what were fundamentally relationships of convenience.

Thus we find S.T.C. eulogising the relationship of Charles and Mary Lamb: "She is all his Comfort—he hers. They dote on each other."[11]

Charles Lamb did indeed dedicate his life to his sister and she, in her turn, was understandably devoted to him; but their lifelong partnership was dictated by the harsh circumstances of insanity and his pledges of guardianship.

The essence of the Romantics was that they, literally, romanticised. An attempt was made to view everything in terms of the heightened chiaroscuro of the picturesque. Their sensibility itself revealed special picturesque characteristics. Because of this the Romantics claimed that it was "a new sensibility."

This New Sensibility embodied not only the sunlit principles of natural simplicity, total integrity and perfectly innocent fraternal love; it embraced too, the dark side of the moon.

An aesthetic theory of the Horrid and the Terrible had gradually evolved during the course of the eighteenth century, assuming identifiable features in compositions such as Walpole's *Castle of Otranto* (1764), and paintings such as Stubbs's *White Horse Frightened By a Lion* (a work of 1770, bearing every stamp of the febrile disquiet characteristic of the Romantic movement as a whole) and finding attempted definition in, for instance, J. and A. L. Aiken's *On the Pleasure derived from Objects of Terror* and the *Enquiry into those kinds of Distress which Excite agreeable Sensations.**

The French writer and novelist, Chateaubriand, advised artists to steep themselves in concepts of sublimity explored to their utmost limits. Acting on this and similar advice, the Romantics delved into the gloomiest profundities and most inhibited areas of the human spirit. Nothing was too painful, or too private, for recovery and exposure. The Romantic conception of sublimity and beauty was enhanced, not marred, by associations of horror. Aesthetic gratification was increased, not destroyed, by objects and subjects which, for other schools of taste, would produce sensations of revulsion, even taboo. The more distressing or disturbing a subject, the greater it was relished. The more terrifying an object, the more it was admired. In short, the New Sensibility was essentially a morbid sensibility.

In writing and painting, where no content of horror or terror excited naturally, the Romantic would forcibly introduce such a content. When S.T.C., for example, on his 1799 tour of the Lake Country with Wordsworth, first saw the district's most dramatic waterfall, Scale Force, he wrote in his inevitable pocket-book:

> The first fall a thin broad white ribbon, from a stupendous Height, un-interrupted tho' not unimpinged by, the perpendicular Rock down which it falls ... the chasm thro' which it flows, is stupendous—so wildly wooded that the mosses & wet weeds & perilous Tree increase the Horror of the rocks which *ledge* only enough to interrupt not stop your fall—& the Tree—O God! to think of a poor Wretch hanging with one arm from it.[12]

**Miscellaneous Pieces in Prose* (London, 1773).

This passage demonstrates perfectly the New Sensibility at work; an intellectual predilection for certain subjects is superimposed upon visual experience. Actuality is heightened and thereby distorted by imaginings of horror.

The popular taste of the period tended increasingly towards the uncontrolled, the macabre, the strange. Hence the flood of novels spinning tales of terror against Gothicised backgrounds. Hence the success of an artist like Henry Fuseli (a Zurich painter who spent most of his life in England) whose fantastic pictures of nightmare fiends, demons, erotic lovers jumping to their deaths clasped in one another's embrace, and so on, became all the rage: "a Brusher up of Convulsia & Tetanus upon innocent Canvas,"[13] S.T.C. aptly called him. In 1794 we find S.T.C. telling Southey that he had an idea for a wild ode which he would write when "I am in a Humour to *abandon* myself to all the Diableries, that ever met the Eye of a Fuseli!"[14]

The themes of painters and poets alike ventured increasingly into the domain of the taboo. This movement did not reach its height until the early decades of the nineteenth century, when the uninhibited visual statements of Goya, Turner, Géricault and Delacroix appeared, to rivet the attention of discomfited beholders. In literature, De Quincey felt free to confess to opium-eating and to discuss murder as one of the fine arts, while Coleridge released at last his *Kubla Khan, The Pains of Sleep* and *Christabel* to an entranced, if mystified public. Of *Christabel*, on the poem's appearance in 1816, Hazlitt, in an article in *The Examiner* of June 2, 1816, commented: "There is something disgusting at the bottom of his subject which is but ill glossed over by a veil of Della Cruscan sentiment and fine writing, like moonbeams playing on a charnel-house, or flowers strewed on a dead body." The lady Geraldine was abandoned by S.T.C. before he had forced her to an ultimate conclusion; his inability to finish the poem seems to have been due to reasons more fundamental even than discouragement, ill-health and morphine. It was all very well to propose to abandon himself to Diableries; but S.T.C. was strongly restrained by Christian inhibition. His confrontation in *Christabel* with lamianism and lesbianism proved too much for him. His nerve failed him:

> "By my mother's soul I do entreat
> That thou this woman send away!"
> She said; and more she could not say:
> For what she knew she could not tell . . .[15]
> *Christabel* II 616-619

The morbidity of the New Sensibility and its cherished conviction of "the divine Right of Passion," together with the fashionable popularity of fraternal love in the guise of the brother-sister relationship, virtually guaranteed that incest must become a topic dear to the Romantics.

Prévost used it as one of the key-themes for his celebrated eight-volume romance, *Cleveland,** most of the material for which he claimed to have collected in London. (The English, then as now, were renowned on the Continent, rightly or wrongly, for their addiction to sadism, flagellation and sexual deviation of all kinds.)

In 1786 there appeared John Moore's *Zeluco,* a notorious book in its day. Its theme of incestuous love set respectable persons everywhere turning its pages with breathless interest. (Byron, typically, was to declare that it had been one of his favourite books as a child.)

Zeluco was followed in 1801 by Chateaubriand's rather different, but equally celebrated *Atala, ou les amours de deux sauvages dans le désert,* which, written during his exile in England, invested incestuous love between brother and sister with poetic charm and a certain, albeit sentimental, dignity, as did also his almost equally famous *René.* It was left for Byron himself, in his rôle as leader of the so-called Satanic School of poets, to imbue the subject of incest with its fullest fascination of forbidden fruit and its most tragic undertones ("great is their love who love in sin and fear"),[16] both in his writing and in the scandal which attached itself to his relationship with his half-sister, Augusta Leigh.

A notebook entry for early November 1803 gives us S.T.C.'s ruminations following a discussion which he and Southey had recently had upon the subject of incest and why great religious horror should attach to it. S.T.C. quoted Paley† at length on the orthodox Christian attitude both to fraternal love (of which Paley approved) and incest and then went on to consider secular (as opposed to religious) horror of incest, a horror greater, thought S.T.C., than that felt for

> Theft, Robbery, Rape, &c—nay, I am not sure whether it does not in common minds excite a degree of Horror ... greater & higher than the Crime against Nature [sodomy]. In many Countries this latter has been, & still is, a bagatelle, a fashionable Levity!—but in no age or country among civilized Nations has Incest‡ been regarded without Horror, or attributed to a man but under the certainty of *blackening* him.[17]

*Antoine François Prévost (1697–1763), *Le Philosophe anglais, ou Histoire de Monsieur Cleveland, fils naturel de Cromwell, écrite lui-mesme et traduite de l'anglais* (Paris, 1731–39).

†William Paley (1743–1805), the well-known archdeacon of Carlisle and a canon of St Paul's; author of several widely read moral, philosophical and theological works; notably, *The Principles of Moral and Political Philosophy* (1785), a collection of his lectures delivered when he was a tutor at Christ's College, Cambridge. Wordsworth particularly disliked Paley, accusing him of excessive pedantry.

‡In England incest was not ranked as a criminal offence, although in 1650 it was made punishable by death as an offence against morals. After the Restoration it was referred to the spiritual courts; bills to make it a criminal offence were several times introduced in Parliament but none was accepted until 1908, when an Act was finally passed making incest punishable with penal servitude.

Romantic insistence, upon the one hand, that brotherly and sisterly love was "tender, graceful, soothing, consolatory, yet . . . perfectly pure"[18] and, on the other hand, the simultaneous obsession of the Romantics with incest as a forbidden territory, may well be seen as symbolic of the dichotomy of the Romantic movement in general. Exquisite refinement, simplicity, innocence and kindred purities of mind and spirit were shadowed at every step by an insatiable inclination towards the morbid and the corrupt.

The New Sensibility inevitably had harmful effects upon its more extreme disciples. As Romantic theory maintained that the best means of expressing passion was to experience passion, Romantic enthusiasts, instead of trying to translate spontaneous acts of life into the realms of art, sought to experience in life the suggestions of imaginations, fed upon obsessively morbid art.

At the same time Romantic insistence was upon purity and innocence, natural simplicity and joyousness. The impossibility of attempting to combine these qualities with raging passions à la Byron, or the indulgences of Chateaubriandesque savages, or the diableries of Fuseli, resulted in personal states of inner conflict which surfaced in manifold nervous symptoms and, not infrequently, complete breakdown.

THE NEW SENSIBILITY II

ALTHOUGH THE WORDSWORTHS were, in so many respects, astonishingly alike (even their handwriting shared characteristics), in one or two important instances brother and sister differed. Dorothy was by nature impulsive. We know that everything about her was quicksilver rapid—her movements, speech, responses. She leaped before she looked.

William, a character of great complexity, combined a deeply passionate nature with an ingrained wariness. (In a moment of unwitting self-revelation he was to write to S.T.C., on December 14, 1799, "Rydale [Water] is covered with ice . . . I have procured a pair of skates and tomorrow mean to give my body to the wind—not however without reasonable caution.")

He was highly sensuous and appreciative of "the pleasures of love," as he expressed it in a letter of June 7, 1802, to John Wilson. Passionate sensuality is revealed in his face and features, in his history, above all in the tone of voice which time and again bursts forth in his poetry. De Quincey described him as a man with "animal appetites organically strong"[19] and S.T.C. (who was jealous of Wordsworth's household of devoted and adoring women) repeatedly referred to him as lustful.

In *The Prelude* Wordsworth touches briefly but firmly on episodes of amorous encounter as a youth in the Lake Country. Out of the mists by a desolate mountain tarn a girl with a pitcher on her head suddenly emerges and a few lines further on the poet is writing of roaming these fells by the tarn in "the blessed hours of early love," the loved one at his side.[20] It is more than probable that William's first love would have been exactly some such young lass, courted during an undergraduate vacation, or during his late school-days. To such a girl, or even to several, we must owe at least part of the inspiration of the mysterious and beautiful Lucy poems.

Again, describing the bucolic social delights of a Long Vacation in the Lake Country, William speaks of a "heartless chase" in a fever of sexual ferment (not in these explicit terms, but with perfect frankness in the context of his poetry and his day):

> It would demand
> Some skill, and longer time than may be spared,
> To paint these vanities, and how they wrought
> In haunts where they, till now, had been unknown.
> It seemed the very garments that I wore

Preyed on my strength, and stopped the quiet
stream
Of self-forgetfulness . . .[21]

He draws a picture of feasts and dances, public revelry, sports and games. We see him participating in the social activities of the rural Lake Country; the feasts and dances were the suppers and revelries of clipping-time (as sheep-shearing is called in those parts) and harvest; the sports and games were the wrestlings and races, cock-fights and fox-hunts that came with the shepherds' meets of early autumn. Wordsworth describes with marvellous accuracy and clarity a dance in some dalehead hamlet, amongst a throng of "maids and youths, old men, and matrons staid, A medley of all tempers":

> . . . gaiety, and mirth, . . .
> Din of instruments and shuffling feet,
> And glancing forms, and tapers glittering,
> And unaimed prattle flying up and down;
> Spirits upon the stretch, and here and there
> Slight shocks of young love-liking interspersed,
> Whose transient pleasure mounted to the head,
> And tingled through the veins.[22]

This is not high society that he is describing, but the world of the statesmen-farmers of the mountain valleys. His participation in it gave to his poetry a lifeblood which he could not have extracted from an exclusively vegetarian diet of daisies, daffodils and celandines. It is splendidly corrective to peer into the past of those Northern summer nights which never quite grow dark and to see William Wordsworth seated at the trestle-table of a clipping-supper, joining in the ancient clipping-time song (during its singing the guests had in turn to obey the commands of the second and third verses. If the glass was not emptied by the end of the refrain the penalty was enforced a second time.)

> Here's a good health to the man o' this house,
> The man o' this house, the man o' this house,
> Here's a good health to the man o' this house,
> For he is a right honest man.
>
> And he that doth this health deny,
> Before his face I justify;
> Right in his face this glass shall fly,
> So let this health go round.
>
> Place the canny cup up to your chin,
> Open your mouth and let the liquor run in;
> The more you drink the fuller your skin,
> So let this health go round.*

*From William Dickinson's *Cumbriana, or, Fragments of Cumbrian Life* (1876).

After which would come the delicious "shock of some young love-liking" with a plump lass in the hay-sweet recesses of a barn, or within the shadows of a hedge.

Neither was life at Cambridge wanting

> ... love that makes
> The day pass lightly on, when foresight sleeps,
> And wisdom and the pledges interchanged
> With our own inner being are forgot.[23]

If this is not a William Wordsworth whom we usually see, it is not because he himself avoided such revelations, but because we have chosen to ignore them.

The Wordsworth who came down from Cambridge in the summer of 1790 without having sat for his degree was a young man with only the vaguest idea of how he might, reluctantly, set about earning a living. Before he turned to making any hard decisions he set off upon a fourteen-week walking tour in France and Switzerland with his friend Robert Jones.

Like all progressive young men at that date William's fervour for France and the Revolution knew no bounds. Fundamentally his knowledge and understanding of radical politics was negligible, his interest in them purely Romantic. France, when he passed through it, was in its initial phase of almost unanimous support for revolutionary movement; the English, whose country was the acclaimed cradle of democracy, were fêted whenever they appeared on French soil. Thus France and the French made an excessively favourable first impression upon William.

Back in England he encountered trouble with his guardians. What did he propose to do with his life, they asked him? He could not remain an idler for ever. There was family discussion: moody on his side, irascible on that of his uncles. Finally it was decided that he should return to France in order to become proficient in the French language, with a hazy view to becoming travelling tutor to some young gentleman.

At that early stage of the Revolution English radicals were crossing the Channel in considerable numbers to see the political situation at first hand. These visitors, especially those who travelled as delegates from the English republican, or patriotic societies, were received tumultuously. Such delegates included enthusiasts like James Losh, a Cumbrian Quaker, who arrived in Paris bearing fraternal messages from the Carlisle Patriotic Club and James Watt (son of the famous engineer) who appeared in Paris in December 1791, as a fraternal delegate from the Constitutional Club of Manchester, to be rapturously applauded by the Jacobin Club when he, in the guise of an anonymous "Constitutional Whig" attended one of their gatherings on December 18. The following April, Watt had the honour, together with his fellow compatriot, Thomas Cooper, of marching (carrying the British flag and a bust of Algernon Sidney, the republican martyr) in a procession through the streets of Paris to fête a group of liberated French mutineers. Another Englishman, Tom Paine, the celebrated seditionist, so involved himself in French politics that he actually became a Paris Deputy, subsequently escaping the guillotine by a mere hair's breadth.

Wordsworth arrived in France in the early winter of 1791, there to remain for the next twelve months, living on an allowance from his uncles, sojourning in Paris, Orleans, Blois, and then returning to Paris, a fascinated, out uninvolved and largely uncomprehending spectator:

> ... amused,
> I stood, 'mid those concussions, unconcerned,
> Tranquil almost, and careless as a flower
> Glassed in a greenhouse, or a parlour shrub
> That spreads its leaves in unmolested peace,
> While every bush and tree, the country through,
> Is shaking to the roots: indifference this
> Which may seem strange: but I was unprepared
> With needful knowledge, had abruptly passed
> Into a theatre . . .[24]

In due course, after he had returned to England, William was to make much capital out of this French interlude, hinting to his democratic friends, albeit vaguely, of his Patriotic activities in France.

There is no doubt that he greatly impressed S.T.C. with talk of this nature. By 1807, at the very latest (but probably in conversations dating from the days of their first acquaintance) Wordsworth had somehow given S.T.C. the firm impression that, somewhere along the line, he had done something at least a little glorious in France. In the first draft of his 1807 poem, *To William Wordsworth* (*written after hearing The Prelude read by its author*), S.T.C. hailed a vision of Wordsworth

> ... abroad,
> Mid festive Crowds, thy Brows too garlanded,
> A Brother of the Feast.

(which in the final draft became,

> For thou wert there, thine own brows garlanded,
> Amid the tremor of a realm aglow . . .)

The Prelude made no such claim of garlanded glory; but S.T.C. was firmly convinced that garlanded glory there had been. We can only conclude that Wordsworth had not been above magnifying, for Coleridge's benefit, his political experiences in France.

As the years passed and those who had been genuinely active in the Revolution vanished from the scene, or had their memories dimmed by time, Wordsworth became increasingly bold in his claims that he had been "pretty hot" in the Revolution, involved, in some never precisely revealed fashion, with the Girondins. He name-dropped: Carra, Gorsas, Roland, Madame Roland, Brissot.

Wordsworth, in *The Prelude*, never described any meetings with Paris Girondins and not a scrap of traceable surviving evidence has so far surfaced to confirm that he knew any of these people. He spoke poor French upon his arrival in France and had never hitherto revealed any interest in politics, apart from superficial undergraduate talk. He belonged to no patriotic societies; he had published no pamphlets, mounted no soap-boxes.

His nephew and biographer, Christopher Wordsworth, in his *Memoirs*, particularises that Wordsworth was intimately connected with the Brissotins, but gives no further details. Brissot, editor of the *Patriote Français*, whose varied career included a debtor's prison in England as well as the Bastille, was noted for his ambition, but scarcely for his firmness of political conviction. Again, there is no available hard evidence to connect Wordsworth with this decidedly shady character.

There was only one way in which he might have gained introductions to French political circles and that was through the English democrats then in France. In fact, he went to France equipped with a letter of introduction to the redoubtable Miss Williams, who had been staying in Orleans just before Wordsworth arrived in that town; he missed her there and although he was presently to be in Paris when she was in residence in the Rue Helvétius, where she held a *salon* on Sundays for English people and French political leaders and journalists, Wordsworth seems never to have called upon her. Had he availed himself of his letter of introduction to her he would then have had admittance to Girondin circles; but in 1814, when Crabb Robinson read some of Wordsworth's poetry to Miss Williams, she remarked that she had never heard his name until then. She would certainly have known it had he visited her in France or been active in any way in Revolutionary Paris.

The only Englishman in Paris with whom Wordsworth made contact was, it seems, James Watt. James Muirhead, when he was writing the biography of Watt Senior, many years later, visited Rydal Mount to learn from Wordsworth, at first hand, something about Watt Junior's activities in Paris. To him Wordsworth made the aforementioned claim that he himself had been "pretty hot" in the Revolution of 1792 and '93. Muirhead left no further details.

"Old men forget." Perhaps the distinguished tenant of Rydal Mount was becoming muddled with age? One can only repeat that *The Prelude* contains no claims that Wordsworth played any revolutionary rôle; indeed the poem states precisely the reverse. Although not published until after his death in 1850, it was largely completed by 1805; Wordsworth's memory was relatively fresh when he wrote it.

In *The Prelude* Wordsworth described, in vivid detail, the one Girondin whom he did get to know with any degree of intimacy. This was Captain Michel Beaupuy, whom Wordsworth met in Blois in 1792. Beaupay was not a politician, but a regular army officer. Wordsworth also drew brilliant *vignette* portraits of the Royalist officers whom he met in Orleans and Blois.

The Prelude is not only marvellous poetry; much of it is also inspired reportage. We need be in no doubt at all that, had Wordsworth known political figures in France, he would have given us portraits of them. *The Prelude* contains none.

Equally there can be no shadow of doubt that, had Wordsworth witnessed the guillotining of the Girondin deputy and journalist, Gorsas, in Paris on October 7, 1793 (as Wordsworth, in 1840 or thereabouts, hinted had been the case to Thomas Carlyle, who recalled the conversation hazily in his *Reminiscences*) *The Prelude* would surely have included an unparalleled account of this incident. We do not get it. Neither is there any shred of factual evidence that Wordsworth revisited France in 1793.

All that Wordsworth hinted in *The Prelude* was that, had he remained in France after the autumn of 1792, he would, in all probability, have felt himself impelled to make "common cause with some who perished," even though he had been assured that he was incapable of playing any more effective ,a part than a landlubber upon the deck of a vessel fighting for survival in a storm.[25]

That Wordsworth romanticised his political experiences in France in order to impress his English stay-at-home acquaintances perhaps does not matter much except in the context of his relationship with S.T.C. Here it is important. When he met S.T.C. Wordsworth, clearly, must have represented himself as having had the nerve to go to France, there to participate in revolutionary activity. S.T.C. had failed to rise to such dizzy peaks of performance; he had lectured, written, forfeited his family ties and jeopardised his future in his devotion to Pantisocracy and democracy; he had gained himself a decidedly awkward reputation as a fiery jacobin. But he had not been garlanded in Paris, a Brother of the Feast.

Wordsworth's self-alleged political courage must have been one of the corner-stones upon which S.T.C. constructed his edifice of adulation for "the Giant."[26] He saw himself as little in comparison with Wordsworth, who was happy to adopt the lofty tones of a kindly, yet manifestly superior, senior brother.[27] As we have already seen, Wordsworth, as a young man, was far from being a good example of steadiness.

In France he had had one adventure of which S.T.C. was not informed;

had he been so we may be certain that his reverence for Wordsworth would have been sadly diminished, if not demolished.

Wordsworth, in Orleans sometime in the opening months of 1792, met a young woman named Annette Vallon* who was staying in Orleans with friends, her home being in not-far-distant Blois. Slightly senior to Wordsworth, she came from a middle-class, strongly Roman Catholic family that for several generations past had produced highly respected surgeons who had worked, successively, at the Hôtel Dieu of Blois, an ancient charitable institution run by nuns.

Annette herself was devout and convent-reared. Her surviving letters are exceedingly warm, ardent and trustingly naive. We immediately know that their writer was an enthusiastic disciple of the New Sensibility, a young woman of that "natural simplicity" which Wordsworth so much admired, in short, a young woman who, in many respects, much resembled his adored Dorothy.

It appears that William was rapidly precipitated into a state of

> ... love that makes
> The day pass lightly on, when foresight sleeps.

As for Annette, her subsequent history was to reveal that she was intrepid by nature, never hesitating to back her principles with action, even when that action exposed her to serious risks. As a young woman of sensibility doubtless she entertained a strong belief in the "right of passion." Under the circumstances it is not very surprising that, by the early spring of 1792, Annette was pregnant by William.

Several theories have been advanced in an attempt to explain why she never married her "Cher Villiams" (as her letters reveal that she called him). One favoured suggestion is that the outbreak of war between England and France in 1793 prevented it. Another is that, at the time of his sojourn in France, William could not marry because he was penniless and professionless and, when at length, several years later, he was in a financial position to wed Annette, he realised that she was not suited to be the wife of a poet.

The real explanation is, surely, very much more simple. We know that William's guardians were entirely opposed to the match when they learned about it (only Dorothy, predictably, encouraged him). Upon Annette's side family disapproval was equally categorical. William Wordsworth was a Protestant Englishman with exactly the kind of morals, or rather lack of them, that French Catholics expect of Protestant Englishmen. He came from out of the blue, penniless, professionless. He had no connections in France to whom he could apply for a character. He had met Annette by chance encounter. The Vallons in all probability saw Wordsworth as an

*For a fuller account of Annette and her extraordinary career, see Emile Legouis, *William Wordsworth and Annette Vallon* (Dent, 1967 ed.).

English adventurer after their sister's dowry (for though not rich, the Vallons certainly could not have been poor).

Annette had made a fool of herself, and worse, over this young man; she must not be permitted to add to idiotic indiscretion the insanity of marriage. The Vallons preferred the expense of putting her child out to nurse and paying for its upkeep and education themselves, which is what they did. Annette and William never married.

We know that, by the early autumn of 1792, Annette's relatives had made it impossible for the young couple to see one another. The lovers contrived a farewell meeting, during which William kissed the clothes in the *layette* of his future child, including the baby's cap. He lingered in either Blois or Orleans, as near Annette as possible, not leaving for Paris until the end of October.

With the September massacres the enthusiasm of most of the English for France and the Revolution came to an end, as we have already seen. Wordsworth was thoroughly frightened by the atmosphere of Paris when he returned there (a perfectly understandable reaction). He stayed on, nonetheless, while his money ran out and the city echoed with the tramp of marching feet and the strains of the "Marseillaise". He kept himself much to himself; with the exception of James Watt he made no attempt to contact any of the other English who still remained. Wordsworth was anxious not to leave France until he received news from Annette; it reached him at last. A daughter, Caroline, had been born at Orleans on December 15. Wordsworth was back in England by the close of the year.

Annette returned to Blois with her child. She lived in her family home, but Caroline, for fear of scandal, was put out to nurse in the outskirts of Blois, where Annette visited her. The young mother at first wrote William many moving letters, one of which, a long double letter of March 20, 1793, was impounded by the French police (because of the war between France and England), to be discovered in the Blois Record Office a century later. Herein Annette speaks of her love for her child and William, of her longing for the day when she and "Cher Villiams" will be reunited and of their future life together. She describes how Caroline wears the little bonnet which her father had kissed.

William had told Annette about Dorothy and her great gifts of heart and sensibility. Dorothy, when William arrived back in England, not only heard all about Annette and Caroline, but also assumed the rôle of mediator between William and his uncles. They were categorical in their disapproval of his behaviour and their opposition to a marriage with Annette. William Cookson would no longer receive his nephew at Forncett once he had learned of the liaison. Dorothy, for her part, sent letters to Annette encouraging her to dream of a life which she, with Caroline, would share with William and Dorothy in a rustic cottage—a Romantic idyll indeed. War put an end to the reception of letters upon either side of the Channel. Annette was left in France with Caroline, to rebuild her life as the widowed Mrs Williams (La Veuve Williams) and to play an active and daring rôle as a counter-revolutionary.

William, in *The Prelude*, disguised this amorous adventure as the story of two lovers of old, Julia and Vandracour. A few close friends of the Wordsworths in due course came to know the real story of William's French romance, but S.T.C. was not numbered among them, as a letter (below) to Sara Hutchinson makes clear. The fact that a well-established tradition was preserved in the Coleridge family that Wordsworth, during his sojourn in France, had, by a young Frenchwoman, had a *son* who in maturity visited his father at Rydal Mount, indicated that S.T.C. had developed suspicions, but had been kept guessing.

Perhaps it would have been too traumatic for Wordsworth to have un-burdened himself to S.T.C. The latter so quickly elevated Wordsworth to a position of deity and Wordsworth so basked in the glory conferred upon him that it would admittedly have been asking a very great deal that he should have climbed down to reveal feet of clay. If S.T.C., in discussing with Wordsworth prominent radicals and atheists, had spoken (as he had to Thelwall) of their villainously sensuous behaviour, declaring roundly that "a Sensualist is not likely to be a Patriot;"[28] if, as an instance of atheistic depravity, S.T.C. had cited to Wordsworth (as, again, he had to Thelwall) the seditionist John Gerrald's desertion of a wife, and if S.T.C. had then gone on to denounce adultery with the vigour which he usually displayed when berating "Men who are hurried into vice by their appetites,"[29] "Your Atheistic brethren [who] square their moral systems exactly according to their inclinations,"[30] Wordsworth, understandably, might well have pre-ferred not to enlighten S.T.C. upon the full extent and nature of his acti-vities in France.

Wordsworth, in 1793, passed through a period of restlessness and depression which at one point seems to have come dangerously close to breakdown. He lost all his early orientation, becoming a complete sceptic:

> ... demanding formal *proof*,
> ... I lost
> All feeling of conviction, and, in fine,
> Yielded up moral questions in despair.
>
> This was the crisis ...
> This the soul's last and lowest ebb ...[31]

In theory he turned extreme republican. His *Letter to the Bishop of Llandaff* (the Bishop was a popular target for republican fire) was a most forceful expression of seditionist sentiment (men had been sent to the Tower for less), but as its author was careful not to publish he was placed in not the slightest jeopardy.

1793, the year in which Wordsworth wrote the *Letter*, saw, also, the publication of his poems, *An Evening Walk* and *Descriptive Sketches*. These caused considerable interest in a limited, but discerning, circle.

During what appears to have been the nadir of his depression William made a solo walking tour to North Wales, his route including Salisbury, Stonehenge, Bristol and Tintern Abbey. Not long after this he and Dorothy, in the spring of 1794, set out to visit the Lake Country together. They were virtually never to separate again.

The Wordsworths spent much of 1794 in Keswick, Cumberland, where William helped to nurse and divert his friend Raisley Calvert, a youth who was dying of consumption.

Dorothy's decision to accompany William upon this lengthy sojourn to the Lake Country evoked strong disapproval from their relations. She was far from being in a situation where William was her sole relative and protector; several homes were open to her, yet she insisted upon joining forces with the black sheep of the family. Her letters to Jane introduce a decidedly Chateaubriandesque note: "Oh Jane the last time we were together he won my Affection to a Degree which I cannot Describe."[32] Dorothy quoted passages from a letter that William had written to her in which he envisaged life with her in a dream-cottage (no mention of Annette) and spoke with lover-like impatience (or so reported Dorothy) of their next meeting: " 'I assure you so eager is my desire to see you that all obstacles vanish. I see you in a moment running or rather flying to my arms'."[33] Thus William to Dorothy.

In *The Prelude* Wordsworth was to pay warm tribute to the support which Dorothy gave him during his period of depression. She was a "companion never lost through many a league:"

> She whispered still that brightness would return,
> She, in the midst of all, preserved me still
> A Poet, made me seek beneath that name,
> And that alone, my office upon earth.[34]

Throughout this period the conviction grew for William that his true life's vocation was poetry and that, furthermore, if he were to realise his full potential as a poet, he must not dissipate his time and energies upon attempting to earn a living.

Nevertheless he could not survive on air. For several months he had been toying with ideas of journalism; but these ideas came to nothing; his heart was not in them. Meantime Raisley Calvert had succumbed to Dorothy's fervent faith in William as a poet who would one day benefit mankind. On

October 23, 1794, Calvert signed a will bequeathing William nine hundred pounds. This did not solve his immediate problems, but it promised basic financial independence in the probably not too distant future.

While at Keswick, William had been working on a long poem which he had started some two or three years earlier as a poem of social protest. He was redrafting it now as *Adventures on Salisbury Plain.* (A lengthy excerpt, entitled *The Female Vagrant*, was subsequently to be included in *Lyrical Ballads.*) *Salisbury Plain* was a diatribe against war and as many social injustices and evils as the author could cram into it (in 1814 Wordsworth was to comment that the poem "was addressed to coarse sympathies").[35] It was highly typical of the humanitarian propaganda in verse that was being written at that time by many young men (Southey in his *Botany Bay*, for instance).

To the female vagrant Wordsworth attributed all the virtues dear to Romantic sensibility: artless simplicity, total innocence, transports of joyous revelling in nature. Into his account of her mating he introduced a fashionably Chateaubriandesque note:

> There was a youth whom I had loved so long,
> That when I loved him not I cannot say.
> 'Mid the green mountains many and many a song
> We two had sung, like little birds in May.
> When we began to tire of childish play
> We seemed still more and more to prize each other;
> We talked of marriage and our marriage day;
> And I in truth did love him like a brother,
> For never could I hope to meet with such another.[36]

When Raisley Calvert died early in January, 1795, and William came into his inheritance,* he and Dorothy took up residence together at Racedown Lodge, Dorset. The house was a country home of the Pinney family and Dorothy wrote to Jane that she found it very well appointed, elegant and pretty. She was fortunate enough to engage as servant a "very nice girl," "strong . . . who could cook plain victuals tolerably well."[37]

William was now able to dedicate himself to poetry, while Dorothy assumed the rôle of chatelaine. It was a fraternal *ménage* which could only enjoy the warmest approval of persons embracing the principles of Romantic Sensibility. Thelwall voiced this Romantic view of the Wordsworths in verses he wrote after visiting them during their subsequent tenancy of Alfoxden. In these lines he described

---

*£400 of this he loaned to Montagu, on the understanding that it would be paid back with interest. Montagu was in no position to pay the interest regularly, although he managed to repay it ultimately; the principal was not repaid until 1814.

Alfoxden's musing tenant, and the maid
Of ardent eye, who, with fraternal love
Sweetens his solitude.*

In order to augment their income a little and also to assist Montagu, the Wordsworths undertook the care of his small son, Basil. As convinced disciples of Rousseau's theory of child training and education (which might be described as a permissive, not to say, passive approach, laying great emphasis on natural behaviour and free expression) they were able to try their patience with little Basil, who, Wordsworth noted, was an incorrigible liar.

The two Pinney sons, John Frederick and Azariah, came to Racedown for a week at Christmas and for a month at a slightly later period. In the company of these young men William and Dorothy enjoyed the pastimes of country gentry; Dorothy told Jane that she and William had been riding, hunting, hare-coursing and cleaving wood with the Pinneys.[38]

A London acquaintance unkindly predicted that the Wordsworths would turn into cabbages.[39]

A childhood friend of Dorothy, named Mary Hutchinson, made a long visit to Racedown from November, 1796, to early March, 1797. This young woman (who, five years later, was to become William's wife) was one of a large family of brothers and sisters, children of a Penrith tobacco merchant. Early orphaned, the little Hutchinsons had been split up between relatives. Mary and her sister Margaret (Peggy)† were brought up in Penrith by their maternal aunt, Miss Elizabeth Monkhouse, and it was in Penrith that they and Dorothy had grown close, although their first meeting dated back to infancy.

Mary has remained an obscure figure. In life she was for many years much overshadowed by her mercurial sister-in-law, Dorothy, and posterity has tended to let her rest in that shade.

According to De Quincey she was tall and plain-featured, with a slight cast in her eye; but she had such a winning expression and manner and such great personal charm that she did in fact exercise all the fascination of beauty. It is clear that men found her extraordinarily attractive. S.T.C., who adored her, called her his "beautiful green willow."[40] Keats, when he met her, described her as "Wordsworth's . . . beautiful wife."[41]

Mary's intelligence, said De Quincey, was not of an active order; her element was to feel and to enjoy in luxurious repose of mind (a neighbour once remarked that she could only say, "God bless you!"). Rather shy and retiring, even solemn-seeming in the presence of strangers, it is possible that she created an impression of being considerably less intelligent than in

*Lines written at Bridgewater, in Somersetshire, on the 27th of July, 1797.
†The other Hutchinson sisters were Elizabeth (Betsy), Sara and Joanna. Peggy died early in 1796.

fact was the case. De Quincey, it must be borne in mind, was comparing her with her rather aggressively ebullient and bustling sister, Sara. In contrast to her (and even more so in contrast to Dorothy) Mary possessed a reposeful personality. It was also an immensely strong one, if unobtrusively so.

Wordsworth certainly does not give an impression of Mary Hutchinson as a solemn young woman. Although she did not, for several years, interest him romantically, being for him no more than "a phantom to adorn a moment,"[42] she was, nonetheless, most welcome and enchanting in that rôle, as one of his famous lyrics tells us:

> She was a Phantom of delight
> When first she gleamed upon my sight;
> A lovely Apparition, sent
> To be a moment's ornament;
> Her eyes as stars of Twilight fair;
> Like Twilight's, too, her dusky hair;
> But all things else about her drawn
> From May-time and the cheerful Dawn;
> A dancing Shape, an Image gay,
> To haunt, to startle, and waylay.[43]

It seems likely that, without making any conscious attempt to be so, Mary was the Romantic ideal of a young woman of perfectly natural simplicity and spontaneity. Wordsworth, in Book Twelve of *The Prelude*, favourably compared her instinctive and unforced appreciation of beauty with the artificial eye which he himself (and therefore, of course, Dorothy) brought to bear upon natural objects, an eye confined by the bondage of approved picturesque taste:

> ... I knew a maid,
> A young enthusiast, who escaped these bonds;
> Her eye was not the mistress of her heart;
> Far less did rules prescribed by passive taste,
> Or barren intermeddling subtleties,
> Perplex her mind; but, wise as women are
> When genial circumstance hath favoured them,
> She welcomed what was given, and craved no more;
> Whate'er the scene presented to her view,
> That was the best, to what she was attuned
> By her benign simplicity of life,
> And through a perfect happiness of soul ...
>   ... methought
> Her very presence such a sweetness breathed,
> That flowers, and trees, and even the silent hills,
> And everything she looked on, should have had
> An intimation how she bore herself

> Towards them . . . God delights
> In such a being; for, her common thoughts
> Are piety, her life is gratitude.

There must have been conversation at Racedown about S.T.C. during Mary's visit; although at this stage William scarcely knew him personally and Dorothy only knew of him through William's talk. Clearly, S.T.C.'s visit was keenly anticipated at Racedown. At last came the moment when Dorothy could write to Mary of the enthusiastic guest who had leapt the gate and bounded down the field, as eager for friendship with the Wordsworths as they were for friendship with him:

> You had a great loss in not seeing Coleridge. He is a wonderful man. His conversation teems with soul, mind, and spirit. Then he is so benevolent, so good tempered and cheerful, and, like William, interests himself so much about every little trifle. At first I thought him very plain, that is, for about three minutes; he is pale and thin, has a wide mouth, thick lips, and not very good teeth, longish loose-growing half-curling rough black hair. But if you hear him speak for five minutes you think no more of them. His eye is large and full, not dark but grey; such an eye as would receive from a heavy soul the dullest expression; but it speaks every emotion of his animated mind; it has more of the 'poet's eye in a fine frenzy rolling' than I ever witnessed. He has fine dark eye-brows and an overhanging forehead.
>
> The first thing that was read after he came was William's new poem *The Ruined Cottage* with which he was much delighted; and after tea he repeated to us two acts and a half of his tragedy *Osorio*. The next morning William read his tragedy *The Borderers*.[44]

S.T.C. in his turn sent Cottle an enthusiastic description of Wordsworth's "exquisite Sister":

> She is a woman indeed!—in mind, I mean, & heart—for her person is such, that if you expected to see a pretty woman, you would think of her as ordinary—if you expected to find an ordinary woman, you would think her pretty!—But her manners are simple, ardent, impressive— . . . Her information various—her eye watchful in minutest observation of nature—and her taste a perfect electrometer—it bends, protrudes, and draws in, at subtlest beauties & most recondite faults.[45]

This was the portrait of one who was the very epitome of Romantic sensibility and taste. We must, of course, bear in mind that S.T.C. was himself seeing her with the eye of that same sensibility. We cannot be certain how much may be taken as reliable description and how much was Romantic hyperbole. This caution applies equally to William's *Tintern Abbey* tribute to her "wild eyes" with their "shooting lights."

If these descriptions bear any resemblance to the truth, they suggest a rather alarmingly febrile personality. The Grasmere Journals indicate that Dorothy had a strong tendency towards hysteria (using this term in its medical, rather than the popular, context). We must not forget De Quincey's penetrating description of her at the age of thirty-six, when he found her short and slight, stooping forward as she walked, her movements all of a glancing quickness, her manner ardent. Her speech often suffered from what De Quincey called "the agitation of her extreme organic sensibility." Her eyes were "wild and startling and hurried in their motion":

> some subtle fire . . . burned within her, which, being alternately pushed forward into a conspicuous expression by the irrepressible instincts of her temperament and then immediately checked in obedience to the decorum of her sex and age and her maidenly condition, gave to her whole demeanor and to her conversation an air of embarrassment, and even of self-conflict that was almost distressing to witness.[46]

This is the portrait of a person heading for ultimate nervous disaster, as indeed such was to prove the case with Dorothy.

When S.T.C. first met her at Racedown the Dorothy of the above description was a decade distant in time. The circumstances which were to produce this painful condition did not as yet prevail; youth was on Dorothy's side; her maidenly state did not yet betoken a middle-aged spinster, but a young woman who, Romantically, was the partner in a relationship of fraternal, instead of matrimonial love.

Constant fell-walking had not yet made Dorothy's gait an "unsexual" stride, as De Quincey was to call it; neither had her out-of-door Grasmere way of life tanned her face to the "Egyptian brown" upon which he also commented (alternatively, a rather acid female acquaintance declared Dorothy's skin to be "as yellow as a duck's foot").[47] Dorothy, however, always tended to a sallow complexion—"what you call wishy-washy," as she had sighed to Jane.[48]

The youthful Dorothy's attraction for her contemporaries lay in her qualities of Romantic ardency and "wildness". The recently discovered silhouette portrait, supposedly of Dorothy, does indeed suggest a person of attractive eagerness and energy. There is a certain quality of alert intentness about the profile that is reminiscent of a moorland pony, scenting the breeze with gaze fixed upon some fascinating distant object.

Certainly she captivated S.T.C., although we sense that at first he was somewhat in awe of one who so perfectly and impressively epitomised the spirit of the age. Before long a profound affection (totally devoid of romantic inflexion) was established between them. It was with William Wordsworth that S.T.C. fell headlong in love. In Dorothy's company S.T.C. admiringly revelled; before William he adoringly grovelled:

I speak with heart-felt sincerity & (I think) unblinded judgement, when I tell you, that I feel myself *a little man by his* side; & yet do not think myself the less man, than I formerly thought myself— ... T. Poole's opinion of Wordsworth is—that he is the greatest Man, he ever knew—I coincide.—[49]

The "unblinded judgement" was gross self-delusion on S.T.C.'s part; he was infatuated and completely dazzled by this new sun in his firmament. So overwhelmed was he that, for instance, he wrote to assure Cottle that Wordsworth's drama, *The Borderers*, compared favourably with Shakespeare.

This enthusiasm for Wordsworth's attempt at drama was symptomatic of the over-all Coleridgean ecstasy during this first visit to Racedown. The Wordsworths for their part exhibited almost equal enthusiasm for S.T.C. Wordsworth was good enough to speak so highly of *Osorio* that S.T.C. hurled himself into the conclusion of it, reading to his new "strict & almost severe critic"[50] the passages as they came from his pen. S.T.C. already heard the applause of Drury Lane.

On June 28 he returned to Stowey. Doubtless he gave both Sara and Tom Poole tremendous accounts of Racedown. Almost immediately S.T.C. returned there, reappearing in Stowey on July 2, with the Wordsworths in tow. Charles Lamb was shortly coming to stay; S.T.C. could not wait to introduce Wordsworth to him. Indeed, S.T.C. was desirous that the whole world should meet this miraculous man, "—The Giant Wordsworth—God love him!"[51]

CHAPTER NINE

INDULGENT SKIES

(July–September 1797)

> . . . beloved Friend!
> When looking back, thou seest, in clearer view
> Than any liveliest sight of yesterday,
> That summer, under whose indulgent skies,
> Upon smooth Quantock's airy ridge we roved
> Unchecked, or loitered 'mid her sylvan combs . . .
> When thou dost to that summer turn thy thoughts,
> And hast before thee all which then we were . . .
> . . . the buoyant spirits
> That were our daily portion when we first
> Together wantoned in wild Poesy.[1]

THE NOTE OF nostalgia for that wonderful summer so strongly pervades these lines from *The Prelude* that we find ourselves longing for some wizard's wand to transport us back to that evening of July 2, 1797, when the Wordsworths arrived at S.T.C.'s cottage.

The calvacade that made its way up sleepy and dusty Lime Street, Nether Stowey, consisted of a one-horse chaise with Dorothy and little Basil Montagu as passengers and S.T.C. driving. Wordsworth, we must suppose, followed on horseback. Doubtless faces peered at windows and heads poked out from doorways as the Stowey populace strove to see what their strange jacobin neighbour, Mr Coleridge, was about now.

S.T.C. had driven over to Racedown in the chaise (which, it seems, he was able to procure "free of expence") and had "brought back Miss Wordsworth over forty miles of execrable road" without mishap (S.T.C. had recently had practice at driving and was "now no inexpert whip").[2]

The guests, given a cheerful welcome by Sara Coleridge, squeezed into the Esteesian abode which, they declared, was precisely the kind of place that they themselves were trying to find. Their tenancy of Racedown expired at midsummer and they had been indulging in "some dream of happiness in a little cottage."[3]

On his previous visit to Stowey, in April, William had discovered Alfoxden House (a large manor in a deer park) three miles from Nether Stowey, and had then asked Poole to apply for it to the lessee, John Bartholomew of Putsham (the owner was Mrs Anna Maria St. Albyn, widow of the Reverend Lancelot St. Albyn). Nothing, however, had come of this scheme.

The Lambs were expected to join the Coleridge house-party any day.

S.T.C. planned a week of roving the Quantocks with his guests. Poetry and the beauties of nature were to be the restorative libations proffered to the beloved visitor from London. But when the Lambs arrived, upon July 7, it was to discover their host confined to a couch, unable to walk, Sara having accidentally emptied a skillet of boiling milk on his foot (this episode had occurred on the second day of the Wordsworths' visit). As a result all the excursions about the countryside had to be made without S.T.C., who consoled himself, during the absence of his friends, with the company of Tom Poole in the arbour of Poole's garden. Here, one evening, S.T.C. composed what was his finest poem to date; *This Lime-Tree Bower My Prison.*

In this the poet sees, in his mind's eye, his friends roaming the "hill-top edge" without him; he imagines them wandering delighted, admiring the sunset which he, in turn, admires from his couch of confinement in the tree and foliage-filled garden, until, in the thickening nightfall the black ivy leaves

> . . . gleam a lighter hue
> Thro' the last twilight.—And tho' the rapid bat
> Wheels silent by and not a swallow twitters,
> Yet still the solitary bumble-bee
> Sings in the bean flower.[4]

Finally the poet concludes (with commendable philosophy) that his scalded foot was a species of blessing in disguise, for

> 'Tis well to be bereav'd of promis'd good
> That we may lift the soul, contemplate
> With lively joy the joys we cannot share.[5]

The poem embodies a special and tenderly touching tribute to Charles Lamb, here quoted from the 1834 text:

> . . . Yes, they wander on
> In gladness all; but thou, methinks, most glad
> My gentle-hearted Charles! for thou hast pined
> And hungered after Nature, many a year,
> In the great City pent, winning thy way
> With sad yet patient soul, through evil and pain
> And strange calamity!

(Against the note to this poem in a copy of the 1834 *Poems* S.T.C. wrote: "Ch. and Mary Lamb—dear to my heart, yea, as it were my Heart.— S.T.C. Æt 63; 1834–1797–1834=37 years!"[6])

One can imagine the joy of Charles Lamb when he arrived back at the cottage and had this poem read to him. Perhaps, too, Sara was equally delighted (not to say relieved) that Samuel's scalded foot had resulted in an exceedingly fine poem which he would certainly not have written had he not been confined to Tom Poole's garden.

To suppose that the accident in any way betrayed an unhappy friction between the pair would be quite wrong. There is a mass of testimony to reveal that their marriage, now almost in its fourth year, was gaining in depth and happiness as it progressed. Clearly it had its ups and downs and fair share of fights, as have most true marriages (indeed, the strength of a marriage may be gauged by the vicissitudes which it contrives to survive). The young Coleridges had already experienced many vicissitudes and were so far surviving very well. Sara, at the time of this summer house party, was in the first weeks of a new pregnancy, about which she and S.T.C. seem to have been content.

The mood of this house party was one of tearing high spirits. The Lambs and the Wordsworths appear to have liked one another passably well at this initial meeting. The Lambs, however, were never at any stage to join the cult of Wordsworth idolatory. Mary Lamb, herself a most remarkable woman, was wholly different in personality from Dorothy, while Charles Lamb's acute sense of the ridiculous made it impossible for him not to detect, from the first, the comic aspects of William Wordsworth's character.

Between the Lambs and Sara Coleridge there quickly developed a warm affection. In his letter of thanks written to S.T.C. after the visit (he had managed to leave his greatcoat behind) Lamb spoke of "you and your dear Sara—to me also very dear, because very kind."[7]

The Wordsworths, before going to Stowey, must have heard from S.T.C. upon the subject of his Sally (his letters, in those early years, contain innumerable proud and loving references to her). On arrival at Stowey the Wordsworths were met by a happy, exceedingly pretty little hostess of decidedly chirpy disposition who was everyone's darling, the pet of Tom Poole and his mother, in warm favour with the Lambs when they arrived and gallantly, albeit jocularly, courted by an admiring Thelwall when *he* arrived. S.T.C. was an unabashedly doting spouse; the seraphic Hartley beamed from Sara's arms.

That a violent mutual jealousy existed between Dorothy Wordsworth and Sara Coleridge over the greater part of their long acquaintance is undeniable. It is highly probable that Dorothy was the first to experience these pangs; initially Sara had no reason to be envious of Dorothy, but the latter had very real cause to envy Sara.

Fraternal love may be a rare and precious thing, but maternal love stirs deeper, more primeval instincts in a woman. Dorothy doted upon infants and children. Great as was her devotion to William, we must suppose that she would, at the age of twenty-six, still have married had a desirable suitor appeared. But none approached. Her increasing absorption in William must have placed her in a position where a man, even had he been romantically

243

inclined, would have hesitated to intrude upon a relationship of such obvious significance to both brother and sister. Moreover, Dorothy was not growing younger; she had no dowry to bolster physical charms. Her marital chances were patently becoming slender by the time she visited Stowey and although she may well have felt that her relationship with William was compensation for the lack of a conjugal love, she must have already suspected, with heaviness of heart, that she would never know the satisfaction of maternal love.

During the fortnight that the Wordsworths were staying with the Coleridges they discovered that Alfoxden House* was still vacant. They applied for it and, on July 14, William Wordsworth and Bartholomew, with Poole as witness, signed an agreement giving Wordsworth immediate possession for a year from the previous Midsummer's Day, at an annual rent of twenty-three pounds, taxes included.[8]

S.T.C. sent a loud hurrah to Southey: "I had been on a visit to Wordsworth's . . . I brought him & his Sister back with me & here I have *settled* them."[9]

Dorothy, with zest, reported to Jane that Alfoxden was "a large mansion with furniture enough for a dozen families like ours."[10]

The very day that they signed the lease the Wordsworths moved into their new residence and, as the Lambs had left to return to London that day, S.T.C. and Sara were able to follow the Wordsworths to Alfoxden without delay "for a change of air."[11] The Coleridges were back in Stowey by July 17 to welcome their new guest, John Thelwall.

The celebrated seditionist turned out to be a stout, short, bespectacled, amazingly jolly little man in a round white hat (Josiah Wade, who entertained him to dinner at Bristol in early August, confided to S.T.C. that: "Some people would accuse him of too much levity").[12] Although S.T.C. and Thelwall had become energetic pen-friends they had never hitherto met in the flesh. Despite the fact that they disagreed upon almost every topic that they discussed, they discovered that they liked one another "uncommonly well." Thelwall was a "very warm hearted honest man," decided S.T.C., noting (there could be no higher recommendation) that: "He is a great favourite with Sara."[13]

Within twenty-four hours of Thelwall's arrival the Wordsworths had left their seat and were at Stowey. The flavour of the gathering was distinctly jacobin; all present addressed one another as "Citizen," or "Citizeness." Thelwall, writing to his wife Stella, to tell her that he had slept the night at "Coleridge's cot," added, "Faith, we are a most philosophical party . . . the enthusiastic group consisting of C. and his Sara, W. and his sister, and myself . . . An old woman, who lives in an adjoining cottage, does what is required for our simple wants."[14]

*Now known as Alfoxton it was, in S.T.C.'s day, usually spelled Alfoxden; S.T.C., to Southey, wrote it as pronounced locally, All-foxen.

Thelwall's visit lasted some ten days; he was at first at Stowey and then, at the week-end, removed with the Coleridges to stay at Alfoxden. There was much roaming the countryside and never-ending talk. S.T.C. was to remember:

John Thelwall had something very good about him. We were once sitting in a beautiful recess in the Quantocks, when I said to him, "Citizen John, this is a fine place to talk treason in!"—"Nay! Citizen Samuel!" replied he, "it is rather a place to make a man forget that there is any necessity for treason!"[15]

Alarming rumours began to spread in and about Stowey. An agitated Cousin Charlotte confided to her journal:

We are shocked to hear that Mr Thelwall has spent some time at Stowey this week, with Mr Coleridge and consequently with Tom Poole. Alfoxden house is taken by one of the fraternity—To what are we coming?[16]

On Saturday July 22 it seems that Tom Poole was requested by S.T.C. to dispatch to Alfoxden a forequarter of lamb (kindly provided by old Mrs Poole) as there was to be a party. S.T.C.'s note concluded with an invitation to Poole to come over to Alfoxden "if possible by eleven o'clock that we may have Wordsworth's Tragedy read under the Trees—."*[17]

Following the reading under the trees on that July Sunday, fourteen people sat down at table to discuss the forequarter of lamb. We do not know who they all were: Poole must certainly have been present, and Thelwall, perhaps Cottle, very possibly Montagu. A local man named Jones was hired to wait at table; from him derives our information about this dinner party. He noted particularly, among those present "a little Stout Man with dark cropt Hair . . . [who] wore a White Hat and Glasses" (Thelwall). After dinner this little man made an "inflamed political speech" that thoroughly frightened Jones, according to Jones's own testimony.[18]

Thelwall remained at Stowey until the first days of August and (apart from the fact that he had lost his trunk, which had been sent on in advance by Parson's Bath wagon but had never arrived) the visit was an unmitigated success. The bustle and activity, to be sure, was almost certainly responsible for the miscarriage which Sara suffered at the end of July, "but in so very early a stage, that it occasioned but little pain, one day's indisposition and no confinement."[19]

Meantime: "My little Hartley grows a beautiful child,"[20, 21] "Hartley sends a grin to you! He has another tooth!"[22]

S.T.C.'s foot took a long time to heal; he walked on it too soon. However by mid-August he was able to go to Bristol for a few days. He was due to

*Griggs dates this note as *circa* July 17, but Moorman suggests, and it seems probable, that the forequarter of lamb belonged to the dinner party of Sunday, July 23.

return to Stowey on August 18, but missed the coach. He tried for the coach again next morning, but it was completely full; so he walked back to Stowey, a full forty miles, arriving home in the evening (apparently not over-fatigued) to find Richard Reynell at the cottage, on a visit. Reynell had been suggested to the Coleridges as a possible lodger in the place of Lloyd, which would "at least provide my immediate household expenses,"[23] as S.T.C. remarked to Estlin. In spite of the fact that Reynell seemed much to enjoy his visit (he sent a long and detailed account of it to his sister, including a vivid description of S.T.C. as so "very very happy" in his domestic life)[24] he did not become a lodger at Stowey.

S.T.C. was once more facing problems of livelihood. His rôle as a self-supporting agriculturalist had long since been abandoned; his garden was lush with weeds. With his guests gone he pressed on to conclude *Osorio* which, he optimistically supposed, would soon solve all his financial difficulties.

The presence of the Wordsworths as neighbours both stimulated poetic activity and at the same time prevented work. By day they (and often S.T.C. with them) wandered about the countryside on picturesque scenic excursions, armed with their camp-stools and notebooks. At night they walked moon-gazing.* A fragment belonging to Alfoxden describes the increasingly Chateaubriandesque approach of the Wordsworths during this period:

> In many a walk
> At evenings or by moonlight, or reclined
> At midday upon beds of forest moss
> Have we to Nature and her impulses
> Of our whole being made free gift, and when
> Our trance had left us, oft have we, by aid
> Of the impressions which it left behind,
> Looked inward on ourselves, and learned, perhaps,
> Something of what we are![25]

In addition to these picturesque excursions, Wordsworth would sit for hours with S.T.C. under the sea-wall, discussing philosophy (it was now that the two men compared their data and found it dissimilar).

Meantime, the local populace was plunged into a galvanising spy-scare. As is so often the case, the suspects themselves were the last to become aware of this furore.

The Wordsworths had arrived in Stowey under the aegis of S.T.C. Although he liked to think that local suspicion of himself had been wholly

---

*A fashionable pastime with the Romantics and the subject of two of the best-known pictures of the German Romantic painter Caspar David Friedrich (1774–1840): *Two Men Gazing at the Moon* (Dresden), and *Man and Woman Gazing at the Moon* (Nationalgalerie, Berlin).

allayed, such in fact was far from being the case. The Wordsworths, as friends of "the vile jacobin villain"[26] Coleridge, were bound to be suspect. Following their removal to Alfoxden a surreptitious, but close, watch was kept on them. Chief among those who studied them was one Mogg, a former servant at Alfoxden. The Wordsworths' northern speech (most strange to Somerset ears) and their dark colouring suggested to the worthy Mogg that here were French people; she discovered that they washed and mended their clothes on a Sunday, sure proof that they were Papists; furthermore, their *ménage* had an atmosphere of typical Gallic immorality, in as much as the Master of the house had "no wife with him, but only a woman who passes for his sister."[27]

The arrival of Thelwall added to the excitement. Jones's reports of the Alfoxden dinner-party and the republican speeches and toasts thereat finally convinced Stowey that they had a jacobin nest in their midst. Mogg confided her accumulated fears to another former Alfoxden domestic, now in service at Bath, who repeated the tale to her employer, a Dr Lysons. He in turn informed the Home Secretary, at that date the Duke of Portland. As the result of Lysons' report, together with the complaints of other reputable persons in the Stowey neighbourhood (Charlotte Poole's prattle should be recalled in this context) the Home Office dispatched to Stowey a Government agent named Walsh, who placed the activities of the Wordsworths and S.T.C. under strict observation.*

Their habit of walking about the countryside carrying notebooks in which they wrote detailed observations, together with the night expeditions, not unnaturally gave Walsh much food for thought. However his final conclusion was that the suspects were not French, but "a mischievous gang of disaffected Englishmen."[28] No action was taken against the suspects, but they were made to feel uncomfortable in local society. When Thelwall, who had formed an immense fancy for Stowey and the democratic company there, wrote to S.T.C. asking him to find a cottage for the Thelwalls, S.T.C. had to point out the undesirability of this:

> Very great odium T. Poole incurred by bringing *me* here—my peaceable manners & known attachment to Christianity had almost worn it away—when Wordsworth came . . . You cannot conceive the tumult, calumnies, & apparatus of theatened persecution which this event has occasioned round about us. If *you* too should come, I am afraid, that dangerous riots might be the consequence . . . Add to which, that in point of *public interest* we must put into the balance the Stowey Benefit Club—/of the . . . utility of this T. Poole thinks highly.[29]

Poole's Benefit Society was an early experiment in workers' compensa-

---

*For further details of this episode see H. Eaglestone, "Wordsworth, Coleridge and the Spy," *Coleridge: Studies by Several Hands* (1934).

tion and insurance.* This work of serious social reform was put at hazard by the jacobin antics of the Alfoxden circle. Poole himself was clearly becoming wary of Wordsworth for various reasons and attempted to wean S.T.C. from excessive enthusiasm for "Alfoxden's musing tenant."

Thelwall, with the hard practicality of a man who had seen the inside of the Tower, took S.T.C.'s advice and found himself a cottage in Wales.

Thus passed the wonderful summer of 1797, with almost ceaseless laughter and high-spirits, constant visits, talk and sociability, love and warm happiness, excitement and buoyancy. There is no hint that at any time between mid-June and the end of August did S.T.C. experience ill-health. He was temporarily released from pressure (always the vital factor where his illnesses were concerned) and the weather was warm and dry, which greatly agreed with him.

In view of his drug history we can only suppose that he must have had some recourse to opium during this period (happy doses to keep him happy). The Wordsworths probably became aware, during those first months of friendship, that S.T.C. took opium; this drug was in favour with the New Sensibility and S.T.C.'s habit would have been seen by the Wordsworths as exceedingly "interesting." (If we may believe Southey, Poole, and Mrs Coleridge, the Wordsworths encouraged his opium habit rather than otherwise;[30] it was not until much later that S.T.C.'s slavery to the drug became a grievous burden for them.)

From that summer's blue skies of unblemished sympathy, friendship, talk and laughter there stirred a current of new poetry:

> Thou in bewitching words, with happy heart,
> Didst chaunt the vision of that Ancient Man,
> The bright-eyed Mariner . . .
> . . . I, associate with such labour . . .
> Murmuring of him who, joyous hap, was found,
> After the perils of his moonlight ride
> Near the loud waterfall; or her who sate
> In misery near the miserable Thorn . . .[31]

*Similar societies were being launched up and down the country at the close of the eighteenth century. By 1801 it was estimated that some 7,200 societies were in existence; most of them, like Poole's, being purely local and drawing their membership from a single village or restricted area in a large town.

CHAPTER TEN

WANTONING IN WILD POESY

(September 1797–October 1798)

> Like the Gossamer Spider, we may float upon air and
> seem to fly in mid heaven, but we have spun the slender
> Thread of our fancies, & it is always fastened to some-
> thing below.—[1]

> A great Poet must be . . . a profound Metaphysician . . .
> he must have the *ear* of a wild Arab listening in the
> silent Desart, the eye of a North American Indian
> tracing the footsteps of an Enemy upon the Leaves
> that strew the Forest—; the Touch of a Blind Man feel-
> ing the face of a darling Child.[2]

THE HEART OF the author of *The Ancient Mariner* was not so happy, it seems, as Wordsworth was subsequently to recall in *The Prelude*.

We know that by the early autumn of 1797 S.T.C. was once more engulfed in financial anxieties and fears for the future. In a letter to Estlin dated December 30 of that year S.T.C., retracing the events of his previous three months, wrote: "At the commencement of this period I began to feel the necessity of gaining a regular income by a regular occupation."[3]

Earlier letters reveal that S.T.C. became unwell at the end of August.[4] At the start of September he visited Bowles at Shaftsbury, taking with him *Osorio*, now all but completed. S.T.C. was back at Stowey (and ill with a sore throat) by September 15.

On either September 15 or 16, John and Tom Wedgwood* and possibly also James Tobin (of the family of the Bristol firm of Pinney and Tobin) arrived at Alfoxden for a five day visit (Charles Lloyd was there briefly, also).

Tom Wedgwood had come to reside temporarily with his brother John at Cote House, in order to be a patient of Dr Beddoes. One of Tom

---

*The Wedgwoods were an ancient family of potters; Josiah Wedgwood Senior (1730–1795) was the youngest child of Thomas, of Burslem, Staffordshire. Josiah was an exceptionally skilful potter who, with great success, specialised in ornamental wares, manufacturing them at his factory, Etruria (named after his famous Etruscan ware), at Hanley. His eldest son John, a banker, lived at Cote House, near Bristol. Josiah Junior succeeded as head of the family potteries, while Thomas, a chronic invalid, was a brilliant dilettante (he invented "heliotypes," the forerunners of photographs and was also a distinguished metaphysician). John and Josiah married sisters, the Misses Allen. A third Miss Allen married James Mackintosh, whose first wife was sister of Daniel Stuart (1766–1846), who became editor of the *Morning Post* in 1795.

Wedgwood's many interests was what we today would call "progressive education;" he was currently planning a nursery-school for geniuses.[5] Wordsworth, as a disciple of Rousseau, at this period in time professed an ardent interest in radical social reform and education. Either Tobin or Montagu suggested to Tom Wedgwood that he might find Wordsworth's views on education of interest.[6]

The visit to Alfoxden was an unproductive one so far as the Wedgwood-Wordsworth encounter was concerned. Tom Wedgwood, like James Mackintosh, formed but a very indifferent opinion of Wordsworth. This visit, however, did result in the introduction of S.T.C. to the Wedgwoods.

The problem confronting S.T.C. in the autumn of 1797 was his by now only too familiar chain-reaction of irregular income, financial pressure, anxiety, ill-health, and opium.

By removing to Stowey he had contrived a temporary escape from this escalating pattern of disaster, but now he was once more faced with it. He resumed the desperate occupation of musing over schemes whereby he might earn a living. The one-man enterprise as an agriculturist had proved to be nothing but a bucolic dream. S.T.C. still cherished the idea of starting a school of his own, this time in partnership with Montagu, but the school would require capital and neither S.T.C. nor Montagu possessed a penny.[7] The Unitarian Ministry offered S.T.C. a livelihood, but he was fundamentally loath to don the Unitarian cloth. There remained literature; but S.T.C. now knew his chances of earning a steady income with his pen to be negligible. Nevertheless, he still entertained a faint lurking hope that he might win popular favour as an author of extravagantly imaginative writing. Not novels, but long narrative poems or ballads at that time were an increasingly profitable form of Romantic literary endeavour, prompted by the interest aroused in Thomas Percy's *Reliques of Ancient English Poetry*, published in 1765.

This anthology of traditional ballads had a profound influence upon the work of both S.T.C. and Wordsworth; the latter discovered in the ballads that directness of language and appeal to common understanding that he was anxious to achieve in his own poetry, while S.T.C. found Percy to be a source of stimulating ideas and atmospheric effects.

Imitations of these ballads were becoming increasingly popular with the public, particularly those of Gottfried August Bürger (1747-94), who specialised in supernatural variations upon the old ballad themes, embellishing his poems with macabre horrors wholly in the taste of the New Sensibility. His most successful ballad, *Lenore* (in which a soldier returns from the dead to carry off his living bride on horseback) was first introduced to English readers in translation, as *Ellenore*, by William Taylor, in the *Monthly Magazine* for March 1796 (several other translations rapidly appeared in its wake).

A host of eager authors now leapt upon the Romantic ballad bandwagon, including the indefatigable M. G. Lewis with his blood-curdling *Alonzo the Brave*, and the young Walter Scott who was subsequently to leave all his rivals far behind. Scott's first ballads, *The Chase* and *William and Helen*, published in 1796, were unabashedly drawn from Bürger.

Wordsworth, at Racedown, had attempted a ballad in this genre, *The Three Graves*, a story of a curse. Wordsworth's heart was not in this kind of thing, however, and he abandoned the ballad half-way through.

By the autumn of 1797 both he and S.T.C., their funds low, together directed their attention to this increasingly lucrative market; these popular ballads looked easy enough to write. As S.T.C. was to observe to Wordsworth, *à propos* of Scott, all a man had to do was to "jog on . . . between a sleeping Canter and a Marketwoman's trot . . . [he] must be troubled with a mental strangury, if he could not lift up his leg six times at six different Corners, and each time piss a canto."[8]

S.T.C. had already contributed verse to the *Monthly Magazine* (which paid five pounds for a long Romantic ballad).

Purchas was yet once more taken up and studied as a source for ideas and imagery. A notebook entry for this period, transcribed by S.T.C. from Rubruquis' *Travels into Tartary*,

Article the first, in the Third Part of Purchas his Pilgrimes . . .

Cublai Chan began to reign, 1256 the greatest Prince in Peoples, Cities, & Kingdoms that ever was in the World[9]

strongly suggests that, in the fall of 1797, Cublai Chan was the subject favoured by S.T.C. for his five-pound ballad-mongering.

Osorio also had to be finished.

The cottage at Stowey was too confined and animatedly noisy for intensive literary labour. ("Hartley is well—& *will not* walk or run, having discovered the art of crawling with wonderful ease & rapidity!")[10] S.T.C., in search of total seclusion, retired to a "lonely farmhouse" near Culbone Church, between Porlock and Lynton. The October scenery of the tree-filled coombes on the edge of Exmoor, with the Bristol Channel washing the bleached quay of Porlock Wier within short distance, is perfectly described by the lines which S.T.C. gave to Alhadra, the Moorish woman in *Osorio*:

> The hanging Woods, that touch'd by Autumn seem'd
> As they were blossoming hues of fire & gold,
> The hanging woods, most lovely in decay,
> The many clouds, the Sea, the Rock, the Sands . . .[11]

The date of this retreat to Culbone seems almost certainly to have been at the commencement of October, 1797. We know that S.T.C. was at Stowey on September 15. In a letter to Thelwall, written on or about

October 14, S.T.C. remarked that he had been "absent for a day or two."[12] This corroborates S.T.C.'s own statement, made in a note added to an autograph copy of *Kubla Khan*, that he retired to the farmhouse "in the fall of the year, 1797."[13]

In his 1816 note to *Kubla Khan* S.T.C. explained: "In consequence of a slight indisposition, an anodyne had been prescribed." In the aforementioned note to the autographed copy of the poem S.T.C. enlarged upon this: "two grains of Opium, taken to check a dysentry."

We may, however, confidently discount S.T.C.'s excuse that the Culbone opium was taken for strictly medicinal reasons. S.T.C., when he retired to the seclusion of the farmhouse, was under stringent financial pressure; he was faced with the dire necessity of a stint of strenuous, bread-winning literary labour. He succeeded, apparently, in finishing *Osorio*; but with the five-pound ballad for the *Monthly Magazine* he got no further than the opening lines. Instead of working, S.T.C. at Culbone turned to the escape and solace of opium and dreams. The habit which had commenced at Cambridge can be traced, unmistakably, via Newgate Street, Bristol and Nether Stowey, to Culbone.

Everything about S.T.C. at this period of time conforms to the classical portraiture of the narcotics addict. S.T.C.'s reading, his philosophising, his dreaming, much of the substance of his letters, his behaviour, all fit the pattern perfectly. Highly typical was his reading, during the winter of 1796, of Jones's translation of *Institutes of Hindu Law*. Of this work S.T.C. had commented to Poole: "The first chapter contains sublimity—."[14] Neither was the study of Spinoza wholly unrelated to opium, one suspects. The sensation that *"all things* counterfeit infinity" is a drug-turned-on, as well as a pantheistic, experience. It is interesting and significant to note how often, in this drug-honeymoon period, S.T.C. would, when under pressure, withdraw to his study with Spinoza and opium and let the outside world go by unheeded.

Lines written, it almost certainly seems, at Culbone and again given to the Moorish Alhadra, reveal S.T.C.'s mood at the farmhouse:

> It were a lot divine in some small skiff
> Along some Ocean's boundless solitude
> To float for ever with a careless course . . .[15]

A letter to Thelwall, written, it seems, shortly after S.T.C.'s return to Stowey from Culbone, is redolent with opium:

My Mind feels as if it ached to behold & know something *great*—something *one & indivisible*, and it is only in the faith of this that rocks or waterfalls, mountains or caverns give me the sense of sublimity or majesty! But in this faith *all things* counterfeit infinity!—"Struck with the deepest calm of Joy" I stand . . . [here he quotes from *This Lime-Tree Bower*] It is but seldom that

I raise & spiritualize my intellect to this height—& at other times I adopt the Brahman Creed, & say—It is better to sit than to stand, it is better to lie than to sit, it is better to sleep than to wake—but Death is the best of all!—I should much wish, like the Indian Vishna [Vishnu], to float about along an infinite ocean cradled in the flower of the Lotus, & wake once in a million years for a few minutes—just to know that I was going to sleep a million years more.[16]

We see S.T.C. at Culbone, seated in the farmhouse parlour, ostensibly at work on his ballad, with Purchas open on his knee at the passage:

In Xanadu did Cublai Can build a stately Palace, encompassing sixteene miles of plaine ground with a wall, wherein are fertile Meddowes, pleasant Springs, delightfull Streames, and all sorts of beasts of chase and game, and in the middest thereof a sumptuous house of pleasure, which may be removed from place to place.[17]

The world knows what allegedly happened next. The poet fell asleep (a comfortable euphemism for succumbing to narcosis) and,

continued for about three hours in a profound sleep, at least of the external senses, during which time he has the most vivid confidence, that he could not have composed less than two to three hundred lines: if that can be called composition in which all the images rose up before him as things, with a parallel production of the correspondent expressions, without any sensation or consciousness of effort. On awakening he appeared to himself to have a distinct recollection of the whole . . . and instantly and eagerly wrote down the lines that are here preserved. At this moment he was unfortunately called out by a person on business from Porlock, and detained by him above an hour, and on his return to his room, found . . . that though he still retained some vague and dim recollection of the general purport of the vision, yet, with the exception of some eight or ten scattered lines and images, all the rest had passed away . . . Yet from the still surviving recollections in his mind, the Author has frequently purposed to finish what had originally, as it were, been given to him.[18]

It should be remembered that opium-dreams are, so to speak, subconsciously managed or directed by the dreamer himself (*"the marvellous velocity of Thought & Image in certain full Trances"*, S.T.C. called it).[19] He would have been perfectly able to have had a vision based upon Purchas's Cublai Chan had he so desired. At this stage of his drug history his dreams, or visions, were happy, beautiful and wholly gratifying, so that the vision of Xanadu was in every respect enchanting.

Certainly the substance of such a vision would have made perfect material for the projected ballad and we may well accept that S.T.C. attempted to jot down all that he remembered upon coming out of his trance. But dreams resemble those miraculously-coloured fish that dwell in the deeps and which, when brought to the surface, shimmer in all their beauty for a moment and then fade. This, as S.T.C. makes clear, is what happened to Kubla Khan.

But S.T.C.'s published claim was not simply that he had had a vivid dream, part of which he had used as material for his poem. He was to maintain that: "This fragment, with a good deal more, not recoverable, was composed in a sort of Reverie," and "that he could not have composed less than from two to three hundred lines" of which, on awakening, he "wrote down the lines that are here preserved."

It is not at all rare for drug addicts to claim that, during a trance, or trip, they have effortlessly written a long and marvellous poem, or story. The poem or story, if any attempt is made to commit it to paper, proves to be no more than a few garbled lines of jabberwocky. Instances of S.T.C.'s verse written under the influence of drugs or alcohol, or both, are scattered throughout the notebooks. They are never more than poor doggerel.

Kubla Khan was not published until 1816, despite the fact that, according to S.T.C., it was "given" to him in 1797. Ever since its first appearance *Kubla Khan* has enjoyed immense popularity, yet S.T.C., if we can believe him, kept these magical lines unpublished for nearly twenty years, during which time he published much verse. *Kubla Khan* seems never to have been considered either for *Lyrical Ballads* or S.T.C.'s projected third edition of poems in 1798. When he was scraping the barrel for verse to send to the *Morning Post, Kubla Khan* made no appearance.

Copies of poems with which he was pleased were always sent in letters to his friends. *Kubla Khan* seems not to have been sent to anyone. Thelwall received lines from *Osorio* in the letter of October 14;[20] if S.T.C. had indeed received a miraculous gift of such extraordinary, subtle and effective poetry as *Kubla Khan* one would have supposed that he would certainly have informed Thelwall, yet this he did not do. Dorothy makes no mention of *Kubla Khan* at this time of its alleged writing. S.T.C. had had this incredible experience, resulting in a poem with which he must surely have been delighted; yet he kept the entire matter to himself. This behaviour is peculiarly out of key.

Until 1802, by which time he was becoming seriously disorientated by his drug and poetry had deserted him, S.T.C. never claimed that his poems came to him miraculously; he did not try to conceal the fact that he worked hard at them and was much involved in problems of technique. In 1802 he produced a poem, *Hymn Before Sunrise in the Vale of Chamouni* which, he claimed, he had poured forth involuntarily like a psalm, while on the summit of Scafell. His notebook entries describing the ascent of Scafell make no mention whatever of such an incident, neither does the long and detailed letter which he wrote, while on the summit, to Sara Hutchinson. The lines seem not to have been committed to paper by S.T.C. until three weeks after his ascent of the mountain and they are not of his own inspiration, but are in part a translation, in part an expansion of an ode by Friederica Brun. This hoax was never confessed to by S.T.C.; it was finally exposed by De Quincey.

In 1802, when S.T.C. passed off this *Hymn* as a miraculously inspired poem of his own, his powers of concentration and thus of composition were already ravaged by morphine. By 1816, when he published *Kubla Khan* as lines given him in an opium-dream, S.T.C. was barely emergent from the nadir of morphine reliance. Bearing in mind the history of the *Hymn*, we should be exceedingly reluctant to accept the poet's account of the miraculous conception of *Kubla Khan*.

What we may feel inclined to accept is that certain glimpses, or snatches, of *Kubla Khan* possibly derive from that dream. It seems almost certain that *Kubla Khan* was started as a projected picturesque ballad at Culbone; that S.T.C. abandoned composition for opium and dreamt out his ballad instead of working on it. He was left with a handful of remembered fragments of his dreaming and these, at some unspecified date, he welded together, using all his incredible skill to produce a magical song, a miracle of vision-like verse.

Close scrutiny of *Kubla Khan* tends to confirm this theory. The opening stanza has a wonderfully compulsive, singing metre that bears all the stamp of having "come" as the opening lines of a poem do so often arrive, as if by impetus of their own. Instances spring to mind:

> I wander'd lonely as a cloud
> That floats on high o'er vales and hills . . .[21]
>
> I wonder by my troth, what thou, and I
> Did, till we lov'd? were we not wean'd till then?[22]
>
> Ah, sun-flower! weary of time,
> Who countest the steps of the sun . . .[23]
>
> In Xanadu did Kubla Khan
> A stately pleasure-dome decree;
> Where Alph, the sacred river, ran
> Through caverns measureless to man
> Down to a sunless sea.

But after the sweet initial upsurge of a poem must always follow the considered development and working-out. This one certainly would not expect to find in a poem that was simply a fragment of spontaneous vision, but the second passage of *Kubla Khan* is a brilliantly controlled and organised development (carefully using, it should be noted, all the material that S.T.C. had been reading and absorbing and which he now employed in a subtly organised, apparently effortless build-up of images—a technique which he was to use with even greater mastery in *The Ancient Mariner*):

> So twice five miles of fertile ground
> With walls and towers were girdled round:
> And there were gardens bright with sinuous rills
> Where blossomed many an incense-bearing tree;
> And here were forests ancient as the hills,
> Enfolding sunny spots of greenery.
>
> But oh! that deep romantic chasm which slanted
> Down the green hill athwart a cedarn cover!
> A savage place! as holy and enchanted
> As e'er beneath a waning moon was haunted
> By woman wailing for her demon-lover!

The last five lines quoted above have all the carefully selected ingredients beloved by Romantics, while the imagery of a "woman wailing for her demon-lover," though admirably Bürgeresque, is quite out of place in the "instantaneous dream" context; it is a thought-out image, custom-made for the *Monthly Magazine*:

> And from this chasm, with ceaseless turmoil seething,
> As if this earth in fast thick pants were breathing,
> A mighty fountain momently was forced:
> Amid whose swift half-intermitted burst
> Huge fragments vaulted like rebounding hail,
> Or chaffy grain beneath the thresher's flail:
> And mid these dancing rocks at once and ever
> It flung up momently the sacred river.

Again most precise and, one would have hazarded, carefully thought-out imagery. The "chaffy" and "momently" are highly Coleridgean and wholly in the poetic vein that he was at that period pursuing; they are self-conscious words. The stanza continues:

> Five miles meandering with a mazy motion
> Through wood and dale the sacred river ran,
> Then reached the caverns measureless to man,
> And sank in tumult to a lifeless ocean:
> And 'mid this tumult Kubla heard from far
> Ancestral voices prophesying war!

This is not only absolutely beautiful but also marvellously clever, while the last two lines are as skilfully designed a piece of sign-posting as one could hope to find anywhere.

Then comes the sudden change in mood, metre and subject-pattern which is always assumed to indicate opium-influence—a sub-conscious, working at random:

> The shadow of the dome of pleasure
> Floated midway on the waves;
> Where was heard the mingled measure
> From the fountain and the caves.
> It was a miracle of rare device,
> A sunny pleasure-dome with caves of ice!

The first four lines of this stanza convey perfectly an impressionistic, hypnotic dream-cadence. But the final two lines are disconcertingly different. They are not spontaneous impression, but considered comment. The visionary poet is taking a step back from his vision to remark what an excellent vision it is!

In the succeeding stanza he repeats the process, with even greater disillusionment:

> A damsel with a dulcimer
> In a vision once I saw:
> It was an Abyssinian maid
> And on her dulcimer she played,
> Singing of Mount Abora.

Why, if these lines were given to S.T.C. spontaneously during the course of an opium-vision, was it necessary for him, during the course of receiving the lines during that vision, to step back and explain to some third party that this damsel with the dulcimer had once been seen in a vision? The whole set-up, so to speak, is hereby exposed as a confidence-trick; *Kubla Khan* was miraculously delivered to S.T.C. with a reader in mind who, likely to be confused by the sudden appearance of the Abyssinian damsel, required the reassurance of, "Don't worry that this poem is rather inconsequential; I dreamt it all."

However, under normal circumstances the reader of *Kubla Khan* is not permitted time to explore the *bona fide* of the poem. He is swept forward, with breath-taking, thought-suspending flexibility and bravura, upon waves of new rhythm,

> Could I revive within me
> Her symphony and song,
> To such a deep delight 'twould win me
> That with music loud and long,
> I would build that dome in air,
> That sunny dome! those caves of ice!
> And all who heard should see them there,
> And all should cry, Beware! Beware!
> His flashing eyes, his floating hair!
> Weave a circle round him thrice,
> And close your eyes with holy dread,
> For he on honey-dew hath fed,
> And drunk the milk of Paradise.

The haunting final lines, a total *non sequitur* so far as the preceding stanzas are concerned, by their utter inconsequentiality are imbued with the spirit of mystery which heightens the magic of the poem as a whole.

Certainly S.T.C. was turned on when he wrote *Kubla Khan*, but turned on with a controlled touch which suggests that mysterious but undeniable force, the creative imagination of the artist, rather than any substance from the druggist.

Herein lies the secret of the effectiveness of the fraud of *Kubla Khan*. The brilliance of the poetic imagination allied with a superlative technique have resulted in a poem which, with its sudden switches in rhythm and abrupt changes in subject-matter, exactly resembles what persons ignorant of the true nature of material written under drugs and of the extreme control and unrelenting concentration required for poetry of the calibre of *Kubla Khan*, believe an opium-poem would be like.

The Romantic Age was not only highly impressionable, it was also highly credulous. It was an era so susceptible to forgeries and frauds that it virtually begged to be hoodwinked. The forgeries of the boy poet, Chatterton, with his allegedly discovered "curious manuscripts," and James Macpherson's "translations" of the Ossianic poems expose the eager gullibility of the period. In their avidity for extreme sensation people were prepared to accept the most blatant of fakes, so long as the end results were Transports of Rapture, Dejection and Horror. Indeed the ultimate mood of the period was virtually a cult of the fake; a Romantic deception which in turn prompted false reactions of appreciation and a consequent train of artificial emotions which in turn could only breed a sequence of wholly artificial social stances.

In such a climate it was neither exceptional nor difficult for S.T.C. to pass off a poem like *Kubla Khan* (a *tour de force* of musicality that obviously must have been processed through draft after draft) as an opium vision experienced in immediate, perfect verse. *Kubla Khan* is a small masterpiece of confidence trickery; this in no way detracts from the fact that it is also a uniquely beautiful and strangely moving poem.

S.T.C., upon his return to Stowey, sent a completed copy of *Osorio* to William Linley, Sheridan's brother-in-law. Two days later another copy was sent to Sheridan himself, via Bowles. But S.T.C. was no longer optimistic about the drama. "I have no hopes of its success—or even of it's being acted,"[24] he told Thelwall, glumly.

The prospect before S.T.C. was closing in. "I suppose that at last I must become a Unitarian minister as a less evil than starvation—for I get nothing by literature—& Sara is in the way of repairing the ravages of war, as much as in her lies."[25]

Despite this reluctant decision, or at this stage half-decision, to enter the

Unitarian ministry, S.T.C., together with Wordsworth, still continued to nurture schemes for a Bürger-like success in the *Monthly Magazine*. Although S.T.C.'s datings are somewhat confused and unreliable, it seems that a joint composition was attempted now; this was *The Wanderings of Cain*, a tale in the manner of Gessner's *Death of Abel*. But this effort was soon abandoned; "the whole scheme . . . broke up in a laugh; and *The Ancient Mariner* was written instead."[26]

Early in November S.T.C. and the Wordsworths made a walking-tour to Lynton's so-called Valley of the Rocks (already becoming a noted attraction for tourists). As S.T.C. was to tell Hazlitt, later, that this had been the proposed setting for *The Wanderings of Cain* it seems that the poets were still projecting that poem at the time of this tour.

A week after having returned to Stowey from Lynton the party of three set out again, at about four o'clock in the afternoon of November 13. They walked some eight miles, towards Watchet; according to Dorothy the evening was dark and cloudy. As they walked, S.T.C. and Wordsworth planned the outline of a supernatural ballad "in the *style* as well as . . . the spirit of the elder poets," which would recount the adventures of a doomed seaman (an Old Navigator as they, mindful of Shelvocke, called the Ancient Mariner at that stage), condemned forever to circumnavigate the oceans of the world, accompanied by two spectres playing dice for his soul (a theme, it seems, derived from the legend of Falkenberg). Some crime was needed to bring this curse down upon the Old Navigator. The polar imagery of icebergs, floes, fogs and "that giant bird Vuokho," the albatross, already thronged S.T.C.'s mind, together with the spirits drawn from Crantz's *History of Greenland* and used in *The Destiny of Nations*. Wordsworth now made a vital suggestion: "Suppose you represent him [the Old Navigator] as having killed one of these birds on entering the South Sea and that the tutelary Spirits of these regions take upon them to avenge the crime."[27] Wordsworth also suggested the navigation of the ship by dead men. "I . . . do not recollect that I had anything more to do with the scheme of the poem,"[28] he was subsequently to comment.

The poets started to compose the ballad that evening, probably at Watchet, and continued to work on it during the tour; but the theme, from the start, held a peculiar fascination and excitement for S.T.C. and, totally seizing his imagination, quickly carried him headlong into a millrace of composition, so that Wordsworth, feeling himself to be a "clog,"[29] left *The Rime of the Ancyent Marinere* to Coleridge. By November 20 or thereabouts he had composed some three hundred lines;[30] a completed version was ready by March 23, 1798.[31] It was not sent to the *Monthly Magazine* but was used instead to provide the nucleus for *Lyrical Ballads*.

The Ancient Mariner originated as a Gothic foray into the supernatural and the macabre, wholly within the taste of the New Sensibility, but, as S.T.C. worked on it, the poem developed into something very different.

The theme of the two spectres playing dice for the Mariner's soul diminished to a mere passing detail of plot; the true action of the poem became a circumnavigation not only of the globe, but of Samuel Taylor Coleridge, indeed of Man himself. The moral and spiritual implications of the poem are profound, with "a very serious moral and spiritual bearing upon human life."[32] It is one of the foremost instances of a work of genius so far in advance of its day that it was wholly misunderstood and undervalued by contemporary opinion, defying real comprehension until the twentieth century, with its expanded grasp of associational psychology, discovered in the poem what S.T.C.'s contemporaries and immediate successors had been unable to discern.

In essence it now emerges as an essentially autobiographical poem; the salient difference between S.T.C.'s masterpiece and Wordsworth's auto-biographical *Prelude* being that Wordsworth presented his growth of a poet's mind in the form of a detailed looking-back upon a chronological sequence of recollected experiences,

> ... things that may be viewed
> Or fancied in the obscurity of years[33]

and described how he learned from these things.

Coleridge, in *The Ancient Mariner*, foretold the progressive development of the conscious awareness of his "I Am." In other words, *The Prelude* traces in retrospect an expanded state of knowing; *The Ancient Mariner*, by a species of clairvoyance, traces an expanding state of Being. The poet of *The Prelude* searched the past for important landmarks in his process of "knowing what we have learnt to know;" the poet of *The Ancient Mariner* stood perched high on his own ship's masthead, peering into the fog of the future, distinguishing, spread ahead of him in a track of eerie light, the passage-to-be of his I-Am-ness.

Can opium be identified as the medium behind this remarkable act of clairvoyance? Lowes has demonstrated beyond dispute that opium had no connection with *The Ancient Mariner*; neither did S.T.C. ever claim that this poem came to him entire, as a vision. He made no secret of the planning, hard work and time put into its composition.[34] The highly complicated and subtle organisation of the poem (six hundred and fifty-eight lines in all upon its first appearance in *Lyrical Ballads*), its immense technical expertise and, above all, its unrelaxing, yet brilliantly integrated imagery, the manifold sources of which have been traced by the indefatigable Lowes, put opium completely out of the question in the context of *The Ancient Mariner*.

S.T.C., when he wrote the poem, had never made a sea voyage, yet so intensely had he experienced his readings of travellers' tales that his descriptive passages in the poem contain the very essence of ice-fields and fog-banks, storms and tropical calms. The idiom of the poem itself is a feat of assimilation; it is exactly the tone of voice and turn of phrase found in Purchas. It is an Old Navigator who relates this tale, not Coleridge.

All this requires a supreme gift of imagination; but imagination alone cannot explain the uncanny mystery of those passages, particularly in Book IV of the poem, where S.T.C. gives to the Mariner the overwhelming sensations of guilt, despair, isolation and utter desolation which were to be his own experience during the nadir of his drug reliance, but which he had certainly not experienced in 1797. The total aridity of spirit, the awful benumbed sensation of being all alone in an immense expanse of ocean, where no one, not even God, will take pity on him, is a classical plight of the morphine-victim. S.T.C. wrote these lines nearly six years before he arrived at that stage of drug experience.

The same is true of S.T.C.'s symbolic use of the albatross, which, throughout the poem, is far more than a bird, alive or dead. S.T.C. first gives the albatross a moral significance by attaching to it Christian attributes:

> And an it were a Christian Soul,
> We hail'd it in God's name.[35]

> In mist or cloud on mast or shroud
> It perch'd for vespers nine.[36]

As the poem progresses the bird becomes a symbol of a deed of unspeakably wicked betrayal and the destruction of something most precious, a leaden weight of guilt, an inescapable and unbearable reproach constantly staring the Mariner in the face and stinking in his nostrils, until at last the dead bird becomes a torture, a crucifixion:

> Instead of the Cross the Albatross
> About my neck was hung.[37]

Guilt and torment of this dreadful degree S.T.C. was to know, but he had not known it in 1797 when he wrote these lines.

There could be no respite for the Mariner until he had experienced a complete change of heart and, shedding all his arrogance, had humbled himself by submitting to the realisation that the least of God's creatures, even "slimy things" that crawled were, in reality, miracles of creation, possessing great beauty of their own and deserving love and consideration. The realisation of the truth that

> He Prayeth best who loveth best
> All things both great and small:
> For the dear God, who loveth us,
> He made and loveth all.[38]

261

is the pivot upon which the redemption of the Mariner swings. The moment when he sees the amorphous and repulsive "slimy things" as individual and incredibly beautiful water-snakes each swimming in a track of golden fire and he loves them for their integrity and beauty and blesses them, the load of guilt falls from the Mariner:

> O happy living things! no tongue
>   Their beauty might declare:
> A spring of love gusht from my heart,
>   And I bless'd them unaware!
> Sure my kind saint took pity on me,
>   And I bless'd them unaware.
>
> The self-same moment I could pray;
>   And from my neck so free
> The Albatross fell off, and sank
>   Like lead into the sea.[39]

Even so, the Mariner was not yet shrieved of his great sin of betrayal and destruction:

> ... the man hath penance done,
> And penance more will do.[40]

This penance took the form of eternal, compulsive, abrasive confession:

> "O shrieve me, shrieve me, holy Man!"
>   The Hermit cross'd his brow—
> "Say quick", quoth he, "I bid thee say
>   "What manner man art thou?"
>
> Forthwith this frame of mine was wrench'd
>   With a woeful agony,
> Which forc'd me to begin my tale
>   And then it left me free.
>
> Since then at an uncertain hour,
>   Now oftimes and now fewer,
> That anguish comes and makes me tell
>   My ghastly aventure.
>
> I pass, like night, from land to land;
>   I have strange power of speech;
> The moment that his face I see
> I know the man that must hear me;
>   To him my tale I teach.[41]

The above, 1797–8 version of the poem, should be compared with the gloss, or marginal commentary, not published until 1817 (though S.T.C. may have written it considerably earlier). This is written in the character of a God-fearing antiquarian of the early seventeenth century. The gloss on the above verses reads:

> The ancient Mariner earnestly entreateth the Hermit to shrieve him; and the penance of life falls on him.
>
> And ever and anon throughout his future life an agony constraineth him to travel from land to land;
>
> And to teach by his own example, love and reverence to all things that God made and loveth.

> every Thing has a Life of it's own, & . . . we are all *one Life.*[42]

The triumph of *The Ancient Mariner* is that it portrays the salvation of an individual I-ship through an awareness of "All is One and One is All." It is true that no attempt is made to explain the process of salvation; it is left to the Wedding Guest to understand and accept, or reject, the Mariner's message. He, it will be recalled

> . . . went, like one that hath been stunn'd
> And is of sense forlorn:
> A sadder and a wiser man
> He rose the morrow morn.[43]

It would be wrong to attempt to draw parallels throughout the poem between the symbolic experiences of the Mariner and the actual experiences of S.T.C. Yet there is no escaping the strange fact that the poet's own life-story did closely follow the experiences of the voyaging Mariner.

Clairvoyancy or "second sight" is a phenomenon which, although it has been recorded often enough, has never been explained. Neither can we explain that mysterious power known as creative invention, which turns certain people on far more effectively than can any drug. The highest form of imagination is a kind of instinct, or, as S.T.C. himself would have expressed it, an apprehension, rather than a comprehension.

S.T.C. seems never to have been aware that *The Ancient Mariner* was "the great work to be of benefit to mankind" that his friends were always begging him to write. In early April, 1797, S.T.C. told Cottle:

> I should not think of devoting less than 20 years to an Epic Poem. Ten to collect materials and warm my mind with universal science. I would be a

tolerable Mathematician, I would thoroughly know Mechanics, Hydrostatics, Optics, and Astronomy, Botany, Metallurgy, Fossilism, Chemistry, Geology, Anatomy, Medicine—then the *mind of man*—then the *minds of men*—in all Travels, Voyages and Histories. So I would spend ten years—the next five to the composition of the poem—and the last five to the correction of it.

So I would write haply not unhearing of that divine and rightly-whispering Voice, which speaks to mighty minds of predestined Garlands, starry and unwithering.[44]

Apropos of this Cottle was to observe, in his *Reminiscences*:

How much is it to be deplored, that one whose views were so enlarged as those of Mr Coleridge, and his conception so Miltonic, should have been satisfied with theorizing merely; and that he did not, like his great Proto-type, concentrate all his energies, so as to produce some one august poetical work, which should become the glory of his country.

It is ironic that the first publisher of *The Ancient Mariner* never recognised that this poem was a work which would become one of the glories of the English language.

Lowes has given ample evidence that the process of collecting material and warming up his mind, half conscious as the process was, may have taken S.T.C. all of ten years and more. The first edition of the poem took five months, not five years, to complete, but during the ensuing thirty-six years S.T.C. was to subject the poem to repeated alterations and improvement. First published in 1798, *The Ancient Mariner* is the supreme example of the way in which S.T.C. worked and reworked his poems. From the first reprint of *The Ancient Mariner* in 1800 up to the final version of 1834 there is no edition of the poem which does not contain amendments, some of them of vital importance.

For the 1800 edition of *Lyrical Ballads* S.T.C. thoroughly revised the poem, removing the more blatant archaisms. Further important improvements, among them inclusion of the marginal gloss, had been made in the poem when it appeared in *Sibylline Leaves* in 1817. The marvellous marginal commentary "No twilight within the courts of the sun" (appended to the lines commencing, "The Sun's rim dips; the stars rush out") was not inserted until 1828.

By the end of November 1797, S.T.C. and Wordsworth were thinking of printing *The Ancient Mariner* together with other poems, mainly by Wordsworth, thereby making a small volume of joint work, rather than trying to sell the long poem to the *Monthly Magazine*. In January S.T.C. was so desperately short of money that he was once more speaking of selling *The Ancient Mariner* separately.[45] In February, 1798, and again in mid-March, he was discussing with Cottle plans for an enlarged third edition of his *Poems on Various Subjects*, in which *The Ancient Mariner* would be included. No such third edition materialised; instead Cottle was approached by S.T.C. and Wordsworth jointly with the suggestion that he should publish their tragedies in one joint volume, with a second small volume of verse by Wordsworth. A series of negotiations took place over the next few weeks during which Cottle, showing active interest, visited Alfoxden for discussion.

While these negotiations were in progress Wordsworth experienced a great outburst of frenetic creative energy.

He and S.T.C. were now working to a dual plan of composition; Wordsworth choosing subjects, characters and incidents from ordinary life, to which he proposed to give "the charm of novelty . . . by awakening the mind's attention from the lethargy of custom, and directing it to the loveliness and the wonders of the world before us," while S.T.C. directed his endeavours to "persons and characters supernatural, or at least romantic," to be used in poems composed with a regard for "human interest and a semblance of truth sufficient to procure for these shadows of imagination that willing suspension of disbelief, for the moment, which constitutes poetic faith."[46]

The poetic rôle allotted to Wordsworth within this framework wholly suited him. It enabled him to explore and work through his theory of poetic diction and to experiment with "poetry . . . not unimportant in the multiplicity and the quality of its moral relations."[47] S.T.C.'s assignment of supernatural and romantic subjects placed him, on the other hand, in an untenable position.

Anything that he might have attempted in that *genre* would have come as an anticlimax in the wake of *The Ancient Mariner*. The short poems which he wrote that spring of 1798, the exquisite and contemplative *Frost at Midnight* and the "conversational" poem, *The Nightingale*, reveal the superlative pitch which S.T.C. was now attaining in this kind of direct and intimate blank-verse—an experiment in spontaneous philosophical soliloquising. S.T.C. dissipated his own great leap forward as a poet in attempting Gothic-style ballads in which he did not really believe. His technical expertise and powers of imagination were of a calibre to ensure that what he wrote would be interesting, often arresting (in the case of *Christabel* the result was brilliant) but he could finish none of the several ballads which he attempted at this time, not even Christabel; they either dried up or turned sour on him.

In short, while S.T.C. undoubtedly owed much of his gigantic breakthrough in poetry to the stimulus of Wordsworth's company and conversation, actual partnership in the production of a volume of poems written to a scheme proved to be an abortive experience for S.T.C. In 1818 he was to speak of Wordsworth's "cold praise and effective discouragement of every attempt of mine to roll onward in a distinct current of my own,"[48] and though S.T.C. was here doubtless specifically referring to developments belonging to a later date, even so early as 1798, working in conjunction with Wordsworth, S.T.C.'s attempts to roll on in a distinct current of his own were inhibited. *The Ancient Mariner* and the conversational soliloquies were the true Esteesian philosophical current—not *The Three Graves* and *The Ballad of the Dark Ladie*, not even *Christabel*, however much that beautiful blood-curdler has been admired.

Because S.T.C. could not complete any of the supernatural poems projected as his contribution, the planned volume of poems became but a slender one, with *The Ancient Mariner*, originally thought of as the nucleus of the joint work, standing isolated; "an interpolation of heterogenous matter" as S.T.C. was to say in a note of 1817.

Cottle visited Stowey in late March or early April, apparently with an offer to publish the work of the two poets separately; this they refused. In May it was decided to make up a single volume out of poems already written.

Among the poems written by Wordsworth during the Alfoxden period are two exceedingly significant ones, neither of which found a place in *Lyrical Ballads*. The first, originally called *Travelling*, and later entitled *This Is The Spot** is known to have been addressed to Dorothy:

> This is the spot:—how mildly does the sun
> Shine in between the fading leaves! the air
> In the habitual silence of this wood
> Is more than silent; and this bed of heath—
> Where shall we find so sweet a resting-place?
> Come, let me see thee sink into a dream
> Of quiet thoughts, protracted till thine eye
> Be calm as water when the winds are gone
> And no one can tell whither. My sweet Friend,
> We two have had such happy hours together
> That my heart melts in me to think of it.

The second, never published in Wordsworth's lifetime, was discovered in his Alfoxden notebook for 1798:

> Away, away, it is the air
>   That stirs among the withered leaves;
> Away, away, it is not there,
> Go, hunt among the harvest-sheaves,

*The last six lines are included in the second part of the *Ode to Lycoris* (Dorothy), written in 1817 (P.W. IV. 97).

There is a bed in shape as plain
As from a hare or lion's lair
It is the bed where we have lain
In anguish and despair.

Away, and take the eagle's eye
   The tyger's smell,
Ears that can hear the agonies
And murmurings of hell:
And when you there have stood
By that same bed of pain,
The groans are gone, the tears remain.
Then tell me if the thing be clear,
   The difference betwixt a tear
Of water and of blood.

Blood is thicker than water? Is this poem a confession, in heavily veiled terms, that the innocent fraternal love of Chateaubriand's *Atala*, when practised in real life at Alfoxden, had brought in its train the "agonies and murmurings" of a hell which neither brother nor sister had anticipated in their initial fervour for the New Sensibility's favourite relationship? It may well have been so.

By November, 1797, S.T.C. had given up all hope of *Osorio*. No word had been heard from Sheridan; as S.T.C. said, he had not received even common courtesy from that quarter. To divert himself, S.T.C. wrote a group of parodies, *Sonnets attempted in the Manner of Contemporary Writers*. These caused a serious rift between Lamb, Lloyd, Southey and S.T.C., who, disguised as Nehemiah Higginbottom, had, with the sonnets, severely damaged the susceptibilities of these three fellow poets. While the Higginbottom furore was in progress S.T.C. was obliged to make his Hobson's choice of the Unitarian ministry as a future full-time occupation. He approached his Unitarian friends, soliciting their help in finding him a congregation. Fate now intervened on S.T.C.'s behalf, first in the shape of Mackintosh, who persuaded Daniel Stuart to give S.T.C. a trial as a regular weekly contributor to the *Morning Post*, at a guinea a week, this salary to be increased if the connection proved agreeable to both parties. (Mackintosh may also have influenced the Wedgwoods in their decision to help S.T.C. though upon this point there is no direct evidence.)[49]

S.T.C. accepted the offer from Stuart and commenced his weekly contributions on December 7, 1797.

Events of a most complicated and wholly Esteesian character began to crowd one upon the other.

On Christmas Day S.T.C. received two letters, one offering him the chance to become Unitarian minister at Shrewsbury, the other containing a draft for a hundred pounds from Josiah and Tom Wedgwood. S.T.C. was placed in a quandary of indecision. Poole strenuously urged him to accept the draft and finally, on December 27, S.T.C. wrote the Wedgwoods a letter of acceptance. He had no sooner done so than there arrived a letter from Shrewsbury officially requesting S.T.C. to become minister there. This offer was largely due to the efforts of Estlin, and S.T.C. could not bear to think of the disappointment it would cause in that quarter if he now refused the offer. On the other hand, if he changed his mind about the Wedgwood draft, S.T.C. would run the risk of losing their interest and esteem. After a week of further desperation, S.T.C. returned the draft to the Wedgwoods.

S.T.C.'s reason for this decision was, he explained, that, although the sum of a hundred pounds would enable him to live for the next two years in leisure and comfort, writing what he chose to write rather than what would sell, "anxiety for the future would remain & increase, as it is probable that my children will come fast on me . . . and Anxiety, with me, always induces Sickliness, and too often Sloth" (sloth here being an obvious euphemism for opium).[50]

Thus, it was to be the Unitarian ministry. The decision taken, S.T.C. set about borrowing money from friends in order to pay off twenty pounds in small debts, among them a quarter's rent at two guineas, sundry small tradesmen's bills, and the maid's wages of one guinea.[51] On Saturday, January 13, S.T.C. set off for Shrewsbury, leaving behind him a baffled and despondent Poole.

A second letter from the Wedgwoods arrived at Stowey a few hours after S.T.C. had left for Shrewsbury. Poole (who in S.T.C.'s absence handled his friend's affairs) opened it and at once forwarded it to S.T.C., with an enclosed note urging S.T.C. to accept the proposal here put forward. This was that S.T.C. should accept an annuity for life of a hundred and fifty pounds, no conditions whatsoever being annexed to it. "Thus," wrote Josiah Wedgwood, "your liberty will remain entire, you will be under the influence of no professional bias, & will be in possession of a 'permanent income not inconsistent with your religious & political creeds' so necessary to your health & activity."[52]

Hazlitt, whose father was a Dissenting Minister at Wem, not far from Shrewsbury, has left us a most succinct portrait of S.T.C. at this crossroads:

in the year 1798 . . . Mr Coleridge came to Shrewsbury, to succeed Mr Rowe in . . . charge of a Unitarian congregation there. He did not come until late on the Saturday afternoon before he was to preach; and Mr Rowe, who himself went down to the coach . . . could find no one at all answering the description but a round-faced man, in a short black jacket (like a shooting-jacket) which hardly seemed to have been made for him, but who seemed to be talking at a great rate to his fellow-passengers. Mr Rowe had scarce returned to give an account of his disappointment when the round-faced man in black entered, and dissipated all doubts on the subject by beginning to talk. He did not cease while he stayed; nor has he since, that I know of . . . I had heard a great deal of his powers of conversation, and was not disappointed. In fact, I never met with anything at all like them, before or since . . . He told me in confidence that he should have preached two sermons before he accepted the situation at Shrewsbury, one on Infant Baptism, the other on the Lord's Supper, shewing that he could not administer either, which would have effectually disqualified him for the object in view.[53]

S.T.C., as probable successor to Mr Rowe, paid a courtesy visit to Hazlitt Senior, dined at his house and spent the night. When young Hazlitt came down to breakfast in the morning he found that S.T.C. had just received the letter from the Wedgwoods containing the offer of the annuity. Coleridge, observed Hazlitt, "seemed to make up his mind to close with this proposal in the act of tying on one of his shoes."[54]

When Poole learned that S.T.C. had accepted this offer his joy knew no bounds; he was so happy, he told S.T.C., that, he "went to a party . . . and was never so cheerful; never *sung* so well, never so witty, never so agreeable, —so I was told ten times over! They little knew the cause which made joy beam from every feature and action."[55]

One result of the Wedgwood generosity was that S.T.C. was now able to turn his thoughts to the project, so long dear to him, of resuming his university studies. "I . . . have just knowledge enough of most things to feel my ignorance of all things,"[56] he had told Estlin. The Wedgwood annuity would enable S.T.C. to go to Jena, there to pursue the course of study that he had first outlined to Poole two years previously.[57] S.T.C. would take his family with him.

The Wordsworths began to talk of accompanying the Coleridges. Mrs St Albyn had positively refused to renew the Wordsworths' tenure of Alfoxden; they found themselves without a home. Wordsworth, in a letter of March 11 to James Losh, said that he and Dorothy were thinking of going to Germany for two years to learn German and natural science. They would live, they hoped, in a village near a university. Wordsworth suggested that Losh and his wife might join the party which would be, said Wordsworth, a "little colony."[58]

In April S.T.C. paid a brief visit to Ottery. In April, too, was published Lloyd's novel, *Edmund Oliver*, which at first greatly distressed S.T.C. The novel brought in its wake an outbreak of gossip, quarrelling and discord. S.T.C., as a result, became seriously estranged from Lamb (the friendship was not resumed until early in 1800). Lloyd wrote malicious letters to all and sundry, including one to Dorothy, calling S.T.C. a villain. Dorothy, in tears, showed the letter to S.T.C.; he had the strength of mind to laugh at it.[59] Lloyd's behaviour, S.T.C. perceived, "was not that of a fiend, only because it was that of a madman."[60] On the other hand S.T.C., rightly or wrongly, traced Lloyd's attacks back to the smouldering animosity of Southey; Lloyd's infirmities, S.T.C. decided, had been made "the instruments of another man's darker passions."[61]

On May 14 Sara was safely delivered of a fine boy, who was named Berkeley, in honour of the Bishop. Hartley, at this time, was ill with an ugly cough and temperature; the anxious parents feared the whooping-cough, but decided at last that it was teething trouble.

Hazlitt came upon a three-week visit to Stowey (*circa* May 20 to June 11). S.T.C. and his friend Chester marched Hazlitt to Lynton and back. After Hazlitt's departure S.T.C. went to visit the Wedgwoods at Stoke, near Cobham in Surrey. Meantime the Wordsworths, upon their removal from Alfoxden, stayed with Sara Coleridge at Stowey until July 2 and then made a visit to Tintern followed by a walking-tour up the Wye, returning to lodgings at Bristol, where they remained in order to see *Lyrical Ballads* through the press.

S.T.C., after visiting the Wedgwoods, travelled to London. Finally back in Bristol and reunited with the Wordsworths he suggested to them, apparently upon the spur of the moment, that they should go with him to pay a flying visit to Thelwall in Wales. Next morning at six o'clock the trio set off. A week was spent with Thelwall at Llyswen in Brecknockshire.

By this time S.T.C. was beginning to have second thoughts concerning the practicality of taking Sara and two infant children with him to Germany. Neither, it seems, was Sara's heart set upon the scheme.[62] It was decided, therefore, that S.T.C. should go without her. She would remain with her children at Stowey, under Poole's watchful and affectionate eye.

Lyrical Ballads was printed and a few copies distributed by Cottle during that summer; the impression, for reasons not wholly clear, was subsequently transferred to J. and A. Arch, a firm of London booksellers, who published the book on October 4 of that year.[63] By this time S.T.C. and the Wordsworths were in Germany. The first reviews were unenthusiastic and sales were meagre. Wordsworth's poems, upon the whole, were not unkindly treated by the leading reviewers, but *The Ancient Mariner* was ill-received. Southey, in the *Critical Review* for October 1798 declared dourly: "Genius has here been employed in producing a poem of little merit."

CHAPTER ELEVEN

EPITAPHS

(September 1798-June 1799)

ON SEPTEMBER 16, S.T.C., John Chester and the Wordsworths set sail for Germany from Yarmouth.

The passage to Cuxhaven lasted forty-eight hours and was a rough one. The Wordsworths and Chester became sea-sick immediately that the packet moved from harbour into the open sea: "Chester began to look Frog-coloured and doleful—Miss Wordsworth retired in confusion to the Cabin—Wordsworth soon followed."[1] They suffered throughout the entire voyage. Dorothy was the worst afflicted, "vomiting, & groaning, unspeakably! And I neither sick nor giddy, but gay as a lark,"[2] reported S.T.C. triumphantly.

It was the first time that the author of *The Ancient Mariner* had ever made a sea voyage. S.T.C. noted in his pocket-book:

> The Ocean is a noble Thing by night—the foam that dashes against the vessel, beautiful. White clouds of Foam roaring & rushing by the side of the vessel with multitudes of stars of flame . . .[3]

> . . . & every now and then light Detachments of Foam dart away from the vessel's side with their galaxies of stars, & scour out of sight, like a Tartar Troop over a Wilderness!—.[4]

While the sea-sick passengers lay in misery below, the good sailors congregated on deck to talk and be sociable. The time, so far as S.T.C. was concerned, "passed merrily."[5] Because he was dressed in black his companions supposed him to be a priest. S.T.C. explained that he was a philosopher. He then proceeded to behave most philosophically, becoming rather drunk and enjoying himself immensely, with

> excellent wine . . . Grapes & part of a pine-apple . . . Every now and then I entered into the feelings of my poor friends below, who in all their agonies of sea-sickness heard us most distinctly, spouting, singing, laughing, fencing, dancing country dances—in a word being Bacchanals.[6]

At four o'clock in the morning of September 18 S.T.C. was awakened from a nap by shouts of "Land! Land! . . . It was an ugly Island Rock . . . called Helgoland."[7] About nine they sighted the dreary, flat-coasted mainland; at eleven they berthed at Cuxhaven.

A few passengers went ashore; the captain of the packet agreed to take the rest up the Elbe to Hamburg for ten guineas all told. (S.T.C.'s share of this came to half a guinea. The total cost of his journey from Yarmouth to Hamburg was six pounds fourteen shillings and sixpence, including porterage, provisioning and tips to the crew.) When night fell the packet anchored, for the Elbe was perilous to navigate. S.T.C. seized the opportunity to write home: "Over what place does the Moon hang to your eyes, my dearest Sara? To me it hangs over the left bank of the Elbe." The letter ended lovingly: "Good night, my dear, dear Sara!—'every night when I go to bed & every morning when I rise' I will think of you with a yearning love, & of my blessed Babies!—Once more, my dear Sara! good night—." Then, with practical affection: "Did you receive my letter, *directed* in a different hand with the 30£ Bank Note?—"[8]

On Wednesday, September 19, the travellers arrrived at Hamburg, which proved to be "an ugly City that stinks in every corner,"[9] or so S.T.C. found it. Lodgings were scarce and expensive (however, excellent claret could be obtained for a trifle).*

Within ten days S.T.C. and the Wordsworths had decided to separate. There is no reason to suppose that the friends had fallen out (whatever Wordsworthian reservations there might have been concerning the Bacchanalian revelries aboard the packet). The ostensible reason for the separation was that Germany was a great deal more expensive than the travellers had anticipated: S.T.C., although Wedgwood-financed, had to abandon all thoughts of going to either Weimar or Eisenach; he decided to settle for three or four months in Ratzeburg instead. The Wordsworths "determined to go on, & seek lower down, obscurer & cheaper Lodgings without boarding."[10] As a result of their decision, they went to Goslar.

In England the news of this separation of S.T.C. and the Wordsworths was greeted with joy by the friends of the former. Poole wrote to S.T.C., on October 8, 1798: "The Wordsworths have left you—so there is an end to our tease about amalgamation, etc. etc. I think you both did perfectly right."[11]

Josiah Wedgwood confided to Poole that he hoped that Wordsworth and S.T.C. would continue separated: "I am persuaded that Coleridge will derive great benefit from being thrown into mixed society."[12]

Lamb, in a letter to Southey, allowed himself a touch of rare malice: "I hear that the Two Noble Englishmen have parted . . . but I have not heard the reason—possibly, to give novelists an handle to exclaim, 'Ah me! what things are perfect?' "[13]

An aura of mystery, never yet really dispelled, hangs over the Words-

*S.T.C. documented his German tour fully in letters to Sara and to Poole and in a journal that he kept for them as augmentation of the letters. Part of this journal was revised and published as *Satyrane's Letters* (*The Friend*), 1809, and *Biog. Lit.* 1817.

worths in Germany. S.T.C. himself, closer to them at that date than anyone else, seems to have been at a loss to explain their behaviour. He must have been considerably dismayed when they, who had decided to travel with him to Germany not only (ostensibly) to learn German but to retain his company, shortly after arrival there deliberately cut themselves off from his society and chose oblivion, exclusively in one another's company.

The Wordsworths dropped out of reach and cognizance like two ravens locked in love embrace dropping out of the sky.

They departed for Goslar on October 3. On November 8 S.T.C. told Sara: "We have not heard from the Wordsworths—to my great Anxiety & inexpressible Astonishment. Where they are, or why they are silent, I cannot even guess."[14] On November 20, however, S.T.C. informed Poole that he had at last heard from Wordsworth, who had been at Goslar for the past six weeks. Wordsworth explained that his violent hatred of letter-writing had caused his ominous silence. (It was S.T.C. who named it ominous. As Lamb was later to point out, Wordsworth was only a reluctant letter writer when he chose to be.)

William's voiced intention upon leaving England was a mastery of the German language, but his behaviour in Germany made a nonsense of this as a serious reason for the visit. In order to learn German fluently, constant social intercourse was a necessity. The Wordsworths knew but a smattering of German and had no introductions; their one hope of meeting and conversing with Germans lay in their remaining with S.T.C., who was in a far better position than they to make social contacts. Instead, brother and sister deliberately lost touch with S.T.C. and placed themselves in a position of total isolation and seclusion.

In Goslar the Wordsworths obtained rooms in the house of a linen-draper. S.T.C., in the letter of November 20, repeated to Poole some of William's comments,

> provisions very cheap, & lodgings very cheap, but no Society—and therefore as he did not come into Germany to learn the Language by a Dictionary he must remove: which he means to do at the end of the month . . . Dorothy says—'William works hard, but not very much at the German.'— This is strange—I work at nothing else, from morning to night—[15]

In reply to William, S.T.C. offered advice upon the problem of social intercourse for the Wordsworths in Germany:

> You have two things against you: your not loving smoke; and your sister. If the manners at Goslar resemble those at Ratzburg, it is almost necessary to be able to bear smoke. Can Dorothy endure smoke? Here, when my friends come to see me, the candle nearly goes out, the air is so thick.[16]

Dorothy herself observed that "in Germany a man travelling alone may do very well, but, if his wife or sister goes with him, he must give entertainments."[17] The Wordsworths could not afford entertainments but neither, it seems, did they desire them. Despite their total isolation in Goslar, and their avowed intention of leaving by the end of November, they remained there until mid-January.*

The winter of 1798–99 was the coldest of the century. The Wordsworths, immured by the weather, their frugality, their *unseekingness* (as S.T.C. called it) and their total absorption in each other, scarcely stirred, it seems, from their lodgings. William would occasionally venture out after donning a "fur gown and a black fur cap in which he looks like any grand signior,"[18] as Dorothy dotingly reported.

During these long weeks of winter in Goslar, William exploded into another great, creative upsurge. From his pen flowed the wonderful boyhood passages of *The Prelude*, the mysteriously beautiful and unique Lucy poems, *Ruth* and the Matthew poems.

S.T.C. commented to Sara,

> [Wordsworth] . . . seems to have employed more time in writing English than in studying German—No wonder! for he might as well have been in England as at Goslar, in the situation which he chose, & with his *unseeking* manners . . . His taking his Sister with him was a wrong step—it is next to impossible for any but married women . . . to be introduced to any company in Germany. Sister is considered as only a name for Mistress . . . however *male* acquaintance he might have had . . . but W., God love him! seems to have lost his spirits & almost his inclination for it.[19]

The sojourn of the Wordsworths in Germany becomes increasingly remarkable the more it is scrutinised.

Let us accept that they, in perfectly good faith, decided to go to Germany to learn the language and to enjoy the company of S.T.C. and that, upon arrival there, they found that this would involve them in too great expense, whereat, in the interests of economy, they plunged themselves into the obscurity of Goslar; and that William, seized by inspiration, abandoned his attempts to learn German and gave himself instead to composition. Reading what he wrote in Goslar, we come across lines *Writen in Germany, on one of the coldest days of the Century*. These describe the misfortunes of a wretched fly who, seduced by the heat from the stove in the Wordsworths' living-room, crawled forth from his "winter retreat" to fumble about the

---

*They had quitted Goslar by January 14, 1799; on the twenty-seventh day of that month they arrived in Nordhausen. (In April they were to pass through Göttingen on their way back to England. Where they had been or what they had been doing between their arrival in Nordhausen and their appearance in Göttingen is not known to us.)

oven top and, after much dismal creeping back and forth, stopped stock-still, bemazed. The poet compared the fly's lot with his own:

> No brother, no friend has he near him,—while I
> Can draw warmth from the cheek of my love:
> As blest and as glad in this desolate gloom,
> As if green summer grass were the floor of my room,
> And woodbines were hanging above.

This seems explicit enough.

We can, if we choose, urge poetic licence, point out that convention demanded that a simple philosophic versifier must have his innocent love against whose cheek he might press his own, recall that few readers would appreciate that the poet who wrote these lines was living exclusively in the company of his sister. All these explanations may, and should be, put forward. Once again we should remind ourselves of the fashionable posturing of disciples of the New Sensibility; of the divergence, so often revealed, between what the Wordsworths preached and what they practised; we must make every allowance for Romantic hyperbole.

Yet, when all this is said, we are still up against the incontestable fact that the Wordsworths, by choice, sequestered themselves for months on end, under most intimate living conditions, in a country where nobody knew them and where, resultantly, they were not exposed to the consequences of gossip. While living together, thus, Wordsworth wrote poetry in which he referred to his sister as if she were his mistress.

The spate of great poetry which flowed from William in Goslar is explained (even more so than was the Alfoxden upsweep into passionate creative energy) by the close presence of his Muse, Dorothy. At Goslar William and his White Goddess were one. The immense chords now heard in Wordsworth's song are not those of a man who occasionally gave his Muse a chaste peck on the cheek or a pat on the hand.

Wordsworth, discussing in later life with De Quincey the intensity of reception of impressions and the phenomena of imagination and total recovery of memory, remarked that he had discovered that his senses and feelings were particularly impressionable in the first relaxed moments following an effort of concentration.

One does not need to be a poet to know that there are certain moments in a love affair when the mind is opened up as effectively as by any drug; concentration relaxes, strange curtains are drawn back and a brilliant light streams into the recesses of closeted memory, revealing every detail of a room once well known but now far distant: a childhood playground, a seashore or a stable-loft, a garden with bee-hives, a narrow lane with butterflies, a kitchen, a school-room. Unbidden they return, allowing time for astonished and delighted exploration in every detail (the polar-bear-skin rug, the holiday trunk, the dolls in the corner, the china on the dresser, the pink saucer with the brown sugar in it; yes, dear objects, all are there). Wordsworth's mind was opened at Goslar; there returned the glimmering lake; the smooth green turf where the woodcocks ran; the little boat tied to the willow tree. Out of the mists came the girl with the pitcher on her head, not, as yet, to take her place in *The Prelude*, but to inspire verses written in commemoration and celebration of a child of Nature—the Lucy poems* and *Ruth*.

The girl haunting the poet in the Lucy poems is a spirit of wild places and dream-love, a vagrant wraith of Romantic imagination. What little tangibility she possesses seems to stem from that first love whom Wordsworth discovered in the fell-country landscape of

> ... bare common
> A naked pool that lay beneath the hills,
> The beacon on the summit.

The 1799 MS of *'She Dwelt Among Th'Untrodden Ways'* tells us that Lucy lived but a brief life:

> And she was graceful as the broom
> That flowers by Carron's side;
> But slow distemper checked her bloom,
> And on the heath she died.

Again, in the fourth poem of the group, *'Three Years She Grew'*, we are told:

> How soon my Lucy's race was run!
> She died, and left to me
> This heath, this calm and quiet scene:
> The memory of what has been
> And never more will be.

It is perhaps worth bearing in mind that tuberculosis was rife in the Lake Country during the eighteenth and nineteenth centuries; there was a particularly high mortality rate among the young. Wordsworth's first love may well have been one such victim.

These rare moments of verisimilitude sound here and there in the dreamy strange music of the Lucy poems, all four of which are laments, but laments of a peculiarly haunting, mysterious nature, not so much for one specific girl, or love, but reminiscent rather of those Highland (or Breton) laments which one hears played upon bagpipes in a lonely evening place—laments

*'*Strange Fits of Passion I Have Known'*, *'She Dwelt Among Th'Untrodden Ways'*, *'A Slumber Did My Spirit Seal'*, *'Three Years She Grew in Sun and Shower'*.

for all transient beauties, all the inevitable destructions of ravaging time. The poems culminate in the incredible lines:

> A slumber did my spirit seal;
> I had no human fears:
> She seemed a thing that could not feel
> The touch of earthly years.
>
> No motion has she now, no force;
> She neither hears nor sees,
> Rolled round in earth's diurnal course
> With rocks and stones and trees.

Wordsworth sent a copy of these lines to S.T.C. who found them "most sublime."[20] Being a poet himself, he knew the total fatuity of the layman's eternal demand for elucidation. Sensing in the passion and mystery of these lines experience too deep to be dredged up for pat exposition, S.T.C. fobbed Poole off when that worthy tanner, shown Wordsworth's "sublime epitaph," requested an explanation. Whose epitaph was it? enquired Poole. S.T.C.'s reply was calculatedly vague; he could not say if the lines had "any reality . . . Most probably, in some gloomier moment he [Wordsworth] had fancied the moment in which his sister might die."[21]

The choice of the name "Lucy" for the girl in these poems is of no real significance; we should not conclude that William's first love was named Lucy. This was a name much favoured by English Romantic poets for their rustic heroines. Wordsworth, on occasion, referred to Dorothy as "Lucy"; this was when he wished to present her in the guise of natural simplicity. Emma (another Romantic name) was also his soubriquet for Dorothy. At Goslar he used the name Lucy in several of his poems: in the famous verses which are placed together under that name, in the ballad *Lucy Gray* and in the fragment, *Nutting*.

Although Dorothy herself was not the actual Lucy of these poems, she was in some measure the inspiration behind them, for it was surely her intimate presence which inspired Wordsworth in Goslar. S.T.C. seemed to have been of the opinion that Wordsworth might have written these poems as well in England as in Germany.[22] It is doubtful, however, whether Wordsworth could have discovered the precise alchemy, had he remained in England. We almost certainly would have had the opening books of *The Prelude* in some form (perhaps lacking some of their marvellously vivid impact) but we very possibly might never have had the Lucy poems.

It is important not to allow reverence for the Wordsworths to suspend our powers of judgement. Viewing their relationship objectively, we must admit that every fact that we know about them indicates an incestuous relationship; indeed, there is more hard factual evidence to support the allegations of such a relationship than can possibly be brought forward to refute it. Only the pious belief that the Wordsworths "were not that kind of person" can be reiterated, finally, as refutation of their incest. But upon what grounds can we maintain that they were not "that kind of person?" Incestuous relationships are of far greater occurrence, in all walks of life, than is usually assumed. The Wordsworths themselves have supplied abundant written testimony of their mutual infatuation. We may, if we insist, attribute it all to poetic licence and Romantic exaggeration, or consider it as manifestation of a particularly rare understanding between brother and sister. In adopting this partisan and prejudiced stance we can only fail to understand the Wordsworths.

The very core of William Wordsworth, both as poet and man, vibrated for and with Dorothy. She reciprocated with all her heart. They were obsessed with one another.

There seem to be two major reasons for this tragic state of affairs. The first was, undoubtedly, that they rediscovered one another at a most dangerous time—late adolescence. The second reason, in all probability, was their conditioning by the climate of the New Sensibility.

Is it possible for a man who (at first perhaps purely for voguishly intellectual reasons) professes an ecstatic "fraternal" love for his sister and in due course comes to address her poetically as he would his mistress, to avoid developing incestuous feelings for her? Is it possible for a woman to reside in intimate proximity with such a man, knowing that he refers to her in effect as his mistress, without her coming, at last, to see herself in that rôle? Once these two persons have viewed one another in the fantasy rôle of lover and mistress will they, living together in privacy and intimacy, be able to avoid acting out the fantasy situation? And was not that fantasy situation initially based upon desire? The fact that the desire was taboo, impossible to avow openly, accounted for the necessity of inventing a fantasy situation in the first place. The players, once acclimatised to the full implications of the fantasy situation, may then move on to a plane of active reality.

It seems virtually certain that such was the predicament of the Wordsworths. It was tragedy indeed. Their moments of delight were always counterbalanced by moments of anguish. The relationship only too obviously became agonising for them both; as each was to make very clear. Their lives were often rendered unbearable by their love. (It is more than probable that Dorothy's sanity was ultimately sacrificed in the cause of attempting to come to terms with it.)

Ratzeburg, whither S.T.C. and Chester had removed upon September 30, proved an agreeable town with plenty of society. S.T.C., never troubled with difficulties when it came to making friends, was soon being invited to parties, dinners, balls and concerts galore: "I am pressed by all the Ladies to dance . . . But . . . I am in no dancing mood,"[23] he told Sara in a letter of November 26.

His dejection was due to lack of letters from home. On October 20 we find him imploring Sara: "God bless you, my love! write me a very, very long letter—write me all that can cheer me—all that will make my eyes swim & my heart melt with tenderness!"[24] So great was his homesickness that he himself could not take pen in hand without tears.[25] A month later he was becoming even more desperate for news from home: "My beloved Poole—How comes it that I hear from none of you?—Since yours of the 8th of October, there has been a dreary Silence . . . and no hour passes in which my anxiety about you does not for a few minutes turn me away from my studies."[26]

To Sara ever more frantic pleas were addressed:

Another and another, and yet another Post day; and still Chester greets me with, 'No letters from England!' . . . How is this my Love? Why do you not write to me?—Do you think to shorten my absence by making it insupportable to me?—Or perhaps you anticipate that if I received a letter, I should idly turn away from my German to *dream* of you—of you & my beloved babies!—Oh yes!—I should indeed dream of you for hours and hours; of you, and of beloved Poole, and of the Infant that sucks at your breast, and of my dear dear Hartley—You would be *present* . . . and . . . with what leaping and exhilarated faculties should I return to the objects & realities of my mission.—But now—nay, I cannot describe to you the gloominess of Thought, the burthen and Sickness of heart, which I experience every day.[27]

The inevitable happened; S.T.C. became feverish, with a throbbing head, "rheumatic heats,"[28] enormously swollen eye-lids and insomnia. "I have taken physic"[29] all too obviously means laudanum.

When news at last came from Sara it was to tell S.T.C. that the infant Berkeley had been dangerously ill following a smallpox injection. Rightly or wrongly, Sara poured out all her feelings in this letter, which concluded with the happier assurance that the child was at last recovering.

On receiving this news the overwrought S.T.C. burst into floods of tears: "I cried myself blind . . . when I ought to have been on my knees in the joy of thanksgiving."[30] "When I read of the danger and the agony—My dear Sara!—my love! my Wife!—God bless you & preserve us . . . believe and know that I pant to be home with you."[31]

Poole, who had not wanted S.T.C. to be told about Berkeley's illness, quickly followed Sara's letter with a bluff morale-raiser: "Berkeley was, as you have heard, well-peppered with the smallpox, but never in any danger . . . He is a delightful boy, and we begin to think him very like you . . . Hartley speaks everything, and knows two or three letters."[32]

Adverse winds meant that this letter (written on November 24) did not reach S.T.C. until January 4 of the new year (1799). During December he received no mail from home. His anxiety for his family was allayed by Sara's joyful hopes of little Berkeley's speedy and full recovery, an optimism born of the poignant smile that her "sweet Berkeley" had given her upon wakening from his healing sleep after turning the point of recovery from the smallpox, a smile of total rapport between mother and child, a smile which Sara would remember always.[33]

During the final weeks of 1798 S.T.C. regained much of his tranquillity of mind and, consequently, his health. Social gaieties were resumed, including skating upon the now frozen lake. S.T.C. was unwise enough to send Dorothy an account of this new amusement. It drew a stiff reprimand:

> You speak in rapture of the pleasures of skaiting . . . in the North of England amongst the mountains whither we wish to decoy you, you might enjoy it with every possible advantage. A race with William upon his native lakes would leave to the heart and the imagination something more Dear and valuable than the gay sight of Ladies and countesses whirling along the lake of Ratzeberg [sic].[34]

Mere fragments have survived of the correspondence between S.T.C. and the Wordsworths while in Germany, but there is sufficient to reveal that there had now commenced a tug-of-war between Wordsworth and Poole for possession of S.T.C. The Wordsworths were dreaming of living in the north when they returned to England; Dorothy had openly admitted their intention of "decoying" S.T.C. thence, while Wordsworth, as inducement, informed S.T.C. that he thought that he might procure a house near Sir Wilfred Lawson's library in the Lake Country.

Poole had told S.T.C.: "I will not part from you if you will not part from me."[35] S.T.C., torn between his two friends and desirous of hurting neither, seems to have promised each that he would not desert them. To William S.T.C. wrote: "I am sure I need not say how you are incorporated into the better part of my being; how, whenever I spring forward into the future with noble affections, I always alight by your side."[36] To Poole S.T.C. wrote: "[Wordsworth] cannot think of settling at a distance from *me*, & I have told him that I *cannot* leave the vicinity of Stowey."[37] S.T.C. asked Poole to look out for a new house for him near Stowey; he could not remain in the old cottage, which was too small either for work or comfort.

With the New Year the wind changed, bringing mail once more from England. The first letter to arrive was from Poole, but S.T.C. was by now in a fever of impatience for news from Sara. When at length her letter arrived S.T.C. held it in his hand, stupidly, making no attempt to open it. "Why don't you read the letter?"[38] asked the puzzled Chester. S.T.C. read it.

Sara sent deeply disquieting news about Berkeley. Although Poole had seen fit to gloss over the child's smallpox, explained Sara, she had felt, and still felt, that it was best to tell S.T.C. the truth. Berkeley had indeed been very seriously ill and in spite of his initial appearance of recovery was, in fact, still causing her great concern. Soon after seemingly having mended from the smallpox he had succumbed, sharply and alarmingly, to a feverish cough. Sara made no attempt to conceal her anxiety (although at this stage she seemed not to suspect the dread "consumption"). S.T.C., in a great surge of distress and sympathy wrote back without a moment's delay to his "dearest Love":

> Ah little Berkley [sic]—I have misgivings—but my duty is rather to comfort you, my dear dear dear Sara! . . . I am well; but my spirits have left me—I am completely home-sick . . . I entreat & entreat you! take care of yourself —if you are well, I think I could frame my thoughts so that I should not sink under other losses.—You do right in writing me the Truth—Poole is kind—but you do right, my dear! In a sense of *reality* there is always comfort—the workings of one's imagination ever go beyond the worst that nature afflicts us with . . . Enough, that you write me always the whole Truth . . . If God permit . . . I hope, on May day, to be once more at Stowey . . . O God! I do languish to be at home! . . . O my Babies!—my Babies!—[39]

Sara and Tom Poole shared all the letters that came from S.T.C. When he learned the contents of this one Poole became exceedingly alarmed. On January 24 another strong-minded missive was dispatched in Poole's hand:

> Once more . . . let me entreat you not to over-interest yourself about family and friends here: not to incapacitate yourself by idle apprehension and tender reveries of imagination concerning us . . . I do not mean to check tenderness, for in the *folly* of tenderness I can sympathize—but be *rational*, I implore you.[40]

To appeal to S.T.C.'s rationality was always a forlorn hope, but in this instance the letter did not even reach him for over two months. The onset of the cruellest mid-winter within living memory choked the mouth of the Elbe with ice; no mail could reach S.T.C. from England and neither could he send any out.

On February 6, 1799, S.T.C. and Chester left Ratzeburg for Göttingen. S.T.C. was working on a projected study of Lessing and German literature and to further his research for this he proposed to enroll as a student at Göttingen University. The journey between Ratzeburg and Göttingen took nearly a week in the cumbersome and slow German coaches. "In England I used to laugh at the 'Flying Waggons' but compared with a German Post Coach the metaphor is perfectly justifiable, & for the future I shall never meet a flying Waggon without thinking respectfully of its speed."[41](S.T.C. to Sara, March 10 1799.)

The second night of S.T.C.'s journey to Göttingen, that of February 7,

1799, was the coldest night of the century. So far S.T.C. had not suffered greatly from the exceptional cold (if dry, it did not disagree with him), but, *"that Night—My God*! [Now] I know what the *Pain* of Cold is."[42] S.T.C. and Chester spent *that Night* in a wretched old stage-coach rolling slowly across "a flat objectless hungry heath."[43] They arrived in Hanover on the evening of Saturday, February 9, and left on the following Monday noon, to arrive at Göttingen the next morning, Tuesday, February 12.

In Bristol, over that same week-end, tragedy fell upon Sara. She had gone with her children to Bristol for Christmas and at first the change of air had seemed to improve Berkeley's health a little. But he soon relapsed, the cough returned, he lost weight steadily; it became clear that he was in a rapid consumption. His mother nursed him devotedly, but the case was a hopeless one. Berkeley Coleridge died on Sunday, February 10. A brief, broken-hearted little note arrived at Stowey:

> *Monday, Noon.*
>
> Oh, my dear Mr Poole, I have lost my dear, dear child! At one o'clock on Sunday morning a convulsive fit put an end to his painful existence. Myself and two of his aunts were watching by his cradle. I wish I had not seen it, for I am sure it will never leave my memory . . . I shall not yet write to Coleridge, and when I do, I will pass over all disagreeable subjects with the greatest care, for well I know their violent effect upon him—but I account myself most unfortunate in being at a distance from him at this time, wanting his consolation as I do, and feeling my grief almost too much to support with fortitude. I suppose you will have received from Coleridge the promised letter for me. I long for it, for I am very miserable.[44]

Edith and Robert Southey, without hesitation, removed Sara and little Hartley to their own home at Westbury, where they did everything they could to help the unhappy mother. Southey made, and paid for, all the funeral arrangements.

Poole was at first insistent that S.T.C. should not be told about Berkeley's death until he returned to England. But, after some further consideration and consultation with Sara, it was decided that S.T.C. had better be informed, and on March 15 Poole wrote a letter carefully breaking the news. This letter was sent to Sara, who read it and forwarded it to S.T.C., on March 18; on the 24th of that month she followed Poole's cautious preliminary epistle with one of her own.

These letters did not reach S.T.C. until the first days of April.

At Göttingen S.T.C. was finding both town and University congenial. He enjoyed the prestige of an introduction to Von Brandes, Secretary of State and Governor of the University, and this brought him the privilege (which usually only the professors enjoyed) of being able to borrow any number of books that he chose from the University library.

He and Chester found lodgings in the Burg Strasse; these S.T.C. described to Sara as "very neat"[45] but a notebook entry reads, probably with greater truth: "Chester and S.T.C. in a damn'd dirty hole in the Burg Strasse."[46]

A number of compatriots quickly introduced themselves. These included three Cambridge men, one of them Anthony Hamilton, a former St. John's undergraduate and an old acquaintance of S.T.C. Doubtless recalling S.T.C.'s undergraduate reputation as a roaring boy, Hamilton took him and Chester, together with Charles and Frederick Parry (brothers of Sir William Parry, the Arctic explorer) to the Saturday Club, an exclusive student meeting place, where there ensued a highly convivial party: "embracing, fighting, smashing bottles & glasses against the wall, singing— in short, such a scene of uproar I never witnessed before, no, not even at Cambridge,"[47] commented S.T.C. later. In describing the occasion to his wife he naturally assured her that he had drunk nothing.*

But company and reading could not altogether banish his anxiety and homesickness. S.T.C. once again became dangerously dejected:

> I languish after Home for hours together, in vacancy, my *feelings* almost wholly unqualified by *Thoughts*. I have, at times, experienced such an extinction of *Light* in my mind, I have been so forsaken by all the *forms* and *colourings* of Existence, as if the *organs* of Life had been dried up; or if only simple BEING remained, blind and stagnant!—After I have recovered from this strange state, & reflected upon it, I have thought of a man who should lose his companion in a desert of sand where his weary Halloos drop down in the air without an Echo—I am deeply convinced that if I were to remain a few years among objects for whom I had no affection, I should wholly lose the powers of Intellect—Love is the vital air of my Genius.

(This was to Sara in a letter of March 10; the Elbe was still ice-choked, but S.T.C. was too impatient and homesick to go longer without attempting to send a letter. He had not yet heard of Berkeley's death.) The letter concluded: "My dear Hartley!—My Berkley [sic]—how intensely I long for you! My Sara—O my dear Love!"

The state of mind described here was one of serious depression. The letters of this period provide ample evidence that opium was taken in quantity to combat this trough of despair. Particularly significant is a comment at the conclusion of this letter: "I am apt to be costive & wakeful,"[49] unmistakable symptoms of opium. (The evidence of these letters fully

*This Goslars ale is strong & staunch,
Yet sure twas brewed by Witches:
For ere you think, 't has reach'd the Paunch
Odd's fish! tis in your Breeches![48]
S.T.C. notebook entry; translation of an accompanying verse in German, *Es ist zwar ein recht gutes Bier.*

supports the assertion, allegedly made by Benecke, to the anonymous author of an article, *Gottingen in 1824*, which appeared in Putnam's Magazine, viii, 600, 1856, that S.T.C. "took opium when at Göttingen." It would, of course, have been markedly more noteworthy had the addicted S.T.C. *not* have taken opium at Göttingen.)

The mysterious telepathy which so often exists between intimately bonded couples kept Berkeley and his mother constantly in S.T.C.'s heart and thoughts. Some time close upon the death of the infant (about which S.T.C. as yet knew nothing) a fellow Englishman at Göttingen requested the poet to write an epitaph on an infant that had died a few weeks before its baptism. S.T.C. obliged, but "While I wrote it, my heart with a deep misgiving turned my thoughts homewards."[50]

> Be rather than be call'd a Child of God!
> Death whispered. With assenting Nod
> It's head upon the Mother's breast
> The baby bow'd, and went without demur,
> Of the Kingdom of the blest
> Possessor, not Inheritor!—[51]

The lines were in truth an epitaph for Berkeley.

Spring at last cracked the ice and the mail-packets could once again enter the Elbe. Poole's first letter to arrive, that of January 24, brought "the livelier impulse and the dance of thought"* as S.T.C. put it, but the second letter broke the news of the death of Berkeley, couched by Poole in terms of cautious restraint. The child's death had occurred under circumstances that were purely natural, stressed Poole, "such as probably no human foresight could have averted." Poole continued, perhaps somewhat too breezily:

> Mrs. Coleridge was much fatigued during the child's illness, but her health was very good, and she very wisely kept up her spirits . . . The truth is, my dear Col, it is idle to reason about a thing of this nature . . . Only let your *mind* act, and not your *feelings*. Don't conjure up any scenes of distress which never happened. Mrs. Coleridge felt as a mother . . . and, in an examplary manner, did all a mother could do. *But she never forgot herself.* She is now perfectly well, and does not make herself miserable by recalling the engaging, though, remember, mere instinctive attractions of an infant a few months old. Heaven and Earth! I have myself within the last month experienced disappointments more weighty than the death of ten infants . . . Let us hear from you . . . let us hear that you are happy . . . We long to see you. But still I say, don't come till you have done your business.[52]

Fears In Solitude.

S.T.C. read the letter with calmness, after the first intake of breath: "Death—the death of an Infant—of one's own Infant!" He finished reading, folded the letter and walked out into the open fields, oppressed not by his feelings, but by riddles: "Oh! this strange, strange, strange Scene-shifter, Death! that giddies one with insecurity, & so unsubstantiates the living Things that one has grasped and handled!" And he found himself repeating: "A Slumber did my spirit seal." The letter which he presently wrote to Poole was a perfectly tranquil one: "I cannot truly say that I grieve—I am perplexed—I am sad."[53]

He found the letter to Sara difficult to write. For once in his life he seems to have been almost at a loss for words. On April 8 he at last steeled himself to address a sheet of blank paper, "If I do not send off this letter now, I must wait another week:"[54]

It is one of the discomforts of my absence, my dearest Love! that we feel the same calamities at different times—I would fain write words of consolation to you; yet I know that I shall only fan into new activity the pang which was growing dead and dull in your heart—Dear little Being!—he had existed for me for so many months only in dreams and reveries, but in them existed and still exists so livelily, so like a real Thing, that although I know of his Death, yet when I am alone and have been long silent, it seems to me as if I did not understand it.

Thereafter he stuck. So he moved into his best sermonising strain, calling upon Sara to consider the use to which God put His power. So absorbed did S.T.C. become in his theme that he was soon informing her: "I confess that the more I think, the more I am discontented with the doctrines of Priestley. He builds the whole and sole hope of future existence on the words and miracles of Jesus—yet doubts or denies the future existence of Infants—only because according to his System of Materialism he has not discovered how they can be made unconscious." It was not the letter to send to a bereft young mother.

In conclusion S.T.C. did his best to convince Sara that even this heavy cloud had a silver lining:

I trust, my Love!—I trust, my dear Sara! that this event which has forced us to think of the Death of what is most dear to us, as at all times probable, will in many and various ways be good for us—To have shared—nay, I should say—to have divided with any human Being any one deep sensation of Joy or Sorrow, sinks deep the foundations of a lasting love—When in Moments of fretfulness and Imbecility I am disposed to anger or reproach, it will, I trust, be always a restoring thought—"We have wept over the same little one—with whom am I angry? with her who so patiently and unweariedly sustained my poor and sickly Infant through his Pains—with her —who, if I too should be called away, would stay in the deep anguish over my death-pillow! who would never forget me!"—Ah, my poor Berkley! [sic][55]

(One sentence in this letter is important to note within a different context: "When in Moments of fretfulness and Imbecility I am disposed to anger or reproach." Sara Coleridge has been handed down to posterity as a virago, thanks to the portrait drawn of her in S.T.C.'s later letters. The earlier letters, however, contain several open admissions by S.T.C. to a hotly irascible temper of his own. We need have no doubts that the Coleridge fights were full-blooded, two-sided, stand-up battles-royal of the kind that have formed a solid foundation for many a successful marriage. Tragically, in the case of the Coleridges, their fighting was to become bedevilled by a factor which drastically changed the entire climate of their relationship.)

The letters of both Poole and S.T.C. upon the occasion of Berkeley's death reveal how little either of them understood a woman. Poole's ignorance was pardonable; he was a confirmed bachelor with but a son's experience of the opposite sex. S.T.C., less pardonably, seemed at least in part to share Poole's comfortable conviction that Sara was quickly able to forget Berkeley; that "the pang . . . was growing dead and dull" in her heart. Like Poole he chose to suppose that Sara would not for long recall "the engaging attractions of an infant a few months old."

Sara Coleridge was a character of exceptional courage; she had gallantry, she put a gay face on things; she "kept up her spirits." But this was far from meaning that she did not feel deeply, or that she forgot easily. To S.T.C. she wrote: "To behold the death of a child—it is a suffering beyond conception . . . I have seen him twice at the brink of the grave, but he has returned and recovered and smiled upon me like an angel."[56] (On the back of this letter, many years after, she wrote: "No secrets herein. I will not burn it for the sake of my sweet Berkeley.") Till the end of her life she never forgot those smiles which her "sweet Berkeley" had given her from his cradle. Each year she was to note the date of his birthday and to remark upon the age that he would have been had he lived. As if to mock Poole (albeit quite unconsciously) she, long years after Berkeley's death, was still referring to the infant in her letters to the good man. For Sara Coleridge "sweet Berkeley" survived as all lost infants survive in the memories of mothers; for ever.

Some time in mid April the Wordsworths passed fleetingly through Göttingen on their way back to England. They were "melancholy and hipp'd . . . dear Wordsworth appears to me to have hurtfully segregated & isolated his Being / Doubtless, his delights are more deep and sublime; / but he has likewise more hours, that prey on his flesh & blood,"[57] S.T.C. told Poole (with greater insight than perhaps he realised).

Sara's account of Berkeley's death (written on Easter Sunday) so affected S.T.C. that his first impulse was to pack up and return to England with the Wordsworths. But he still had a great deal of reading to do in Göttingen and a lot of lost time for which he must somehow make up: "it is . . . impossible that I can collect what I have to collect, in less than six weeks from this day; yet I read & transcribe from 8 to 10 hours every day," he assured Sara, in the letter of April 23,[58] an extraordinary document that commenced not with his usual "My dearest Love," but with a cool, "My dear Sara."

Sara, in her letter breaking the news of Berkeley's death, had possibly piqued S.T.C. a little by repeating Southey's unfavourable opinion of *Lyrical Ballads*, but S.T.C.'s sudden desire to hurt her had deeper causes than this by far.

Of all the emotions which rack the morphine addict, guilt is the strongest and cruellest. Unable to bear this burden, the addict inverts his guilt sensation and attacks those very persons whom he has already most distressed by his drug-habit. To relieve his own self-torturing remorse he tortures those nearest and dearest to him.

Guilt prompts not only displays of sadism; it likewise prompts gestures of masochism. S.T.C., secretly weighed down by the knowledge of opium indulgence in Germany and his resultant idling and furthermore feeling that he should have returned to Stowey upon first hearing of Berkeley's illness, soon had convinced himself, however irrationally, that he was responsible for the loss of his child.

"There are moments when I have such a power of life within me, such a conceit of it, I mean—that I lay the Blame of my Child's Death to my absence—not *intellectually*; but I have a strange sort of sensation, as if while I was present, none could die whom I intensely love,"[59] he was to tell Poole (in a letter almost certainly written under the influence of opium: see below).

S.T.C.'s outrageous letter of April 23 to Sara provides exceptionally rewarding material for those interested in subconscious thought association. Here was no consciously organised attempt to make wounding remarks; the letter, on the contrary, was an unbridled self-indulgence in spontaneous sado-masochistic expression. It may properly be seen as an early exercise in the ranting, raging monologues of wild accusation, repudiation and brutal, bloody, verbal assault that the morphine-addict hurls in vituperative frenzy at his family.

The letter contained, in the first part, certain passages of tenderness, but each happy or gentle comment was immediately mirrored by a disturbing reflection, or image:

This day in June I hope & trust, that I shall be in England—!—O that the Vessel could but land at Shurton Bars . . . then & after a lonely walk of three miles . . . to see you . . . It lessens the delight of the thought of my Return, that I must get at you thro' a tribe of *acquaintances, damping* the freshness of one's Joy!—My poor little Baby!—at this moment I see the corner of the Room where his cradle stood—& his cradle too—and I cannot help seeing *him in* the cradle. Little lamb! & the snow would not melt on his limbs!

He followed this with an account (which he knew Sara would like) of traditional family celebrations in Germany.* This was followed by a long passage on the superstitions of German Catholics; from thence he progressed to baptismal fonts, from fonts to graves and graveyards (asking Sara if she recalled Jeremy Taylor's passage from *Holy Dying* "and the Summer brings briars to bud on our graves"). From graves he got, via shepherds, to perches for owls, from perches to gallows, concluding with a Goyaesque description of the Göttingen gallows: "three great Stone Pillars, square-like huge Tall chimneys, connected with each other at the top by three iron bars with hooks to them—& near them is a wooden pillar with a wheel on the top of it, on which the head is exposed, if the Person instead of being hung is beheaded." Around the gallows, he continued, was a multitude of bones; he had been frightened at first, supposing them the bones of men, but then he had discovered that it was the custom for the country folk to deposit their dead domestic animals at the gallows' foot as a kind of tithe to the hangman and a knacker's yard combined: "Drowned Dogs, & Kittens, &c are thrown there; in short, the Grass grows rank, & yet the Bones overtop it.—The fancy of human bones must, I suppose, have arisen in my ignorance of comparative Anatomy.—

God bless you, my Love!—I will write again speedily."

The sado-masochistic undertones of this letter are unmistakable. He had to hurt Sara; he had to hurt himself.

Yet he ended by enclosing an enchanting set of verses which he had written for her in Ratzeburg (in imitation of the German nursery song, *Wenn ich ein Voglein war*); verses written, he said, with "a yearning, yearning, yearning *Inside*—for my yearning affects more than my heart—I feel it all within me."

> If I had but two little wings
> And were a little feath'ry Bird,
> To *you* I'd fly, my Dear!
> But Thoughts, like these, are idle Things—
> And I stay here.
>
> But in my sleep to *you* I fly,
> I'm always with you in my sleep—
> The World is all one's own.
> But then one wakes—and where am I?
> All, all alone!

*Published, almost without any editing at all, in *The Friend*, No. 19, December 28, 1809.

Sleep stays not tho' a Monarch bids,
So I love to wake ere break of Day;
For tho' my Sleep be gone,
Yet while 'tis dark, one shuts one's lids,
And still dreams *on!*[60]

Writing out these verses for Sara melted him; his dagger was sheathed. He concluded in a rush of love: "God bless you, my dear dear Wife, & believe me with eagerness to clasp you to my heart."

A letter to Poole, written on May 6, seems almost certainly to have been written under the influence of opium:

My dear Poole, my dear Poole! I am homesick . . . O my God! how I long to be at home—My *whole Being* so yearns after you, that when I think of the moment of our meeting, I catch the fashion of German Joy, rush into your arms, and embrace you—methinks, my *Hand* would swell, if the whole force of my feeling were crowded there.—Now the Spring comes, the vital sap of my affections rises, as in a tree!—And what a gloomy Spring! . . . There are a multitude of Nightingales here/poor things! they sang in the snow/—I thought of my own verses on the Nightingale, only because I thought of Hartley, my *only* child!—Dear Lamb! I hope, *he* won't be dead, before I get home.

And S.T.C., with another despairing cry "O Poole! I am homesick," enclosed what he himself described as a "hobbling Ditty" on homesickness (Poems, i. 314), adding, "my poor Muse is quite gone."

The letter switched abruptly from subject to subject: a detailed account of a peculiarly horrible suicide pact between two Teutonic lovers, whether parchment might not be made out of old shoes, whether *aqua fortis* might not be extracted from cucumber, a new discovery for heating rooms with moistened quicklime enclosed in tightly screwed tins, a pricelist for meat in Hanover for the month of May, 1799. Finally, exhausted, S.T.C. exclaimed:

[A Stupid] letter—I believe, my late proficiency in Learning has somewhat stupefied me but live in hopes of one better worth the postage . . . My dear Poole! don't let little Hartley die before I come home.—That's silly—true—& I burst into tears as I wrote it.[61]

In view of the evidence of opium during this Göttingen period it is doubtful if there was much truth in his pious assurance to Poole: "I read & transcribe from morning to night . . . never in my life have I worked so hard."[62] This labour was connected with the study of Lessing, upon which S.T.C. was now pinning his usual extravagant hopes; the work would not only make money to clear all his debts (he had already overdrawn the Wedgwood annuity for that year by some fifty pounds),[63] but would establish his reputation for "industry & erudition, certainly; & I would fain

hope, for reflection & genius—."[64] "Reputation gets money—& for reputation I don't care a damn, but money—yes—Money I must get, in all
honest ways."[65]

On May 11, S.T.C. and Chester set off on a walking tour in the Hartz
mountains (much admired for their scenery and mines by the Romantics;
mines were, interestingly, considered to be immensely picturesque). The
walking party consisted of the two Parry brothers, Clement Carlyon (a young
physician), Charles Bellas Greenough, geographer and geologist and a
youth named Blumenbach, a natural historian.

The tour lasted a little over a week* and included an ascent of the Great
Brocken. The party was energetic by day (the distance walked daily aver-
aged a good twenty-five miles) and convivial at country inns in the evening.
Back in Göttingen S.T.C. succumbed to fresh, desperate homesickness, but
for a month he worked on collecting the last of his notes for the study of
Lessing; or so he was to maintain. How far morphine had, in fact, by now
sapped his resolution and energy and, inevitably, involved him in lying and
subterfuge, is best demonstrated by the complicated story of Josiah Wedgwood and the history of the Bauers; a classical case of deception by a
morphine addict.

In early January, 1799, S.T.C. was assuring Josiah Wedgwood and Poole
that he was proposing to send the former, within "a few days," "a most
voluminous letter, or rather series of letters, which will comprise a history
of the Bauers, or Peasants."[66] The first of these was written and posted to
Wedgwood in February. It is almost a certainty that the remainder were
never written.

S.T.C., upon arrival back in Göttingen after the tour of the Hartz
mountains, his return to England imminent, found himself faced, it seems,
with the problem not only of unwritten completion of the history of the
Bauers,[67] but without the material even having been properly assembled.[68]
He told Wedgwood (in a letter written on May 21 1799):

I have lying by my side six huge *Letters*, with your name on each of them/&
all excepting one have been written for these three months. About this time
Mr Hamilton, by whom I send this & the little parcel for my wife, was as it
were, setting off for England: & I seized the opportunity of sending them
by him, as without any mock-modesty I really thought that the expence of
the Postage ... would be more than their Worth.—Day after day, & Week
after week, was Hamilton going/& still delayed—and now that it is absolutely
settled that he goes tomorrow, it is likewise absolutely settled that I shall go
this day three weeks/& I have therefore sent only this & the Picture by him/
but the letters I will now take myself—/for I should not like them to be lost,

*For S.T.C.'s account of this tour see CL 280–282 and "Over the Brocken"
(*Amulet*, 1829). Carlyon's account of it appeared in his *Early Years and Late
Reflections*, 4 vols (1836–58). For Greenough's description of the tour, see E. J.
Morley, *Coleridge in Germany: Wordsworth and Coleridge* ed. Griggs (1939).

as they comprize the only subject, on which I have had any opportunity of making myself thoroughly informed.

S.T.C. continued:

> What have I done in Germany?—I have learnt the language ... I have attended the lectures on Physiology, Anatomy, & Natural History with regularity ... I have read & made collections for an history of the Belles Lettres in Germany before the time of Lessing—& ... very large collections for a Life of Lessing. ... For these last 4 months, with the exception of last week in which I visited the Harz I have worked harder than, I trust in God Almighty, I shall ever have occasion to work again.[69]

Such avowals of frenetic hard-work are themselves suspicious. (One recalls similar avowals to George Coleridge at the time of Esteesian idling at Cambridge and like protestations to Southey at Bristol after a period of idleness that drew reproaches from Lovell.) It is worth noting here that the much-heralded book on Lessing was never written. Nor were any letters upon the history of the Bauers handed to Wedgwood on S.T.C.'s return to England; indeed, no mention of these letters was made over the next eighteen months. On November 1, 1800, S.T.C. (then settled in Keswick, morphine-reliant and desperate both for money and for a tangible achievement with which to placate the Wedgwoods) wrote to Josiah to say that these letters, together with other material relating to the German tour, were in a printer's hands; S.T.C. having, so he alleged, made up a volume out of his journeys. But this book never appeared and no more was ever heard of the Bauer letters. Had they existed we may be almost sure that they would have made an ultimate appearance in *The Friend*.

On June 24, 1799 S.T.C. and Chester set off on the first lap of their return journey to England. With Greenough and Carlyon they walked to Clausthal and from thence over the Brocken to Elbingerode, Wolfenbüttel and Braunschweig. On July 3, the parties separated, S.T.C. and Chester travelling to Helmstedt, Greenough and Carlyon returning to Göttingen.

The walk to Helmstedt was made in broiling sun; stripped to the waist and hatless, S.T.C. marched for seven hours without stopping, the ever loyal Chester pounding behind. They arrived at their destination both severely sunburned. Chester literally fell on to his bed at the inn and was asleep immediately, such was his state of exhaustion. The hypermanic S.T.C. washed and dressed himself properly and went off with a letter of introduction to call on Hofrath Bruns, with whom he spent a very agreeable evening, mainly in the arbour of the Hofrath's garden; they drank *Bütterbrot* and talked of literature and of Oxford, where Bruns had once resided for a few years. It transpired, during the conversation, that he had known some of S.T.C.'s father's friends. (Of S.T.C.'s command of German he himself now said that it was fluent enough but his pronunciation was hideous: "it must be a *torture* for a German to be in my company.")[70]

At eleven-thirty the evening broke up; at ten the next morning Bruns arrived to do further honours of the town. Next day the travellers went to Brunswick. S.T.C. had lost his luggage—a chest and portmanteau sent in advance:

> My Stars! What shall I do!—Last night I sprinkled my shirt with [water?] hung it up at the window, & slept naked—for my *one* clean shirt I *must* keep till I get to Hamburg.—Heaven! I stink like an old Poultice!—I should mislead any pack of Foxhounds. ... Put a Trail of Rusty Bacon at a Furlong Distance & me at a mile, and they would follow *me*—I should hear a cry of Stop Thief close at my ears with a safe Conscience—but if I caught only the Echo of a Tally Ho! I should climb up into a Tree! ... Marry,—and my Books—I shall be ruined—on the Debtor's Side in Newgate, just 5 yards distant from Sodomy, Murder & House-breaking—Soul of Lessing! hover over my Boxes![71]

This to Greenough, written at Brunswick at half-past eight in the morning, Saturday, July 6, 1799. Shortly after penning this light-hearted farewell to Greenough "and eke Carlyon, and Charles Parry, & little Fred," S.T.C. and Chester, the latter still afire with sunburn, climbed on the coach ("the Kaufman had forgotten to take places so we go with the Packages")[72] and rumbled away to Hamburg.

CHAPTER TWELVE

FIRE AND BRIMSTONE:
THE THIRD BOLT

(July–December 1799)

S.T.C. HAD LEFT England while the air was still thick with the vapours of *Edmund Oliver*, Lloyd's gossip and intrigue, Southey's rancour, Lamb's satirical laughter.

Sara Coleridge, however kindly and generously received into the home of Edith and Robert Southey, had found herself in a climate still vibrating with animosity towards her husband.

The breach between S.T.C. and Southey had been exploited and accentuated by Lloyd until it bore, as a topic for gossip and a stimulus of ill feeling, no resemblance to the actual attitudes of S.T.C. and Southey themselves. S.T.C. had become persuaded that Southey nursed a "deep & implacable enmity"[1] towards him, while Southey was convinced that S.T.C. harboured a profound hatred of him. In fact, S.T.C.'s feelings for Southey were still fundamentally those of "respect & affection"[2] and although Southey seems to have been somewhat more fixed in his sensations of resentment towards S.T.C. (as was only to be expected of such an inflexible personality) he certainly did not feel that the breach between himself and S.T.C. put reconciliation out of the question.

No such reconciliation had as yet been effected, however, and Sara, staying with the Southeys, had been placed in an exceedingly awkward situation. *Lyrical Ballads* were pulled to pieces; Sara was challenged upon S.T.C.'s present political convictions. To Poole she wrote, on April 2, 1799: "It is very unpleasant to me to be often asked if Coleridge has changed his political sentiments, for I know not properly how to reply. Pray furnish me."[3]

It would have been difficult for anyone to have stated with confidence what S.T.C.'s politics were at that stage of his career; possibly he himself did not know. In a letter to Sara of May 17 he described how the evenings in the Hartz mountains were spent by him and his companions in singing rounds of English songs, of which *God Save the King* and *Rule! Britannia!* were prime favourites; for, "being abroad makes every man a Patriot & a Loyalist—almost a Pittite!"[4] Southey, if this were reported to him, must have been hard-pressed to conceal a sardonic smile at the thought of the not-so-long-since seditionist seated outside some German inn, bellowing *God Save the King* at the top of his voice.

To add to Sara's humiliation during her stay with the Southeys, she was so short of money that she had to borrow.[5]

Upon his arrival home, therefore, S.T.C. was greeted by a chagrined Sara's recitals of what had been said about him by the Southeys. Little Hartley, too, prattled about his uncle Southey, albeit, in a more innocent vein. S.T.C. must have found this all very irritating, to say the least.

The letters to and from Germany confirm how dearly and deeply the Coleridges were attached to one another. Yet, by the end of July, within a few short weeks of his return, S.T.C. and Sara had become involved in serious fighting.

To attempt to attribute this conflict wholly to S.T.C.'s hurt over Southey's alleged attitude towards him, or to Sara's frayed temper, would be only in part to explain it. The quarrelling had a very much more serious cause.

S.T.C.'s happy honeymoon period with morphine was drawing to a close; unmistakable danger signals were making their appearance. There are numerous indications that S.T.C. was now showing an increasing disregard for the truth (a classical symptom of morphine addiction); he himself noted a decline in his general health (another symptom); his Muse had most tellingly deserted him; and every fact that we know about the Coleridge marriage from this date onward is entirely in keeping with a background of an addict's descent into the hell of true reliance, which is invariably accompanied by a sudden and tragically appalling deterioration in his close personal relationships.

Galled by Sara's accounts of Southey's criticism, in debt to the Wedgwoods, worried by a housing problem, torn between Poole and the Wordsworths (the latter were now in the north), privately ashamed of his increasing opium habit, his health suffering, S.T.C. was in no state to maintain a serene temper. He became beset by "Moments of fretfulness and Imbecility . . . disposed to anger . . . [and] reproach,"[6] such as he had assured Sara that in future he would not suffer. She, in all probability somewhat exhausted by the ordeal through which she had recently passed, could not have had limitless reserves of nervous endurance and patience at her disposal. Temper clashes flared between the couple, a form of "domestic affliction"[7] that pressed hard upon S.T.C. (who could never stand quarrels, incessantly as he came to provoke them).

This was precisely the kind of situation which would have prompted him increasingly to opium. Sara, dismayed by this evidence of an intensifying drug-habit, without doubt would have reproached and upbraided him. He, guilty, ashamed and sulky, would just as certainly have taken more opium to escape from the pressure of marital strife. So commenced their tragic tarantism

> of arguing in a circle
> and so we whirl round & round in perpetual
> & vertiginous agitation—agitation and vertigo[8]

At last S.T.C. wrote to Southey in an attempt to clear the air and effect a reconciliation in that quarter; while Sara, Hartley and the nursemaid, Fanny (Nanny having left Sara's service in April) travelled along the coast to Minehead, a small watering place on the edge of Exmoor, where Edith and Robert Southey had gone for a holiday. Sara proposed to join them in a short tour of Lynton, Lynmouth and the Valley of the Rocks. It seems that, at that juncture, she found their company more congenial than that of S.T.C.

Southey did not yield immediately to S.T.C.'s overture. Poole was called upon to affirm to Southey that S.T.C. had never thought or spoken of Southey with anything but respect and affection throughout the unfortunate affair with Lloyd (of whom "it would be cruel to attribute his conduct to anything but a diseased mind"). [9] Southey responded as S.T.C. and Poole had hoped; instead of going to the Valley of the Rocks he and his little party returned to Stowey. Here the Southeys remained for a short but amicable stay; reconciliation had not only been effected between S.T.C. and Southey but between S.T.C. and Sara also.

In September the two families went into Devonshire together for a holiday, visiting Ottery, where the Southeys, as well as the Coleridges, stayed for a few days. This Ottery visit passed off excellently well, "all love & attention," [10] S.T.C. reported to Poole. The Southeys, when they left, went to Exeter where they took lodgings; the Coleridges prolonged their visit at Ottery. S.T.C. found that he had neither tastes nor feelings in common with his brothers, though George and James were "good men . . . very good men." S.T.C., a guest at the table of "a Clergyman and a Colonel," and replete with "Roast Fowls, mealy Potatoes, Pies & Clotted Cream . . . bless the Inventors thereof!" kept the peace and drank to Church and King when James gave the toast. Thus all was harmony. [11]

Harmony, too, with Sara, in serene autumn weather beside "the blue waters of the 'ROARING SEA!' "[12] as Hartley called it. The leaves fell gently from the trees; S.T.C., walking with his wife and child, noted the aromatic smell of the poplars, [13] a smell which he was to meet again five years later in exile in Sicily, when, engaged in a lively and guilty flirtation with the prima donna, he walked at night to the Syracuse opera house:

> Amid cruelly unlike Thoughts as I was passing up the green Lane . . . on my way to the Theatre . . . the aromatic smell of the Poplars came upon me! What recollections, if I were worthy of indulging them. [14]

In Devonshire there were ash-tree dells, rocks, waterfalls and pretty rivers. With Southey, S.T.C. made a five-day walking tour; he was impressed by the views of Totnes and Dartmouth. Meantime Sara stayed in Exeter with Edith; they were joined by their sister Eliza. Southey and S.T.C. returned to make up a pleasant family party. This was rudely disrupted by the discovery that Hartley was scratching himself incessantly; apparently he had caught the Itch (Scabies). Treatment for this highly contagious infection was drastic in those days, involving isolation, applications of brimstone, frenzied fumigations, tubbings, washings and scrubbings of every item of clothing and bedding in sight. Poor Sara, overcome by the misfortune, gave way to what her husband a little unkindly dubbed "hypersuperlative Grief;"[15] nevertheless a very real anxiety was felt lest Edith or Eliza should have become infected. Hartley, who at this age always referred to himself as Moshes (Moses), was hurried back to Stowey by his parents. Fanny was dispatched to her own home as a form of quarantine. Hartley was smothered with brimstone; he was very merry during the first application, singing and chanting: "I be a funny fellow, And my name is Brimstonello."[16] After which he had an excellent night's sleep.

For the next few days the cottage was in an unspeakable confusion of sulphur, soap, water, fumigations and Mercurial Girdles; these last prescribed by the apothecary to be worn as preventatives by Sara and S.T.C.: "Our little Hovel is almost afloat—poor Sara tired off her legs with servanting—the young one fretful & noisy with confinement exerts his activities on all forbidden Things—the house stinks of Sulphur."[17] Arrayed in his mercurial girdle S.T.C. went for a walk and marched himself into a furious perspiration: "O Christus Jesus!—how I stunk!"[18] As a result he caught a chill and succumbed to excruciating rheumatic pains. Lulled by laudanum he shut himself away with his Spinoza and contrived to "remain as undisturbed as a Toad in a Rock"[19] while Sara, likewise sweating and reeking in her "Cest of the Caledonian Venus"[20] struggled, single-handed, to rid the house of any possible harbourage of *sarcoptes scabei*. Hartley maintained a non-stop performance of getting into trouble and getting in the way.

S.T.C., unable to bear his girdle any longer, flung it off. He blamed it for the excruciating pains that shot through him like "hot arrows headed with adders' Teeth . . . I would rather have old Scratch himself, whom all the Brimstone in Hell can't cure, than endure them! . . . You'd laugh to see how pale & haggard I look—& by way of a Clincher, I am almost certain that Hartley has not had the Itch—."[21]

Under these circumstances it was not surprising that conjugal tempers flared again. Sara obviously must have expressed herself with vehemence upon the subject of a husband who left his wife to deal single-handed with a house in turmoil while he retired into a privacy of philosophy and opium. Finally S.T.C. rushed off to visit his patrons at Upcott (the temporary home of Josiah Wedgwood) while Sara with rudimentary assistance, completed the task of getting "the house, sheets, blankets, and cloaths washed, and the latter buried."[22]

S.T.C.'s rheumatism was too painful for him to remain comfortably at Upcott; he returned to the "little Hovel" in Lime Street to find Hartley in good health and the embrimstonement concluded; "but the scent still remains,"[23] as Sara sighingly told Mrs George Coleridge.

Rheumatic pains continued to harass S.T.C. in his head and shoulders, but, he wrote to Southey:

> when the Pain intermits, it leaves my sensitive Frame *so* sensitive! My enjoyments are so deep, of the fire, of the Candle, of the Thought I am thinking, of the old Folio I am reading—and the silence of the silent House is so *most & very* delightful—that upon my soul! the Rheumatism is no such bad thing.[24]

The hypersensitivity here described must undoubtedly have been attributable to morphine rather than to rheumatism. The experience is of a kind well known to addicts who are happy with the drug. For S.T.C. opium was still the milk of Paradise; but he was nearing the bottom of the glass.

Additional symptoms of opium addiction which S.T.C. mentioned in the same letter were sleeplessness, indigestion and loss of appetite.

Sara must have been deeply perturbed to see him thus withdrawn in a seclusion of alleged severe pain and only too apparent opium. The family finances were by now precarious; the Coleridges were considerably in debt, the Wedgwood annuity obviously required supplementation by S.T.C.'s own efforts and activity, yet he had been home for over three months and no effort had been made. S.T.C. had plans enough: he would take boarding-pupils on "very advantageous Terms;"[25] he thought of writing a school-book[26] which he was certain would be a "lucrative speculation;"[27] "I will set about *Christabel* with all speed . . . but my money-book I *must* write first—."[28] He and Southey on their tour had drawn up an outline for an eight-book poem in hexameters on Mahomet, but this was never written: "I am not in a poetical Mood / & . . . am resolved to publish nothing with my name till my Great Work."[29]

The Great Work S.T.C. at this time envisaged as a poem of Spinoza. In his notebook he jotted:

> If I begin a poem of Spinoza, thus it should
> begin/
> I would make a pilgrimage to the burning sands of
> Arabia, or &c &c to find the Man who could explain
> to me there can be *oneness*, there being infinite
> Perceptions—yet there must be a *oneness*, not
> an intense Union but an Absolute Unity, for &c[30]

Nothing was written; nothing was done.

Sara began to reproach and upbraid him constantly; he responded with petulant outbursts of temper and self-pity. "The Wife of a man of Genius who sympathises with her Husband in his habits & feelings is a *rara avis* with me; tho' a vast majority of her own sex & too many of ours will scout her for a *rara piscis*," he grumbled to Southey.[31]

Reconstructing from the evidence contained in letters of S.T.C. and Poole it seems almost certain that Sara took her troubles to Poole and probably requested that he should have a word with S.T.C. in an attempt to get him to stop taking laudanum and pull himself together. This Poole did (with such drastic results that he was to vow: "in future when I see errors and inconsistencies in those whom I love, where I can't sympathize I will at any rate be silent").[32]

S.T.C., bruised by criticism from his wife and best friend, announced to Sara that he must go at once to Bristol to search for his still-missing chest and portmanteau. If he could not find this lost luggage in Bristol, he said, he would then go to London to look for it. Accordingly on, or about, October 20, S.T.C. quit Stowey.

Two days later the missing luggage arrived, unexpectedly, at the cottage. Sara, it seems, sent a message to this effect to Bristol. She then closed the cottage and with Hartley, "now in all respects perfectly well," she went to stay with friends at Old Cleeve, near Watchet. She heard nothing from S.T.C. but was apparently none too dismayed; she was accustomed to his unreliable habits. "I am going to Stowey tomorrow and hope to find him safe at Mr Poole's," Sara wrote to Mrs George Coleridge on November 2. "I expect when I return to Stowey, if Coleridge is not there, to find a letter inviting me and the Child to Bristol, for as I have no maid I cannot remain in the house alone."[33]

But S.T.C. was not at Poole's; neither was there any letter from him inviting Sara to Bristol. On that day of November 3 when she arrived back in Stowey and went to Poole's house hoping to find Samuel safely there he, in fact, was at Grasmere in the Lake Country, with Wordsworth.

In Bristol S.T.C., smarting from Sara's tongue and Poole's lecturing, had sought the congenial company of uncritical friends. (It was during those few days that he was probably first introduced to the youthful Humphrey Davy who, for the past twelve months, had been in charge of the laboratory at Dr Beddoes' Pneumatic Institution. Between Davy and S.T.C. a close and warm friendship rapidly sprang up.)

Almost certainly however, S.T.C. had not gone to Bristol with the pure and simple intention of looking up friends and lost luggage. In spite of what he had told Sara, Bristol on this occasion had been no more than the first leg of a journey to Sockburn, near Hurworth-on-Tees, County Durham, where the Wordsworths were staying with the Hutchinsons. Although S.T.C. was subsequently to make the excuse that he was "called up to the North by alarming accounts of Wordsworth's health"[34] (an excuse which he was to employ upon more than one occasion), Wordsworth's health was perfectly good at the time and it is impossible to avoid the suspicion that S.T.C., in his inability to say "No" either to Wordsworth or Poole, had at some point (perhaps in Goslar) promised the former that, when circumstances permitted, he would join him in the North. The present visit was to be a form of preliminary reconnaissance of the Lake Country.

Cottle (who was about to retire from publishing) was contemplating a visit to Wordsworth in order to discuss the disposal of the copyright of *Lyrical Ballads*. S.T.C. persuaded him to share the trip to Sockburn and, on October 22, the two men left Bristol together. They were at Sockburn by October 26.

Mary Hutchinson had heard a great deal about S.T.C. from Dorothy and William; he, too, had heard much talk about Mary. (It should be stressed that there was, at this time, no thought of romance between Mary and William.)

"Few moments in life so interesting as those of an affectionate reception from those who have heard of you yet are strangers to your person,"[35] S.T.C. jotted in his eternal notebook. The well-meaning, but always rather idiotic Cottle, after the tea that had been served upon the travellers' arrival, asked Mary, point-blank: "Pray, what do you think of Mr Coleridge's first appearance?" S.T.C. laughed loudly, amused, but immediately afterwards the question made him melancholy.[36] Was he suddenly disturbed by memories of that first, meteor-like visit to the tea-table of the Frickers, five years prior to this "most important journey to the North?"[37]

Mary, for her part, was excited, confused, delighted by the presence of the famous Mr Coleridge who, if we judge by her reaction, must already have been giving her some admiring glances. She, naive, shy, yet warmly sweet, responded with:

> Curiousity of true love* respectfulness, yet eager look of kindness—& when turned away to do any thing, to fetch any thing, the rapidity of motion, & of eagerness—a relief to the strong Feelings, which . . . respect due to a Stranger made it necessary to repress or chasten.—O dear Mary . . . never shall I forget your [. . .] manners.[38]

Although it has been supposed that S.T.C. fell in love with Sara Hutchinson during this visit to Sockburn, the evidence of the notebooks indicates clearly enough that it was Mary, not Sara, who first enchanted him.

Mary, as aforesaid, charmed men. Possibly it was true, as De Quincey spitefully observed of her, that "though liberally endowed with sunshiny temper and sweetness of disposition, [she] was perhaps a person weak intellectually beyond the ordinary standards of female weakness."[39] Men

---

*S.T.C. uses the term "true love" here in the "refined sensibility" meaning of the phrase: an innocent, but deep and spontaneous sympathy.

do not give intellectual qualities paramount importance when reckoning the attractions of a woman and S.T.C., like Wordsworth himself, was won to Mary by

> ... her exulting outside look of youth
> And placid under-countenance ...
> ... that meek confiding heart.[40]

Mary, said Wordsworth, speaking of himself and Coleridge, was "reverenced by us both."[41]

The day after their arrival at Sockburn, S.T.C. and Cottle set out with Wordsworth upon what S.T.C. gaily called "a picteresk Toor" of the Lake Country.[*][42] With Cottle on horseback (an old leg-injury making walking difficult for him) the trio travelled to Temple Sowerby where they were joined by John, Wordsworth's sailor brother. ("Your Br. John is one of you; a man who hath solitary usings of his own Intellect, deep in feeling, with a subtle Tact, a swift instinct of Truth & Beauty. He interests me much,"[43] wrote S.T.C. to Dorothy.)

At Temple Sowerby Cottle left the party to return to London where he had business appointments to keep (one with Longman and Rees of Paternoster Row, to whom he sold all his copyrights). S.T.C. and the two Wordsworths continued to Bampton, Haweswater, Hawkeshead, Windermere and Grasmere. Here they remained for a few days confined by bad weather (they contrived, nonetheless, to climb Helvellyn). William, who had loved Grasmere since boyhood, began to dream of living there with Dorothy. Perhaps they might build a house by the lake shore? John would give them forty pounds to buy the ground. Alternatively there was a small house empty which they might rent: "but of this we will speak,"[44] William wrote to Dorothy.

S.T.C. declared that the beauty of the scenery kept his eyes dim with tears; it was "a vision of a fair Country." "Why were you not with us Dorothy? Why were not you Mary with us?"[45]

At Grasmere John left the party. S.T.C. and Wordsworth continued their tour, visiting Keswick, Embleton, Lorton and Buttermere, Ennerdale, Wasdale Head, over the Sty to Borrowdale, from Borrowdale to Ullswater by way of Threlkeld and Matterdale Commons and finally to Eusemere, where lived Wordsworth's friend Thomas Clarkson, the abolitionist. Here, on Monday, November 18, Wordsworth and S.T.C. parted company, William remaining at Eusemere while S.T.C. walked to Sockburn.

At Sockburn, on this occasion, S.T.C. further flirted with Mary and,

---

*For accounts of this tour see Vol. 1, *Coleridge Notebooks* ed. Coburn; G. H. B. Coleridge, "Samuel Taylor Coleridge discovers the Lake Country," *Wordsworth and Coleridge* ed. E. L. Griggs (1939). For a study of S.T.C.'s walking in the Lake Country see Molly Lefebure, "The First of the Fell-Walkers;" *Cumberland Heritage* (1970).

too, with the twenty-four-years-old Sara, the second daughter of the Hutchinson family.

The young Sara Hutchinson is little known to us. We find innumerable morphine-distorted references to her in the Coleridge notebooks, but these tell us nothing of the real woman. We get fleeting glimpses of her in some of the Wordsworth and Coleridge letters; but nowhere is she truly revealed, until in 1808 or thereabouts, when she began to fight her way from under the calamitous camouflage-net that S.T.C. had cast over her. We begin, then, to meet a flesh-and-blood Sara through the medium of her own surviving letters.

It was S.T.C.'s tragic conviction that it was "the perfection of every woman to be characterless."[46] The perfect woman was a devoted slave, without mind or personality of her own; she might then be moulded into that twin soul, that projection of himself, that sublimated *döppelganger* for whom he always yearned and searched:

> My nature requires another Nature for its support, & reposes only in another from the necessary Indigence of its Being—Intensely similar, yet not the same; or may I venture to say, the same indeed, or dissimilar, as the same Breath sent with the same force, the same pauses, & with the same melody pre-imaged in the mind, into the Flute the Clarion shall be the same soul diversely incarnate.[47]

This twin-soul, needless to say, must neither argue nor criticise. She must think as he thought; wish as he wished; dream as he dreamed. She must be his echo; the flute ever repeating the *leit-motif* of his clarion.

Sara Coleridge could not fulfil such a rôle; she was a wife, a flesh-and-blood reality. There was no place for reality in S.T.C.'s dream of "the same soul diversely incarnate."

At Sockburn in 1799 S.T.C. was not yet in that psychotic state where fantasy ousted reality, when Asra (as he was to call Sara Hutchinson) was to become his supporting *döppelganger*, who might be totally identified with himself, yet, being outside himself, would still stand upright when he had fallen flat on his back, a *döppelganger* who would be there to raise him and prop him up when his own limbs had given way. Opium and Asra alike were to be his crutches.

In 1799 the time was not yet ripe for Asra. Instead S.T.C. found himself laughing and teasing with Sara who was a very short (only a little over five feet in height), dumpy, ungraceful, plain-featured young woman, what she herself described as a true Hutchinson: "her hair brown and her under chap . . . forward"[48] (this last feature is very marked in Sara's silhouette portrait). De Quincey was to recall her abundant chestnut-brown hair as her one beauty.

More extrovert than Mary, she combined an innocent gaiety with good sense and a native shrewdness; she enjoyed a certain reputation as a wit.* She seems to have been, at all times, quite without malice, but given to that rather pithy humour which certain spinsterish women cultivate (the larger the heart, the sharper the tongue). From the first she had a sturdy, down-to-earth, almost dogmatic no-nonsense strain, demonstrated excellently in this excerpt from a letter to her cousin, John Monkhouse, in 1800. Monkhouse was in London, and Sara wished him to buy for her:

> a *Chip Hat or bonnet* of the very *newest* fashion—I would have it cold pea-green else lilac I would prefer a useful size—that is one to shade the face but not too large as you know that would be out of proportion ... mind no flowers or kickshaws about it let it be very modest—not hemm'd with Ribband or anything but simply the Hat itself don't give an extravagant [price?].[50]

According to De Quincey, Sara Hutchinson had real distinction of mind and character. As a child she had lived in the house of her relative, James Patrick of Kendal, who was known as "the intellectual Pedlar." (It is thought that Wordsworth's Wanderer in *The Excursion* was intended as a portrait of Patrick, drawn largely from Sara's reminiscences of him.) Sara always said that "the best part of her education was gathered from the stores of that good man's mind."[51] Certainly she possessed a discerning taste in poetry (she enjoyed transcribing poems for her friends in an even and beautiful hand). In course of time she was to make both Wordsworth and S.T.C. a valued amanuensis.

The supposition that S.T.C. fell hopelessly in love with her at this first meeting is demonstrably false upon his own evidence. He flirted with her, as he flirted with every young woman he met (save, it seems, Dorothy Wordsworth). The often-quoted retrospective notebook entry of October 1803, describing Sunday, November 24, 1799, speaks of an evening of conundrums and puns, stories and laughter standing round the fire; S.T.C. pressed Sara's hand behind her back for a long time and "then Love first wounded me with a light arrow-point, poisoned alas, and incurable."[52]

The analogy here is not that of Cupid's shaft, shot from a bow and precipitating the bewildered target into headlong love instantaneously; it is rather that of a poison-tipped arrow projected by a blow-pipe and is almost certainly drawn from Stedman's narrative of an expedition to Surinam,†

---

*The letters of her middle years are full of somewhat tartly humorous comments; for instance, of the death of Lady Diana Fleming in 1816: "Lady Diana ... will be placed in the same grave with her husband; a situation which in her life-time I guess, she would have shuddered to think of."[49]

†J. S. Stedman, *Narrative of a Five Years' Expedition against the Revolted Negroes of Surinam, in Guiana, on the Wild Coast of South America, from the Year 1772 to 1777* 2 vols (1796).

which S.T.C. had recently been recommending to Southey.[53] The venom from a light arrow-point does not take effect immediately. In a letter to Crabb Robinson, of March 12, 1811, S.T.C. wrote of "Long and deep Affection suddenly, in one moment, flash-transmuted into Love."[54] The circumstances of S.T.C.'s infatuation for Sara Hutchinson seem to confirm that he did not develop his obsession until many months after the Sunday evening of puns and conundrums.

S.T.C. would seem to have been in an overwrought and hypersensitive condition during this visit. His philandering may have been somewhat more reckless than usual, as an unconscious reaction against Mrs Coleridge. Bursting with wild high spirits he reduced Jack Hutchinson and his naively innocent and delighted sisters to helpless laughter with conundrums and jokes of which he has left specimens in the notebooks:

Two old women on a Fir Apple—A Cone under'em[55]

—What is a foetus in a bottle of spirits?
—A young *Pickle*[56]

Always intensely aware of the integration of sensation and thought, the wholeness and oneness of existence, that each and every facet of experience is inextricably involved with every other, forming a reticulated series of patterns, as miraculously intricate as a python's skin,* S.T.C. absorbed the details of the room at Sockburn, committing all to memory:

Print of the Blackwall Ox; of Darlington—so spot-sprigged/Print, how interesting—viewed in all its moods, unconsciously distinctly, semiconsciously with vacant, with swimming eyes—a thing of nature thro' the perpetual action of the Feelings!—O God! when I now think how perishable Things, how imperishable Ideas—what a proof of My Immortality—What is Forgetfulness?[57]

In 1803 he added the note:

so far was written in my b. pocket [book] Nov. 25th 1799—Monday Afternoon, the Sun shining in upon the Print, in beautiful Lights—& I just about to take Leave of Mary—& having just before taken leave of Sara.—I did not then know Mary's and Williams's attachment /†
The lingering Bliss,
The long entrancement of a True-love kiss.[58]

---

*For instance:—"Seem to have made up my mind to write my metaphysical works, as *my Life* & *in* my Life—intermixed with all the other events / or history of the mind & fortunes of S. T. Coleridge." (Notebook entry, 1515 4.86.Sept.–Oct. 1803).
†On William's own evidence (EWL 256) no such attachment existed at that date.

When, four years later, S.T.C. recalled this episode of farewell by visualising in his mind's eye that sunlit print, he felt "instantly the trains of forgotten Thought rise from their living catacombs!" He noted, also, that "Opium, probably by its narcotic effect on the whole seminal organization, in a large Dose, or after long use, produces the same effect on the *visual, & passive* memory."[59]

S.T.C. arrived back in London from Sockburn on Wednesday, midnight, November 27, to find the great city a "harsh contrast"[60] with the fair places that he had left behind him. He was now to remain in London. Daniel Stuart* had offered him regular work on the *Morning Post* and he had accepted. He had no idea of the whereabouts of Mrs Coleridge. He wrote to Cottle, in an attempt to trace her:

> If Mrs. Coleridge be in Bristol, pray desire her to write to me immediately ... I have written to Stowey, but if she be in Bristol, beg her to write to me by return of post, that I may immediately send down some cash for her travelling expenses, &c. We shall reside in London for the next four months.[61]

We do not know what kind of financial provision (if any) S.T.C. had made for Sara during his absence of nearly six weeks. He certainly left her without telling her his true destination; as she does not seem to have communicated with him during his absence we can only assume that she did not at any time know where to find him.

By bolting from Stowey and Sara in this way S.T.C. had inflicted upon her the same punishment of anxiety and distress that he had inflicted upon his mother at the time of the Ottery flight, when he had remained out all night, "thinking ... with inward & gloomy satisfaction, how miserable my Mother must be!" The punishment had been echoed by Comberbache, George Coleridge having then been the chief victim of Esteesian retribution. Now it had been Sara Coleridge's turn; presumably S.T.C., during his sojourning in the North, had had moments when he had indulged in gratifying thoughts of how miserable Sara must have been.

We do not know what Sara wrote to him when at last she received his London address, nor what S.T.C. said to her; although, as an essential ingredient in the pattern of these bolts was a masochistic orgy of remorse on his part in the final act, we must suppose that he abased himself. We do know that by December 19, Sara and Hartley were installed with S.T.C. in lodgings at 21, Buckingham Street, Strand (conveniently near the *Morning Post* office), and that Sara was very soon pregnant again.

---

*Daniel Stuart (1766–1846) was owner editor of the *Morning Post*, raising the paper into eminence. He was subsequently equally successful with the *Courier*.

CHAPTER THIRTEEN

"GOD KNOWS WHERE WE CAN GO"

(December 1799-July 1800)

THE NECESSITY OF making some money had driven S.T.C. into newspaper work (he was now overdrawn upon the Wedgwoods by a hundred-
and-fifty pounds). He quickly proved to be an outstandingly brilliant
journalist.

Between December 7, 1799 and April 21, 1800, S.T.C. wrote forty
political leaders* for the *Morning Post*; he also contributed miscellaneous
features and verses. The political writing necessitated occasional attendance
at the House of Commons in order that he might report on the debates. As
usual, when at last he screwed himself to a job, he did it with complete pro-
fessionalism, working "from 9 in the morning to 12 at night—a pure
Scribbler;"[1] "yesterday I went [to the House] at a quarter before 8, and
remained till 3 this morning—& then sate writing, & correcting other men's
writing till 8—a good 24 hours of unpleasant activity!"[2] When not spending
the evening reporting debates he went to the theatre in the capacity of
drama critic. It was intended that he should write a series of essays for his
newspaper on the Drama, both generally, and specifically in relation to the
contemporary English theatre.

S.T.C. also accepted from Longman a commission to translate Schiller's
five-act drama, *The Piccolomini, or The First Part of Wallenstein*, and *The
Death of Wallenstein* (also in five acts). This was work of the sheerest
drudgery; for it Longman paid a mere fifty pounds. A third play, *Wallenstein's Camp*, and an *Essay on the Genius of Schiller*, both promised in the
advertisement to *The Piccolomini*, never appeared.

This translation S.T.C. described as "irksome and soul-wearying;"[3] "a
Bore—never, never, never will I be so taken in again—Newspaper writing is
comparative extacy."[4] Indeed, although he complained constantly in his
letters of the long hours and the not-infrequent tedium of newspaper work,
there is abundant proof that he, in fact, enjoyed it rather than otherwise.
Throughout this period his health remained good; it is probable that he
took no more than a minimum of opium. (He must certainly have taken
some.) "Thank God, I have *my Health perfectly* & I am working hard . . .
Life were so flat a thing without Enthusiasm—that if for a moment it leave
me, I have a sort of stomach-sensation attached to all my Thoughts, like
those which succeed to the pleasurable operation of a dose of opium,"[5] he
wrote to Tom Wedgwood at the New Year.

*See *Essays On His Own Times*

A professional writer to the core, S.T.C. nursed no dilettante fears of possible damaging effects which newspaper work might have upon him: "by being obliged to write without much elaboration I shall greatly improve myself in naturalness & facility of style."[6] He informed Josiah Wedgwood: "I am not ashamed of what I have written."[7] He mused, with satisfaction: "it is not unflattering to a man's Vanity to reflect that what he writes at 12 at night will before 12 hours is over have perhaps 5 or 6000 readers?"[8]

With his opium consumption reduced, his health improved and a regular income relieving his anxieties, S.T.C. now found his marriage amicable again. He still had moments when he permitted himself a grumble to Southey, sighing that Sara's everyday self and minor interests did not harmonise with his own occupations, temperament, or weaknesses,* but, "we cannot be happy in all respects . . . (as everything mellows) I am content, indeed, thankful!"[9]

Among the lesser-known poems of S.T.C. there is this exceedingly moving one written for Sara Coleridge. The date of writing is uncertain, perhaps somewhat later than Buckingham Street (though it would scarcely have been written after 1802); but whatever the date, it expresses wonderfully the storms and calms of marriage:

THE HAPPY HUSBAND

Oft, oft methinks, the while with Thee
    I breathe, as from the heart, thy Dear
    And dedicated name, I hear
A promise and a mystery.
    A pledge of more than passing life,
    Yea, in that very name of Wife!

A pulse of love, that ne'er can sleep!
    A feeling that upbraids the heart
    With happiness beyond desert,
That gladness half requests to weep!
    Nor bless I not the keener sense
    And unalarming turbulence

Of transient joys, that ask no sting
    From jealous fears, or coy denying;
    But born beneath Love's brooding wing,
And into tenderness soon dying,
    Wheel out their giddy moment, then
    Resign the soul to love again;—

---

*The letters contain repeated evidence, of this somewhat indirect yet unmistakable nature, that it was S.T.C.'s opium-habit that was the chief bone of contention between the Coleridges.

"God Knows Where We Can Go"

A more precipitated vein
   Of notes, that eddy in the flow
   Of Smoothest song, they come, they go,
And leave their sweeter understrain
   It's own sweet self—a love of Thee
   That seems, yet cannot greater be!

A lasting bond between the Coleridges was their great love of their children. Hartley, or Moshes, was the apple of their mutual eye, a constant delight to them (though perhaps not so much to their friends). The Coleridges were now seeing a good deal socially of the Godwins and on one occasion Hartley gave "Mr Gobwin" such a rap on the shins with a ninepin that the author of *On Political Justice* (and advocate for anarchy), dancing in agony, severely lectured Sara Coleridge on the need of discipline for her anti-socially boisterous son. "Moshes is somewhat too rough and noisy," allowed S.T.C., "but the cadaverous silence of Godwin's Children is to me quite catacomb-ish."[10]

Pleasant as his London social life was proving (there had been a full reconciliation with Lamb, among other congenial happenings), lucrative and often gratifying as was the newspaper work, S.T.C. had decided that he would quit full-time journalism and London at the end of four months. We may be virtually certain that, during the "pikteresk Toor," he had promised Wordsworth that, having done a stint of newspaper work sufficient to clear his financial situation, he would remove to the North, there to be Wordsworth's neighbour.

On Friday, December 20 William and Dorothy, in practical pursuance of this mutual pact with S.T.C., had moved into Dove Cottage at Grasmere (the cottage that William had discovered during the "pikteresk Toor"). On Christmas Eve, 1799, William wrote a long letter to S.T.C. describing the journey that he and Dorothy had made, on foot, from Wensleydale to Kendal, where they had bought and ordered furniture; they then had completed, in a post-chaise, the remainder of their journey from Kendal to Grasmere. Dorothy has left us an inimitable retrospective account of their arrival at Dove Cottage in the dark damp cold of midwinter:

> The evening before the shortest day Molly [the servant] came in in her brisk way to shake hands with me at six o'clock, the time when we arrived here 6 years ago. "Aye," says the poor old creature, "I mun never forget t'laal striped gown and t'laal straw Bonnet, as ye stood here" (by the parlour fire). It was a miserable dark chimney with a handful of reddish cinders in it, for you must know Molly had kept fires in the house for a fortnight with *two bushels of coals* that it might be dry and comfortable to receive us.[11]

Despite Molly's admirable efforts William and Dorothy, not altogether surprisingly, caught troublesome colds in their damp and empty house and

307

Dorothy was soon also racked with toothache, brought on by an evening walk in icy wind. She, confined thereby indoors, sat "absolutely buried"[12] in needlework; bed-curtains and window-curtains in the making piled in folds of material over and about her (from which she must have peered like a bright-eyed mouse). Meanwhile the chimneys smoked (as Wordsworth chimneys always smoked) and brother and sister hoped that John Wordsworth might join them any day and that Coleridge, in the spring, would arrive, successfully decoyed, to be their neighbour.

S.T.C. now found himself in an extremely difficult, albeit typical, predicament.

It cannot be stressed too often that the contemporary view of the Coleridge-Wordsworth friendship was mainly one of rank and mounting disapproval. S.T.C. himself was only too aware of this. He had returned to London expressly, it seems, with the object of quickly making enough money to clear his debts and of arranging guarantees of free-lance work which would enable him to install himself in the North with a fair measure of security. However, he knew only too well that any announcement of his intention to settle in the Lake Country with Wordsworth would evoke an uproar of disapproval from his friends and from his patrons the Wedgwoods. Therefore, while doggedly plugging on with fulfilment of his scheme, he exerted himself to delude everyone into believing that the furthest idea from his mind was the intention of moving northward. Poole, Southey, the Wedgwoods, Sara: all entertained distinct views upon where S.T.C. should settle and to their chorus Daniel Stuart soon added his voice. S.T.C., committed by his emphatic "Yes" to Wordsworth, found himself in his everlasting dilemma of being unable to say "No" to anyone else and thus, in no time, he was involved in a complicated strategy of deception which almost defies analysis.

The Wedgwoods were, perhaps, the easiest dealt with. S.T.C. explained to Thomas: "I shall remain in London till April—the expences of my last year made it necessary for me to exert my industry; and many other good ends are answered at the same time. Where I next settle, I shall continue: & that must be in a state of retirement & rustication . . . In April I retire to my greater work—the Life of Lessing."[13] To Josiah he wrote: "I work from Morning to night; but in a few weeks I shall have accomplished my purpose —& then adieu to London for ever!"[14]

With the Wedgwoods it was possible to be ambiguous. Poole, however, was another matter.

Poole's enthusiasm for the Wordsworths had rapidly waned once they had become his neighbours. S.T.C.'s bolt to Sockburn had convinced Tom Poole, finally and conclusively, that Wordsworth exerted a positively dangerous influence over Coleridge. The flight to the North, made without a word of explanation to Poole who, with Sara, had been left in absolute ignorance and silence, had angered and injured that most staunch and loving of friends. Poole had been the support and stay of Sara Coleridge during S.T.C.'s absence in Germany; his purse, as well as his loyal friendship, had been at the disposal of S.T.C.'s wife and children. This generous gesture was regarded as perfectly natural by Poole himself; he asked for no praise. What he certainly had not anticipated was that S.T.C., on his return from Germany, would (by what Poole could only see as self-indulgent behaviour and idolatry of the Wordsworths) open a gaping breach where before had been such seemingly solid ground. He could not quickly recover from the trauma of S.T.C.'s bolt and in February was still reproving him: "I think you treated me with unmerited silence."[15] He doubted the continuing strength of S.T.C.'s affection for him.

S.T.C.'s reply was warm with fond chiding: "How could you take such an absurd idea into your head that my affections have weakened towards you?"[16]

Protestations of affection on S.T.C.'s part naturally encouraged Poole to hope that S.T.C. would return to Stowey to live, once he had finished his necessary work in London. S.T.C., quite unable to tell Poole his true plans, plunged into discussion of possible accommodation in, or near, Stowey, where, he declared, he would beyond all doubt settle, so long as he could get a house large enough for him to have a study beyond earshot of domestic sounds and with a garden. He was, he swore to Poole, "Stowey-sick." If he could not find a suitable house by midsummer in the Stowey locality, then he, Sara and Hartley would take lodgings at Minehead or Porlock.

Mollifying messages of love were sent, including "Sara's Love—'and my Lub—Hartley Cöidge's Lub'."[17]

Presumably S.T.C. sounded Sara on the subject of the North and the Wordsworths, but after the bolt she, too, must have been at least a little prejudiced against both the Lake Country and these two particular inhabitants thereof. S.T.C. became petulant again:

> God knows where we can go; for that situation which suits my wife does not suit me, and what suits me does not suit my wife. However, that which is, is,—a truth which always remains equally clear, but not always equally pleasant.[18]

Southey, meanwhile (not at all well at this point in time, suffering from what seems to have been nervous exhaustion brought about by too long and intensive writing hours), was speaking wistfully of forming a little colony overseas—not, now, upon the banks of the Susquehannah, but in Italy or the South of France. A good deal of correspondence about such a scheme passed between himself and S.T.C., who pictured a happy little band: the Southeys, the Wordsworths, Davy, Tobin, the Coleridges. "Precious Stuff for Dreams—& God knows, I have no time for them!"[19] When came to serious schemes of residence, said S.T.C.:

I am as unfixed as yourself—only that we are under the absolute necessity of fixing somewhere—& that somewhere will, I suppose, be Stowey—there are all my Books, & all our Furniture.—In May I am under a kind of engagement to go with Sara to Ottery—My family wish me to fix there, but *that* I must decline, in the names of public liberty and individual Free-agency. Elder Brothers ... are subjects of occasional Visits, not temptations to a Co-township. But ... Sara ... must be settled in a house by the latter end of July, or the first week in August ... O my dear Southey! I would to God, that your Health did not enforce you to migrate—we might most assuredly contrive to fix a residence somewhere ... Alfoxden would make two houses.[20]

This was not precisely lying but neither was it an exact regard for the truth. S.T.C. must have known that Alfoxden would never again be let to "one of the fraternity," yet he constantly reverted to the theme. *"I have a huge Hankering for Alfoxden."*[21] It was a safe place for him to hanker after, for he could scarcely hope to get it.

Stuart, learning that S.T.C. was determined to leave him in April, commenced exerting pressure on him to change his mind. S.T.C. told Poole:

If I had the least love of money, I could make almost sure of 2000£ a year/ for Stuart has offered me half shares in the two Papers, the M.P. & Courier, if I would devote myself with him to them—but I told him, that I would not give up the Country, & the lazy reading of old Folios for two Thousand Times two thousand Pound—in short, that beyond 250£ a year, I considered money as a real Evil—at which he stared.

He continued:

I would to God I could get Wordsworth to retake Alfoxden—the Society of so great a Being is of priceless Value—but he will never quit the North of England—his habits are more assimilated with the Inhabitants there—there he & his Sister are exceedingly beloved, enthusiastically ... Certainly no one neither you, or the Wedgewoods [sic] ... ever entered into the feeling due to a man like Wordsworth—of whom I do not hesitate in saying, that since Milton no man has *manifested* himself equal to him.[22]

It made Poole decidedly angry to hear S.T.C., whose brilliant gifts had now led him to the threshold of an immensely successful career, blithely announcing firstly, that beyond a bare pittance he regarded money as an evil (without doubt Poole was bearing in mind that until now S.T.C. had had to rely upon the charity of his friends for even that bare pittance) and, secondly, to hear him so fulsomely praising an individual who was, in Poole's estimation, inferior to S.T.C. not only in genius but also as a man. He took Coleridge to task in a letter of some asperity, charging him with prostration before Wordsworth. This further irritated S.T.C. The breach between the two men became yet a little wider.

It is significant that Poole seems to have been one of the first to have commented upon character changes in S.T.C.[23] He attributed these changes to the unfortunate influence of Wordsworth; they were, in fact, attributable to morphine.

In our own day of intravenous heroin the changes both in the personality and appearance of an addict are rapid and dramatic; in S.T.C.'s day the process was necessarily very much more gradual. It is possible that the ten months' absence in Germany had made the personality changes in his case more readily apparent to lovingly discerning eyes when he returned. Attentive study of the letters for this period, within a morphine context, reveals subtleties of ambiguity; S.T.C. was becoming increasingly slippery. Disturbing nuances, as it were, are discernible in the tone of his voice. We find him at times having to strain for the old, happy, ringing manner. A lack of confidence may at times be detected where once he would have been all sublime bounce. He was taking offence more easily. There is also significance in the way in which, with certain correspondents (Tom Wedgwood, Humphrey Davy), S.T.C. made free allusion to opium in a context unconnected with medicine.

Tom Poole's accusations of a changed manner were based upon something more tangible than the sore imaginings of a hurt and jealous heart.

On March 2, Sara and Hartley left London to stay for a month with friends at Kempsford. S.T.C. moved to 36 Chapel Street, Pentonville, Islington, the address of "the Agnus Dei & the Virgin Mary,"[24] as S.T.C. called Charles and Mary Lamb. On the evening of Sara's departure, a Sunday, S.T.C. and the Lambs visited Godwin at his delightfully named villa, 'Polygon', in Somers Town (then a flowery-gardened village). S.T.C., liberated from Sara's watchful eye, first drank wine, then took punch and became very tipsy, with the result that he had a violent argument, approach a brawl, with Godwin (whom he never genuinely liked, despite a brave show of friendship; he could neither forgive nor forget Godwin's atheism). Next day S.T.C. wrote to apologise—a letter worth quoting at length, because it tells us so much about S.T.C. and explains why his friends found him so deeply lovable, despite his many blemishes:

> *Mr Lamb's No/36 Chapel Street Pentonville—*
> *8, Monday Morning   3 March 1800*
>
> Dear Godwin,
>   The Punch after the Wine made me tipsy last night—this I mention, not that my head aches, or that I felt after I quitted you, any unpleasantness, or titubancy—; but because tipsiness has, and has always, one unpleasant effect —that of making me talk *very* extravagantly/& as when sober, I talk extravagantly enough for any *common* Tipsiness, it becomes a matter of nicety in discrimination to know when I am or am not affected.—An idea starts up in

my head—away I follow it thro' thick & thin, Wood & Marsh, Brake & Briar —with all the apparent Interest of a man who was defending one of his old and long-established Principles—Exactly of this kind was the Conversation, with which I quitted you / I do not believe it possible for a human Being to have a greater horror of the Feelings that usually accompany such principles as I then supported, or a deeper conviction of their irrationality than myself —but the whole Thinking of my Life will not bear me up against the accidental Press & Crowd of my mind, when it is elevated beyond its natural Pitch /.—

We shall talk wiselier with the Ladies on Tuesday—God bless you, & give your dear little ones a kiss a piece for me—

The Agnus Dei & the Virgin Mary desire their kind respect to you, you sad Atheist—!

> Your's with affectionate/Esteem
> S. T. Coleridge[25]

Despite his hard stint in journalism, S.T.C.'s financial situation at the close of the four months on the *Morning Post* was no better than it had been at the start. He was still overdrawn on Wedgwood; he was in debt to Poole's friend Purkis, from whom he had borrowed sums of ready cash upon his first arrival in London from Sockburn. In mid-March, 1800, S.T.C. was given an advance of a hundred pounds by Longman for an account of his recent "pikteresk Toor," but this money seems to have been quickly spent: on April 21, he was obliged to confess to Josiah Wedgwood[26] that he had drawn a draft of twenty pounds on him (without at the time informing him) in order to pay back an old debt of twenty pounds to Cottle, who was now winding up his affairs as a bookseller. (Wedgwood behaved very understandingly and two months later S.T.C. paid him back the twenty pounds.) Nevertheless, S.T.C. was still adamant in his determination to quit full-time work for Stuart (and to go North); he buoyantly informed Purkis: "I can with tolerable ease get 300£ a year by my pen,"[27] —this in a free-lance capacity. As a bald factual statement this was true enough; but Purkis, for one, must have privately recognised that though S.T.C. *could* do so, the chances were remote that he *would* do so.

By April 10, S.T.C. was in Grasmere assisting Wordsworth to prepare a second edition of *Lyrical Ballads*. The Wordsworths were now well settled at Dove Cottage; their brother John was with them on a protracted visit. Mary Hutchinson was also with them for six weeks from the end of February until early April. Dorothy explained to Jane how they managed to accommodate visitors in so small a house:

> We have made a lodging-room [bed-chamber] of the parlour below stairs. The bed, though only a camp-bed, is large enough for two people to sleep in. We sit in a room above stairs and we have one lodging-room with two single beds, a sort of lumber room and a small low unceiled room, which I have

papered with newspapers and in which we have put a small bed without curtains.[28]

John Wordsworth had arrived at Dove Cottage at the end of January. He had not seen Dorothy for several years and seems to have been shy of meeting her again; twice he approached Dove Cottage on the evening of his arrival, put his hand on the latch, stopped, then turned away again without the courage to enter (he was not by nature a timid man). Finally he went to the inn and sent word round to Dove Cottage that he had arrived.

Once the ice of meeting was broken he delighted in the cottage and, with a sailor's practicality, busied himself continuously making various improvements for the comfort of the place and helping to plant the garden. The little we know of him suggests an impressive combination of the artist and the businessman, a successful blending of the sensibilities of William and Dorothy with the sense of Christopher and Richard. The life of a sailor merchantman was therefore particularly suited to him.

It is possible that Mary Hutchinson's presence kept John at Dove Cottage for longer than he might otherwise have stayed. Dorothy was subsequently to recall: "John used to walk with her everywhere, and they were exceedingly attached to each other."[29]

William, after John's death at sea in 1805, was to say:

he found in his Sister and me and Coleridge and in my Wife and a Sister of hers whom at that time he had an opportunity of seeing much of, all that was wanting to make him completely happy . . . He encouraged me to persist in the plan of life which I had adopted; I will work for you was his language and you shall attempt to do something for the world . . . (observe this was long before my marriage and when I had no thought of marrying and also when we had no hope about the Lowther debt).[30]

This remark, coupled with S.T.C.'s masochistic notebook entries (p. 430) and a comment of his in a letter to Stuart (CL 682) have led to the supposition that John and Sara Hutchinson were privately betrothed. Close examination of the relevant material in no way supports this theory. Several factors have to be borne in mind. The most important is that if Sara Hutchinson and John Wordsworth had indeed been engaged, this would have meant that for the best part of four years S.T.C. was importuning with protestations of love the fiancée of a man whom he professed greatly to love and admire and who was, moreover, the brother of his two dearest friends, both of whom were well aware of S.T.C.'s infatuation for Sara and neither of whom made any apparent attempt to prevent Sara and S.T.C. meeting (indeed, Dorothy, in the enthusiasm of her sensibility clearly encouraged the romance). It is impossible to believe that such a situation would have prevailed. S.T.C.'s main reason for making Sara the obsessive object of his opium-dreaming rather than Mary seems to have been that, once he was aware of the attachment between Mary and William, he placed a taboo upon Mary. It, is almost certain that he, in the strict, albeit idiosyncratic code of honour which he heroically strove to adhere to throughout the nadir of his drug experience, would have placed a similar taboo upon Sara had she truly been betrothed to John.

It was always necessary for his masochistic gratification to visualise the woman of his dreams in another man's arms. Thus S.T.C. visualised Sara as John's wife; he also visualised her as William's wife in the case of Mary's death, as this notebook entry reveals:

SICKLY Thoughts about M. mort. & W. ÷ Sa—[31]

This note was made *before* John Wordsworth's death.

It is possible that, once Mary had become betrothed to William, Dorothy may have permitted herself castles-in-the-air in which she saw Sara married to John and with him settled at Grasmere. Had Dorothy had such dreams she would doubtless have voiced them aloud and, such being the attitudes of the New Sensibility, once a fancy was voiced aloud it virtually became accorded all the serious consideration of established fact. To quote Jane Austen again:

> Elinor ... knew that what Marianne and her mother conjectured one moment, they believed the next—that with them, to wish was to hope, and to hope was to expect. She tried to explain the real state of the case to her sister ... Marianne was astonished to find how much the imagination of her mother and herself had outstripped the truth.
>
> "And you really are not engaged to him!" said she.[32]

William's remark to James Losh (above) that John had an opportunity of seeing much of "my Wife and a Sister of hers . . . observe this was long before my marriage and when I had no thought of marrying" was written five years after John's visit. It does not seem, in fact, that John had nearly so good an opportunity of getting to know Sara during his sojourn in the Lakes as he had of becoming acquainted with Mary; Sara did not stay at Dove Cottage until November 17, 1800, when she came on a long visit; John had left on September 29 to go to sea. Although he was to return to England between voyages on more than one occasion before his death he never again visited the Lakes, nor saw Sara Hutchinson, which he surely would have done had he been betrothed to her. There is strong indication, however, that Mary's betrothal to William may have been one important reason why John did not accept Dorothy's further pressing invitations to come to Grasmere.

S.T.C., on his way to Grasmere at the end of March, called on the Hutchinsons and saw Sara, with whom he doubtless resumed what seemed an amusing and harmless flirtation. He seems to have left with a little of her hair in his pocket.³³ This kind of gallantry was something that he could never resist and we must suppose that she, naive and young, was flattered by his light-hearted advances (which at this stage were regarded by everyone as an entertaining pleasantry). At Grasmere, where S.T.C. arrived on April 6, it is possible that he saw Mary before she left for home.

The reviews of the first edition of *Lyrical Ballads* had, generally speaking, been favourable and the book had gradually gathered momentum as a success; it was *The Ancient Mariner* which had drawn most of the critical fire, principally because it had been almost universally misunderstood. (Lamb, alone, stood as its unqualified champion and admirer.) In deciding to bring out a second edition of *Lyrical Ballads* Wordsworth planned that this should be in two volumes; the first edition forming the first volume, the second volume to be made up of new poems and the entire work to be published under his name only. To all this S.T.C. agreed.

On May 4, S.T.C. returned South. He had arranged to see Stuart in London, undoubtedly to discuss further work with him. (Knowing S.T.C. it is possible that he had not yet had the courage to tell Stuart categorically that he would be giving up full-time newspaper work. Certainly Stuart had wished to discuss further free-lance work in detail.) S.T.C., obviously unable to face direct confrontation with Stuart, ducked the London encounter and went to Bristol.³⁴ Here he apparently arranged for Biggs and Cottle to print the new edition of *Lyrical Ballads*; he also made an agreement on Wordsworth's behalf for their publication by Longman; for the copyright of this edition Longman paid eighty pounds. Davy agreed to look over the proof sheets when they were ready. This last point suggests that S.T.C. did not anticipate being in, or near Bristol by that date; in fact, he extended a tentative invitation to Davy to stay with him at Keswick "in the fall of the year."³⁵

S.T.C., while in the Lake Country with the Wordsworths, had seen and virtually decided upon Greta Hall, a then recently built house standing upon an eminence about a furlong from Keswick* and commanding extensive and wonderful views of Derwentwater, Bassenthwaite Lake, Skiddaw, Borrowdale and the Derwent Fells. The pretence of house-hunting in the Quantocks and Exmoor indulged in by S.T.C. when he got back to Stowey at the end of May should therefore be seen as a purely token gesture. Even as he made it S.T.C. was writing to Godwin, describing the house at Keswick:

a house of such prospect, that if, according to you & Hume impressions & ideas *constitute* our Being, I shall have a tendancy to become a God.³⁶

To Godwin, also, went an invitation to visit Keswick in the autumn.

*The town has now grown around Greta Hall, which today is part of Keswick School.

There is more than a whiff of opium about these last weeks in the West Country, "a sense of wearisomeness & disgust" which unfitted S.T.C., he said, for anything "but sleeping or immediate society."[37] This he overtly attributed to the finishing of the Schiller translation; but his disgust was probably more correctly self-disgust. S.T.C. was wantonly deceiving Poole, to whom he insisted that he would prefer Stowey above all places for the sake of Poole's society. But "there was no suitable house, and no prospect of a suitable house."[38]

The Coleridges removed from the West Country to the Lake Country in mid-June; S.T.C. allegedly parted from Poole with "pain & dejection."[39] The first part of the journey North was made from Bristol to Liverpool, by chaise. The Coleridges stayed in Liverpool for eight or nine days, during which period S.T.C. caught a severe "cold from wet."[40] By the time he and his small family arrived at Grasmere on Sunday, June 29, he was very ill; the Wordsworths were determined to take him sailing on Rydal Water in William's boat and this they did, but immediately afterwards S.T.C. retired to bed "with a rheumatic fever almost"[41] which kept him in bed for several days and left him tired and listless. (Laudanum would have been taken medicinally.) His eyelids became painfully inflamed and swollen; he could write no letters, nor was he in the mood.

On Wednesday, July 23, S.T.C. left for Greta Hall; Sara and Hartley followed next day. The evening before S.T.C.'s departure* there was a picnic on the island of the lake:

> our kettle swung over the fire hanging from the branch of a Fir Tree, and I lay & saw the woods, & mountains, & lake all trembling, & as it were *idealized* thro' the subtle smoke which rose up from the clear red embers of the fir-apples which we had collected. Afterwards, we made a glorious Bonfire on the Margin, by some alder bushes, whose twigs heaved & sobbed in the uprushing column of smoke—& the Image of the Bonfire, & of us that danced round it—ruddy laughing faces in the twilight—the Image of this in a Lake smooth as that sea, to whose words the son of God had said, PEACE![42]

Had S.T.C. but known it, he stood on the verge of his life's great sea of stormy waters; over a decade and a half of fearsome passage lay ahead.

---

*Dorothy gives the date of this picnic as Friday, July 18, and the occasion of the bonfire as Sunday, July 20; but she did not write up her journal for the Coleridges' visit until a day or two after they had left.

PART THREE

Shooting the Albatross

"God save thee, ancient Mariner!
From the fiends, that plague thee thus!
Why look'st thou so?"—With my cross-bow
I shot the Albatross . . .

Ah! well a-day! what evil looks
Had I from old and young!
Instead of the cross, the Albatross
About my neck was hung.

The Ancient Mariner I and II (1834)

This I long ago observed, is the dire Curse of all habitual Immorality, that the impulses wax as the motives
wane—like animals caught in the current of a Sea-
vortex, (such as the Norwegian Maelstrohm) at first
they rejoice in the pleasurable ease with which they
are carried onward, with their consent yet without any
effort of their will—as they swim, the servant gradually
becomes the Tyrant, and finally they are sucked onward against their will: the more they see their danger,
with the greater and more inevitable rapidity are they
hurried toward and into it—.

S.T.C. to R. H. Brabant (CL 959)

CHAPTER FOURTEEN

LAND OF ICE AND FEARFUL SOUNDS

(July 1800–May 1801)

And now there came both mist and snow,
And it grew wondrous cold:
And ice, mast-high, came floating by,
As green as emerald.

And through the drifts the snowy clifts
Did send a dismal sheen:
Nor shapes of men nor beasts we ken—
The ice was all between.

The ice was here, the ice was there,
The ice was all around:
It cracked and growled, and roared and howled,
Like noises in a swound!

The Ancient Mariner I (1834)

FRIDAY, JULY 15, 1800, found S.T.C. writing ecstatic letters about his new home to as many friends as he could manage to find time to send greetings:

> From the leads on the housetop of Greta Hall, Keswick, Cumberland, at the present time in the occupancy and usufruct-possession of S. T. Coleridge, Esq., Gentleman-poet and Philosopher in a mist.[1]

"Here I am," he told Tobin, "with Skiddaw at my back; the Lake of Bassenthwaite . . . on my right hand; on my left, and stretching far away into the fantastic mountains of Borrowdale, the Lake of Derwentwater; straight before me a whole camp of giants' tents."[2] These were the Newlands fells; to Davy the excited S.T.C. repeated: "before me there is a great Camp of Mountains—Giants seem to have pitch'd their Tents there —each Mountain is a Giant's Tent—and how the light streams from them —and the Shadows that travel upon them!"[3] S.T.C., endeavouring to encourage Davy to keep his promise of a visit, declared: "My dear fellow, I would that I could wrap up the view . . . in a pill of opium and send it to you!"[4]

S.T.C. sat writing on the leads while the nearly eight months pregnant Sara dealt with the manifold chores of settling into a new home. At last, however, she discovered Samuel's whereabouts: "My wife will not let me stay on the Leads—I must go, and unpack a trunk for her—she cannot stoop to it—thanks to my late Essay on Population!"[5]

319

To Southey (destined one day to be a tenant of Greta Hall himself) S.T.C. sent a detailed description:

Our house stands on a low hill, the whole front of which is one field and an enormous garden, nine-tenths of which is a nursery garden. Behind the house is an orchard, and a small wood on a steep slope, at the foot of which flows the river Greta, which winds round and catches the evening lights in the front of the house. In front we have . . . an encamped army of tent-like mountains, which by an inverted arch gives a view of another vale. On our right the . . . wedge-shaped lake of Bassenthwaite; . . . on our left Derwent-water and Lodore in full view, and the fantastic mountains of Borrowdale. Behind us is the massy Skiddaw, smooth, green, high, with two chasms and a tent-like ridge in the larger. A fairer scene you have not seen in all your wanderings.[6]

S.T.C.'s landlord was a retired carrier named William Jackson, who had so prospered in his business that he had been able to build himself this almost over-impressively large, fine new house. Half of it he lived in himself, with his housekeeper Mrs Wilson (the Coleridge children's beloved "Wilsy" and S.T.C.'s "old love God and be cheerful").[7] Mr Jackson, very fond of reading and with a library of nearly five hundred books, was so proud of having a literary man as his tenant and was so happy to have Hartley's company (he was a bachelor and both he and Mrs Wilson missed bairns about the house) that he "absolutely refused to receive any rent for the first half year" and from thereon charged a mere peppercorn rent. "Hartley quite *lives* at the house—& it is as you may suppose no small joy to my wife to have a good affectionate motherly woman divided from her only by a Wall."[8] Thus S.T.C. to Josiah Wedgwood, adding: "for two thirds of the year we are in complete retirement—the other third is alive & swarms with Tourists of all shapes & sizes, & characters."[9] To Wedgwood S.T.C. also protested how sadly he missed Poole: "I feel what I have lost— feel it deeply—it recurs more often & painfully, than I had anticipated . . . I used to feel myself more at home in his great windy Parlour, than in my own cottage. We were well suited for each other—my animal Spirits corrected his inclinations to melancholy; and . . . my mind freshened in his company, and . . . acquired . . . more of substance and reality . . . Yet when I revise the step, I have taken, I know not how I could have acted otherwise."[10]

S.T.C. had to tread carefully with the Wedgwoods; he knew that neither of them approved of his removal to the North and the near company of Wordsworth. In spite of his protestations of nostalgia for Poole, S.T.C. was reluctant to write to him; the breach between them lay on his conscience.

S.T.C., upon his arrival at Keswick, was faced with a heavy programme of professional writing and a sea of financial embarrassment. There is no doubt that he could have extricated himself from the latter and have earned a lucrative livelihood with his pen had he now addressed himself to a hard and steady work routine. Stuart was only too anxious to receive articles from him. The account of the German tour for Longman (for which S.T.C. had received an advance) would in all probability have sold well. S.T.C. was furthermore under an obligation to Phillips, from whom he had accepted an advance for a "bookseller's compilation;" he was also under a moral responsibility to write the long promised life of Lessing, for Wedgwood.

Instead, once S.T.C. had sufficiently recovered from the illness that had beset him upon his arrival in the Lake Country, he neglected everything to devote himself to the *Lyrical Ballads* and the interests of Wordsworth, at whose disposal S.T.C. almost wholly placed himself during the latter half of 1800. In addition to extensively rewriting *The Ancient Mariner*, S.T.C. rewrote his poem, *Love*, to take the place of Wordsworth's poem, *The Convict* and, in a stupendous outburst of creative energy, composed the second part of *Christabel* which, it was planned, should conclude Volume Two of the *Ballads*. S.T.C. himself transcribed many of Wordsworth's poems. He prepared the sheets and wrote complicated and detailed directions to the printers, concerning lay-out, order of the poems and so forth. Furthermore, he discussed with Wordsworth the latter's celebrated preface to this edition of the ballads, talking it over in the utmost detail: indeed, S.T.C. was subsequently to claim, no doubt with justice, that much of the preface was his own brain-child. During this period of working for Wordsworth S.T.C.'s own work, upon which he and his family largely depended for their income and upon which S.T.C. wholly depended for furtherance of his own reputation, fell into almost total abeyance. His friends' fears of Esteesian prostration before Wordsworth were alarmingly justified.

Certainly Southey's well-known criticism of the Wordsworths would seem to contain at least an element of truth:

> Wordsworth & his sister who pride themselves upon having no selfishness, are of all human beings whom I have ever known the most intensely selfish. The one thing to which W. would sacrifice all others is his own reputation, concerning which his anxiety is perfectly childish ... & so he can get Coleridge to talk his own writings over with him, & criticise them & (without amending them) teach him how to do it,—to be in fact the very rain & air & sunshine of his intellect, he thinks C. is very well employed & this arrangement a very good one.[11]

During the month of August, 1800, there was much coming and going between Dove Cottage and Greta Hall and much work was done upon *Lyrical Ballads*.

S.T.C.'s struggles with *Christabel* were initially intense and exhausting, but towards the end of August he got the poem moving.* Once he had got it

*It is uncertain how much faith should be placed in S.T.C.'s account to J. Wedgwood (CL 362) of how he managed to get Part II to go: "immediately on my arrival

to go, he commenced his exploration of the fells. The ambiguous Gothic background of Part I of *Christabel* became, in Part II, scattered with Lake Country names. Even so, the country in which Christabel and the blood-freezing Geraldine confronted one another was never really the English Lakes. The serious writing about the Lake Country which S.T.C. now began to do is to be found in his notebooks, not in *Christabel*, and it was in prose that he wrote, not in verse.

S.T.C. was walking in the fells now as a solitary and, indeed, a pioneer fell-walker. His attitude to mountains was far in advance of his day. The Romantics enjoyed mountainous scenery as a tangible expression of the sublime, but they never regarded mountains as a physical challenge. The picturesque tourists, when they came to the Lake Country, confined themselves mainly to the valley bottoms. The few who did venture upon the hills went as sightseers and not as fell-walkers and they always employed guides: even Wordsworth, so far as we know, never ventured alone upon the major tops.

S.T.C. had not been in the Lake Country long before discovering the ridiculous discrepancy between the exaggerated awe with which the picturesque tourists approached the hills and the confident manner in which the dalesfolk lived and worked in these reputedly hair-raising regions. For the dalesman, securely at home in the land of his forefathers, the region held few of the terrors which kept the Romantics agog.

At the end of August 1800 (we do not know the exact date) Coleridge set off alone to explore Saddleback. He jotted a running commentary in his notebook as he went. The joy of fell-walking (and he was insistent upon stressing the word "joy") lay for him not only in the physical satisfaction of leaping, bounding and flashing over the heights (these are the words he used to describe his progress) but also in the stimulation which he received, as an artist, from the landscape. His notes became exercises in an experimental technique of writing which would simultaneously and exactly record impressions of scenery and natural objects as they greeted his eye. He was training himself in the course of working out this technique, not only to see with exactitude (something which few people, in fact, ever learn to do) but to put what he saw—shapes, lights, textures—making them true and putting them rightly, the most difficult technique of all for the writer. S.T.C. roamed daily and incessantly upon the fells, analysing sunsets, mists and storm-clouds, lights viewed over the lake, and asking himself questions

---

in this country I undertook to finish a poem . . . entitled Christabel . . . I tried and tried, & nothing would come of it . . . many a walk in the clouds on the mountains did I take; but all would not do—till one day I dined out at the house of a neighbouring clergyman, & some how or other drank so much wine, that I found some effort & dexterity requisite to balance myself on the hither Edge of Sobriety. The next day, my verse making faculties returned to me, and I proceeded successfully."

which in turn were to obsess painters like Turner, Corot and Monet: how does morning light differ from evening? Is the difference in the mind, or is there a physical cause? And if a physical cause, how can that be defined and put on paper? As Kathleen Coburn has remarked of S.T.C.'s work in this very important field: "The frequent conjunction of more than one kind of sensory awareness in moments of acute experience . . . involved him in heroic efforts to find new words to describe these apperceptions, with results that sometimes suggest a much later development in the history of painting and poetry."[12]

Obviously a companion of any kind would have been a distraction to S.T.C. in the fells. "I *must* be alone," he wrote, "if either my Imagination or Heart are to be enriched."[13]

August 29 again found him on Saddleback; he walked to Mungrisedale, spent the night there and next day explored Bannerdale Crags, Bowscale, Mosedale, Drycomb Beck. The day following his return from Mungrisedale he set off again; this time to Dove Cottage, via Helvellyn. He climbed Whitepike from Threlkeld Common, then took the now classical route southward over the tops: Calfhow Pike, Great Dod, Stybarrow Dod, Raise and Helvellyn. S.T.C.'s enthusiasm heightened with every fresh summit and every fresh view: "O Joy for me!"[14] he exclaimed in his notebook when, arrived on Stybarrow Dod, he saw Ullswater. The summit of Raise evoked another burst of enthusiasm and spate of notes.

S.T.C. had started out late, his walk was a long one and night was now falling, but it was a clear night and the moon was almost at the full. His notes reveal that by the time he had arrived on the summit of Helvellyn he was in a state of near intoxication from the excitement and the beauty of the walk. The twilit, utterly solitudinous scene made a thrilling and tremendous impression upon him. Above all he was overawed by Striding Edge, "that prodigious Precipice of grey stone with deep Wrinkles facing me."[15] He stood for a long time staring silently about him, before making a perilous descent by Nethermost Pike (perilous because of the poor light and the bad ground); a slanting downward route, it seems, across Birk Side and Seat Sandal. The moon was now above Fairfield, and "O! my God! how *did* that opposite precipice look—in the moonshine—its name Stile Crags."[16] (Steel Fell).

He jogged down the final stretch of Dunmail Raise and reached Dove Cottage at eleven. William and John Wordsworth had gone to bed, but Dorothy was browsing in the garden, enjoying the moonshine. On hearing the voices of his sister and their friend, William came down in his dressing-gown; the trio sat talking about the mountains and Helvellyn in particular and Coleridge then read them the draft of *Christabel* Part II that he had carried with him over Helvellyn, in his pocket.

Dorothy's ensuing *Journal* entries convey to us some of the magic of Dove Cottage at that period:

September 1st, Monday Morning. We walked in the wood by the Lake. W. read *Joanna*, and the *Firgrove*, to Coleridge. They bathed. The morning was delightful, with something of an autumn freshness. After dinner, Coleridge discovered a rock-seat in the orchard. Cleared away the brambles. Coleridge obliged to go to bed after tea. [While he was in bed the Wordsworths visited a neighbour to borrow some bottles for bottling rum] The evening somewhat frosty and grey, but very pleasant. I broiled Coleridge a mutton chop, which he ate in bed. Wm. was gone to bed. I chatted with John and Coleridge till near 12.

September 2nd, Tuesday. In the morning they all went to Stickel [sic] Tarn. A very fine, warm sunny, beautiful morning. I baked a pie etc. for dinner— . . . The fair-day . . . My Brothers came home to dinner at 6 o'clock. We drank tea immediately after by candlelight. It was a lovely moonlight night. We talked much about a house on Helvellyn. The moonlight shone only upon the village. It did not eclipse the village lights, and the sound of the dancing and merriment came along the still air. I walked with Coleridge and Wm. up the Lane and by the Church, and then lingered with Coleridge in the garden. John and Wm. were both gone to bed, and all the lights out.

Next day William, John and S.T.C. climbed Helvellyn again, accompanied by the Reverend Joseph Simpson, the vicar of Wythburn. S.T.C. parted from his friends on the summit and loped back to Keswick along the mountain range over which he had originally come.

His solitary moonlight expedition over Helvellyn from a direction entirely new to him was, both in concept and daring, quite as remarkable as his subsequent celebrated ascent of Scafell.

A week after his return from Grasmere, on September 9, S.T.C. struck out for the Coledale Fells; exploring Stoneycroft Gill, High Moss, Coledale, Grisedale Pike and the grand ridge-walk of Eel Crags, Crag Hill, Sail, Scar Crags and Causey Pike, a walk today rated as one of the classics. S.T.C. must have been one of the first, if not the first, to have done it purely as a walk and not as part of a sheep-gathering or fox-hunt. Within a decade of his first treading it the excursion up Causey Pike and along the ridge had become a popular one with tourists, but they were advised never to try it without a guide. (S.T.C. strode along it in the carefree style of a twentieth-century Youth Hosteller.)

The splendid Grisedale Pike-Causey day was followed by a break both in S.T.C.'s fell-walking and his visiting at Dove Cottage. His second surviving son, Derwent, was born on September 14. The child was a "very large" one and mother and infant at first did well; on September 17, S.T.C. wrote to Tobin, proudly, that Sara "dined & drank Tea up, in the parlour with me, this day— . . . There's for you!"[17] But the baby caught a chill and became so ill that he was not expected to live. Sara's distress was violent. She wept, while "the child, hour after hour, made a noise exactly like the creaking of a door which is being shut very slowly to prevent its creaking."[18]

Meantime S.T.C. attempted to catch up with some of his work for Stuart.

S.T.C. did not believe at that time in infant baptism, but the good Mr Jackson and Mrs Wilson insisted that the apparently dying child should be baptised and so, on September 27, he was christened Derwent Coleridge. Had the baby been a girl she would have been named after the Greta.

At Dove Cottage, William's old walking-tour friend, Robert Jones, came to stay from September 19 to 26. S.T.C. arrived on the twenty-third, and left with Jones. On Sunday, September 28, the Wordsworths drank tea and supped with Charles Lloyd who, now married, had settled with his wife at Old Brathay, Clappersgate: "on that day heard of the Abergavenny's arrival," noted Dorothy in her *Journal*. This was John's long awaited ship and next day he left Grasmere to join her. He walked over Grisedale Hause to Ullswater; William and Dorothy accompanied him as far as the tarn near the top of the pass. There they said their farewells and, after he had left them, "stood till we could see him no longer, watching him as he *hurried* down the stony mountain."[19]

Due to the birth of Derwent and the child's subsequent illness S.T.C. was not at Grasmere between September 26 and October 24. The Wordsworths consequently saw more of Charles Lloyd (whom S.T.C. still tried to avoid); Dorothy's *Journal* for October 2 tells us that she, William and Lloyd walked to Easedale (which the Wordsworths called "The Black Quarter"): "We had a pleasant conversation about the manners of the rich —avarice, inordinate desires, and the effeminacy, unnaturalness, and the unworthy objects of education."

During this period of S.T.C.'s absence Wordsworth was also much preoccupied with problems arising, as he saw it, from *The Ancient Mariner*.

As aforesaid, the reviews of the first (1798) edition of *Lyrical Ballads* were, generally speaking, favourable to all the poems but *The Ancient Mariner*; this was almost universally misunderstood and consequently attacked. Wordsworth (who himself never comprehended the poem) soon came to feel that S.T.C.'s masterpiece endangered the succcess of the *Ballads* as a whole. In June, 1799, Wordsworth was already writing to Cottle, saying that should the poems come to a second edition, he would put in the Mariner's place some little things which would be more likely to suit the common taste. When the time came for a second edition, Wordsworth discussed with S.T.C. the possible exclusion of *The Ancient Mariner* and S.T.C., in his anxiety to please Wordsworth, agreed to the poem's suppression. Against this Wordsworth finally decided, mainly because the omission of such a long poem would have affected the length of the book. However, Wordsworth retained his mistrust of the poem and when the time came (*circa* October 1) to post off to Biggs and Cottle the last two paragraphs of the preface to *Lyrical Ballads* Wordsworth, as well as including a long note defending his poem, *The Thorn*, also added a long and apologetic comment on *The Ancient Mariner*:

I cannot refuse myself the gratification of informing such Readers as may have been pleased with this poem, or with any part of it, that they owe their pleasure in some sort to me; as the Author was himself very desirous that it should be suppressed. This wish had arisen from a consciousness of the defects of the poem, and from a knowledge that many persons had been much displeased with it. The Poem of my Friend* has indeed great defects [Wordsworth then went on to detail them; chiefly, that the Mariner had no distinct character; that he did not act but was rather constantly acted upon and, lastly, that "the imagery is somewhat too laboriously accumulated".] Yet the poem contains many delicate touches of passion, and indeed the passion is everywhere true to nature . . . It therefore appeared to me that these several merits . . . gave to the poem a value which is not often possessed by better poems. On this account I requested of my Friend to permit me to republish it.

It seems exceedingly probable that S.T.C. was never shown this note before it was dispatched to the printer and knew nothing about its appearance until he actually saw it in print. Upon its appearance this gratuitous note of Wordsworth's drew furious fire from Charles Lamb: "For me, I was never so affected with any human tale. After first reading it, I was totally possessed with it for many days . . . I am hurt and vexed that you should think it necessary with a prose apology to open the eyes of dead men that cannot see."[20] Whether because of Lamb's spirited objection or not, Wordsworth withdrew this note from *Lyrical Ballads* after 1802.

On October 4, S.T.C. went over to Grasmere with the completed *Christabel*, Part II. What happened may best be left to Dorothy to describe, in the words of her *Journal*:

October 4th, 1800, Saturday. A very rainy, or rather showery and gusty, morning . . . Coleridge came in while we were at dinner, very wet—we talked till 12 o'clock. He had sate up all the night before, writing Essays for the newspaper. His youngest child had been very ill convulsion fits [sic]. Exceedingly delighted with the second part of Christabel.

October 5th, Sunday Morning. Coleridge read a 2nd time *Christabel*; we had increasing pleasure. A delicious morning. William and I were employed all the morning writing an addition to the preface . . . Coleridge and I walked to Ambleside after dark with the letter. Returned to tea at 9 o'clock.

October 6th, Monday. A rainy day. Coleridge intending to go, but did not get off . . . Determined not to print Christabel with the L.B.

On the face of it, S.T.C. appeared to accept with equanimity the decision to reject *Christabel*. He wrote most objectively about it to Davy, on October 9, explaining that Wordsworth had decided not to include the poem "be-

*The reader is reminded that this edition of *Lyrical Ballads* appeared under Wordsworth's name only.

cause it was in direct opposition to the very purpose for which the *Lyrical Ballads* were published."[21]

This was a correct decision in accordance with Wordsworth's observation in his preface to this second edition that the *Lyrical Ballads* were an attempt to counteract the "degrading thirst after stimulation" of Romantic Gothicism. But it should be borne in mind that this had become the aim of *Lyrical Ballads* in this second, Wordsworth-orientated edition; *Lyrical Ballads* had started out as a partnership between two poets, each of whom approached a specific problem from a different angle; Wordsworth sought to "give the charm of novelty to things of everyday" while S.T.C.'s endeavours were to be directed to giving "persons and characters supernatural, or . . . romantic . . . a semblance of truth."[22] (p. 265). *Christabel*, although both supernatural in content and wholly Romantic in key, nonetheless is completely convincing, inasmuch as it fulfils the purpose of all fantasies and fairy tales and compels the listener (or reader) to suspend his critical powers and believe the impossible during the course of the narrative.

Thus, although the decision to exclude *Christabel* was the correct one if the poem were to be subjected to the criticism expounded in Wordsworth's preface, from the point of view of the original concept of *Lyrical Ballads* it was a wrong decision.

In confrontation together the two poets contrived to keep their controversy cool. S.T.C. approved the decision about *Christabel*: the Wordsworths damned the poem with faint praise; it was not without merit, but they "were abundantly anxious to acquit their judgements of any blindness to the very numerous defects,"[23] as S.T.C. subsequently was to comment. He appeared to take their criticism in good part; he had pride, but no conceit. Yet, despite an overtly calm initial reaction to Wordsworth's rejection of *Christabel* this, together with the earlier serious disparagement of *The Ancient Mariner*, inflicted the gravest possible trauma upon S.T.C. In fact it perhaps would not be exaggeration to see this rejection of Coleridge's poetry by Wordsworth as the mortal blow which precipitated S.T.C.'s calamitous collapse and destruction.

The heroin addict of today faces virtually certain death within a foreseeably not too distant future. The nature of his drug and its intravenous administration ensures speed and fatality. In S.T.C.'s day morphine was slowly, albeit surely, destructive but this destruction, although deeply distressing in its consequences, was not necessarily fatal. The morphine habit, once acquired, could not be broken but, in properly treated cases, it might be controlled (De Quincey was a case in point). It is possible, therefore (although admittedly not very probable) that S.T.C., maintained upon a reasonably even keel by friendship and sympathetic support, might have progressed throughout the years, encountering increasing chronic illness from his rheumatic disease and resorting always to regular, controlled, opium, but avoiding outright catastrophe. This, with good fortune, might have been his lot. But such was not to be his destiny. Wordsworth's rejection of him as a poet precipitated the always perilously high-wire-balanced S.T.C. into a profound dejection combined with a fatal loss of self-confidence. Dejection meant an opium jag; opium meant further neglect of work and more domestic fighting; these brought anxiety and guilt; anxiety and guilt in turn meant more opium; more opium spelled illness and so the tragic carousel revolved and, in this instance, evolved into a spiral of overwhelming and complete disaster.

S.T.C.'s dejection upon his return to Greta Hall from Dove Cottage is made clear enough by this letter to Stuart, written on October 7:

> If I know my own heart . . . I have not a spark of ambition . . . This is no virtue in me, but depends on the accidental constitution of my intellect in which my taste in judging is far, far more perfect than my power to execute —and I do nothing, but almost instantly its defects and sillinesses come upon my mind, and haunt me, until I am completely disquieted with my performance.[24]

This kind of dejection inevitably meant that his laudanum bottle would be taken up. But upon this occasion, to add to his distress, dunning letters arrived in his study. His finances were desperate; he was now in danger of becoming half demented with the realisation of how fearfully behind he had fallen in his own work: "the endeavour to finish *Christabel* . . . threw my business terribly back—& now I am sweating for it,"[25] he told Poole.

S.T.C. had agreed to write contributions to Wordsworth's group of verses, *Poems on the Naming of Places*, but he did not do so. When Wordsworth went to Keswick in mid-October, presumably to collect these, it was to discover, as Dorothy noted in her *Journal* (perhaps with a slight touch of resentment): "Coleridge had done nothing for the L.B. Working hard for Stuart." Again, she notes for October 22: "Coleridge came in to dinner. He had done nothing." (She goes on to describe how they were nonetheless all very merry together. In the evening Mr and Miss Simpson came with potatoes and plums and John Stoddart called.)

These desperate efforts of S.T.C. to redeem his own work situation were inevitably doomed to failure as dejection and opium together tightened their grip upon him. His ability to concentrate deserted him; he became oddly benumbed. A notebook entry for October 30 reads, tragically:

> He knew not what to do—something, he felt, must be done—he rose, drew his writing-desk suddenly before him—sate down, took the pen—& found that he knew not what to do.[26]

All his usual symptoms of opium now appeared; his eyes became severely inflamed, thereby rendering reading and writing scarcely possible. He took to his bed with rheumatic pains in the back of his head and limbs; a surgeon-apothecary was called, Mr John Edmundson.* He applied leeches repeatedly to the patient's temples and the inflamed eyes recovered but, to harass the patient "almost beyond endurance," boils appeared upon his neck. The weather became cold and wet; the house was exceedingly damp and draughty; S.T.C. kept to his bed during the greater part of November, quite unable to do any work. "For the last month or more I have indeed been a crazy machine,"[27] he told Poole. A letter to Davy is more revealing; with him S.T.C. could be frank upon the subject of opium:

Did Carlisle† ever communicate to you, or has he . . . published, his facts concerning *Pain*, which he mentioned when we were with him? It is a subject which *exceedingly interests* me— . . . I want to read something by somebody expressly on *Pain*, if only to give an *arrangement* to my own thoughts . . . For the last month I have been tumbling on through sands and swamps of Evil, & bodily grievance. My eyes have been inflamed . . . and strange as it seems, the act of poetic composition, as I lay in bed, perceptibly affected them, and my voluntary ideas were every minute passing, more or less transformed into vivid spectra . . . Amid all these changes & humiliation & fears, the sense of the Eternal abides in me, and preserves unsubdued
My chearful Faith that all which I endure
Is full of Blessings!
At times indeed I would fain be somewhat of a more tangible utility than I am, but so, I suppose, it is with all of us—one while cheerful, stirring, feeling in resistance nothing but a joy & a stimulus; another while drowsy, self-distrusting, prone to rest, loathing our own Self-promises, withering our own Hopes . . . the vitality & cohesion of our Being!—[28]

At the close of this letter S.T.C. assured Davy that he proposed to publish *Christabel* by itself. This scheme was but another of S.T.C.'s withering self-promises; *Christabel* remained unpublished.

By November 15, S.T.C. seemed better. Wordsworth arrived at Greta Hall on that day and Dorothy joined him on the 17th; the purpose of the visit was chiefly to collect Sara Hutchinson, who was coming to Grasmere for a long stay. William met her at Threlkeld (whither she had been chaperoned by her brother) on the 17th and she and the Wordsworths remained at Greta Hall until Saturday, November 22 when they returned to Grasmere.[29] On the following Friday S.T.C. walked to Grasmere (a distance of some fourteen miles); he was very unwell, with great boils on his neck, and during the walk he got very wet. On the night of his arrival he

---

The Universal British Directory for 1790 gives Keswick surgeon-apothecaries as Joseph Brown, John Edmundson, John Tyndal, and Christopher Williamson.
†Sir Anthony Carlisle (1768–1840); a noted surgeon.

awakened the Dove Cottage household with his screams, as he struggled in fearful nightmare:

> Friday night, Nov. 28, 1800, or rather Saturday morning—a most frightful Dream of a Woman whose features were blended with darkness catching hold of my right eye & attempting to pull it out—I caught hold of her arms fast—a horrid feel—Wordsworth cried out aloud at hearing my scream— heard his cry & thought it cruel he did not come/but did not wake till his cry was repeated a third time—the Woman's name was Ebon Ebon Thalud— When I awoke, my right eyelid swelled—[30]

He spent most of the ensuing five days in bed, with rheumatic symptoms; he returned to Keswick in a chaise, too ill to walk, on December 2. Yet by the 4th he was staggering back to Dove Cottage; there was pressing work to be done still on behalf of Wordsworth and *Lyrical Ballads*.

The rest of the month passed with almost non-stop illness and equally non-stop back-and-forth visiting by S.T.C. and the Wordsworths. In spite of his wretched ill-health S.T.C. was now extending himself by writing letters to distinguished persons who might be influential in obtaining good reviews for *Lyrical Ballads*: some of these letters (among them one to William Wilberforce and another to Fox) purported to come from Wordsworth but, needless to say, they were written for him by S.T.C. He also wrote to all his personal acquaintances who were likely to have any influence in pushing *Lyrical Ballads*. "I am especially pleased that I have contributed nothing to the second volume, as I can now exert myself loudly and everywhere in their favour without suspicion of vanity or self-interest," he told Longman masochistically.[31]

In this same letter S.T.C. regaled his publisher with a farrago of lies typical of the morphine addict who has fallen down on a job of work, or failed to keep an appointment, or in any other way has proved, as the morphine victim always proves to be, utterly and devastatingly unreliable:

> I will explain to you the delay in my manuscript ... After I had finished the work ... I was convinced by a friend that a long account which I had given of the Illuminati would raise a violent clamour against me & my publisher ... at the same time Mr Wordsworth who had been in a different part of Germany offered me the use of his Journal ... I immediately resolved to throw my work into Chapters instead of Letters, & substitute my friend's account of Germany farther south than I had been instead of the obnoxious Letters. This however would have taken so little time that you would have had the copy, within a week or ten days at most later than the day appointed —but at that time a complaint seized my head & eyes, which made it impracticable for me even to read.

Then followed an account of weeks of illness (which at least was true) followed by the assurance:

330

you may depend on it that from the first of January to the printing of the last page your Printer shall not have to complain of an hour's delay.

This account of the tour, needless to say, had not even been attempted. It was never attempted for Longman.

As for S.T.C. and poetry, "I have altogether abandoned it," he wrote to Thelwall, "being convinced that I never had the essentials of poetic Genius, & that I mistook a strong desire for original power."[32] To Wrangham S.T.C. declared: "Wordsworth . . . is a great, a true Poet—I am only a kind of Metaphysician."[33]

The close of the year found S.T.C. at Dove Cottage for Christmas, with his wife and Derwent. S.T.C. devoted the last days of 1800 to copying out the first two hundred and sixteen lines of Wordsworth's poem *Michael* for the printers.

The New Year of 1801 saw S.T.C. succumb to severe fever and rheumatic pains, to which was added the violent discomfort of an hydrocele (an accumulation of fluid between the epididymus and the body of the testicle, as S.T.C. explained to Davy: "*how* learned a Misfortune of this kind makes one").[34] His financial situation was desperate to brood upon, with money owed in all directions (including twenty-five pounds to Phillips in advance for a manuscript not yet written and over which Phillips now threatened to sue). S.T.C. was already overdrawn by forty pounds on the Wedgwood annuity for the coming year. Panicky and distraught, S.T.C. wrote to Poole, who replied with a loan of eighteen pounds and much loving counsel and encouragement: "be *calm* . . . I will, remember, *at any time*, if you are very ill, or have any particular wish to see me, come and see you." Poole added, perhaps correctly: "I bitterly regret your leaving Stowey. I fancy if you had continued here this would not have happened."[35]

S.T.C. resorted, during his illness, to reading philosophy, and when, on February 1, he felt himself better, he wrote to Poole that he hoped soon to be able to look back on his illness "only as a Storehouse of wild Dreams for Poems, or intellectual Facts for metaphysical Speculation. Davy in the kindness of his heart calls me the Poet-philosopher—I hope, Philosophy & Poetry will not neutralize each other, & leave me an inert mass. But I talk idly—I feel, that I have power within me."[36]

Power he most certainly had, but he could not control the machinery. His slight recovery was soon followed by another relapse: opium was almost certainly the cause. To Poole, S.T.C. explained that during this period of indifferent, yet nonetheless improved health, he had applied himself to philosophy, making a close examination of Locke's position in relation to Descartes. This study resulted in the four philosphical letters dispatched during February to the Wedgwoods; Tom Wedgwood, however, was too ill to read them, while Josiah, who was not a metaphysician, had no interest whatever in them. As a method of impressing S.T.C.'s patrons, therefore, and compensating for the lack of the life of Lessing, these philosophical letters were a failure. Nevertheless, they were of some academic importance inasmuch as they revealed Coleridge as among the first to demonstrate Locke's indebtedness to Descartes and to reject English empiricism; a stance which S.T.C. was subsequently to say had done him much damage in his own country. Poole (who had been sent copies of the letters) reacted with alarm: "Think before you join the Little-ists, who, without knowing in what way Locke is defective, wish to strip the *popular mind* of him, leaving in his place *nothing*."[37]

In connection with his studies, particularly Newton's work on optics, S.T.C. made, so he claimed, a multitude of minute experiments with light and form, which left him so nervous and feverish that he could not sleep and what sleep he did have was so confused that it brought him no refreshment. To Poole he stated that these experiments, involving his own sensations and senses, seemed to have done injury to his nervous system. These experiments are, in fact, not very convincing. The notebooks contain no serious mention of them, as one would expect had S.T.C. truly carried them out. The only direct allusion to any such experiment seems to be in a letter to Godwin; here S.T.C. remarked that his hands were scarred from scratches received from a cat whose coat he had been rubbing in the dark to see whether sparks from it were refrangible by a prism.[38] In short, we are left with the strong suspicion that S.T.C. was using hypothetical experiments as an excuse for the morphine-engendered general restlessness and sleeplessness that had now gripped him, together with an inability to compose poetry or do any serious literary work of his own.

"The Poet is dead in me—my imagination . . . lies, like a Cold Snuff on the circular Rim of a Brass Candle-stick, without even a stink of Tallow to remind you that it was once cloathed & mitred with Flame . . . I was once a Volume of Gold Leaf, rising & riding on every breath of Fancy—but I have beaten myself back into weight & density, & now I sink in quick silver, yea, remain squat and square on the earth amid the hurricane, that makes Oaks and Straws join in one Dance, fifty yards high in the Element."[39] "My Sickness has left me in a state of mind, which it is scarcely possible for me explain to you—one feature of it is . . . an extreme Disgust which I feel at every perusal of my own Productions, & which makes it exceedingly painful to me not only to revise them, but . . . even to look on the Paper, on which they are written."[40]

All this spells opium and well S.T.C. knew it was opium. He had turned to metaphysics primarily in order to take his mind not only from his physical pain, but from the constant self-disgust and despair which his opium habit was now causing him—"Sands and swamps of Evil," as he wrote to Davy. In metaphysics he had sought a refuge from bodily pain and "mismanaged sensibility" (his stock euphemism for opium). "Sickness and some other & worse afflictions, first forced me into *downright metaphysics.*"[41] "I attribute . . . my long & exceedingly severe Metaphysical Investigations . . . partly to Ill-health, and partly to private afflictions which rendered any subject, immediately connected with Feeling, a source of pain & disquiet to me."[42]

His desire was to retreat from feeling; to retreat above all from feelings of guilt, despair and remorse.

The restlessness and the troubled nights, and now the "gout" and stomach trouble which soon followed this period of "experiments" and metaphysics, resulted almost certainly directly from opium and, of course, induced him to repair to further opium for alleviation:

> O dear Poole! the attacks of my stomach, & the nephritic pains in my back . . . they were terrible! The Disgust, the Loathing, that followed the Fits & no doubt in part too the use of the Brandy & Laudanum which they rendered necessary . . . Disgust, Despondency, & utter Prostration of Strength.[43]

He added that he had decided that if a course of iron tonic, followed by a summer of "Prudence" (surely another euphemism), "regulated Diet & regulated Exercise" did not markedly improve things, he would have to try wintering in a warmer climate; Captain Wordsworth had recommended the Azores.

The excuse for his opium slavery most favoured by S.T.C. later in life was, of course, the much quoted:

> By a most unhappy Quackery after having been almost bed-ridden for six months with swoln knees & other distressing symptoms of disordered digestive Functions, & thro' that most pernicious form of Ignorance, medical half-knowledge, I was *seduced* into the use of narcotics.[44]

He enlarged upon this by explaining that, during the course of this long period of illness at Keswick, he had borrowed a pile of old medical journals from Mr Edmondson* and in them had read of a case apparently precisely identical to his own, in which a cure had been obtained by rubbing in laudanum on the swollen joints, while at the same time taking an internal dose. S.T.C. had tried this; he was to claim that it had acted like a charm, thereby seducing him into the accursed habit.

This explanation has been widely accepted by posterity. The excuse of seduction is, of course, an ancient and favoured one in all cases of temptation and human frailty. Few people, if we may believe them, ever get with child, or turn junkie, or involve themselves in escapade or felony of their own volition. Seduction, nine times out of ten, is the allegation. The individual, understandably, ever seeks to evade total blame.

*S.T.C.'s more usual, and indeed the common, spelling of this name.

The evidence that has now come to light in the form of Coleridge letters and, above all, in the notebooks, makes it certain beyond all possible doubt that S.T.C.'s morphine addiction dated back years before the Keswick *débacle*. He was an addict long before he borrowed Mr Edmondson's medical journals. It is possible that these journals may have first introduced S.T.C. to the celebrated Black Drop (App. I), an opium preparation somewhat stronger than laudanum and which, although well known in the North of England, was then little known in the South; S.T.C. may have read an advertisement for it in one of these journals. We know that he was presently taking opium which he obtained from Kendal (the town where the Black Drop was manufactured). We know that S.T.C. was most certainly using the Black Drop at a later date; we find him referring to it amicably as Old Black. It is not unreasonable to suppose, therefore, that S.T.C. began to take the Black Drop during this first winter at Keswick. The fact that he resorted to this stronger preparation, in ever-increasing quantity, may have suggested to him that his subsequent slavery to the drug was directly attributable to the Black Drop.

This, however, in no way affects the total falsity of his submission that, at Keswick, he was seduced into the use of narcotics. Upon his own written evidence he had used them constantly throughout the previous decade.

In the light of our present-day knowledge of morphine reliance, we can refute his allegation that a few months of opium usage at Greta Hall would have resulted in his bondage to the drug. Today, morphine reliance may be established within a period of months; in S.T.C.'s era, when the drug was taken in vastly adulterated form, orally, such speedy development of reliance was out of the question.

Another important point to be borne in mind is that he could not have tolerated the large doses of opium that he took during that first winter at Keswick without a long build-up of tolerance to the drug beforehand.

S.T.C.'s winter of engulfment in true morphine reliance must necessarily have been preceded by a long history of progressive opium consumption. The evidence now exists, abundantly, of precisely such a history.

Again, S.T.C.'s own written testimony in notebooks and letters can leave us in no doubt that, despite his subsequent passionate protests to the contrary, he resorted to opium not only for medicinal reasons but for purposes of purely sensory gratification.

In any case, niceties of whether the drug was taken to allay pain and tension or to promote pleasurable sensory experience do not matter; we know sufficient about the reasons for drug-addiction to understand that these stem from personality troubles too deep to be facilely dismissed as weak indulgence.

One of the most distressing aspects of morphine addiction is the drug victim's inevitable and at last almost total social isolation. A classical symptom of morphine addiction is a growing lack of concern for the feelings and welfare of others; a total loss of any sense of family and social responsibility. As reliance upon the drug deepens, so does the ability to sustain personal relationships atrophy, until at last the addict cannot cope with them at all.

Inescapably there is destruction of all friendships, all family, parental and marital ties. Morphine is the force behind the tornado of disruption that whirls the family unit away into a hell of violent discord, usually finally resulting in rejection of the addict by his family, or rejection of the family by him. There will almost always be scenes of reconciliation and attempts to "cure" the addict; but soon the quarrelling will begin all over again. So the pattern repeats itself, heartbreakingly and exhaustingly.

In desperation the parents or spouse of the addict increasingly heap him with reproach. He retaliates with accusations of every kind of neglect and cruelty, flaying those whom he most truly loves with arraignments of coldness, spite, selfishness, temper and total lack of feeling.

More and more the addict withdraws from contact with his domestic situation, finding comfort instead with some small handful of "in-group" persons upon whom he can rely for uncritical sympathy and condolence—a support-group, in fact. When this group finally becomes critically impatient with him (as is invariably the case, for the simple reason that the drug-addict tries beyond endurance the tolerance of every acquaintance and quarrels with everyone in the end) then the drug-victim retires completely into the world of psychotic delusion which, by this time, will be progressively enshrouding him in its net of fantasy.

The delusional personalities who inhabit his shadowy world may be based upon actual individuals; these are launch-pads for fantasy characters. The actual individual will be avoided, once the fantasy figure has been set up; or, if encountered, will be seen as a shadow lurking behind the fantasy, if recognised at all. Reality has become something with which the drug-victim can no longer cope. He evades coming to terms with it.

Although he has lost touch with what the outer world calls truth, he frequently believes that he is in pursuit of a Holy Grail of inner significance and spirituality. This sensation of privileged perception gives him feelings of immense superiority. His family, in particular, appears to him to be sunk in attitudes of hypocritical materialism and insensitivity. It is now that, in turning to seek an alternative support-group, he discovers for himself (invents, would perhaps be a better word) a guru, or gurus; a person, or persons of special wisdom, special understanding and almost godlike endowments.

Viewed apart from the context of morphine, S.T.C.'s progressive idolatry of the Wordsworths seems almost inexplicable. It puzzled and infuriated his friends; it has bemused posterity. When, however, we view this infatuation within a drug context, it falls into the classical pattern of the addict's behaviour. Wordsworth became S.T.C.'s guru, with the women of the Dove Cottage coterie as acolytes. For S.T.C. each member of the immediate Wordsworth circle was bathed in a species of heavenly light. They were nonpareils.

Wordsworth, said S.T.C., had descended on him like the Light from Heaven and, by showing him what true poetry was, had made him know that he himself was no poet.[45] Wordsworth, in years to come, would be recognised as "the first & greatest philosophical Poet."[46] S.T.C. looked forward to Wordsworth's projected (and never fully realised) poem, *The Recluse*, as "the *first* and *only* true philosophical poem in existence."[47]

Wordsworth was guru; Dorothy and the two Hutchinson sisters, Mary and Sara, formed the accompanying, magical, support-group. To this little circle S.T.C. applied his favourite symbol of perfect love:

The spring with the little tiny cone of loose sand rising & sinking at the bottom, but its surface without a wrinkle—W.W. M.H. D.W. S.H.[48]

Prompted no doubt by some perfectly natural, if regrettable, jealousy of their beloved Coleridge's wife, the Wordsworths were prepared to listen to all S.T.C.'s complaints about Sara and the increasing domestic strife of Greta Hall.

The reader should objectively consider Sara Coleridge's plight. Removed to a part of the world where she had no friends, settled in a large, draughty, damp, improperly heated house among rain-swept mountains, breast-feeding an infant, tending a sick five-year-old (Hartley had got jaundice), short of money and beset by duns and, above all, confronted by a bed-ridden, opium-hooked husband who was, by his own confession, "fretful & splenetic," Sara's was a winter which would have moved a saint to discontent.

Naturally she upbraided S.T.C. for idling on opium when he should have been bestirring himself, for prostration before the Wordsworths, for repeatedly making himself ill by travelling over to Grasmere in the wet and for putting her in such an intolerable position.

Deteriorating health and private alarm at his drug predicament makes the morphine-victim extremely irascible, over-sensitive and resentful, in short, virtually impossible to live with. S.T.C. responded to Sara's up-braiding by flying into fearsome rages. She raged back. He raced away to Grasmere, to seek comfort with the Wordsworths. Growing jealousy of them added to Sara's acrimony. S.T.C. resented her reaction. He turned with even greater alacrity to the Wordsworths. Sara became more miserable, more jealous, more distraught. She saw the Wordsworths as an increasingly damaging influence upon S.T.C. Her perfectly natural and wholly understandable response to her predicament is mirrored in Southey's summing-up of the situation:

They [the Wordsworths] have always humoured ... [S.T.C.] in all his follies,—and listened to his complaints of his wife,—& when he has complained of the itch, helped him to scratch, instead of covering him with brimstone ointment, & shutting him up by himself.[49]

The more the Coleridges fought, the more S.T.C. took opium to soothe himself; the more opium he took, the more the situation deteriorated; the further the situation deteriorated, the more opium he took. Sara stormed at him; he stormed at her. Greta Hall resounded to the desolate tumult of strife between two people who loved each other.

It must not be supposed that S.T.C. did not appreciate the hardship and strain which he was placing upon his family. To Godwin, in early December, 1800, S.T.C. confessed that he had become "fretful & splenetic."[50] To Thelwall he spoke of his "poor Wife and children."[51] To Poole, in a letter of April 18, 1801, S.T.C. described his wretchedness, not simply because of physical pain, but also because of the effect that his chronic ill-health was having upon his family—"the gloom & distress of those around me for whom I ought to be labouring & cannot."[52]

On one point only, in these letters, did S.T.C. remain reticent: opium was never identified as the real berg upon which his marriage was foundering.

CHAPTER FIFTEEN

BEWARE OF PITY

(May 1801–March 1802)

By MAY 1801 the puzzled Mr Edmondson had diagnosed S.T.C.'s case as one of irregular gout with nephritic symptoms. S.T.C. complained incessantly of swollen knees, knotty fingers, "loathing stomach, & a dizzy head."[1] His trouble was chronic rheumatic heart disease and morphine addiction, but Edmondson was no Gillman and his extraordinary patient was not of a sort commonly encountered in Keswick.

Meanwhile, "scarce a day passed without a scene of discord between me & Mrs Coleridge,"[2] as S.T.C. reported. She has left us no account of Samuel, but he has left vivid impressions of her:

> Ill-tempered Speeches sent after me when I went out of the house . . . Ill-tempered Speeches on my return, my friends received with freezing looks, the least opposition or contradiction occasioning screams of passion, & the sentiments, which I held most base, ostentatiously avowed . . . the utter negation of all that a husband expects from a Wife . . . & the consciousness that I was myself growing a worse man . . . no one can tell what I have suffered. I can say with strict truth, that the happiest half-hours, I have had, were when all of a sudden, as I have been sitting alone in my Study, I have burst into Tears.[3]

Elsewhere, however, he has admitted that he criticised her endlessly, not only when they were alone together, but when the Wordsworths were present,[4] comparing her, to her disadvantage, with Dorothy and with Mary and Sara Hutchinson. His outbursts of temper were furious and frequent; he gave way to "offensive vehemence of manner, look, & language."[5]

In his saner moments he, with his keen psychological insight, was still able to analyse the situation. "In all perplexity there is a portion of fear," he mused, "which predisposes the mind to anger."[6]

Sara was understandably both bewildered and frightened by the changes in S.T.C. and the resultant consequences. Hitherto, when they had quarrelled, it had been speedily to make it up. Now, S.T.C.'s black mood persisted, week in, week out. He seemed only to be happy in the company of the Wordsworths and the Hutchinsons, whose society he obviously preferred to hers. He stumbled from one bout of illness to the next, his boon companion the laudanum bottle. He did no work; he earned no money. The begging women and children who came to the door of Greta Hall[7] must have struck chilling chords in Sara's heart. She had no one to whom she could turn to pour out her woes; all her friends were four hundred miles away.

The morass of opium and misery, marital breakdown and despair in which S.T.C. now floundered was the kind of situation which could only evoke the most avid interest in disciples of the New Sensibility. It was precisely this word, "interest," which Dorothy applied to the long recitals of suffering with which S.T.C. now interminably regaled the Wordsworths: "Had some interesting melancholy talk about his private affairs," reads one typical comment from her *Journal*.[8]

Naturally the Wordsworths, especially Dorothy, accepted all S.T.C.'s criticism of his wife. A letter from Dorothy to Mary Hutchinson, dated April 29, 1801, is immensely revealing of the Wordsworth attitude to the tragic domestic drama of Greta Hall. The Wordsworths, with Sara Hutchinson, arriving there on April 19 for a seven-day stay, found S.T.C sitting in the parlour, looking very pale; he was largely bed-ridden at this time, but had got up to greet his friends. To quote Dorothy:

> He was very, very unwell in the way that Sara can describe to you—ill all over, back and stomach and limbs and so weak that he changed colour whenever he exerted himself at all. Our company did him good and the next day he was much better. Since that time he has been upon the whole greatly improved in his looks and strength but he was never quite well for more than an hour together during the whole time we were there, tho' he began to form plans and schemes for working but he was unable to do anything . . . We should have stayed longer at Keswick but our not being so new did not do him so much good as at first, and then we are never comfortable there after the first 2 or 3 days. This of course we do not mind while we are of any essential service to him, but the same cause which makes us uncomfortable at Keswick prevents him from having all the good from us that he otherwise would have. Mrs. C. is in excellent health. She is indeed a bad nurse for C., but she has several great merits. She is much very much to be pitied, for when one party is ill matched the other necessarily must be so too. She would have made a very good wife to many another man, but for Coleridge!! Her radical fault is want of sensibility and what can such a woman be to Coleridge? She is an excellent nurse to her sucking children (I mean to the best of her skill, for she employs her time often foolishly enough about them). Derwent is a sweet lovely Fatty—she suckles him entirely—he has no other food. She is to be sure a sad fiddle faddler. From about $\frac{1}{2}$ past 10 on Sunday morning till two she did nothing but wash and dress her 2 children and herself, and was just ready for dinner. No doubt she suckled Derwent pretty often during that time.[9]

(It seems never to have occurred to Dorothy that Sara Coleridge may have dawdled her time away upstairs with her children in order to avoid the company of the visitors.)

Orientated as the Wordsworths were towards sympathy for S.T.C., even they sometimes wearied. In a joint letter of theirs, dated May 22, an involuntary sigh escapes from Dorothy:

> God bless you! dear Coleridge we are sadly grieved for your poor eyes and the rest of your complaints ... Oh, for one letter of perfect uncomplainingness![10]

The sad changes now becoming apparent in S.T.C., not only in his health but in his very character, were remarked upon by almost all who knew him well. Godwin was one who commented upon S.T.C.'s withdrawal into complaints and self absorption, with a diminishing interest in, or affection for, his friends. S.T.C.'s reply constitutes a significant and classical description of the state of mind induced by morphine reliance:

> Partly from ill-health, & partly from an unhealthy & reverie-like vividness of Thoughts, & ... a diminished Impressibility from Things, my ideas, wishes, & feelings are to a diseased degree disconnected from motion & action.

This is penetrating and exact. But S.T.C. was not prepared to confess to opium; therefore he now shrugged off further analysis of his trouble with a false, but facile: "In plain & natural English, I am a dreaming & therefore an indolent man." He added, more revealingly than perhaps he intended:

> I am a Starling self-incaged, & always in the Moult, & my whole Note is, Tomorrow, & tomorrow, & tomorrow. The same causes that have robbed me to so great a degree of the self-impelling self-directing Principle, have deprived me too of the due powers of Resistance to Impulses from without. If I might so say, I am, as an *acting* man, a creature of mere Impact. 'I will' & 'I will not' are phrases, both of them equally, of rare occurrence in my dictionary.—This is the Truth—I regret it, & in the consciousness of this Truth I lose a larger portion of Self-estimation than those, who know me imperfectly, would easily believe—I evade the sentence of my own Conscience by no quibbles of self-adulation; but I confess, that this very ill-health is as much an effect as a cause of this want of steadiness & self-command; and it is for mercy I ask, not for justice.—[11]

S.T.C.'s shrinking grip on reality, his "diminished Impressibility from Things," was now to have increasingly tragic impact upon his personal life. Sara Coleridge and he were drifting farther and farther apart; it was as if they, who had once shared a raft, now had it sundered in two halves becoming every moment more distant one from the other. S.T.C. watched the process with a strangely cold eye; he could see that Sara was acutely distressed by his withdrawal of love, but this distress he attributed to chill, materialistic motives:

by an habitual absence of *reality* in her affection I have had an hundred instances that the being beloved, or the not being beloved, is a thing indifferent: but the *notion* of not being beloved—that wounds her pride deeply.[12]

From this stance it was easy for S.T.C. to move on to allegations of Sara's lack of feeling and finally to see her as a person without feelings at all. He exclaimed that Sara suffered from "coldness . . . & paralysis in all *tangible* ideas & sensations . . . all that forms *real* self . . . Nothing affects her with pain or pleasure as it is but only as other people will *say it is*." She was "all as cold & calm as a deep Frost." "Sara is uncommonly *cold* in her feelings of animal Love,"[13] he grumbled, overlooking her continuing lack of reluctance to become pregnant by him, her intensely passionate delight in her children, her joyful breast-feeding and fondling of them. But morphine benumbed him, locking up his understanding:

> To love is to know, at least, to imagine that you *know* (not always indeed *understand*), what is strange to you, you cannot love (Mrs. C. is to be all *strange*, & the Terra incognita always lies near to or under the frozen Poles).[14]

In any event, as aforesaid, his understanding of women was never better than minimal. His attitude towards them was generalised, combining contemptuous condescension with a species of holy veneration. (When, at last, Sara presented him with a daughter, he was astonished: "the words child and man child were perfect Synonymes in my feelings—however I bore the sex with great Fortitude.")[15]

He was firmly convinced that:

> A woman's head is usually over ears in her heart. Man seems to have been designed for the superior being of the two; but as things are, I think women are generally better creatures than men. They have, taken universally, weaker appetites and weaker intellects, but they have much stronger affections. A man with a bad heart has been sometimes saved by a strong head; but a corrupt woman is lost forever.[16]

His weakness for letting his "Wishes make Romances out of men's characters"[17] was even more pronounced when women's characters were involved. This he correctly attributed largely to his upbringing in a single-sex school:

> to a man brought up in a Wilderness by unseen Beings . . . how beautiful would not the first other man appear, whom he saw . . . /he would . . . attribute to the man all the divine attributes of humanity, tho' haply it should be a very ordinary or even almost ugly man, compared with a hundred others. Many of us have felt this with respect to women, who have been bred up where few are to be seen.[18]

His ideal of a perfect woman was "a compassionate Comforter . . . most innocent and full of love—"[19] (This the distracted and accusing Sara Coleridge of the long, wild winter of 1800–1801, had most decidedly ceased to be.)

S.T.C.'s paramount emotional need, however, was for a döppelganger:

My heart plays an incessant music/for which I need an outward Interpreter[20]

That to be in love is simply to confine the feelings prospective of animal enjoyment to one woman is a gross mistake—it is to associate a large proportion of all our obscure feelings with a real form.[21]

In other words, the woman he loved should not be an individual in her own right, but a projection of himself.

"In love," said S.T.C., "each strives to be the other, and both together make one whole."[22] But, as his partner had to be a projection of himself, the other which he strove to be was but a reflection of Esteesee; Love, for him, was a self-embracement, which meant, in effect, that he had to cross no frightening frontiers of another's personality; he was always on *terra cognita*.

It did not matter very much upon whom he fixed his choice as partner in this Siamese-twin exercise; he had not the slightest intention of making true acquaintance with a flesh-and-blood woman. All that he required was some tangible form around which he might weave his fantasies: he could then allow himself to drift away, constructing his opium streamy daydreams about a really "very ordinary" woman whom he would, in his dreaming, invest with "all the divine attributes of humanity" and involve in a series of wholly imaginary, but immensely gratifying, sentimental (and frequently masochistic) situations:

if I have not heard from you very recently, & if the last letter had not happened to be full of explicit Love & Feeling, then I conjure up Shadows into Substances—& am miserable/Misery conjures up other Forms; & binds them into Tales & Events—activity is always Pleasure—the Tale grows pleasanter—& at length you come to me/you are by my bedside, in some lonely Inn, where I lie deserted—there you have found me—there you are weeping over me!—Dear, dear, Woman![23]

>My eyes make pictures, when they are shut:—
> I see a fountain, large and fair,
>A willow and a ruined hut,
> And thee, and me and Mary there.
>O Mary! make thy gentle lap our pillow!
>Bend o'er us, like a bower, my beautiful green willow! . . .
>
> Thine eyelash on my cheek doth play—
> 'Tis Mary's hand upon my brow!

> But let me check this tender lay
> Which none may hear but she and thou!
> Like the still hive at quiet midnight humming,
> Murmur it to yourselves, ye two beloved women![24]

These two beloved women were Mary and Sara Hutchinson. The poem, *A Day Dream*, from which the above verses are taken, is an attempt to reproduce an opium dream's time-sequence-free, streamy action, the liberated mind gliding from one imagined sequence to the next. It is a poor poem, but a highly interesting one, for it reveals how inextricably fantasy and reality were intertwined for S.T.C. in this "reverie-like vividness of Thoughts."

The Hutchinson sisters were warm-hearted, excessively naive and deeply impressed by S.T.C.'s charm and reputation. Mary, from the first, had greatly appealed to him. Sara had proved a jolly little girl to be teased and hand-squeezed. He found the company of each light-heartedly diverting and pleasantly flattering.

During the winter and spring of 1801 events occurred, however, which thrust S.T.C. towards Sara Hutchinson.

The Wordsworths, at Dove Cottage, seem purposely to have surrounded themselves with visitors, as if they sought not to find themselves alone together. They required a third party to blunt the tension of their necessary physical discipline. We can do no more than cautiously speculate upon the extent of their physical experience together; we do have unmistakable evidence in the Grasmere *Journal* that, at Dove Cottage, brother and sister endured an agonising frustration of full physical expression of their love. Their dilemma, as we see it, was founded upon one or other of two possibilities; if Alfoxden and Goslar had been a period of shared full sexual experience then such experience must never be repeated again. If, alternatively, Alfoxden and Goslar had seen no more than poetry and Romantic posturing, nonetheless real embers had smouldered beneath this stance and smouldered still, requiring constant vigilant control to prevent conflagration.

In an extraordinarily passionate and beautiful poem, *'Tis Said That Some Have Died For Love*, written in 1800 for the second edition of *Lyrical Ballads*, Wordsworth, exploring the emotions of a man who killed himself following the loss of his sweetheart, engenders an atmosphere of almost unbearable intensity: "His love was such a grievous pain."

> 'Oh! what a weight is in these shades! Ye leaves,
> When will that dying murmur be suppressed?
> Your sound my heart of peace bereaves
> It robs my heart of rest.
> Thou thrush, that singest loud and loud and free,
> Into yon row of willows flit,

Upon that alder sit;
Or sing another song, or choose another tree . . .'

The man who makes this feverish complaint
Is one of giant stature, who could dance
Equipped from head to foot in iron mail.
Ah gentle Love! if ever thought was thine
To store up kindred hours for me, thy face
Turn from me, gentle Love! nor let me walk
Within the sound of Emma's voice, or know
Such happiness as I have known today.

The Grasmere *Journal* reveals that, at Dove Cottage, William and Dorothy were more deeply in love than ever, but with a ripening tenderness and understanding. It is impossible to avoid the impression that here was a truly wedded couple whose first sexual ardour had been consumed, but who had discovered, after the initial explosion of leaping flames, a glowing and steady fire. Tragically, the moments of physical fervour which intermittently shot forth from this well-established hearth of love had to be firmly controlled; a species of draught-excluder had to be drawn, shutter-wise, between the kindling coals and the fanning winds.

It was an intolerable situation that could not be extended indefinitely. William found himself sexually attracted by Mary; Dorothy herself comprehended that he must have a wife.

It seems that William, in this dilemma, took S.T.C. into very full confidence (possibly before commencing with Dorothy the "affecting" and "tender" conversations in which brother and sister together explored the realities and necessities of the predicament). In a long notebook entry for May 12, 1808, S.T.C. reveals that he played a decisive part in Wordsworth's decision to marry:

> when in my bed—I then ill—continued talking with Wordsworth the whole night thru' till Dawn of the Day, urging him to conclude in marrying [Mary Hutchinson: name heavily deleted in manuscript] a blessed marriage for him and for her it has been.[25]

The chronology here is interesting to trace. A letter from S.T.C. written on February 24 1802, to Mrs Coleridge, explains that Mary and William were planning to marry as early in that year as possible (in the event, they did not marry until October, because Annette had to be informed about William's marriage plan and visited). It seems that S.T.C. may have had his night-long conversation before September 1801, because, in a notebook entry for that month, S.T.C. writes of the pulsating love-spring (p. 336) and groups the initials thus: W.W. M.H. D.W. S.H., which speaks for itself. We know that Mary spent a long stay at Dove Cottage from October

1801 until mid-January 1802; it is possible that William may have definitely proposed to Mary, or at least have arrived at some understanding, on November 25, 1801; Dorothy's *Journal* for that date describes how she stayed at home and baked pies and bread while William and Mary walked to Clappersgate; a showery morning had set in to a rainy afternoon, with a high wind in the evening, which made Dorothy concerned for Mary and William, but: "They came in at nine o'clock, no worse for their walk, and cheerful, blooming, and happy."

The all-night conversation between S.T.C. and William must have occurred during a Wordsworth visit to Greta Hall in the spring of 1801. It may have been in late April that S.T.C. had his warm and affectionate feelings for Sara Hutchinson "flash-transmuted"[26] to love. This, if we may rely on a poem for factual evidence (a rather dangerous expedient with S.T.C.'s poetry), occurred at Greta Hall on Greta side, at the bottom of the garden. In *Recollections of Love* (written *circa* 1807) speaking of Asra, (as S.T.C. came to call Miss Hutchinson, especially when referring to her within the context of döppelganger), he invoked her as "a maiden mild:"

> . . . when those meek eyes first did seem
> To tell me, Love within you wrought—
> O Greta, dear domestic stream!—

This is speculation. What is fact is that Coleridge was definitely obsessed with Sara Hutchinson by early September 1801. By that time, too, he knew that William had decided upon betrothal to Mary, which placed her out of bounds as a *döppelganger* for S.T.C.

We know that by early July, 1801, S.T.C. had come to the "heart-withering Conviction" that he could not be happy without his children and "could not but be miserable with the mother of them."[27] He began to plan a bolt overseas.

His predicament was stringent. "Marriage is indissoluble,"[28] he had written categorically to Thelwall in 1796. To this he held. Furthermore, sexual intercourse outside marriage was lust and lust he abhorred. This attitude was ingrained in him by virtue of his Christianity. At the same time his inherent personality problems demanded a complementary partner: "every generous mind . . . feels its Halfness," he wrote, "and cannot *think* without a Symbol—neither can it *love* without something that is at once to be its Symbol, & its other half."[29] Again and again we find him propounding this theme.

Sara Hutchinson-Asra was beyond physical reach. This was one of her chief attractions for him, if not the greatest. She satisfied all his masochistic inclinations:

Why we two made to be a Joy to each other, should for so many years constitute each other's melancholy—O! but the melancholy is Joy—.[30]

345

It is fascinating to analyse the alchemy which transformed Sara Hutchinson into the character Asra. From the first S.T.C. viewed her through distorting spectacles: "the mild & retired kind," he thought her. Yet inspection of Sara Hutchinson's aggressive, lively profile and perusal of her letters and the events of her life reveal a woman who was bustling, busy, practical, gregarious, talkative and dearly fond of managing the lives of those about her. She was forever circulating from one household to another: "I am . . . the real jaunter,"[31] she once told her cousin, Mary Monkhouse. Everywhere she went, she instantly took control of every problem, became acquainted with all the gossip, overflowed, herself, with witty comment and shrewd counsel.

Her letters to her farming brothers reveal her intense and practical interest in livestock, hay crops, pasturage and agricultural prices. She was very fond of riding and followed hounds with zest.[32] But she could also enjoy books, letter-writing and quiet: "I am . . . a good *bider* of solitude."[33] Highly literate and with a real feeling for poetry, she was receptive in mind and amenable to S.T.C.'s attempts to fashion her in his own intellectual image:

> Endeavouring to make the infinitely beloved Darling understand all my knowledge I learn the art of making the abstrusest Truths intelligible; & interesting even to the unlearned.[34]

As a present he gave her, early in their friendship, a copy of his beloved Bartram's *Travels*, telling her:

> This is not a Book of Travels properly speaking; but a series of poems, chiefly descriptive, occasioned by the objects which the traveller observed.— It is a *delicious* Book; and like all *delicious* things, you must take but a *little* of it at a time.[35]

To Daniel Stuart, who had "somehow or other been led to misunderstand" her character, S.T.C. expostulated:

> If Sense, Sensibility, sweetness of Temper, perfect Simplicity and unpretending nature, joined to shrewdness & entertainingness, make a valuable woman, Sara H. is so—[36]

It would be interesting to know what alternative view of her had been given to Stuart and by whom.

As aforesaid (p. 301) there is every indication that S.T.C. had a deeply depressing effect upon Sara Hutchinson, which seems to have resulted in her recession into a species of personality eclipse during the first years of the nineteenth century. This may, in part, have contributed to the fact that his view of Miss Hutchinson was so greatly at variance with the portrait of her which emerges from her letters and the evidence of her later years.

Sara Hutchinson's nature was not that of a *femme fatale*; the rôle of "other woman" was one which she seems to have slipped into by a combination of immense innocence and inexperience, buttressed by a very human susceptibility to flattery and great natural good-heartedness. S.T.C., in the wake of William's betrothal to Mary, reached towards Sara Hutchinson with increasing avidity. Clearly, she was soon out of her depth with him. Yet she was reluctant to retract from the friendship lest she should further hurt a man who insisted that he was already desperately miserable and ill as a result of his wife's allegedly unfeeling treatment of him.

S.T.C.'s pining for a love which she could not give him convinced her, finally, that his attachment to her had been the curse of his happiness. S.T.C. accused the Wordsworths of planting this notion in her mind. William responded:

> So far from our having done this the very truth is the reverse. They [Mary and Dorothy] did not pretend to deny . . . that your passion was a source to you of much misery; but they always told her that it was a gross error to appropriate this to herself . . . telling her that your mind [?must] have had such a determination to some object or other, that she was not therefore the cause, but merely . . . the innocent occasion of this unhappiness, that in fact so far as *you* were concerned she might congratulate herself; had this passion fixed upon a [   ]* of a different kind what might you not have suffered?[37]

Had Dorothy and Mary not reasoned with Sara Hutchinson in this wise she might well have terminated her relationship with S.T.C. years before she finally did so. The depression and nervous illnesses from which she suffered during the years of this relationship, together with a growing repugnance, which she could not conceal, for S.T.C.'s physical company, combine to create an unmistakable portrait of a woman placed in an intolerable position which pity alone inspires her to maintain.

Significant in this context are Sara's observations to her cousin, Thomas Monkhouse, in a letter of February 28, 1818. He was suffering from an unrequited love and had written to Miss Hutchinson for advice; she told him:

> as I find that absence has had no salutary effect, but has made, & will continue to make you more susceptible at any chance meeting, I would not avoid but seek opportunity of being in Her society—habit may enable you to meet her with firmness if not with indifference & . . . as you feel that she does not dislike you (for how can she knowing how much you admire her & *have not intruded upon her much less persecuted her with your attention*)† perseverence may secure her.[38]

There can be no doubt that S.T.C. both intruded upon Sara Hutchinson and persecuted her with his attention.

*Space left in MS.
†Present author's italics.

In July, 1801, S.T.C. paid a visit to Sara and her brother George at their farm at Bishop's Middleham, near Durham. The ostensible purpose of the visit was that S.T.C. might obtain books from Durham cathedral library. S.T.C. arrived at the farm on July 16. The stay was a merry one; George had a reputation as a humorist and made "very droll verses in the northern dialect." After a short visit here S.T.C., together with Sara, went to Gallow Hill to see Mary and Tom Hutchinson. Present also were Joanna,* the youngest of the Hutchinson sisters, and her friend Miss Isabella Addison (she later married John Monkhouse). S.T.C., in his element with all these young women, flirted, teased, joked, jabbered and laughed nonstop. It seems that, as a married man, he was permitted a certain degree of special licence; it was understood that his advances were a form of innocent larking.[39]

However, there occurred during this stay one episode of incredible, indeed outrageous, innocence. One evening Mary and Sara, while seated with S.T.C. on what he described as a "lazy-bed"[40] (a kind of *chaise-longue*) by the light of a candle and a decaying fire, were regaled by him with a long recital of his marital woes. Possibly he wept. Probably he told them how they and the Wordsworths alone understood him. Mary, in the warmth of her sympathy, took his head upon her lap and stroked his brow, Sara pressed herself against him and embraced him. Thus they lay, a trio barely two centuries distant in time, yet utterly incomprehensible to our post-Freudian era. Coleridge described the episode both in notebook form and in verse (as a stanza in an early draft of *Ode to Dejection* and in *The Day Dream*):

> Prest to my bosom & felt there—it was quite dark. I looked intensely towards her face—& sometimes I *saw* it—so vivid was the spectrum, that it had almost all its natural sense of *distance* & *outness*—except indeed that, feeling & all, I felt her as a *part* of my being—twas all spectral—But when I could not absolutely *see* her, no effort of my fancy could bring out even the least resemblance of her face.—Lazy Bed—Green . . . the fits of L & D from the Candle going out in the socket . . . that last Image how lovely to me now.[43]

The stanza in *Ode to Dejection* shows this notebook jotting transformed into verse:

> It was as calm as this, that happy night
> When Mary, thou & I together were,
> The low decaying Fire our only Light,
> And listen'd to the Stillness of the Air!
> O that affectionate & blameless Maid,
> Dear Mary, on her lap my head she lay'd—

---

*Joanna barely figures in these pages as she thought poorly of Grasmere[41] and even less of Dove Cottage[42] and avoided going there.

Her Hand was on my Brow,
Even as my own is now;
And on my Cheek I felt thy eye-lash play.
Such Joy I had, that I may truly say,
My Spirit was awe-stricken with the Excess
And trance-like Depth of its brief Happiness.

It seems that Asra did not yet feel that physical repugnance for him that she was soon to find impossible to conceal. Yet, even in the summer of 1801, he could scarcely have been a physically attractive man:

I have a very large Boil on my neck . . . & it is poulticed—in consequence whereof I smell so exactly like a hot Loaf, that it would be perilous for me to meet a hungry blind man—But it has broke, & is easy.[44]

Without doubt, Sara Hutchinson was moved to show tenderness for Coleridge by pity; that sentiment which has moved more women to avowals of love than men would care to know.

S.T.C. had returned to Keswick by September 7, his head and heart full of symbolic sexual-intercourse sequences with Asra. He received a stinging reception from Sara Coleridge. In vain he attempted to put his case; it was hopeless. To his notebook he confided:

A lively picture of a man, disappointed in marriage, & endeavouring to make a compensation to himself by a virtuous & tender & brotherly friendship with an amiable Woman—the obstacles—the jealousies—the impossibility of it—[45]

It seems that, sometime that autumn, Sara Coleridge sent Sara Hutchinson an anonymous letter; we do not know what she said in it, but we do know that S.T.C. discovered that she had sent it and, understandably, resented it.[46]

The Southeys came to stay at Greta Hall during September; S.T.C. did not enjoy the visit so much as he had expected. The incessant bickering of himself and Sara spoiled it.[47] The Southeys were not accustomed to marital discord (S.T.C. was to record that the only time he ever saw Southey angry with Edith was on the occasion of her sportively putting a little milk on his mash; a drop or two fell on his jacket and he feared a stain. He rebuked her with a frown, which apparently went unnoticed by her. S.T.C. attributed the harmony of the Southeys to the fact that Southey did not mind if his wife lacked sensibility.)[48]

In late autumn, S.T.C., unable to winter abroad since Poole would lend him no more money, escaped from marital disharmony by going to London to work for the *Morning Post.* He had made up his mind to devote his months of absence to "self-discipline" (which meant an attempt to give up opium) and then to make one more trial of marriage (this decision reveals his understanding of the root cause of his marital trouble). If his marriage could not be repaired, then he and Sara must live apart. It is possible that the Wordsworths were already advocating this latter step. S.T.C. was subsequently to tell George Coleridge:

> The few friends who have been witness of my domestic life, have long advised separation as the necessary condition of everything desirable for me.[49]

S.T.C. sighed to Southey:

> If my wife loved me, and I my wife, half as well as we both love our children, I should be the happiest man alive—but this is not—will not be![50]

In London S.T.C. saw much of Davy; worked well for the *Morning Post*; enjoyed a bachelor existence at Number 10, King Street, Covent Garden and met with social success in London drawing-rooms. After Christmas he went to stay with Poole who, during this visit, clearly must have remonstrated with S.T.C. upon the subject of his opium habit; S.T.C. did not take offence this time, but attempted to stop the opium, with the result that, on his return to London, he was seized with what was without doubt a violent withdrawal attack while dining with Southey. S.T.C., not understanding the nature of this abrupt illness, attributed his diarrhoea and shivering (classical withdrawal symptoms) to the greens and apple-pie that Edith Southey had served.[51]

An attempt was now made by him, in letters, at a reconciliation with Sara Coleridge. ("Poor Mrs C. has suffered a great deal from rheumatism lately," S.T.C. confided to Miss Hutchinson; he sent his wife brisk advice to make herself flannel drawers and to take mustard pills.)[52] His main message to her was that he hoped to return to her in love and peace. "It is my frequent prayer . . . that we may meet to part no more—& live together as affectionate Husband & Wife."[53]

S.T.C. returned North at the start of March, 1802, apparently full of hope for happier times with Sara Coleridge. Instead of going direct to Keswick he stopped off at Gallow Hill to see Sara and Mary Hutchinson. On arrival back at Greta Hall he was received by an unenthusiastic Sara Coleridge, who took a poor view of his visit to Gallow Hill and remarked caustically of Sara Hutchinson that she could see nothing extraordinary in her.[54]

S.T.C. was precipitated into a new abyss of dejection and opium. During this he wrote Sara Hutchinson a letter of such despair that it made her ill. She took to her bed.

It is possible that her family now began to think that she should perhaps be removed from S.T.C.'s easy access; there was talk that she and Tom

Hutchinson might farm in the Wolds after Mary's marriage.[55] Nothing came of this scheme. What is certain is that Miss Hutchinson now increasingly found herself the unhappy victim of that most dangerous of all responses of the human heart—pity.

CHAPTER SIXTEEN

THE PAINS OF SLEEP

(March 1802–July 1803)

DOROTHY WORDSWORTH's GRASMERE *Journal* is very different from the self-consciously picturesque one of Alfoxden, which was shown and read to friends. At Grasmere Dorothy was writing privately, partly for William, providing him with material which later he incorporated in his poetry, partly for herself, using the *Journal* as confidant. In its pages she achieved the stature of one of the most remarkable prose-writers in the English language.

The picture that emerges from the pages of the Grasmere *Journal* is one of a woman deeply in love with a man who reciprocates her love to the full, but is forced to marry another. The struggle of the lovers to accept this harsh fate and the tensions arising from their struggle (tensions intensified by the fact that the frustrated pair live intimately together) result in constant physical distress, severe headaches, nausea and insomnia. Dorothy records incident upon incident of heartbreak:

William's head was bad ... I petted him on the carpet.[1]

We sat by the fire, and were happy, only our tender thoughts became painful. Went to bed ½ past 11.[2]

Wm. out of spirits and tired. After we went to bed I heard him continually, he called at ¼ past 3 to know the hour.[3]

The Wordsworths, as aforesaid, early in 1802 were discussing with S.T.C. by letter a scheme whereby, soon after S.T.C.'s projected return from London to the Lake Country in the spring, William would marry Mary Hutchinson, following which they and Dorothy, together with the Coleridges, would remove for a year or two to a place of warm climate; Montpellier was envisaged. S.T.C. hoped that the Southeys might also join the party, which would set sail from Liverpool for Bordeaux in July.[4]

In the event, the Wordsworth-Hutchinson marriage did not take place so early as at first planned, principally, it seems, because Annette Vallon had to be taken into consideration. The temporary cessation of hostilities between France and England meant that Annette was able to make contact with William again. She no longer retained any desire to marry him; but he was the father of her child and it was thus correct to keep in touch.[5] It was decided that, before his marriage to Mary, William together with Dorothy, should visit France to see Annette and little Caroline.[6]

Mary must have been informed about Annette and Caroline; when, is uncertain (perhaps it was in mid-February, when William went to Penrith for a few days). During William's absence Dorothy slept in his bed, "and I slept badly, for my thoughts were full of William."[7] On February 16 he returned: "his mouth and breath were very cold when he kissed me. We spent a sweet evening. We went to bed pretty soon and we slept better than we expected and had no bad dreams."[8]

S.T.C., as described, was back in Keswick early March. Mrs Coleridge was soon once more pregnant, but neither husband nor wife was made happy this time by the discovery of her condition. "Mrs Coleridge . . . is breeding again / an event, which was to have been deprecated," S.T.C. told Poole, grumpily.[9]

Before long he and Sara Coleridge were fighting—if anything, worse than previously. It was now that S.T.C. sent Sara Hutchinson the epistle of intense despair that made her so miserable that she was obliged to take to her bed:

> . . . I wrote thee that complaining Scroll
> Which even to bodily sickness bruis'd thy Soul![10]

William, learning of S.T.C.'s wretched state, went to Keswick. Dorothy, once again bereft of his company, vowed to her *Journal*:

> I *will* be busy. I *will* look well, and be well when he comes back to me. O the Darling! Here is one of his bitten apples. I can hardly find in my heart to throw it into the fire . . . full of thoughts about my darling. Blessings on him.[11]

William returned on Sunday, March 7. On March 9 he read Dorothy "a beautiful poem on Love" by Ben Jonson. "We then walked. The first part of our walk was melancholy."[12]

Poetry, love, heartbreak; the *Journal* tells the tragic tale:

> Tuesday [March 16] . . . After dinner I read him to sleep. I read Spenser while he leaned on my shoulder.
> Wednesday [March 17] . . . After dinner we made a pillow of my shoulder . . . I read to him and my Beloved slept . . . [Later she went for an evening walk alone: by Rydal Water she met William] . . . I saw the shape of my Beloved in the road at a little distance . . . [They sat together on a wall as night fell. Presently William "kindled" and began to compose. They returned to the cottage; took cloaks into the orchard where William composed some more. Dorothy, "tired to death" at last went to bed; later William] "came down to me, and read the Poem to me in bed."

William, in 1802, was gripped by another great stir of poetry: he composed incessantly, wearing himself out with the nervous strain involved.

The intense emotional stress under which he laboured must additionally have contributed to his exhaustion. That spring of 1802, with its tragic incestuous love, its quiet but kindling interest in Mary, its nostalgic thoughts of Annette and its miraculous explosion of poetry must surely have been one of the most incredible passages in this incredible man's life.

On March 14 William composed rapidly, over breakfast, his poem *The Butterfly*. This was the first of several poems in a spontaneous, fluid, almost impressionistic style, in which he suddenly at this time began to write. Wordsworth was in a wholly new poetic mood, seeing, feeling and transmitting quite differently from hitherto.

The reality of the way in which a poet works is immensely different from anything that the public ever supposes. On Friday and Saturday, March 26 and 27, William Wordsworth was much absorbed by the problems of, firstly, obtaining a load of dung for the garden and, secondly, of digging it in. Yet, during these two earthy days, he composed some of his most celebrated spiritual poetry. Dung was the subject engrossing him during the day upon the evening of which he wrote:

> My heart leaps up when I behold
>   A rainbow in the sky;
> So was it when my life began;
> So is it now I am a man;
> So be it when I shall grow old,
>   Or let me die!
> The Child is Father of the Man;
> And I could wish my days to be
> Bound each to each by natural piety.

These lines, *The Rainbow*, served as the introductory theme of the great ode, *Intimations of Immortality*, which he began to compose the next morning at breakfast; after which the dung arrived "and Wm went to work in the garden"[13] while his mind and heart beat with strophes:

> There was a time when meadow, grove and stream,
> The earth, and every common sight,
>   To me did seem
>   Apparelled in celestial light,
> The glory and the freshness of a dream.

The following day the Wordsworths rode over to Keswick. There they remained for a week, during the first part of which Dorothy was unwell. Otherwise the visit went pleasantly enough, with walks and a good deal of Keswick party-going and gossip. On the evening of Sunday, April 4, the day before the Wordsworths were to leave, the Greta Hall folk took tea (in those days an evening ceremony) with the Calverts at Greta Bank. Here

Dorothy repeated some of William's verses to the company, including lines from the new ode (which William may well already have recited himself to Coleridge on Skiddaw, the previous day):

Our birth is but a sleep and a forgetting:
The Soul that rises with us, our life's Star,
   Hath had elsewhere its setting
    And cometh from afar:
    Not in entire forgetfulness,
    And not in utter nakedness,
But trailing clouds of glory do we come
   From God, who is our home:
Heaven lies about us in our infancy!
Shades of the prison-house begin to close
   Upon the growing Boy,
But He beholds the light, and whence it flows,
   He sees it in his joy;
The Youth, who daily further from the East
   Must travel, still is Nature's Priest,
    And by the vision splendid
    Is on his way attended;
At length the Man perceives it die away,
And fade into the light of common day.

When he got back to Greta Hall from Greta Bank S.T.C. withdrew to his study and his laudanum bottle. Weeping, he stayed by his window for a long time, watching the sunset glow and fade and brooding upon the heart-rending knowledge that his powers as a poet were fading too, as rapidly and as inevitably as the setting sun.

S.T.C. was no longer capable of either the concentration or the lift of imagination required for poetry. Morphine had doused the sap of his poet's centre—"the force that through the green fuse drives the flower."[14] These days, when S.T.C. flickeringly kindled to write a poem, his ideas "Beat up Game of another kind," as he himself put it:

instead of a Covey of poetic Partridges with whirring wings of music, or wild Ducks *shaping* their rapid flight in forms always regular ... up came a metaphysical Bustard, urging its slow, heavy, laborious, earth-skimming Flight over dreary & level Wastes.[15]

(S.T.C., of course, overtly blamed his wife, not opium, for his inability to compose poetry: "discord between me and Mrs Coleridge ... quite incapacitated me for any worthy exertion of my faculties by degrading me in my own estimation.")[16]

While his powers of poetry waned to vanishing point, S.T.C. was obliged to undergo the experience of witnessing Wordsworth's marvellous further burgeoning of genius.

On that memorable Sunday, April 4, 1802, the lines of Wordsworth's new ode must have struck into Coleridge's soul like an implement of torture. He watched the sun set over the Coledale Fells and the new moon come up with the old moon in her lap, reminding him of the ancient Scots ballad of Sir Patrick Spens:

> Late, late yestreen I saw the new Moon,
> With the old Moon in her arms;
> And I fear, I fear, my Master dear!
> We shall have a deadly storm.

S.T.C. took up his own pen and moved into the opening lines of the ode which subsequently (in carefully censored guise) was to become famous as *Dejection*; in its original draft an unparalleled example of the self-torturing long-drawn-out howl of anguish and recrimination which the morphine-addict hurls at the world.

Because Sara Hutchinson was, at this time, the kernel of his fantasy-spinning, the symbolic Wailing Wall against which he wept, S.T.C.'s ode, in its first draft, took the form of a letter to her. But he did not keep it a private poem; on April 21, at Grasmere, S.T.C. repeated it to the Wordsworths and, subsequently, a much-polished draft was addressed to William. On May 7, S.T.C. was telling Poole: "I ought to say that on the 4th of April I wrote you a letter in verse; but I thought it dull & doleful—& did not send it—."[17] This, of course, was an utter lie, no doubt told to keep Poole happy in the thought that his beloved Col remembered him.

Dejection: an Ode (now addressed to *Edmund*, a Romantic soubriquet for Wordsworth) was finally given to the world in the *Morning Post* on October 4, 1802, Wordsworth's wedding-day and the seventh anniversary of S.T.C.'s wedding. The appearance of the poem on this particular date could surely not have been purely coincidental. The ode, by this time, was very different from the sado-masochistic, opium-impregnated draft that had first gone to Sara Hutchinson (The version which, invoking some anonymous *O Lady!* appeared in *Sibylline Leaves* in 1817 was even more impeccably polished.)

The original draft that went to Sara Hutchinson is the version of the ode which most merits our attention here. The opening stanza begins soberly, if sombrely, enough, but with the first lines of the second stanza we are with morphine:

> A Grief without a pang, void, dark, & drear,
> A stifling, drowsy, unimpassion'd Grief
> That finds no natural outlet, no Relief
> In word, or sigh, or tear . . .

As he continued composing S.T.C. became progressively high (or, in this instance, more correctly low) on his drug. The discipline gradually seeped from the writing, the tension of the poem was lost and the metre, bereft of internal spring, began to trudge. Only an innate technical prowess kept S.T.C. moving as he recalled the fire-side incident of the lazy-bed, from thence to move on to a sadistic lip-licking at the thought of the distress he had recently caused Asra with his complaining letter:

> And must I not regret, that I distress'd
> Thee, best beloved! who lovest me the best?
> My better mind had fled, I know not whither,
> For O! was this an absent Friend's Employ
> To send from far both Pain & Sorrow thither ...
> I read thy guileless letter o'er again—
> I hear thee of thy blameless Self complain—
> And only this I learn—& this, alas, I know—
> That thou art weak & pale, with Sickness, Grief & Pain—
> And *I—I* made thee so!

The note of sadistic satisfaction in these lines is quite unmistakable.

The poem (designed to distress Sara Hutchinson even more than previously, if possible) continued with its whining, its repining, its searing allusions to his household of "Indifference or Strife," his "coarse domestic Life," his half-wish that his children had never been born. Every image of anguish was lovingly taken out and ardently embraced, including the Eolian Lute, that once played exquisite music to himself and his other Sara at their honeymoon cottage at Clevedon, but which now sobbed and screamed in his Greta Hall window. He brooded, enviously, over the happiness of Mary, William and Dorothy, then returned to the satisfactory spectacle of Sara Hutchinson, made as miserable now as he was:

> But O! to mourn for thee ...
> To know that thou art weak & worn with pain,
> And not to hear thee, Sara! not to view thee—
> Not sit beside thy Bed,
> Not press thy aching Head,
> Not bring thee Health again—
> At least to hope, to try ...
> Nay, wherefore did I let it haunt my Mind
>   The dark distressful Dream!
> I turn from it, & listen to the Wind
> Which long has rav'd unnotic'd! What a Scream
> Of agony by Torture lengthen'd out
> That Lute sent forth! O thou wild storm without! ...
> Mad Lutanist! that in this month of Showers,
> Of dark brown Gardens, & of peeping Flowers,

357

Mak'st Devil's Yule . . .
Thou Actor, perfect in all tragic Sounds!
Thou mighty Poet, even to frenzy bold!
   What tell'st thou now about?
'Tis of the Rushing of an Host in Rout—
And many Groans from men with smarting Wounds—
At once they groan with smart, and shudder with the Cold!
'Tis hush'd! there is a Trance of deepest Silence;
Again! but all that Sound, as of a rushing Crowd
And Groans & tremulous Shudderings, all are over—
And it has other Sounds, and all less deep, less loud! . . .
   'Tis of a little Child
   Upon a heathy Wild,
Not far from home—but it has lost its way—
And now moans low in utter grief & fear—
And now screams loud, & hopes to make its Mother hear!

The effect which this ode had upon the unhappy Sara Hutchinson has not been recorded. We know that it had, not surprisingly, a miserable one upon the Wordsworths when S.T.C. recited it to them on April 21. Dorothy recorded that:

> Coleridge came to us and repeated the verses he wrote to Sara. I was affected with them and . . . in miserable spirits. The sunshine—the green fields and the fair sky made me sadder; even the little happy sporting lambs seemed but sorrowful to me.[18]

The discord at Greta Hall now mounted to a crescendo.[19] At length S.T.C. decided to follow the advice of the Wordsworths that he and Sara Coleridge should part. The struggles of his mind upon this issue were so violent that his health deteriorated again rapidly (massive opium dosage was no doubt resorted to with desperation) and his "sleep became the valley of the Shadows of Death."[20] He steeled himself to broach the subject of separation to Mrs Coleridge; she reacted furiously. Their quarrel reached such a pitch that S.T.C. collapsed. Sara, terrified, flung herself upon him and begged forgiveness. The result was that each made a pact with the other to try to give up fighting. Sara promised "to set about an alteration in external manners & looks & language . . . her inveterate habits of . . . Thwarting & . . . Dispathy." S.T.C. "promised to be more attentive to all her feelings of Pride . . . and to try to correct . . . [his] habits of impetuous & bitter censure."[21]

Both parties now made a desperate and heroic attempt to save their marriage. Sara kept her "solemn promise of amendment" beyond all S.T.C.'s expectation and, he said, began "to feel as a Wife ought to feel."[22]

Of course, as he hinted darkly to Southey, Sara had only mended her ways because his collapse had so scared her:

> the fears of widowhood came upon her . . . these feelings were wholly selfish, yet they made her *serious*—and that was a great point gained—for Mrs. Coleridge's mind has very little that is *bad* in it—it is an innocent mind—; but it is light, and *unimpressible*, warm in anger, cold in sympathy—and in all disputes uniformly *projects* itself *forth* to recriminate, instead of turning itself inward with a silent Self-questioning. Our virtues & our vices are exact antitheses—I so attentively watch my own Nature, that my worst Self-delusion is, a compleat Self-knowledge . . . mixed with intellectual complacency . . . my quickness & readiness to acknowledge my faults is too often frustrated by the small pain, which the sight of them gives me, & the consequent slowness to amend them. Mrs. C. . . . shelters herself from painful Self-enquiry by angry Recriminations . . . Alas! I have suffered more, I think, from the amiable propensities of my nature than from my worst faults & most erroneous Habits . . . But as I said—Mrs. Coleridge was made *serious*—and for the first time since our marriage, she felt and acted as beseemed a Wife & a Mother to a Husband, & the Father of her children . . . I have the most confident Hopes that this happy Revolution in our domestic affairs will be permanent, & that this external Conformity will gradually generate a greater inward Likeness of thoughts, & attachments, than has hitherto existed between us. Believe me, if you were here, it would give you a deep delight to observe the difference of our . . . conduct towards each other, from that, which, I fear, could not but have disturbed your comforts, when you were here last.[23]

S.T.C.'s relief at recovering domestic harmony is revealed by the way in which he reported upon it to all his friends who had known of the disharmony. To Estlin he wrote that "*at home all is Peace & Love.*"[24] Even Asra was given the glad tidings: "the wind has risen, Darling! it blows this way a strong & steady gale, & I see already with the eye of confident anticipation the laughing blue sky, & no black thick Cloud!"[25]

Sara Coleridge obviously now exerted herself to the utmost to demonstrate her loving concern for Samuel. The reader will judge for himself whether she had in truth offended, or had been more offended against, in this marriage. Dorothy Wordsworth, however, had no hesitation when it came to this question. Writing to Mary and Sara Hutchinson, during a three-day stay that S.T.C. paid to Dove Cottage, arriving there on June 10, Dorothy roundly declared:

> Mrs Coleridge is a most extraordinary character—she is the lightest weakest silliest woman! She sent some clean clothes on Thursday to meet C. (the first time she ever did such a thing in her life) from which I guess she is determined to be attentive to him—she wrote a note . . . all in her very lightest style . . . Is not it a hopeless case? So insensible and so irritable she

never can come to good and poor C! but I said I would not enter on this subject, and I will not.[26]

The Wordsworths, at this time, were looking for more extensive accommodation to move to after William's marriage; S.T.C. suggested that they should share Greta Hall with him and his family, but Dorothy was certain that the plan would not work and the idea was dropped. She was equally opposed to a suggestion put forward by the Hutchinsons that she and William should move to Gallow Hill. "I made a vow that we would not leave this country for Gallow Hill," she confided to her Journal.[27] Fate was forcing her to share her beloved William; she was not going to relinquish her beloved Lake Country too.

That "sweet spring, the best beloved and best,"[28] turned into summer; the time was fast coming when brother and sister would no longer be alone together, seated, William's head on Dorothy's shoulder, "deep in silence and Love,"[29] or lingering in their orchard, reciting William's verses to one another, or sharing the vigils of nights tortured by despair and memories. The moonlight stretched across the floor; Dorothy, to soothe William to sleep, sat by his bed and recited to him at his request, over and over again: "This is the spot:" (p. 266).

> We two have had such happy times together
> That my heart melts in me to think of it.

In June the Wordsworths learned that William, Lord Lowther (the new heir to James Earl of Lonsdale, who had recently died) was prepared to pay the Wordsworths the debts outstanding to them by the Lowther family. Brother and sister, at first almost dazed by this information, walked together on White Moss Common: "We talked sweetly together about our riches. We lay upon the sloping Turf. Earth and sky were so lovely that they melted our very hearts."[30]

On Friday, July 9, they left Grasmere on the first leg of their journey to France. They went to Keswick; here they stayed the week-end. Dorothy was ill as, too, was S.T.C. He was, it seems, in a sorry state of exclusion and dejection.

The full facts behind the reason for the Wordsworths' visit to France had been withheld from him. All the surviving evidence points to the fact that S.T.C. was never told the true identity of Annette and Caroline. A spiteful epigram of his, *Spots in the Sun*, written in reference to Wordsworth at this time (obviously inspired by jealousy of William's happiness with Mary) refers to Annette as a "lovely courtesan". We can only suppose that S.T.C. was jumping to wild conclusions; Annette was a Frenchwoman and that, for S.T.C., almost automatically spelled courtesan.

During the Wordsworths' absence in France S.T.C. endeavoured to pump Sara Hutchinson: "Dear little Caroline*:—Will she be a ward of Annette?—Was the subject too delicate for a letter?—I suppose so."[31] This comment is the only known reference to Annette and Caroline discoverable in Coleridge's letters.

Miss Hutchinson seems not to have enlightened him; perhaps she did not know the full facts herself.

The Coleridge family for long nursed a rumour that Wordsworth had had an illegitimate son in France who, continued this rumour, as a young man subsequently visited his parent at Rydal Mount.[31] Clearly, although S.T.C. had harboured strong suspicions, the Wordsworths had never fully confided in him upon this matter.

On Monday, July 12 the Wordsworths and S.T.C. walked together across Matterdale Common to the foot of Ullswater. S.T.C. accompanied the Wordsworths as far as the seventh milestone. Here the three friends rested by the roadside. They sat in silence, their thoughts, perhaps, going back to that sunny morning at Racedown, almost precisely five years since, when S.T.C., in his eagerness to meet the Wordsworths, had leapt over the gate to cut off a corner and had run across the field to them.

At last, the Wordsworths rose to their feet to walk on to Eusemere, S.T.C. rose, too, to return to Keswick. Theirs was a "melancholy Parting."[32]

The Wordsworths paid a visit to Mary Hutchinson before travelling to France. On their way to Gallow Hill brother and sister crossed Stanemoor in the rain on the outside of a coach; William buttoned the two of them together inside his greatcoat "and we liked the hills and the Rain the better for bringing [us] so close to one another."[33]

So journeyed these two tragic people.

Their visit to Gallow Hill was brief, then on to London, then to Dover. The Wordsworths arrived at Calais at four o'clock on Sunday morning, July 31. They went ashore and found Annette and Caroline at "chez Madame Avril dans la Rue de la Tête d'or."[34]

William and Dorothy stayed in France a month; they returned to London on August 30. They remained in the South of England until September 22. During that time they saw their brothers, including John, who had just returned from his third voyage in the *Abergavenny*. He "was grown fat and looked very handsome" noted Dorothy.[35] Mary Hutchinson had written to him about her intended marriage. He sent a brief note in reply:

I have been reading your Letter over and over again My dearest Mary till tears have come into my eyes and I know not how to express myself, thou

*The name, Caroline, is heavily inked out in the MS.

art [a] kind and dear creature But what ever fate Befall me I shall love [thee] to the last and bear thy memory with me to the grave.

Thine affte

JOHN WORDSWORTH[36]

Dorothy and William arrived back at Gallow Hill on September 24. It is best to let Dorothy describe the rest of this episode of William's marriage:

> Mary first met us in the avenue. She looked so fat and well that we were made very happy by the sight of her ... the garden looked gay with asters and sweet peas. I looked at everything with tranquillity and happiness—was ill on Saturday and on Sunday and continued to be so during most of the time of our stay ...
>
> On Monday, 4th October, 1802, at Brompton, my Brother William was married to Mary Hutchinson. I slept a good deal of the night and rose fresh and well in the morning. At a little after 8 o'clock I saw them go down the avenue towards the church. William had parted from me upstairs. I gave him the wedding ring—with how deep a blessing! I took it from my forefinger where I had worn it the whole of the night before—he slipped it again onto my finger and blessed me fervently ... I kept myself as quiet as I could, but when I saw the two men running up the walk, coming to tell us it was over, I could stand it no longer and threw myself on the bed where I lay in stillness, neither hearing or seeing anything, till Sara came upstairs to me and said "They are coming." This forced me from the bed where I lay and I moved I knew not how straight forward, faster than my strength could carry me till I met my beloved William and fell upon his bosom. He and John Hutchinson led me to the house and there I stayed to welcome my dear Mary.[37]

William, Mary and Dorothy returned to Dove Cottage on Wednesday evening, October 6. To quote Dorothy once more:

> Molly was overjoyed to see us, for my part I cannot describe what I felt, and our dear Mary's feelings would I dare say not be easy to speak of.[38]

During their absence S.T.C., considerably better and happier than he had been for many months, made his famous ascent of Scafell, part of a very strenuous week's walking in the fells. His experiences upon Scafell, left him in a state of thrilled rapture: "Oh how I wished for health and strength that I might wander about for a month together in the stormiest month of the year among these places, so lonely and savage and full of sounds!"[39] "Of all earthy things which I have beheld, the view of Sca'fell & *from* Sca'fell ... is the most heart-exciting."[40]

His prose account in the notebooks and in letters to Sara Hutchinson are unrivalled writing, but this was not enough for him. He longed to be able to compose a poem to commemorate the occasion, but he could not. His power as a poet was disintegrated. Subsequent events were tragic. On September 11, 1802 there appeared in the *Morning Post* a poem ostensibly by S.T.C., *Hymn Before Sunrise, in the Vale of Chamouni*. This, S.T.C. told his friends, had been composed by him on Scafell (it should be observed that the note-books make no reference whatever to his having composed any poetry during his tour. He wrote a letter to Sara Hutchinson while on the summit of Scafell; then he hastily descended by Cam Spout into Upper Eskdale, driven from off the tops by a thunder-storm). Yet to Sotheby, among others, S.T.C. declared that,

> I involuntarily poured forth a Hymn in the manner of the Psalms, tho' afterwards I thought the Ideas &c disproportionate to our humble moun-tains—& accidentally lighting on a short Note in some Swiss Poems, con-cerning the Vale of Chamouny, & its Mountains, I transferred myself thither, in the Spirit, & adopted my former feelings to these grander external objects. You will soon see it in the Morning Post.[41]

The *Hymn* was criticised by Wordsworth on the grounds of artificiality; why should S.T.C., who had never been to the Vale of Chamouny in his life, transfer to the Swiss Alps a poem written upon Scafell? S.T.C.'s excuse to Wordsworth doubtless resembled the explanation (above) prof-fered to Sotheby.

The true story of the poem's origin did not emerge until much later (see pp. 254–5).

Wordsworth's marriage had ejected S.T.C. from out of the Dove Cottage orbit back into the anti-Wordsworth camp. The drug-addict (like every seriously disorientated person) tends to swing with abruptness from one sphere of influence to another and S.T.C. was a perfect case in point. With the Wordsworths gone he had no sympathetic Dorothy to encourage his complaints about his wife and therefore he gradually found less to complain about. The Lambs came to stay at Greta Hall on August 9 and their three weeks visit had a highly therapeutic effect upon S.T.C., who delighted in showing them all the splendours of the Lake Country. Following their departure he was in such good spirits that, for the first time in months, he was able to address himself to regular feature-writing for the *Morning Post*. S.T.C. told Thomas Wedgwood that he was devoting three days a week to newspaper work.

S.T.C. was now once more full of ambitious literary schemes; he spoke of a two volume critical history of English prose, which, "if my life and health remain" (this had now become a very popular phrase with him) & I do but write half as much and as regularly, as I have done during the last six weeks . . . will be finished by January next—& I shall then put together my memorandum Book on the subject of poetry."[42] He was even thinking of starting work on his poetic *magnum opus* (being tragically unaware that he had already written it); this was to be an heroic poem on the Seige of Jerusalem by Titus. S.T.C. confided to Tom Wedgwood that he had meditated on this since his twentieth year: "But I never think of it except in my best moods."[43]

Of course nothing came of any of this. He was no longer capable of such work.

It seems that during this good patch of health and spirits S.T.C. attempted to go without opium; on September 21 he was suddenly seized with what he thought to be a "nervous Fever"[44] but which was almost undoubtedly a withdrawal attack.

S.T.C. convalesced in his study, from one of the windows of which he lovingly watched his children playing in the garden[45]—the adorable two-year-old, fat Derwent, "a thorough Coleridge in his whole cast,"[46] and the thin six-year-old Hartley, a wonderful elfin child, "a spirit of Joy dancing on an Aspen leaf,"[47] marred only, ruminated the proud parent, by a villainously low forehead, bequeathed to the child by his mother. In the windy, bright autumn weather the two small boys rollicked on the grass:

> where the Gusts blow most madly—both with their Hair floating & tossing, a miniature of the agitated Trees below which they were playing / inebriate both with the pleasure—Hartley whirling round for joy—Derwent eddying half willingly, half by the force of the Gust—driven backward, struggling forward, & shouting his little hymn of Joy.[48]

By the end of October S.T.C. felt so fit and optimistic that he offered himself to Tom Wedgwood as a travelling companion. Wedgwood, without hesitation, at once invited S.T.C. to Cote House, with a view to travelling to France soon after. S.T.C. was game, though, "you are aware, that my whole knowledge of French does not extend beyond the power of limping slowly, not without a Dictionary Crutch, thro' an easy French Book; & that as to Pronunciation, all my Organs of Speech, from the bottom of the Larynx to the Edge of my Lips, are utterly and naturally Anti-gallican."[49] Wedgwood was not put off by this and S.T.C. left for London on November 4.

Unfortunately he spent a day with Sara Hutchinson in transit (she was visiting her aunt at Penrith). This he confessed nervously to Mrs Coleridge, by letter from London. He concluded, doubtless in an attempt to ward off her anticipated annoyance: "My dear Love—write as chearfully as possible. I am tenderer, & more fluttery, & bowel-weak, than most—I can not bear any thing gloomy, unless when it is quite necessary.—Be assured, I will bring back (come home when I will) a pure, affectionate, & husbandly Heart."[50]

As he had anticipated, Sara Coleridge was made angry and thus their first flurry of correspondence following their parting was acrimonious. With her scolding ringing in his ears, S.T.C. set off with Tom Wedgwood not upon a tour of France but, instead, a brief preliminary trip to Wales. They first stayed at St Clear, in Carmarthenshire, and on November 17 S.T.C. walked alone to Laughan, drawn there by who knows what strange anticipation of future poetry to be written in the shadow of the "fine richly ivied Castle close upon the sea."[51]

S.T.C. arrived at low tide and wandered round the bay, gazing across the expanses of exposed sand and salt-marshes while, from the distance, came "the murmur of the main Sea / & the Barking, yelping, whining, wailing of the various Sea fowls."[52] The furze bushes were in blossom and white petals still lingered on the yellow tansy heads.

In Laughan itself he found a number of handsome, well-kept houses; one with two large cages suspended outside it, with a screaming parrot in each cage. On top of the cages were perched barnyard fowls, including a cock with a "bold brave old England face."[53] S.T.C. waited for him to crow; but the bird failed to oblige and S.T.C., at last tired of waiting, wandered down to the "White Church with grey Steeple a furlong or so from the Town near the bottom on a Hillside—."[54] Here, where one day another poet was to lie, S.T.C. examined the tombstones, copying some of the naive and touching inscriptions into his pocket-book. Half-seated, half-stooping over "a square Tomb . . . where the Tom Tits with their black velvet caps showered down the lovely yewberries,"[55] he read the commemorative verses for the wife and daughters of Evan Jones who, outlasting his family by forty-one years, died at ninety-six: so much space had been devoted to verses for those who had predeceased him that, as S.T.C. noted, there was "no room even for one couplet on the old man."[56]

> And I am dumb to tell the lover's tomb
> How at my sheet goes the same crooked worm.[57]

During his travels and absences S.T.C.'s mind and heart invariably turned towards Sara Coleridge. How desperately these two struggled to save their marriage is proved by the surviving documentary evidence. S.T.C.'s letters to his wife, during this period, vibrate with a determination to attempt to make their marriage work:

My dear Love! let me in the spirit of love say two things / I owe duties, & solemn ones, to you, as my wife; but I owe equally solemn ones to Myself, to my Children, to my Friends, and to Society . . . I can neither retain my Happiness, nor my Faculties, unless I move, live, & love, in perfect Freedom, limited by my own purity & self-respect . . . That we can love but one person, is a miserable mistake, & the cause of abundant unhappiness. I can & do love many people, dearly—so dearly, that I really scarcely know, which I love the best . . . Would any good & wise man, any warm & wide hearted man marry at all, if it were part of the Contract—Henceforth this Woman is your only friend, your sole beloved! all the rest of mankind, however amiable & akin to you, must be only your *acquaintance*!—? . . . I have a *right* to expect & demand, that you should to a certain degree love, & act kindly to, those whom I deem worthy of my Love.—If you read this Letter with half the Tenderness, with which it is written, it will do you and both of us, GOOD & contribute it's share to the turning of a mere Cat-hole into a Dove's nest!

Then, anxious that, with this last remark, he might have gone too far:

You know, Sally Pally! I must have a Joke—or it would not be me![58]

Clearly Sara replied to this letter with a warmth and generosity of feeling that he had not dared to hope for. He replied to it, in his turn, upon the very night of his having received it:

My dearest Love
. . . I was affected by your Letter with such Joy & anxious Love . . . overpowered by it . . . God love you & have you in his keeping, my blessed Sara! —& speedily restore me to you.—I have a faith, a heavenly Faith, that our future Days will be Days of Peace, & affectionate Happiness.— . . . my dearest dearest Sara!—my wife & my Love, & indeed my very Hope / May God preserve you![59]

Upon first setting out with Tom Wedgwood S.T.C. had not only anticipated, but had hoped for a long absence. He had no idea where he might find himself; Tom Wedgwood was as vague a character as himself. They might go to "Cornwall, perhaps, or Madeira . . . I don't see any likelihood of our going to the Moon, or to either of the Planets, or fixed Stars."[60] But now S.T.C., anxious only to return to Greta Hall, contrived to persuade Tom Wedgwood that a tour of the Lake Country was what he required. Sara was told that S.T.C. and their guest would be at Keswick by New Year's Day.

She had put S.T.C. in a fever of anxiety at one point by writing to say that she, now eight months pregnant, had had a fainting fit. He begged her "INSTANTLY to get a Nurse . . . get somebody immediately, have a fire in your Bedroom . . . If you are seriously ill, or unhappy at my absence, I will return at all Hazards."[61]

The baby was expected at the New Year and, as Christmas approached, S.T.C. wrote with alarming suggestions for names—Bracey or Crescelly, should the infant be a boy (which he more or less took for granted), Algretha, Rotha or Lovenna, should it be a girl. He proposed that Sara

Hutchinson should be procured as nurse while Sara Coleridge was lying-in, that the latter might learn to know the former, "as she really is . . . much of our Love & Happiness depends on your loving those whom I love."[62]

As it transpired, S.T.C. had not reached Greta Hall when the child arrived on December 23. At Grasmere, where S.T.C. and Wedgwood called on December 24, they were greeted with the news that Sara had given birth to a daughter; both mother and child were safe and well. The sex of the new arrival was a shock, as S.T.C. confessed to Southey. Sara was selected as the infant's name.

The year of 1803 thus started with promise. But there could be no truly happy prospect for S.T.C., nor for his marriage, unless opium could be abandoned—a forlorn hope.

Indeed, in the company of Tom Wedgwood, himself an opium-eater, there was active encouragement to continue with the drug. "I am fully convinced, & so is T. Wedgwood, that to a person, with such a Stomach and Bowels as mine, if any stimulus is needful, Opium . . . is incomparably better in every respect than . . . any *fermented* Liquor—nay, far less pernicious even than Tea,"[63] S.T.C. informed Sara Coleridge in one of his many justifications for the continuance of his habit.

Illness laid S.T.C. low again at Greta Hall in the New Year, following an injudicious crossing over the Kirkstone Pass on foot in a fearful storm.[64] The thought of death now haunted him continually and with it guilt-ridden visions of a penniless, unprotected widow and children. Spurred on by these spectres of disaster, S.T.C. persuaded Robert Southey to consider sharing Greta Hall for a while. The Southeys, now the parents of an infant daughter delightfully known as The Passionate Pearl, favoured the thought of a secluded country residence. There was only one disadvantage to the plan and that was that the Southeys might bring with them the unhappy Mary Lovell; a possibility which Sara welcomed even less than did S.T.C., if that were possible.

S.T.C. proposed to insure his life as a further step towards procuring security for his dependents. This, too, he discussed with Southey. "I fear I must *rouge* a little,"[65] commented S.T.C., wryly. Speaking of his death, he explained that his fear was only for Sara: "nothing would give me greater pleasure on my Death bed, than the probability of her marrying a second time, happily."[66]

S.T.C. was determined that everything that now lay within his power to secure Sara comforts and tranquillity should be done. "In an evil Day for me did I first pay attentions to Mrs Coleridge; in an evil day for me did I marry her; but it shall be my care & my passion, that it shall not be an evil day for her; & that whatever I may be, or may be represented, as a Husband, I may yet be unexceptionable, as her Protector & Friend.—"[67]

He was now, once again, upon the point of setting off with Tom Wedgwood, it was supposed to the Mediterranean. But Wedgwood, whom chronic invalidism and drugs had rendered as disorientated as S.T.C., suddenly changed his mind about having Coleridge as travelling companion; he contemplated taking Tobin instead. S.T.C., as a preliminary step to his anticipated travels, had gone to stay with Poole at Stowey; here he learned of Tom Wedgwood's change of mind. S.T.C., determined to try a warmer climate for his health, began pondering upon how he might raise the money to travel alone.

During this period of uncertainty he learned from Davy that Tom Wedgwood was most anxious to sample some Indian hemp (cannabis resin), then popularly known as Bhang (or Bang). Davy could not obtain any; S.T.C. came to the rescue and procured some through the good offices of Samuel Purkis. The Bang arrived at Stowey on February 17.

S.T.C. and Poole were already proposing to visit the Wedgwoods at Gunville; S.T.C. now wrote gaily to Tom Wedgwood that he would bring the Bang with him, rather than entrust it to the post:

> the Stowey Carriers of Letters ... are a brace of as careless & dishonest Rogues, as had ever claims on that article of the Hemp & Timber Trade, called the Gallows.

S.T.C. then went on to prophesy, with relish:

> We will have a fair trial of *Bang*—Do bring down some of the Hyoscyamine Pills—& I will give a fair Trial of opium, Hensbane, & Nepenthe. Bye the bye, I always considered Homer's account of the Nepenthe as a *Banging* lie.—[68]

On February 18, S.T.C. and Poole left Stowey for Gunville (it is more than doubtful that Tom Poole was aware that S.T.C. and Tom Wedgwood were planning a drug session together; such matters can be, and are, skilfully concealed from the innocent).

Whether it was the Bang, or indeed whatever the cause, Tom Wedgwood suddenly changed his mind about travelling abroad with S.T.C.; plans were made for the two to leave together for France without delay. S.T.C. was fitted out with a wardrobe at the Wedgwoods' expense and departure was imminent, when there came a severe war scare. In the end Tom Wedgwood left for France, the scare over; but he travelled with another friend, Underwood, instead of with S.T.C. and, in the event, war with France did once again break out and Wedgwood and Underwood hastened back to England on May 16.

Meanwhile S.T.C. returned to Keswick on April 8, full of good intentions but with little hope. He had now insured his life under an Equitable Assurance Policy T20743. It cost him thirty-one pounds the first year and twenty-seven each succeeding year; drowning, hanging and suicide were not covered. To his honour he never permitted this policy to lapse.

Greta Hall, Keswick. S.T.C.'s study, with two aspects, on right-hand of first-floor.
(*George Fisher Collection*)

Dove Cottage, Grasmere, in its subsequent guise as a shrine.
(*George Fisher Collection*)

Sara Hutchinson: *c.* 1815. Silhouette by artist unknown.
(*Courtesy Dove Cottage Trustees*)

Mrs Sara Coleridge, aged thirty-nine: a miniature portrait
painted by Matilda Betham in 1809.
(*By Permission of Mr A. H. B. Coleridge*)

The Exile: S.T.C. in Rome, 1805. Unfinished portrait by Washington Allston. (*Courtesy of the Fogg Art Museum, Harvard University, Loan – The Washington Allston Trust*)

On the way back to Keswick he caught influenza from an old man on the mail-coach (an epidemic was raging). The whole of the Greta Hall household was laid up with influenza, Hartley excepted. It was not a happy homecoming for S.T.C. He treated himself with "opium taken with Camphor & Rhubarb"[69] but, in spite of these precautions, he developed a bout of rheumatic fever.

In due course he recovered somewhat and spent June and July mainly in drafting grand literary schemes which came to nothing. (His ideas included a philosophical work which would be an introduction to his ultimate *magnum opus*. He also outlined, for Southey, a *Bibliotheca Britannica*, or *History of British Literature*, in which Longman seemed interested; but the idea was shelved.) During this period visitors came to Keswick; Hazlitt appeared, to be followed by Sir George and Lady Beaumont. Sir George, a distinguished patron of the arts, disliked S.T.C. when first he met him[70] (later the acquaintance was to ripen into a friendship of mutual regard). S.T.C., for his part, was cool in his first feelings for Sir George and penetrating in his appraisal of Lady Beaumont, telling the Wordsworths (whom the Beaumonts much wished to meet): "I can describe her to you in a few words—She is a miniature of Madame Guion /

> A deep Enthusuast, sensitive,
> Trembles & cannot keep the Tears in her eye—
> Such ones do love the marvellous too well
> Not to believe it. You may wind her up
> With any Music.—*

but *music* it must be, of some sort or other."[71]

The Wordsworths seem to have taken this advice to heart; they were to become highly adept at winding up Lady Beaumont.

To Sir George, S.T.C. spoke glowingly of his future writings; especially at this time did he talk about his philosophical work, outlined already to Godwin as "Investigations relative to the omne scibile of human Nature— *what* we *are*, & *how we become* what we are; so as to solve the two grand Problems, how, being acted upon, we shall act; how, acting, we shall be acted upon."[72] To Southey S.T.C. confessed: "the sense of responsibility to my own mind is growing deeper & deeper with me from many causes— chiefly, from the knowledge that I am not of no significance, relatively to, comparatively with, other men, my contemporaries."[73]

"The sense of responsibility" to his own mind had dawned too late. When he wrote these words to Southey, S.T.C. had not yet grasped the full extent of his tragedy. He certainly realised that he had extinguished the fire of his

---

Osorio II, i, 32–36. Poems, ii, 536.

poetry, but he still believed that his powers of reasoning, his gifts of speculative intelligence, remained intact, if grown a little rusty. He decided to
recondition his mind with "Thoughts" that would be his "Guides,
Guardians, and Comforters."[74] With the aid of these thoughts he would
fortify his intellect; intellect would fortify will-power; fortified will-power
would vanquish the opium habit.

S.T.C.'s generation knew even less about the working of the mind than
we do. The supposition that mind and body were distinct one from the
other was firmly entertained by S.T.C. A question asked by himself in the
notebook for mid-June 1803 is revealing:

> What is the *Detail* of the Causes in consequence of which Ill-health weakens
> the Understanding; in cases, where the faculties themselves are not appar-
> ently or suddenly attacked?[75]

"The faculties" were, in his concept, aloof from the rest of his person.
"The blood & the secretions—are no parts of my Knowledge,"[76] he observed to Sir George Beaumont. Man was departmentalised.

This belief in a departmentalised self led S.T.C. into the error (a common one that is still voiced today) of supposing that the intellectual performance of Esteesee could be isolated from his opium.

By 1803 S.T.C. had become fully morphine-reliant. No control of thought,
no force of will-power could reverse that physical fact. His conscious self
still refused to contemplate the terrifying truth that he could not abandon
opium; still less would he recognise that he had eroded his powers of
intellect beyond repair. But his subconscious mind now began to bombard
his conscious self with a horrible array of realities disguised as phantoms.

S.T.C.'s opium reveries, of which he was the semi-conscious but nonetheless always present helmsman (like a lone sailor who still guides the
rudder even when half asleep), were, as he agitatedly noted, becoming
increasingly difficult to manage; again and again they veered towards
images which, instead of giving pleasure, brought distress. His recurrent
opium dreams of happiness with Asra in turn prompted him to dreams of
Sara Coleridge's death. These so horrified him that he had to taboo them.
He confided to his notebook:

> There is one thing out of my Power. I cannot look forward with the faintest
> pleasure of Hope, to the Death of any human Being, tho' it were, as it seems
> to be, the only condition of the greatest Imaginable Happiness to me, and
> the emancipation of all my noblest faculties that must remain fettered during
> that Being's Life—I dare not, for I cannot: I cannot, for I dare not. The very
> effort to look onward to it with a stedfast wish would be suicide, far beyond

what the dagger or pistol could realize—absolutely suicide, cœlicide, not mere viticide.—[77]

By struggling hard he managed to keep some grip on his daytime opium reveries. At night his predicament was very different; adrift in the immense Pacific waters of sleep S.T.C. lost control. His nights had, for many months past, been disturbed by restlessness and strange, flitting dreams; occasionally he had had nightmares of particular intensity and unpleasantness. One early dream, experienced after his return to Keswick following the Gallow Hill incident of the lazy-bed, had been that he and his wife were dead and were seeking their children. This had troubled, rather than frightened him (he had no fear of death itself, his conviction of personal survival was too strong); but a few months later he began to have true nightmares of a most violent and distressing nature:

My Dreams uncommonly illustrative of the non-existence of Surprize in sleep—I dreamt that I was asleep in the Cloyster at Christs Hospital & had awoken with a pain in my hand from some corrosion / boys & nurses daughters peeping at me / On their implying that I was not in the School, I answered yes I am / I am only twenty—I then recollected that I was thirty, & of course could not be in the School—& was perplexed—but not in the least surprized that I could fall into such an error / So I dreamt of Dorothy, William and Mary—& that Dorothy was altered in every feature, a fat, thick-limbed & rather red-haired—in short, no resemblance to her at all—and I said, if I did not *know* you to be Dorothy, I never should *suppose* it / Why, says she—I have not a feature the same / & yet I was not surprized—

I was followed up & down by a frightful pale woman who, I thought, wanted to kiss me, & had the property of giving me a shameful Disease by breathing in the face /

& again I dreamt that a figure of a woman of a gigantic Height, dim & indefinite & smokelike appeared—& that I was forced to run up toward it—& then it changed to a stool—& then appeared again in another place—& again I went up in a great fright—& it changed to some other common thing—yet I felt no surprize.[78]

The nightmares were, at first, irregular in their visitation. By the spring and early summer of 1803 they began to trouble S.T.C. with increasing frequency; soon they were making three nights out of five intolerable for him; he regularly woke the household with his screams.

The dreams all followed much of a same pattern; one, in the early hours of December 13, 1803, serves as a representative example:

Wednesd. Morn. 3 o'clock, Dec. 13, 1803. Bad dreams / How often *of a sort* / at the university—a mixture of Xts Hospital Church / escapes there—lose myself / trust to two People, one Maim'd, one unknown / insulted by a fat sturdy Boy of about 14 . . . who dabs a flannel in my face (or rather soft hair brown Shawl stuff) (was this a flannel Night-cap?) he attacks me / I call to my Friends—they come & join in the Hustle against me—out rushes a university Harlot, who insists on my going with her / offer her a shilling—seem to get away a moment / when she overtakes me again / I am not to go with another while she is "biting"—these were her words / —this will not satisfy her / I sit down on a broad open plain of rubbish with rails & a street beyond & call out—whole Troops of people in sight— . . . In the early part of the Dream, Boyer, & two young Students, & R. Allen: Legrice & I quizzing / N.B. Arrogant sense of intellectual superiority under circumstances of depression, but no envy . . .

. . . in an after Dream / a little weak contemptible wretch offering his services, & I (as before afraid to refuse them) literally & distinctly remembered a former Dream, in which I had suffered most severely, this wretch leaping on me, & grasping my Scrotum / —I therefore most politely assured him of the 3 guineas, but I meant only to get rid of him / —Again too the slight pain in my side produced a fellow knuckling me there / —My determination to awake, I dream that I got out of bed, & volition in dream to scream . . . in an half upright posture struggling, as I thought, against involuntary sinking back into Sleep, & consequent suffocation / twas then I screamed, by will / & immediately after really awoke /[79]

Examination of the several dreams described in great detail in the notebooks reveals again and again images of maiming and distortion, fears of being spied upon, especially in a sexual context, fears of getting lost, of being abandoned. Above all there are repeated incidents of violent sexual aggression, proffered, it should be noted, by persons of both sexes.

That S.T.C. should connect sexual activity with shame was natural, bearing in mind the strong Christian indoctrination of his childhood. What is unexpected however, is the persistence in these dreams of violent sexual encounters with males. It is impossible to avoid the supposition that he might have experienced forcible homosexual seduction when a young boy at Christ's Hospital.

The drug-honeymoon period of beautiful dreams does not and cannot last; it is inevitably displaced by horror. The articulate junkie will explain that this is because, for the dreams to be good, they must be approached in the right frame of mind. The dreamer must be happy, guilt-free and wholly receptive. If, instead, he approaches the drug with sensations of guilt, fear, or a desire in any way to reject, then his dreams will be chaotic and very frightening, a "mismanaged experience."

S.T.C. detailed his mismanaged dreams in *The Pains of Sleep*:

> Deeds to be hid which were not hid,
> Which all confused I could not know,
> Whether I suffered, or I did:
> For all seemed guilt, remorse or woe,
> My own or others still the same
> Life-stifling fear, soul-stifling shame.[80]

Sensations of guilt, remorse and terror and a desire to escape the drug rather than to embrace it are inexorably part of the progressive morphine process. Once the victim has become reliant he is fated to explore not only the fair places but also the fiends of drug experience.

By 1803 S.T.C.'s approach to opium was made in thrall and was deeply guilt-ridden. He knew that he had betrayed innocents whose trust was in him. Above all, he had betrayed his own immense gifts of intellect and poesy.

In his nightmares he approached splendid destinations which, when glimpsed, evaded him and were lost: "the wanderings thro' Streets, the noticing the Complex side of a noble Building, & saying to my Guides—'it will be long before I shall find my way here—I must endeavour to remember this'/."[81]

Thus, in his sleep, with no control upon the helm, S.T.C. confronted the truths of his fearful bondage. Awake, he still huddled in terror of the moment when he would have to acknowledge to himself, in full consciousness, that not only was he now in full bondage to his drug but furthermore that he, who had been endowed with pinions of the mind which could have carried him to altitudes of intellectual achievement far beyond the reach of most men had, by his own hand, destroyed his genius. It was he, and no other, who had slain the albatross.

CHAPTER SEVENTEEN

THE FRIGHTFUL FIEND

(July–September 1803)

WORDSWORTH'S FIRST CHILD, John, was born on June 18, 1803, and baptised on July 15; S.T.C., Richard and Dorothy Wordsworth were godparents.

Dorothy absolutely worshipped this infant from the instant of his arrival. To her delight he had inherited an unmistakably Wordsworthian appearance, having his father's "very fine head" and "noble nose." Ecstatic descriptions of John were sent to all her friends: "I long to shew you our dear little child."[1]

From the first Dorothy referred to the child as "ours." William's legitimate children were her children because they were William's. She had not been able to bear them herself, but, reading Dorothy's letters, we feel that she had done what Rachel had done when, unable to conceive children for her husband, she had gone to him and said: "Behold my maid Bilhah, go in unto her; and she shall bear upon my knees, that I may also have children by her."

Once Mary Wordsworth and the infant were seen to be strong and thriving, William and Dorothy set about their plans for putting into practice a long-cherished scheme of making a tour of the Highlands of Scotland with S.T.C. This they would now do in August. Sara Hutchinson was to come to stay at Dove Cottage to keep Mary company.

The plan at first had been to make the tour a pedestrian one, with a pony for Dorothy; then the tourists became more ambitious and settled on a jaunting-car and a horse. The jaunting-car was purchased from a Devonshire acqaintance of S.T.C.'s who made himself sound so poor that S.T.C. was placed in the awkward position where he could not well offer less than fifteen pounds for it. A horse was even more difficult to procure: "Dearest dearest dearest Friends—I will have 3 dearests, that there may be one for each—(and Godson John shall have one for himself)," wrote S.T.C. to Dove Cottage. "I begin to find that a Horse & Jaunting Car is *an anxiety*."[2] Keswick, S.T.C. explained, was not the place to obtain a horse (it is difficult to avoid the suspicion that he had not tried very hard; horses were plentiful in the region in those days). However, one was procured by August 11, "aged but stout & spirited."[3]

A spell of wet weather at this juncture made S.T.C. ill; he began to have private second thoughts about "the safety & propriety" of travelling through Scotland in an open carriage and he approached Mr Edmondson upon the advisability of the scheme. Mr Edmondson was confident that, should S.T.C.'s health suffer from the tour, it could quickly be restored with Carminative Bitters; he added that in his opinion S.T.C. would find the exercise highly beneficial.[4] Sara also urged him to go. Unable to persuade either his wife or his apothecary to take his illness as seriously as he thought it deserved to be, S.T.C. sought sympathy from Southey:

> I have been very ill ... Of my disease there now remains no Shade of Doubt; it is a compleat & almost heartless case of Atonic Gout. If you would look into the Article Medicine, in the Encyc. Britt. Vol. xi, Part 1— No 213—p. 181— ... you will read almost the very words, in which, before I had seen this Article, I had described my case to Wordsworth ... Mr Edmondson, whom I have consulted ... on my tour ... recommends it. He is confident—O that I were—that by the use of Carminative Bitters I may get rid of this truly poisonous, & body—&—soul—Benumming Flatulence and Inflation; and that ... the Exercise & the Excitement will be of so much service as to outweigh the chances of Injury from Wet or Cold. I will therefore go; tho' I never yet commenced a Journey with such inauspicious Heaviness of Heart before.

S.T.C. went on to detail his symptoms so that Southey might repeat them to Dr Beddoes, who had sponsored a new gout medicine that S.T.C. was anxious to try "whatever the expence be." S.T.C.'s list of symptoms included capricious appetite, indigestion, "costiveness that makes my evacuation at times approach in all the symptoms to pains of Labour—viz —distortion of Body from agony, profuse & streaming Sweats, & fainting —at other times looseness with griping—frightful dreams with screaming— *breezes* of Terror blowing from the Stomach up thro' the Brain ... frequent paralytic Feelings ... three times I have wakened out of these frightful Dreams, & found my legs so *locked* into each other as to have left a bruise ... My mouth is endlessly full of water." He further went on to describe swelling of the hands and feet. The letter concluded that, if after trial, the new gout medicine were to prove a failure, "I then, by God! go off to Malta or Madeira/Madeira is the better place; but Stoddart is gone to Malta with a wife ... and has given me a very kind invitation."[5]

The symptoms thus outlined to Southey were largely attributable to S.T.C.'s consumption of opium; but, as the above letter reveals, this truth S.T.C. had not yet recognised. Reading between the lines of his letters and some of the notebook entries, a growing alarm is discernible; he had discovered that opium was living up to its reputation as a habit-forming drug and the habit was proving a devil to break. ("Is not *Habit* the Desire of a Desire? ... How far is Habit congenerous with Instinct?" he asked, in a long, opium-saturated notebook entry, written in the weeks prior to the tour.)[6]

To his wife, who was becoming increasingly convinced he was caught in the coils of the notorious opium-habit, S.T.C. vehemently insisted that nothing of the kind was occurring. These denials were to be repeated with increasing frequency not only to her but to the growing number of friends who, now aware of his addiction and alarmed by the signs of its mounting hold upon him, voiced their concern and plied him with warnings.[7]

Classically, he denied the very symptoms in himself that were now privately beginning to scare him dreadfully. From the world at large he still attempted to conceal the very fact that he took opium; with those too close to him to be deluded on that score, he shifted his ground to maintain that the drug in no way endangered him.

The situation of the morphine victim becomes additionally complicated by the psychotic element which is introduced into his condition as his reliance becomes established. The saturating effect of the drug produces an organic psychosis which results in delusions; fact and fantasy become inextricably interwoven until the one can no longer be differentiated from the other by the victim. S.T.C., with his poet's imagination and natural tendency to fantasy, was inherently a character whose feet, in comparison with those of others, had never been over-firmly planted on the ground. As his drug reliance progressed and the psychotic element entered increasingly into his relationships, he began to involve all those around him in his fantasy-building. Finally, fantasy so overtook reality for him, that normal relationships with him were no longer possible.

The jaunting-car was delivered to Grasmere sometime in mid-August. Judged an eccentric vehicle by all who saw it, the car was to become well known in the Lake Country in due course, for the Wordsworths promoted it to the rôle of family carriage. S.T.C. described it in detail to Southey; it had room for three persons on either side, sitting benchwise on long seats placed back to back; there was a dicky-box for the driver and "a space or hollow in the middle, for luggage—or two or three Bairns . . . Your feet are not above a foot from the ground . . . you may get off & on while the Horse is moving without the least Danger."[8]

Keswick had its first view of the jaunting-car upon Thursday, August 11, when the aged but spirited horse appeared clip-clopping alongside the Greta; Wordsworth perched on the dicky, driving; Dorothy and Mary Wordsworth, S.T.C., the Coleridges's nursemaid, Hartley, Derwent and the infant Johnny comprised the passengers (on Sunday, Mary, Sara Hutchinson, and Johnny were taken part of the way back to Grasmere in it, with Mrs Coleridge, her children and the nursemaid as joy-riders).

The horse was kept in exercise; upon the following day, at twenty minutes past eleven in the forenoon, the three tourists departed for Scotland. Sara Coleridge reported to Southey:

W. is to drive all the way, for poor Samuel is too weak to undertake the fatigue of driving—he was very unwell when he went off, and was to return in the *Mail* if he grew worse ... My husband is a good man—his prejudices —and his prepossessions sometimes give me pain, but we all have a somewhat to encounter in this life—I should be a very, very happy Woman if it were not for a few things—and my husband's ill health stands at the head of these evils![9]

Meantime the jaunting-car travelled merrily enough, "up the steep hill to Threlkeld—turned off at the White Horse, under Saddleback* to Grisedale . . . [and] so on to Carrock, and Hesket Newmarket," there to spend the night at the Queen's Head, where S.T.C. noted with exactitude:

The sanded stone floor with the spitting Pot full of Sand Dust, two pictures of Young Master & Miss with their round Birds' Eyes & parlour Dress, he with a paroquet on his hand, horizontal, the other hand pushed forward just below it—she with a rose in her uplifted perpend. hand, the other hand grasping it to support it in that Posture. The whole Room struck me as Cleanliness quarrelling with Tobacco Ghosts—.[10]

The following morning the party set off for Carlisle where they dined and afterwards walked on the ancient city walls. John Hadfield, the notorious forger and bigamous husband of the Beauty of Buttermere, was then imprisoned in Carlisle castle, under sentence of death (App. II); he had in fact been sentenced at eight o'clock that very morning. It was possible in those days for people of rank or distinction to obtain interviews with celebrated felons if they so had the fancy; Dorothy insisted now that William and S.T.C. should have an interview with Hadfield. S.T.C. wrote in his notebook:

visited Hatfield [sic], impelled by Miss Wordsworth—*vain*, a hypocrite / It is not by mere Thoughts, I can understand this man†[11]

The rather unpleasant interview over, and reported upon to Dorothy, the trio travelled on to Longtown, where they slept at the Graham Arms. Next day they crossed the Border and proceeded to Dumfries, where William and Dorothy visited Robert Burns's grave. The night was spent at an inn in the Nith Valley; here they had trouble procuring beds for three persons. S.T.C. "cut the knot by offering . . . to sleep on the chairs in the Parlour."[13] He further jotted in his notebook, in criticism of Wordsworth's

*This was the old mines road which ran from Lonscale mine to Carrock mine, traversing Saddleback along and behind the fell-wall. This road was the quick route from Keswick to Mungrisedale.
†S.T.C., when some months later he was introduced to Sheridan, commented that his manners were "startlingly like those of Hatfield," adding, "I could take that man in; but, I'll be damned, if he could take me in.—"[12]

conduct in connection with the incident: "Feckless . . . & wants dignity & courage / . . . wants kindness & stateliness & gentlemanly Dignity."[14]

Uncomfortable upon his chairs, S.T.C. fell asleep thinking hard things about his travelling companions; he reflected: "how little there was in this World that could compensate for the loss or diminishment of the Love of such as truly love us / and what bad Calculators Vanity & Selfishness prove to be in the long run—"[15]

The party was only three days out, but already things were going wrong. S.T.C. disliked the jaunting-car; he could not keep dry when it rained; he feared for his health; the sound of the wheels grating interminably upon the rough stony road-surfaces grated correspondingly upon his nerves. Obviously he complained a good deal, especially about the damp and his health.

Wordsworth seems, so far, never to have upbraided S.T.C. upon his opium habit. It was Wordsworth's creed to "convey all the truth he knows without any attack on what he supposes falsehood, if that falsehood be interwoven with virtues or happiness,"[16] as S.T.C. had reported to Estlin. Opium had been interwoven for S.T.C. in its early stage with all the virtues of the New Sensibility and all the happinesses of spots of "inchantment [sic] . . . in the very heart of a waste of Sands."[17] We need have little doubt that the permissive Wordsworth of this period would have contemplated S.T.C.'s opium-habit with equanimity; if S.T.C. sought gratification in opium, let him do so. It was not Wordsworth's business to criticise.

But inevitably a point was to be reached where even Wordsworth could no longer refrain from criticism and advice. All the evidence indicates that, somewhere in the region of the Border, Wordsworth reached this moment of truth.

We need not doubt the Wordsworths had to listen to their fellow-passenger in the jaunting-car repeat to them all the rigmarole he had already inflicted upon Southey—a dissertation upon the state of mind necessary to the "most important phaenomena of Sleep & Disease / it is a transmutation of the *succession of Time* into the *juxtoposition of Space* . . . a clue to the whole mystery of frightful Dreams, & Hypochondriacal delusions."[18] The Wordsworths were surely regaled, too, with atonic gout and Dr Beddoes's new gout medicine. Not a word did S.T.C. ever say to indicate that opium might contribute to his sad state of health; gout was the trouble and damp the root cause of the gout: "The effects of the weather are to the full as palpable upon me, as upon the little old Lady & Gentleman in the weather Box."[19]

At last, it seems, Wordsworth spoke his mind, in all probability saying outright to S.T.C. what he was to repeat at intervals throughout the coming years:

one thing is obvious, that . . . resolution, self-denial, and well-regulated

378

conditions of feeling, are what you must depend upon . . . and that Doctor's stuff has been one of your greatest curses . . . You must know better than . . . any Surgeon what is to do you good; what you are to do, and what to leave undone.[20]

The result was fatal and instantaneous. S.T.C. was flooded with bitter resentment against Wordsworth, which took the form of incessant carping complaint and criticism (the notebook for this period is peppered with it). Wordsworth, in the face of S.T.C.'s resentment, withdrew into himself, no doubt wisely deciding that silence was the best policy. (S.T.C. was to report peevishly to Poole that William in Scotland was "a brooder over his painful hypochondriacal Sensations . . . not my fittest companion".)[21] Thus the tables were turned on William, who had dared to suggest that S.T.C.'s atonic gout might be due to causes other than damp. In his notebook S.T.C. wrote:

The exquisite Affectability of my Skin, & the instant sympathy of my Stomach and mesenteries with the Affections of the Skin . . . my miserable barometrical Dependence of my Stomach Sensations on the *weather*, especially damp & wet-stormy weather, forms a specific distinction between my Complaint, & William Wordsworth's Hypochondriasis.[22]

Angry with his companions and struggling privately all the time with his opium appetite ("The still rising Desire still baffling the bitter Experience, the bitter Experience still following the gratified Desire")[23] S.T.C. sat huddled in the jaunting-car, or trudged disconsolately, leading the horse. He did not like the Scots; he didn't think much of Scotland. Groundsel everywhere in the hedges, he noted grumpily, instead of foxgloves and "other *Englishmen*."[24] He adversely compared the way in which the Scots went barefooted with the way in which the Germans did so:

In Germany . . . the Class that go bare-footed . . . always have their Shoes in their Hands or on their Heads / In Scotland Cabin Gowns, white Petticoat, all tawdry fine, & naked Legs, & naked Splaid-feet & gouty ancles.[25]

With the keen and often sardonic humour that never deserted him S.T.C. noted the delightful discrepancy between the huge boredom of a small girl acting as guide to the rapturising Dorothy at the Cora Lynn Falls.[26] But his laughter never lasted for long now; he tortured himself with the absence of Asra and then with pangs of jealousy that William should have Dorothy while he had to travel alone. At Loch Lomond Dorothy's habit of reciting snatches of William's poems whenever appropriate occasion presented itself brought a notebook wail from S.T.C.:

What? tho' the World praise me, I have no dear Heart that loves my Verses

379

—I never hear them in snatches from a beloved Voice, fitted to some sweet occasion of natural Prospect, in Winds or Night—[27]

The tour continued according to itinerary: the Trossachs, Rob Roy's cave (the guide to which S.T.C. crossly dubbed "a Jacobin Traitor of a Boatman," perhaps meaning Jacobite)[28] and Loch Katrine: "a fine body of water . . . but the mountains were all too dreary and not very impressive."[29]

The tourists, accustomed to the more populated Lake Country, struck out for the Trossachs, through scenery totally wanting in "cultivated Land & happy Cottages."[30] Their road wound "thro' the most luxuriant Heaths, the purple, the white, the pale purple, the deep crimson, or rose-coloured Purple,"[31] which gave "a sort of feeling of Shot silk and ribbon finery."[32] The edges of the mountain sky-line became "wildly broken."[33] Rocks, blasted trees and rushing mountain torrents added to the Romanticism of the expedition. But the day was wearing on and soon the travellers, having made enquiries from a native, discovered that their Expedition to the Trossacks [sic] was "rashly undertaken / we were at least 9 miles from the Trossacks, no Public House there or here / it was almost too late to return, & if we did, the Loch Lomond Ferry boat uncertain. We proceeded to the first House in the first Reach, & threw ourselves upon the Hospitality of the Gentleman, who after some demur . . . did offer us a Bed / & his Wife . . . made Tea for us most hospitably. Best possible Butter, white Cheese, Tea, & Barley Bannock /."[34]

This kind pair proved to be Mr and Mrs James MacAlpin and very greatly appreciated was their hospitality, though Mrs MacAlpin "perfectly puzzled" the English trio with her Scots speech, particularly when she spoke of a "fearful wild beast," which proved to be her way of describing an eagle.[35]

On the following morning the trio retraced their steps to the ferry-house. Resentful envy of Wordsworth continued to torment S.T.C., who felt "little ugly Touchlets of Pain & little Shrinkings Back at the Heart . . . Saw the faults of . . . [Wordsworth] & all that belonged to . . . [Wordsworth] & detested himself dwelling upon them."[36]

The time was approaching when S.T.C. would bolt, withdrawing himself from a situation which he could no longer face. He was not, however, quite ripe for this and had to content himself with a token withdrawal. When they reached the ferryman's little house by the grey misty loch S.T.C. declined to get into the boat with Wordsworth. Miserable mental soliloquising upon the subject of Wordsworth's alleged blemishes of character resulted now in S.T.C.'s actual physical vision of his friend becoming strangely distorted, as if by a trick mirror. S.T.C. was long to carry within himself the memory of that moment, as he stood by the water's edge, gazing down at Wordsworth who, already seated in the boat, stared back at S.T.C. with an "up, askance, pig look."[37] S.T.C. turned away and plunged into the hills, to spend the day exploring the head of the loch in the heart of the Trossachs. At one point he leaned against an ash-tree and gazed at the "visionary Scene;" comparing it with his beloved Borrowdale. Now that he was alone the beauty of the landscape enchanted him. "I must see it again!"[38] In the evening he returned to the ferry-house where he was soon joined by the Wordsworths and an artist from Edinburgh. The ferryman, Gregor MacGregor, and his wife provided accommodation for the night.

The ferry-house was a small and primitive croft, the interior "black & varnished & glistening with peat smoak, the Fowls roosting in the chimney amid the cloud of smoke."[39] The visitors had a merry meal;* the fire, stirred and fed to burn and leap brightly, was a marvel of life and light; S.T.C., whose shoes were sodden with wet, thrust them exceedingly close to the blaze, with the result that they caught fire. S.T.C. found himself with badly damaged shoes, a singed heel and an inflamed left leg.

After a wildly hilarious evening

we slept in the Barn upon the Hay / My Friend & the Artist had a sort of Hay Bed with Blankets spread on the Ground / but I preferred the Hay Rick.[40]

Dorothy slept in the loft.

Next day they went by boat to the end of the Lake and from there they walked to the ferry-house by Loch Lomond. There was no ferry as the boat had taken the local populace "to the Preaching;" as a result the tourists were obliged to spend the day in the ferry-house, a "comfortless Hovel," while outside the rain fell. At length the boat returned, crowded with Highlanders and their children, returning from the Preaching; they were disembarked and the English tourists were taken aboard, to be ferried to East Tarbet;[41] it rained all the time. The damp, chill S.T.C. was now quarrelling with Wordsworth again:

My words & actions imaged on his mind, distorted & snaky as the Boatman's Oar reflected in the Lake / —.[42]

At Arrochar on the following day, Monday, August 29, the Wordsworths and S.T.C. parted company. S.T.C.'s excuse made to them was that sitting in the open jaunting-car in the rain had given him rheumatism in the head and if persisted in would be death to him. To Poole he wrote that he found himself "a burthen" on the Wordsworths.[43] This last, no doubt, was the nub of the matter.

S.T.C. and the Wordsworths divided their money; they took twenty-nine guineas and S.T.C. six, since he would require less than they. Then brother and sister drove away in their equipage, while the solitary S.T.C. returned

*See Dorothy Wordsworth's account of the Highland Tour for a detailed description of this episode.

to East Tarbet on the ferry. It was still raining: the pale surface of the loch as the ferry crossed it was agitated by the raindrops dancing on the water like "an army of Spirits, or Faeries, on a wilderness of white sand."[44]

The Wordsworths were scarcely to blame for what had happened. It was inevitable. They were to resume their friendship with S.T.C. after the Highland tour, but Arrochar marked the beginning of the end.

The actual notebook itself speaks almost unbearable volumes upon the Wordsworth-Coleridge rupture. This Highland tour notebook is small, shabby, misshapen from having been squeezed, damp, into a wet coat pocket. The entries are mainly in pencil; finger-marks and mud and rain-smears have smudged them. Some of the entries are difficult to decipher, partly because they have faded with time, but often because, obviously, they were written as the jaunting-car bumped over the uneven roads. The entries at the ferry-house and Arrochar had distraught annotations interpolated by S.T.C. on June 5, 1812, when his rupture with Wordsworth had become profound and complete. Where S.T.C. describes sleeping-accommodation at the croft—"My Friend and the Artist had a sort of Hay Bed"—"Friend" is ringed round and after it has been interjected: "O me! what a word to give permanence to the mistake of a Life!" With other added cries of woe, S.T.C. concludes (after the entry, "Tuesday, Aug 30, 1803—am to make my own way alone to Edingburgh [sic]"), "(O Esteesee! that thou hadst from thy 22nd year indeed made *thy own* way & *alone!*)".

A small slip of paper has been very neatly inserted between the pages here, gummed in place; on it is written, equally neatly, in the widowed Mrs Ann Gillman's gentle hand:

Heart breaking for such a Being—

Immediately that S.T.C. found himself alone in the Highlands he was happy. He decided against returning direct to Edinburgh and instead set out on a pedestrian tour of his own—Glen Coe, Loch Ness, Aviemore, Kingussie, Loch Tummel, Kenmore, Perth—two hundred and sixty three miles in eight days.

He travelled light, having sent all his things on in advance to Edinburgh by carrier from East Tarbet. His burned shoes gave him trouble, resulting in severe blisters; he could not find another pair to buy until he reached Perth ("there are none ready made").[45] He sent Sara Coleridge an S.O.S. asking her to post money to Perth for him ("you must contrive somehow or other to borrow £10"); he was running desperately short of cash. In spite of his sore feet he was, by day, happy, "having Nature with solitude & liberty; the liberty natural & solitary, the solitude natural & free!"[46]

Yet, though his days were pleasurable, his nights were now more dreadful than ever before. Terrorised by his nightmares, S.T.C. resolved not to sleep; he struggled to lie awake, but at last succumbed, slept and "blest the scream which delivered . . . [him] from . . . Dreams . . . of Guilt, Rage, unworthy Desires, Remorse, Shame, & Terror."[47]

At Fort William, after a long day of good, stout, fast walking S.T.C. was seized with an intense and abrupt fatigue and torturing pain in his limbs. He required support from a passer-by to reach an inn; this was full and he was directed to another. Here he collapsed in a fit of frantic hysterical weeping, followed by violent diarrhoea, to "the unutterable consternation and *bebustlement* of the Landlord, his Wife, children, & Servants, who all gabbled Gaelic to each other, & sputtered out short-winded English"[48] to S.T.C. He was treated with the utmost kindness by his bewildered hosts; he washed, crawled into bed, was brought a basin of hot tea and was soon asleep. "30 miles was perhaps too much for one day."[49] Yet he maintained that the real reason for his attack was a drink of cold water that he had had from a burn, shortly before reaching Fort William. This, he told Sara Coleridge, had brought on acute stomach gout. According to his letter to her, his attack was the third such in his experience; the former two, however, had resulted from "agitated Feelings."[50]

Obviously these were withdrawal attacks, resultant upon abstinence from the drug on which his body had now come to rely. It is more than possible that this attack at Fort William was the outcome of an attempt to take Wordsworth's advice of "resolution [and] self-denial;" in other words, to give up opium. S.T.C., despite his overt resentment of criticism and warnings, wished passionately to break free from what he privately recognised now as a desperate habit, wished to please those who loved him, to win their approval and, at the same time, demonstrate his will-power. But, inevitably, attempts to go without opium could only result in frightening seizures which only more opium could allay.

All the time he was ever building up greater resistance to morphine, which meant that, to reap benefit, larger and ever larger doses were necessary. On September 3 (the day after the attack at Fort William), feeling threatenings of yet more "Stomach Gout" he was "frightened" into taking "a violent Stimulus" which kept him "half-awake the whole night,"[51] "weeping—vomiting . . . in a sort of stupid sensuality of Itching from my Head to my Toes,"[52] as he described it to Sara. "Intoxication by a narcotic," he called it.

At this time he still had not grasped that withdrawal of opium promoted what he now called "hysterical attacks." When at last he came to understand the true nature of these attacks, he gave an account of them (to Estlin, December 3, 1808) which cannot be bettered as a revelation both of his sufferings and his dilemma:

From the disuse [of narcotics] my spirits and pleasurable feelings used gradually to increase to the very Hour, when my circulation became suddenly disturbed, a painful and intolerable Yawning commenced, soon followed by a violent Bowel-complaint.

He became convinced that if he continued without recourse to the drug he would die, so he had recourse to another dose; but, as he had no medical confirmation of the danger of going without drugs, he was never sure that, by having further recourse to them in order to allay the symptoms of withdrawal, he was not acting guiltily:

> Lur'd by no fond Belief,
> No hope that flattered Grief
> But blank Despair my Plea,
> I borrowed short relief
> At frightful usury![53]

As yet he had not experienced the full horror that would envelop him once he had realised beyond all possible doubt that he was chained by a habit which he could not break and which could only have more and more frightful consequences. He was still doing his best to avoid this truth; but it was now dogging his steps and threatening to overtake him, quicken his stride from it as he might:

> Like one, that on a lonely road
>   Doth walk in fear and dread,
> And having once turn'd round, walks on
>   And turns no more his head:
> Because he knows, a frightful fiend
>   Doth close behind him tread.[54]

S.T.C. had written those lines five years previously. Did they haunt him now as he followed the empty roads through the cloud-lowering Highland glens?

S.T.C. found tragic news awaiting him when he reached Perth; Southey's little daughter, the Passionate Pearl, had died (from what was then diagnosed as "water on the brain from teething"[55] but was, almost certainly, tubercular meningitis). The grief-stricken parents were already on their way to Keswick, to seek comfort in the company of the Coleridges. S.T.C. at once replied:

My dearest Southey ...
    Whatever Comfort I can be to you, I will ... I will not stay a day in

Edinburgh—or only one to hunt out my clothes. I can [not] chit chat with Scotchmen, while you are at Keswick, childless. Bless you, my dear Southey! I will knit myself far closer to you than I have hitherto done—& my children shall be yours till it please God to send you another.—56

With this letter S.T.C. enclosed a copy of his first draft of *The Pains of Sleep*.

S.T.C. felt himself drawn closer to Sara Coleridge by the dark skies which seemed to be closing upon every side. He included a postscript to her in this same letter, written with the frankness of disillusioned, rock-bottom affection which reads more heartrendingly than any of the notebook addresses to Asra:

as all things propagate their Like, you must not wonder, that Misery is a Misery-maker. But do you try, & I will try; & Peace may come at last, & Love with it . . . O Sara! dear Sara!—try for all good Things in the spirit of unsuspecting Love / for miseries gather upon us . . . Good night, my sweet Children!57

CHAPTER EIGHTEEN

THE MARINER BECALMED

(September–December 1803)

Down dropt the breeze, the Sails dropt down,
  'Twas sad as sad could be
And we did speak only to break
  The silence of the Sea.

All in a hot and copper sky
  The bloody sun at noon,
Right up above the mast did stand,
  No bigger than the moon.

Day after day, day after day,
  We stuck, ne breath ne motion,
As idle as a painted Ship
  Upon a painted Ocean.
        The Ancient Mariner Part II (1798)

S.T.C. ARRIVED BACK at Greta Hall on Thursday, September 15, in the afternoon, just in time for dinner at three o'clock (the popular dining-hour in those days). He found not only the Southeys in residence, but also Mary Lovell. Southey, though overpowered when he spoke of his lost child, generally seemed in better heart than S.T.C. had anticipated;[1] Edith appeared drooping, but not so greatly as might have been expected.[2] S.T.C. suspected that she might already be pregnant again.[3]

A large "Cag"* of the dubious gout medicine advocated by Dr Beddoes and the invention of a Mr Welles (who hoped that it would immortalise him)[4] was delivered to Greta Hall; S.T.C. at first felt that he derived benefit from it. He began to think that his whole complaint was nothing more than "flying Gout with a little Gravel."[5]

Hazlitt came to stay; he painted portraits of the inmates of Greta Hall. There was conversation and tramps over the Borrowdale fells. The weather was good; S.T.C. felt much improved. After Hazlitt's departure for Manchester, S.T.C. and Southey set out, on September 29, on a projected walking tour—Caldbeck, Cockermouth, Lorton, Ennerdale; with exploration of Saddleback, Bowscale and Caldbeck fells; Uldale fells, the Loweswater fells, the Ennerdale fells, the Steeple, Pillar and Gable complex, Red Pike, High Stile and High Crag, Scarf Gap, Buttermere. It was a glorious itinerary, but Southey was weary and homesick by the time S.T.C. had

*Zummerzetshire for "Keg".

marched him to Caldbeck and the Howk; he had not yet recovered his full buoyancy following the death of the Passionate Pearl. The two men returned to Keswick.

An atmosphere of tension and apprehension had gripped the country; the autumn of 1803 found England threatened by French invasion. Urgent preparations were made to repulse Bonaparte; volunteers were drilled and beacon fires were constructed ready to light should the enemy land. S.T.C. announced (and meant it with every fibre of his body) that, should the "Corsican Tippoo Saib" set foot in England, he, Esteesee, would sally forth: "If . . . I find the Country in real Danger, I will stand or fall with it—and I trust, I should not be found in my Study if the French remained even 10 days on British Ground."[6]

Since the return of the Wordsworths from Scotland the great friendship had been resumed; on the surface the well of mutual love was tranquil enough again, but the spring that bubbled up from the depths was now, upon S.T.C.'s side, deeply tinctured with feelings which he himself had at first, by Loch Lomond, ascribed to envy but which (in a long passage of analysis recorded in his notebook for mid-October) S.T.C. finally and no doubt correctly diagnosed as resentment. Referring to himself as A and Wordsworth as B, S.T.C. wrote:

> he saw the faults of B . . . and detested himself dwelling upon them . . . Then, A took himself to Task respecting B.—It is very true that B is not so zealous as he might be, in some things—and overzealous to himself—But what is he on the whole? What compared with the mass of men? It is astonishing how powerfully this Medicine acted—how instantly it effected a cure/ . . . one important part of the Process in the growth of Envy is/ . . . Self-degradation . . . dim notion that our nature is suddenly altered for the worse. &c &c.—Deeplier than ever do I see the necessity of understanding the whole complex mixed character of our Friend—as well as our own.[7]

This was admirable, but it did not prevent S.T.C. from grumbling peevishly to Poole:

> I now see very little of Wordsworth: my own Health makes it inconvenient . . . for me to go thither one third as often, as I used to do—and Wordsworth's Indolence, &c keeps him at home. Indeed, were I an irritable man, and an unthinking one, I should probably have considered myself as having been very unkindly used by him—for I was at one time confined for two months, & he never came in to see me / me, who had ever paid such unremitting attentions to him. But we must take the good & the ill together; & by seriously & habitually reflecting on our own faults . . . we shall then find little difficulty in confining our attention as far as it acts on our Friends' characters, to their good Qualities.—Indeed . . . the concern, which I have felt in . . . *crying* instances, of Self-involution in Wordsworth, has been almost wholly a Feeling of friendly Regret, & disinterested Apprehension—

I saw him more & more benetted in hypochondriachal Fancies, living
wholly among *Devotees*—having every the minutest Thing, almost his very
Eating & Drinking, done for him by his Sister, or Wife—& I trembled lest
a Film should rise, and thicken on his moral Eye.—[8]

This passage not only affords a fascinating glimpse of the Dove Cottage
ménage; it tells us a great deal about Esteesian subtleties. In this passage
S.T.C. succeeds in reading a small sermon to Poole, that he should reflect
upon his own faults before criticising the characters of his friends (S.T.C.);
he makes himself sound above envy and resentment (while in fact succumbing to it) and finally, in labelling Wordsworth a victim of hypochondriacal
fancies and in danger of losing his moral vision, S.T.C. almost undoubtedly
levels at Wordsworth the indictments which Wordsworth, on the Highland
tour, had levelled at him.

On Sunday, October 9, Wordsworth rode over to Keswick to seek advice
from Mr Edmondson upon the health of Sara Hutchinson who, then
staying at Dove Cottage, was "in a bad hysterical way."[9] This, given the
circumstances, was scarcely surprising. Asra had been placed under prolonged and obviously intolerable pressure by S.T.C. He was still plaguing
her with letters and if these resembled the bosom-beatings of his notebook
supplications to her, then they must indeed have been refined torture to
have received.

At home at Greta Hall he and Sara Coleridge seem to have been living
with a fair degree of tranquillity. S.T.C., in writing to Poole, allowed himself a little wretched spite at her expense, but the fact that they were not
quarrelling tells us more than this:

We go on, as usual—except that tho' I do not love her a bit better, I quarrel
with her much less. We cannot be said to live at all as Husband & Wife / but
we are peaceable Housemates.[10]

Explosions of temper, when they occurred, seem to have been between
the three sisters, with Mrs Lovell as the chief source of friction. Both Edith
Southey and Mary Lovell were in "miserable Health," Edith being in the
early stages of pregnancy, while Mary, according to S.T.C., could never
be well while there existed "such things as Tea, and Lavender & Hartshorn
Slops, & the absence of religious, & the presence of depressing, passions."
In short: "Mrs S & Mrs Lovell are a large, a very large Bolus!" S.T.C.
comforted himself with the thought: "it is astonishing, how one's Swallow
is enlarged by the sense of doing one's Duty . . . But scarcely can even the
Sense of Duty reconcile one to taking Jalap regularly instead of Breakfast,
Ipecacuanha for one's Dinner, Glauber's salt in hot water for one's Tea, &
the whole of the foregoing in their different Metempsychoses after having
passed back again thro' the mouth, or onwards through the Bowels, in a
grand Maw-wallop for one's Supper."[11]

His own health still seemed to be improving, thanks, he thought, to the gout medicine. But at this juncture the weather began to turn wild; the wind rushed across Keswick Vale from Newlands, to hurl itself against the windows of Greta Hall. October 19, 1803, had been proclaimed a general Fast Day, "all hearts anxious concerning the Invasion." It was also the day before the date which S.T.C. always, erroneously, supposed to be his birthday; his annual Day of Atonement. "This is Oct. 19, 1803. Wed. Morn. tomorrow my Birth Day, 31 years of age!—O me! my very heart dies!—This year has been one painful Dream / I have done nothing!—O for God's sake, let me whip & spur, so that Christmas may not pass without some thing having been done."

October 19 was, in every respect, as he said, a day of storm both within Greta Hall and without. He dosed himself with rhubarb and opium and stared from his window at:

> the vale, like a place in Faery, with the autumnal colours ... Beeches & Birches, as they were blossoming Fire & Gold!—& the Sun in slanting pillars, or illuminated small parcels of mist, or single spots of softest greyish Light, now racing, now slowly gliding, now stationary / —the mountains cloudy—the Lake has been a mirror so very clear, that the water became almost invisible—& now it rolls in white Breakers, like a Sea; & the wind snatches up the water, & drifts it like Snow / —and now the Rain Storm pelts against my Study Window!—

And, weeping, he commenced his favourite lament, epitome of morphine and despair (and yet, all the time he lamented, clutching to himself in ecstasy the instrument of self-torture):

> O Asra Asra why am I not happy! why have I not an unencumbered Heart! these beloved books still before me, this noble Room, the very centre to which a whole world of beauty converges, the deep resevoir [sic] into which all these streams & currents of lovely Forms flow—my own mind so populous, so active, so full of noble schemes, so capable of realizing them / this heart so loving, so filled with noble affections—O Asra! wherefore am I not happy! why for years have I not enjoyed one pure & sincere pleasure!—one full Joy!—one genuine Delight, that rings sharp to the Beat of the Finger! all cracked, & dull with base Alloy!—Di Boni! mihi vim et virtutem / vel tu [. . .] eheu! perdite amatio! (Trans. O God! to me [it has been] strength and courage, but whether to you ... alas! this hopeless love!)[12]

He spent the greater part of his supposed birthday copying out the original Sockburn notebook entries, followed by long analyses of the characters of Southey and Wordsworth. These two men, in spite of their faults, he felt he could love, for both had counterbalancing "excellencies ... of Head & Heart." But, continuing, he could not apply these criteria, he said, to Davy and Cottle; if he could, "I should love them as well as ever / but to all the

Questions of Importance relative to what they *are* I find myself compelled to answer so gloomily, that their actions, base as many of them are base & foul, sink into insignificance.—May I not be mistaken?—Certainly I may. But as without any faulty passions of my own, of which I am conscious . . . I find myself incapable of thinking otherwise . . .—I am quite justified in shunning such men. They are unfit to be my acquaintances."[13]

(We know that Cottle had criticised S.T.C. at the time of asking for his old debt to be repaid. Davy must have offended too, although no details of this appear to be discoverable.)

By October 24, Hazlitt had returned to complete S.T.C.'s portrait. On that date Wordsworth, also, was at Greta Hall and in the afternoon there was a most unpleasant dispute between Hazlitt and Wordsworth (both atheists) on the one hand and S.T.C. on the other. S.T.C. listened to their arguments against the existence of an Almighty God, based apparently on the theme that were there a God, he would not have created a world of so much vice and misery. They spoke so "irreverently so malignantly of the Divine Wisdom, that it overset"[14] S.T.C., who gave vent to a passionate contempt for their argument. Hazlitt flew into a furious rage; S.T.C. likened him to phosphorus: "it is but to open the Cork, & it flames—but to love & . . . Friendship, let them, like Nebuchadnezzar, heat the Furnace with a 7 fold Heat, this Triune Shadrach, Mesach, Abednego, will shiver in the midst of it."[15] And S.T.C. dismissed Hazlitt with a benevolently pitying, "Peace be with him!" But William was a different matter:

> dearest Wordsworth . . . What if Ray, Durham, Paley, have carried the observation of the aptitudes of Things too far, too habitually—into Pedantry? —O how many worse Pedantries! . . . Dear William, pardon Pedantry in others & avoid it in yourself . . . surely always to look at the superficies of Objects for the purpose of taking Delight in their Beauty, & sympathy with their real or imagined Life, is as deleterious to the Health & manhood of Intellect, as always to be peering & unravelling Contrivances may be to the simplicity of the affections, the grandeur & unity of the Imagination.—O dearest William! Would Ray, or Durham, have spoken of God as you spoke of Nature?[16]

On October 27, S.T.C. sat to Hazlitt for completion of the portrait.* During the course of the sitting he elucidated the origin of evil satisfactorily to his own mind and forced Hazlitt to confess that the metaphysical argument reduced itself to: "Why, in short, did not the Almighty create an absolute infinite number of Almighties?" The resultant portrait, though Wordsworth was to describe it as the best resemblance of S.T.C., feature for feature, that he had ever seen, gave him (again according to Wordsworth) a dreadfully funereal and lugubrious, if not downright tragic expression. S.T.C. was, at the time of sitting, attempting to solve "the Question of

*Long since lost.

Evil—woe to the man, to whom it is an uninteresting Question,"[17] and furthermore, it seems, was privately summing up Hazlitt as "*Worthless, Soul*-less, *God*less."[18] A smiling visage might scarcely be the anticipated result of such a confrontation between accusative subject and metaphysically cornered portrait-painter.

After the sitting S.T.C. retired to his study, to sleep early:

> A sad night—went to bed & in about 2 hours absolutely summoned the whole Household to me by my Screams, from all the chambers—& I continued screaming even after Mrs Coleridge was sitting & speaking to me!—O me! O me!—[19]

He lit his candle, rekindled his fire and sat awake into the small hours, composing a suitable counter argument to Hazlitt and Wordsworth.

Hazlitt seems not to have prolonged his visit after completion of the portrait. Greta Hall settled quietly into the late autumn. Southey worked at his writing-table with impressive industry, relaxing himself with daily strolls with S.T.C., these punctuated by the latter's sudden disappearances behind walls and bushes: "Walked with Southey to Braithwaite . . . I had a violent Motion (in the field under an oak by a Fence with the Brook on the other side)."[20] Following which, S.T.C. observed to himself that if only he had as housemate one whom his Soul loved, his diarrhoea would increase rather than decrease his happinesss.

These anal-sadistic disturbances of daytime were exchanged after dark for hideous nocturnal shrieking:

> Nov. 10th, 1/2 past 2 o'clock. Morning. Awoke after long struggles & with faint screaming from a persecuting Dream. The Tale of the Dream began in two *Images*—in two Sons of a Nobleman, desperately fond of shooting—brought out by the Footman to resign their Property, & to be made to believe that they had none / they were far too cunning for that / as they struggled & resisted their cruel Wrongers, . . . I became they—the duality vanished—Boyer, & Christ's Hospital became concerned— . . . and I was conjuring him . . . to have pity on a Nobleman's Orphan, when I was carried back to bed, & was struggling up against an unknown impediment, some woman on the other side about to relieve me—when a noise of one of the Doors, strongly associated with Mrs Coleridge's coming in to awake me—the first thing, I became conscious of, was a faint double scream, that I uttered—.[21]

He became seriously unwell again as the autumn grew more melancholy: "so mere a Slave to the Weather. In bad weather I can not possess life without opiates."[22] He shut himself away in his study for hours on end, alone with his drug, once more enclosed like the toad in the rock: "dead to everything,"[23] "all one blank Feeling, one blank idealess Feeling,"[24] "despondent, sick at heart."[25] And he opium-drowsed and awakened to scribble despairingly in his notebooks, then to drowse again, until day and night became one protracted, opium-impregnated, unimaginably hopeless, rudderless dream, himself utterly becalmed, caught in the irons of morphine:

Novemb. 20th—Midnight.—O after what a day of distempered Sleeps, out of which I woke, all sense of Time & Circumstance utterly lost / of fever, rheumatic pain, & loads of stomach-sickness.—I got up / am calm, like one *lownded*—/as I lifted up the sash, & looked out at the Sky, for the first minute I thought it all dark, a starless Sky; the wind, all the summer swell lost, & the winter Hollowness & Whistle not yet come, mixed its sea-like solemn roars with *the Rustle* from the yet remaining half dry Leaves on all the Trees —/—but I looked again at the Sky—& there were so many Stars, so dim & *dingy*, that they might have put into Paracelsus's Fancy his whim of the Astra tenebricosa, that radiated cold & darkness, with hollow rays, tube-like as Hairs, ensheathing the rays of Light & Heat, & so producing cold & darkness—
Monday Morning, 9 o'clock—Cold Rain in the valley, which is Snow upon the Mountains—[26]

Night after night he woke to look from his window:

Sat. Morn. Oct. 29, 1803. Three o'clock. The Moon hangs high over the Greta, & the Bridge, on the first step of her Descent, & three hours at least from the Mountain, behind which she is to sink: nearly full—not a Cloud in Heaven, the Sky deep sable blue, the Stars many & white in the height of the Sky, but above around, & beneath the Moon, not a Star; she is starless as the Sun ... The Mountains are dark, low, all compact together, quiet, silent, asleep—the white Houses are bright throughout the vale, & the evergreens in the garden. The only Sound is the murmur of the Greta, perpetual Voice of the Vale—[27]

Wednesday Midnight, one o'clock or near it—after much excitement, very very far short of intoxication, indeed not approaching to it to the consciousness of the understanding, tho' I had taken a considerable quantity of ... [laudanum] I for the first time in my life felt my eyes near-sighted,—& tho' I had 2 Candles near me, reading in my bed, I was obliged to magnify the letters by bringing the Book close to my Eye—I then put out the Candles, & closed my eyes—& instantly there appeared a spectrum, of a Pheasant's Tail, that altered thro' various degredations into round wrinkly shapes, as of Horse Excrement, or baked Apples—indeed exactly like the latter—round baked Apples, with exactly the same colour, the same circular intra-circular Wrinkles—I started out of bed, lit my Candles, & noted it down ...
I went to the window to empty my Urine-Pot, & wondered at the simple grandeur of the View.[28]

Southey, during this period, seems to have been surprisingly sympathetic in his attitude towards his wretched brother-in-law, whom he watched "quacking himself for ailments that would teaze anybody into quackery."[29] Gradually, however, Southey saw with increasing clarity which way the wind blew. He, too, began to utter warnings. S.T.C. was evasive in his explanations and excuses. The bad weather made him ill; he could not survive his illness without opiates, but "with what aversion I take them!" He continued: "I can not hitherto detect any pernicious Effect of it . . . nothing certainly compared with the effect of Spirits."[30]

Loudly he insisted that it was the damp that made him so desperately unwell: "in fine weather I have not a Feeling about me that ever reminds me that I have been ill."[31]

He now recommended his earlier insistence: "I must go into a hot climate."[32]

There is, however, abundant if somewhat obscure evidence that it was not really the climate which was driving him from England. He was now faced with the terrifying knowledge, which he kept a close personal secret, that he had become a true victim of the dread "opium-habit." If he remained in England this would become generally known; his name would be bandied about as an opium-eater and a smearing reputation would be earned for himself which would ruinously dog him and his family. There was only one course open to him; he must leave the country and fight opium among strangers. If he succeeded in overcoming the habit, he would return to England. If he failed, then he would die out of sight, his secret of shameful weakness (for such he believed it to be) unknown. At all cost his family name must not be dragged in the mud.

S.T.C. possibly unburdened himself to Wordsworth upon the details of this plan; Sara Coleridge also knew the real reason for the journey to a warm climate in pursuit of what was euphemistically called "restored health."

Necessary as it had become in S.T.C.'s view that he should go, his heart sank at the thought of leaving his home; to quit Keswick was like tearing away part of his heart: "For I love the place with a perfect love."[33] More so, he hated to leave his beloved bedroom-study, where he and opium had circumnavigated great globes together:

When in a state of pleasurable & balmy Quietness I feel my Cheek and Temple on the nicely made up Pillow in *Celibe Toro meo*, the fire-gleam on my dear Books, that fill up one whole side from ceiling to floor of my Tall Study—& winds, perhaps are driving the rain, or whistling in frost, at my blessed Window, whence I see Borrodale [sic], the Lake, Newlands—wood, water, mountains, omniform Beauty—O then as I . . . sink on the pillow . . . what visions have I had, what dreams—the Bark, the Sea; all the shapes & sounds & adventures made up of the Stuff of Sleep & Dreams, & yet my Reason at the Rudder / O what Visions . . . & I sink down the waters, thro' Seas & Seas—yet warm, yet a Spirit—/.[34]

Most agonising was it to leave his children, seven-year-old Hartley, "An utter Visionary! . . . If God preserve his life for me, it will be interesting to know what he will be— . . . all who have been with him, talk of him as a thing that cannot be forgotten . . . Derwent . . . a fat large lovely boy,"[35] who loved a joke—"when he had scarce a score of words in his whole Tonguedom comes holding up a pair of filthy Pawlets, & lisps—Here's *clean white* Hands!—& then laughed immoderately.—"[36] He was a child for whom all meals were "a time of Rapture and Jubilee, and any story that has no Pie or Cake in it, comes very flat to him."[37] Last, but not least, there was little Sara: "a darling little Thing with large blue eyes"[38] . . . "a remarkably interesting Baby . . . she smiles as if she were basking in a sunshine, as mild as moonlight, of her own quiet Happiness."[39] "O bless them! next to the Bible, Shakespeare, & Milton, they are the three Books from which I have learnt the most . . . and with the greatest Delight."[40]

A fragment of a letter written to Sara Coleridge five years later best speaks of the tragedy of husband and wife:

> . . . known any woman for whom I had an equal personal fondness, that till the very latest period, when my health & spirits rendered me dead to everything, I had a PRIDE in you, & that I never saw you at the top of our Hill, when I returned from a Walk, without a sort of pleasurable Feeling of Sight . . . some little akin to the delight in a beautiful Flower joined with the consciousness—'And it is in *my* garden.'[41]

CHAPTER NINETEEN

THE BIG BOLT

(December 1803–April 1804)

S.T.C., TAKING DERWENT with him for the first leg of the journey, left Keswick for Grasmere upon the eve of Christmas. He had planned but a short stay at Dove Cottage. However, almost immediately upon his arrival he fell ill: "for days altogether so weak, as scarcely to be able to smile with tenderness & thanks on Mrs Wordsworth & Dorothy, who have nursed me with more than Mother's Love."[1]

Within Dove Cottage all was noise, overcrowding, discomfort. Outside the rain swept through the valley in vast curtains, drawn across the lake and fells as if by an invisible hand: "the Rooms . . . so small & the Rain so incessant."[2] "Rain, soaking Rain."[3]

S.T.C. was "lame with the gout, stomach-sick, haunted by ugly dreams, screamed out in the night, durst not sleep etc. etc. . . . Mary had a very bad cold most of the time . . . Molly was poorly, Coleridge continually wanting coffee, broth or something or other—the bed was moved into the sitting room night and morning, and with Derwent and the liveliest of Johnny's you may think we were busy enough in our small house."[4] Dorothy, here, says all that need be said.

By day S.T.C. lay in the sitting-room, brooding on his afflictions, sending yet more detailed accounts to poor Southey:

on the slightest action of an uncongenial Air, from without, on the skin, or of distressing disquieting Thoughts on the Digestive Organs from within, the *Secretories* of the skin commence a diseased Action / if the *Absorbents* become languid, I have swellings, with moveable Fluid, in my knees and ancles / & am bed-ridden / if by means of opiates I revivify the action of the Absorbents, I have no swellings nor eruptions—no bad knees, no Boils in my neck, & Thighs, no little agony-giving ulcers in my mouth, et super Scrotum / but *then* the diseased Action of the Secretories of the Skin seems to be propogated into the Stomach, unless I so far increase the Dose, as to enabel the Stomach to repel it—in which case the whole System obtains a *Temporary* Peace by the Equipoise of hostile Forces. How dim & dusky all this is, I feel as strongly as you can . . . Mrs Wilson was for many years according to her own account in a state of bad Health almost to identity like mine/miserable Dependence on the weather, continual craving for stimulants . . . affrightful Dreams, & epileptic Breezes from the Stomach & still lower up to the Brain &c &c—after many years burst out a burning Eruption on her Skin . . . & since that time she has been well . . . if I can pass a year, a whole year, in a hot climate, I feel a deep confidence, that I shall . . . recover

395

my Health / & gladly should I purchase it at the price of an Eruption, that would kill all Love not purely spiritual.[5]

By night he was tortured with dreams; Dorothy and Mary took turns to sit up with him, in order to wake him at the first indication that he appeared to be having a nightmare. If they failed to wake him and he did dream, his shrieks were bound, in due course, to rouse the whole household:

> I dreamt among other wild melancholy Things, all steeped in a deep dejection but not wholly unmingled with pleasure, that I came up into one of our Christ Hospital Wards, & sitting by a bed was told that it was Davy in it, who in attempts to enlighten mankind had inflicted ghastly wounds on himself, & must henceforward live bed-ridden. The image before my Eyes instead of Davy was a wretched Dwarf with only three fingers ... I ... burst at once into loud & vehement Weeping, which at length ... awakened me / My cheeks were drowned in Tears, my pillow & shirt collar quite wet.[6]

A series of notebook entries for this period (made in very bad, loose, irregular handwriting) speak volumes:

> What a beautiful Thing Urine is, in a Pot, brown yellow, transpicuous, the Image, diamond shaped of the of the [sic] Candle in it, especially, as it now appeared, I having emptied the Snuffers into it, & the Snuff floating about, & painting all-shaped Shadows on the Bottom.[7]

> Purple *Streams** in manifold Shapes, but *angular*—& then white or flesh-coloured Streaks with Dark Streak / or Darkness streaked with Life & Flesh.[8]

> angle—angular—yet a doubt whether I have spelt the word/ the nature of memory / the Effort in writing—compare this writing with sober writing—the diminished Facility of Volition, whatever that Faculty be.[9]
> I will at least make the attempt to explain to myself the Origin of moral Evil from the *streamy*† Nature of Association, which Thinking—Reason, curbs & rudders / how this comes to be so difficult / Do not the bad Passions in Dreams throw light & shew proof of this Hypothesis?—Explain those bad Passions: & I shall gain light, I am sure—A Clue! A Clue!—an Hetacomb a la Pythagoras, if it unlabyrinths me—Dec. 28, 1803—Beautiful luminous Shadow of my pencil point following it from the Candle—rather going before it & illuminating the word, I am writing. 11 o'clock /—[When his eye must have fallen upon the face of the slumbering child, Derwent, who shared his

*Colours seen with the eyes shut, or in the darkness, while under opium; akin to the colour sequences of an acid-trip.
†Here he uses "streamy" as an adjective to describe the apparently spontaneous thought-association process of the opium dream, a day-dream which seems to conduct itself wholly independently of the person dreaming it, yet is *his* dream. The above is one of S.T.C.'s many notebook attempts to analyse and describe the opium experience.

room] But take in the blessedness of Innocent Children, the blessedness of sweet Sleep &c &c: are these or are they not contradiction to the evil from *streamy* association?—I hope not: all is to be thought *over* and *into*—but what is the height, & ideal of mere association?—Delirium.—But how far is this state produced by Pain & Denaturalization? And what are these?—In short, as far as I can see any thing in this Total Mist, Vice is imperfect yet existing Volition, giving diseased Currents of association, because it yields on all sides & yet is—So think of Madness: O if I live! Grasmere, Dec. 29, 1803.[10]

In preparation for his proposed journey to Madeira, S.T.C. had written to Thelwall, now living at Kendal, asking him to go to the best druggist in Kendal,* there to purchase for S.T.C. "an Ounce of crude opium, & 9 ounces of Laudanum, the latter put in a stout bottle & so packed up as that it may travel a few hundred miles with safety." The cost of this purchase S.T.C. estimated at about half a guinea.[11]

Although Dorothy and Mary knew that S.T.C. took "stimulants" (as Dorothy, with rare discretion, referred to his brandy and opium) it is doubtful if they appreciated the extent of his problem. Wordsworth (though ignorant of the true implications of drug reliance and sincerely believing that S.T.C. could break his opium habit with will-power) was aware of the enormity of S.T.C.'s habit and of the frightful hold that it had upon him. "Wordsworth alone knows . . . the full extent of the Calamity,"[12] said S.T.C.

Wordsworth knew the extent of the calamity, certainly; in the *Prelude* he wrote of it as "a private grief, keen and enduring."[13]

This last visit of S.T.C. at Dove Cottage was, then, anything but a happy one. At last, however, the rain stopped and S.T.C. felt himself recovering. He convalesced by taking walks with the Wordsworths, walks during which S.T.C. was saying a silent farewell to his beloved Lake Country which he privately believed he would never see again.

With Wordsworth, S.T.C. visited his favourite places: Easedale (The Black Quarter) and Greenhead Gill (where lay the ruins of Michael's sheepfold). The weather had now become sweet and gentle, lyrical almost, as it often does in the Lake Country at the turn of the year:

*Kendal druggists:
Bailey's Northern Directory, 1784 list only—Mason, George
The Universal British Directory, 1790 lists—

Brookbank, John	chemist and druggist
Tobey, John	master of dispensary

Unfortunately there is no discoverable directory for Kendal which covers the dates 1802–1816 specifically.

On this blessed calming Day—sitting on the very Sheepfold dear William read to me his divine Poem, Michael.—The last day of the year.[14]

As William read, S.T.C. gazed and gazed at the view, attempting to commit it, in total detail, to memory:

The two Nesses, dispated . . . ask Dorothy for a word /—the Helm Crag central / Easedale Tarn Rocks (Steel Fell the expanse to our Right) to the left of Helm Crag Sour Milk Force, Langdale Pikes, Elterwater Quarries & Coniston Fells—/—the foot path so even on the steep breast, of the Mountain, with such a precipice beneath & the tumultuous Brook at the bottom / but as you turn round & come out upon the vale, O my God! the whole white vale, from Steel Fell this way, from the Force on Easedale the River with the Mountain Islanding the half almost of the vale, Butterlip How, the Church / & O! just in sight close down beneath me that House with dark slates & dingy white walls!—O remember it—

The eye—let it be a spectrum in my feverous brain! The connection by Intakes of the smooth bowling Green Vale with the steep Mountain, & of the sides of the mountain with its craggy castle-ruin-like Top / —Road between Walls—the Lake with three walls rising each above the other—the Bridge with 2 arches—/—the smoke a perfect pillar / —the whole River from the Force to the quiet Lake.[15]

He wrote direct into his notebook as he sat by the fold. He had now developed a special technique of writing down (putting into words on paper) the Lake Country scenery, using a method derived from musical scoring. To readers unacquainted with the Lake Country these notes read as obscurely as a musical score for a person who has not learned how to read music; for the person who knows the Lake Country S.T.C.'s notes make marvellously informative reading. Thus, this view looking down from high up in Greenhead Gill:

High up on the Gill, sublime Lines of simple sublime by Helm Crag centrally fronting / indescribable in idea / the Tune, the Music only can be given— 2 Nesses, then a gap, then three mountain steps horizontal—.[16]

On January 4, 1804 William read to S.T.C. his recently completed books of *The Prelude*:

Wednesday, Jan. 4th/in the highest & outermost of Grasmere Wordsworth read to me the second Part of his divine Self-biography—3 basons—/ misty Tarn / satting dove colour painted Petticoat rocks / & a slope /.[17]

Snow fell; the scenery whitened; on Friday, January 5 he wrote a long and beautiful note (CNB 1812 16.196, too long to quote here) on scenery seen from the terrace wall in Easedale and then during a walk down Grasmere Vale to Rydale. The snowy weather lasted for four days. Then:

Monday Morning, Jan. 9, 1804 in the Dark with my eyes shut / a loud Thaw wind. Derwent asleep in the other bed, God love little dear Heart—& Dorothy, in the Parlour, O dear Dorothy—& O dear Sara Hutchinson.[18]

And opium obtrudes again: "Images in sickly profusion."[19] He went on to attempt to analyse the difference between love and lust; musing upon his penis: "an organ acting with what an intensity of personal Life / compare it with the Eye & Ear / then at a less distance with the smell, still less with the Taste."[20]

Opium: he lay with his candle and the drug, drifting away into dreams and half-sleep; waking; more of the drug. "Images of my own self, which appeared to gain their existence by the narrowing of a [perpendicular] into a [horizontal] so as to gain in Latitude what it loses in length (one might express it by the Horizontalizing of the Perpendicular)."[21]

He mused upon his illness and on the possible benefits from removal to a warmer climate:

What if it brought out a deforming Eruption on my Face and Body, leaving my inner life sound and full of faculty?—O I should rejoice. My Soul she would always love, the faithfully Beloved!—and I could more than pardon her aversion from my bodily Presence.[22]

Finally, in those last hours at Dove Cottage, he picked up William's copy of Purchas and read once again from Rubriquis' *Travels into Tartary*:

Cublai Chan began to reign, 1256 the greatest Prince in Peoples, Cities, & Kingdoms that ever was in the World.[23]

On Saturday, January 14, 1804, S.T.C. made one of his incredible lightning recoveries. He left Grasmere on foot for Kendal, walking nineteen miles in just under five hours, which included a rest for lunch. As he was often to describe, he was capable, within a single hour, of changing from a state "which seemed next to Death . . . to a state of Elastic health . . . Wordsworth has . . . [said] 'I could not expect anyone to believe it who has not seen it—'."[24]

On arrival at Kendal S.T.C. wrote to Tom Poole (who was in London, on Rickman's invitation, assisting with a statistical report to the House of Commons on pauperism, based on figures supplied by parish overseers). S.T.C., writing on Sunday, January 15, assured Poole that he expected to arrive in London the following Friday, January 20, at six o'clock, at the Saracen's Head, Snow Hill. Poole accordingly arrived at the Saracen's Head at the time appointed and waited there, in vain, until past midnight. S.T.C. arrived at the White Horse Cellar, Piccadilly, at seven in the evening of Tuesday, January 24, having spent almost a week with his acquaintance,

Dr Crompton, at Liverpool. From Piccadilly S.T.C. took himself and his luggage in a Hackney coach to the long-suffering Poole's lodgings in Abingdon Street, Westminster. Here he found Poole ("drest so grand!"),[25] who gave S.T.C. a loving welcome, despite the Saracen's Head. He had found a very comfortable bed for S.T.C. at Waghorn's Coffee House, next door to the House of Lords; Waghorn's was "a quiet domestic place," kept by a Mrs Segur; here Poole and S.T.C. breakfasted daily at half-past eight; Poole then went off to his Parliament office and his report, where he worked until four in the afternoon, while S.T.C. occupied the parlour in Abingdon Street.[26]

Here he proposed to slog at a Work, tentatively to be entitled *Consolations and Comforts from the exercise and right application of the Reason, the Imagination, and the moral Feelings, addressed especially to those in Sickness, Adversity, or Distress of mind*:

> I want only one fortnight's steady Reading to have got *all* my materials before me—& then I neither stir to the Right or to the Left, so help me God! till the work is finished.[27]

It was never finished.

In addition to the *Consolations* (as he called this work) S.T.C. had a volume on "the whole plan" of his life ready to be written,[28] he assured Poole; a series of essays on various subjects virtually drafted in his mind ready for the writing, and a gargantuan study of Shakespeare projected.[29] All that he needed was to regain his health and then: "I have a cheering . . . Confidence that I shall make an active & perseverant use of the faculties & acquirements, that have been entrusted to my keeping,"[30] he told Tom Wedgwood, Sara Coleridge and the Beaumonts, among others.

Before embarking upon the fortnight's steady reading S.T.C. wrote several long letters to friends, mainly about his health. For Sara he reserved intimate details which were, in due course, censored from the letter which contained them; all that remains is one intriguing, typical, Esteesian half-line:

> to put a Sock over it on the pit of my Stomach.—[31]

S.T.C. was overjoyed to be once again living a bachelor's existence, or, as he termed it, to be *loose* in London.[32] He dined with Davy, with Stuart, was merry with Godwin at Somers Town and with Lamb at Pentonville. But his enemy would suddenly steal upon him unawares.

On Saturday, January 28, he suffered a definite withdrawal attack while dining with Stuart; S.T.C. had barely sat down to dine when he burst into a sweat "like a tropical Rain,"[33] followed by violent vomiting, diarrhoea and prostration. He recovered quickly, doubtless after taking more opium. A notebook entry mentions a terrible night of dreams and screaming prior to this attack and, on the morning of the 28th, "pain & tightness at the chest, puffing & involuntary yawning;" these, however, were classical heart disease symptoms.[34]

He began to worry lest there might be "unpleasant speculation"[35] about his state of health. This indeed was the case. He had by now acquired a bad reputation for breaking engagements. At dinner-parties it was noticed that he frequently drank more than was wise and as a result became obtrusive in conversation. His excuses were profuse and fluent, basing the blame upon the three D's; Damp, Diarrhoea and Depression. All London now knew that damp gave S.T.C. diarrhoea and depression and that depression made him drink, but undoubtedly there were several persons who suspected something other than damp as the root cause of his fluctuating health and behaviour.

Rickman, for one, had by now formed a poor opinion of S.T.C., describing him in a letter to Southey as hypersensitive and suffering from a sulky imagination, due to want of regular work and application. Southey agreed; his own cautiously euphemistic diagnosis of S.T.C.'s troubles was "want of management."[36]

S.T.C. sensed the suspicions surrounding him and in what seems to have been a forlorn attempt to throw people off his own scent, he commented insistently and foolishly upon the wretched George Burnett's by this time well-known opium addiction.[37]

I met G. Burnet [sic] the day before yesterday in Linc. Inn fields—so nervous, so helpless—with such opium-stupidly-wild eyes—O it made the place, one calls the Heart, feel as if it was going to [break].[38]

The febrility of S.T.C.'s behaviour, the hunted tone in his letters, suggests that he, privately, now knew himself doomed. Yet he still endeavoured to convince the world that he resorted to opiates from free choice, in order to control illness from damp and anxiety. In a warm dry climate and free of all worries he would abandon opiates: "I am resolved to be tranquil. Spite of everything, I have certainly been, on a long Average, better & more tranquil for the last two months than before—and when I have once *set to*, I expect to be wholly tranquil,"[39] he wrote to Southey on March 12. There is a ring of defiance in this.

His friends noticed that he had become quarrelsome, quick to take offence (which he formerly had never been), highly inflammable, in fact. On February 2, while supping at "Polygon" with the Godwins and the Lambs, S.T.C. made a "disgraceful scene,"[40] as he afterwards called it, quarrelling violently with Godwin over reviews. According to Godwin's own account of the evening, S.T.C. "thundered and lightened with frenzied Eloquence"[41] for nearly an hour and a half; Godwin did not think S.T.C. tipsy, but saw, clearly, that something unusual ailed him and that he had not been his "natural Self" the whole evening. Next morning, at half-past eight, S.T.C. wrote Godwin an urgent note of apology, blaming his condition on a large glass of punch that Mary Lamb had given him (or so he alleged) before he and the Lambs had left for Somers Town.

It was ominous that a coolness had once again sprung up between S.T.C. and Tom Poole; S.T.C., as a result, moved away from Poole and lodged instead with James Webbe Tobin. To Southey S.T.C. hinted at defects in Poole's character, including lack of generosity: "no doubt he was very fond of my *conversation* & the instruction he derived from it / but I had to pay for all my lodgings, & 7 shillings a day for dinner—never once did he offer to pay for me . . . Of course, I broke off, and went to Tobin's."[42] The true cause of the breach must almost certainly have been unwelcome warnings and advice from Poole.

Tobin became critical of S.T.C. in his turn, making it alarmingly clear that he had penetrated S.T.C.'s secret, *"advising and advising"*[43] against the dangers of habit-forming indulgence. Nonetheless S.T.C. continued to lodge with Tobin for the simple reason that he could not afford to go anywhere else.

The tentative plan to reside in Madeira was now abandoned by S.T.C. in favour of a definite scheme to go to Malta. George Bellas Greenough had strongly recommended a sojourn in Sicily and S.T.C. had become fired by the ambition to climb Mount Etna.

Stoddart* had gone to Malta, as Admiralty Advocate, and had extended to S.T.C. an invitation to stay with him there. Malta was an excellent launching place for Sicily and, therefore, S.T.C. now decided to take up Stoddart's invitation.

Sotheby had given S.T.C. a cheque for a hundred pounds (Wordsworth standing as security) to go towards defraying the expenses of Mediterranean travel. The Beaumonts (who were proving most kind to S.T.C. and had invited him, in mid-February, to their seat at Dunmow, in Essex) insisted upon his accepting a similar sum from them, while Stuart was generosity itself in allowing S.T.C. to draw upon him well beyond a sum which S.T.C. had deposited with him to defray all Keswick expenses on behalf of Mrs Coleridge during her husband's absence abroad.

On February 21, S.T.C. suddenly received a heavy and damaging blow from a wholly unanticipated quarter. A letter arrived from Sara Hutchinson (it has not survived) making it very clear that she wished their painful association to cease. In the evening of that day S.T.C. was taken ill at Rickman's, a notebook entry marked the episode enigmatically, but poignantly:

Will you ask the maid to get me a Hackney coach?

*Sir John Stoddart (1773–1856) a prominent journalist: The King's and the Admiralty Advocate at Malta, 1803–7. His sister, Sarah, married William Hazlitt.

Later S.T.C. dated this entry and filled in the details a little:

Rickman's, Tuesday Night, Feb. 21, 1804, 11 o'clock / the Receipt of that heart-wringing Letter from Sara, that put Despair into my Heart, and not merely as Lodger, I fear, but as a Tenant for Life.[44]

As a result of this letter S.T.C.'s health suffered (who can doubt that on receipt of such a letter he must have resorted heavily to opium?). On February 28 he explained to Rickman: "I have been very unwell for the last day or two—& rather roughly treated not by the Weather alone—."[45] A week later he sent Lady Beaumont a letter of excuses for his not having written: "I have been ill & in a sort of Stupor."[46]

Sara Hutchinson's increasing aversion to his company had been becoming apparent to him for some months past. His departure to the Mediterranean must have seemed to her, understandably, an excellent opportunity to bring to an end a relationship that had proved a desperately unhappy one for them both. It was a fair and eminently wise request. S.T.C., however, could not see the letter in this light; he tortured himself with "the continuance of the same appetiteless heart-gnawing passion"[47] for Asra and contemplated writing an *Ode on a Suicide for Love*.[48]

In the midst of his despair he had to continue to attend to the practical details of the voyage to Malta. This would be made in convoy, because of the war with France. S.T.C. hoped to travel on a Royal Naval vessel but, owing to what appears to have been one of his typical muddles of procrastination and last-minute, frenzied planning, he finished by booking a passage on a merchant vessel, *Speedwell*, a hundred-and-thirty-ton brig that was sailing in a Mediterranean convoy at the end of March. Her destination was Trieste; she would touch at Malta. Her captain, John Findlay, was a Scot, "a short, well-bellied man."[49] *Speedwell* had the reputation of being a fast ship but travelling in convoy would slow her voyage, which would take eight or nine weeks, inclusive of a week at Gibraltar.

The passage money was thirty-five guineas, S.T.C. to find his own wine and spirits and bedding[50] and the Captain everything else.

However, the Captain obligingly procured all the bedding but the counterpane. He could get the things cheap, he said; the cost of everything (counterpane excluded) would not exceed three pounds ten shillings.

A list of S.T.C.'s personal requirements for the voyage read:

A Jacket & Hood to fit on to my green Bag / to sleep in
Umbrella—
Pencils for presents—
Portable Soup. Mustard
Get Jacket & Trousers at Malta /
A pair of *strong* Boots made *large*: High half-Boots—
Eau de Luce—[51]

The Governor of Malta was Sir Alexander Ball.* Sotheby, at S.T.C.'s request, conciliated the Governor's protection for him; it was to prove a wise step. Mackintosh had suggested to S.T.C. that, if he had any sort of influence with Ball, he might without difficulty procure some small appointment on his staff that would at least, by its remuneration, liquidate S.T.C.'s travelling expenses. "If I should see any opening, when abroad, I shall not be prevented from engaging your good offices in my Behalf," wrote S.T.C. to Sotheby on March 13, 1804,[52] after he had booked his passage.

Sometime in March, S.T.C. sent Sara Hutchinson a copy of the third edition (1658) of Sir Thomas Brown's *Pseudodoxia Epidemica*, bound up with reprintings of *Religio Medici*, *Hydriotaphia*, and *The Garden of Cyrus* and annotated by S.T.C. himself. Lamb had bought it and given it to S.T.C. on March 10; Sara Hutchinson inscribed it: "Given by S.T.C. to S. Hutchinson March 1804." It was doubtless intended as a farewell gift to her (being an Esteesian present the book subsequently found its way back into his own possession). Sir Thomas Brown, as S.T.C. told Sara in a covering letter, was among his first favourites.

Between March 18 and 20, S.T.C. went down with yet another violent diarrhoeal attack "of incessant fury for 10 hours."[54] This he diagnosed as "cholera morbus, which is now going about."[55] He saw that he "could not get over it without / so . . . [he] sent for some Laudanum, & took it drop by drop." He made a recovery, though remaining very weak.[56]

The kind-hearted Beaumonts took him into their Grosvenor Square home for a brief recuperative stay. How much Sir George knew about S.T.C.'s opium-habit at this stage we can but surmise; rumours had possibly reached him. S.T.C., ignorant himself of the extent of Sir George's knowledge of this, had written a cautious letter which would signify nothing to Sir George if he were ignorant of S.T.C.'s opium addiction, but which should go far to mitigate his disapproval if he suspected the habit:

I was hardly used from infancy to Boyhood; & from Boyhood to Youth most, MOST cruelly / yet 'the Joy within me' which is indeed my own Life and my very Self, was creating me anew to the first purpose of Nature, when other & deeper Distress supervened—which many have grieved, but Wordsworth alone knows to the full extent of the Calamity / Yet even this I shall master—if it please the Almighty to continue in me the Thoughts, that have been my Guides, Guardians, and Comforters, for the last 5 months.—[57]

This is ambiguous; as of course it was intended to be (the reader can

---

*Sir Alexander Ball (1757–1809), a distinguished naval officer, had forced the capitulation of the French garrison at Malta in 1800 following a two-year blockade. He had been appointed Civil Commissioner for Malta and was generally referred to as Governor of the island, although in fact he was never actually officially recognised as such.[53]

judge for himself the truth of these allegations of hard usage in infancy to boyhood).

The "Thoughts that have been my Guides" are not made explicit either in the letters or the notebooks of this period. It is probable that S.T.C. was now working his way back to an acceptance of orthodox trinitarian Christianity (see pp. 128–131).

When the time came for S.T.C. to leave the Beaumonts and Grosvenor Square he did so laden with gifts: wines, medicinal foods, soups, an elegant little portable desk, complete with "the concisest dictionary and grammar" that money could buy (Lady Beaumont's idea; she knew that authors cannot function without dictionaries and especially would S.T.C. require a grammar) and, perhaps the most thoughtful gesture of all, a packet of James's powders. S.T.C., examining this little *escritoire* when he got on board ship, felt his heart seized by "a hundred Tentacula of Love & affection & pleasurable Remembrances. How could it be otherwise? Every thing had been so manifestly placed there by the Hand of affectionate Solicitude!"[58]

On Saturday, March 24, he was informed that *Speedwell* had gone to Gravesend and was due at Portsmouth by Tuesday; S.T.C. must leave for Portsmouth on Tuesday at the latest. Accordingly he went to the Angel Inn, behind St Clement's Church in the Strand (from whence the Portsmouth mail set out) and booked a place on the mail-coach for Tuesday evening at seven. He made his hasty departure an excuse for not saying personal farewells, but in fact he was now half-stupefied with large quantities of laudanum, doubtless taken to deaden his emotion at leaving. On Sunday, March 25, he sat to James Northcote for a sketch from which a portrait could be made for Beaumont (this is now in the possession of Jesus College, Cambridge). It was not considered a good likeness by those who knew him; Dorothy rather bluntly commented on it to Lady Beaumont that:

the whole face, when seen all at once, seems to *me* scarcely to resemble Coleridge, though the forehead and outline of the *shape* of the face are very much like him.[59]

It is scarcely surprising that the portrait was not an unmitigated success; S.T.C. had had to break off the sitting because he had been, he told Davy, on the point of "falling into distempered sleep."[60] This, to Davy, he had blamed on the weather, but a notebook entry made sometime that same week-end read:

Opium always in the day-time increases the puffing Asthma, eye closing, & Startlings.[61]

The letter to Davy was an attempted message of love, appreciation and farewell: "I would to God I thought of myself, even as you think of me but—"[62] Here it broke off. Davy's good-bye note to S.T.C. had pleaded, "Do not in any way dissipate your noble nature / Do not give up your birthright—."[63]

A few essential farewell letters were written from Stuart's *Courier* office on Tuesday afternoon; they included a skimpy note to Poole:

Tuesday, March 27, 1804

Dear Poole

I will write to you from Portsmouth. At present, weak as I am & daily tottering into relapses, it would not be wise—scarcely safe—for me either to write to you at full & [or?] to take leave of you in person.—May the Almighty guide you onward where ever and when ever the Road leads to Happiness & that sole Virtue which is in FAITH not in the OUTWARD WORKS.

S. T. COLERIDGE[64]

(In 1835, a year after S.T.C.'s death, Poole wrote of this note:

I cannot read this affecting farewell without deep feeling, being conscious that the intimate dear, and to me most valuable intercourse, which had existed between us for the preceding ten years, formed the happiest period of my hitherto life.)[65]

On Tuesday evening, March 27, S.T.C. left London on the Portsmouth mail. Sir George Beaumont's valet had packed all S.T.C.'s things for him, sent everything off for him, and now accompanied him to the Angel Inn. Also there to see S.T.C. off were Tobin, Lamb and Stuart. Tobin was full of last-minute admonitions and advice. He "continued *advising* . . . to the last moment. O God! he is a good fellow, but this rage of *advising* . . . and (as almost all men of strong habitual health have the trick of doing) of finding out the cause of everybody's ill health in some one malpractice or the other." S.T.C. was, as he put it, "low to sinking" by the time he reached the Angel; Tobin did not improve matters for him. Just as S.T.C. was on the point of taking his seat on the coach Tobin reminded him of a ten-pound debt. S.T.C., made furiously angry by this, began calling on Stuart, to ask him to pay the sum for him. Tobin immediately fervently restrained S.T.C. from doing anything of the sort.[66] In this turmoil of last-minute distraction, hot temper and misery, S.T.C. climbed into the coach, amidst a farewell hubbub from his distracted friends. The whip cracked, the horn blew, hooves clattered, wheels grated on the cobbles; the mail-coach clattered out of the inn yard into the Strand; S.T.C.'s biggest and best-bruited bolt was away.

Twelve-and-a-half hours later the Mail arrived at Portsmouth, at the Crown

Inn. *Speedwell* had not yet made Portsmouth; the wind was against her.
S.T.C., after a few days staying at the "dirty dolefull Inn,"[67] found himself
cheap lodgings in the town; he took all his meals, however, at the house of a
Mr Mottley, a Portsmouth bookseller and newspaper proprietor, to whom
S.T.C. had been given an introduction by Stuart. Mottley proved friendly,
generous and helpful to a degree. He showed S.T.C. round Portsmouth:
"the whole Town is a huge Man of War of Brick & Mortar."[68] From his
house S.T.C. wrote his farewell letters; to Southey: "O Southey! from
Oxford to Greta Hall—a spiritual map with our tracks as of two Ships that
left Port in Company—;"[69] to Stuart, with deepest thanks for all his generosity and kindness; to Sir George Beaumont; to the Wordsworths: "O
dear Friends! I love you, even to anguish love you." The letter contained a
despairing private message to William (who, knowing its full import, must
have read it with a very heavy heart):

> O dearest & most revered William! I seem to grow weaker & weaker in my
> moral feelings / and every thing, that forcibly awakes me to Person & Con-
> tingency, strikes fear into me, sinkings and misgivings, alienation from the
> Spirit of Hope, obscure withdrawings out of Life, and . . . a wish to retire
> into stoniness & to stir not.[70]

A painful letter of farewell, full of love and friendship, came from Poole.
S.T.C. wrote of it contemptuously to Southey: "Good God! to believe &
to profess that I have been so & so to him, & yet to behave as he has done
. . . 3 years long did I give my mind to this man / exclusive of introductions
&c &c—."[71] This is classical morphine recrimination and ranting and
almost word for word resembles S.T.C.'s railing against Wordsworth at a
later date.

S.T.C. sent to Hartley and Derwent a farewell present of Spillekins. To
his wife went a letter which is both agonised and agonising in its attempt at
total honesty. The word "love" is avoided scrupulously:

> My dear Sara! the mother, the attentive and excellent Mother of my chil-
> dren must needs be always more than the word friend can express when
> applied to a woman / I pray you, use no word that you use with reluctance / .
> Yet what we have been to each other, our understandings will not permit our
> Hearts to forget!—God knows, I weep Tears of Blood, that so it is!—For
> I greatly esteem & honour you / Heaven knows, if I can leave you really com-
> fortable in your circumstances, I shall meet Death with a face, which I feel
> at the moment I say it, it would rather shock than comfort you to hear . . .
>
> My very dear Sara, / May God Almighty
> bless you / & your
>
> affectionate
> S. T. COLERIDGE[72]

There is little doubt that he believed that these were final farewells. To Southey he had written: "if I return, we shall be Friends: if I die, as I believe I shall, you will remember me."[73]

Clearly, he was hoping for death. He was in terror of the future and his enslavement by opium; he wanted to die in oblivion, overseas, rather than to slide down the slope of total degradation in full public view, amongst those who had once admired him and had looked to him to accomplish so many great things.

Speedwell reached Portsmouth on the evening of April 3. Captain Findlay presented himself to S.T.C.; he was full of splendidly nautical information. *Leviathan** a man-of-war of seventy-four guns, was to convoy them; she had not yet received her orders, but would probably receive them next day. At present the wind was south-westerly, point-blank against them and in an obstinate corner.

This intelligence was of the good, hard, technical kind which always delighted S.T.C. He repeated it with obvious gusto to the Wordsworths in his final farewell letter to them, dated April 4. Thursday, April 5, he was due to go aboard *Speedwell*, but the gale blew too strong. Next morning he was bundled on board; at noon he wrote a final note to Rickman: "I am off—pray, write to Southey & tell him I am off, am well, & bless them all!"[74] But it was a false start; the wind swung westerly again; S.T.C. informed the Beaumonts: "our Commodore, Captn H. W. Bayntun, of the Leviathan . . . is to sail with the first Puff that wins a point & a half on the hither Side of Impossibility. We *hope* to go tomorrow: we may be here this day fortnight . . . I am better, than I was."[75] Physical activity always stimulated him; stimulation always heartened him. Notebook entries describing the actual departure vibrate with excitement:

> Saturday, April 7th / quite calm / beautiful sight / Isle of Wight, & the Ships below it / and on the other side 9 men of war in . . . [diagram] zigzag semicircle, & in the interspaces all sorts of smaller Ships, some with sails reefed, others all flying—the Sun on some, some in shade . . . The different Signals, Drums, Guns, Bells, & the sound of Voices weighing up & clearing Anchors. Wind all against us / Saturday, went on shore / but slept aboard. Dined on board on Sunday.
> Monday, April 9th, really set sail.[76]

---

*Leviathan was on her way to join Nelson's fleet at Toulon. She was to win herself fame and glory at Trafalgar.

PART FOUR

The Courts of the Sun

No twilight
within the
courts of
the sun

The Sun's rim dips; the stars rush out:
At one stride comes the dark;
With far-heard whisper, o'er the sea
Off shot the spectre-bark.

At the
rising of
the Moon

We listened and looked sideways up!
Fear at my heart, as at a cup,
My life-blood seemed to sip!
The stars were dim, and thick the night,
The steersman's face by his lamp gleamed white;
From the sails the dew did drip—
Till clomb above the eastern bar
The horned Moon, with one bright star
Within the nether tip.

The Ancient Mariner Part III (1817)

CHAPTER TWENTY

"HOW THE MARINERE SAILED FORTH ..."

(April–May 1804)

> With sloping masts and dipping prow,
> As who pursued with yell and blow
> Still treads the shadow of his foe,
> And forward bends his head,
> The ship drove fast, loud roared the blast,
> And southward aye we fled.

The Ancient Mariner Part I (1817)

S.T.C. FOUND HIS first night at sea somewhat uncomfortable, but next morning, up on deck, with the waves rolling rough and high and thirty-five other ships of the convoy sailing in wide-flung company, the lonely gulls fishing among the ships, the blue land falling away on his right, he experienced something of his old exhilaration, as he exulted first in the beauty of the entire seascape, then in that of a single wave.

Speedwell, deeply laden with eighty-four cannon for Trieste in her hold, rode "like a Top Bough on a Larch Tree in a wind / pitching and rocking."[1] She lived up to her reputation of being a fast brig and was always either sailing abreast of the Commodore, *Leviathan*, or well up in her wake.

S.T.C., his second night out, rocking furiously back and forth in his bunk, discovering to his immense satisfaction that he was as good a sailor as ever:

> thought of a Lullaby Song to a Child on a Ship / giant rocking Cradle ... Creak of Main Top Irons, Rattle of Ropes, & Squeak of the Rudder Rope running on the Block / And so play at bopeep with the Rising Moon, and the Lizard Light /—There is thy native Country, Boy!—Whither art thou going.[2]

The ship's company was small; in weighing anchor the men had grumbled aloud, saying that *Speedwell* had not half her complement of crew. Of two sailors pressed in the Downs, one, a rascal of a one-armed cook, had run away, but he was no great loss. Now *Speedwell* was left with "Captain, Mate, 2 boys, 4 men, 3 passengers, one sheep, 3 pigs, several Ducks & Chicken, 1 Dog, a Cat and 2 Kittens."[3]

S.T.C.'s two fellow-passengers, although not exactly congenial companions, provided him with considerable diversion. They were a man and woman, travelling as individuals, not as a pair. The man was "a gross

411

worldly minded fellow, not deficient in sense or judgment, but inert to every thing except Gain & eating."[4] The woman, a retired housekeeper, was:

> A creature with a horrible Superfluity of Envelope, a Monopolist & patentee of flabby Flesh ... Mrs Carnosity ... She eats everything by a choice / 'I must have that little potatoe'—(baked in grease under the meat) 'it looks so smilingly at one.'—'Do cut me if you please' (for she is so fat, she cannot help herself) 'that small bit—just there, Sir!—a leetle tiny bit *below*, if you please.'—'Well! I have brought plenty of pickles, I *always* think &c / I have always three or four jars of brandy cherries with me; for with boil'd rice ... I always think &c'—and true enough, if it can be called thinking, she does always think upon some little damned article of eating that belongs to the Housekeeper's Cupboards and Locker. And then her plaintive Yawns ... And she said to me this morning, 'How unhappy, I always think, one always is, when there is nothing & nobody, as one may say, about one to amuse one. It makes me so nervous.'[5]

S.T.C., with much "pomp of promise"[6] drew up a strict itinerary for himself aboard ship, dividing his day into strenuous sessions of Italian study, essay writing and composing. "No Health or Happiness without Work."[7] Needless to say, having planned this timetable, he at once abandoned it. Instead he spent much of his time jotting in his notebook a running commentary on the voyage, seated on deck, whenever weather permitted, using the rudder-case as his desk and a duck-coop as a stool.

Five days out, a brisk gale sprang up with a high sea. S.T.C., although still not actually seasick, was miserable enough to feel intense sympathy for the wretched sheep which, tethered on deck in the lee of a boat:

> yesterday cropt its hay cheerfully—flashes of Lightning from the Tops & dimples of the gentle waves, & the sweet murmur might have awakened the sensations of dewy grass in sunshine, & the murmur of its Trees—but now / kneeling its poor face to the Deck, its knees black, worn, & sore /—up it starts, a great wave rushing over the ship—& staggers—& trembles under the Boat, with another on the Top of it, by the side of the Pump, a Gun close before it / (the Boat a Pig Stye) alas! it came from flat peaceable meadows—/ Had it come from ... Helvellyn ... the dreadful Tempest of Sound, its Shelter behind the Rocks, the Snatching up of water, & of the waterfalls &c &c[8]

Then the storm dropped; "the weather was heavenly."[9] S.T.C., feeling once more uncommonly well, luxuriated in the sunshine and occupied himself by analysing the elements of the picturesque in a man-of-war (the *Leviathan*, in this case):

> 1. Its height upon a flat surface / if a Steeple be so uniformly pleasing on a diversified meadow, how much more the Masts of a man of war, referring as with a finger to the sky, on this vast Level?

2. The proportion of the solid Height to the Height above the Hull, about as 40 to 160, made graceful and right by the strongly felt Lightness & Airiness of the Sails / while yet

3. The elliptical figure of the Hull & its kindred motion prevent all abrupt or harsh contrast between the wood & the Canvas . . .

4. The height of the naked mast above the sails, connected however with them by Pennant & Vane, associated, I think, with the human form on a watch-tower . . .

5. The harmony of the Lines—the ellipses & semi-circles of the bellying Sails & of the Hull, with the variety from the permanence of the one & the contingency of the other /

6. The terminating Lines of the Sails forming a similar curve with the sail, yet by its determinateness producing a threefold effect / 1. of a strongly felt variety in the Canvassage of the Vessel /2. Secondly . . . its stiffness & determinateness always mingles a notion of natural Straightness which seems to form a link of union with the masts, & so thro' the masts with the Hull making one whole of the whole Vessel / while the mast above the Sails connects it with the beholder by obscure resemblance of the human form as seen at a distance or on a height. / 3. This determinateness of the stiff rope-hemm'd Edge Line of the Sails, not dying away into each other, weakening the *sensuous beauty* raises it to the picturesque, giving the whole a greater facility of connecting itself with other Ships as Forms, & of forming an interesting part of a common whole: which if it were a complete visual whole in itself, as a circle with its radii, &c it could not so easily do—

7thly / Every one of these sails is *known* by the Intellect to have a strict & necessary action & reaction on all the rest, & that the whole is made up of parts, each part referring at once to each & to the whole /—and nothing more administers to the Picturesque than this phantom of complete visual wholeness in an object, which visually does not form a whole, by the influence ab intra of the sense of its perfect Intellectual Beauty or Wholeness.—To all these must be added the Lights & Shades, sometimes *sunshiny*, sometimes *snowy*; sometimes shade-coloured, sometimes dingy—whatever effect distance, air tints, reflected Light, and the feeling connected with *the* Object (for all Passion unifies as it were by natural Fusion) have in bringing out, and in melting down, differences and contrast, accordingly as the mind finds it necessary to the completion of the idea of Beauty, to prevent sameness or discrepancy.—Of a Fleet of Ships more may be said: & probably more will suggest itself & of less obvious kind, on after quiet Looking: now that the Intellect has done its main business & rests.[10]

The resting of the artist's intellect, after the preliminary analytical work, was regarded by Coleridge as being of paramount importance. When the time arrived for the analytical material to be used, it was done not by working from the actual notes, but by writing from a memory organised and disciplined by the intellectual spadework. Thus, the *Leviathan* appears in all her splendour in this passage from a letter to Southey, written, it seems, two days after the above notes:

413

our Commodore, the Leviathan of 74 guns, the majestic & beautiful Creature / sailing right before us . . . with two or at most three Topsails, that just bisect the naked masts, as much naked masts above as below, upright, motionless, as a church with its Steeple—.[11]

These passages need to be quoted at length, for they, and the many like them with which the notebooks abound, must be seen not only as the most important and profoundly original experimental prose-writing of that epoch, anticipating by a hundred years the work of twentieth-century innovators, but also, perhaps even more significantly, as the foundations of our modern theories of the nature and function of criticism. To quote R. P. Blackmur: "Coleridge began the whole business of the special techniques of modern scholarship and criticism of poetry: all the expansions into the psychology of language and imagination."

It was not possible for Coleridge's contemporaries to recognise the tremendous importance of this aspect of his work, simply because he was moving so far ahead of them. Even truer of Coleridge himself was the comment which he made to Tom Wedgwood and Mackintosh in defence of Wordsworth: "He strides on so far before you that he dwindles into the distance!"[12]

On the morning of April 16, shortly before nine, the coast of Portugal came in sight and S.T.C., flinging on his greatcoat, hurried shoeless on deck to stare at a country which was so strongly associated in his mind with Southey. Portugal presented warm yellow-green mountains patterned with large black cloud-shadows. S.T.C. gazed long and in rapture, then commenced a letter to Southey: "Well! I need not say, that the Sight of the Coast of Portugal made it impossible for me to write to anyone before I had written to you, I now seeing for the first time a country, you love so dearly."[13]

S.T.C. wrote at length and discursively, with news of himself, his health, the ship, the convoy, his fellow passengers. The letter was intended as much for Sara Coleridge as for Southey: "If Mr S. be absent, Mrs Coleridge will open the letter."[14]

S.T.C. was careful, in this letter, to make subtle reference to James Tobin, who had detected S.T.C.'s opium-habit and had warned him of its dangers. S.T.C. knew that Tobin was a great gossip and that, without doubt, details of his experience of S.T.C.'s drug-taking would in due course reach Keswick. S.T.C. was always anxiously assuring Southey and Sara Coleridge (and indeed everyone of his acquaintance) that opiates did him no harm and were not habit-forming with him. He was still deluding himself that he could delude the world.

I took out with me some of the finest Wine . . . in the Kingdom . . . Brandy, & Rum . . . & excepting a pint of Wine which I had mulled at two different times . . . I have touched nothing but Lemonade from the day we set sail, to the present Hour. So very little does anything grow into a Habit with me. This I should say to poor Tobin, who continued *advising* and *advising* to the last moment. O God! he is a good fellow, but this rage of *advising*, & of *discussing characters* and (as almost all men of strong habitual health have a trick of doing) of finding out the cause of everybody's ill health in some one malpractice or other . . . renders him a sad Mischief-maker, & with the best intentions a manufacturer & propagator of Calumnies.[15]

This passage speaks tragic volumes.

On April 19 at ten in the morning S.T.C. found himself with the Spanish coast on his left hand and the Barbary coast of Africa on his right. "Mount behind Mount . . . three or four behind like chimneys in the Clouds—and one old stooping Giant looking in upon us 20 leagues inland."[16] At forty-four minutes past two, he noted with excited exactitude, the Rock of Gibraltar came into view.

A sudden sensation of great distance from home was the cause, perhaps, of an attack of Asritis which seized him at this point:

What change of place, Country, climate, company, situation . . . ever is that one feeling at my Heart / felt like a faint Pain, a spot which it seems I could lay my finger on /—I talk loud or eager, or I read or meditate the abstrusest Researches, or I laugh, jest, tell tales of mirth / and ever as it were, within & behind I think, & image you / and while I am talking of Government or War or Chemistry, there comes ever into my bodily eye some Tree, beneath which we have rested, some Rock where we have walked together or on the perilous road edging, *high above* the Crummock Lake / where we sate beneath the rock, & those dear Lips pressed my forehead /—or that Scale Force in its pride, as we saw it—when they laughed at us for two lovers./[17]

On this occasion S.T.C. was saved from prolonged dejection because *Speedwell* anchored in the harbour at Gibraltar and on the morning of August 20 he went ashore, to find himself plunged into a kaleidoscope of new impressions. He jostled in a noisy crowd of muleteers, goats, porters, Moors, Jews with:

Bumbazine Dresses, & of fine family face . . . Spaniards, dirty dogs, with their cloaks, falling down very elegantly . . . Greek Women, pretty Dowdies! . . . English officers & Ladies, & Soldiers of all Regiments & Runaway Sailors . . . Geranium with pink flowers climbing down the walls . . . here and there huge plants of prickly Pear . . . I walked calmly, slowly, happily . . . Reluctantly I returned to a noisy dinner of 17 Sea Captains, indifferent Food, &

Burning Wines . . . [At length] I . . . forced home my now very tipsy Capt—
whom I left still drinking in his own Cabin with 3 other Masters of Merchant
Vessels, & went to bed.[18]

Next day S.T.C. again ventured on shore further to explore the Rock,
climbing to the highest point. As he toiled upward in the heat he wondered
at the ramparts with "their huge artillery—hollow Trunks of Iron where
Death and Thunder sleep;"[19] at "gardens in deep Motes between lofty &
massive walls;"[20] at mansions and Moorish towers. At length he reached
the eastern side of the Rock, uninhabited, except by the apes.

Here, in fascination, S.T.C. spent much of his time the next few days:

scrambling about . . . among the Monkeys: I am a match for them in climbing, but in Hops & flying Leaps they beat me.[21]

S.T.C. discovered, in addition to the apes, St Michael's Cave, a

perfect Gothic Extravaganza / . . . chambers within chambers, the bottom of
which no one has yet reached, tho' many have descended 300 & 400 feet, till
the Smoke of their Torches has become intolerable—O if we do not sail till
Thursday, surely, surely, I will try to go someway down it /[22]

It is pleasant to linger with a vigorous and happy S.T.C., clambering
among the apes, or seated alone, high on "the striding edge" of Gibraltar,
musing in the sunshine upon:

a multitude of almost discordant complexity of associations—the Pillars of
Hercules, Calpe, Abbila, the Realms of Massinissa, Jugurtha, Syphax—
Spain, Gibraltar, the Dey of Algiers, dusky Moor & black African / and O!
how quiet it is to the Eye, & to the Heart when it will entrance itself in the
present vision, & know nothing, feel nothing, but the Abiding Things of
Nature, great, calm, majestic, and one.[23]

Among several letters of introduction which S.T.C. had been given to
English residents in Gibraltar was one to a Major Adye, a quondam pupil of
George Coleridge. Adye proved most hospitable, entertaining S.T.C. to
dinner and conducting him on sightseeing tours of the Rock. In this manner
time passed pleasantly, in spite of the fact that S.T.C. suffered what was in
all probability a mild heart attack: "Heart . . . gnawing, & palpitation—
strange sense of Stopping."[24]

On Wednesday, April 25, *Speedwell* was once more under weigh and
Gibraltar dropped astern. S.T.C. had a speedy relapse. He found himself
back with the fiendish crowd of shapes and thoughts by night, unwholesome dozings and optical illusions by day, languor and a general oppression
and misery. He took more and yet more opiates to deaden his despair.

Speedwell ran into calms and head-winds. Her captain looked for a Jonah (or Jonas) in the convoy. S.T.C. reflected that here, indeed, was one advantage of sailing in convoy: "On a single Vessel the Jonas must have been sought out amongst ourselves."[25] And who would have been Jonas? Surely, Samuel Taylor Coleridge, now, by that mysterious alchemy which may make the poet and his subject one, metamorphosed into the Ancient Mariner; voyaging, under dire curse, across a wide wide sea.

The notebook entries for this period reveal how obsessed S.T.C. became with the feeling, mounting to inner conviction, that he had become his own prophetic creation: "that ancient man, The bright-eyed Mariner."[26]

The poem, within the context of seamen's superstitions, had become a subject of conversation between S.T.C. and *Speedwell*'s captain.

"Damn me!" said good Captain Findlay. "I have no superstition. I had as soon sail on Friday as on Saturday; but this I must say, that Sunday is really a lucky day to sail on; indeed to begin any sort of business upon."[27]

Speedwell plied wearily to the windward off Carthagena: "wet foggy oppressive Weather, with the wind impotent or against us!"[28] sighed S.T.C.

Captain Findlay muttered darkly: "Top sails and top gallant sails and royals: the Devil has helped him to a Commadore's [sic] share. Aye! aye! the Devil knows his relations!"[29]

S.T.C. noted that: "Vexation, which in a Sailor's mind is always linked on to Reproach and Anger, makes the Superstitious seek out an Object of his Superstition, that can feel his anger—Else the Star, that dogged the Crescent of my 'cursed be the last Look of the waning moon' were the better."[30]

> A gust of wind sterte up behind
>   And whistled through his bones;
> Thro' the holes of his eyes and the hole of his mouth
>   Half-whistles and half-groans.
>
> With never a whisper in the Sea
>   Off darts the Spectre-ship;
> While clombe above the Eastern bar
> The hornéd Moon, with one bright Star
>   Almost between the tips.
>
> One after one by the hornéd Moon
>   (Listen, O stranger, to me!)
> Each turned his face with a ghastly pang
>   And cursed me with his ee.*

The notebook becomes anguished reading:

*From the 1805 version of the *Ancient Mariner* III, 197–209.

417

Tuesday Afternoon, one o'clock, May Day—We are very nearly on the spot, where on Friday last about this same Hour, we caught the Turtles—And what are 5 days' toiling to Windward just not to lose ground, to almost 5 *years*! Alas! alas! what have I been doing on the Great Voyage of Life since my return from Germany but fretting upon the front of the Wind— well for me if I have indeed kept my ground even![31]

Wednesday May 2nd/1804 . . . desperately sick, abed, one deep dose [?doze] after another . . . Poet. interesting Thought of May 2nd & Thursday before May Night / Alas! how dear do these Thoughts cost you, Coleridge?—[32]

Specimens of verse and prose genuinely written under opium during this period, should be compared with *Kubla Khan*:

> Bravo, Captain Findlay
> Who foretold a fair Wind
> Of a constant mind
> For he knew which way the wind lay.—
> Bravo! Captain Findlay!

> A Health to Captain Findlay!
> Bravo! Captain Findlay!
> When we made but ill Speed with the Speedwell,
> Neither Poet, nor Sheep could feed well
> The Poet ate Muffin, the Sheep eat its Hay
>   [the above line erased]
> And Poet & Pig! how [?grief] rotted Liver
> And yet Malta, dear Malta as far off as ever
> Bravo! Captain Findlay—
> Foretold to a fair wind
> Of a constant mind,
> For he knew which way the Wind lay.[33]

By purpler Pimples gemm'd the Face one purple Blotch / or Chin, Nose, Cheek, Brow one purple Blotch By purpler Pimples gemm'd where two black shining Eyes forever shine and shine /—And shine and shine, and as they shine for ever will shine on, Till what with Brandy, what with Rum, the Liver's fairly gone! Eyes that like watch *lights* shine, as if they were there not for themselves to see with, but as a *sight* for others to avoid.[34]

On May 6 the convoy ran into a storm which even Captain Findlay disliked. *Speedwell*'s foremost yard was carried away. S.T.C. opium-dozed in his bunk.

These last days in my frequent sudden awakings I have been much struck with the conversions of Forms & lines into Human Faces, & Head Dresses . . . a flower on the curtain expanded with the outlines of petals marked by brown lines, & a polyandria Polygynia Tuft of yellow in the center with a bud beside turned into a very sweet Lady's Face & Head Dress, & arm extended & gently curved in a resting posture /.³⁵

S.T.C., deep in the miasma of a prolonged opium jag, now succumbed to one of the inevitable results of the drug, severe constipation:

Tuesday Night, a dreadful Labor, & fruitless Throes, of costiveness— individuated faeces, and constricted Orifices. Went to bed & dozed & started in great distress—Wednesday Morning, May 9th—a day of Horror—tried the sitting over hot water in vain / after two long frightful, fruitless struggles, the face convulsed, & the sweat streaming from me like Rain, the Captn. proposed to send for the Commadore's Surgeon ... but by Calm & one thing or other it was late evening before he could speak to him. The Surgeon instantly came, went back for Pipe & Syringe & returned & with extreme difficulty & the exertion of his utmost strength injected the latter. Good God! What a sensation when the obstruction suddenly *shot* up!—I remained still three-quarters of an hour with hot water in a bottle to my belly (for I was desired to retain it as long as I could) with pain & Sore uneasiness, & indescribable desires—at length went / O what a time! equal in pain to any before / Anguish took away all disgust, & I *picked out* the hardened matter & after awhile was completely relieved. The poor mate who stood by me all this while had the tears running down his face.—A Warning!³⁶

The rumour spread through the convoy that one of the gentlemen passengers aboard *Speedwell* had died.
S.T.C. might almost have welcomed death. He was under no delusions:

this is not the Time for me to begin my aweful Duty of considering and investigating the real state of my Health. Yet my voyage in rough weather from Hamburgh forces itself upon my recollections painfully! Whither have my Animal Spirits departed? My Hopes—O me! ... I have many thoughts, many images; large Stores of the unwrought materials ... but ... the power to do, the manly effective *Will*, that is dead or slumbers most diseasedly ...

O there are Truths below the Surface in the subject of Sympathy, & how we *become* that which we understandably behold & hear, having, how much God perhaps only knows, created part even of the Form.—[? and so] good night—³⁷

And now, weird echo of the albatross, a poor exhausted hawk alighted on *Speedwell*'s bowsprit. The sailors shot at it. The bird, utterly fatigued, did not stir. Again the men fired. The bird circled in the air, then returned to the bowsprit. Five times it was thus shot at, gyred, returned to the bowsprit. At last it flew to another vessel. More shots were taken at it. The bird perished. "Poor Hawk! O Strange Lust of Murder in Man."³⁸
And that burden which hung, albatross-wise, about S.T.C.'s own neck?

Pain without gloom & anxious Horror, & from causes communicable openly to all, rheumatism, &c. O it is a sport!—but the Obscene, or the disgustful—the dull quasi finger-pressure on the Liver, the endless Flatulence, the frightful constipation when the dead Filth *impales* the lower Gut—to weep & sweat & moan & scream for the parturience of an excrement . . . for Sleep a pandemonium of all the shames & miseries of the past life from early childhood all huddled together, & bronzed with one stormy Light of Terror & Self-torture / O this is hard, hard, hard!—O dear God give me strength of Soul to make one thorough Trial—if I land at Malta / spite of all horrors to go through one month of unstimulated Nature—yielding to nothing but manifest Danger of Life!—O Great God! Grant me grace truly to look into myself, & to begin the serious work of Self-amendment . . . let me live in Truth . . . I am loving & kind-hearted & cannot do wrong with impunity, but O! I am very, very weak—from my infancy have been so—& I exist for the moment!—Have mercy on me, have mercy on me, Father & God! omnispresent, incomprehensible, who with undeviating Laws eternal yet carest for the falling of the feather from the Sparrow's Wing.—Sunday Midnight, May 13th, 1804.[39]

CHAPTER TWENTY-ONE

"... AND OF THE STRANGE THINGS THAT BEFELL."

(May 1804-June 1805)

AT FOUR IN the afternoon of Friday, 18th May, 1804, *Speedwell* dropped anchor in the harbour of Valetta and S.T.C. disembarked.

At first all went splendidly. S.T.C.'s host, Dr Stoddart, conducted S.T.C. on a sightseeing tour of Valetta and he enjoyed a wonderful sensation of wellbeing. "Found myself light as a blessed Ghost,"[1] he wrote in his notebook on May 19; his thoughts still concentrated upon his *döppelganger*, the Ancient Mariner:

> I mov'd and could not feel my limbs,
> I was so light, almost
> I thought that I had died in sleep,
> And was a blessed Ghost.[2]

On Sunday, May 20, S.T.C. attended chapel; afterwards he presented his letters of introduction to Sir Andrew Ball and to General Vallette, Commander-in-Chief of the troops in Malta. Both men received him courteously, Ball particularly so, but S.T.C. gained the impression, at this first meeting with the Governor, that there would be no chance of a salaried minor administrative post such as he had hoped for.

It quickly proved otherwise. Ball almost immediately succumbed to Coleridge's charm, conversation and company. S.T.C., for his part, discovered Ball to be "a very extraordinary man—indeed a great man."[3] This mutual esteem rapidly ripened into friendship. As a result, S.T.C. within two months of his arrival on the island was appointed private secretary to Ball and, shortly afterwards, as acting Under-Secretary for Malta.

The Public Secretary, Alexander Macauley, was, at eighty, past effectively fulfilling his duties. Almost the entire burden of office fell upon the Under-Secretary, Edmond Chapman, at this time absent from Malta. Thus S.T.C., without premeditation or design, stepped into a job of real responsibility.

That he should be instantly and strikingly successful in his new rôle was to be expected; the work, which largely consisted of writing reports and memoranda, was of a nature that he could do brilliantly well without the least difficulty. But the other side of his moon was dark; his attempt to survive without opiates met with total, and inevitable, disaster.

For his first week or so in Malta S.T.C. kept very well, but he was then abruptly seized with what appeared to be a raging fever: "My whole body & heart panting & shivering like an ague fit of Love."[4] He was dining out at the time; he returned to Stoddart's immediately and retired to bed without disturbing anyone, although scarcely in his right senses. At ten o'clock a servant discovered him and called Stoddart. S.T.C. was able to rally himself sufficiently to direct Stoddart to give him thirty drops of laudanum in a large tumbler of warm lemonade: "in about 20 minutes I was manifestly and greatly better—& soon after fell into perspiration and a gentle Sleep."[5]

This, a classical withdrawal attack, was thus quickly controlled; but the sworn attempt to go at least a clear month without opiates had had to be abandoned, almost before it had begun.

In a letter to Sara Coleridge of June 5, S.T.C. also mentioned an oppression in his breathing "so that I walk up and down like a Leopard in his Den."[6] This breathlessness, mentioned by him from now on with increased frequency, was almost certainly a symptom of valvular damage to the heart due to his chronic rheumatic disease.

Following his appointment as Ball's secretary, S.T.C. left the Stoddarts, to become domiciled with the Governor and Lady Ball. S.T.C. now spent much of his time at the Governor's country residence, the Palace of Saint Antonio, four miles out of Valetta. In Valetta S.T.C. had a suite at the Governor's Palace. "A Parent could not be kinder to me than Sir A. Ball," S.T.C. told the Beaumonts, in a letter of August 1, 1804.[7]

S.T.C.'s mood in Malta was subdued, his public behaviour decorous. Lady Ball was disappointed in him:

> At Malta ... I have earned the general character of being a quiet well meaning man, rather dull indeed—& who would have thought, that he had been a *Poet*! "O very wretched Poetaster, Ma'am! As to the reviews, it is well known, he half ruined himself in paying cleverer fellows than himself to write them" &c—[8]

According to one Underwood (a clerk in the Malta Treasury) S.T.C. was "exceedingly enamoured" of Lady Ball.[9] This should not be taken too seriously. Lady Ball was a charming woman and doubtless S.T.C. was always extremely polite and attentive to her, with suitable little touches of gallantry, but this was his habitual behaviour towards women. There are indications in his notebooks that, privately, he found Lady Ball rather silly.

Her comment that "The Catholic Religion is better than none" certainly infuriated S.T.C., who was not even prepared to concede that Roman Catholicism *was* a religion. He gave vent to a sarcastic notebook blast:

> Sugar of Lead / Well! better than no Sugar. Put Oil of Vitriol into my Sallad —well, better that than no oil at all ... well! we must get the best we can— better that than none!—So did not our noble ancestors reason, or feel—or we should now be Slaves.[10]

Their religion and their propensity for violent noise apart, S.T.C. liked
the Maltese; but of the island itself he commented that, although the
climate was delightful, "a drierier Place Eye never saw."[11]

Very different was his opinion of Sicily, which he visited from August 10
until November 7, 1804. His base was Syracuse, where his hosts were
Gould Francis Leckie, the British consul, and his beautiful young wife.
S.T.C. found the Leckies and their sociable household most congenial. He
had no chance to be lonely or to mope; when he was not being diverted
socially he was kept busy with semi-official work for Ball. In addition,
S.T.C. exerted himself to explore as much as he could of the island.

According to a letter to Sara Coleridge, he ascended Etna twice, the first
time on August 19, the second, it seems, on August 25. Etna was somewhat
of a disappointment; the fatigue of ascending it was the only thing that had
not been exaggerated, S.T.C. told Sara.

Sicily was still both wild and primitive; for example, at Cava Secchia, on
October 18, 1804, a boy saw ten wolves.[12] S.T.C., roaming the countryside,
noted undrained marshes, stone-filled fields where men toiled with oxen
and primitive wooden ploughs, roadways choked by fallen walls. He visited
strange and ancient places: Tremiglia, where Neptune was said to be
buried "under a large Bay Tree, with vines wreathing about it / Sleep,
Shade, & Quiet!"[13] "The Point of Plemmyrium where Alcibiades &
Nicias landed . . . that round Bason . . . the rushing of subterraneous
water,"[14] Timoleon's villa, Pysma and the Temple of Jupiter. Fallen
columns, brambles, lizards sunning themselves:

> Glide across the sunny walk like shooting Stars, green, grey, speckled /
> exquisite grace of motion / all the delicacy of the Serpent and a certain dignity
> from even just the increasing erectness of it to its hind paws— . . . firmness
> of its *stand-like* feet, where the Life of the *threddy* Toes makes them both
> seem & be so firm, so solid—yet so very, very supple / one pretty fellow,
> whom I had fascinated by stopping & gazing at him as he lay in a thick net-
> work of Sun & Shade, after having turned his head from me so as but for the
> greater length of its Tail to form a crescent with the outline of its body—
> then turned his Head to me, depressed it, & looked up half-watching, half-
> imploring, at length taking advantage of a brisk breeze that made all the
> Network dance & Toss . . . darted off as if an Angel of Nature had spoken
> in the Breeze—Off! I'll take care, he shall not hurt you /—I should like if I
> could know what they eat, or if they eat bread, to tame one /[15]

The notebook for this period vibrates with vivid impressions: three
midnight horsemen, loaded with beehives, clattering by in the moonlight;
wild, hairy-legged women washing clothes in a mountain torrent; groves of
ancient olive trees like twisted old pillars; the aged Marquis of Casalia, in
order to prove his memory and knowledge of English, learning a very
complex dance of more than eighty-six steps and dancing it without a single
mistake.

But, for S.T.C., above all other fascinations and delights was the opera.

Opera, in Syracuse, was the rage. The arias sung with immense *bravura* within the opera house were fully audible in the street outside, where, after the second or third representation of an opera, they were repeated by "the ragged boys and girls . . . with wonderful accuracy & agility of Voice."[16] S.T.C., always passionately fond of music, swiftly succumbed and was soon writing of the opera with a veteran's appreciation:

> Of a Quintette in the Syracuse Opera / and the pleasure of the Voices—one, and not one, they leave, seek, pursue, oppose, fight with, strengthen, annihilate each other, awake, enliven, soothe, flatter, and embrace each other again, till at length they die away in one Tone. There is no sweeter Image of wayward yet fond Lovers, of Seeking and Finding, of the love quarrel & the making up, of the losing and the yearning Regret, of the doubtlet then compleat Recognition, and of the total melting union. Words, not interpreters, but fellow-combatants.[17]

There were attractions other than the singing. S.T.C. met and rapidly became involved in an ardent flirtation with the Prima Donna, Cecilia Bertozzoli, who formed what he called " a sincere vehemence of attachment"[18] for him. Evening after evening he went to the opera house, walking along a green lane past poplars whose aromatic smell brought back memories cruelly unlike the unworthy thoughts (to use his own description) in which he now indulged. His flirtation with the Prima Donna prompted many whispers of his conscience; but they were whispers in vain. He continued to make assignations with her.

One visit to la P.D. (as S.T.C. called her in his notebook), occurred on October 12. His following notebook entry was particularly philosophical, no doubt in an attempt to quell his conscience: "do not too harshly quarrel with your present Self: for all Virtue subsists in and by Pleasure."[19] But: "I remain faithful to you and to my own Honour in all things," he was able to write to Sara Coleridge,[20] subsequently.

Upon matters connected with sex S.T.C.'s notions of honour were pathologically nice. He was prepared to philander with any woman who attracted him and to carry on the affair indefinitely, so long as it involved no sexual compromise and therefore satisfied his definition of "innocence." With a woman like Sara Hutchinson—naive, virgin, and rigidly bound by a convention of chastity—he could get away with this kind of behaviour, teasing both himself and her to the utmost of his masochistic and sadistic inclinations; but with the hot-blooded and doubtless experienced Prima Donna, things were different. La Bertozzoli, in her Sicilian "vehemence of attachment," succeeded in luring S.T.C. to her bedside, with the clear intention of seducing him. S.T.C. fled.

(This incident, however, must almost certainly have occurred during his second visit to Sicily; it is difficult to believe that even S.T.C. would have returned to pay court to a woman from whom he had bolted at the moment of truth.)

Part of Sicily's appeal for S.T.C. may have lain in the fact that narcotics were easily and cheaply available there. In his notebook he mentions a projected report "On the culture of Hemp and its effects in Sicily;"[21] he does not tell us whether this report was to be written at the behest of Ball, or for his own diversion.

Poppies, grown for opium, were a crop with more than an academic interest for S.T.C. He detailed, in a private note:

> The white poppy seed, sown in the months of October & November . . . one poppy produces from three or four to ten heads . . . from each head from six to 20 Incisions may be made . . . [from] many of Incisions I have taken away 2 or 3 grains.[22]

In Syracuse, in mid-October, he succumbed to a bout of dejection and opium, occasioned almost certainly by his birthday, which he celebrated, if that be the right word, with his customary lamentations and bosom-beating:

> So help me Heaven! . . . so completely has a whole year passed, with scarcely the fruits of a month . . . O Sorrow & Shame! I am not worthy to live—Two & thirty years.—& this last year above all others!—I have done nothing!—O no! still worse . . . body & mind, habit of bedrugging the feelings, & bodily movements, & habit of dreaming without distinct or memorable . . . [rest of passage obliterated, probably in post-Coleridge censorship].[23]

S.T.C.'s plan was to go from Syracuse to Messina in early November; but on November 7 he was obliged to return to Malta unexpectedly, upon official business.

During his absence his suite at the Palace had been given to Commissioner Otway; S.T.C. was therefore now temporarily accommodated in "a sort of Garrets in the Treasury,"[24] where he had a tiny slip of a chamber with a magnificent painted ceiling depicting four vomit-faced winds of heaven, each spewing white vapour in the direction of a central mariner's compass. Beneath the unheeding gaze of this quartette of cloud-beruffed, "curly-wigged *Nobodies*"[25] S.T.C. fought long and lonely battles against opium and despair.

At first, back upon Malta, his health and spirits seemed reasonably good. "I use my faculties, not indeed as once, but yet freely."[26] Ball, increasingly confident in S.T.C., proposed to send him to the Black Sea on a corn commission (speaking, on November 26,[27] as though the matter were definitely decided).

S.T.C. mentioned this assignment in a letter of December 12 to Sara Coleridge, saying that he had agreed to the proposal in a fit of despair, when life had appeared a burden to him. His anguish was due, he explained, to the almost total failure of letters.[28]

War and natural hazards combined to make communication between England and Malta exceedingly difficult. S.T.C. had received virtually no letters from home; neither did mail which he attempted to send to England meet with good fortune; for instance, letters entrusted by S.T.C. to the *Arrow*, the *Acheron* and a merchant vessel were thrown overboard with other documents when these ships were captured by French craft; a packet of mail entrusted by S.T.C. to Major Adye (whom he had re-encountered while in Sicily), perished when the Major died of plague upon his arrival back at Gibraltar (where an epidemic was raging) and all papers in his possession were automatically destroyed as a precaution against further contagion.

S.T.C. was to make much of distress occasioned by lack of communication with home; referring to it as a major cause of his deplorable deterioration in health and morale in 1805. This deterioration in health, in turn, he put forward as part excuse for his failure to return to England that spring: "accidents, partly of an excess of official Labour and anxiety, partly at distress of mind at my not hearing from my friends and knowledge that they could not have heard from me . . . has produced sad alteration in me for the worse," he wrote to Stuart on May 1, 1805,[29] asking him to pass on this information to Mrs Coleridge. But in the previous December S.T.C. had already tried to warn Sara: "O God! O God! if that, Sara! which we both know too well, were not unalterably my Lot, how gladly would I prefer . . . Life in England."[30]

By December, 1804, S.T.C. had become finally convinced of the fearful truth that opium was unalterably his lot.

Abysmally wretched and ill, sleepless, much of the time either intoxicated or opium-dreaming, S.T.C. passed the Christmas period of 1804 alone in his sky-chamber, intermittently scrawling in his notebook a running commentary upon his tortured vigil. Largely incoherent, these maudlin and fragmented notes, haphazard as they are, convey, almost unbearably, "the meaning of the injured mind."[31] S.T.C. had lost himself, but somewhere in the engulfing fog still survived the essential Esteesee, distressingly aware of his failure, cruelly jibing at himself:

> one might make a very amusing Allegory of an embryo Soul up to Birth!— Try! it is promising!—You have not above 300 volumes to write before you come to it—& as you write perhaps a volume once in ten years, you have ample Time, my dear Fellow!—Never be ashamed of scheming—you can't think of living less than 4000 years, & that would nearly suffice for your present schemes—/To be sure, if they go on in the same Ratio to the Performance, there is a small difficulty arises / but never mind! look at the bright side always—& die in a Dream! OH![32]

Yet, peering at himself, he affirmed:

The Best remains! Good God! wretched as I may be bodily, what is there good and excellent which I would not do—?—But this is written in *involuntary* Intoxication. God bless all![33]

Then, abruptly, from these distracted pages bursts an appeal which surely no reader of the actual, battered little pocket-book can encounter without having the vision suddenly blurred by tears. S.T.C., defying the barriers of time, manifests himself, speaking urgently and directly:

If I should perish without having the power of destroying these & my other pocket books, the history of my own mind for my own improvement, O friend! Truth! Truth! but yet Charity! Charity![34]

On December 27, S.T.C. confided to his notebook, writing in his new numerical cypher: "No night without its guilt of opium and spirits."[35]

Not infrequently he exclaimed aloud in his agonies of despair: he was heard only by the *Nobodies* on the ceiling and by his taper, whose flame was "sometimes frightened of its perpendicular by my groans."[36]

Early in January a convoy arrived from England. It stood off the island for several days, unable, because of unfavourable wind, to beat into harbour. On January 11 a boat put out from Valetta to pick up mail. There were several letters for S.T.C., including one from Southey, but nothing from Sara Coleridge. This filled S.T.C. with such dread that he could not bring himself to open any of his letters for three or four days: he tortured himself with half-dreams that "one of the children had died," or that she herself had been ill—"for so help me God! most ill-starred as our marriage has been, there is perhaps nothing that would so frightfully affect me as any change respecting her Health or Life."[37]

There appears in his notebook for this period a highly significant and illuminating note upon Dread:

It is a most instructive part of my life the fact, that I have been always preyed on by some Dread, and perhaps all my faulty actions have been the consequence of some Dread or other on my mind.[38]

Dread, he insisted, involved him, above all, in chronic procrastination.[39] This throws significant light upon his constant condition of acute anxiety.

At last S.T.C. summoned sufficient courage to open Southey's letter, written the previous October. This contained the shattering news that Mr Jackson was trying to sell Greta Hall.[40] (Dorothy Wordsworth is worth quoting here: on October 14, 1804, she had written to Mrs Clarkson that Mr Jackson was preparing to sell Greta Hall to "Mr White, that worthless

Fellow who brought his wife with him [to Keswick] and a *Mistress* in Boy's Clothes.)[41]

S.T.C.'s shock on reading Southey's news was such that he had to take a walk and write to Sara Coleridge before he could compose himself sufficiently to do any more letter reading. "My dear Study! . . . to belong to Mr White! Oh how could Mr Jackson have the heart to do it!"[42]

In the end Mr Jackson did not do it; but S.T.C., for some months to come, remained in ignorance of the reprieve and his disturbance over this crisis was added to all his other innumerable anxieties and woes.

In letters written to England early in 1805, S.T.C. expressed his intention of leaving Malta by the end of the coming March. He would have been devastated had he known the Wordsworths' reaction to this news. Dorothy told Mrs Clarkson (in April): "We look forward to Coleridge's return with fear . . . indeed I dare not look to it—I think as little as I can of him."[43]

S.T.C.'s talk of leaving came to nothing. On January 18, at five in the morning, during a tremendous storm of thunder and lightning, old Mr Macauley died, "like a sleeping Baby—without sigh or motion."[44] As Chapman was still absent, S.T.C. was temporarily appointed Public Secretary for Malta.

S.T.C. was now second in civil dignity to the Governor. Because he preferred not to involve himself in the responsibilities of Treasurer, he drew only half of the salary which the post usually carried. Nonetheless he had sufficient work to keep him fully employed during regular office hours: "subscribing, examining, administering Oaths, auditing &c &c."[45]

As "Segretario Publico dell' Isole di Malta, Gozo, e delle loro dipendenza,"[46] he was able to put up at least a passable show of energy and efficiency; but the notebooks reveal a steady deterioration in his health, private habits and morale. On Feburary 16, during a long, sleepless vigil in the small hours, he groaned aloud:

Me miserable! O yes!—Have Mercy on me, O something *out* of me! For there is no *power*, (and if that *can* be, less *strength*) in aught *within* me! Mercy! *Mercy*!

Sat. Morn. 2 o'clock. S.T.C.[47]

The next entry must have been written within hours, if not less:

Worse and worse! "Why will ye die?" The Soul is smitten with despair, and fears to form a resolution / Even to resolve is a lie at the Heart, a Blasphemy![48]

The nightmares now returned again, in force: "disgust and terror with remorse,"[49] "the *idea* and *sensation* of actual grasp or touch contrary to *my* will:"[50]

8 March 1805—
But yesternight I pray'd aloud
In Anguish and in Agony—
Help Lord! or I perish.[51]

9th 1 o'clock Sunday Morning—, 1805
O keep me from utter Despair! ah what Hope? S.T.C.[52]

Mr Chapman not yet arrived! and I am to stay another 2 months at least! /
O God, guide me aright![53]

Sunday Evening, March 17, 1805. A Day of Evil . . . O a groan / deep &
almost of moral despair![54]

Not only opiates and spirits involved him in patterns of temptation and
guilt. Here was a man in the prime of life gripped in the irons of self-
imposed celibacy. "Can I wonder that good men have joined in the cry
of the Vileness of Human Nature!"[55] he exclaimed, at half-past two in the
morning of March 21, when he rose from bed and made an (unspecified)
vow aloud: "O me! that I ever should have had need to make such a Vow!"[56]
He wrote a long, confused notebook entry:

Merciful God! grant that this rising out of my Bed may be a Resurrection
to my better Spirit!—I rose for this cause / I felt myself in pleasurable bodily
feeling half-asleep and interruptively *conscious* of being sweetly half-asleep /
and I felt strongly, how . . . the Pressure of the Husband's Hand or swelling
chest on the bosom of the beloved Wife shall appear as strictly and truly
virtuous, as *Actively* virtuous, as the turning away in the heat of passion
from the Daughter of Lust or Harlotry. O best reward of Virtue! to feel
pleasure made more pleasurable, in legs, knees, chests, arms, cheek—all in
deep quiet, a fountain with unwrinkled surface yet still the living motion at
the bottom, that 'with soft and even pulse' keeps it full—& yet to know that
pleasure so impleasured is making us more *good* . . .
  But I, Sara! [?Asra] But I am not worthy of you / I shall perish!—I have
not goodness enough to hope enough / and tho' I neither game nor ever connect myself with Woman . . . yet my bodily infirmities conquer me, and the
cowardice of pain, or rather of danger of Life, drives me to stimulants that
cannot but finally destroy me. O me / let me return!—Awake! awake!—[57]

Spring arrived. Pinks appeared, growing in pots on walls and balconies; the
orange trees were laden with bright fruit and pale flowers, simultaneously,
while peach, apricot and almond blossom glowed on bare branches. S.T.C.
noticed these things; but privately he moved in chaos, and he began
thinking of suicide:

Virtue a path of Thorns and Vice an Impossibility—to die! to die! . . . the
consequences of Suicide O endless indefinite yearning thro' infinity.[58]

On Sunday, March 31, 1805, a little after one o'clock, the Governor sent for S.T.C. who, not being able to find Sir Alexander in his study, went to the drawing-room, which was full of visitors. Here Lady Ball told S.T.C. the news of John Wordsworth's death at sea. S.T.C. was just able to falter a few correct words and retire from the room; he was followed by Sir Alexander, upon a business matter, and a Dr Sewell, who wanted to invite S.T.C. to dine with him. Once outside the drawing-room S.T.C., almost strangled with shock and emotion, managed to say to the Governor: "I have just heard of the death of a dear friend, sir! excuse me!"[59] He was led back to his suite supported by the sergeant and followed by a solicitous Sir Alexander. The rest of the day S.T.C. spent alone, overwhelmed. At eleven at night he wrote a detailed notebook account of how Lady Ball had broken the news to him. He followed this account with a wild outburst of grief:

> O William, O Dorothy, Dorothy!—Mary—& you loved him so!—and O blessed Sara, you whom in my imagination at one time I so often connected with him, by an effort of agonizing Virtue, willing it with cold sweat-drops on my Brow! ... O God have pity on us! O may Almighty God bless you, my Friends![60]

This notebook entry states plainly that S.T.C.'s behaviour in Lady Ball's drawing-room, in the face of this disastrous news, had been controlled and seemly. He makes no mention of an hysterical collapse; nor have any of the several people present at the time left any evidence of such a collapse. But, in July, S.T.C. sent Sara Coleridge a dramatic account of how, upon learning of John Wordsworth's death: "I ... attempted to stagger out of the room (the great Saloon of the Palace with 50 people present) and before I could reach the door fell down on the ground in a convulsive hysteric Fit / —I was confined to my room for a fortnight after /—."[61]

The notebook leaves no doubt that this was simply not the case. Within two or three days of March 31, S.T.C. went on a tour of Cevita Vecchia, which he recorded in the liveliest detail. The story of dramatic drawing-room collapse and subsequent prostration was one which he circulated when he arrived back in England. It is more than probable that, in the end, he came to believe in this version himself.

After returning to Valetta from Cevita Vecchia, S.T.C., in delayed reaction to John's death, abandoned himself to an unrestrained opium bout that seems to have extended over the week-end of the fifth to the eighth of April. Hour after hour he lay supine, lost in opium reveries, many of which were sexual in content and revolved upon an Asra axis. He carefully directed these sex fantasies away from physical encounters, which were equally tempting and repulsive to him; instead, he sublimated them into spiritual consummations between twin Souls. These communions approximated to

God, because: "The best, the truly lovely, in each & all is God. Therefore the truly Beloved is the symbol of God to whomever it is truly beloved by!"[62] The essence of loving Asra was "the grandeur of loving the Supreme in her—."[63]

In spite of his every effort to preserve Asra in a "pure" context in his day-dreams, which were "cautiously built," S.T.C. was obliged to confess that fancy and imagination "stream on," and impure images are "forced into the mind by the feelings that arise out of the position of the state of the Body and its different members."[64]

Masturbation increasingly became an obsession. His own culpability made him closely observant of others:

> Many a man's Secret Harm (to some favoured Beings secret even to themselves) may be discovered by observing where they place their hand or hands when lost in thought, or vacant / & What is their commonest posture in Sleep.[65]

S.T.C.'s nightmares continued to be erotic in content, connected, as almost always with school. In a disturbed and disturbing dream of April 9:

> There was a Desk, like that of a Master's at the upper end of a School / for School & Desk &c it always will be . . . and Middleton . . . was there and received me kindly—with him was blended a series of images entirely dependent, as I found on awakening, on the state in which Flatulence had placed the different parts of my Body—he went away—& I lay down at the bottom of the Desk, & heard a Clergyman quoting aloud a text from St Paul . . . the next instant it was St Paul himself . . . Then Middleton returned & reproved me severely for taking Liberties on the slightest encouragement, & sitting thus by *his Fire* / Till that moment it had been the bottom of a Desk, & no Fire / but now there was a little obscure Fire-place—all this without surprize —& I awoke—.[66]

In his sleep the image of Asra, and those whom he most deeply loved and revered, remained undesecrated, as he put it. But in one dream, S.T.C. and Asra actually reached, or had reached, the point where they "solemnized the long marriage of our Souls by its outward Sign & natural Symbol."[67] This was the end of:

> a long Dream, of my Return, Welcome, &c. full of *Joy & Love*, wholly without *desire*, or bodily Inquietude, tho' with a most curious detail of images, and imagined actions, that might be supposed absolutely to *imply* awakened Appetite. A Proof this . . . that by vigorous unremitting Purity of our Thought, when awake, joined with the unremitting Feeling of intense *Love*, the imagination in Sleep may become almost incapable of combining base or low Feelings with the Object of that Love.—[68]

He steeled himself to take courage and write a full confession of all his sins and weaknesses, "& try to lighten my chest, my Brain / the something that weighs *upon* and *against* my Eyebrows! O Asra! Miserere mei, Domine!"[69]—that "decrease of Hope and Joy, the Soul in its round & round flight forming narrower circles, till at every Gyre its wings beat against the *personal Self*."[70]

No confession materialised: instead, he made a memorandum "to attempt to *understand* that craving after indefinite sensations of comfort . . . the *manner* of its domination."[71] But this attempt at understanding produced no startling or novel revelations or conclusions, only "the old old Methusalen Law, that Evil produces Evil—One error almost compels another / tell one lie tell a hundred,"[72] one of those Truisms "so true that they lose all the privileges of Truth,"[73] he sadly reflected.

From the dates appended to the notebook entries it becomes clear that he cultivated the habit of remaining fairly self-controlled and steady during the week, when he was "incessantly employed in official tasks,"[74] but at week-ends he regularly closeted himself with opiates, spirits, dreams, his notebook and remorse. This last was an essential ingredient; he derived deep satisfaction from his violent outbursts of self-recrimination, which at times reached a climax of physical self-chastisement. In one notebook entry for that period S.T.C. spoke of:

> the Blows given by a person to himself, to his hands, breast, or forehead in the paroxysms of *Self-reproof* . . . so as to make the body itself feel the *condemnation* which the mind feels so deeply.[75]

The public excuse put forward by S.T.C. for his overfrequent periods of confinement to his room was recurrent illness due to excessive sensibility. This was decidedly the right line to take with Lady Ball: "your strong feelings are too great for your health,"[76] she commented sympathetically. It is hard to believe, however, that Sir Alexander had not, by this time, discovered what was truly amiss with his Public Secretary. However, S.T.C. was Establishment; the matter was kept decently concealed.

S.T.C. himself, in letters home and in his subsequent journalism and talk, zealously nurtured a fiction that Ball had remained his most ardent admirer to the last, unable to bear the thought of losing him and virtually attempting to bribe him to remain in Malta, making him extravagant offers of office and income. But, in a letter of November 30, 1806, to George Coleridge, S.T.C., off his guard, afforded a glimpse of a strained, indeed most uncomfortable, relationship between himself and Ball:

> I had determined to return to England in [the] Spring . . . However, April came; but Mr Chapman had not returned, & it was as uncertain as ever, when he *would*. Sir A. Ball *intreated* me not to leave him: I could not say, no! I did not *say*, *yes*! but I sullenly complied with him, and from that month

lost all the little Spirits and Activity of mind, which I had hitherto retained. I will not tire you with the Detail.[77]

The details of those final tragic months in Malta may be gleaned from the notebooks. It is obvious that S.T.C., from mid-April onwards, underwent a shockingly rapid decline. News arrived of the death of John Tobin, the dramatist, whom S.T.C. had liked and esteemed and, much more distressingly, of Robert Allen. Poor Allen, who had lost his young wife after a long illness, had subsequently gone to Portugal as Assistant Surgeon to the Second Royals. Across S.T.C.'s inner vision now flashed a kaleidoscope of memories: Christ's Hospital, kindnesses to Comberbache, gifts of tea and cash and sugar and tearful visits of brotherly affection, wild undergraduate laughter, negus and revelry:

O when we are young we lament for Death only by sympathy or with the *general* feeling for which we grieve for Misfortune / . . . but there comes a time, (and this year is the time that it has come to me) when we lament for Death, as *Death*, when it is felt for itself . . . Then comes the grave-stone into the Heart.[78]

He sank ever deeper into a Lethe of opiates and brandy; mourning, above all else, his wasted genius, his "sense of stifled Power."[79] Then, appalled by a sudden flashing revelation of the prospect before him, he gave a shriek:

O this is that which made poor Henderson, Collins, Boyce, &c &c &c— *Sots!*—awful Thought—O it is horrid!—Die, my Soul, die!—Suicide— rather than this, the worst state of Degradation! It is less a suicide![80]

27 June 1805: Malta.

To God.
Thou who the weak and bruised never breakest,
Nor ever triumph in the Yielding seekest /
Pity my weak estate, o now or never /
I ever yet was weak, and now more weak than ever.
S.T.C.—The Fish gasps on

the glittering mud, the mud of this once full stream, now only moist enough to be glittering mud / the tide will flow back, time enough to lift me up with straws & withered sticks and bear me down into the ocean. O me! that being what I have been I should be what I am!—[81]

How shall I plead I plead not / I dare mention no good quality, no palliation of the Bad—sure only this, the earnest wish to be better / to be good for goodness' sake without a phantom of Vanity, "without a Daydream of Praise & Admiration" / But finally, it is a Darkness, or a Mercy which I understand not. Yet still the something within cries, Mercy![82]

433

"... IN WHAT MANNER THE ANCYENT MARINERE CAME BACK TO HIS OWN COUNTRY."

(June 1805–October 1806)

THE SUMMER BLAZED more fiercely; S.T.C. declared that the great heat agreed with him. But his moods of wellbeing never lasted long; depression, boils, erotic dreams were soon making him miserable again. His homesickness, his sense of isolation, his desolation, became more unbearable than ever, if such a thing were possible. "It seems as if I should see no more the faces of those whose blessed Countenances are the Light of Life to me."[1] The yearning for return to England was always followed by the desperate realisation: "Yet if I go, whither am I to go?"[2]

Morphine so distorts the moral vision and so erodes all real emotional capacity of its victims that normal criteria cannot be applied when considering their behaviour. In spite of the fact that S.T.C. was now writing to his wife with apparent tenderness—"My dear Sara! . . . be assured, I shall never, never cease to do everything that can make you happy"[3]—he was, simultaneously, privately nursing an almost obsessive determination to separate from her for good and all, once he returned to England.

Divorce was literally unobtainable and in any case S.T.C. would not have sought it, for he firmly believed that marriage was indissoluble; but he did desire a situation whereby both his wife and his friends would accept that a final matrimonial separation had taken place, so far as cohabitation was concerned. Sara would still be his lawful wife, but he need have nothing more to do with her, other than arrange for her to live in as much comfort as he could procure for her. He would retain access to his children.

Fundamentally he could no longer handle any close relationship that could not be sublimated out of all resemblance to harsh reality. As in all cases of morphine reliance, toleration of reality had been forfeited as part of the price paid for toleration of the drug. There is no reality more real than a flesh-and-blood spouse under the same roof; S.T.C.'s intention was to contrive irreversible escape.

Yet, in severing himself from Sara, he knew within his heart that he was severing himself from the one sure, rocklike physical entity in his life. To leave her would be, also, to leave forever Greta Hall, his study, all that was implied for him by the word home. He became increasingly disorientated; insomnia beset him. He walked out late or lay, wretched, in his bed, tormented by the sounds of Maltese hot-weather night-life.

434

". . . in what manner the Ancyent Marinere came back to his own Country."

The many dogs, who slept fitfully all day in meagre patches of shade, revived at night to race about the streets in packs, diverting themselves in combat with the innumerable pigs cooling themselves in the moonlit gutters of Valetta. The impassioned choruses of enraged swine repulsing the frenziedly yapping canine hordes in the square between the Treasury and the Hall of Archives, moved S.T.C. to contemplate composing a *Piggiad*. And, when dawn came and dogs and pigs subsided into quiescence, S.T.C. shudderingly awaited:

> that accursed Reveillee, the horrible Crash, and persevering malignant Torture of the Parade Drum, [that] will attack me, like a party of yelling drinking N.A. Indians attacking a crazy Fort with a tired Garrison.[4]

On September 6 Mr Chapman returned to Malta: "At last!"[5] exclaimed S.T.C., like a man reprieved. He quitted Malta for good on Monday, September 23, at twelve noon and arrived at Syracuse next morning.

He remained there but briefly, staying with the Leckies for just short of a week, leaving for Taormina on September 30. It is probable that the Prima Donna, to whom he had hastened to resume paying his respects, had a part in speeding his departure.

It seems likely that, sometime during this second visit to Syracuse, there occurred the incident which he described later in a notebook entry for October 22, 1808, when he was living at Allan Bank, Grasmere, with the Wordsworths and Sara Hutchinson.

Miss Hutchinson, in middle-age, developed a penchant for large and decidedly aggressive caps. Her only known surviving portrait shows her arrayed in a formidably pugnacious head-piece. It must have been in some similar creation that she appeared on that October morning:

> Astonishing effect of an unbecoming cap on Sara H.—in the strictest sense of the word frightened me and even continues to do so—in a less degree, producing a painful *startle*. Whenever she turned her head suddenly round on me or I mine, and when I force myself to remain looking a while, the effect is perhaps yet more unpleasant, for then it has the distressing character of one of those dreams . . . in which all the features, stature etc. all being altered, the person is still known—and familiar. It is really quite shocking. I am conscious that I have said a great deal too much in the presence of others: I ought to have taken no notice of it *noticeably*, but alone, to have tried to convince Sara how very much I really most unaffectedly and involuntarily suffer. If she believed one tenth part of what is the fact, she would not play these tricks with her angel countenance . . . Gracious Heaven! when I call to mind the heavenly vision of her face which came to me as the Guardian Angel of my innocence and peace of mind at Syracuse, at the bedside of the too fascinating Siren against whose witcheries Ulysses's wax would have proved but a half-protection—poor Cecilia Bertozzoli! . . . I tremble to think what I was at that moment on the very brink of being

435

surprised into by the prejudices of the *shame of sex* as much as by the *force of its ordinary impulses*. And I was saved by that vision, wholly and exclusively by it, and sure I am that nothing on earth but it could at that time have saved me. I may well say saved, for earth could not have contained a more utter wretch than myself. Remorse and the total loss of self-esteem would have been among the strongest knots of the *cords* by which I should have been held. For o! the incalculable importance to the self-dissatisfied spirit to have some one spot of cloudless and fixed sunshine in the memory of conscience.

Although he was ostensibly so eager to return to England, S.T.C., now that the time had arrived, dallied on a circuitous and loitering route. His subsequent excuse for his long delay in getting back was that he had left his return too late in the year for him to take either an overland route through Italy and Germany, or travel direct by sea. But this can scarcely be seen as a viable explanation; the truth was that he dreaded the return as greatly as he desired it and so, in his customary fashion, he procrastinated. He lingered in Sicily during October, sightseeing, making Messina his base. As usual, he spent October 20 in wild lamentation, supposing it to be his birthday. A few days earlier he had made "the melancholy observation"[6] of having a prominent abdomen, apparently the first time that he had noticed this ominous sign of deteriorating condition and fleeing youth.

In many respects a Peter Pan personality, S.T.C. loathed the idea of growing up, let alone of becoming old:

the Truth . . . came upon me . . . under the melancholy dreadful feeling of finding myself to be a *Man*, by a distinct [?progression] from Boyhood, Youth, and "young man"—Dreadful was the feeling—before that Life had flown on so that I had always been a Boy.[7]

Washington Allston, the American painter, in the unfinished portrait for which S.T.C. sat in Rome, caught something of this not quite vanished youth. Allston captured, too, with immense sensitivity, the incredible paradoxical quality of his subject; the tragic loneliness of this amiable genius so far from home, the incurable sense of the comic, veiled by profound melancholy—an imperishable optimist facing almost certain defeat, a mariner inexpressibly weary, yet proudly brave, a battered man-of-war with (to the discerning eye) impressive reserves of fight still left in him.

S.T.C., whose financial situation was by now precarious in the extreme, intended to winter in Naples, as a guest of George Noble, the brother of a Malta acquaintance. Instead, Thomas Russell, a young art dilettante from Exeter and a friend of the Ottery Coleridges, who was touring Italy, invited S.T.C. to accompany him to Rome, all expenses paid. S.T.C. accepted.

Intent upon travelling light, he left all his private papers, manuscripts and part of his wardrobe at Naples, in care of Noble, to whose villa S.T.C. proposed to return before long. But:

> I had not been ten days in Rome before the French Torrent rolled down on Naples—all return was impossible . . . After two months sickening anxiety I received certain tidings that Mr N. had decamped (having admirably out-maneuvred the French) with all my papers and effects; but whether to Malta or Sardinia was not known.[8]

In fact these possessions went with Noble to Messina and subsequently, in all probability, to Stoddart in Malta; it is thought that they were among the books and manuscripts which S.T.C. retrieved from Stoddart, not without difficulty and acrimony, in December 1807.

On May 18, 1806, S.T.C. and Russell left Rome, the advancing French army making it dangerous for them to stay longer. (There is no available evidence to support the oft-quoted statement, allegedly originally made by S.T.C. to Cottle and repeated by Cottle in his *Reminiscences*, that Cardinal Fesch personally warned S.T.C. to leave Italy as soon as possible, because S.T.C. had offended Napoleon by his political articles, and that S.T.C. accordingly quitted Rome in the suite of the Cardinal. On the contrary, everything points to the fact that S.T.C. and Russell left Rome together and proceeded, without any real appearance of hasty flight, to Florence, Pisa and Leghorn. A full month and more elapsed between their departure from Rome and their farewell to Italy.)

S.T.C., towards the close of this tour, entered a period of illness and acute dejection, during which he had undoubted suicidal moods. His inner dread of returning to England overwhelmed him. At Leghorn, in an entry dated June 7 (ominously a Saturday night) he released his feelings in a disjointed notebook confession:

> O my Children, my Children! . . . I could commit Suicide but for you, my Darlings (of Wordsworths—or Sara Hutchinson / that is *passed*—or of remem-bered thoughts to make a Hell of) O me! now racked with pain, now fallen abroad & suffocated with a sense of intolerable Despair / & no other Refuge than Poisons that degrade the Being, while they suspend the torment, and which suspend only to make the Blow fall heavier / . . . I live . . . to die minutely.[9]

And at Pisa, during a night of electric storm, he wished passionately for death (significantly, death in as *spiritual* and unrepugnantly corporeal guise as possible):

> Repeatedly during this night's storm have I desired that I might be taken off, not knowing when or where / but a few moments past a vivid flash passed

437

across me, my nerves thrilled, and I earnestly wished, so help me God! like a love-longing, that it would pass through me!—Death without pain, without degrees, without the possibility of cowardly wishes, or recreant changes of resolve / Death without deformity, or assassin-like self-disorganisation / Death, in which the mind by its *own* wish might seem to have caused its own purpose to be performed, as instantaneously and by an instrument almost as spiritual, as the Wish itself / !—

> Come, come, thou bleak December Wind,
> And blow the dry Leaves from the Tree!
> Flash, like a Love-thought, thro' me, Death
> And take a Life, that wearies me.[10]

Russell and S.T.C. sailed together from Leghorn on June 22 in an American vessel, *Gosport,* her master a Captain Derkheim (again, Cottle gives an incredible version: a tale of a forged American passport and a surreptitious boarding of the ship; S.T.C. disguised as a steward and carrying a basket of vegetables). They were fifty-five days at sea; S.T.C.'s sufferings during the voyage were, he was to claim, unremitting and frightful; from pain, costiveness, loathing of food, insomnia and depression. Both Russell and Derkheim had been "seriously alarmed"[11] for his life.

They entered quarantine at Stangate Creek on August 11, according to S.T.C.'s dating. He finally leaped ashore on to English soil on Sunday afternoon, August 17, at Halstow in Kent, near a "curious little Chapel,"[12] into which he rushed, to offer up fervent thanksgivings for being once more on dry land.

S.T.C. had dreamed of returning from Malta with his debts paid off, with copious material for journalism and literature, with recovered health and freed from drug slavery. Instead he had lost* nine-tenths of his papers and manuscripts, had no more than two or three guineas in his pocket, no decent hat to his head, nor shoes to his feet. He was in worse health and greater servitude to morphine than when he had left England. He had no home to go to.

Stuart, who was on holiday with his family at Margate, offered S.T.C. the temporary use of his own town house. "There are acts of friendship where it is better not to give birth even to the whole of the inward feelings appropriate to them,"[13] wrote S.T.C., in a letter of thanks.

Stuart had been more than generous in advancing money to S.T.C. during his long absence in Malta. In a letter of August 15, S.T.C. had already attempted to express something of what he felt:

---

*So he alleged. It is impossible to avoid the suspicion that "losing manuscripts" was a favoured excuse with him for the non-production of anticipated work.

". . . in what manner the Ancyent Marinere came back to his own Country."

God bless you, my dear Sir! I have yet cheerful Hopes that Heaven will not suffer me to die degraded by any other Debts, than those which it ever has been & ever will be, my joy & pride to pay & still to owe, those of a truly grateful Heart—& to you among the first of those to whom they are due.[14]

Stuart followed up the offer of his town house with an invitation to S.T.C. to join him at Margate. But S.T.C. preferred to remain in London; he was half expecting Wordsworth to arrive in Town, to welcome him back. Meanwhile, he sought refuge with the Lambs.

S.T.C. was no sooner installed in Islington than he commenced lobbying his friends for their support in persuading Sara Coleridge to agree to a separation.

S.T.C. was, understandably, concerned for his reputation, which was by no means secure. He realised that his opium habit had been exposed in certain London circles prior to his departure for Malta; neither could he hope that Ball's circumspection would entirely prevent reports of Coleridgean drug habits in Valetta from leaking back to England. S.T.C. could not afford to add to the stigma of opium-eating the odium of wanton desertion of his wife.

It is significant that, as early as August 22, 1806, S.T.C. had written a letter to Stuart which was, in effect, special pleading on his own behalf. Detailing the long years of domestic strife with Sara Coleridge, S.T.C. blamed "this perpetual Struggle, and endless *heart-wasting*," for all his "irresolution, procrastination, languor, and former detestable habit of poison-taking."[15]

The word "former" should be noted; Stuart (and London) had to be persuaded that S.T.C. had turned over a new leaf. The story must also be spread abroad, diplomatically, that S.T.C.'s failures and transgressions were due solely to an unhappy marriage, rendered thus unhappy by Mrs Coleridge's choleric disposition. Stuart, one of London's leading newspapermen, seemed an excellent choice as recipient of such inside information; he could not be expected to put it in a leading article, but his journalist's instincts might surely be relied upon to see that the story leaked. S.T.C., no mean journalist himself, understood perfectly well the gentle art of planting gossip.

He lacked the nerve to approach Sara direct upon the subject of separation. Instead, he persuaded the Lambs to attempt to persuade Wordsworth and Southey to coax Sara into an agreement to separate.

The Agnus Dei and the Virgin Mary had suffered enough tragic vicissitudes in their own lives to be humbly tolerant of the sins and omissions of others, but they were both fond of Sara Coleridge and, although Mary Lamb wrote at S.T.C.'s request to Wordsworth and Southey on August 28, "anxiously longing . . . [them] to endeavour to bring Mrs C. to consent to a separation,"[16] she almost instantly had serious qualms over the matter.

439

On August 29 she confessed, in a letter to Dorothy Wordsworth, that:

> today ... I think of the letter I received from Mrs Coleridge, telling me, as joyful news, that her husband is arrived, and I feel it very wrong in me even in the remotest degree to do anything to prevent her seeing her husband— she and her husband being the only people who ought to be concerned in the affair.[17]

Dorothy herself balked, at least at this stage, at the notion of the Coleridges finally separating:

> Poor soul! he had a struggle of many years, striving to bring Mrs C. to a change of temper, and something like communion with him in his enjoyments. He is now, I trust, effectually convinced that he has no power of this sort ... If he *can* make use of the knowledge which he has of the utter impossibility of producing powers and qualities of mind which are not in her, or of much changing what is unsuitable to his disposition, I do not think he will be unhappy: I am sure, I think he ought not to be miserable! While he imagined he had anything to hope for, no wonder that his perpetual disappointments made him so! But suppose him once reconciled to that one great want, an utter want of sympathy, I believe he may live in peace and quiet. Mrs C. has many excellent qualities ... she is unremitting in her attention as a nurse to her children, and indeed I believe she would have made an excellent wife to many persons. Coleridge is as little suited for her as she is for him, and I am truly sorry for her.[18]

S.T.C.'s own profound discomfort over the course of action that he was adopting is indicated unmistakably, if obliquely, by a notebook entry made during this 1806 period of residence with the Lambs:

> Let me try—that I may have at least one good thought to alleviate the pang of dying away—to pursue steadily the plan of opening the eyes of the public to the real situation of Needle-workers, and of women in general. Mary Lamb has promised me Facts in abundance.[19]

It was not, surely, "to alleviate the pang of dying away" that he desired to do something to help "women in general," but to alleviate his sense of guilt and remorse towards one woman in particular.

While Mary fed S.T.C. with preliminary facts about distressed needle-women, Charles gave S.T.C. support in quite another context.

Charles Lamb may correctly be described as the first enthusiastic critic of *The Ancient Mariner*. He must often have discussed with S.T.C. the poem and its reception and Wordsworth's subsequent reaction to it and S.T.C., equally, must often have repeated passages from the poem to Lamb, who liked nothing better than to hear Col recite his own compositions. In that small household in Islington there was now hammered out one of the most tremendous and moving stanzas of the poem; the coda, as it were, to S.T.C.'s own voyaging.

The first draft of this revised draft of the close of the third part of *The Ancient Mariner* is given in S.T.C.'s notebook (as an entry for October 1806):

> With never a whisper on the main
> Off shot the spectre ship:
> And stifled words & groans of pain
> Mix'd on each murmuring lip /
> We look'd round & we look'd up
> And Fear at our hearts as at a Cup
>   The Life-blood seem'd to sip
> The Sky was dull & dark the Night,
> The Helmsman's Face by his lamp gleam'd bright,
>   From the Sails the Dew did drip /
> Till clomb above the Eastern Bar
> The horned moon, with one bright Star
>   Within its nether Tip.
> One after one, by the Star-dogg'd moon,
>   &—[20]

These lines were further worked through to the final draft (quoted on p. 409), which first appeared in 1817—lines which shudder with a blood-chilled note of agonised apprehension. Neither did that other tremendous passage of terror—

> With sloping masts and dipping prow,
> As who pursued with yell and blow,
> Still treads the shadow of his foe,
> And forward bends his head ...[21]

appear until the 1817 edition. The gloss, or prose commentary, with its doom-laden, Bunyanesque strophes, also made its first appearance then.

This does not mean that these additions were not written (perhaps long) before 1817 (as were the lines first worked upon at Lamb's, in 1806). It does mean that these additions were post-Malta.

Prior to Malta S.T.C. was not capable of writing them; he had not, until Malta, had the knowledge of that degree of fear.

The notebooks reveal how essential a part the opium-haunted, dreadful voyage to Malta and the torments in the sky-chamber played in S.T.C.'s subsequent revisions to *The Ancient Mariner*. True, he had, with incredible gifts of prophecy, written the main body of the poem five years before he sailed for Malta under an opium curse; the inspired improvements that he was to make to the poem after Malta substantiate, as it were, the anticipatory insights of the first version of the poem.

PART FIVE

Alone on a Wide Sea

Alone, alone, all all alone
Alone on the wide wide Sea;
And Christ would take no pity on
My soul in agony.

The many men so beautiful,
And they all dead did lie,
And a million million slimy things
Liv'd on—and so did I.

The Ancient Mariner IV (1798).

INTERLUDE:

PORTRAITURE

DE QUINCEY'S DESCRIPTION of S.T.C. as he appeared in 1807:

he seemed to be five feet eight inches (he was in reality about an inch and a half taller) ... His person was broad and full, and tended even to corpulence; his complexion was fair ... his eyes were large and soft in their expression, and it was by the peculiar appearance of haze or dreaminess which mixed with their light that I recognised my object. This was Coleridge; I examined him steadily for a moment or more, and it struck me he neither saw myself, nor any other object in the street. He was in a deep reverie.

Tait's Magazine I–II (1834–5)

Southey introduced Coleridge to Madame de Staël in October 1813. He was one of the very few people with whom she, for a change, could not get a word in edgeways:

"Pourtant, pour Monsieur Coleridge, il est tout à fait un monologue!"

Southey *Letters* ii, 332n.

S.T.C. upon himself as a monologue:

There are two sorts of talkative fellows whom it would be injurious to confound / & I, S. T. Coleridge, am the latter. The first sort is of those who use five hundred words more than needs to express an idea—that is not my case—few men, I will be bold to say, put more meaning into their words than I or choose them more deliberately and discriminatingly. The second sort is of those who use five hundred more ideas, images, reasons &c than there is any need to arrive at their object / till the only object arrived at is that the mind's eye of the bystander is dazzled with colours succeeding so rapidly as to leave one vague impression that there has been a great Blaze of colours all about something. Now this is my case —& a grievous fault it is / ... to go on from circle to circle till I break against the shore of my Hearer's patience, or have my Concentricles dashed to nothing by a Snore—.

CNB 2372 21.552.

S.T.C. on the subject of lice, picked up by him on the Birmingham to Liverpool coach (familiarly known as "the lousy Liverpool") in February 1812:

Don't spake to henny wun, if u plaze, about them there two Lousses, as I caut on my nek—becaze they may take the *Licence* to zay, has how I has more of the first sillybull in my ed, than the last.

From a letter to the Morgans, CL 854.

CONVERSATIONS WITH THE DEAD

(October 1806–October 1810)

S.T.C. DELAYED FOR over two months before at last summoning the necessary resolve to travel to the Lake Country.

The letters which he sent to Sara Coleridge during that period were affectionate enough and expressed his eagerness to be with her and the children. (His excuses for delay in London ranged from swollen ankles to the necessity of planning a series of lectures. S.T.C. told Sara that he did not think that Providence would enable him to live long enough to put more serious literary work into practice. His best scheme, therefore, was to raise immediate money by lecturing. His private conviction was, almost without doubt, that he could no longer write anything of a sustained nature. Henceforth he must rely upon talk for a livelihood.)[1]

Sara wrote with impatience; she could not understand why Samuel tarried in his return to Keswick. Meanwhile the Wordsworths urged S.T.C. to come to them at Grasmere; but he did not come. William thought of travelling south, to S.T.C., but feared to miss him on the road. All was "distraction," "doubt," and "painful conjectures" at Dove Cottage.[2]

S.T.C. had a desire to see the Wordsworths and not to see them, to resume his old involvement with them and not to resume it, just as he had a desire to be parted from Sara and yet to be reconciled with her. He was no longer a man on firm ground, but a shipwrecked mariner, tossed by waves, carried this way and that by unseen currents.

He had, of course, arrived at a most advanced stage of morphine reliance; his condition was now one of organic psychosis. His body's chemistry was radically altered by his drug, completely orientated to morphine and thus totally disorientated to all else. His world was now the junkie's exclusive world of irrational, irrelevant delusion. The exterior world was no longer viable for S.T.C.; it had become one aching, eternal weariness peopled by the dead; his chief desire was to have as little contact with it as possible:

> I closed my lids, and kept them close,
> And the balls like pulses beat;
> For the sky and the sea, and the sea and the sky
> Lay like a load on my weary eye,
> And the dead were at my feet.[3]

When these dead attempted to resurrect themselves and to grapple with

447

him, pulling him down to them, mouthing their now meaningless messages, S.T.C. either responded by turning his face away, or by opening and shutting his own mouth like a puppet, while a voice, blurting out from the recesses of his social persona's dusty booth, quacked all the old cliché lines dredged up from the debris of the years. Something to say, anything to say by which to extricate himself from talk with the dead: dust to their dust, ashes to their ashes, then to escape back into his private world.

This private world was by no means synonymous with what the outside world called a private life. S.T.C. no longer had that kind of private life; indeed, the more intimately dear to him people, places, thoughts and memories the greater his desire now to reject them, to turn his face from them and to stare instead at the impersonal. The pain and stress of all true association had become unendurable. His private world was one of isolation, delusion, introspection and morphine.

His condition was exceedingly serious and could only continue to deteriorate, as long as he continued without skilled medical assistance. Medical knowledge was limited in S.T.C.'s day; the full effect of drugs upon a victim was not appreciated. Nonetheless, as both De Quincey's history and Gillman's subsequent handling of S.T.C.'s case were to demonstrate, under medical supervision an opium addict's consumption of the drug could be controlled and a measure of effective health and energy restored. (S.T.C.'s predicament was bedevilled by his progressive chronic heart-disease; he was a seriously sick man without the additional complication of drug reliance.)

As is almost invariably the case with a drug-victim (even today) those about S.T.C. insisted upon approaching him and his problems from the standpoint of the perfectly normal and rational, applying to him and his situation criteria which, for him, no longer possessed any validity whatsoever. Classically, the result could only be one of confusion and frustrated disillusionment on the part of the would-be supporters and ultimate withdrawal from the scene by the victim.

It seems that when S.T.C. alighted from the mail-coach at Penrith at the end of October, 1806, (having travelled there, typically, by a circuitous route via Bury St Edmunds and Cambridge), he was more than half intending to proceed to Keswick without attempting to see the Wordsworths. But at Kendal he felt himself drawn by nostalgia in the direction of his erstwhile *döppelganger*, Asra. So he went to seek her and learned that she had left home, but half-an-hour previously, to go to Kendal, there to join the Wordsworths who were leaving the Lake Country to winter at Coleorton, the country home of the Beaumonts. This disappointment drained S.T.C. of what little energy and resolve he possessed; his one sole desire was now to stagger back to Greta Hall, there to collapse in the kennel of his study. He sent a message to the Wordsworths at Kendal, telling them that he was on his way to Keswick. This news alarmed them; they surmised that once back with Sara Coleridge and the Southeys, all S.T.C.'s determination to part from Mrs Coleridge would ebb and he would be lost. The Wordsworths "resolved to see him" at all costs and sent a special messenger to Keswick, bidding S.T.C. to come at once to them in Kendal. This, however, was unnecessary; S.T.C., having made up his mind to go to Keswick, had at once boarded the next coach to Kendal. Upon the evening of Sunday, October 26, S.T.C., at Kendal, installed himself at an inn and sent a messenger to fetch William Wordsworth, who speedily arrived accompanied by Dorothy, Mary and Sara.[4]

"Never," Dorothy told Catherine Clarkson, "did I feel such a shock as at the first sight of him . . . He is utterly changed; and yet sometimes, when he was animated in conversation concerning things removed from him, I saw something of his former self. But never when we were alone with him. He then scarcely ever spoke of anything that concerned him, or us, or our common friends . . . except we forced him to it."

Forced to speak of things which he no longer cared to think about, let alone discuss in conversation, S.T.C. proceeded to declaim in his puppet's voice. The Wordsworths were above all anxious that he should take a firm stand over his marriage. The puppet thereat rattled out all the old phrases; his wife's temper and general tone of feeling were incompatible with an endurable life, and precluded all chance of his ever developing the talents with which his Maker had entrusted him.[5] In short, he must either part from Mrs Coleridge, or die leaving his children destitute.[6]

The Wordsworths listened to this recital with all their old ready sympathy. They assured S.T.C. that, if he parted from Mrs Coleridge, he and his boys would always have a home awaiting them with the Wordsworths. They would all move together into a larger house (Dove Cottage was already bursting at the seams). S.T.C. would regain his tranquillity and thus be enabled to apply himself to "some grand object connected with permanent effects" as Dorothy put it. With their scheme S.T.C. agreed. The Wordsworths then departed for Coleorton and S.T.C. for Keswick.[7]

Here, at Greta Hall, Sara Coleridge and the children were all joyful excitement at the thought of seeing him. Sara scurried round the house collecting extra pillows for his bed (he always demanded several). Derwent gave up his pillow readily, declaring that he was prepared to sleep on straw for his father. Mrs Coleridge laughed and was happy.[8]

S.T.C. arrived; his talk was all of separation. The laughter dissolved into argument, temper and tears.

Sara objected most strongly to the idea of formal, bruited separation. To all intents and purposes she and Samuel were already separated; there had been, and was, gossip on this score (a "buzz"), but so far it had been possible for her to maintain the social fiction that his professional work in London and, more latterly, his health, had necessitated Coleridge's long absences from home. Now he was asking that the world should be informed that he and his wife were formally separating on the grounds of inequality of temper.

At some point in the discussion S.T.C. further informed Sara that the Wordsworths had offered both himself and the boys a home with them and that he had accepted the offer. Against this Sara raised impassioned and far from unreasonable objection. If Samuel wished to reside with the Wordsworths, then let him do so without taking the boys and without announcing the fact to the world at large. To let everyone know that he was leaving her forever to live with the Wordsworths (only fourteen miles distant) and to depart thence with the boys would expose her to malicious gossip that she had not only been a bad wife but also a bad mother. She had been treated most cruelly as it was; why must she be exposed to this additional unkindness?

Talk was pointless. S.T.C. had made up his mind, such as his mind now was. Sara's arguments revealed "an indelicacy and artifice . . . which tho' they did not . . . lessen my anguish, yet made . . . me see . . . without the possibility of a doubt, that mere selfish desire to have a *rank* in life . . . was at the bottom of all. Her temper, her selfishness, her manifest dislike of me (as far as her nature is capable of a *positive* feeling) and her self-encouraged admiration of Southey as a vindictive feeling in which she delights herself as satirizing me &c &c,"[9] he reported ramblingly to Dorothy. Against this warped attitude the unhappy Sara was powerless. On Wednesday, November 15, S.T.C. noted in his pocket-book that the separation had been finally agreed upon.[10] The boys were to go to school as weekly boarders; they would spend their week-ends with him and their holidays with their mother, with whom Sara *fille* would remain. This determined, S.T.C. retired to his room and the consolations of opium.[11]

A few days before Christmas S.T.C. left Keswick for Coleorton, taking Hartley with him. It was arranged that, in the spring, Mrs Coleridge and the children should, with S.T.C., visit Ottery as a social gesture designed to establish that the separation was free from all stigma, save an incompatibility of temper.

The Wordsworths received the news with relief. Dorothy now envisaged a life-saving therapy for S.T.C. Where his wife had failed to help him, the Wordsworths would succeed. Dorothy wrote buoyantly to Lady Beaumont:

> if he is not inclined to manage himself, *we* can manage him, and he will take no harm, while he has not the temptations which variety of company leads him into of taking stimulants to keep him in spirits while talking.

Dorothy also reported that Mrs Coleridge had been "outrageous," but now appeared, from what Coleridge had written to them, to have become tolerably reconciled to the arrangements for separation:

I had a letter from her last week, a strange letter! She wrote just as if all things were going on as usual, and we knew nothing of the intentions of Coleridge. She gives but a very gloomy account of Coleridge's health, but this in her old way, without the least feeling or sense of his sufferings.[12]

Sara Coleridge, knowing her Samuel, must have realised that after all the talk things would in fact go on just the same as usual. She decided, therefore, to make no mention of the proposed formal separation; it would soon be forgotten. The Wordsworths, on the other hand, were determined to make it as well known as possible. When S.T.C. arrived at Coleorton Wordsworth advised him to disclose to all his relations and friends his intention of parting from Mrs Coleridge; otherwise she would never give up the hope of making him retract.[13] To speed the good work, the Wordsworths lost no time in acquainting all their own friends with the news.

There was, as Dorothy called it, a buzz. Everyone was writing about it to everyone else. Southey found himself applied to for confirmation. To Rickman, for instance, he replied rather grimly: "What you have heard of Coleridge is true, he is about to separate from his wife . . . His present scheme is to live with Wordsworth—it is from his idolatry of that family that this had begun . . . I myself, as I have told Coleridge, think it highly fit that the separation should take place, but by no means so that it should ever have been necessary."[14]

That the Wordsworths (and perhaps especially Dorothy) had gradually come to feel themselves involved with Sara Coleridge in a species of tug-of-war over S.T.C. is revealed most clearly in this comment of Dorothy's to Mrs Clarkson:

Coleridge often talks of you and wishes to write; but he never writes any letters but of necessity and I believe will not be able to do so till he has seen Mrs Coleridge again and parted from her for ever—by for ever I mean made it public and taken up his home elsewhere. It is his wish that she should be in such a state of mind as to be able to visit her in a friendly way.[15]

The Wordsworths were soon disillusioned about their supposed ability to be able to save S.T.C. from "stimulants."

Over the New Year he had seemed cheerful and improved; William read to the assembled company his now completed *Poem on the Growth of an Individual Mind* (subsequently entitled *The Prelude*) and S.T.C., to whom the poem was dedicated, was so moved by it that he succeeded in composing a quite excellent short poem in reply. But this recovery did not last. William's masterpiece had the result, soon, of flooding S.T.C. with new remorse at the thought of his own tragic failure, while envious resentment of William's prowess as a poet further added to Esteesian distress.

Not only was S.T.C. jealous of William the poet; he was becoming increasingly jealous of William the man. S.T.C. had arrived at Coleorton hoping for and indeed expecting the loving society of Asra. He seemed to have forgotten the letter that Sara Hutchinson had sent him before his departure to Malta. Miss Hutchinson, however, had lost all desire to play *döppelganger* to S.T.C. The notebooks for this period at Coleorton abound with despairing comments that confirm that she now found highly repugnant S.T.C.'s constant importuning for a love which she could not give. She did her best to avoid finding herself alone with him; she avoided his touch and even his gaze.

S.T.C.'s notebook analysis of the situation was both penetrating and despairing:

> You never *sate* near me ten minutes in your life without showing a restlessness and a thought of *going*, etc.—for at least five minutes out of the ten. Some things incomprehensible to me in Sara's feelings concerning me and her evidently greater pleasure in gazing on William, supposing a real preference of love to me. But how much her love is Pity? Humane Dread of inflicting Anguish? Dignified sense of consistency and faith?[16]

Sara Hutchinson had now become very much a member of the Wordsworth household. There existed a warm mutual attachment of esteem and affection between herself and William (the Master, as the ladies of his household always called him: themselves they invariably spoke of as "we females"). S.T.C. had long been jealous of Asra's obvious fondness of William, and now, at Coleorton, he began to watch the couple with a newly attentive and increasingly suspicious eye.

It seems that he voiced some complaint of Asra's coolness towards him, not in discussion of the matter with her, but with William who, apparently, responded by telling S.T.C. bluntly that it was neither becoming for Miss Hutchinson to make open expressions of love for S.T.C. nor reasonable of S.T.C. to demand that she should. This prompted an hysterical notebook outburst from S.T.C. (in the form of Latin verse addressed to William):

> Dost thou command me to endure Asra's neglect and look on my Asra's averted eyes? And to know that she is false & cruel who was always so dear to me and always will be? . . . Ah, let him perish who can make use of reasoning in love! Ah let him perish who loves other than utterly! . . . What is and is not becoming, let those judge whose minds are sound . . . Asra . . . lives, forgetful of me.[17]

Balked in his attempts to thrust his substanceless hopeless passion upon Sara Hutchinson, S.T.C. grew more and more dejected and distracted until, at last, he became convinced that he had seen her and William Wordsworth in bed together. The notebook burst into frenzied wails of anguish:

O that miserable Saturday morning! The thunder-cloud had long been gathering, and I had been now gazing, and now averting my eye from it, with anxious fears, of which I scarcely dared to be conscious. But *then* was the first Thunder-peal!

But a minute and a half with *me*—and all that time evidently *restless* & going. An hour and more with [W.W.] & *in bed*—O agony! & yet even . . .[18]

(Here two pages have been cut out of the notebook.)

Coleridge's friendship with Wordsworth was now completely jeopardised. It could only be a matter of time before the cleavage surfaced. William certainly noticed S.T.C.'s change in manner and was deeply hurt by it.

George Coleridge had written suggesting that S.T.C. might contemplate settling with his family at Ottery. George, of course, knew nothing of the impending marital separation when he made this proposal. After much anguished consideration S.T.C. decided to accept it; the more mileage now placed between himself and the Wordsworths, the better[19] (it should be noted that he continued to give the Wordsworths the impression that his intention was to live with them).

In writing to tell George that he was prepared to return to live at Ottery S.T.C. also confessed that he proposed to separate from his wife. He added that he hoped, before the separation was made final, to bring Sara and the children to Ottery for a visit.

This letter appalled the Ottery Coleridges. George sent S.T.C. an agitated reply making it abundantly clear that S.T.C. and his family would not be received at Ottery.

George's letter was written on April 6 but it was not read by S.T.C. until June 6, by which time Sara Coleridge and the children, together with S.T.C., were assembled as guests of Tom Poole at Nether Stowey, as a first leg on the anticipated journey to Ottery. George's letter had been in S.T.C.'s possession for several weeks before he had opened it (S.T.C. had now fallen into the habit of leaving letters unopened and unanswered for weeks, sometimes months, on end).

S.T.C., upon at last reading George's letter, was furiously hurt and upset by the contents. Sara maintained her poise, but must privately have been much dashed; while the children asked awkward questions about why they were not now going to visit their "Father's Mamma?"[20] They were told, as was Poole, that illness prevented the visit. To the Wordsworths S.T.C. wrote that he had neglected telling his brothers of his intention of visiting them and so they had all gone to a watering-place.[21]

Sara and the children remained at Stowey until July 30; nothing was said about the separation. Another guest staying in the house at the time, a young naturalist, found Sara a "quiet, unaffected, pleasant lady," perhaps made a little "uncomfortable by the habits of a man of learning."[22]

After Sara and the family had returned to Bristol S.T.C. lingered with

Poole until mid-September. Poole noted that his old friend's health was weaker than formerly and his procrastination increased. "The tide of life which gives joy does not exist," sighed Poole. He did all he could to urge S.T.C. to exert himself in using the great gifts with which he had been endowed; S.T.C. miserably scribbled his response to this on a piece of old torn envelope:

> "Let Eagle bid the Tortoise sunward soar,
>   As Vainly Strength speaks to a broken Mind!"[23]

His notebook entries read despairingly:

> My path becomes daily more rugged and mazy, a cloud dwells upon my eyes, my heart is sick, and hope is dead & yet the deep Yearning will not die, but lives & grows as in a charnel house—and all my Vitals are possessed by an unremitting Poison.[24]

Yearning for opium and yearning for Asra had become inextricably entwined. The memory of her in bed with William, though doubtless founded upon delusion, was entirely real for S.T.C. and it haunted him and hounded him incessantly:

> O agony! O the vision of that Saturday Morning—of the Bed /—O cruel! is he not beloved, adored by two—& two such Beings—/ and must I not be beloved *near* him except as a Satellite? . . . O No! no! no! no! he does not—. . . he does not love, he *would* not love, it is not the voice, not the duty of *his* nature, to love *any* being as I love you . . . I alone love you so devotedly, & therefore, therefore, love me, Sara! Sara! love me!
>   Awakened from a dream of Tears, & anguish of involuntary Jealousy, ½ past 2 / Sept. 13, 1807.[25]

Nonetheless, when he rejoined Sara Coleridge in Bristol, she found him "in such excellent health and improved looks, I thought of days 'lang syne' and hoped and prayed it might continue,"[26] she told Poole. It did not; he grew ill again, although husband and wife remained together for another three weeks. She then returned to Keswick with the three children and chaperoned by De Quincey.

The celebrated separation was becoming a subject of some embarrassment to the Wordsworths. They had bruited it with enthusiasm, only to see the Coleridges spend a good part of the summer together, apparently quite amiably. Now, with winter approaching and "Coleridge not knowing how to manage with the Boys or where to place them," Sara was returning to Greta Hall with all her children as though positively no separation agreement had been drawn up at all.

From this autumn onward S.T.C., it seems, ceased telling his friends that he proposed separating from his wife; Dorothy complained that he lacked "the resolution to persist in declaring it." Sara Coleridge, visiting at Grasmere with her children on the way back to Keswick, was tackled on the subject by Dorothy and Mary; Sara retorted flippantly: "Well, he may stay away if he likes I care nothing about it if he will not talk of it." Dorothy, defeated, henceforth changed her tune: "Of course, the part that we, and all the friends of both parties, should take is this; to keep silence, and if the subject is ever discussed in our presence, to say we know nothing about it."[27] (This was indeed a policy of shutting the stable door after the horse was out.)

Dorothy's letters reveal that there was much avid correspondence that autumn and winter between herself, Catherine Clarkson and Sara Hutchinson, concerning S.T.C.'s lamentable "irresolution respecting his wife" and his failure to put "it out of her power to torment him any more."

Oddly, Sara Coleridge seemed to be disposed to be more friendly than ever with the Wordsworths (perhaps to prove a point with S.T.C.). Dorothy commented: "if she had not so little feeling I should pity her very much for having been so often put into disagreeable situations." Dorothy seemed to remain unaware that she herself had helped to create these situations.

S.T.C., in London, was about to commence a course of lectures. Dorothy feared that his health would suffer from the bustle and fatigue. "I shall be very anxious to hear regularly from him. He had been detained more than a fortnight at Bristol by illness brought on by having got wet after dining out and drinking wine which turned sour upon his stomach." She, at least, still believed his explanations and excuses. Indeed, she still believed in him in every respect:

> The best news contained in his letter was that he had been going on with Christabel, and had written allmost as much as we have already seen, and *re*written his tragedy. If he has no more to do with Mrs C. in the way of discussion, arrangements, or disputes, and comes hither in a mood to continue to compose verses, I shall have yet hopes that he may fulfil the promise of his great endowments, and be a happy man.[28]

Needless to say, none of this writing had been done.

His financial position was at this time a little easier; De Quincey had made S.T.C. an "anonymous" gift of three hundred pounds. Although De Quincey's given reason for doing this was that he entertained an enormous admiration for S.T.C.'s work (which undoubtedly he did), he may well have been motivated to this generosity by his own opium experience. De Quincey could recognise a sufferer who needed urgent help.

Another friend who now came to S.T.C.'s assistance was John Morgan of Bristol, whom S.T.C. had first met in 1795. Morgan had subsequently married Mary Brent, whose sister, Charlotte, made her home with them.

Morgan was a man of large private means and had a deep and warm affection and most sincere admiration for S.T.C., who had stayed at the Morgans' house in Bristol after leaving Nether Stowey in September and saying good-bye to Mrs Coleridge when she had returned to Keswick with the children. Henceforth S.T.C. was to see much of the Morgans.

S.T.C. now settled for several months in London, living a life of intermittent journalism, lecturing, opium, attempts to give up opium, violent withdrawal attacks, hopeless consultations with medical men who could do nothing for him, debts, despair, deception and disintegration. He lodged in the Strand, in the attics above the *Courier* office (Stuart's new paper, part-owned with Street, for which S.T.C. worked). S.T.C. was cared for (somewhat haphazardly it seems) by an old woman named Mrs Bainbridge, to whom he would bawl from his attics when in need of service, she having her dwelling in the subterranean regions of the building.

S.T.C.'s first course of lectures at the Royal Institution commenced on January 15, 1808. This course was not so successful as he had hoped, or perhaps more correctly, as his friends had hoped (the disruptive attacks of illness, the postponements and procrastinations could scarcely have surprised S.T.C. himself). Soon after commencing the lectures he was taken frightfully ill with bowel attacks (possibly he had decided to cut down on his opium during his lectures, with, of course, dire results). Unable to receive visitors, S.T.C. was confined to his bed and the ministrations of Mrs Bainbridge. From this arose a rather delightful incident, which S.T.C. described to Morgan:

> The most flattering Compliment I have received for a long time was from my old woman—During my illness a Mr Lanseer [sic] (an Engraver, I hear ...) called; but of course could not see me ... When a little recovered, seeing his Card among many others I asked the old woman, who is Mr Lanseer (for I had never heard the name before). I am sure I don't know (replies she) but from what he said, I guess, he is a sort of *Methody Preacher* at that Unstitution, where you goes to *spout*, Sir.[29]

The Morgans were now taking the place which had once been reserved in S.T.C.'s heart exclusively for the Wordsworths. S.T.C. carried in his vest pocket locks of hair given him by Mrs Morgan and Miss Brent and small medallions, or lockets, bearing their profiles. It seems that he even went so far as to attempt to recreate an Asra situation, this time involving Charlotte Brent (who had "dear meek eyes," a "sweet chin and mouth, & a general *Darlingness* of Tones, manners, & Person").[30] He flirted with her playfully and, sometime in February 1808, sent her a species of love-letter (probably precisely the same kind of bosom-beating, imploring, despairing missive with which he had once tortured, and woo'd, Asra). Obviously, in this case, it was a highly injudicious step; we find him back-pedalling furiously:

I intreat dear Miss Brent to think of what I wrote as the mere *light-headedness* of a diseased Body, and a heart sore-stricken— ... I love her most dearly! O had I health and youth, and were what I once was—but I played the fool, and cut the throat of my Happiness, of my genius, of my utility, in compliment to the merest phantom of overstrained Honour![31]

The Morgans were now bombarded, as the Wordsworths once had been, with bitter complaints about Sara Coleridge. At this point in time (early 1808) husband and wife were exchanging a remarkable correspondence; he, full of self-pity, wrote long letters assuring her of his imminent death; she, obviously (and understandably) utterly tired of the whole situation, responded in a manner calculated to drive him to near frenzy, as he described to the Morgans:

I wrote her 3 letters, the last of them, almost a farewell to her & to my Children—written with great effort during Pain and desperate weakness, in which I assured her of my forgiveness & begged her's in return for whatever pain I had wilfully caused her—in short, I will venture to say, that that letter would draw Tears down the face of your Servant—this day I received the answer ... 'Lord, how often you are ill! You must be MORE careful about Colds!'[32]

The Morgans, not being disciples of the New Sensibility, were able to handle S.T.C. with compassion wisely tinctured with objectivity. They suggested that he should come to stay with them in Bristol, where he might place himself in the hands of Dr Beddoes. But S.T.C. hesitated at this: "what right ... have [I] to make your House my Hospital?"[33]

But, as he despairingly mused aloud to them, where else could he go?

To Keswick, The *sight* of that Woman would destroy me. To Grasmere?— They are still in their Cottage ... they have not room scarcely for a Cat ... And shall I stay here?—Alas! it is sad, it is very sad.[34]

A poignant episode occurred during that sad springtime. One April evening, at the close of a Coleridge lecture, a lady, who had been seated in the audience, approached the distinguished speaker and introduced herself as Mrs Todd, the former Mary Evans. The polite, right things were said; a social invitation was extended by Mrs Todd to Mr Coleridge and accordingly, a few evenings later, S.T.C. visited her and her husband.

To his horror it rapidly became apparent that Mary's marriage had been an even greater disaster for her than his had been for him. The Todd *ménage*, beneath the social veneer, was clearly that of an ill-matched pair. S.T.C. spent an exhausting evening being polite to an (at all events in the Esteesian view) thoroughly objectionable Fryer Todd* and, upon arriving

---

*Todd subsequently lost his fortune and the home was broken up.

back at his lodgings flung himself down on his bed, where he lay awake weeping for the greater part of the night, haunted by memories and imaginings of what might have been.

S.T.C. was now fundamentally in a state of total social and emotional isolation.

A soliloquy with his notebook for this period speaks volumes of his tragic predicament:

> Ah! dear Book! Sole Confidant of a breaking Heart, whose social nature compels *some* Outlet . . . every generous mind . . . feels its Halfness—And cannot *think* without a Symbol—neither can it *love* without something that is at once to be its Symbol, & its *other half* . . . Hence, I deduce the habit, I have most unconsciously formed, of *writing* my inmost thoughts. I have not a soul on earth to whom I can reveal them—and yet 'I am not God, that I should stand alone' and therefore to you, my passive, yet sole true & kind, friends I reveal them. *Burn you I certainly shall*, when I feel *myself dying*; but in the Faith, that as the Contents of my mortal frame will rise again, so that your contents will rise with me, as a Phoenix from its Pyre of Spice and Perfume.[35]

In March Wordsworth had travelled down to London to see S.T.C., disturbing reports having reached Grasmere about his health. S.T.C. had seemed happy enough to see William and had voiced the resolve of travelling north to take up residence with the Wordsworths as soon as they had moved into a larger house. The friendship with Wordsworth, serene as it now seemed once again to be, seethed under the surface with strange and troubled currents of which William himself knew but little. S.T.C. had never dared to accuse him outright of the bedroom scene with Asra: "that is too sore a point."[36] But the memory of that thunderbolt moment did not leave S.T.C.,; it was seared upon his memory. At midnight on May 12, 1808, S.T.C., led away by opium, brandy and dejection, permitted himself to write a deeply insulting letter to William:

> I for the first time suffered murmurs, and more than murmurs, articulate complaints, to escape from me, relatively to [Wordsworth's] conduct towards me . . . summed up courage and dared tell him how highly I disapproved of his cowardly mock-prudence relatively to his Friends . . . I did not mention the affair of [?Asra] because that is too sore a point and, I am sure, will some how or other occasion him a *public* Pain which will prove the *imprudence* of this over-prudence . . . In a mind so good and wise, what are the causes of it?

There followed a long and incoherent analysis of Wordsworth's character: "High self-opinion pampered in a hot bed of moral intellectual sympathy

... The connection of it in his mind with calculating Foresight, with no pride of intellect that can controll the present feeling." It was a rigmarole of classical drug self-pity, scrawled and erased. But finally came the underlying reason for this long dirge of complaint:

> let but a poem be disliked, and indignation is called forth which had slept or dozed, when his dearest friend was called, or treated as a villain, etc. The day before I wrote to George Coleridge—In short, I have summoned courage ... to give vent to my stifled heart—to let in air upon it! Cruelly have I been treated by almost every one ... but above all by Wordsworth ... Oh God! if it had been foretold me, when ... I ... [urged] him to conclude in marrying [Mary Hutchinson] ... But O! wedded Happiness is the intensest sort of Prosperity, & all Prosperity, I find, hardens the Heart—and happy people become so *very prudent* & far-sighted ... I tremble, lest my own tenderness of Heart, my own disinterested enthusiasm for Others, and eager Spirit of self-sacrifice, should be owing almost wholly to my being and having been, an unfortunate unhappy Man.[37]

The actual letter which S.T.C. sent to Wordsworth has not survived, although the letter to George Coleridge has. It, too, is a wild outpouring of pent-up resentment, pitched in a tone intended to convey that this was to be the last communication made to George by S.T.C., (which, of course, it was not). Neither has Wordsworth's actual letter of reply to S.T.C. survived; it is probable that one was never sent. There do remain, however, two drafts of a reply which William prepared. This reply was remarkably restrained; William did permit himself the perceptive comment that S.T.C.'s letter had obviously come from a man in a lamentably insane state of mind.[38]

In June the Wordsworths moved into their new home, Allan Bank, Grasmere. The house had been built very recently by a Mr Crump (App. II) and the Wordsworths, finding it a frightful eyesore, had not been able to say rude enough things about it. When, however, Mr Crump made it known that he intended letting it William sagely observed that, if there is an offensive house within eyeshot, rather than to have to see it, one should move into it oneself and look out from it. The Wordsworths accordingly moved into Allan Bank.

The house commanded delicious views, but it was at that time a very trying domicile because of the extremely smoky chimneys. As a result everything was always smothered with smuts and Dorothy (in spite of the fact that there were now three servants) complained that she and Mary never stopped cleaning. Sara Hutchinson who, because of poor health, was not permitted to do housework, has left a vivid portrait of Allan Bank, given in a letter written in October 1808:

> you can have no conception of the uncomfortableness, not to say *misery*, of

this House ... not a chimney will draw the Smoke! and one day we could not have a fire except in the Study & then you could not *see* each other. In the rest of the rooms the fire was actually blown out of the Grates—We have at last got the Chimney doctor who has begun his operations in the kitchen ... but I fear it will be an age before they are cured.[39]

To add further to their discomfort the Wordsworths had a painful insufficiency of furniture and carpets for such a large house.

The reason for taking a place of this size had been, of course, that the Wordsworths had expected S.T.C. to live there with them; but time passed, they heard nothing from him and the suspicion began to form in their minds that perhaps it would be better for them if he did not come. Dorothy explained to Mrs Clarkson:

> When we engaged this house it was under the idea that Coleridge, with his two Boys would come and live with us ... We do not, however, now think that Coleridge will have the resolution to put this plan in practice; nor do we now even think it would be prudent for us to consent to it, C. having been so very unsteady in all things since his return to England ... we had long experience at Coleorton that it was not in our power to make him happy; and his irresolute conduct since, has almost confirmed our fears that it will never be otherwise; therefore we should be more disposed to hesitation; and fear, of having our domestic quiet disturbed.[40]

However, S.T.C. did finally arrive, on Thursday, September 1, 1808. He seemed in unexpectedly good health and spirits and announced that he had given up opium: "I left it off all at once."[41] This, of course, was an impossibility, as he soon discovered; nonetheless, with the help of medical supervision, he did succeed in reducing and controlling his consumption of the drug for a while.

He was anxiously determined to work, to keep well, to impress the Wordsworths with his manly resolve.

Hartley and Derwent, now at school at Ambleside, spent their week-ends at Allan Bank during term-time. S.T.C. visited Greta Hall and was given a kind and friendly reception by Mrs Coleridge. He brought Sara *fille* back to Allan Bank with him for a short stay. In tearing high spirits he rollicked and played with the children (of whom there were three of his own and four little Wordsworths, though Catherine, the youngest Wordsworth, was merely a newly arrived infant). Sara Hutchinson remarked that, with the children, S.T.C. made "enough racket for twenty."[42]

At Allan Bank Sara Hutchinson, with something approaching real dedication, became S.T.C.'s amanuensis for the great literary project upon which he embarked in an astonishingly determined attempt to show the Wordsworths (and the world) that he was still to be reckoned with as a literary force. He addressed himself to the task of producing a weekly subscription journal, *The Friend*, which consisted chiefly of essays written by himself.

Without Sara Hutchinson's help he could not possibly have succeeded as he did with this project; it seems that she unstintedly gave him her time and labour in an attempt to compensate for the love which she could not offer him. This situation in part gratified S.T.C.: "He likes to have her about him as his own, as one devoted to him,"[43] observed Dorothy. But the notebooks, with their despairing supplications to Asra, their self-pitying exclamations and impassioned complaints, reveal that Miss Hutchinson's practical and wholehearted demonstration of regard for him was not enough; S.T.C. sought avowals of a kind which she could not give, protestations of feelings which she did not entertain for him. He did not confine these prayers and protestations to the notebooks alone; he "intruded upon . . . and persecuted her" with his attentions.[44] "He harassed and agitated her mind continually, and we saw that he was doing her health perpetual injury,"[45] Dorothy told Catherine Clarkson.

Against the backcloth of this abortive relationship with its melancholy posturings, erosive demoralisation and nervous illness, *The Friend* was produced, most of it dictated by S.T.C. to Miss Hutchinson.

After a vast deal of trouble obtaining subscribers (a task with which all S.T.C.'s friends and acquaintances assisted) and even more time-consuming difficulties with paper, printing, collecting subscription money and so forth, S.T.C. published the first number of *The Friend* on June 1, 1809.

Wordsworth had gloomily remarked that it would be better if S.T.C. were never to succeed in getting the first number out and distributed, since he would, of a certainty, never carry the project further than a few issues and failure of this kind could only be injurious to him; but upon this occasion Wordsworth was misplaced in his pessimism. S.T.C., aided, encouraged and goaded by Sara Hutchinson, produced *The Friend* (with incredible regularity considering the nature of the writing and the practical difficulties) for ten months, twenty-seven numbers in all appearing, the last upon March 15, 1810.

By then he had exhausted himself. Additionally, he was reduced to despair by the stark realisation that *The Friend* was not going to reward him financially for his labour any better than had *The Watchman*, twelve years previously.

S.T.C. relapsed into dejection and huge quantities of opium. Sara Hutchinson attempted not only to spur him on to continuation with *The Friend*, but also, it seems, to restrain him from the drug. The inevitable resulted; S.T.C. quarrelled with her.

By February, 1810, Sara had decided to leave Allan Bank. Her brother, Tom, together with her cousin, John Monkhouse, had taken a farm in Radnorshire and for some time past it had been her plan to pay them a long visit as soon as *The Friend* would permit. Probably because she was aware that S.T.C. would attempt to prevent her leaving, Sara departed from Grasmere abruptly, surreptitiously and without even saying good-bye.

S.T.C., cast into the deepest dejection, withdrew himself to his room with his drug and remained there, doing no work, weeping and calling upon his notebook to bear witness to Asra's cruelty. His heart turned against both Dorothy and Mary, for he was convinced (no doubt correctly) that they had aided Sara in her unheralded and swift departure.

The spring weather was beautiful; Dorothy constantly urged S.T.C. to take a walk, to delight in it, but he remained closeted with his opium and despair. Dorothy once more wrote to Mrs Clarkson:

> do not think that it is his love for Sara which has stopped him in his work—do not believe it: his love for her is no more than a fanciful dream—otherwise he would prove it by a desire to make her happy. No! . . . when she stood in the way of other gratifications it was all over.[46]

With Sara Hutchinson gone, there was little temptation for S.T.C. to linger at Allan Bank. He was fond of comfort; the Wordsworths were never greatly concerned with it. Random observations of visitors have survived to provide us with unnerving glimpses of the Wordsworth *ménage*. Sara Coleridge *fille* was to recall of Allan Bank: "Smoke, dirt, irregular Scotchy ways, the mischief of the children, who were chid and cuffed often enough, yet far from kept in good order."[47]

Dorothy herself was to confess to unpapered walls, half-carpeted floors and half-furnished apartments. Southey, after having paid a visit of inspection to Allan Bank, observed that the Wordsworths made but a dolorous appearance in good rooms.

There was now talk of quitting Allan Bank and of living like simple cotters. This would scarcely have appealed to S.T.C. who, as he grew older, found warmth and a certain degree of cossetting essential.

Mrs Sarah Walker (the little Sally Greene whom the Wordsworths employed at Allan Bank as a nursemaid), recalled in later life that the Wordsworths had lived very plainly, but that their friends had always been welcome to visit, so long as they had been prepared to live plainly likewise. This they all were, except "that Mr Coleridge, he was a plague . . . he often wanted different things; roast potatoes and cold meat at supper, for instance, while the Wordsworths only had small basins of new milk from their cow and a loaf of bread."[48]

Dorothy, too, found him tiresome; there was his fire to light, his bed always to be made at unreasonable hours, requests for gruel, toast and water, eggs, a constant demand for attention. In addition there was his opium, his increasing sulky melancholy and withdrawn misery. He was virtually impossible to live with; the household was distressed and distracted by his presence. The scales fell from the eyes of the Wordsworths;

they saw him at last as Sara Coleridge had for so long seen him. Dorothy wrote:

> We have no hope of him—none that he will ever do anything more than he has already done. If he were not under our Roof, he would be just as much the slave of stimulants as ever; and his whole time and thoughts, (except when he is reading and he reads a great deal), are employed in deceiving himself, and seeking to deceive others . . . This Habit pervades all his words and actions, and you feel perpetually new hollowness and emptiness.[49]

Mary was expecting another child within weeks; S.T.C. welcomed this as an excuse to leave. He returned to Greta Hall and Sara Coleridge. There he remained for the next five months.

He was now fully back in the irons of opium and by October he had formed the resolve to go to Edinburgh, there to place himself under medical supervision in a whole-hearted attempt to cure his addiction. At this time the Montagus were visiting Grasmere and, hearing of S.T.C.'s proposed scheme, they suggested as an alternative plan that he should accompany them to London, stay with them and place his case in the hands of their friend and physician, Anthony Carlisle. S.T.C., after some demur, agreed.

Before the Montagus and S.T.C. left for London Wordsworth, speaking from sad personal experience, took it upon himself to persuade Montagu that "mutual dissatisfaction"[50] could be the only result if he attempted to house Coleridge under his own roof. Montagu remained unconvinced; so William bluntly informed him of the real nature of S.T.C.'s habits. "Montagu then perceived that it would be better for C. to have lodgings near him"[51] rather than to reside with him.

This was the Wordsworthian (and no doubt the most reliable) version of the incident.

S.T.C. was at Greta Hall at the time of this conversation and knew nothing of it. He did not arrive back at Allan Bank until October 18, the day of departure for London. Wordsworth was subsequently to claim that he had had no time in which to discuss the matter with S.T.C.

Farewells were said; S.T.C. and the Montagus left Grasmere in good spirits in a chaise. They arrived in London on October 28 and Montagu then imparted to S.T.C. the gist of his conversation with Wordsworth. There exists no exact record of what Montagu said to S.T.C., but surviving letters and Crabb Robinson's diary have preserved some of the more objectionable expressions which S.T.C. was to allege had been used. Montagu explained that Wordsworth had advised him not to have S.T.C. in the house with him, going on to say that "Wordsworth *has commissioned* me to tell you that for years past [you] had been an ABSOLUTE NUISANCE in the Family" and that "he has no Hope of you." According to S.T.C., Montagu also added that Wordsworth had referred to S.T.C. as a "rotten drunkard" who was "rotting out his entrails with intemperance."

This onslaught fell upon S.T.C. like a bombshell: "the moment Montagu had ended his account—O this is cruel! this is *base!*—"[52] burst forth from S.T.C. Furiously angry, with great dignity he instantly walked out of Montagu's house and went to Hudson's Hotel, Covent Garden. Meantime the Morgans, who were now living at Hammersmith, were warned by a friend of Montagu's to be on their guard against S.T.C. Morgan repaired without delay to S.T.C., told him that he had enemies at work blackening his character, and insisted that S.T.C. should at once repair to Hammersmith with him. This S.T.C. did.

When Montagu wrote to the Wordsworths to tell them of S.T.C.'s precipitate departure from his house they did not at first appreciate the extent of the damage that had been done to their relationship with S.T.C. By degrees, however, it transpired that S.T.C. regarded the friendship as over. In his opinion Wordsworth had behaved traitorously.

Wordsworth was insistent that, though he had spoken to Montagu about S.T.C.'s habits, it had been simply to prevent an intimacy which he knew could only have resulted in painful consequences for both parties. He strenuously denied having used any of the phrases attributed to him and he most vehemently denied having commissioned Montagu to pass on home truths to S.T.C. on his behalf. He suggested that S.T.C. himself had invented the alleged objectionable phrases. This S.T.C. equally vehemently denied. Montagu was too vague to be a reliable witness of what had or had not been said.

Viewing the famous quarrel in retrospect it seems reasonable enough that Wordsworth should have deemed it advisable to warn Montagu of S.T.C.'s unsuitability as a member of his household. It seems unlikely that he would have commissioned Montagu to pass on these home truths for him. We must accept that the interview between Montagu and S.T.C. did occur (Montagu made no attempt to deny this) and we may believe that Montagu most indiscreetly repeated Wordsworth's blunt confidences about S.T.C.'s habits, including the fact that Wordsworth no longer had any hope of him. But, bearing in mind S.T.C.'s psychotic condition of delusions and hallucinations, we should be prepared to agree with Wordsworth that S.T.C. had invented (or imagined) at least some of the more sensationally objectionable remarks.

In any case, S.T.C. had been moving towards just such an open breach with Wordsworth ever since the interlude of the Highland tour. Morphine made a rupture between these two men as inevitable as all the other ruptures which had successively destroyed S.T.C.'s loves, friendships and family ties. Ultimately the morphine victim will always find himself alone.

"O GOD SAVE ME ... FROM MYSELF ..."

(November 1810–September 1814)

S.T.C., ON NOVEMBER 3, 1810, barely a week after his traumatic interview with Montagu, flung back his head and howled: "what many circumstances ought to have let me see long ago, the events of the last year, and emphatically of the last month, have now forced me to perceive—no one on earth has ever LOVED me."[1]

This to his notebook. It was the classic cry of the morphine-victim.

To the world at large, and his notebook in particular, S.T.C. lamented his lacerated heart. He repeated again and again the wounding words: "Wordsworth has given me up. *He* has no hope of me—I have been an absolute Nuisance in his family—."[2] Darkly, S.T.C. reminded himself of:

> T. Wedgwood's farewell Prophecy to me, respecting W., which he made me write down, & which no human Eye ever saw—but mine—[3]

What this prophecy was, S.T.C. never disclosed, but in 1810 he seemed to think that it had been fulfilled.

To Poole S.T.C. declared that all former afflictions in his life were "less than Flea-bites" in comparison with the sufferings arising from the difference between himself and Wordsworth.[4]

Over the course of the next two years the quarrel between the two poets became a literary *cause célèbre*. As neither man would communicate direct with the other, mutual friends in turn acted as third party (among them principally Charles Lamb and Crabb Robinson); but these attempts to bring about reconciliation were all in vain.

Although the Wordsworths were at first astonished and baffled by Coleridge's reaction to his interview with Montagu (and professedly surprised by Montagu's indiscretion), by the spring of 1811 they were revealing an intelligent and perceptive understanding of S.T.C.'s behaviour. Dorothy outlined the Wordsworthian standpoint with admirable clarity to Catherine Clarkson. Saying that, were anyone to judge from S.T.C.'s allegations, William had been guilty of the most "atrocious treachery or cruelty," Dorothy continued:

> but what is the sum of all he did? he privately warned a common friend disposed to serve C. . . . that C. had one or two habits which might disturb his tranquillity, he told him what these habits were, and a greater kindness could hardly have been done to C., for it is not fit that he should go into houses

where he is not already known. If he were to be told what was said at Penrith after he had been at Anthony Harrison's, then he might be thankful to William. I am sure we suffered enough on that account and were anxious enough to get him away. I say that at first I was strong with indignation at S.T.C.'s allegations of treachery by William but *that* soon subsided and I was lost in pity for his miserable weakness. It is certainly very unfortunate for William that he should be the person on whom he [S.T.C.] has to charge his neglect of duty—but to Coleridge the difference is nothing, for if this had not happened there would have been somebody else on whom to cast the blame. William . . . would not write to C. himself as he had not communicated his displeasure to him . . . If he seek an explanation William will be ready to give it, but I think it is more likely that his fancies will die away of themselves—Poor creature! unhappy as he makes others how much more unhappy is he himself![5]

In a letter of a few weeks later Dorothy added:

It has been misery enough, God knows, to me to see the truths which I now see. Long did we hope against experience and reason; but now I have no hope, if he continues as he is. Nothing but Time producing a total change in him can ever make him a being of much use to mankind in general, or of the least comfort to his Friends . . . I . . . grieve at the waste and prostitution of his fine genius, at the sullying and perverting of what is lovely and tender in human sympathies, and noble and generous . . . I grieve whenever I think of him.[6]

S.T.C., following upon his initial trauma of the interview with Montagu, seems to have lost himself in opium. He abandoned the scheme of consulting Dr Carlisle (on the grounds of the latter's professional indiscretion; however, according to Southey, Carlisle had found S.T.C.'s case "utterly hopeless"),[7] and spoke of becoming, instead, the patient of John Abernethy, but failed so to do. For some weeks S.T.C. wrote to no one and did nothing; there was "a suspension of all conduct"[8] on his part; he was, as he told Godwin, in "a very low way."[9] During this period of nihility S.T.C. was with the Morgans, at Hammersmith; but, true to junkie form, he fled from that refuge at the end of December, after unspecified trouble (probably the attempts of the Morgans to wrest him from his opium).[10] A letter from S.T.C. to the Morgans, written on December 21, 1810, is significantly revealing:

My dear Friends,
    I am at present at Brown's Coffee House, Mitre Court, Fleet Street: my Objects are, to settle something by which I can secure a certain sum weekly, sufficient for Lodging, Maintenance, and Physician's Fees—and in the mean time to look out for a suitable Place near Gray's Inn [in order to become a patient of Abernethy] . . . For indeed, it is not only useless, but unkind and

ungrateful to you & all who love me, to trifle on any longer: depressing your
spirits, and in spite of myself gradually alienating your esteem & chilling
your affection towards me . . . Dear dear Mary! dearest Charlotte!—I entreat
you to believe me, that if at any time my manner toward you has appeared
unlike myself, this has arisen wholly either from a sense of Self-dissatisfaction,
or from the apprehension of having given you offence—for at no time and
on no occasion did I ever see or imagine any thing in your behaviour which
did not awaken the purest and most affectionate Esteem & . . . the sincerest
Gratitude. Indeed, indeed, my affection is both deep and strong toward you:
& such too that I am proud of it—

> And looking t'ward Heaven, that bends above you,
> Full oft I bless the lot, that made me love you!—[11]

For much of the period between Sunday, October 28, 1810, the date
upon which he walked out of Montagu's house in Frith Street, Soho, and
Monday, April 15, 1816, when he arrived upon the doorstep of Dr Gillman's house in Highgate, S.T.C. resided with the Morgans and it would
probably be no exaggeration to say that without their devoted friendship
and support he could not have survived.

S.T.C., describing to Wordsworth (in 1812) how Morgan had come to
his aid at Hudson's Hotel, after the exit from Montagu's, said:

> He came to me instantly . . . and pressed me to leave the Hotel & to come
> home with him—with whom I have been ever since, with exception of a few
> Intervals when from the bitter consciousness of my own infirmities & increas-
> ing inequality of Temper I took lodgings against his will & was always by
> his zealous friendship brought back again.[12]

The kindness, tolerant generosity and selfless devotion of the Morgans
was quite remarkable. S.T.C. sponged on them and lied to them; he made
promises to them and broke them. With them he tried and tried again,
desperately and without avail, to free himself from the bondage of "Old
Blacky, alias Opium."[13] They took his opium from him and did all that
they could to prevent his access to more; but, with the cunning of the
addict, S.T.C. outwitted them. He tricked them and insulted them; he fled
from them; he returned to them. He was undignified and unjust and un-
seemly and must at many times have distressed them greatly and have been
very hard to love; yet they continued to solace, comfort and support him.
S.T.C. was to say of them:

> If it be allowed to call any one on earth, Saviour, Morgan & his Family have
> been my Saviours, Body and Soul.[14]

Between *circa* December 20, 1810, and March 14, 1811, S.T.C. resided,
after leaving Brown's Coffee House, at 34 Southampton Buildings, Chancery Lane. He seems to have done some writing for the *Courier*; he also

devoted considerable time and energy to trying to collect money from dilatory subscribers to the late *Friend.*

S.T.C.'s fighting spirit had now reasserted itself. In what seems to have been a brave Cavalier gesture in the face of threatening total defeat he had "his hair dressed and powdered every day," behaved "very chearful" and looked "like Bacchus, Bacchus ever sleek and young."[15] The Wordsworths, receiving reports of these things from the Montagus and the Lambs, waxed indignant. "We hear nothing better of poor dear Coleridge than that he has his hair dressed and powdered," Dorothy told Mrs Clarkson, adding: "One thing is certain, that he is in great want of money."[16] William stated that S.T.C.'s wearing of powder was "proof positive"[17] that he could not be suffering any real pain of mind from the Montagu affair.

S.T.C.'s precarious, albeit courageous attempt at independence, was shattered in February of the New Year, 1811, by the news of George Burnett's wretched death as a pauper in the Marylebone Infirmary. For months prior to his death Burnett, virtually starving, had survived by writing begging-letters: Lamb, Southey, Crabb Robinson and Rickman had been among those who had assisted him. Shortly before his death he had once more applied to the kind-hearted Lambs; Charles on this occasion had been obliged to refuse help, pointing out that Burnett had not long since "received relief from him, with a promise not to apply again for six months."[18]

The news of Burnett's death so upset Mary Lamb that she suffered one of her attacks of insanity. For S.T.C., too, the event spelled fresh disaster, triggering an inevitable sequence of "incurable depression of Spirits, Brooding, Indolence, Despondence, thence Pains & nightly Horrors, & thence the Devil & all his Imps."[19] As a result, on March 14, S.T.C. decided to return to the Morgans: "I shall put myself in the Hammersmith Stage this evening—as I am not fit to be in Lodgings by myself."[20]

By May S.T.C. had recovered sufficiently to resume his journalism. Between May 7 and September 27 of that year he contributed some fifty or so political articles to the *Courier.*

Following the reappointment of the Duke of York as Commander-in-Chief of the Army, S.T.C. wrote a piece strongly criticising the appointment. Despite some editorial hesitation, the article appeared in the *Courier* for July 5. It was suppressed by the Treasury after some ten thousand copies had been run off.

Stuart's compliance with the Treasury in this matter so incensed S.T.C. that he tried to find employment with *The Times* instead.[21] When work for *The Times* did not materialise, S.T.C. (temporarily) withdrew from journalism as protest against Stuart.[22]

We now enter the vexed and paradoxical territory of S.T.C.'s integrity. On the one hand (above all within the pages of the notebooks) we see an S.T.C. given to perpetual probing enquiry and analysis, constantly reasoning, testing, involved in tireless endeavour to expose the very essence of whatever subject he had in hand. He was content neither with outward appearances nor prevalent theories. His was a profoundly penetrating, subtly original, and above all synthesised mind. The discovery and establishment of the truth stood for him as intellectual activity of paramount importance. His genuine attachment to truth, his horror of falsity, were essential cornerstones of his ingrained Christianity.

On the other hand we see an S.T.C. who, during his lifetime, earned a reputation for hopeless unreliability in both word and deed and who was a recognised plagiarist. Today Coleridge's plagiarisms stand exposed not only extensively but also in great detail.

In the autumn of 1811, S.T.C. gave a course of lectures which not only tell us much about him as a plagiarist but may help us to understand something of the insurmountable predicament with which he was confronted.

In all he gave a course of fifteen lectures that autumn in London, on Shakespeare, Milton and the Principles of Poetry. In preparation for these lectures S.T.C. wrote to Crabb Robinson, on November 6, saying that he was very anxious to see a copy of Schlegel's "Werke" (*Vorlesungen*).*

The lectures were delivered on Monday and Thursday evenings, between November 18, 1811, and January 27, 1812, at the London Philosophical Society, Scot's Corporation Hall, Crane Court, Fetter Lane.

Following a lecture on *Romeo and Juliet*† a German member of the audience, a Herr Krusve, introduced himself to S.T.C. and "after some courteous Compliments said, Were it not almost impossible, I must have believed that you had either heard or read my Countryman Schlegel's Lecture on this play . . . the principles, thought, and the very illustrations are so nearly the same." S.T.C. replied that he "had not even heard of these Lectures, nor had indeed seen any work of Schlegel's except a volume of Translations from Spanish Poetry."[23]

The untruth here is blatant.

S.T.C. found it necessary, following these Shakespeare lectures, to write at least one letter (CL 845) defending himself against allegations of plagiarism. Crabb Robinson's comments, given below, provide additional evidence of such allegations.

Robinson, who attended and made notes of the lectures, himself read Schlegel's *Vorlesungen* in February, 1812, and he then remarked that although "Coleridge . . . did not disdain to borrow observations from Schlegel . . . the coincidences between the two lecturers are for the greater part

*The lectures of A. W. von Schlegel (1767–1845) were given in Vienna in 1808. The first two volumes of his *Ueber dramatische Kunst und Litteratur. Vorlesungen* appeared in 1809; the third volume, containing his lectures on Shakespeare, was published late in 1810.
†S.T.C.'s seventh and eighth lectures, given on December 9 and 12 respectively, both dealt with that play.

coincidences merely."[24] The salient phrase of this observation (made by a Coleridge protagonist) is "for the greater part."

There is no doubt that S.T.C. stood in unacknowledged debt to Schlegel, upon whom he had relied for a not inconsiderable substance of these Shakespeare lectures. There were now times, however (and they recurred with ever increasing frequency) when S.T.C.'s condition was such that he was totally incapable of original thought or composition.

In the autumn of 1811, S.T.C.'s financial situation had made it imperative that he should earn money quickly. In mid-October, beset by duns and utter desperation, he had made yet another bolt from the Morgans. The letters (CL 831 and 832) that he wrote to Morgan from Southampton Buildings on this occasion excellently demonstrate morphine's annihilation of the appreciation of truth. It will be noted that the deception here is not of Morgan alone. S.T.C., too, is victim of his own inescapable lying; the most cruel lie of all being that he is inherently incapable of telling a deliberate falsehood:

> on . . . Tuesday Night . . . a letter found me, in addition to one received the day before—It is no odds, what. Suffice it was such as made me desirous not to see you: for I knew, I must either tell you falsehoods, which would answer no end, could I have endured to tell a deliberate falsehood—& if I had told you the Truth, it would . . . have made you . . . attempt for me what . . . I could not have received from you— . . . There are not those Beings on earth, who can truly say that having professed affection for them, I ever either did or spoke unkindly or unjustly of them . . . My present distracting difficulties, which have disenabled me from doing what might have alleviated them, I must either get thro', or sink under, as it may happen. Some Consolation— nay, a great Consolation—it is, that they have not fallen on me thro' any Vice, any extravagance, or self-indulgence; but only from having imprudently hoped too highly of men.

This letter (CL 831) concluded tragically: "think of me as one deceased who *had been* your sincere Friend."

The above letter, written on, or about, October 12, was enclosed in a second, written three days later, when S.T.C.'s better self was once more in ascendancy. It was again addressed to Morgan:

> I intreat (and beg you to intreat for me) Mrs Morgan's and Charlotte's forgiveness for the gross disrespect, which my absence & silence render me guilty of . . . I can only palliate it by saying what is the Truth & the whole Truth, that my intentions have not been guilty—that the agitation & distraction of my mind have been the causes—that it was intolerable to me to bring back to your House of Peace & Love a spirit so disquieted.

A post-haste message to Morgan, dispatched during this same period, is brutally exposing:

470

Pray send the books &c: for something I must make up in a hurry—for I have tried in vain to compose anything new. To transcribe is the utmost of my power.[25]

To Stuart S.T.C. had written earlier:

perpetual Struggle, and endless *heart*-wasting . . . turned me away . . . from political and moral disquisition, poetry, and all the flowers & herbs that grow in the Light and Sunshine—to be a Delver in the unwholesome quick-silver mines of abstruse Metaphysics.[26]

"A delver in the unwholesome quick-silver mines" speaks tragic volumes. "Quick-silver" is a particularly subtle and revealing term. It denotes, simultaneously, a short-cut to both intellectual material and financial reward. It indicates also that the substance delved for was not genuine ore, but a poisonous substitute. "Delver," as it is used here, is surely also a derogatory word—"a delver," as opposed to a thinker; a manual labourer who retrieves and brings to the surface that which is already in existence, available material ready to hand, yielding to simple muscular exertion.

In May and June, 1812, S.T.C. lectured on drama at Willis's Rooms, St James's Square, following a visit to Keswick. The Wordsworths had obviously expected that S.T.C. would see them during his stay in the Lake Country, but they had been disappointed. Despite his self-alleged distress brought about by estrangement from Grasmere (S.T.C. was to say that he had experienced such a "fever and irritation about the Wordsworths" that he had wished that he had not left London),[27] he departed from Keswick for the South on March 26 without having made any overtures to William and Dorothy.

In London S.T.C. rejoined the Morgans, who had now moved to a house in Berners Street. S.T.C.'s improved appearance and spirits delighted all his friends in Town. He was temporarily full of hope: "A more favourable Star seems rising for me."[28] His new course of lectures promised well. Gale and Curtis arranged to publish *The Friend* as a volume, upon "the most liberal Terms."[29] "Every thing, my dear! goes on as prosperously as you yourself could wish," he told Sara Coleridge in a letter of April 24.[30]

Wordsworth's arrival in London at the end of that same month changed S.T.C.'s optimism to dramatic dejection. Having heard the hard things that S.T.C. had said about him while at Keswick, Wordsworth was determined that S.T.C. should without delay be confronted by Montagu and himself, with Josiah Wedgwood present as mediator. Alternatively, said Wordsworth, if S.T.C. declined this confrontation he must cease forthwith to discuss the affair.

S.T.C. was outraged by the proposal for confrontation with Montagu:

"I cannot endure . . . to stand a trial with him which of us is a liar."[31] Discussing the matter with Charles Lamb, S.T.C. announced dramatically: "If . . . Montagu solemnly declares to my face that he did not say what I solemnly aver that he did—what must be the consequence, unless I am a more abject Coward than I have hitherto suspected, I need not say."[32]

Wordsworth made it known that all he wanted was to bring the parties for once and for all to a naked and deliberate statement upon the subject. To hope for naked and deliberate statements from S.T.C. was to ask the impossible. The latter sent Wordsworth a lengthy letter on May 4, concluding: "Whatever be the result of this long delayed explanation, I have loved you & your's too long & too deeply to have it in my power to cease to do so."[33] On May 8 Wordsworth called unexpectedly upon Crabb Robinson, asking him to convey a message to S.T.C. that: "He, Wordsworth, denied most positively having ever given to Montagu any commission whatever to say anything as from him, Wordsworth, to Coleridge; that he had said nothing to Montagu with any other than a friendly purpose towards both Coleridge and Montagu." Wordsworth further denied ever having used the phrase "rotten drunkard" (adding the typically Wordsworthian rider that "such an expression he could not, as a man of taste, merely, have made use of"). Neither, claimed Wordsworth, had he ever said that Coleridge had been a nuisance in his family. Finally, he no longer wished to confront Coleridge together with Montagu. Wordsworth was content to leave undetermined the question of who had erred, but "he expected from Coleridge that when he, Wordsworth, had made this declaration, he, Coleridge, would give him credit for the truth of it."[34]

S.T.C. received this message with emotion but no great satisfaction. He kept repeating: "Had Wordsworth *at first* denied using the language employed by Montagu . . . the . . . affair would have been as a cobweb between Wordsworth and my love of him."[35] Nonetheless he agreed to produce "a dry statement" of the assertions of Montagu. This statement was penned and conveyed by Crabb Robinson to Wordsworth, who prepared a lengthy reply, the gist of which was Wordsworth's assurance to S.T.C. that Montagu's statements contained "Absolutely NOTHING of the spirit of the truth."[36] S.T.C. replied with assurances of his faith in Wordsworth's word; the breach between the two men was patched, rather than healed. As S.T.C. confided to Poole, in February 1813:

> the *Feeling*, which I had previous to that moment, when the ¾ths Calumny burst like a Thunder-storm from a blue Sky upon my Soul—after 15 years of such religious, almost superstitious, Idolatry & Self-sacrifice—O no! no! that I fear, never can return.[37]

Sara Coleridge was left to have the last word, also in a letter to Poole:

> I think I may venture to say, there will never more be *that* between them

which was in days of yore—but it has taught C. one useful lesson; that even his dearest & most indulgent friends, even those persons who have been the great means of his self-indulgence, when he comes to live *wholly* with them, are *as* clear-sighted to his failings, & much *less* delicate in speaking of them, than his Wife, who being the Mother of his children, even if she had not the slightest regard for himself, would naturally feel a reluctance to the exposing of his faults.[38]

In August of that same year S.T.C.'s health took a sudden sharp turn for the worse. His right leg, ankle and foot swelled alarmingly and he was confined to bed with a painful oppression in his chest. Robert Gooch, a well-known physician, was called; he diagnosed "Indigestion, & Erysypelatous Inflammation" and prescribed rest. S.T.C. placed his whole general case in Gooch's hands "without the least concealment" and Gooch professed "strong hopes" that S.T.C. would either wholly emancipate himself from opium or, failing that, would bring himself to a regulated use of narcotics that would not very materially affect either his health or longevity. An attempt was accordingly made to diminish S.T.C.'s opium intake, little by little. This attempt, however, met with no success.[39]

The oppression in the chest and swollen limbs were, in fact, a stage in the classical progression of S.T.C.'s rheumatic heart disease. Yet, in spite of this serious illness, S.T.C., in dire need of money once again, was busy re-writing his drama, *Osorio*; henceforth to be known as *Remorse*. A fresh series of lectures was delivered at the Surrey Institution on Tuesday evenings between November 3, 1812 and January 26, 1813.

Shortly after the commencement of this course of lectures S.T.C. received a letter from Josiah Wedgwood, delicately intimating that he wished to discontinue payment of his half of the Wedgwood annuity of one hundred and fifty pounds.

Thomas Wedgwood* in his will, dated June 13, 1805, had settled his portion of the annuity upon S.T.C. for life. This seventy-five pounds (amounting yearly to sixty-five pounds ten shillings after income-tax had been deducted) went to Mrs Coleridge: "it is all she receives for supporting herself, her daughter, and two boys at school:—the boys' expenses amounting to the whole," Southey was to confide to Cottle.[40] Annual payment of the premium upon his life insurance was as much as S.T.C. could otherwise reliably manage. Southey subsidised Mrs Coleridge and Sara *fille*.

As it turned out, S.T.C. was able to send much-needed extra money to his family in the New Year of 1813; *Remorse* was produced at Drury Lane on January 23 and played for twenty consecutive nights (an excellent run, in those days). But fresh troubles pressed thick and fast. In the spring of 1813, Morgan's health began to fail; in the summer of that year he crashed financially.

*He had died during S.T.C.'s absence in Malta.

473

It was now S.T.C.'s turn to give the Morgans assistance, through efforts extending from pawning all his books (in September 1813) to lecturing in Bristol in the late autumn.

Morgan was obliged to find refuge in Ireland in order to escape from his creditors. The house at Berners Street was let; the two ladies took lodgings in Fitzroy Square. S.T.C. departed for Bristol, there to organise lectures and arrange practical help for Morgan among his friends. Writing from Bristol to Mary Morgan on October 25, S.T.C. reported, stoutly: "This Evening, I trust, all will be settled that can be, in this place: & for the future, we will rely on our own efforts."[41]

The first series of (eight) lectures was given in Bristol between October 28 and November 23. The first of a series of four, to be delivered in Clifton, at Mangeon's Hotel, was given on November 10. A second was given seven days later. The two intervening Clifton lectures S.T.C. had to cancel on the grounds of ill-health.

He had contrived, so far, to be a perfect tower of strength to Mary Morgan and her sister. His letters to them reveal an unexpected grasp of financial matters; they are full of sound and shrewd advice. Actual pecuniary assistance was also generously sent: "I doubt not, that I shall be able to supply you regularly with whatever is necessary for your immediate expenses,"[42] S.T.C. told Mary (who was ailing) on November 5.

This was S.T.C. at his bravest and best. But he could not sustain this pitch. November 9 found him penning a midnight, opium-impregnated letter to poor Mary and Charlotte; upbraiding them for not writing to him and for not entertaining a just appreciation of his affection for them. He feared that he had affronted them, feared that they were ill, feared for everything. Five days later he was writing to apologise for his "peevish and querulous letter." He described an illness of frightening sickness and griping. Then, picking up heart again, he went on to practicalities: that they should all lodge together at Clifton, pending Morgan's return, that Charlotte must go to the pawnbroker's and redeem for S.T.C., "40 Books, Watch, Snuff Box, in for 6£—the Duplicates in the Watch Fob of my old whity-coloured Small Clothes."[43]

It is obvious that, although S.T.C. enjoyed, rather than otherwise, the feeling that the sisters now needed his help, his fundamental reliance upon them remained enormous. In spite of this, because they were women he insisted upon addressing them as if they were two enchanting, yet weak-minded, children. His affectionate regard for them was undoubtedly sincere, yet when they failed to accord with his every plan, or meet his every voiced wish, he became petulant and spiteful and made wretched personal digs at their intelligence, accomplishments and sex. The following lines, addressed specifically to Mary but intended for both sisters, is an admirable example:

You write a good-hand, & express yourself naturally & like an unaffected Gentlewoman . . . [not] too blue-stocking fine & correct . . . [in literary style] . . . So help me Conscience! I should always anticipate a more natural Letter, more really wise, & more unaffectedly affecting, the more ill-spelt Words there were in it . . . You yourselves *cannot* write half as sweetly & heart-touchingly, as with *your* thoughts & feelings you would have done, if you had never heard of Grammar, Spelling, &c.—O curse them—at least as far as Women are concerned. The longer I live, the more do I loathe in stomach, & deprecate in Judgement, all, *all* Bluestockingism. The least possible of it implies at least two *Nits*, in one egg a male, in t'other a female—& if not killed, O the sense of the Lady will be *Licence*! Crathmo—crawlo!—[44]

This particular onslaught was because the "Ideas & Intentions" of the sisters had not been "such, as on the whole . . . [he] could have wished them."[45]

By November 25, S.T.C. was back in Fitzroy Square with Mary and Charlotte, all disagreements forgotten, all love again. "The flurry of Joy at seeing me has precluded all conversation that could enable me to settle anything with my Protégées here: and of course all information of my own plans.—Mrs Morgan has been far, far worse than they thought proper to let me know—& out of London she must go immediately, somewhere or other.—By Saturday we shall have decided—,"[46] S.T.C. wrote to Wade.

S.T.C. was due to give a further series of lectures at Bristol, commencing on December 7. It was proposed that he should escort the sisters to Ashley, near Box, some four miles from Bath, settle them there in comfortable lodgings and then proceed himself to Bristol. This was done; Mary and Charlotte were installed at "Mrs Smith's, Grocer."[47] But the journey, far from being a pleasant one, was nightmarish.

S.T.C. was once more resorting to enormous doses of laudanum "besides great quantities of liquor."[48] Every attempt to withdraw from the drug resulted in "a dreadful *falling-abroad* . . . intolerable restlessness & incipient Bewilderment."[49] He was rapidly approaching the brink of total disaster.

At some point on this journey to Ashley it seems that his alarming opium consumption drew remonstrance from the ladies. There was a painful scene; S.T.C. retired further into opium and spirits.[50]

The details of this crucial episode (for such it proved to be) are scanty. To Morgan S.T.C. subsequently hinted at: "excess of cruelty to Mary & Charlotte, when at Box, and both ill—(a vision of Hell to me when I think of it!)."[51] What exact form this cruelty took we can only surmise; remembering his treatment of his wife we must envisage violent outbursts of peevish and furious temper, brutal verbal assault, ranting and raging followed by blank withdrawal into seclusion and more opium, at those very moments when his assistance was most required.

S.T.C., subsequently attempting to placate the sisters through the medium of Morgan, explained: "I know, it will be vain to attempt to per-saude Mrs Morgan, or Charlotte, that a man, whose moral feelings, reason, understanding, and senses are perfectly sane and vigorous, may yet have been *mad*—And yet nothing is more true."[52] And, again:

> I scarce know what to say or bid you to say to Mary or Charlotte—for I can-not, of course, address myself to the reason of Women—& all that common sense, their experience, & their feelings, suggest to them, must be irreversably against me. Nevertheless, strange as it must appear to them & perhaps in-credible, it is still true, that I not only have loved ever, and still do *love* them; but that there never was a moment, in which I would not have shed my very blood for their sakes—At the very worst, I never neglected them but when in an hundred fold degree I was injuring myself. But this I cannot expect women to understand or believe—& must take the alienation of Mary's & Charlotte's esteem & affection among the due punishments of my Crime—[53]

S.T.C. was wrong about Mary and Charlotte; they continued to give him their esteem and affection. But he was correct in suggesting that his condition now resembled insanity. Subsequently he was to write:

> By the long long Habit of the accursed Poison my Volition (by which I mean the faculty *instrumental* to the Will, and by which alone the Will can realize itself . . .) was compleatly deranged, at times frenzied, dissevered itself from the Will, & became an independent faculty; so that I was perpetually in the state, in which you may have seen paralytic Persons, who attempting to push a step forward in one direction are violently forced round to the opposite.[54]

We have no precise details of S.T.C.'s behaviour at Box, nor at Bath, whence he went from Box. Nonetheless we may accept that his "Volition . . . was compleatly deranged . . . frenzied, dissevered . . . from the Will."

At the Grey Hound, Bath, where he put up *en route* for Bristol, he seems to have experienced a violent crisis which apparently lasted for at least the greater part of a week. On December 8, the day following that scheduled for the first lecture of his new Bristol series, S.T.C. was still at Bath and writing to Wade to blame failure to appear at Bristol in part upon "the passions and pride of Women,"[55] and in part upon a violent cold: "since my arrival at the Grey Hound, Bath, I have been confined to my Bedroom—almost to my Bed.—"[56] This was followed by two lines now heavily inked out in MS (a subsequent censoring by some hand other than his). More was surely disclosed to Wade than the passions and pride of women and a violent cold. We may buttress our surmise with the wild cries which ensued from S.T.C. in conclusion to this letter:

> Pray for my recovery . . . for my infirm wicked Heart, that Christ may medi-ate to the Father to lead me to Christ, & give me a living instead of a reason-ing Faith!—and for my Health as far only as it may be the condition of my Improvement & final Redemption.—

476

The evidence of the letters points to the fact that at Bath S.T.C. underwent a terrifying physical reaction to excesses of opium and alcohol. He was "driven up and down for seven dreadful days by restless Pain, like a Leopard in a Den."[57] "From the Sole of my foot to the Crown of [my h]ead* there was not an Inch in which I was not [contin]ually in torture ... no [sleep] ... visited my Eyelids."[58] "For seven days consecutively I never swallowed a morsel."[59]

Upon his "almost friendless Sick-bed"[60] S.T.C. suffered unspeakably. "The Terrors of the Almighty have been around & against me—."[61]

A Dr Parry was called; he, it turned out, was the father of Charles and Frederick Parry, S.T.C.'s friends at Göttingen. This was pure (and remarkable) coincidence; Parry was "called in by accident (for I was too wild with suffering to direct any thing myself)."[62] S.T.C.'s condition approached dementia: "the anguish & remorse of Mind was worse than the pain of the whole Body.—"[63] He became suicidal: "Such was the direful state of my mind, that ... the razors, penknife, & every possible instrument of Suicide it was found necessary to remove from my room!"[64]

> You have no conception of what my sufferings have been, forced to struggle and struggle in order not to desire a death for which I am not prepared ... O how I have prayed even to loud agony only to be able to pray! O how I have felt the impossibility of any real *goodwill* not born anew from the Word and the Spirit! O I have seen far, far deeper and clearer than I ever saw before the ground of pernicious errors! O I have seen, I have felt that the worst offences are those against our own souls! ... O God save me—save me from myself.[65]

Parry's devoted care restored S.T.C. to a condition in which he was enabled to travel to Bristol by chaise on December 9. At Bristol he stayed with Wade. It was not until April that S.T.C. was able to give a course of six lectures on Milton, *Paradise Lost*, Poetic Taste and, as the sixth lecture, a philosophical analysis of *Don Quixote*.

It was during this period of the lectures that S.T.C. had the correspondence and conversations with Cottle detailed above (pp. 36–41).

S.T.C. was now back upon large daily quantities of laudanum, in spite of all his vows and prayers and the attempts of Wade to restrain him from the drug.† His one desperate wish was for two hundred pounds: "half to send to Mrs Coleridge & half to place myself in a private madhouse, where I could procure nothing but what a Physician thought proper & where a medical attendant could be constantly with me ... then there might be Hope! Now there is none!"[66] Cottle's plan to raise a subscription for S.T.C. was demolished by the remonstrances of Southey (p. 39): "This, Cottle, is

---

*Given in CL as "[my h]eart".
†Lectures for April 29 and May 3 had to be cancelled.

an insanity which none but the Soul's physician can cure. Unquestionably restraint would do for him as much as it did when the Morgans tried it, but I do not see the slightest reason for thinking it would be more permanent."[67]

At last, through the kindness of William Hood, Henry Daniel, a Bristol physician, was called. S.T.C. was bluntly frank with him:

> At his [Daniel's] second call I told him plainly (for I had sculked out the night before and got Laudanum) that while I was in my own power, all would be in vain—I should inevitably cheat & trick him . . . that I must either be removed to a place of confinement, or at all events have a Keeper.[68]

A "strong-bodied but decent, meek, elderly man" was engaged to superintend S.T.C., under the guise of valet. All in Wade's house were forbidden to fetch anything to S.T.C., but by the doctor's order. These measures appeared to work. To Morgan (who had now returned from Ireland and was at Box) S.T.C. reported on May 14, 1814 that:

> Daniel . . . already from 4 & 5 ounces a day [of laudanum] has brought me down to four tea-spoonfuls in the 24 hours—The terror and indefinite craving are gone—& he expects to drop it altogether by the middle of next week . . . Daniel is *sanguine* respecting my total recovery.[69]

S.T.C. declared, of his experiences between November 29, 1813 and May 13, 1814 that:

> I had been crucified, dead, and buried, descended into *Hell*, and am now, I humbly trust, rising again, tho' slowly and gradually.[70]

In spite of every precaution to prevent S.T.C. from obtaining laudanum he continued, with the unbelievable cunning of the addict, to succeed in so doing. His longing to break the habit was passionate, his struggles to do so intense and sincere; but such was the degree of his body's reliance upon morphine that to eschew the drug entirely proved an impossibility. Reading between the lines of letters for this period of May and June, 1814, S.T.C. was still duping his friends, his doctor and even his guard-valet. On June 16, S.T.C. was telling Morgan that, though his laudanum doses were greatly reduced and in vigour of mind and general activity he was much improved, he was nonetheless "subject at times to strange Relapses of Disquietitude" and, on one occasion, became "thoroughly be-belzebubbed."[71]

At length, overcome by remorse for his deception of Wade, S.T.C., sometime between June 16 and 26, bolted from Bristol to the Morgans. To Wade he wrote abjectly (above, p. 40):

> Dear Sir,
>   For I am unworthy to call any good man friend—much less you, whose hospitality and love I have abused . . .[72]

S.T.C. was back with Wade in Bristol by June 29 and under Daniel's care again. He remained at Bristol until mid-September; the desperate struggle against opium once again resumed. "O I have had a new world opened to me, in the infinity of my own Spirit!—Woe be to me, if this last Warning be not taken!" S.T.C. had cried, from his room at the Grey Hound, Bath:

O I have seen, I have felt that the worst offences are those against our own souls! That our souls are infinite in depth, and therefore our sins are infinite, and redeemable only by an infinitely higher infinity; that of the Love of God in Christ Jesus. I have called my soul infinite, but O infinite in the depth of darkness, an infinite craving, an infinite capacity of pain and weakness, and excellent only as being passively capacious of the light from above. Should I recover I will—no—no may God grant me power to struggle to become *not another* but a *better man*—[73]

THE ANCIENT MARINER ESCAPES IN THE PILOT'S BOAT

(September 1814-April 1816)

THERE ARE SOME lives in which a single brief point of intense experience may be seen as the fulcrum of the entire existence of the individual concerned. All that went before was but a prelude to the crucial point; all that follows stems from it.

The seven days and nights of Esteesian agony at the Grey Hound, Bath, formed the culminating point of horror of the long years, stretching from late adolescence to early middle age, during which S.T.C. had become sucked further and ever further into the current of the vortex of morphine-reliance.

He was drawn at last to the brink of the heart of the maëlstrom; he looked into its terrifying depths. "O I have seen far, far deeper and clearer than I ever saw before." "The Terrors of the Almighty have been around & against me."

And S.T.C. swore the great oath of his life: "Should I recover I will"— then calculated resolution changed to humble supplication—"no—no may God grant me power to struggle to become *not another* but a *better man.*"

During the months immediately following crisis point at the Grey Hound S.T.C. made no real progresss in the fight against his drug, but his prayers for "a living instead of a reasoning Faith" became "incessant" and "fervent." He was still inclined to adopt an intellectual approach to religion, as his theological letters to Joseph Cottle amply demonstrate; therein he fluently expounded the logical reasoning which might be applied in illustration of the Trinity as "the grand article of faith, and the foundation of the whole christian system."[1] But it was a very different Esteesee who, in the privacy of his despair, drummed on the gate of Heaven with urgent fists, imploring:

> in agony of Spirit, and for hours together . . . O! only for the merits, for the agonies, for the cross of my blessed Redeemer! For I am nothing, but evil—I can do nothing, but evil! Help, Help!—I believe! help thou my unbelief!—[2]

Before the Grey Hound S.T.C. had looked to what little will-power that he possessed, buttressed by the wisdom of medical men, to save him. After the Grey Hound he still looked to medical men, but his faith in his will-power was virtually gone; instead he sought strength from spiritual sources.

His experience at the Grey Hound had radically changed his whole attitude towards both himself and the way in which he must live his life, (above p. 477):

> O how I have felt the impossibility of any real *good will* not born anew from the Word and the Spirit! . . . our sins are infinite, and redeemable only by . . . the Love of God in Christ Jesus.

This realisation in turn led him to the discovery that:

> the faith, which saves and sanctifies, is . . . a total act of the whole moral being . . . its living sensorium is in the *heart*.[3]

The importance of his seven days' agony was best expressed by S.T.C. in a letter written to Stuart on September 12, 1814:

> Even now, that both in mental & bodily Health I am on the whole better than I have been for at least 12 years, the very Retrospect of what I suffered is such, as leaves me struggling against the immoral Wish to have died at the commencement of my Sufferings . . . We *know* nothing even of others, till we know *ourselves* to be as nothing! . . . From this *Word* of Truth, which the sore Discipline of an almost friendless Sick-bed has compacted into an indwelling Reality; from this article formerly of *speculative* BELIEF, but which Embarrassment, & Grief, and Miserableness and Desertion have *actualized* into *practical* FAITH; I have learnt to counteract Calumny by Self-reproach . . . This is among the salutary effects even of the Dawn of actual Religion on the mind, that we begin to reflect on our Duties to God and to ourselves as permanent Beings, and not to flatter ourselves by a superficial auditing of our negative Duties to our neighbors, or mere Acts in transitu to the transitory. I have too sad an account to settle between my Self that is & has been & my Self that *can* not cease to be, to allow a single Complaint.[4]

S.T.C. had charted a course of redemption for his Ancient Mariner in 1798. It was perhaps scarcely surprising that, when the time came for him to seek redemption himself, he should have followed that same course.

The besetting sin of man was identified by S.T.C. in *The Ancient Mariner* as arrogant self-pride. The shooting of the albatross upon one level of interpretation is certainly a symbolic gesture of that arrogance; there is no arrogance greater than man's assumption that he is superior to, and therefore entitled to destroy, living creatures which he in his overweening, blind pride, supposes to be of less account than himself in the scheme of the Universe (a message that is of immensely greater importance to us today than it was when Coleridge penned it in 1789).

Man, to be redeemed, must first lose his arrogant sense of superiority ("We *know* nothing even of others, till we know *ourselves* to be as nothing!"). The Ancient Mariner lost all his sense of superiority when, overwhelmed with self-disgust, he equated himself with:

> Slimy things [that] did crawl with legs
> Upon the slimy sea.[5]

The next redemptive step, as identified by Coleridge in this poem, is the realisation that there is beauty and Divine significance in everything (even in slimy crawling things), an awareness of the importance of the greatest and the meanest objects in the Universe (of which we are part and which is part of us), from the heavenly bodies in the sky to the plankton in the seas—a realisation which brings an overwhelming sensation of delight and joy.

The experience of discovering this truth of Life and Creation forms the great central passage upon which the entire poem of *The Ancient Mariner* revolves.

After seven days and seven nights of agonised, prayerless awareness of the curse in the eyes of all the dead men lying staring fixedly at him from the deck at his feet, the Ancient Mariner, exhausted, at last looks up and gazes about him. The gloss to the poem tells us:

> In his loneliness and fixedness he yearneth towards the journeying Moon, and the stars that still sojourn, yet still move onward; and everywhere the blue sky belongs to them, and is their appointed rest, and their native country and their own natural homes, which they enter unannounced, as lords that are certainly expected and yet there is a silent joy at their arrival.

The accompanying verse reads:

> The moving Moon went up the sky
>   And no where did abide;
> Softly she was going up
>   And a star or two beside—
>
> Her beams bemocked the sultry main
>   Like April hoar-frost spread;
> But where the Ship's huge shadow lay,
> The charmèd water burnt away
>   A still and awful red.

[By the
light of the
Moon he
beholdeth
God's crea-
tures of the
great calm.]

> Beyond the shadow of the ship
>   I watched the water-snakes:
> They moved in tracks of shining white;
> And when they reared, the elfish light
>   Fell off in hoary flakes.
>
> Within the shadow of the ship
>   I watched their rich attire:
> Blue, glossy green, and velvet black
> They coiled and swam; and every track
>   Was a flash of golden fire.

[Their
beauty and
their
happiness.]
[He blesseth
them in his
heart.]
[The spell
begins to
break.]

O happy living things! no tongue
   Their beauty might declare:
A spring of love gusht from my heart,
   And I blessed them unaware!
Sure my kind saint took pity on me,
   And I blessed them unaware.

The self-same moment I could pray;
   And from my neck so free
The albatross fell off, and sank
   Like lead into the sea.'[6]

(These verses are taken from the version of 1805; the gloss did not appear in print until 1817 (above p. 264); it explicitly underlines Coleridges' intention behind the verses themselves.)

But prayer alone was not sufficient to save the Ancient Mariner; he had further to do penance and to be shrived through confession, thereafter to roam, preaching his message of redemption.[7]

After the Ancient Mariner's vessel had been sunk by the magic agency of the Polar Spirit who "loved the bird that loved the man Who shot him with his bow," the Mariner escaped in a pilot's boat. Upon reaching his native shore: as gloss and verse tell us.

The ancient Mariner earnestly entreateth
the Hermit to shrieve him: and the penance
of life falls on him.

And ever and anon throughout his future
life an agony constraineth him to travel
from land to land;

And to teach by his own example, love
and reverence to all things that God
made and loveth.

I pass, like, night from land to land;
   I have strange power of speech;
The moment that his face I see
I know the man that must hear me;
   To him my tale I teach . . .

Farewell, farewell! But this I tell
   To thee, thou wedding-guest!
He prayeth well who loveth well
   Both man and bird and beast.

He prayeth best who loveth best
   All things both great and small:
For the dear God, who loveth us,
   He made and loveth all.[8]

Like all paramount works of genius, *The Ancient Mariner* was far in advance of its own day. The baffled attitude of its contemporary readers was typified by Mrs Barbauld's complaint that the poem had no moral. To this S.T.C. replied that the poem had too much moral: "the . . . chief fault . . . was the obtrusion of moral sentiment so openly on the reader as a principle or cause of action in a work of such pure imagination."[9]

For today's critics the poem has a "very serious, moral and spiritual bearing upon human life" (above, p. 260). Yet even so late as 1948 Tillyard was able to level the (at that time) perfectly valid criticism at the poem's "rebirth theme" that, *"The Ancient Mariner* is unlike the most satisfying works that render the theme, for instance the *Oresteia* or *Lycidas*, in that the renovation brought about is less powerful than the thing from whose destruction it has sprung . . . the haunting terror of the destructive experience remains the dominant theme of the poem."[10]

Now, almost thirty years later, we see that *The Ancient Mariner* is in every respect a poem for us. The haunting terror of the destructive experience is the dominant theme of the second half of the twentieth century. The Mariner's crime, his guilt, his psychological predicament, strike chords for us which could not sound for Mrs Barbauld. Neither she, nor her contemporaries, had knowledge of the kind of experiences which give our era a nightmare quality and often, it seems, presage engulfing darkness to come. Today, we can understand *The Ancient Mariner* almost too well. Each reader will have his individual response to the central verses of Book IV of the poem; but he will have a response. He cannot possibly dismiss these lines, as Southey did, as "absurd . . . unintelligible."[11]

> Alone, alone, all all alone
> Alone on the wide wide Sea;
> And Christ would take no pity on
> My soul in agony.
>
> The many men so beautiful,
> And they all dead did lie!
> And a million million slimy things
> Lived on—and so did I.
>
> I looked upon the rotting Sea,
> And drew my eyes away;
> I looked upon the ghastly deck,
> And there the dead men lay.
>
> I looked to Heaven, and tried to pray;
> But or ever a prayer had gusht,
> A wicked whisper came and made
> My heart as dry as dust.
>
> I closed my lids and kept them close,
> Till the balls like pulses beat;

> For the sky and the sea, and the sea and the sky
> Lay like a load on my weary eye,
>   And the dead were at my feet.[12]

Had S.T.C. written these lines after, let us say, 1810, we should marvel at the way in which he had succeeded in expressing the essence of his personal predicament and sufferings. Had he written the poem after 1813 we would at once recognise the significance of:

> Seven days, seven nights I saw that
>   curse,
> And yet I could not die.[13]

Yet all this verse quoted above was written in 1798, fifteen years before S.T.C. reached the Grey Hound, Bath, and some four or five years before he had first tasted the haunting terror of his own destructive experience.

The Malta notebooks reveal how closely S.T.C. came to identify himself with his Ancient Mariner. Wordsworth's comment upon the birth of the poem (p. 259) indicates that, from the first, S.T.C. had felt himself to be in remarkable sympathy with both theme and Old Navigator. In short, he had been carried away, composing in a spirit of what may be seen, inexplicably, but not incorrectly, as the *déjà vu*.

Cottle has left us what we may accept as at least the gist of an important conversation with S.T.C. that seems to have taken place in Bristol in the spring of 1814:

> Mr Coleridge ... entered into some observations on his own character ...
> He said that he was naturally very arrogant; that it was his easily besetting sin.[14]

By the autumn of 1803, at the latest, S.T.C. had perceived his full danger from opium. He had contrived to keep his dreadful knowledge private to himself, although both Wordsworth and Sara Coleridge had known the extent of his habit. Neither of them, however, had understood the true nature of it; nor as yet had S.T.C. himself fully comprehended the true horror of his predicament. All parties had firmly believed that deficient will-power alone prevented S.T.C. from breaking the habit. What he had long appreciated (which the others did not) was the fundamental weakness of his personality as a factor beyond his alteration and control. Determined, nonetheless, to make a brave and manly bid to exert his will and vanquish opium or die, S.T.C. had travelled to Malta. During the voyage out he had made an assault upon his drug habit and had fallen back, defeated. By the time he had reached Malta S.T.C. had had degrading and horrible experiences which had done much to erode his natural arrogance:

the Obscene . . . the disgustful . . . the frightful constipation when the dead
Filth *impales* the lower Gut—to weep & sweat & moan for the parturience of
an excrement . . . Sleep a pandemonium of all the shames & miseries of the
past life . . . all huddled together & bronzed with one stormy Light of Terror
& Self-torture / O this is hard, hard, hard! . . . O Great God! Grant me grace
truly to look into myself, & to begin the serious work of Self-amendment
. . . let me live in Truth . . . Have mercy on me, have mercy on me, Father
& God! omnipresent, incomprehensible, who with undeviating Laws eternal
yet carest for the falling of the feather from the Sparrow's Wing.—[15]

In Malta S.T.C.'s attempt to make "one thorough Trial"[16] of abandonment of the drug had failed and he had returned to England an utterly
vanquished man. Thereafter he had slipped steadily down the steep slope
of degradation. To his son, Hartley, he had written in 1808, with complete
sincerity:

my dear, anxiously beloved Child . . . think of God, & what *worms* we all are,
& how likely to be wrong in any case, how sure to be wrong in many.[17]

1808 had seen, too, this strangely moving confession in his notebook:

My inner mind does not justify the Thought, that I possess a Genius.
—My Strength is so very small in proportion to my power . . . and yet, I
think, I must have some *analogon* of Genius; because, among other things,
when I am in company . . . I feel like a Child—nay, rather like an Inhabitant
of another Planet—their very faces all act upon me, sometimes as if they were
Ghosts, but more often as if I were a Ghost, among them—at all times, as if
we were not consubstantial.

ah me![18]

At length S.T.C.'s tragic journey took him to the Grey Hound, with its
cathartic agony, remorse and revelations. From thereon, with progressively
obsessive dedication, S.T.C. followed his course of redemption, prayer,
penance, shriving, preaching.

The essence of his effort was to abandon opium as a crutch and, instead,
to derive support from a living religious faith, "which saves and sanctifies"
(above, p. 481). The saving of his "I-ship," his essential and immortal
self, involved him, of necessity, in one gigantic final bid to free himself from
the bondage of opium.

S.T.C. knew now that he was right in supposing that he must place himself under complete restraint and skilled supervision in some medical institution; this would cost money. In an attempt to earn sufficient to pursue his
goal, S.T.C. took up his pen. Successful professional writing in itself
demanded drug discipline:

Should I have success in my . . . [literary] enterprises as to be able to say—
'for six months to come I am not under the *necessity* of doing any thing!' I
have strong hopes that I should emancipate myself altogether from this most
pitiable Slavery . . . In my present circumstances . . . all I can do is be quite
regular, and never to exceed the smallest dose of Poison that will suffice to
keep me tranquil and capable of literary labour.[19]

S.T.C. outlined his daily routine:

I breakfast every morning before nine—work till one—& walk or read till 3—
thence till Tea time chat or read some lownge-book—or correct what I have
written—from 6 to 8, work again—from 8 to bed time play whist, or the
little mock-billiard, called Bagatelle, & then sup & go to bed.[20]

This routine probably bears a fair relation to the truth, for S.T.C. was
now living with the Morgans again (first at Box, then at Calne in Wiltshire)
and they had sufficient influence over him to see that he kept a steady
regimen.

His domicile with them was one important additional reason why he had
to earn money; it was essential that he should contribute to the slender
finances of the joint household.

From August 1814 onward S.T.C. addressed himself to writing with an
industry that would have been commendable in any author but which, in
the case of a drug-addict (who, in addition, was now seriously sick with
progressive heart-disease) was nothing short of miraculous.

One is speaking, here, of the sheer physical labour and application involved. The question of what S.T.C. was actually producing confronts us
afresh with plagiarism.

In August 1814 he wrote, for *Felix Farley's Bristol Journal*, a series of
essays upon the Fine Arts.* These, to quote from Wellek, "follow the
distinctions drawn in Kant's *Critique of Judgment* at times so closely that
Coleridge takes over Kant's anecdotes and illustrations."[21] These essays
were followed by a project for translation work for Murray (which fell
through chiefly because Murray objected to S.T.C.'s very reasonable stipu-
lated terms), political journalism for Stuart, a volume of S.T.C.'s collected
verse (*Sibylline Leaves*, published 1817), a Dramatic Entertainment, *Zapolya*,
published in 1817 as *A Christmas Tale*, in two parts, the publication of
Christabel, *Kubla Khan* and *The Pains of Sleep* (1816), tentative work on a
contemporary arrangement of *The Beggar's Bush* by Beaumont and Fletcher,
an uncompleted tragedy, the alleged commencement of work on his projected *magnum opus*, at this stage titled *LOGOSOPHIA* (the ultimate
manuscript, *Opus maximum*, still for the most part unpublished, contains
extensive borrowings from Kant and Mendelssohn), and the *Biographia*

On the Principles of General Criticism concerning the Fine Arts

Literaria, containing, in chapters twelve and thirteen, long, literally verbatim quoted passages from Schelling and Maas, as well as sections taken
from S.T.C.'s own earlier writings.

It will be seen from this that the bulk of S.T.C.'s work in these first
years of his renaissance as a literary man was not original writing; he was
either engaged in reassembling, arranging and publishing earlier work of
his own, or in incorporating and borrowing the work of others.

McFarland has put up a far from unconvincing defence for the Coleridge
borrowings: "the very multiplicity of instances [of borrowing]—far more
than at first charged, and by no means as yet all identified—suggests the
explanation, bizarre though it may seem, that we are not faced with
plagiarism, but with nothing less than a mode of composition—composition
by mosaic organization."[22]

It is possible that, during the latter years of his literary life, Coleridge,
liberated from his necessity for large quantities of morphine and much
restored in mental, if not in physical condition, did develop just such an
idiosyncratic technique, employing "borrowings so [to] honeycomb his
work as to form virtually a mode of composition" (to quote McFarland
again). But, in the early period of his attempted re-emergence as a "literary
giant," there can be little doubt that S.T.C.'s borrowings were motivated
by a desperate need to produce a body of work which would earn him quick
money, yet which would be of sufficiently high intellectual calibre to fend
off criticism that opium had destroyed his former powers.* To achieve
this end, S.T.C., his intellectual capacity in truth as hopelessly eroded by
morphine as it ever was, resumed his delving in the German quick-silver
mines.

The struggle to settle the account between "my Self that is & has been
& my Self that *can* not cease to be" now became paralleled with a second,
somewhat more worldly, yet not unworthy aim; that of being able to hold
up his head with pride again, both socially and professionally (fundamentally a different thing from holding up one's head in arrogance):

> I have a great, a gigantic effort to make & I will go through with it or die.
> Gross have been the calumnies concerning me; but enough remains for
> Truth to enforce the necessity of considering all other Things as unimpor-
> tant compared with that of *living them down.*[23]

How intensely S.T.C. desired recapture of his former pre-eminence is
revealed by the comment (made in the New Year of 1816): "From several
causes my literary Reputation has been lately on the increase."[24]

*Mr R. H. Brabant, a Devizes surgeon, was told by S.T.C.: "every year I compose
more slowly and with greater effort;" S.T.C. added, hardly convincingly: "not from
any decrease in the stream of my thoughts . . . but from the increasing difficulty of
satisfying myself."[25]

The work which S.T.C. was publishing did not exactly match this brave statement; the albatross was certainly hoisted aloft again, but as yet at no great altitude; the creaking of his wings might be heard, and he was relying upon borrowed plumes to assist his laboured flight.[26]

The borrowed plumes might be seen by critical observers as scarcely compatible with the aims of a man who was avowedly intent upon saving his immortal soul. Plagiarism is not an edifying pursuit. Yet, in fairness to S.T.C., it is only right to ask ourselves if he, genuinely disorientated from truth by morphine as he was at this period, regarded these unacknowledged borrowings in the same light as we do.

Aware as he was that charges of plagiarism had been made against him, following the lectures, and that similar allegations would probably be repeated after publication of *Biographia Literaria*, S.T.C. went to some lengths in the ninth chapter of that book to defend himself in anticipation of such attacks. To quote McFarland once more, the "curious mixture of frankness and of plain deceit in this passage[27] leads . . . into a veritable labyrinth of paradox."[28] It is precisely from this curious mixture of frankness and plain deceit, this labyrinth of paradox, that S.T.C.'s statements made in his own defence derive their classical features of the self-excuses of an articulate junkie. One moment the feet of the defendant appear firmly on the ground and all is cohesive persuasion; the next, the feet are waving wildly in the air and the defendant's case is, likewise, exposed as farcical. Coleridgean jabberwocky reads well, but it is jabberwocky nonetheless:

Whether a work is the offspring of a man's own spirit, and the product of original thinking, will be discovered by those who are its sole legitimate judges, by better tests than the mere reference to dates.[29]

In the following passage we may (again quoting McFarland) discern both "plausibility and disingenuousness in almost equal proportions:"[30]

Suppose myself & Schlegel . . . nearly equal in powers, of similar pursuits & acquirements, and it is only necessary for both to have mastered the spirit of Kant's Critique of the Judgment to render it morally certain, that writing on the same Subject we should draw the same conclusions by the same trains [of reasoning] from the same principles, write to one purpose & with one spirit.[31]

It is difficult to believe that any man with S.T.C.'s subtlety of intellect could expect this kind of thing to be accepted; that he did may be seen as one more indication of his disorientated grasp of reality.

Yet, appreciating how far morphine had removed him from the realm of

truth, we should be willing to concede at least a spirit of total sincerity to
these lines written in his notebook:

> to have fixed on the partic. instances in which I have really been indebted to
> these [German] Writers would have [been] very hard, if possible, to me who
> read for truth & self-satisfaction, not to make a book, & who always rejoiced
> & was jubilant when I found my own ideas well expressed already by others
> ... & lastly, let me say, because ... I seem to know, that much of the matter
> remains my own, and that the Soul is *mine*. I fear not him for a Critic who
> can confound a Fellow-thinker with a Compiler.[32]

Paraphrasing this, we might say that S.T.C.'s hovering spirit need fear
no critic who can confound an advanced case of morphine-reliance with a
man in his right mind.

To those who insist upon judging S.T.C. according to merits which he no
longer possessed, the sight of this Esteesian albatross struggling, lopsidedly,
to propel himself a few illusory feet into the sphere over which he had
once had effortless mastery will appear as squalidly fraudulent. To those
who find themselves able to understand and sympathise with S.T.C.'s
tragic dilemma, the spectacle of this drug-crippled genius fighting to become air-borne again after years of floundering in the mire will appear both
tragic and valiant.

Coleridge was no insensitive clod who could make a spectacle of himself
without feeling the hard eyes of the crowd bearing upon him. The reverse
was the case. S.T.C. was abnormally sensitive to adverse criticism and
malicious gossip; in 1814 there was much of both.

Whatever the means by which he hoped to achieve his ends, it might
surely be conceded an act of immense courage on S.T.C.'s part to launch
an attack upon recovery of his name and literary reputation. Once his
attempted renaissance had been bruited, every eye was upon him, watching
his every move. It was understood that his goal was regeneration. As nobody understood the true nature of drug reliance, every glimpse of his
relapse into weak indulgence (as his opium habit was considered to be) was
greeted with (as he called it) fresh calumny. No charity was accorded him.
His was a cruel audience, as well as an attentive one.

In November 1815 S.T.C. succumbed to a "sudden and alarming illness"[33] which, lasting for the best part of six weeks, utterly exhausted
and incapacitated him. This must almost certainly have been occasioned
by his heart disease. During this period he wrote to Morgan saying that
he could do nothing in the way of work, but was "Thinking, Planning,
and Resolving to resolve—& praying to be able to execute—."[34]

He recovered: he resumed his struggle. It was now that he wrote to

Brabant saying that, should he have success with his dramatic enterprises, he had strong hopes of emancipating himself from "this most pitiable Slavery, the fetters of which do indeed eat into the Soul."[35]

Here was a man of most remarkable heart. We perceive that he had much in common with his brother Francis, whose gallant conduct at the siege of Seringapatam had won him commendation from Lord Cornwallis "in the presence of the army."[36] The Coleridges were fighters; S.T.C. was as determined and courageous as any. In spite of all set-backs and weaknesses, he staggered to his feet after each defeat, to launch a fresh attack.

The financial assistance which S.T.C. had given the Morgans kept him as impoverished as ever he had been. In January, 1816, the Literary Fund voted him thirty pounds in reply to an application for assistance made on his behalf by Sotheby. The latter also made application to Byron, who sent S.T.C. a hundred pounds and interested himself in publication of *Christabel*. Earlier S.T.C. had received assistance from Gutch and Le Breton, while Hood remained consistently generous in his gestures of help.

During the early months of 1816, S.T.C. was deeply immersed in getting *Sibylline Leaves* and *Biographia Literaria* through the press. At the close of March he went to London to offer his *Christmas Tale* to Covent Garden and, he hoped, to see Byron. S.T.C. had no sooner arrived in London than he was taken desperately ill with another bout of heart disease. He sent to Morgan to come to him:

My heart, or *some part* about it, seems breaking, as if a weight were suspended from it, such is the *bodily feeling*, as far as I can express it by words.[37]

Morgan was with S.T.C. by April 6 and called in "an old acquaintance,"[38] Dr Joseph Adams. To this physician S.T.C. laid bare his opium history and asked if there were any possible chance of a cure; adding, with perfect seriousness, that he was prepared to die in the attempt.

Dr Adams pointed out what S.T.C. already knew; that cure might only be hoped for if S.T.C. were willing to place himself entirely within the care and jurisdiction of a medical man. Dr Adams recommended Mr Gillman, a surgeon, of Highgate. S.T.C. asked Dr Adams to approach Mr Gillman on his behalf. Accordingly, on April 9, Dr Adams took up his pen and commenced a letter of introduction for S.T.C.:

Dear Sir,
A very learned, but in one respect unfortunate gentleman, has applied to me . . .

S.T.C.'s opium bondage was drawing to a close. At Highgate a door would open upon release.

THE KENDAL BLACK DROP

THIS CELEBRATED PREPARATION, a solution of opium in vegetable acids, was popularly supposed, in Coleridge's day, to possess four times the strength of 'common' laudanum; but, according to Robert Christison (the era's foremost expert in medical jurisprudence and toxicology), its strength was greatly exaggerated and he thought it had not more than "twice the strength of laudanum."

The Black Drop was originally an almost exclusively North of England drug, little known beyond the confines of Westmorland and North Lancashire, where it enjoyed a reputation of legendary potency as a "Great Cure-all," acting both as a narcotic in cases of pain or over-excitement and as a stimulant for "drooping energies."

The *Lonsdale Magazine* for March, 1821, refers to it as the "Lancashire Black Drop," in an article culled from another publication called the *Gazette of Health*. According to this article (written by a Dr Cassels), the Black Drop became well known in Lancashire during the latter half of the eighteenth century. He gave two recipes for this early preparation; one a solution of opium in "spirit of wine," the other in vegetable acid.

Neither of these preparations was new. Jones, in *Mysteries of Opium Revealed*, mentioned a solution of opium in vegetable acid very similar to Dr Cassels' second recipe, naming it *laudanum liquidum cydoniacum*. Quincey, in his Dispensatory of 1722, gave the same recipe and added others for tinctures of opium with various aromatics.

The *Lonsdale Magazine* offered its readers a further, improved recipe, using "best Turkey opium dried," saffron and cloves, strong acetic acid and rectified spirit; the mixture to be left to stand for a week.

The claimants to the original recipe for the Black Drop were three in number, all Quakers. The first, John Airey Brathwaite (1758–1810), a Lancashire surgeon, marketed his product under the name of "The Lancashire Genuine Black Drop." It was advertised by him as possessing "in the fullest degree, all the desirable power of opium, in relieving pain, soothing irritation, and procuring repose" while being deprived, "by a chemical process," of all the deleterious effects of laudanum, such as restlessness, headaches, sickness and debility.

The Black Drop, read Dr Brathwaite's advertisement,

is particularly eligible in nervous and spasmodic affections, as pains of the head and stomach, depression of mind, anxiety, and irritability; in the gout, in wounds, inflammation, and mortification; in chronic rheumatism, especially when affecting the teeth and face; in coughs, asthmas, consumptions, and other complaints of the chest, and in the numerous diseases which produce pain and deprivation of sleep.

This preparation is highly concentrated, one drop being nearly equal to four of common laudanum. When a full dose is required for the suspension of a cough, at bedtime, to relieve pain of any description, or to procure sleep, Six or Eight Drops to an adult, and from One to Three Drops to a younger person, in proportion, will be sufficient.

In diseases which are uniformly present—as complaints, and continually painful diseases, Two or Three Drops, or more, may be repeated every four hours during the day, and, if possible, in the night. Sweet wine is the best medium for taking it in general.

If it be exhibited for pain in the stomach and bowels, mint-water will be the proper vehicle; and in the commencement of a fit of asthma, a teaspoonful of ether may be added to a full dose of Black Drop, in simple water. The dose may be gradually increased to any moderate number, Ten, Twenty, Thirty, or Forty Drops, according to the circumstance of the case, and the patient's habit of employing it.

After the death of Dr Brathwaite the recipe and manufacture of the Black Drop passed into the hands of his sister, Margaret (Peggy) Brathwaite who, together with her brother Thomas and his wife, ran an ironmongery business in Kendal and also manufactured chimney-pieces from marble obtained locally in Hawes Wood; this manufactory was carried out at their workshop in Capper Lane. To the manufacture of chimney-pieces they added the Black Drop. Following Margaret Brathwaite's death in 1825 her sister-in-law, now widowed, gave up the ironmongery and chimney-piece trade and relied upon the Black Drop for a very excellent livelihood. Together with her spinster daughter, Hannah, she manufactured the mixture in an atmosphere of well-publicised secrecy; never divulging the ingredients which she used, apart from the all-essential opium, but letting it be known that the brew was simmered for four weeks, during which time it was stirred at dead of night by herself and Miss Hannah, wearing masks, "otherwise the fumes from the heated liquid would seriously impair the complexion". The mixture sold at the then extortionate price of eleven shillings for a small phial of about four ounces, including one shilling duty. It is not surprising to learn that when Mrs Brathwaite died she left her daughter a fortune of at least £10,000.

Miss Hannah carried on the Black Drop business and with accumulating profits, shrewd investments, and frugal living, upon her decease in 1872 left a sum twice as much again.

According to the *Kendal Mercury* (from which the above material about the Brathwaites is drawn) the "original recipe" was deposited in a sealed packet in the hands of Hannah Brathwaite's executors and was rumoured to have been put up for sale by public auction.

In 1802 another Kendal Quakeress, named Ann Todd, had set up business in opposition to the Brathwaites, claiming in an advertisement in the *Lancaster Gazette* that she had "long been in possession of the original recipe for preparing the celebrated Black Drop . . . superior in quality to the article advertised as the Black Drop by a member of the Royal College of Surgeons." She marketed her product at one shilling and sixpence a bottle, about a tenth of the price charged by Dr Brathwaite. Ann Todd continued to sell her rival mixture, which she publicised as "The Genuine Quaker's Black Drop," until her death in 1820. A year later another Quakeress, Hannah Backhouse, put an advertisement in the *Westmorland Gazette* to announce the sale of her "Original Black Drop," claiming that the recipe derived from "a medical practitioner, one of the Society of Friends, who resided at Bishop Auckland, in the county of Durham, upwards of one hundred years ago." Miss Backhouse embellished her advertisement with a view of Kendal Castle; Dr Brathwaite favoured Lancaster Castle as his trademark. There survives no discoverable record of when Miss Backhouse ceased to market her mixture.

We find Coleridge, in a notebook entry for September–October, 1807 (3161 12.22), unearthing a recipe for a solution of opium in quince-juice. He mused: "I guess that the gutta Asiatica or black Drop is=the Laudanum Helmontii Junioris . . . When in Malta, I might have easily tried it with Lemon Juice, instead of Quinces."

Bibliography:

The Brathwaite Will Cause and The History Of The Black Drop. The Black Drop and the Brathwaites—Miss Brathwaite's Will (Reprinted with additions from the Kendal Mercury)—Editorial comments, comp. and ed. J. S. Campbell, December, 1872. (Kendal: Rawson Briggs Lee, "Mercury Office").
Kendal Mercury. Lancaster Gazette. Westmorland Gazette.
CHRISTISON, ROBERT, M.D. *A Treatise on Poisons in relation to Medical Jurisprudence, Physiology, and the Practise of Physic* Edinburgh: 1829.

JOHN HADFIELD

JOHN HADFIELD (not Hatfield, as the *Newgate Calendar* and S.T.C. misspelled it), son of William and Betty Hadfield, of Craddenbrook, Mottram-in-Longdendale, Cheshire, was baptised at Mottram, near Stockport, on May 24, 1759; his father, a man in good circumstances, is described in the church register as a clothier. John Hadfield grew up to be a handsome, well-spoken, plausible con-man and forger. Shortly after coming of age he married the illegitimate daughter of the second son of the third Duke of Rutland. Hadfield, having got his hands on her dowry, deserted her; she died not long after.

When Hadfield had exhausted her money, he supported himself by shady financial deals, confidence-trickery and forgeries; posing as an Army officer, an intimate connection of the Manners family. He is thought to have obtained release from debtors' prison on two occasions by persuading the Duke of Rutland (possibly by threatening him with blackmail) to pay off his creditors.

In 1792 Hadfield received an eight-year prison sentence for swindling hotels; he was rescued by a Devonshire heiress named Michelli Nation who, it was said, occupied rooms facing the prison and fell in love with the interesting and handsome captive at whom she gazed as he paced behind bars. She cleared the money that he owed; he was released and married her within twenty-four hours of regaining his freedom. The pair went to live near Dulverton.

Two years later, as a result of further frauds, Hadfield absconded from Dulverton with as much of his wife's cash as he could obtain. Posing as Colonel the Honourable Alexander Hope, M.P. for Linlithgowshire and brother of the third Earl of Hopetoun, he travelled to Keswick where, in July 1802, he stayed at the Queen's Head. He cultivated the friendship there of Mr John Gregory Crump; a rich Liverpool merchant living at Grasmere (later Wordsworth's landlord), who, flattered by such aristocratic acquaintance, named one of his offspring "Augustus Hope" in honour of the Honourable.

Hadfield (alias Hope) became "betrothed" to the wealthy young ward of a picturesque tourist, Colonel Nathaniel Montgomery Moore, who approved highly of Colonel the Hon. Alexander Hope, but embarrassingly insisted that Lord Hopetoun himself should be asked to give official sanction to the betrothal.

Meanwhile, under pretext of riding over to Buttermere to fish for char, Hadfield was ardently courting Mary Robinson, the pretty daughter of the landlord of the Fish Inn at Buttermere. Mary had been popularised as a picturesque attraction by Joseph Budworth who, some ten years earlier, had given the then fourteen-year-old girl a glowing Romantic write-up in his guidebook, *A Fortnight's Ramble to the Lakes in Westmorland, Lancashire, and Cumberland*, by A Rambler (London, 1792). Mary, in her rôle as the rustic Beauty of Buttermere, lucratively drew the tourists in wagon-loads from Keswick to the Fish, formerly a very humble pot-house.

On Friday, October 1, Hadfield sent a letter by hand to Colonel Moore, asking him to cash a (forged) draft for £30, drawn upon Mr Crump; the letter explained that the supposed M.P. for Linlithgowshire had received a sudden and urgent call to Scotland. Colonel Moore cashed the draft and dispatched the £30 and an extra ten of his own to "Colonel Hope" in Buttermere. Next morning "Colonel Hope" and Mary Robinson were (bigamously) married by special licence at Loweswater church; immediately after which they were off to the Border and a honeymoon.

This was interrupted by a letter from the Reverend John Nicholson, the Loweswater priest who had married them, kindly letting the "Colonel" know that wicked rumours were being spread in Keswick to the effect that he was an imposter. Doubtless, thought the clergyman, "Colonel Hope" would wish to return at once to clear his good name. Hadfield, with all the reckless daring of a psychopath, immediately returned to Buttermere with his bride, arriving there on October 12. Next day he went to Keswick with Mr Nicholson; there the "Colonel" was dramatically unmasked by a visitor at the Queen's Head, a barrister named George Hardinge, who happened to know the real Colonel Augustus Hope. Hadfield was accordingly arrested. However he continued to remain cool, protesting that the whole thing was a preposterous mistake. He ordered dinner for himself and Mr Nicholson and then asked if he might be allowed to take a final stroll down to Derwent Water, in the company of the constable, of course. The obliging constable consented and down to the lake the little party ambled. Arriving at the boating-station on the shore, "Colonel Hope" asked the constable if he might be permitted one last fishing trip on the lake? The constable (doubtless himself a keen fisherman and probably a private sympathiser with the "Colonel", who had made himself very popular in Keswick) agreed to this request; the "Colonel" got into a boat, manned by one Birkett, who had acted as his faithful factotum since his arrival in Keswick in July, and the ardent angler was rowed up the lake, in the direction of the Jaws of Borrowdale.

The October afternoon closed in, it grew dark; but the "Colonel" failed to return; perhaps to the consternation of the waiting constable, perhaps not.

The story was too good a one to be missed by as instinctive a journalist as S.T.C.; he wasted no time in writing it up, captioned, *A Romantic Marriage*. The *Morning Post* carried it on October 11, 1802.

"Colonel Hope's" true identity was quickly discovered; allegedly by the unhappy Mary herself, who is said to have found a packet of revealing letters in the dressing-case that her "husband" had left behind.

Hadfield evaded arrest until early November. Guided by Birkett, he had travelled, under cover of darkness, up Borrowdale to Stonethwaite, thence up the Langstrath and over Stake Pass into Langdale: rough going for an October night, or indeed any night. From Langdale he crossed to Eskdale and down to Ravenglass, where he hid for a while, disguised as a seaman, in a moored and deserted sloop. From Ravenglass he presently made his way to Ulverston. From there he journeyed to Chester, where early in November he was recognised at the theatre. Once again he escaped arrest and fled to Norwich, where all trace of him was lost. A nationwide description of him was published in the press, together with the announcement of a £50 reward for information of his whereabouts. Hadfield was finally arrested at an inn near Swansea, in South Wales. After a fortnight in Brecon gaol, he was removed to London; he appeared at Bow Street magistrate's court before Sir Richard Ford, on December 6, 1802. His true wife travelled up from Devonshire with their two infant children and spent Christmas Day with Hadfield in Bridewell prison.

Two further articles by Coleridge, dealing with the case, had appeared in the *Morning Star* for October 22 and November 5 respectively (these three pieces were subsequently reprinted in *Essays on His Own Times*).

In the New Year Hadfield was moved to Newgate; he was not sent north to stand trial at Carlisle until May, 1803. He appeared at the August Assizes there on the 15th of that month, when he was arraigned before Sir Alexander Thompson. Hadfield stood charged upon three indictments; two, for forgery, being capital offences; the third, for franking letters as a member of Parliament and thereby defrauding the Post Office, was punishable by seven years' transportation. The three principle witnesses for the prosecution were George Wood, landlord of the Queen's Head, Keswick; the Rev. John Nicholson, and Mr Crump.

The trial lasted from eleven in the morning until seven in the evening; the jury took ten minutes to find a verdict of guilty. Hadfield was brought back to Court at 8 o'clock next morning to be sentenced to death.

On that same day, August 16, Wordsworth and S.T.C. had their interview with him. Although it has often been stated that Hadfield refused to see S.T.C. on account of the *Morning Post* articles, S.T.C.'s notebook entry (1432 16.10) and his letter to Robert Southey of March 28, 1804 (CL 589) make it clear that such was not the case; he, with Wordsworth, met Hadfield, "impelled" by Miss Wordsworth.

The case was a notorious one at the time: Dorothy might well have been irresistibly fascinated by the idea of Hadfield as Romantic hero. Here was a desperado under sentence of death; seducer, imposter, daredevil; forty-three years of age but still active, handsome, strong-limbed; his thick black brows contrasting fascinatingly with his unpowdered fair hair with a patch of grey over the right temple; his complexion fresh; his manners allegedly entirely those of a gentleman (but S.T.C. noted that he was vulgar and that his grammar was faulty). Hadfield dressed well, did not hesitate to pay compliments and had a suspiciously honest manner of placing his hand on his heart in a gesture of spontaneous sincerity when he spoke (persons who appear with frequency in the dock develop a habit of swearing themselves in, so to speak, every time that they tell a lie).

Romantic curiosity apart, Dorothy, together with William and S.T.C., had a strong personal interest in his case. They all three knew Mr Crump; they had met Mary of Buttermere; in all probability they knew many others of the local people involved in the Hadfield case. Furthermore S.T.C. had valid professional reasons for seeking to interview the condemned man (although, if we may rely upon his notebook entry, neither he nor William had seemed avid for the interview).

As it turned out, the meeting made a profound impression upon S.T.C. It is said that he had Hadfield much in mind when, subsequently, he came to make his studies for critical analysis of the character of Iago.

Hadfield was hanged on Saturday, September 3, 1803, at Harraby, Carlisle's time-honoured execution place. He died bravely.

Mary of Buttermere had given birth to a still-born child that June. In due course she married a Caldbeck farmer, Richard Harrison; by him she had seven children, five of whom survived into adulthood. Once her youth was past Mary grew fat; nonetheless, so long as she lived at Buttermere she remained an object of interest for tourists, only sinking at last into obscurity when Richard Harrison removed her to Caldbeck.

Bibliography:

John Hadfield (1803). Trial of Henry Fauntleroy and other Famous Trials for Forgery ed. Horace Bleackley, Notable British Trials, Edinburgh: Hodge, 1924.
LYNN LINTON, E. *The Lake Country* London: Smith, Elder and Co., 1864.

REFERENCES

Key To References

AM   *The Rime of the Ancient Mariner*
BL   *Biographia Literaria*
BM   *British Museum*
CL   Coleridge, S. T., *Collected Letters* (ed. Griggs)
CNB   Coleridge, S. T., *Notebooks* (ed. Coburn)
DWJ   Wordsworth, Dorothy, *Journals* (ed. Moorman)
ELG   Griggs, Earl Leslie
EWL   Wordsworth Letters, *The Early Years* (ed. Selincourt)
HCR   Robinson, Henry Crabb
KK   *Kubla Khan*
LB   *Lyrical Ballads*
LL   Lamb, Charles and Mary, *Letters* (ed. Lucas)
MWL   Wordsworth Letters, *The Middle Years* (ed. Selincourt)
Pre   Wordsworth, William, *The Prelude*
PW   Coleridge, S. T., *Poetical Works* (Coleridge, E. H., 1912)
Rec   Cottle, J., *Early Recollections*
Rem   Cottle, J., *Reminiscences*
S   Sandford, Mrs H., *Thomas Poole and His Friends*
SC   Coleridge, Sara (Mrs), *Letters to Thomas Poole* (ed. Potter)
SCL   Southey, Robert, *Life and Correspondence* (ed. Southey, C.C.).
SHL   Hutchinson, Sara, *Collected Letters* (ed. Coburn)
TT   Coleridge, S. T., *Table Talk* (ed. Coleridge, H. N.)
WPW   Wordsworth, William, *Poetical Works* (ed. Selincourt and Darbishire)
WW   Wordsworth, William

PROLOGUE: *Enter Samuel Taylor Coleridge*
1 CL 1002n
2 Gillman, *Life*
3 CL 1002

INTRODUCTION: 1. *"God Protect Me From My Friends . . ."*
1 CL 1028
2 LL ii
3 BM MSS
4 SC 13
5 STC Pref. KK (1816)
6 STC Pref. *Christabel* (1816)
7 STC Pref. KK (1816)
8 KK 3–5
9 SHL 21.11.1825
10 *Tait's Mag.* I–II (1834–5)
11 Hare, J. C., *Brit. Mag.* vii (1835)

12 SHL 10.1.1835
13 Carlyle, T., *Life of John Stirling*
14 HCR *Diaries*
15 *Rem*
16, 17, 18, 19, 20, 21 *Ibid.*
22 CL 651
23 *Rem*
24, 25, 26, 27, 28 *Ibid.*
29 MSS N.Y. Pub. Lib., CL 918n
30 *Rem*
31 CL 927
32 *Rem*
33 *Ibid.*
34 CL 919
35 *Ibid.*
36 *Rem*
37 *Ibid.*
38 CL 920

39 CL 921
40 CL 922
41 *Rem*
42 CL 935
43 *Rem.*, CL 921n2
44 *Rem*
45 CL 439
46 CL 956
47 *Rem*
48 *Ibid.*

INTRODUCTION: II. *The Tyranny of the Body*
1 *Extempore Effusions*
2 Gillman, *Life*
3 CNB 1898 16.243
4 Gillman, *Life*
5 BL
6 CL 947
7 BL
8 CL 983
9 CL 24
10 CNB 1825 16.208
11 CL 179
12 Graves, R. P., *Afternoon Lectures* (1869)
13 CL 999n3
14 CL 971
15 Watson, L. E., *Coleridge at Highgate* (1925)
16 *Ibid.*

INTRODUCTION: III. *The Bondage of Opium*
1 CL 927
2 CNB 2368 21.548
3 BM Add. MS 74519
4 CNB 273 G.270
5 AM (1797–8) iv 224–31
6 CNB 2543 17.101
7 CL 238
8 CNB 7.1.18
9 KK 37–8
10 CL 919
11 CL 719
12 CL 927
13 *Ibid.*
14 CL 931
15 CNB 2086 15.52
16 CL 444
17 CL 717
18 Calkins
19 Mackintosh, R. T., *Life of Sir James Mackintosh*

20 TT 1.5.1830
21 CL 493
22 CL 492
23 CL 493
24 CL 25
25 CL 36
26 *Pre* vi 308–14
27 *Ibid.*
28 CNB 2398 21.564
29 CL 717
30 CNB 2990 11.59
31 AM (1797–1834) ii 138–42

INTRODUCTION: IV. *The Shaping Years*
1 CL 174, 179, 208, 210, 234
2 Gillman, *Life*
3 Lowes, J. L., *The Road to Xanadu*
4 KK 49–52
5 TT 27.9.1830
6 CL 409
7 CNB 1416 4.155
8 TT 16.8.1832
9 CL 2
10 *Ibid.*
11 CL 1
12 CNB 1176 6.151
13 Gillman, *Life*
14, 15 *Ibid.*
16 TT 16.8.1832
17 Gillman, *Life*
18 *Ibid.*
19 CL 2
20 TT 27.5.1830
21 CL 597
22 CL 943
23 *Pre* vi 250–1
24 CL 2
25 LL ii 21
26 CNB 2516 17.81
27 CL 3
28 CL 10
29 CL 401
30 STC *On Leaving School*
31 STC *Youth and Age:* 1st **draft** (1823)
32 AM i 21–8

CHAPTER ONE: *Jesus Man*
1 CL 8
2 CL 9
3 *Ibid.*
4 CL 8

5 CL 9
6 CL 10
7, 8, 9 *Ibid.*
10 CL 11
11 *Ibid.*
12 CL 12
13 *Ibid.*
14 CL 11
15 CL 12
16 CL 14
17 CL 17
18 *Ibid.*
19 CL 16
20 CL 20 (Tr. Griggs)
21 CL 36
22, 23 *Ibid.*
24 CL 21 (Tr. Griggs)
25 CL 23
26 *Ibid.*
27 CL 25
28 CL 28
29 PW i 84
30 Williams, H. M., *Letters*
31 *Pre* xi 79–80
32 Hazlitt, W., *First Acquaintance with Poets* (*Plain Speaker*, 1823)
33 CL 101
34 *Col. Works* 3
35 CL 15
36 CL 25
37 TT 30.7.1831
38 CL 238
39 CL 535
40 CL 679
41 CL 11
42 *Pre* vi 754–5, 765
43 *Ibid.* ix 385–9
44 Soboul
45 *Pre* x 263–303
46 TT 23.7.1822
47 *Ibid.*
48 *Ibid.*n
49 Gillman, *Life*
50 CL 44
51 CL 26
52, 53 *Ibid.*
54 CL 30
55 *Ibid.*
56 CL 36
57 CNB 2398 21.564
58 CL 814
59 CNB 2398 21.564
60 CNB 1913 9.33

61 CNB 2398 21.564
62 CL 68
63 CL 55
64 CL 36
65 CL 210
66 CL 36
67 CL 32
68 *Ibid.*

CHAPTER TWO: *An Indocile Equestrian*
1 Watson, V., *Coleridge's Army Service*, T.L.S. 7.7.50
2 *Rem, Ibid.*
3, 4 *Ibid.*
5 Gillman, *Life*
6 CL 35
7 *Rem*
8 CNB 2290 15.133
9 CL 32
10 *Ibid.*
11 CL 33
12 CL 34n
13 CL 34
14 CL 36
15 CL 33n, 34, 37
16 CL 35
17 CL 36
18 CL 38
19 CL 39
20 CL 41
21 *Ibid.*
22 CL 42
23 *Ibid.*
24 CL 43
25 CL 44n
26 CL 44
27 T.L.S. 7.7.50
28 CL 46
29 CL 47
30 CL 48

INTERLUDE: *Data: The Adorable I Am*
1 CL 248
2 CL 164
3 TT 2.7.1830
4 STC *Philosophical Lectures*
5 Sartre, J. P., *L'Existentialisme est un Humanisme* (1946)
6 *Gedenkausgabe* x 730–1
7 *Pre* vi 638–40
8 CL 248
9 Hazlitt, *First Acquaintance With Poets*

10 CL 459
11 BL
12 CL 634
13 CNB 921 21.121
14 CNB 2860 16.357
15 BL
16 TT 1.3.1834
17 Arnold, M., *Essays in Criticism; First Series*
18 Priestley, J., *Appeal* (1771)
19 TT 23.6.1834
20 CL 55
21 CL 536
22 CL 44
23 CL 74
24 CL 57
25 CNB 174 G. 169
26 CL 380–4, 307–8
27 CL 387
28 S ii 34
29 BM MSS
30 CL 387
31 CL 634
32 HCR *Diary* i 394–401
33 BL
34 McFarland
35 Coleridge, Sara *fille*: *Memoir and Letters* i
36 Watson, L. E.
37 CL 44

CHAPTER THREE: *The Pantisocrats I*
1 CL 81
2 MSS Bod.
3 STC *To The Rev. George Coleridge*
4 CL 66
5 CL 49
6 CL 93
7 S i
8 CNB 2398 21.564
9 CL 50
10 CL 51
11 *Ibid.*
12 CL 51, 52
13 CL 51
14 CL 61
15 CL 57
16 S i
17, 18, 19 *Ibid.*
20 CL 943
21 BL
22 Keats, *Letters* i 265
23 Griggs, *Coleridge Fille*

24 MSS Hunt. Lib.
25 CL 927
26 CL 783
27 SHL
28 CL 317
29 MWL ii 483
30 CL 176
31 CL 676
32 SHL
33 CL 676
34 *Ibid.*
35 CL 674
36 CL 156
37 CL 248
38 CL 197
39 SCL
40 *Ibid.*
41 CL 470
42 CL 73
43 S i
44 STC *Sonnet: Pantisocracy* (1794)
45 CL 54

CHAPTER FOUR: *The Pantisocrats II*
1 CL 55
2 CL 57
3 CL 59
4, 5 *Ibid.*
6 CL 60
7 CL 73
8 *Anima Poetae*
9 CL 60, 62, 64
10 CL 64
11 CL 63
12 CL 65
13, 14 *Ibid.*
15 CL 73
16 CL 65
17 CL 67
18 CL 69
19 CL 66
20 CL 68
21 CL 65
22, 23 *Ibid.*
24 CL 68
25 CL 67
26 CL 69
27 *Ibid.*
28 CL 93
29 *Ibid.*
30 CL 71
31 CL 73
32, 33 *Ibid.*

34 CL 74
35 CL 75
36 CL 76
37 CL 77
38 CL 78
39 *Rem*
40 CL 78n2
41 CL 680
42 CL 81
43 *Ibid.*
44 CL 93
45 CL 81
46 STC *To the Rev. W. J. Hort*
47 *Ibid.*
48 CL 93
49 *Rem*
50 *Ibid.*
51 CL 93
52, 53 *Ibid.*
54 *Rem*
55 *Ibid.*
56 CL 93
57, 58, 59, 60 *Ibid.*
61 *Rem*
62 CL 105
63 CL 93
64, 65, 66 *Ibid.*

CHAPTER FIVE: *The Eolian Harp*
1 S i
2 *Ibid.*
3 STC *Reflections* 1–4
4 *Ibid.* 28, 30
5 BL
6 CL 91
7 CL 90
8 CL 91
9 *Rem*
10 *Ibid.*
11 CL 91
12 S i
13, 14, 15 CL 93
16 *Rem*
17 CL 93

CHAPTER SIX: *On Watch, But Not On Guard*
1 *Rem*
2 CL 97
3 CL 104
4 *Ibid.*
5 CL 105
6 *Rem*

7 BL
8 *Rem*
9 CL 108
10 *Rec*
11 CL 112
12 *Ibid.*
13 CL 92
14 *Rem*
15 CL 913
16 CL 217
17 STC *Religious Musings* 8–9
18 *Ibid.* 127–32
19 *Ibid.* 194–5
20 *Ibid.* 365–77
21 *Ibid.* 268–311
22 BL
23 Sitwell, E., *Aspects of Modern Poetry* i 45
24 Sitwell, E., *A Poet's Notebook* iii 20
25 CL 116
26 CL 120
27 CL 134
28 *Rem*
29 BL
30 CL 114
31 CL 119
32 BL
33 CL 124
34 CNB 73 G.67
35 CL 124
36, 37, 38 *Ibid.*

CHAPTER SEVEN: *The Feelings of the Moment*
1 S i
2 Coleridge, S. MSS
3 CL 130
4 CL 135
5 CL 140
6 S i
7 CL 176
8 CL 141
9 CL 156
10 CL 142
11 *Ibid.*
12 TT 24.7.1831
13 CL 142
14 TT 27.9.1830
15 CL 142
16 *Ibid.*
17 S i
18 CL 146
19 CL 151

20 CL 146
21 LL i 39
22 CL 143
23 CL 122
24 CL 127
25 CL 133
26 CL 164
27 CL 170
28 *Ibid.*
29 CL 164
30 *Ibid.*
31 CL 144
32 *Ibid.*
33 CL 522
34 *Ibid.*
35 CL 156
36, 37, 38 *Ibid.*
39 CL 159
40 CL 154
41 S i
42 CL 127
43 *Ibid.*
44 CL 164
45 CL 163
46 CL 168
47 CL 170
48 CL 146
49 *Ibid.*
50 CL 148
51 CL 151
52, 53 *Ibid.*
54 CL 152
55, 56 *Ibid.*
57 CL 155
58 CL 154
59 *Rem*
60 S i
61 CL 162
62 CL 158
63 CL 160
64 *Ibid.*
65 CL 163
66, 67, 68 *Ibid.*
69 CL 166
70, 71 *Ibid.*
72 CL 164
73 STC *Ode: To the Departing Year*, 153–61

CHAPTER EIGHT: *Happy Young Man Leaps Over a Gate*
1 SC 17
2 CL 294

3 CL 173
4 CL 176
5 LL i
6 CL 176
7 CL 341
8 CL 204
9 CL 176
10 CL 182
11 CL 183
12 CL 183n1
13 CL 183
14 CL 146
15 CL 177
16 CL 209
17 CL 178
18 STC *The Destiny of Nations* 278–91
19 *Ibid.* 93–5
20 *Ibid.* 78–80
21 *Ibid.* 77
22 *Ibid.* 90–4
23 *Ibid.* 111–15
24 AM v 404–5
25 STC *The Destiny of Nations* 412–15
26 *Ibid.* 470–4
27 CL 124
28 *Rem*
29 Hazlitt, *First Acquaintance with Poets*
30 CL 235
31 CL 866
32 LWL 1584
33 STC *Hexameters* (1799)

INTERLUDE: *The New Sensibility* I and II
1 Selincourt, *D.W. Biog.*
2 CL 195
3 *Tait's Mag.* I–II 1834–5
4 W.W. *Stanzas in the Manner of Thompson*
5 EWL 46
6 *Pre* iii 234–6
7 *Ibid.* xii 110–13
8 Ackermann
9 *Pre* xii 110–45
10 EWL 50
11 CL 77
12 CNB 540 5.118
13 CNB 954 4.79
14 CL 74
15 *Christabel* ii 616–19
16 Byron, *Heaven and Earth* (1822)
17 CNB 1637 21.385
18 *Ibid.*

505

19 *Tait's Mag.* I–II 1834–5
20 *Pre* xii 251–69
21 *Ibid.* iv 291–8
22 *Ibid.* iv 309–19
23 *Ibid.* iii 508–11
24 *Ibid.* ix 85–94
25 *Ibid.* x 221–30
26 CL 235
27 *Pre* vi 310–14
28 CL 127
29, 30 *Ibid.*
31 *Pre* xi 301–7
32 EWL 30
33 EWL 31
34 *Pre* xi 340–9
35 WPW i 334
36 LB (1798)
37 EWL 55
38 EWL 58
39 EWL 60
40 STC *A Day Dream,* 6
41 Gittings, *Keats,* 270
42 *Pre* xiv 269
43 WPW i 342
44 EWL 70
45 CL 195
46 *Tait's Mag.* I–II (1834–5)
47 Selincourt, *D.W. Biog.*
48 EWL 31
49 CL 190
50 CL 191
51 CL 235

CHAPTER NINE: *Indulgent Skies*
1 *Pre* xiv 392–418
2 CL 197
3 EWL 72
4 CL 197
5 *Ibid.*
6 PW 1834
7 LL i
8 EWL 72
9 CL 197
10 EWL 72
11 CL 197
12 CL 200n1
13 *Ibid.*
14 S i
15 TT 27.7.1830
16 S i
17 CL 196
18 Eaglestone
19 CL 200

20 *Ibid.*
21 CL 182
22 CL 201
23 CL 191
24 *Ill. Lond. News* 22.4.1893
25 WPW v 243
26 CL 185
27 Eaglestone
28 *Ibid.*
29 CL 204
30 SCL MS Hunt. Lib.; *Rem*; S ii
31 *Pre* xiv 348–407

CHAPTER TEN: *Wantoning in Wild Poesy*
1 CNB 2166 K.21
2 CL 444
3 CL 216
4 CL 202, 204, 207n3
5 Abinger MS
6 BM Add. MSS 35345 f 83
7 CL 216
8 CL 808
9 CNB 1840 16.223
10 CL 209
11 *Osorio* v i
12 CL 209
13 CL 209n
14 CL 152
15 *Osorio* v i
16 CL 209
17 Purchas, 1617, p. 472
18 KKn 1816
19 CNB 1421 4.108
20 CL 209
21 WW *The Daffodils*
22 Donne, J., *The Good-Morrow*
23 Blake, W., *Ah! Sunflower*
24 CL 209
25 *Ibid.*
26 WPW i 285–92
27 WPW i 361
28, 29 *Ibid.*
30 CL 212
31 DWJ
32 House. 92
33 *Pre* xiii 350–1
34 CL 212, 218, 233
35 AM i 63–4 (1798)
36 AM i 73–4 (1798)
37 AM ii 135–8 (1798)
38 AM vii 647–50 (1798)
39 AM iv 274–83 (1798)

40 AM v 413–14 (1798)
41 AM vii 607–23 (1798)
42 CL 459
43 AM vii 655–8 (1798)
44 CL 184
45 CL 218, 219
46 BL
47 WW LB *Pref* 3rd ed (1802)
48 CL 1155
49 CL 214n4
50 CL 217
51 CL 218
52 CL 222n
53 Hazlitt, *First Acquaintance with Poets*
54 *Ibid.*
55 S ii
56 CL 216
57 CL 124
58 EWL 85
59 Chambers, *A Sheaf of Studies*
60 CNB 3.11.1810
61 CL 248
62 CL 252
63 Foxon, D. F., *The Lib. Ser.* 5 ix (1954)

CHAPTER ELEVEN: *Epitaphs*
1 CL 256
2 CL 254
3 CNB 335.31
4 CL 254
5 *Ibid.*
6 CL 256
7 *Ibid.*
8 CL 254
9 *Ibid.*
10 CNB 346 3.12
11 S i
12 CL 255n1
13 LL i 141
14 CL 259
15 CL 261
16 CL 260
17 EWL 107
18 EWL 105
19 CL 270
20 CL 274
21 *Ibid.*
22 CL 270
23 CL 262
24 CL 257
25 CL 258
26 CL 261
27 CL 262
28 CL 266
29 CL 263
30 CL 296
31 CL 263
32 S i
33 SCL
34 EWL 105
35 S i
36 CL 268
37 CL 269
38 CL 270
39 *Ibid.*
40 S i
41 CL 272
42, 43 *Ibid.*
44 S i
45 CL 272
46 CNB 399 3½.6
47 CL 272
48 CNB 429 3½.39
49 CL 272
50 CL 275
51 PW i 312
52 S i
53 CL 274
54 *Ibid.*
55 CL 275
56 *Letters of S. T. Coleridge*, ed. E. H. Coleridge, 282
57 CL 277
58 CL 276
59 CL 277
60 PW i 313
61 CL 277
62 *Ibid.*
63 CL 283
64 CL 276
65 CL 277
66 CL 269
67, 68 *Ibid.*
69 CL 283
70 *Ibid.*
71 CL 285
72 *Ibid.*

CHAPTER TWELVE: *Fire and Brimstone*
1 CL 287
2 *Ibid.*
3 S i
4 CL 281
5 S i
6 CL 275

7 CL 286
8 CNB 909 21.109
9 CL 287n1
10 CL 291
11,12 *Ibid.*
13 CNB 472 5.14
14 CNB 2245 15.123
15 CL 292
16 *Ibid.*
17 CL 294
18, 19, 20, 21 *Ibid.*
22 CL 298n1
23, 24 *Ibid.*
25 CL 291
26 CL 292
27 CL 294
28 CL 298
29 CL 294
30 CNB 556 5.51
31 CL 298
32 S i
33 CL 299n1
34 CL 300
35 CNB 571 5.66
36 CNB 1537 16.42
37 CNB 1583 21.303
38 CNB 1587 21.310
39 *Lake Poets*
40 *Pre* vi 226–9
41 *Ibid.* vi 230
42 CNB 508 5.101
43 CL 299
44, 45 *Ibid.*
46 TT 27.9.1830
47 CNB 1679 21.407
48 SHL 29.9.1813
49 SHL 14.7.1816
50 SHL 8.8.1800
51 MM DWJ 80n4
52 CNB 1575 21.296(a) and note
53 CL 294
54 CL 814
55 CNB 597 4.13
56 CNB 962 4.137
57 CNB 576 5.71
58 CNB 1575 21.296(a)
59 *Ibid.*
60 CNB 591 4.7
61 CL 301

CHAPTER THIRTEEN: *"God Knows Where We Can Go"*
1 CL 305

2 CL 316
3 CL 332
4 CL 329
5 CL 309
6 *Ibid.*
7 CL 316
8 *Ibid.*
9 CL 317
10 CL 305
11 EWL 292
12 Selincourt, *D.W. Biog.*
13 CL 309
14 CL 316
15 S i
16 CL 318
17 CL 320
18 CL 313
19 CL 308
20 CL 317
21 CL 320
22 CL 328
23 CL 330
24 CL 325
25 *Ibid.*
26 CL 332
27 CL 326
28 EWL 140
29 EWL 255
30 EWL 256
31 CNB 2001 9.107
32 *Sense and Sensibility* iv
33 CNB 718 5½.1
34 CL 338
35 CL 333
36, 37 *Ibid.*
38 CL 341
39 *Ibid.*
40 CL 339
41 CL 340
42 CL 432

CHAPTER FOURTEEN: *Land of Ice*
1 CL 343
2 *Ibid.*
3 CL 342
4 CL 339
5 CL 344
6 CL 392
7 Rawnsley
8 CL 362
9 CL 341
10 CL 362
11 N.Y. Pub. Lib.

12 CNB 5½ 47.502
13 CNB 1610 21.370
14 CNB 798 5½.42
15, 16 *Ibid.*
17 CL 351
18 CL 353n3
19 EWL 272
20 LL i 240
21 CL 356
22 BL
23 N.Y. Pub. Lib.
24 CL 355
25 CL 357
26 CNB 834 4.117
27 CL 367
28 CL 365
29 DWJ
30 CNB 848 4.123
31 CL 368
32 CL 369
33 CL 371
34 CL 374
35 S ii
36 CL 377
37 S ii
38 CL 390
39 *Ibid.*
40 CL 391
41 CL 445
42 CL 449
43 CL 400
44 SHL 7.21.1820
45 CL 390
46 CL 444
47 CL 969
48 CNB 980 21.132
49 N.Y. Pub. Lib.
50 CL 367
51 CL 395
52 CL 394

CHAPTER FIFTEEN: *Beware of Pity*
1 CL 397
2 CL 875
3 CL 464
4 CL 481
5 *Ibid.*
6 BL
7 CL 389
8 DWJ 23.5.1802
9 EWL 160
10 EWL 161
11 CL 432

12 CNB 979 21.131
13 *Ibid.*
14 CNB 1816 16.200
15 CL 478
16 TT 5.5.1830
17 CL 409
18 CNB 2516 17.81
19 CL 667
20 CNB 2053 15.14
21 CL 417
22 TT 27.9.1830
23 CNB 1601 21.361
24 STC *A Day Dream*
25 BM Add. MS 47521
26 CL 814
27 CL 432, 403
28 CL 127
29 BM Add. MS 74519
30 CNB 1394 8.122
31 SHL 27.10.1811
32 SHL 15.10.1820
33 *Ibid.*
34 CNB 984 21.136
35 CL 429
36 CL 682
37 MWL 115
38 SHL
39 CL 410
40 CNB 1331 6.108
41 SHL 27.3.1809
42 SHL 27.10.1811
43 CNB 985 21.137
44 CL 405
45 CNB 1065 21.190
46 CL 437
47 CL 449
48 CNB 1030 6.37
49 CL 642
50 CL 421
51 CL 436
52 CL 428
53 CL 435
54 CNB 1152 6.143
55 DWJ 24.3.1802

CHAPTER SIXTEEN: *The Pains of Sleep*
1 DWJ 31.1.1802
2 DWJ 27.1.1802
3 DWJ 28.1.1802
4 CL 437
5 Legouis
6 DWJ
7 DWJ 14.2.1802

8 DWJ 16.2.1802
9 CL 439
10 STC *Ode: Dejection*
11 DWJ 4.3.1802
12 DWJ 9.3.1802
13 DWJ 27.3.1802
14 Thomas, Dylan
15 CL 444
16 CL 464
17 CL 439
18 DWJ 21.4.1802
19 DWJ 22.5.1802
20 CL 449
21 *Ibid.*
22 CL 464
23 CL 449
24 CL 447
25 CL 454
26 EWL 172
27 DWJ 24.3.1802
28 WW, *A Farewell*
29 DWJ 2.6.1802
30 DWJ 20.6.1802
31 CL 453
32 DWJ July 1802
33, 34 *Ibid.*
35 EWL 177
36 *Ibid.*
37 DWJ Oct. 1802
38 *Ibid.*
39 CL 451
40 CL 452
41 CL 459
42 CL 464
43 *Ibid.*
44 CL 461
45 CL 462
46 CL 440
47 CL 376
48 CL 462
49 CL 465
50 CL 466
51 CNB 1266 8.15
52, 53, 54 *Ibid.*
55 CNB 1267 8.16
56 *Ibid.*
57 Thomas, Dylan
58 CL 470
59 CL 471
60 CL 470
61 *Ibid.*
62 CL 472
63 CL 468

64 CL 484
65 CL 489
66 *Ibid.*
67 CL 491
68 CL 493
69 CL 499
70 CL 591
71 CL 508
72 CL 504
73 CL 509
74 CL 550
75 CNB 1402 4.149
76 CL 546
77 CNB 1421 4.108
78 CNB 1250 21.214
79 CNB 1726 16.122
80 STC *Pains of Sleep*
81 CNB 1726 16.122

CHAPTER SEVENTEEN: *The Frightful Fiend*
1 EWL 190
2 CL 508
3 CL 513
4, 5 *Ibid.*
6 CNB 1421 4.108
7 CL 514, 597
8 CL 513
9 *Ibid.* n1
10 CNB 1426 16.7
11 CNB 1432 16.10
12 CL 589
13 CNB 1434 16.12
14 CNB 1435 16.13
15 CNB 1436 16.14
16 CL 248
17 CL 238
18 CL 513
19 *Ibid.*
20 MWL 157
21 CL 524
22 CNB 1826 16.209
23 CNB 1426 7.9
24 CNB 1437 16.15
25 *Ibid.*
26 CNB 1449 7.2
27 CNB 1463 7.6
28 CNB 1469 7.22
29, 30, 31 *Ibid.*
32 CNB 1471 7.24
33 CNB 1469 7.22
34 *Ibid.*
35 CNB 1666 21.401

36 CNB 1606 21.366
37 *Ibid.*
38 CNB 1471 7.24
39, 40, 41 *Ibid.*
42 CNB 1473 7.26
43 CL 524
44 CNB 1472 7.25
45 CL 515
46 CL 514
47 CL 521
48 *Ibid.*
49 CL 515
50 *Ibid.*
51 CNB 1488 7.38
52 CL 517
53 CL 719
54 AM vi 450–6 (1798)
55 CL 523
56 CL 516
57 CL 517

CHAPTER EIGHTEEN: *The Mariner Be-calmed*
1 CL 520
2 CL 523
3 CL 520
4 CL 518n1
5 CL 525
6 CL 526
7 CNB 1606 21.366
8 CL 525
9, 10, 11 *Ibid.*
12 CNB 1577 21.297
13 CNB 1605 21.365
14 CNB 1616 21.374
15 CNB 1618 21.376
16 CNB 1616 21.374
17 CNB 1622 21.379
18 CNB 1623 21.380
19 CNB 1619 21.377
20 CNB 1644 21.390
21 CNB 1649 21.395
22 CL 533
23 CL 683
24 CL 520
25 CNB 1669 21.404
26 CNB 1674 21.405
27 CNB 1624 21.381
28 CNB 1681 21.409
29 SCL
30 CL 523
31 CL 533
32 *Ibid.*

33 CL 482
34 CNB 1718 16.105
35 CL 525
36 CNB 1645 21.391
37 CL 259
38 *Ibid.*
39 CL 525
40 CL 529
41 CL 683

CHAPTER NINETEEN: *The Big Bolt*
1 CL 536
2 CL 532
3 CL 534
4 EWL 200
5 CL 534
6 *Ibid.*
7 CNB 1766 16.152
8 CNB 1767 16.153
9 CNB 1768 16.154
10 CNB 1770 16.156
11 CL 527
12 CL 550
13 *Pre* xiv 419–20
14 CNB 1782 16.168
15 *Ibid.*
16 CNB 1777 16.163
17 CNB 1801 16.185
18 CNB 1820 16.204
19 CNB 1822 16.205
20 *Ibid.*
21 CNB 1823 16.206
22 CNB 1826 16.209
23 CNB 1840 16.223
24 CL 535
25 CL 537
26 *Ibid.*
27 CL 536
28 *Ibid.*
29 CL 530
30 CL 537, 539, 546
31 CL 537
32 CL 539
33 CL 543
34 CNB 1863 9.14
35 CL 543
36 Sultana
37 CL 560
38 CL 562
39 CL 568
40 CL 551
41 CL 562
42 CL 568

43 CL 597
44 CNB 1912 9.33
45 CL 563
46 CL 564
47 CNB 1913 9.34
48 *Ibid.*
49 CL 568
50 CNB 1964 9.70
51 CNB 1887 9.56
52 CL 569
53 Sultana
54 CL 577
55 CL 578
56 CL 577
57 CL 550
58 CNB 1998 9.104
59 EWL 272
60 CL 581
61 CNB 1977 9.84
62 CL 581
63 Trans. Royal Inst.
64 CL 587
65 S i
66 CL 597
67 CNB 1987 9.93
68 CL 593
69 CL 589
70 CL 592
71 CL 596
72 CL 591
73 CL 583
74 CL 594
75 CL 595
76 CNB 1993 9.99

CHAPTER TWENTY: *"How the Marinere Sailed Forth . . ."*
1 CNB 1966 9.102
2 *Ibid.*
3 CNB 1993 9.99
4 CL 597
5 *Ibid.*
6 CL 599
7 CNB 1993 9.99
8 CNB 2005 9.111
9 CL 599
10 CNB 2012 9.118
11 CL 597
12 Hazlitt, *First Acquaintance with Poets*
13 CL 598
14, 15 *Ibid.*
16 CNB 2029 15.10

17 CNB 2036 15.15
18 CNB 2044 15.18
19 CNB 2045 15.19
20 *Ibid.*
21 CL 599
22 CNB 2045 15.19
23 *Ibid.*
24 CNB 2046 15.20
25 CNB 2060 15.32
26 AM i 19–20
27 CNB 2048 15.21
28 CNB 2060 15.32
29, 30 *Ibid.*
31 CNB 2063 15.35
32 CNB 2064 15.36
33 CNB 2071 15.38
34 CNB 2072 15.39
35 CNB 2080 15.47
36 CNB 2085 15.51
37 CNB 2086 15.52
38 CNB 2090 15.56
39 CNB 2091 15.57

CHAPTER TWENTY-ONE: *". . . of the Strange Things That Befell . . ."*
1 CNB 2100 10.3
2 AM v 297–300 (1805), 299–302
3 CL 601
4 CNB 2126 21.439
5 CL 600
6 *Ibid.*
7 CL 605
8 CNB 2372 21.552
9 Sultana
10 CNB 2324 21.508
11 CL 600
12 CNB 2226 15.90
13 CNB 2217 15.85(a)
14 CNB 2195 15.68
15 CNB 2144 K.35, 37
16 CNB 2235 15.99
17 CNB 2356 21.540
18 CNB 22.10.1808
19 CNB 2210 21.462
20 CL 612
21 CNB 2251 15.110
22 CNB 2189 K.49
23 CNB 2237 21.466
24 CL 612
25 CNB 2370 21.550
26 CNB 2279 21.472
27 MS. Pub. Rec. Off.
28 CL 612

29 CL 616
30 CL 612
31 CNB 2367 21.547
32 CNB 2373 21.553
33 CNB 2367 21.547
34 CNB 2368 21.548
35 CNB 2387 21.599
36 CNB 2388 21.598
37 CL 614
38 CNB 2398 21.564
39 *Ibid.*
40 CL 614
41 EWL 232
42 CL 614
43 EWL 267
44 CNB 2408 21.573
45 CNB 2552 17.110
46 CL 614
47 CNB 2453 17.27
48 CNB 2454 17.28
49 CNB 2457 17.31
50 CNB 2468 17.42
51 CNB 2482 17.56
52 CNB 2483 17.57
53 CNB 2485 17.59
54 CNB 2486 17.60
55 CNB 2495 17.69
56, 57 *Ibid.*
58 CNB 2510 17.75
59 CNB 2517 17.82
60 *Ibid.*
61 CL 618
62 CNB 2540 17.98
63 CNB 2530 17.88
64 CNB 2543 17.101
65 CNB 2747 16.333
66 CNB 2539 17.95
67 CNB 2600 17.211
68 *Ibid.*
69 CNB 2530 17.88
70 CNB 2531 17.89
71 CNB 2534 17.92
72 CNB 2535 17.93
73 *Ibid.*
74 CNB 2552 17.110
75 CNB 2541 17.99
76 CL 2517n
77 CL 636
78 CNB 2554 17.112
79 CNB 2557 17.115
80 *Ibid.*
81 CNB 2606 17.214
82 CNB 2607 17.215

CHAPTER TWENTY-TWO: "*. . . in what manner the Ancyent Marinere came back to his own country.*"
1 CNB 2560 17.118
2 CNB 2536 17.94
3 CL 619
4 CNB 2614 18.196
5 CNB 2665 16.268
6 CNB 2701 16.281
7 BM Add. MS 74519
8 CL 621
9 CNB 2860 16.357
10 CNB 2866 15.242
11 CL 621
12 CL 622
13 CL 623
14 CL 621
15 CL 623
16 LL ii 19–22
17 *Ibid.*
18 MWL 47
19 CNB 2783 11.5
20 CNB 2880 11.12
21 AM ii 45–50 (1817)

CHAPTER TWENTY-THREE: *Conversations With the Dead*
1 CL 630
2 MWL 48
3 AM iv 248–52 (1798)
4 MWL 48
5 CL 642
6 MWL 48
7 *Ibid.*
8 CL 635n
9 CL 635
10 CNB 2935 11.125
11 CNB 2934 11.32
12 MWL 58
13 CL 653
14 MS Hunt. Lib.
15 MWL 67
16 Raysor
17 CNB 3231
18 BM Add. MS 74519
19 CL 642
20 CL 705
21 MWL 80
22 S ii
23 MWL 90
24 CNB 3075 19.26
25 CNB 3148 12.63
26 S ii

27 MWL 90
28 *Ibid.*
29 CL 669
30 CL 677
31 CL 680
32 CL 676
33 CL 680
34 CL 700
35 BM Add. MS 74519
36 BM Add. MS 47521
37 *Ibid.*
38 MWL 115
39 SHL
40 MWL 92
41 CL 717
42 SHL
43 MWL 188
44 SHL 28.2.1818
45 MWL 188
46 *Ibid.*
47 Selincourt, *D.W. Biog.*
48 Coleridge, Sara, *Mem.*
49 MWL 188
50 MWL 223
51 *Ibid.*
52 CL 867

CHAPTER TWENTY-FOUR: *"O God Save Me . . ."*
 1 Raysor
 2 CL 867
 3 CL 888
 4 *Ibid.*
 5 MWL 223
 6 MWL 225
 7 MS Hunt. Lib.
 8 CL 823
 9 CL 811
10 *Rem*
11 CL 812
12 CL 867
13 CL 941
14 CL 867
15 CL 815n1
16 MWL 215
17 CL 856
18 HCR
19 CL 821
20 CL 815
21 CL 828
22 CL 844
23 CL 845
24 *Shakespeare Crit.* ii 221

25 CL 831
26 CL 623
27 CL 858
28 CL 863
29 *Ibid.*
30 CL 864
31 HCR
32 CL 866
33 CL 867
34 HCR
35 *Ibid.*
36 Dove Cottage MSS
37 CL 888
38 SCL
39 CL 875
40 *Rem*
41 CL 895
42 CL 900
43 CL 902
44 CL 905
45 *Ibid.*
46 CL 906
47 CL 908
48 CL 927
49 CL 919
50 CL 908, 927
51 CL 927
52 *Ibid.*
53 CL 928
54 CL 927
55 CL 908
56 *Ibid.*
57 CL 910
58 CL 927
59 CL 910
60 CL 951
61 CL 910
62, 63 *Ibid.*
64 CL 928
65 CL 909
66 CL 919
67 MS N.Y. Pub. Lib.
68 CL 927
69 CL 927, 928
70 CL 927
71 CL 938
72 CL 939
73 CL 909

EPILOGUE
 1 CL 922
 2 CL 928
 3 BL i 84

4 CL 951
5 AM ii 121–2
6 AM iv 257–85
7 AM v 390–403; vi 502–7; vii
8 AM vii 580–4, 604–11
9 TT
10 Tillyard
11 Smith, E., 31
12 AM iv 226–46
13 AM iv 255–6
14 *Rem*
15 CNB 2091 15.57
16 *Ibid.*
17 CL 672
18 BM Add. MS 74519
19 CL 987
20 CL 951
21 Wellek

22 McFarland, i 27
23 CL 984
24 CL 1016
25 CL 1035
26 CL 1016
27 BL i ix 102–5
28 McFarland, i 39
29 BL i ix
30 McFarland, i 38
31 CL 845
32 CNB 2375 21.555
33 CL 993
34 CL 985
35 CL 987
36 CL 179
37 Gillman, *Life*
38 CL 1002

BIBLIOGRAPHY

Annals of Bristol in the Nineteenth Century: Bristol Mercury ed. John Latimer, Bristol: 1887.

ARNOLD, MATTHEW *Essays in Criticism; First Series*, London: 1905.

BATESON, F. W. *Wordsworth: a Re-Interpretation* Longmans, 1954.

BOWRA, C. M. *The Romantic Imagination* Oxford: 1950.

BRANDL, ALOIS *Samuel Taylor Coleridge and the English Romantic School* English ed. Lady Eastlake, London: 1887.

CALKINS, A. *Opium and the Opium Habit* London: Lippincott, 1871.

CAMPBELL, J. D. *Samuel Taylor Coleridge, A Narrative of the Events of His Life* 1894.

CARLYLE, THOMAS "The Life of John Stirling" in *The Works of Thomas Carlyle in Thirty Volumes* Centenary Edition, XI, London: 1899.

CHAMBERS, E. K. *Samuel Taylor Coleridge: A Biographical Study* 1938.

CLARK, COLETTE *Home at Grasmere* Harmondsworth, Middlesex: Pelican, 1960.

COLERIDGE, E. H. *Complete Poetical Works of Samuel Taylor Coleridge* 2 vols, 1912.
(ed.) *Letters of S. T. Coleridge*, 1895.

COLERIDGE, EDITH *Memoir and Letters of Sara Coleridge* 2 vols, 1873.

COLERIDGE, HARTLEY *Letters* ed. G. E. and E. L. Griggs, 1936.

COLERIDGE, S. T. *Anima Poetae* (A Compilation from the Notebooks) ed. E. H. Coleridge 1895.
Bigraphia Literaria ed. J. Shawcross, London: 1907.
Collected Letters ed. E. L. Griggs 6 vols, Oxford: 1956–1972.
Essays on His Own Times ed. S. Coleridge 3 vols, 1850.
Literary Remains ed. H. N. Coleridge *The Literary Remains of Samuel Taylor Coleridge* 4 vols, 1836–9.
Notebooks of Samuel Taylor Coleridge ed. K. Coburn 2 double vols, London: Routledge, 1957–62.
The Table Talk of Samuel Taylor Coleridge ed. H. N. Coleridge 1835.
The Friend 2 vols (*Collected Works*) ed. B. Rooke, London: Routledge, 1968.

COLERIDGE, S. T. and WORDSWORTH, W. *Lyrical Ballads* (1798) ed. H. Littledale, Oxford: 1924.
Lyrical Ballads (1798 and 1800) ed. R. L. Brett and A. R. Jones, London: Methuen, 1963.
Lyrical Ballads (1805) ed. D. Roper, London: Collins, 1968.

COLERIDGE, SARA *Minnow Among Tritons: Letters of Mrs Sara Coleridge to Thomas Poole* ed. S. Potter, London: Nonesuch Press, 1934.

COTTLE, JOSEPH *Early Recollections; Chiefly Relating to the Late Samuel Taylor Coleridge During his Long Residence in Bristol* London: 1837.
Reminiscences of Samuel Taylor Coleridge and Robert Southey London: 1847.

CURWEN, J. F. *Kirkbie-Kendall* Kendal: 1900.

DE QUINCEY, THOMAS *The Collected Writings of Thomas De Quincey* ed. D. Massen, Edinburgh: 1889–90.

FOXON, D. F. *The Printing of Lyrical Ballads*, 1798 The Library Service, 5. IX, 1954.

GILLMAN, JAMES *The Life of Samuel Taylor Coleridge* London: Pickering, 1834.

GODWIN, WILLIAM *An Enquiry Concerning Political Justice, and its Influence on General Virtue and Happiness* London: 1793.

GRIGGS, E. L. *Coleridge Fille* Oxford: 1940.

(ed.) *Wordsworth and Coleridge: Studies in Honor of George McLean Harper* Princeton: 1939.

HANSON, LAWRENCE *The Life of Samuel Taylor Coleridge: The Early Years* 1938.

HAYTER, ALTHEA *Opium and the Romantic Imagination* Faber, 1968.

HAZLITT, WILLIAM *The Complete Works of William Hazlitt* ed. P. P. Howe, after the edition of A. R. Waller and Arnold Glover, London and Toronto: 1930–34.

HOUSE, HUMPHREY *Coleridge, The Clark Lectures:* 1951–2 London: 1962.

HUTCHINSON, SARA *Collected Letters* ed. K. Coburn, Oxford: 1954.

KEATS, JOHN *Letters of John Keats, 1814–1821* ed. Hyder E. Rollins, 2 vols, Cambridge: 1958.

KEGAN, PAUL C. *William Godwin: His Friends and Contemporaries* 2 vols, 1876.

KIERKEGAARD, SØREN *The Journals of Søren Kierkegaard* ed. and trans. Alexander Dru, London, New York, Toronto: 1951.

LAMB, CHARLES and MARY *The Works of Charles and Mary Lamb* ed. E. V. Lucas, London: 1903–5.

LEGOUIS, EMILE *William Wordsworth and Annette Vallon* London: Dent, revised ed., 1967.

LITCHFIELD, R. B. *Tom Wedgwood* London: Duckworth & Co., 1903.

LOWES, J. L. *The Road to Xanadu : A Study in the Ways of the Imagination* London: Constable, 1927.

MACKINTOSH, R. T. *Memoirs of the Life of Sir James Macintosh* London: Moxon, 1836.

MARGOLIOUTH, H. M. *Wordsworth and Coleridge, 1795–1834* Oxford: Home University Library, 1953.

MATHIEZ, A. *La Révolution Française* 3 vols, Paris: 1922–27.

McFARLAND, THOMAS *Coleridge and the Pantheist Tradition* Oxford: 1969.

McLACHLAN, H. J. *Socinianism in Seventeenth-Century England* London: 1951.

METYARD, ELIZA *A Group of Englishmen* (1795–1815) London: Longmans, 1871.

MOORMAN, MARY *William Wordsworth, a Biography* 2 vols, Oxford: 1957–65.

MUIRHEAD, J. H. *Coleridge as Philosopher* London and New York: 1930.

PERCY, THOMAS *Reliques of Ancient English Poetry* ed. H. B. Wheatley, 3 vols, London: Swan Sonnenschein & Co., 1889.

POLLOCK, SIR FREDERICK *Spinoza; His Life and Philosophy* London: 1962.

PRIESTLEY, JOSEPH *An Appeal to the Serious and Candid Professors of Christianity* London: 1771.

Hartley's Theory of the Human Mind, on the Principle of the Association of Ideas; with Essays Relating to the Subject of It London: 1775.

RAWNSLEY, REV. H. D. *Literary Associations of the English Lakes* 2 vols, Glasgow: MacLehose, 1894.

RAYSOR, T. M. *Coleridge and Asra* Studies in Philology, 1929.

(ed.) *Samuel Taylor Coleridge; Shakespearean Criticism* London and New York: 1960.

REED, MARK L. *Wordsworth: the Chronology of the Early Years, 1770–1799* Boston: Harvard University Press, 1967.

ROBINSON, H. C. *Henry Crabb Robinson on Books and Their Writers* ed. Edith J. Morley, 2 vols, 1938.

Diary, Reminiscences, and Correspondence of Henry Crabb Robinson ed. Thomas Sadler, London: 1869.

RUDÉ, G. *The Crowd in the French Revolution* Oxford: 1959.

SANDFORD, MRS HENRY *Thomas Poole and His Friends* 2 vols, 1888.

SARTRE, J. P. *L'Existentialisme est un Humanisme* Paris: 1946.

SCHNEIDER, ELIZABETH *Coleridge, Opium and 'Kubla Khan'* Chicago: 1953.

SELINCOURT, ERNEST DE *Dorothy Wordsworth, a Biography* Oxford: 1933.

SIMPSON, KEITH *Forensic Medicine* London: Arnold, 1968.

SMITH, ELSIE (ed.) *An Estimate of William Wordsworth by his Contemporaries, 1793–1822* Oxford: Blackwell, 1932.

SEBOUL, A. *Les Sans-Culottes Parisiens en l'An II* Paris: 1958.

SOUTHEY, C. C. (ed.) *The Life and Correspondence of the late Robert Southey* 6 vols, 1849–50.

STOCK, J. E. *Memoirs of the Life of Thomas Beddoes, M.D.* 1811.

STUART, D. "Anecdotes of the Poet Coleridge", *Gentleman's Magazine* May–August 1838.

SULTANA, DONALD *Samuel Taylor Coleridge in Malta and Italy* Oxford: Blackwell, 1969.

TILLYARD, E. M. W. *Poetry and its Background* London: Chatto, 1955.

UNITED NATIONS *National Laws and Regulations Relating to the Control of Narcotic Drugs: The Report of the Commission on Narcotic Drugs of the Economic & Social Council of the United Nations* New York: 1967.

WATSON, LUCY E. (née Gillman) *Coleridge at Highgate* Longmans: 1925.

WELLEK, RENÉ *A History of Modern Criticism: 1750–1950* New Haven: 1955.

WORDSWORTH FAMILY *Letters of the Wordsworth Family* ed. L. N. Broughton, Ithaca, New York: 1942.

WORDSWORTH, DOROTHY *Journals* ed. Mary Moorman, Oxford: 1971.

WORDSWORTH, MARY *Letters* ed. Mary E. Burton, Oxford: 1958.

WORDSWORTH, WILLIAM and DOROTHY *Letters: Early Years 1787–1805* ed. de Selincourt, revised Chester L. Shaver. *Middle Years, 1806–1811* ed. de Selincourt, revised Mary Moorman, Oxford: 1937–1970.

WORDSWORTH, WILLIAM *Poetical Works* ed. E. de Selincourt and H. Darbishire 5 vols, Oxford: 1940–9.

The Prelude ed. E. de Selincourt, 1926; revised H. Darbishire, Oxford: 1959.

INDEX

Dunmow, 402
Durham, 348
Dyer, George, 153, 157, 164, 187

Edinburgh, 463
Edmondson, Dr John, 329, 333, 334, 374, 375, 388
Edwards, Rev. John, 178, 179
Edwards, Dr Thomas, 150
Estlin, Rev. John Prior, 121, 124, 180, 186, 246, 249, 268, 269, 359, 378, 383
Etna, Mount, 402, 423
Eton College, 95
Evans family, 82, 92–4, 118, 135, 136; Anne, 94; Eliza, 135; Mary, 63, 82, 83, 92–4, 96, 97, 106, 107, 118, 135, 136, 138, 149, 150, 153, 155; as Mrs Fryer Todd, 457; Mrs Evans, 77, 82, 92–4, 107, 118; Tom, 77, 82
Evans, Mrs, of Darley, 143, 187, 188
Examiner, The, 222
Exeter, 70, 80, 105, 295
Exmoor, 251, 295, 315

Falmouth, 169
Favel, Samuel, 147
Fenner, Rest, 25
Ferrier, J. F., 13, 29
Findlay, Capt. John, (*Speedwell*), 403, 408, 416, 419
Flower, Benjamin, 62, 182, 203; Ed. *Cambridge Intelligencer*—(see under own head)
Ford, Sir Richard, 498
Forncett (Norfolk), 215, 217
Forster, E. M., 58
Foxe, Capt. Luke, *North West Fox*, etc., 181
French Revolution, 98–103, 133, 136, 195, 227–33; Bastille, fall of, 98; as a Romantic cult, 98–100, 102, 227–33, 244, 245; British Radical support for, 98–104, 227, 229, 244, 245; British Radical reaction to war with France, 103, 104, 181; Wordsworth as Patriot, 99,

100, 102, 103, 227–33; prison massacres, 102, 103, 232 (see also S.T.C., Radicalism)
Frend, William, 100, 101, 104, 130, 216
Fricker family, 137, 138, 140, 141, 157, 159, 162, 299; Edith 137, 138, 141, 159, 162, 168 (see also Southey, Edith); Eliza, 137, 295, 296; George, 137, 179; Martha, 137; Mary (see Lovell, Mary); "Old Mrs Fricker", 140, 165, 169; Sara (see also Mrs S.T.C.), 137, 138, 157, 159, 162, 163, 165, 190
Friedrich, Caspar David, 246
Friend, The; 121, 272, 288, 291, 461, 468, 471
Fuseli, Henry, 222

Gillman, James, 13, 42, 46, 48, 49, 69, 70, 76, 77, 79, 83, 133, 145, 338, 448, 467, 491; on S.T.C., 19–21, 34, 42–6, 48, 49, 77; *Life of Samuel Taylor Coleridge*, 42, 48, 79; Gillman, Mrs Ann, 382
Godwin, William, 51, 52, 127, 153, 193, 216, 307, 311, 315, 332, 337, 340, 400–2, 466; *On Political Justice*, 127
Goethe, Johann Wolfgang von, 122, 123
Gooch, Robert, (surgeon), 46, 473
Gorsas, Antoine Joseph, 229, 230
Goslar, 272, 273, 275–7, 298, 343
Göttingen, 274, 281, 282, 284, 286, 287, 289, 290, 477
Goya, 222
Grasmere, 139, 239, 307, 308, 321, 343–5, 348, 352–4, 360, 362, 374, 376, 388, 435, 447, 455, 457, 458–463, 471; S.T.C. at, 298, 300, 312–316, 321, 323–6, 329–31, 336, 356, 358, 359, 367, 395–99, 460–3
Grasmere Journal (see Wordsworth, Dorothy)
Gravesend, 404
Green, J. H., 13, 48, 130
Greene, Sally (Mrs Sarah Walker), 462